Currency Management

Currency Management: Overlay and Alpha Trading

Edited by Jessica James

Published by Risk Books, a division of Incisive RWG Ltd

Haymarket House
28–29 Haymarket
London SW1Y 4RX
Tel: +44 (0)20 7484 9700
Fax: +44 (0)20 7484 9758
E-mail: books@riskwaters.com
Sites: www.riskbooks.com
       www.riskwaters.com

Every effort has been made to secure the permission of individual copyright holders for inclusion.

© Incisive RWG Ltd 2004

ISBN 1 904339 18 2

British Library Cataloguing in Publication Data
A catalogue record for this book is available from the British Library

Managing Editor: Sarah Jenkins
Copy Editor: Andrew John
Editorial Assistant: Tamsine Green

Typeset by Mizpah Publishing Services, Chennai, India

Printed and bound in Great Britain

Conditions of sale
All rights reserved. No part of this publication may be reproduced in any material form whether by photocopying or storing in any medium by electronic means whether or not transiently or incidentally to some other use for this publication without the prior written consent of the copyright owner except in accordance with the provisions of the Copyright, Designs and Patents Act 1988 or under the terms of a licence issued by the Copyright Licensing Agency Limited of 90, Tottenham Court Road, London W1P 0LP.

Warning: the doing of any unauthorised act in relation to this work may result in both civil and criminal liability.

Every effort has been made to ensure the accuracy of the text at the time of publication. However, no responsibility for loss occasioned to any person acting or refraining from acting as a result of the material contained in this publication will be accepted by Incisive RWG Ltd.

Many of the product names contained in this publication are registered trade marks, and Risk Books has made every effort to print them with the capitalisation and punctuation used by the trademark owner. For reasons of textual clarity, it is not our house style to use symbols such as TM, ®, etc. However, the absence of such symbols should not be taken to indicate absence of trademark protection; anyone wishing to use product names in the public domain should first clear such use with the product owner.

Contents

About the Editor	vii
Foreword	ix
List of Contributors	xi
Introduction *Jessica James*	xv

PART 1: INTRODUCTION TO FX MARKETS AND MODELLING

1	Market History and Structure *Neil Record* Record Currency Management	3
2	The Electronic Revolution in Foreign Exchange *James van den Heule* Citigroup	49
3	Risks and Rewards *Jessica James* Citigroup	65
4	Where Overlay Comes In *Arun Muralidhar* FX Concepts, Inc	89
5	The Case for Currency Management *Brian Strange* JPMorgan Fleming Investment Management	101

PART 2: CURRENCY RISK AND HEDGING

6	FX Risk *Jessica James* Citigroup	123
7	Traditional Hedging Methods *Chris Attfield* PaR Asset Management LLP	153
8	Active versus Passive Hedging *Henrik H. Pedersen* CitiFX Risk Advisory Group	175

| 9 | A Framework to Determine a Currency Hedge Ratio for an International Portfolio
Eric Busay
Fixed Income Unit, CalPERS | 209 |

PART 3: DESIGNING AND IMPLEMENTING A TRADING STRATEGY

10	Trading for Profit *Jessica James* Citigroup	229
11	Trading Models *James Binny* ABN AMRO	277
12	Model Building and Testing *Gerben J. de Zwart* Robeco Quantitative Research	301
13	Implementing Currency Management *Ron Liesching* Pareto	325

PART 4: CASE STUDIES

14	Bringing FX Prime Brokerage to Currency Overlay *Philip Simotas* FX Concepts	351
15	Currency Risk versus Return in Global Bond Portfolios: A Policy, not a Benchmark Issue *Charles Dolan* Pareto	357
	Index	369

About the Editor

Jessica James joined the Citibank FX® Risk Advisory Group from Bank One, where she headed their Risk Advisory and Currency Overlay group in Europe. Her group was responsible for the design, marketing and maintenance of currency overlay strategies, and the provision of bespoke research to Bank clients, supporting internal marketing. At Citigroup, she is closely involved in both these areas, working with marketers and clients to uptier relationships. Jessica is well known for her research, with several books to her credit and a regular publication record in the financial press. Additionally, she teaches a number of financial mathematics courses and sits on the board of the *Journal of Quantitative Finance*, and the ICBI finance conference board. She has participated in several government Task Forces and is involved with the Institute of Physics as a member of their governing body and a member of their Industry and Business Board.

The major part of Jessica's current research is in the FX area. Over the last few years she has been at the forefront of development of currency risk management models and overlay strategies, and has pioneered the use of Extreme Value Theory to manage the risk of large FX moves. Additionally, she has a wealth of experience in the practical process of setting up currency overlay as a business unit, including trading strategy testing, design and marketing. At Bank One, she was in charge of trading sheet design and strategy execution, and instigated and specified a continuous testing process to ensure that the strategies performed within the bounds of expectations.

In addition to her FX research, Jessica is known for her work on interest rates, having written an extensive work on modelling and valuation (Interest Rate Modelling, Wiley 2000). She has also published in the credit and risk management areas. Prior to her career in finance, Jessica lectured in physics at Trinity, Oxford, having completed her PhD in Theoretical Atomic and Nuclear Physics in 1994.

Foreword

The currency aspect of international investing and institutional investors' focus on risks and returns that are associated with foreign exchange has increased significantly over recent years. The foreign exchange (FX) market has come to be viewed as an asset class in its own right. Investors who have diversified their portfolios, after receiving lower than expected returns from the traditional asset classes, have established currency management as an effective tool to boost returns (or reduce risk). The field of currency risk management is extremely well established among fixed income managers, who have traditionally viewed their bond and currency decisions in an integrated fashion. However equity managers have had a tendency to neglect this topic, having held the view that the impact of foreign exchange will even out over time. While basic theory states that the long-term expected return of currencies is zero, few managers today have the patience to wait for the currencies to reverse to mean (if indeed this theory holds true). In an environment where every pip counts, and where cross-border returns appear very attractive, fund managers and investors are predicted to become major market participants. Portfolio and currency diversification are now combining to create a buoyant currency market.

Citigroup has been in the FX market for more than a century. Though this experience is undeniably valuable the variability of the world's largest market-place is such that constant study and adaptation is required. This book, created in collaboration with Risk Books, is part of our commitment to our clients to continuously develop better understanding of the currency markets, as well as the role of FX in international investing. We have enlisted contributions from experienced market professionals from some of the world's most successful international investing and currency management firms. We hope readers will gain tremendous insights into the world of FX, currency overlay, currency modelling as well as risk management and trading. Additionally, we thank the contributors for their efforts in clarifying some of the most important issues in this area within this volume and hope that this title becomes a worthwhile addition to the literature and will assist in inspiring debate and developments in the sector.

As markets change and investors demand more from a bank than just a good price, Citigroup has taken pride in being the first in many novel areas. This collaboration with Risk Books represents just one of the recent innovations in the area of FX where we aim to be the premier provider of risk management advice and services.

Lars Olesen
Managing Director
Sales Manager Global Foreign Exchange
Citigroup

List of Contributors

Chris Attfield is a partner in PaR Asset Management LLP, a model-based currency hedge fund, with responsibility for trading model development and risk management. Prior to this, he was the senior analyst for the Strategic Risk Management Advisory group of Bank One (formerly First Chicago), where he worked alongside Dr Jessica James. During a seven-year career at Bank One he was extensively involved in risk analysis work for the Bank's clients. Chris started his career in foreign exchange option structuring; he has given seminars on option theory and risk management and has written articles for *Derivatives Week* and *Quantitative Finance*.

James Binny joined ABN AMRO in London in 2003 as a director of FX Risk Advisory. He has been involved with currency management since 1990, initially as a quantitative analyst and then as an investment manager at Natwest Investment Management. In 1995 he moved to GNI Fund Management, where he developed and managed two leveraged derivative funds – one of which was a currency fund. In addition, he advised other fund managers on risk management techniques and assessed potential leveraged fund managers. Between 1998 and 2003, James was a senior investment manager and currency specialist at Gartmore Investment Management. He specialises in techniques for the management of currency. James holds a BA in engineering science from Oxford University.

Eric Busay is a portfolio manager at CalPERS, with over 20 years currency trading, foreign fixed income, sales and portfolio management experience. Eric is responsible for CalPERS' multi billion US dollar currency overlay program consisting of an internal program and external managers, the International (non USD) Fixed Income program, which is entirely managed by external managers and co manages the (Yankee) Sovereign Portfolio in house. Before joining CalPERS, Eric held positions as a proprietary currency and fixed income trader at Koch Industries, Inc., responsible for the multi billion-dollar company-wide currency exposures. Previously, he held a wide variety of trading, sales and management positions with the Toronto Dominion Bank, including that of Chief Dealer and Director of the Currency Desk. Eric earned his undergraduate degree from The University of British Columbia, in honors economics, and also completed studies at McGill University and the University Of California, Davis. He is a chartered financial analyst.

Charlie Dolan is the senior portfolio manager for Global Bonds at Pareto Partners in Los Angeles. He also directs investment research in a number of areas of quantitative finance including risk management, security screening, and macro economic modelling. Before joining Pareto, Charlie directed research projects at the Hughes Research Laboratories in such areas as knowledge-based systems, natural language processing, database management and information warfare. Charlie is the author of various papers on yield curve modelling, artificial intelligence, cognitive science, neural networks, and genetic algorithms.

Ron Liesching is chief research officer at Pareto Partners, of which he was a founder in 1991. Ron started his career at Hoare Govett 30 years ago, analysing currency and interest rates for institutional investors. In 1976 he joined Chase Bank's New York treasury department, working on hedging the bank's foreign currency and interest rate exposures, before joining Chase Investment Bank. He then worked for NatWest Investment Management as head of quantitative products. Ron developed the currency management approach and introduced institutional currency overlay products. He has written and lectured around the world on currency and risk management and edited the first book on risk budgeting. Ron studied mathematics at Cambridge, and mathematics and economics at Lancaster.

Arun S. Muralidhar joined FX Concepts in 2001 as managing director of investment research from JP Morgan Fleming asset management, where he was managing director, responsible for North American marketing of the currency product, and head of currency research. Prior to this, Arun was a member of the investment management committee and head of the research and analytics group at the World Bank. As a plan sponsor, he developed and implemented an innovative risk-controlled currency overlay program for the World Bank's pension fund. He is the author of the book *"Innovations in Pension Fund Management,"* and of many papers on pension finance. He is currently co-authoring *"Rethinking Pension Reform,"* with Professor Franco Modigliani. Arun serves on the advisory board for the *Journal of Asset Management* and the *Journal of Performance Measurement*. Arun holds a PhD in managerial economics from the MIT Sloan School of Management.

Henrik Pedersen is vice president of the CitiFX Risk Advisory Group. He began this role in 2000 and is responsible for developing financial products, proprietary trading models and enhanced hedging solutions for institutional investors. He has published several articles on risk management and is a frequent speaker at seminars and conferences. From 1997 to 2000, Henrik was responsible for the Emerging Markets FX Sales effort to Citigroup's European client base, and led the initiative to develop risk management models and solutions for emerging market exposures. Henrik also has extensive experience in foreign exchange sales and marketing, which he gained during his tenure with the global corporate FX and options sales teams at Citigroup and Chase starting in 1991. In these positions he managed relationships with key multinational clients, corporate and proprietary risk takers. Before commencing his career in banking, Henrik was with A.P Moller Group (Copenhagen), where he managed the group's FX, cash management and money market risks from 1985. Henrik holds a bachelor of commerce degree from the Copenhagen Business School.

Neil Record is currently the chairman of Record Currency Management (currency overlay specialists) in the UK. Neil founded Record in 1983. Prior to this, he worked at the Bank of England as an economist and at Mars as a commodity and currency buyer/trader. Neil has lectured at the Judge Institute at Cambridge University and has recently published a book on currency overlay. Neil holds an MA degree in philosophy and psychology from Balliol College, Oxford and an MSc in economics from University College, London.

Philip Simotas is president and director of Investment Management at FX Concepts. Here, he heads up all aspects of the firm's investment management activities, which include trading, portfolio administration, client servicing, investment research functions and marketing. In addition, he is also chairman of the product development committee, which is responsible for directing the firm's research efforts with respect to enhancing and creating new trading strategies. Philip began his career in derivatives at Dean Witter in 1986, where he was Foreign Exchange Strategist. From 1987 to 1993, Philip was assistant vice president and senior trader on Dean Witter's foreign exchange desk. He has also served as deputy chief of the foreign exchange department. Philip is a *cum laude* graduate of Yale University.

Brian Strange is a client portfolio manager in the currency management group of JP Morgan Fleming Asset Management. Previously, he worked for Key Asset Management in Cleveland, Ohio, where he was the director of client services for institutional accounts. Prior to this, he founded Currency Performance Analytics, a specialist consulting firm advising on currency overlay management issues, and developing meaningful analytical data to assess currency overlay skill. Brian has spoken frequently at investment conferences and has had articles published by *AIMR Publications, European Fund Manager, European Pension News, Global Investor, Investments & Pensions Europe and Pensions & Investments*. Brian obtained an MBA in international finance from the University of Chicago's

Graduate School of Business and earned a masters degree in applied economics from the University of Louvain, Belgium.

James van den Heule joined Citigroup in 1994, where he traded both spot and forward foreign exchange and worked within the corporate and investor sales teams. In 1998 after introducing the benchmark trading concept he became the inaugural member of the Global FX e-commerce team and has subsequently been central to both the sales efforts and new product developments. After leaving university he worked on specific projects for the Bank of Yokohama and Shell plc. His further studies at the Warwick Business School centred on entrepreneurship and small business, skills later employed with the development of Internet trading within Citigroup Foreign Exchange. James was educated at Warwick University, graduating with a BSc in industrial economics.

Gerben de Zwart is a specialist in quantitative currency forecasting models. He joined Robeco in 1998, first as a student trainee and later as researcher. Gerben has been the chairman of the Robeco currency research taskforce since 2001. He has been involved in several joint research projects with Dutch universities and international investment banks and his other research interests include emerging markets and risk management. Gerben graduated in technical mathematics from Delft University of Technology and was awarded the CFA charter in 2003.

Introduction

Jessica James

Citigroup

For far too long there has been a shroud of mystery over the mechanics of foreign exchange rate trading models. "Do they work?" some people ask, "Have traders and currency overlay companies just been lucky?" and, inevitably, the question arises: "If FX models work, how do they work?"

There is an idea of hugely complex models built by teams of PhDs, which give mysterious signals to buy or sell. Somehow, because the FX markets are complex and unique, they are assumed to be untradable except by some elite.

There is no need for this. For the past 20 years, in some cases, companies have been successfully trading the FX markets with simple models that regularly deliver robust returns. This may seem unnatural – surely this very trading activity would negate such profitable market features? – however, it is in fact because of the distinctive nature of the FX markets. Many FX transactions are not done to make money, but because they have to be done to match other cashflows, or to hedge, or as part of other deals. In the equity market it may be fair to say that the vast majority of transactions occur with profit in mind. In the FX market this is far from true, and thus patterns persist over the years.

Another feature of the markets that makes it feasible for trading patterns to persist is that they are not easily traded to give large amounts of risk-free profit. All trading models have associated risks and require careful implementation. One may have confidence that over the next two or three years a careful modelling approach will yield returns, but not over the next six months. The "available" money in the FX markets is not risk-free, and not of huge size. When models are used to enhance returns in currency overlay situations, then they have, over the years, yielded in the region of 1% per annum. This isn't a pot of gold at the end of the rainbow – it is a persistent set of behaviours, which may be monetised if care is taken.

Thus, the purpose of this book is to expand, in a simple and directly useful manner, on the models in the market, how they came about and how the markets came to be the way they are, and how to implement them. To that end, it is divided into four sections:

SECTION 1 – INTRODUCTION TO FX MARKETS AND MODELLING

One of the very longest-running currency overlay companies in the world is Record Overlay, which has for about 20 years been steadily managing FX risk for clients. Neil Record, in the first chapter of this book, gives a comprehensive overview of market history and structure, highlighting the emergence of FX trading strategies as they became feasible. The markets have changed over the years in more ways than one, and in Chapter 2 James van den Heule of Citigroup takes the reader on a tour of the different ways of dealing and gaining access to the market, which these days is more electronic than human. The unique features of the FX market are identified by Jessica James of Citigroup in Chapter 3, "Risks and Rewards", and Arun Muralidhar of the overlay company FX Concepts explains in Chapter 4 where overlay fits into the market in terms of product and usage. Finally, in Chapter 5, Brian Strange of JP Morgan states the case for overlay and FX alpha trading over the years. Brian has been a pioneer in this field, publishing some of the very earliest comprehensive surveys on the subject, which opened investors' eyes to the fact that overlay and modelling techniques seemed to be "working" and delivering returns.

SECTION 2 – CURRENCY RISK AND HEDGING

The nature of FX risk and how it is managed are dealt with by Jessica James of Citigroup in Chapter 6, and Chapter 7 gives a comprehensive picture of traditional hedging techniques, from Chris Attfield at

PaR associates. Active versus passive hedging is covered by Henrik Pedersen of Citigroup in Chapter 8, exploring the differences between the passive benchmark-driven approach to hedging and the more model-driven active approach, and in Chapter 9 Eric Busay of CalPERS discusses the all-important issue of how much to hedge.

SECTION 3 – DESIGNING AND IMPLEMENTING A TRADING STRATEGY

This is in a sense the heart of the book, where the details of the commonly used market models are laid bare. While we cannot claim to cover every possible type of market model, the fact that most CTA returns may be explained by the used of a simple triple moving average bring home the fact that the majority of models in use are variations on this type of theme. The basic models are covered by Jessica James of Citigroup in Chapter 10, and their performance over the last decade is analysed in detail. James Binney of ABN AMRO covers general modelling techniques and market practice and the categorisation of models in Chapter 11; this is followed in Chapter 12 by model building and testing by Gerben de Zwart from Robeco. Finally, who better to discuss strategy implementation than Ron Liesching of the hugely successful Pareto? This section of the book should leave the reader with a solid grasp of modelling and implementation techniques.

SECTION 4 – CASE STUDIES

To end the book, we have two case studies focusing on specific issues in the FX management/overlay area. Philip Simotas of FX Concepts discusses prime brokerage, and Charles Dolan of Pareto analyses risk and return in global bond portfolios.

The chapters of the book, while forming a coherent whole, nevertheless stand alone in their own right. We envisage that while some readers will enjoy the book as a whole, for others it may tend to fall open at a particularly useful or relevant point. It is one of the very first volumes to tackle this fascinating and fast-growing area, and it is interesting to speculate on how it may be viewed in a decade or so's time. Of one thing we are quite sure – styles and fashions may change, but the FX markets will still be there, and people will still be using models to trade them. Let's see if they are the same ones.

Part 1

Introduction to FX Markets and Modelling

1
Market History and Structure
Neil Record
Record Currency Management

INTRODUCTION

This chapter is designed to give an overview of a unique market – that of the exchange of one currency for another. The impatient reader could probably choose to skip this chapter, and not miss any information vital to the understanding of currency overlay and currency management. However, those readers who do take the trouble to read it will discover that in almost every major aspect, the foreign exchange (FX) market is fundamentally different from every other market they are familiar with. In particular, they may discover that the differences are wider and more fundamental than may appear on the surface.

The FX world as we know it started in 1972–3, and the majority of this chapter will therefore deal with the last 30 years. However, the reader will gain an understanding of how we got to where we are today with a bare minimum of knowledge about conditions prior to 1971. This chapter will also allow the reader to understand *why* the FX market in its current form is only 30 years old.

PRE-1945: THE ROLE OF GOLD

Gold (and to a lesser extent silver) had played a fundamental role in money from the birth of specialised economies – that is the stage at which people did not only consume the products of their own labour. By a process of long evolution, these two precious metals emerged as the prime candidate for *money* – a means of exchange and a store of value. Their qualities made them ideal – at least for a particular stage in economic development – for this role. They are portable; they are not a promise from a government or other agency; they have a limited and reasonably predictable supply; they do not physically degrade; and they are difficult to "forge" – imitations are generally detectable without high technology.

For these reasons, by the advent of the Industrial Revolution, those governments that were presiding over the newly industrialising economies had to deal with a whole lot of new problems related to the massively expanded need for both money and a unit of account for the new capital markets. Fiat money (a paper certificate of deposit with, and therefore a debt on, a government-authorised bank), which was not new but was not widely used until the end of the 18th century, became a major economic element in the 19th century. But throughout the whole of the 19th century, and for the 20th century until 1931 (and even up to 1971 in the US) the idea of notes as money was based on their being a representation of an underlying stock of gold that the government was willing to exchange for the notes at a fixed rate. This belief ran deep for all of this period, and whether or not a currency happened to be "on the Gold Standard" at the time, the public believed, or wanted to believe, that a note (or indeed the next derivative: a statement of account of deposits with a non-government bank – or "bank account") was all ultimately backed by gold.

In the 19th century, this fixing of all the major currencies to the Gold Standard meant effectively fixed exchange rates. If each currency was referenced to a weight of gold, then this was clearly a given – since arbitrage would ensure no wide deviation. In the "golden age" of the Gold Standard (1834–1919), each US dollar was equivalent to 23.22 grains of pure gold, and each pound sterling was equivalent to 112.997 grains of pure gold.[1] (Prior to 1717, the pound sterling was one troy pound weight of sterling silver – a high-purity silver. After 1717, the pound sterling was moved de facto onto the gold, rather than the silver, standard). The conversion values above meant that the US dollar/UK pound sterling exchange-rate parity was 112.997/23.22 = 4.866. This was fixed by the definition of the currency units, and the laws of physics! In the

1870s, the UK and US (plus Canada and Australia) were joined on the Gold Standard by most of the rest of the currencies of the developed world. Between that decade and 1914, the world was one of almost completely fixed exchange rates. It was also a period of higher real growth – but, with high real economy volatility the price for exchange rate, and therefore monetary, stability.

There was, however, an element of self-stabilisation built into the system, and it worked as follows. When demand for one currency exceeded another, or vice versa, the price might drift a little from the gold-weight-equivalent "gold point", but then arbitrage would begin to come in. A currency in excess supply (because its imports exceeded its exports) would be bought a little cheaply by arbitrageurs, converted into gold, the gold shipped to the country where currency was in demand, and the gold converted into expensive currency. This might sound very crude, but it was very effective, and had a certain "ring" to it – deficit countries had to sell and export their gold to finance their deficit. No gold – no deficit possible.

Except not quite: a further mechanism was present, depending on the prevailing political and economic stance of the relevant government. This was the so-called *monetary stabilisation policies* – surprisingly akin to modern-day monetary intervention. Deficit countries could attract arbitrage capital by raising the discount rate. However, higher domestic interest rates would tend to lower domestic demand – provide the stimulus for a cycle of adjustment, via higher unemployment to lower wages and prices. This would feed back into lower export prices, which would stimulate export demand – re-establishing the balance of payments. The interest rate differentials were narrower than was common in the 20th century because there was generally perceived to be no exchange-rate risk.

This was the world until around 1931, when, through a chronic inability to achieve a trade balance, sterling finally abandoned the Gold Standard. The period 1931–8 was famously characterised by economic depression, followed by the economic stimulus of rearmament leading to World War Two. In the US, Roosevelt's popular New Deal softened up economic thinking on deficit finance and direct government spending to stimulate the economy.

This was reflected in the economics of World War Two, which were very important to the subsequent development of international monetary arrangements. At the simplest level, macroeconomists lived through a period when laissez-faire and government inactivity meant depression; government spending, financed by borrowing, meant growth, prosperity and (for the Allies) military success.

Running up to the end of the war, and in its aftermath, it is therefore not surprising that the architects of the "new order", apart from being dominated by Anglo-American thinking (since they were the victors), were also dominated by economists and politicians with a bent towards national economic planning, fiscal lassitude and the responsibility of governments for the regulation of economic activity and cycles.

POST-1945: BRETTON WOODS – PHILOSOPHY AND PURPOSE

In July 1944, before the end of the war, under the auspices of the fledging United Nations, a conference was held at the New Hampshire town of Bretton Woods to redesign the world monetary system in the light of the economic effects of the war, and what was seen as the stability necessary to allow world trade to be re-established and grow. Two international institutions emerged from this conference: the International Monetary Fund (IMF) and the International Bank for Reconstruction and Development (IBRD – colloquially known as the "World Bank"). The latter was a state-sponsored provider of long-term development capital, and has turned, 60 years on, into an aid institution for less developed countries. The IMF was the coordinating institution for the Bretton Woods monetary arrangements.

Without going into the institutional details, the idea was to create currency stability based around the US dollar, rather than gold. Gold was still to play a role, although more minor, as the US Federal Reserve Bank agreed to maintain convertibility of the US dollar into gold at a fixed US dollar price.

Each major currency agreed to peg its currency against the dollar, and also against an artificial unit of account created by the IMF called Special Drawing Rights (SDRs).[2]

The core purpose of these arrangements, although not fully stated, was to replicate what was then seen as the "golden age" of international trade, 1871–1914, when gold was king, the UK was the guarantor and liquidity provider of the international monetary system, and international trade was growing strongly. The Bretton

Woods architects imagined that these arrangements were the best environment for encouraging trade and investment. In particular, they rejected the rather chaotic interwar arrangements, in which confidence in the system had been lost, international trade and capital flows had fallen dramatically and the UK had lost its place as leader of the monetary world order. The alternative, of fully floating exchange rates, was implicitly, if not explicitly, seen as a return to those chaotic arrangements.

Under fixed rates, "currency trading" as we now understand it simply did not exist. There was no opportunity (except for party adjustments – see below) to take currency positions for profit other than the role of commercial bank price-giver.

ROLE OF GOVERNMENTS

The architects of Bretton Woods, intellectually led by John Maynard Keynes, firmly believed that it was the role of governments to conduct international trade at exchange rates fixed by politicians. The implications of this are far reaching, and worth enumerating:

Firstly, governments have to put in place the arrangements for central bank intervention to limit price movements to the agreed bands (and under Bretton Woods they were very narrow bands – ±1%).

Secondly, governments have to decide whether and to what extent they maintain exchange controls to further their ability to control rates and their policy aims.

Thirdly, governments have to ensure that they have sufficient reserves (either in the central bank or in the IMF pool arrangements) to support their own currency.

Fourthly, governments have to take the domestic action necessary to maintain the agreed exchange-rate parity.

At the time of Bretton Woods, the Western powers clearly believed both that governments were in a position to maintain this level of intervention and, more crucially, that the benefits of the fixed-rate structure outweighed the obvious costs and political risks.

The idea that exchange rates should be flexible, to allow price signals to feed through to national economies, was not on the agenda.

CURRENT ACCOUNT STRAINS AND PARITY ADJUSTMENTS

The practical effect of the Bretton Woods regime was that current account deficits, and capital flight, became the direct responsibility of the government in question. Under the Gold Standard this was also true, but the absolute nature of the gold convertibility, and the general belief that the gold parity was sacrosanct, meant that the political will was there to force the domestic economy to adjust. If this meant general falls in price levels, and sharp rises in unemployment, then these were regarded as the natural concomitant of international monetary discipline.

HONG KONG – A 21ST-CENTURY GOLD STANDARD?

There is an interesting parallel between Gold Standard countries in the "golden age", and modern day Hong Kong. Hong Kong stands out as an economy that has demonstrated not only an unshakable political commitment to one parity (HKD/USD = 7.80), but also an ability to adjust price and interest rate levels within the economy to allow the parity level to survive very significant shocks. However, the impact of choosing to make the internal economy the "pressure release valve", rather than the exchange rate, should not be underestimated. The graph below shows HK domestic interest rates in the 1997–9 period, when the parity was under speculative attack:

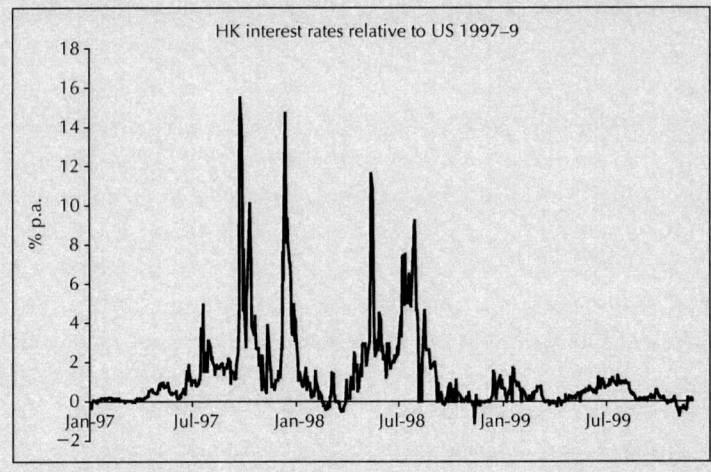

This was in spite of concerted intervention by the HK Monetary Authority and other fiscal measures.

The new social democratic agenda, particularly in postwar UK, ruled out such harsh medicine. The UK had a reforming, nationalising, central-planning-oriented Labour government, who believed in the improvement of the lot of the ordinary people by severely limiting the power of the market. Wage cuts did not form part of that agenda.

The lack of two-way price flexibility in the UK's domestic labour and goods markets meant that the exchange rate had to take the strain of either external shocks or structural weaknesses. The pound was devalued against the US dollar by 30% in 1949, and by 14% in 1967. Among the other major currencies, the French franc was similarly subject to periodic devaluations.

Parity adjustments gave the only opportunity for currency traders (banks; commercial users) to take speculative positions in currencies for prospective gain, although the infrequent nature of devaluations, the limited liquid capital available during this period, and exchange controls (see below) meant that such trading was relatively small scale.

EXCHANGE CONTROLS

The planning and controlling instincts of the Bretton Woods architects extended to exchange controls. Many of the IMF members who maintained fixed exchange rates (vs the US dollar) could do so at acceptable political cost only with the use of exchange controls. For many countries, this found rather bizarre expression in the situation that foreigners were allowed to buy and sell a particular currency at will, but that the citizens of that currency's country were not permitted to do so. Most European countries maintained some exchange controls for residents long after the collapse of the Bretton Woods system, and some were finally demolished only in the run-up to the euro in 1999. Broadly speaking, however, exchange controls had one purpose: to prevent or restrict those who wished to *sell* a currency at the currently prevailing prices from doing so. Most countries with exchange controls (which tended to be those with perennial inflation and/or trade deficit problems) had no desire to prevent anyone from *buying* their currency. In the Bretton Woods era, this asymmetry was more notable than today. Generally speaking, countries under Bretton

Woods were responsible for their currency's potential weakness – not their potential strength. So devaluation was seen as single-country response to poor economic management and performance, whereas the counterpart – the relative appreciation by the remaining countries – was not seen as "their fault", or as an event for which they were responsible.

The exchange control regimes in the UK and France in the 1940–70s meant that it was virtually impossible for residents of those countries to move money into US dollars (or other appreciating currencies) to coincide with devaluations. In the UK, however, there was a parallel FX market, known as the "dollar pool", in which UK institutional investors could buy US dollars for investment purposes, and into which repatriating UK investors could sell US dollars. The pool was, in effect, an auction clearing-house for UK-owned assets already offshore, and freely traded at a significant premium (15–20%) to the normal exchange rate. It did, however, provide a rather esoteric corner of the FX market where traders could exercise their skill and risk their money. The pool abruptly disappeared, with the US dollar premium falling to zero overnight, when the UK summarily abolished all exchange controls in October 1979.

CENTRAL BANK CONTROL

The Bretton Woods system placed central banks at the heart of the foreign exchange market, but not its sole participants. Apart from a small number of highly restrictive countries, the commercial banking sector operated within the constraints of the fixed regime in a symbiotic relationship with the central banks. Bretton Woods defined ±1% bands within which currencies could fluctuate against the SDR (and the US dollar), and central banks had a Treaty obligation to defend these rates.[3] For much of the 1945–71 period it was taken for granted that the parities would be defended with the full vigour and force of not only the governments and central banks of the weaker currencies, but also the combined resources of the IMF – which maintained reserves, subscribed to by its members, designed for exactly this eventuality.

Commercial (money centre) banks were therefore given much more of an administrative role than a market-making role in foreign exchange, and they always knew that they could offload any outstanding unmatched currency with the central bank at the edge of the parity bands at worst. In practice, of course, rates traded well inside parity, as arbitrageurs (in practice the banks) could take stabilising positions near to the bands with (near) impunity. As with the Gold Standard regime 75 years earlier, there were small trends within the bands, which were often indicative of consistent surpluses or deficits putting pressure on one or other side of the band. Usually domestic interest-rate adjustments were used to sort these out (both encouraging capital flows and at least in theory moderating domestic demand one way or the other).

Realignments could be dangerous, of course, to mismatched positions, but mostly these were sufficiently rare, and well flagged, that any position that relied on the parity bands would be unwound prior to an actual devaluation. As with all realignments within fixed-rate systems, however, the shrewd operators had to read the signs. Since no politician can contemplate in public a realignment prior to its happening, this does require a certain awareness of the political and economic tensions.

THE BEGINNING OF THE MODERN ERA – 1972–3
Oil and "oil balances"

This settled state of affairs began to change in the late sixties, and was given a massive spur at the beginning of the seventies with successive oil price rises, which created for the first time very large international liquidity. This sudden appearance of "hot" money started the development of the huge, liquid and unregulated foreign exchange markets that we see today.

Oil was not the cause of the breakdown of Bretton Woods – just a further catalyst to the complete abandonment of attempts at fixed-rate systems. The cause was the same as all breakdowns in planned and controlled economic systems: that regulations and controls, embodied in physical constraints and fixed (artificial) prices, prevented price signals flowing through to all the players in the market.

In the FX market case, countries with weak external trade balances (and in this case it was mainly the US and UK) found themselves unable to finance these without unacceptable domestic consequences, and were unable to depreciate their exchange rates to stimulate export demand.

The timing was instructive: US President Nixon decided to suspend convertibility of the US dollar to gold in August 1971. This

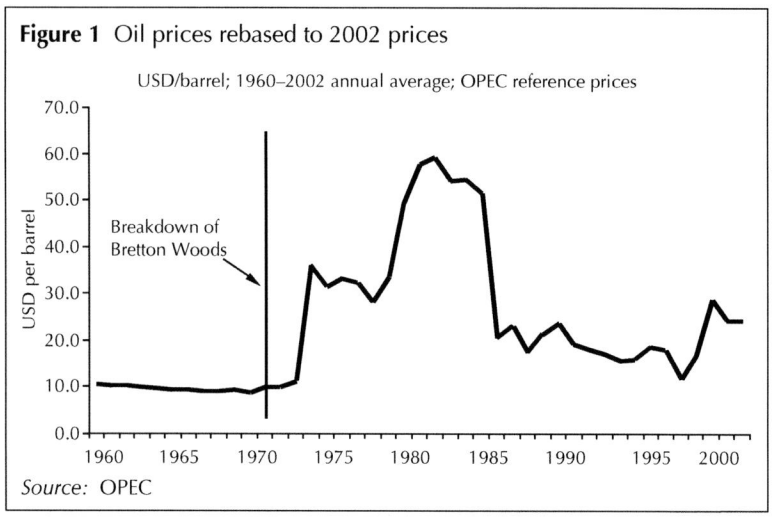

Figure 1 Oil prices rebased to 2002 prices
USD/barrel; 1960–2002 annual average; OPEC reference prices
Source: OPEC

was in response to continuous leakage of US gold, a symptom of a persistent US trade deficit, itself a symptom of persistent overvaluation of the US dollar versus the other major trading countries (particularly Germany and Japan). Figure 1 shows that this was fully two years before the oil price explosion.

However, while oil was not directly implicated in the breakdown, the impact of the massive trade deficits and surpluses generated by the transfer of "resources" (money) in the ensuing years ensured that even the most hardened advocates of a planned international monetary and exchange rate regime could not sustain a return to fixed rates.

The mechanics are important to the development of the FX market, and worked as follows. In 1974, the industrialised economies were suddenly faced with bills for their imported oil, some three times higher than a year earlier. The ability of most of these economies to substitute other energy for oil was very limited in the short term, and so the demand for oil was very inelastic. So, if the industrialised economies had been spending, say, USD 50 billion a year on imported oil before the price rise, after the rise, they would be paying, say, USD 140 billion (not quite three times, but nearly). The extra USD 90 billion per annum was cash straight out of the pockets of Western consumers and into the pockets of OPEC members. The immediate effect in the West was a fall in domestic demand, a massive increase in the trade deficit and inflation. The counterpart of this is that OPEC members, in both private and public sectors, had these huge and ballooning cash balances, and nowhere obvious to invest them, certainly in the short term – their own capital markets were undeveloped, and totally unable to cope with this enormous scale. The only possible investment targets were foreign markets, but most equity markets were very weak on the back of the oil price and subsequent interest-rate rises. Faced with this unprecedented problem, OPEC members did what any investor would do – leave the money in cash. However, when the "cash" is measurable in whole percentages of world GDP, this decision has far-reaching consequences.

Western bank balance sheets ballooned as these balances (which are liabilities from the perspective of the banks) grew. The currencies of original payment of the invoices, (mainly US dollars, but also European currencies and the yen) were not converted into other currencies (which other currency could they be converted into?). The banks had to put this money to work, ie, lend it to the private- and public-sector "owners" of the trade deficit in the Western economies. The circle was thereby squared (as it always will be in international trade) – the West's deficits were financed, and the OPEC countries had a temporary home for their unexpected billions.

However, the OPEC owners of cash balances had the opportunity for the first time to switch between currencies "on a whim". The money was in cash, it was a matter of a moment to ring a bank, and ask for it to be transferred to another currency account. This series of chance events was in effect the start of what for 30 years became known generically as the "Euro-markets".

This chaotic and crises-ridden muddle was the unlikely setting for the foundation of the modern FX market that we see today. For the first time in the post-war era, currency markets began to be the clearing-house for the ever-changing desires of participants – creating ever-changing exchange rates. From this point, currency trading (in the modern sense) began.

"EURO" MARKETS
The expression "Euro-markets" has largely disappeared by the time of writing (2003), but the Euro-markets were a phenomenon

of fundamental importance to many markets, but in particular to FX market development.[4] In simple terms, the Euro-markets were the unregulated, "free" or even "black" markets. They reflected the "real" price, unmuddied by national regulations.

The key to understanding the Euro-markets is the importance of location for the application of national laws and regulations. The "oil balances" of the 1970s and 1980s are a perfect example. These were owned by foreigners when viewed from the perspective of the jurisdictions in which the balances were held. Let us take London as the example jurisdiction. The UK maintained exchange controls over its own citizens until 1979, but was unable to prevent a foreigner who owned sterling from exchanging that sterling for US dollars or Deutschmarks with another foreigner at any rate that was mutually agreeable between the two. Any attempt to impose such control (which would be extremely difficult for a widely held currency like sterling) would immediately cause new foreign investment in sterling to dry up. Since the UK government had every incentive to ensure the continuing attractiveness of not only sterling, but also of London as the foremost location for FX transactions, they made no attempt to control or limit such transactions. In fact, the City of London authorities, and the UK government, made strenuous efforts to continue to attract these types of transaction to London.

In the very strictest sense of the word, a sterling/US dollar transaction between foreigners in London was not a "Euro" deal, because one leg of the transaction (the sterling leg) was in the currency of the host country. A pure "Euro" deal would be a Deutschmark/US dollar deal conducted in London between two non-UK, non-German, non-US residents. In a deal like this, there is no possibility of any legislative control being placed on the deal or its pricing by virtue of the residency of each of the counterparties or the deal location. This is a recipe for free-market pricing.

The "Euro-" or free market in FX, which had always existed in a small way under the influence of the explosion in oil balances, quickly became a huge force in the market that dominated pricing, and eroded to nearly zero the ability of central banks to control pricing. The FX market was always particularly open to this development because at least one of the two legs of an FX deal is always conducted "abroad". To get the best pricing, it is a short step to conduct both legs abroad, or indeed for jurisdictions to recognise this inevitable power of the customer to avoid jurisdiction regulation, and so not bother to attempt to regulate this activity.

Interestingly, in the interest rate markets, which are domestic in nature (therefore much more amenable to jurisdiction control), and also much more politically sensitive, Euro-markets continue to exist. They are defined as the market in a particular currency's interest rate quoted outside that country's jurisdiction, and while the difference between Euro- and domestic market rates has narrowed to near vanishing point for the major currencies (because domestic market restrictions have virtually disappeared), nevertheless the Chicago Mercantile Exchange's Eurodollar futures contract is the world's most actively traded futures contract.[5] The Eurodollar contract is based on the interest rate on a three-month time deposit in a commercial Bank *outside* the US.

So in the early 1970s the FX market as we know it today was born. The two revolutions of that period, the advent of floating rates and the rise to dominance of free (Euro) markets, were the key catalysts for this momentous change.

This large, liquid and volatile new market rapidly attracted the attention of traders who had previously been limited to equity, bond and commodity markets. They came from a wide range of organisations (see the customer's section below), but their common aim was to exploit exchange rate movements for profit. Early in the floating era, traders had little in the way of historical prices to rely on, but by the mid/late-1970s, enough price data had been recorded to allow quantitative FX models to be built for the first time. This development laid the foundations for the active currency management industry, which is the main topic of this book.

The description in the remainder of this chapter of the FX market development is much like the description of the development of the car from 1905 – refinement, sophistication and consolidation – but with the basic structure and design in place.

THE EUROPEAN SNAKE

The advent of floating exchange rates hit an unprepared world in 1971. For 18 months or so until March 1973, the fixed-exchange-rate regime remained fully in place (but in practice moribund), albeit with an 8% devaluation of the US dollar, and wider bands ($\pm 2.25\%$

rather than ±1%).[6] From March 1973, without yet abandoning the legal and treaty structure, all pretence of fixed rates was abandoned.[7]

Meanwhile, European Economic Community (EEC) members, fearful of the loss of control that full floating would bring, agreed among themselves to maintain an exchange-rate "snake", which adopted the ±2.25% variation margin, but applied to each bilateral "central" rate, rather than to the US dollar.[8] This was in effect a narrower limit than the (new but discredited) Bretton Woods margins because it applied to each bilateral rate rather than just to the rate versus the US dollar. The snake was allowed to float against the dollar, hence the name.

In practice the snake was very hard to manage, and it suffered parity changes (and the withdrawal of France and Italy) during its life, which ended in 1979. Its rebirth in the Exchange Rate Mechanism is described below.

THE RISE OF THE YEN

The 1970s also bought a new currency, previously little traded, to prominence. The Japanese economy had been growing very strongly in the 1950s and 1960s, led by even faster export growth. The fixed-exchange-rate regime had in many ways worked in Japanese favour, by allowing their trade surpluses to be absorbed by the stabilisation system, holding down the value of the yen (JPY). This shortage of yen had meant that the yen was not particularly noticeable as an investment currency, and the limitations of technology, of location and the yawning culture gap between Japan and the West meant that the yen remained below the "parapet" both in visibility and in trading volume. While London's *Financial Times* had published spot and forward exchange rates for most major currencies for many decades, the yen was added only in 1979 – an illustration of its previously low profile.

One might have imagined that the abandonment of fixed exchange rates in 1971 exposed the yen to the full force of the free markets. In practice, because of perennial Japanese trade surpluses, and the minor role of the yen, oil balances were not widely held in yen, nor did the OPEC owners regard the yen as a natural home for their money. Japan had little or no oil of its own, so, while the two oil price rises hit the trade balance hard (causing trade deficits in 1973–5 and 1979–81), Japan's economy bounced back rapidly to return to surplus each time. Famously, in the 1980s and 1990s, and even up to the time of writing (2003), Japan remained in large structural trade surplus. By the early 1980s, however, the yen was fully established on the FX market scene, and it quickly became highly important as the Japanese stock market entered a sustained, 10-year bull market, culminating (in 1989) with Japan temporarily overtaking the US as the world's largest stock market.

ERM AND ITS SERIAL CRISES

Meanwhile, in 1979 most EC members, excluding principally the UK, revived the moribund snake into a new fixed-rate regime, the Exchange Rate Mechanism (ERM), within the structure of the European Monetary System (EMS). This included France and Italy, as well as the "surplus" countries (Germany; Netherlands). A complicated system of bands and parities was established around a new EC unit of account (the ECU), with support and intervention mechanisms to be coordinated by the respective central banks. The ±2.25% band for the outer limits of bilateral movement survived, but there were new "indicative" intervention points for rates expressed against the ECU. There was an irritating complication, which was that the pound sterling was not a member of ERM, but it was a member of EMS. This meant that the pound could (and did) vary widely against the basket of European currencies, moving the value of the ECU up and down in such a way that the bilateral rates and the ECU parities became incompatible. In true EC fashion, an "adjusted" ECU was invented, which set the pound at its central rate in the ECU calculation, even if it was trading at a 25% premium or discount to that value.

What was remarkable about the ERM (and the snake before it) was, on the one hand, the similarity to the discredited and abandoned Bretton Woods system (a product of the Depression and World War Two economic planning) and, on the other, the surprising resilience of this dated, creaky and flawed structure. In formal terms, the ERM lasted until 1999, although by 1993 it had been forced to widen its bands to ±15% for all bilateral rates except the Deutschmark and the guilder.

During its 20-year life, the ERM suffered innumerable crises. The most important, disruptive and significant were 1981 (French franc devaluation), 1983 (French franc devaluation), 1992 (sterling, lire and

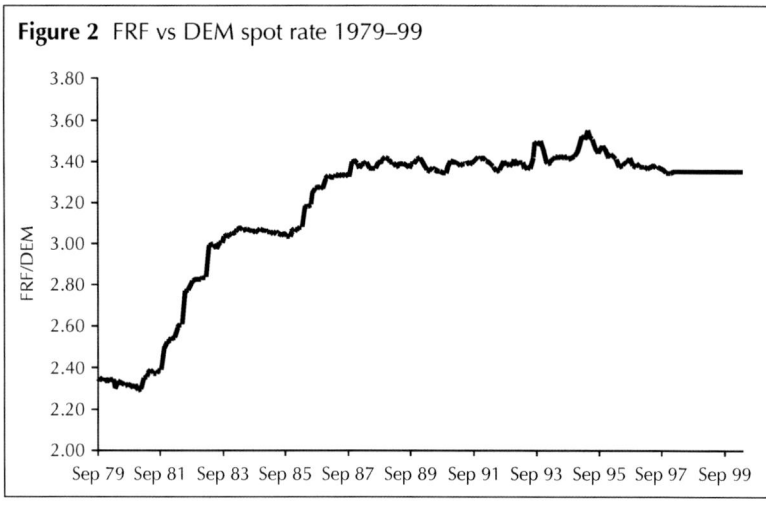

Figure 2 FRF vs DEM spot rate 1979–99

Swedish krone devaluation and forced exit) and 1993 (French franc devaluation and bands widened to ±15%).[9] The tenor of each was mostly the same: high inflation/deficit countries (France and Italy; latterly UK and Sweden) were continually forced to devalue versus their more prudent neighbours. A graph of some of the intra-ERM exchange rates over this period is instructive. Figure 2 shows the French franc (FRF) versus the Deutschmark (DEM) for this period.

The post-1987 period shows that France had begun to adopt a "Franc Fort" policy, but not after significant disruptions in the early 1980s. The Italian lire (ITL) versus the Deutschmark is even more volatile – in fact it is hard to believe from Figure 3 that the ITL was in a fixed-rate regime with the DEM during the entire period covered by this graph!

The chequered history of ERM in the 1980s and early 1990s coincided with a roller-coaster ride for the US dollar, which doubled its value against the DEM in the period 1980–5, and then fell back the whole way in the next three years. These were highly volatile years for exchange rates, which produced tremendous opportunities, and risks, for the currency traders of the period. The frequency of exceptional profits from currency trading (mainly reported by FX market-making banks) is only matched in this period by the frequency of the currency disasters (often from industrial and commercial companies) of those on the other side of these trades.

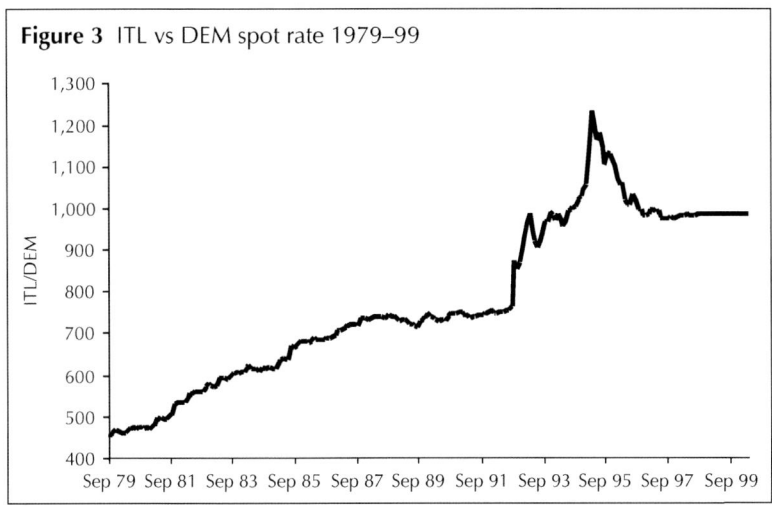

Figure 3 ITL vs DEM spot rate 1979–99

These perennial crises and sequential realignments of the fixed-rate regime came to an end in May 1998, when 11 countries agreed to join a new single European currency, the euro (EUR), and announced the rates at which they would convert their currencies to the euro on 1 January 1999. The legislative framework for the creation of this new currency had been laid in the Maastricht Treaty of 1993, and "kicked into action" by the Dublin Summit of 1996.

From the point of view of the foreign exchange market this had three very important effects:

❏ it signalled the end of any attempt by a group of major industrialised countries to manage their exchange rates within a fixed rate regime;
❏ it removed 11 currencies from the global FX market, many of whom had maintained exchange controls; and
❏ it added one new, large and liquid currency, which had no exchange controls of any sort, and which was not subject to any declared policy of exchange rate management.

THE EURO

The euro is the single currency for 12 EU member states (Germany, France, Italy, Spain, the Netherlands, Austria, Belgium, Finland, Portugal, Ireland, Greece and Luxembourg). The euro was launched in January 1999 with 11 members – Greece did not join initially because it at first failed the economic assessment. It joined in January 2001.

Three EU member states are not members of the euro zone: the UK, Denmark and Sweden. Denmark held a referendum (in September 2000) in which the Danes voted 53–47% not to join the European Single Currency. Sweden held a referendum in September 2003, in which the Swedes voted 56–44% not to join, despite complete "Establishment" support for joining (support from all the main political parties, the unions and the main business organisations). Sweden is technically in an awkward position vis-à-vis the Maastricht Treaty, since, while the UK and Denmark negotiated an "opt-out" of the euro, Sweden did not. It "did not qualify" because of its non-membership of the ERM (and its excessive public debt) at the time of the euro launch, but it "qualifies" now. So the vote to stay out is in breach of Sweden's Treaty obligation to join. This Treaty breach is being swept under the carpet, because it is inconvenient, and because the European Commission does not want to be seen to be "against democracy".

The UK government has famously established five tests to determine whether joining the euro is in the UK's economic interest. In 2003, the government announced that the tests had not been met, and that they could not go forward to a referendum with a recommendation to join. This is likely to delay any referendum on joining until after a 2005 election at the earliest.

The euro is governed by the European Central Bank (ECB), set up under EU Treaties. The ECB has the sole responsibility for monetary policy in respect of the euro. There is a common interest rate across the euro zone, and rules limiting the fiscal flexibility of member states. The principal rule (the Growth and Stability Pact) is that fiscal deficits must not exceed 3% per annum; failure by individual states to meet this target will be met, in theory, by fines, although these have not yet been imposed. Portugal's 2001 public accounts show that it has become the first state to break the 3% limit; and both France and Germany, as well as Portugal, broke the limit in 2002. It appears that France and Germany will again break the limit in 2003, and both governments have not put forward budgets that will pull them back inside the limit in 2004.

At the time of writing, the European commissioner for monetary affairs is considering whether to invoke the excessive-deficit procedure against France, a process that could lead to large fines (about EUR 7.5 billion).

The political difficulty of levying fines on euro zone member states has largely rendered the Stability and Growth pact meaningless. It remains to be seen whether this Achilles' heel in the euro's constitution will prove a real long-term problem for the effective operation of the currency.

Meanwhile, the euro has established itself as the global second currency, behind only the US dollar, on virtually all measures: market liquidity, low cost of dealing and volume of deals in all instruments.

THE BIS SURVEY

In 1986, the Bank for International Settlements (BIS) in Basel, sometimes called the "central bankers' bank", conducted the first official survey of turnover in the foreign exchange market. They did so by asking the central banks of four major FX-dealing centres to poll the banks within their jurisdiction for average turnover in one month – April – of the year in question.

The results showed for the first time the size of the market, as well as its composition (spot, forward, etc). The survey was widely welcomed and the BIS has now established it as a regular triennial event. The latest survey was in 2001, in which 48 central banks participated.[10] The survey results contain a wealth of information about the FX market and its principal instruments. Figure 4 shows a summary of the turnover of the market, and the size of the customer orders that underpin it. We will return to the concept of "customer" later.

One point is immediately notable: just how large this market is. Compare, for example, the FX market's daily turnover in 2001 of USD 1,200 billion with that of the US equity market (NYSE + NASDAQ), which varies widely, but probably averages about USD 70 billion a day. This is partially explained by the distributed nature of the FX market (which is discussed below), but mainly by the very large, natural, two-way demand and supply for currencies from the international trade and investment requirements of the world's businesses and investment pools.

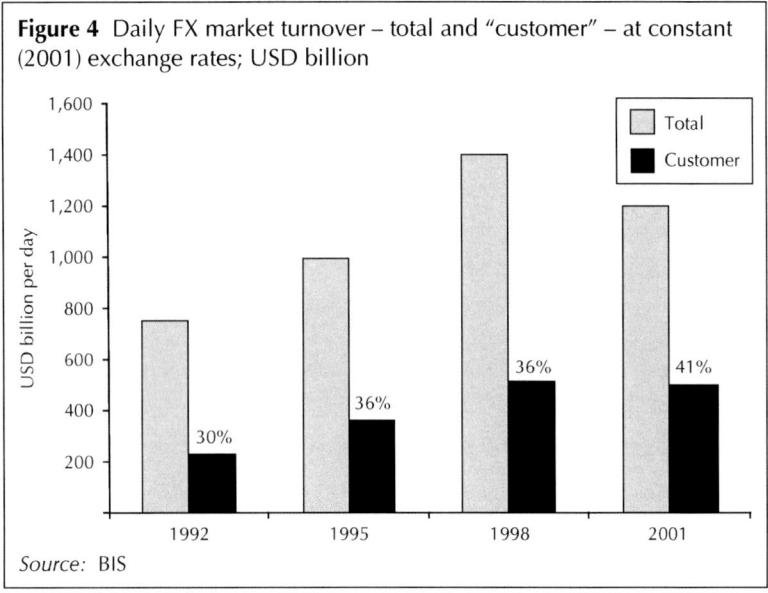

Figure 4 Daily FX market turnover – total and "customer" – at constant (2001) exchange rates; USD billion

Source: BIS

MODERN MARKET STRUCTURE

The modern FX market is not located in one place, nor is it in any tangible sense one "market". So if a TV camera crew want to film, say, the turbulence in the FX market, they cannot go to a defined place, watch what is happening and report from there. Instead, they have to go to a bank dealing room. These are quite photogenic, so our fictional TV crew do not have to worry too much about that. However a bank dealing room is not the FX market: it is one cog in the *machine that makes up* the market.

The bank dealing room is a physical representation of four of the processes in the market:

a. the receiving of customer orders to buy or sell one currency for another;
b. the giving of prices to customers and accepting the deal from the customer (and the currency positions this entails);
c. closing the currency positions either by netting with other deals or by calling other market-making banks, and accepting their prices to offload the risk; and
d. receiving calls from other market-making banks, giving them prices to offload their risk.

The word "calls", can mean telephone calls, or, increasingly likely, other electronic means of communication. Simultaneously with the bilateral communication described above (that is between customer and bank or bank and bank), the private screen networks operated by Reuters and Bloomberg provide all the wholesale users of the market with real-time information on prices across a wide range of currencies and instruments.

Note that "making money out of currency positions" is not included in the functions above. In one sense, of course, "making money" is the only function of the banks that make up the FX market. This will be dealt with later.

In the global FX market, there are numerous bank dealing rooms like that described above, each playing the same role. There is no one else (no clearing house,[11] no regulator,[12] no market committee[13]) in the heart of the market, so the market operates rather like a workstation-based network (distributed processing, all communicating with a server (the price screen networks)), rather than a mainframe-based network, where all the processing and data storage is centralised.

In this structure, deal types c and d are not income-generating to the system as a whole. They simply represent the mechanism for clearing individual bank positions into the global market as a whole. If there were only one bank in the FX market, the surveyed volume would show only customer volume.

This structure was not designed: it evolved. Like biological natural selection, it evolved through the death or demise of competing structures, and by the competitive advantage gained by the technical innovation rewarding the innovators (and punishing the Luddites and laggards). As in all competitive situations, there is an apparent duplication of resources that the central planner may see as unnecessary, and a sitting target for "rationalisation". The elegant thing about duplication, however, is that the customer will continue to pay for duplication only if it is profitable for the customer to do so. The result is continuous operational improvements through competition.

There have been two types of serious competition to this disaggregated/distributed market model.

The first is the *controlled local market*. This still exists in many jurisdictions with exchange controls. In this model, one regulator/market maker (the central bank) makes the rules of the game, but most importantly prevents the local players from accessing the global FX market by imposing controls on the movement of foreign exchange. This type of market can be sustained only by exchange controls, since commercial users would immediately migrate to the cheaper and more liquid global market if allowed to do so.

The other is *currency futures markets*. Futures markets are, at least in theory, very efficient vehicles for the standardising, centralising and clearing of customer orders in liquid, two-way markets. In markets where the local liquidity is poor, or where the commodity dealt is non-standard, or where regulations or tax have been imposed, futures could in theory offer a very attractive alternative. Futures markets have been put head to head with the global FX market on many occasions in the past 20 years, and with one major exception, and some minor exceptions, futures markets have lost out in this competition. The major exception is Chicago Mercantile Exchange (CME), which has established a substantial FX customer base.

Futures markets are most useful to retail and individual users, particularly amateur "FX traders", since access is easy, trading is cheap and the prices are transparent. These are the CME's customers, along with trading houses dealing with other futures contracts. CME accounts for some 70% of the circa USD 12 billion traded daily in FX futures.[14] However, this USD 12 billion accounts for only 2.5% of total FX market customer volume.

INCOME FLOWS

The providers of FX services are supplying a business product, just like the provision of any other goods or services. Contrary to popular myth, the FX market is not the preserve of a "magic circle" of huge multinational banks, although, as we shall see below, they play a particular role within it.

There are a number of niches within the market that provide an attractive business environment, and there are some other rather windswept areas in which the cold wind of competition blows continuously. Broadly speaking, the closer the service provider is to a pure market maker, and the further it is away from the customer, the harsher the environment.

Financial pressures on the providers of FX services take several identifiable forms. On the income side there are two basic categories: volumes of customer orders; and the net profit, in basis points, that the provider is able to make out of that volume. On the expenditure side are the continually rising real (that is inflation-adjusted) pay required to hire and retain highly skilled FX sales and market-making staff; and the cost of technology required (a) to keep up with market standard technology, and (b) to substitute increasingly expensive labour.

Let us concentrate on the income side of the FX business. Any speculative profits or losses I exclude from this analysis, the sector as a whole makes out of position-taking in the market. In practice, over the longer run, these are likely to net out to zero.

The FX market is, except in certain retail segments, a market that operates without commissions. This means that the costs of using the market are on the one hand less visible than, say, the equity market,[15] where there are commissions, but on the other hand the costs are "clean" – the difference between the price to buy and the price to sell (the bid–offer spread[16]) is the only cost that most customers face. There are also no taxes, levies or other costs levied against FX deals.[17]

Figure 5 shows a graphical representation of the spreads that are typically levied by the price-giver in each sector of the market. It needs some elaboration to be understandable. First, it is designed to show the bid–offer spreads charged by the service provider to

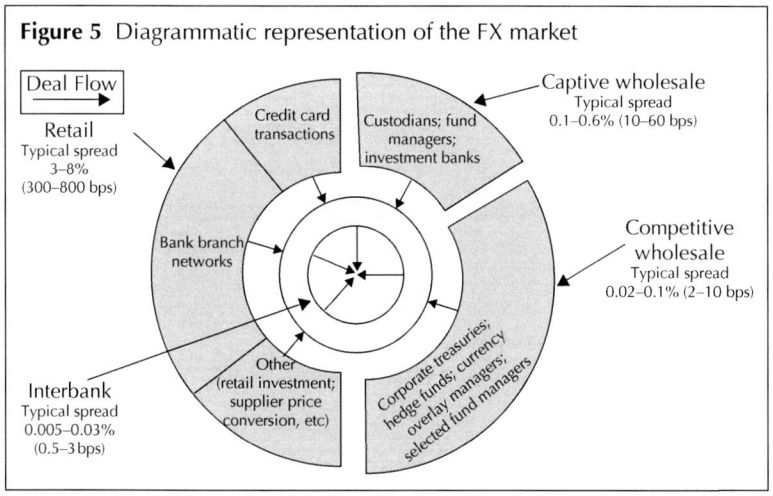

Figure 5 Diagrammatic representation of the FX market

the customer. The definition of a customer is the party who asks for a fixed price in return for being able to deal the amounts, currencies and direction of their choice. The provider is the other party. The deals illustrated in Figure 5 are for spot deals between OECD currencies.[18]

Let us take, for example, the Bank Branch Network. This is where ordinary individuals go to buy their foreign currencies. If a customer wants to buy US dollars with euros, they might get an exchange rate of 1.10 USD/EUR when the mid-price in the FX market at that moment is 1.13. The former is a worse rate for the customer than 1.13 because it means that EUR 100 will buy USD 110 rather than the USD 113 they would have got at the mid-price. Note that there are few firm conventions for quoting exchange rates. Banks (at least in the US, the euro zone and the UK) will tend to quote all exchange rates to their domestic customers with their own currency as the denominator. Hence an American asking to sell euros at their local bank branch would be quoted 0.909 EUR/USD for the same deal, but they would still get USD 100 for their EUR 110. In this example, the spread is $((1.13 - 1.10)/1.10)*2 = 5.45\%$. The distance from the mid-price is multiplied by 2 because the quoted prices are offer to mid, not offer to bid.

This deal (and millions like it) will then be netted by the bank concerned with other deals in the opposite direction, and the net position will be "sent" (electronically) to the FX dealing room of the bank. The net positions (each expressed as single currency positions – the deal above puts the bank "short" of USD 110 and "long" of EUR 100) will be aggregated with all the other deals conducted by the bank that day, and by the end of the business day the bank will ensure that its position in each currency is sold or bought back to (roughly) zero by taking prices (and deals) from the interbank market. In this last role the market-making bank acts as customer – but of course it is also continuously giving prices to similar market-makers, in which they are acting as customer.

This is, of course, a very abbreviated summary of the process, but it gives a flavour of the way in which deals are aggregated, netted and then cleared in the market.

The market will clear when the global sum of desires to buy a currency equals the global sum of desires to sell at any particular moment. The dynamic nature of this equilibrium makes the process quite difficult to visualise and understand, but the principles are identical to any market clearing system – the players in the market will be forced to transact at prices at which they can execute their desires. Those desires change as the price changes (lower price, more demand; higher price, more supply), and this dynamic interaction takes place in real time in the market-making departments of the major FX market-makers.

With the most transitory of exceptions, the FX market is sufficiently large and liquid and unregulated to ensure that there is never a shortage (or surplus) of currency, since the banks will always move prices in such a way as to ensure that every desired deal is executed. The only uncertainty is the price at which "shortages" and "surpluses" can be eliminated.

To get some idea of the scale of each of the segments in Figure 5, we can glean a little more information from the BIS survey. At the first level, the BIS distinguishes between deals with other "reporting" professional counterparties (ie, interbank deals) from customers' deals. This information is shown in Figure 6. The BIS break down the customer segment into only two categories, which they call *non-reporting financial institutions* (including mutual funds, pension funds, hedge

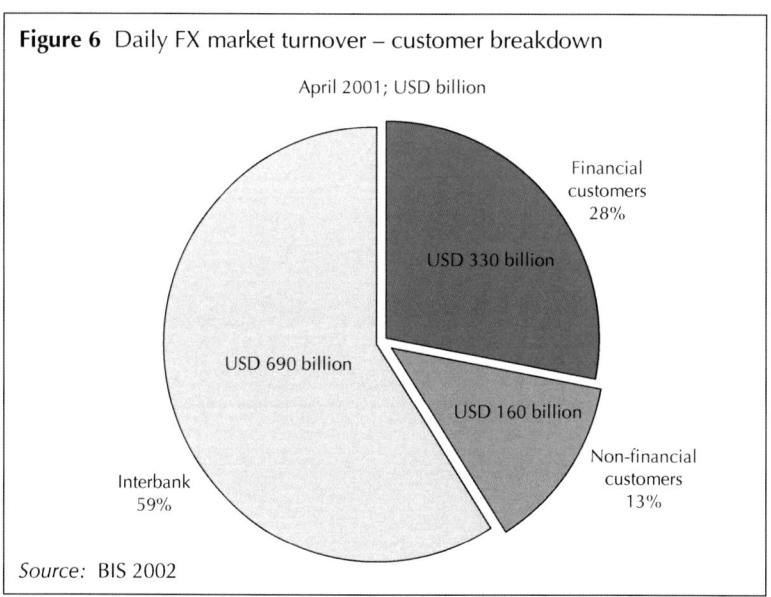

Figure 6 Daily FX market turnover – customer breakdown

April 2001; USD billion

Financial customers 28%
USD 330 billion
USD 690 billion
USD 160 billion
Non-financial customers 13%
Interbank 59%

Source: BIS 2002

funds, currency funds, money market funds, building societies, leasing companies, insurance companies, central banks and those labelled "financial customers" in Figure 6) and non-financial customers (mainly companies – corporate entities and partnerships – and governments). Individuals do not appear as customers because individuals do not have direct FX dealing accounts at reporting banks. Very rich people who wish to deal direct with FX dealing rooms generally have to use corporate vehicles for this purpose.

The interbank segment is the banks' clearing trades between themselves, and, as mentioned above, would fall to zero if there was just one FX market-making bank. Interbank dealing does not make the FX market money – it is just there to clear FX risk.

Concentrating on the financial customers' segment, which is in some ways more varied than the non-financial, it is not possible from the BIS data to unravel what proportion of which categories are retail, captive wholesale and competitive wholesale.[19] However, we can make some educated guesses, and Figure 7, which should be emphasised is speculative (although also based on data from several other sources) sets out a possible split of the financial customer volume. Note that are split from spot deals, and

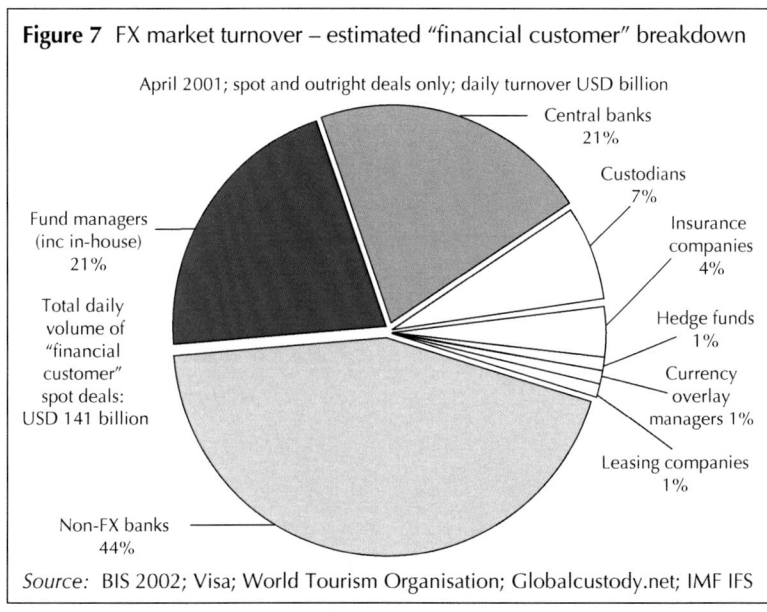

Figure 7 FX market turnover – estimated "financial customer" breakdown
April 2001; spot and outright deals only; daily turnover USD billion

- Central banks 21%
- Custodians 7%
- Insurance companies 4%
- Hedge funds 1%
- Currency overlay managers 1%
- Leasing companies 1%
- Non-FX banks 44%
- Fund managers (inc in-house) 21%

Total daily volume of "financial customer" spot deals: USD 141 billion

Source: BIS 2002; Visa; World Tourism Organisation; Globalcustody.net; IMF IFS

Table 1 Estimates of FX market income for spot trades – financial customers

| | Daily turnover USD billion | Percentage in each category ||| Annual FX market income USD billion |
		Retail (ave spread 5%)	Captive wholesale (ave spread 0.4%)	Competitive wholesale (ave spread 0.05%)	
	A	B	C	D	E[20]
Non-FX banks	60	20%	25%	55%	84.6
Fund managers (inc in-house)	30	0%	25%	75%	5.2
Central banks	30	0%	0%	100%	1.9
Custodians	10	0%	75%	25%	3.9
Insurance companies	5	0%	25%	75%	0.9
Hedge funds	2	0%	25%	75%	0.3
Currency overlay managers	2	0%	0%	100%	0.1
Leasing companies	2	0%	25%	75%	0.3
Total – financial customer	141	8%	23%	69%	97.2

concentrated on the spot deals (which include those reported as "outright" – they have a spot element). FX swaps are "time-shifting" transactions, involve much less market risk for the banks, and therefore attract narrower spreads than spot. They will be left out of this exercise.

Finally, if we make some heroic assumptions about the split of types of business within these categories, we can come up with a table (Table 1) giving a rough estimate of the FX industry income from this sector. The key category, about which we know little, is the "non-reporting banks" (called "non-FX banks" in the table). BIS respondents are asked to categorise their counterparties in this way. However we do not know how they treat, for example, captive business from their own retail branch network. Those aggregated deals will come into the dealing room via a "branch" desk. Since the dealers will not know the ultimate beneficiaries of the branch deals, it is possible that they will record these deals as coming from a non-reporting bank. Credit card

Table 2 Estimates of FX market income for spot trades – all customers

	Daily turnover USD billion	Percentage in each category			Annual FX market income USD billion
		Retail (ave spread 5%)	Captive wholesale (ave spread 0.4%)	Competitive wholesale (ave spread 0.05%)	
	A	B	C	D	E[21]
Financial customers	141	8.5%	22.9%	68.6%	97.2
Non-financial customers	67	0.0%	20.0%	80.0%	10.1
Total – all customers	208[22]	5.8%	21.9%	72.3%	107.2
Memo item – income by client "segment"		75.0	22.8	9.4	107.2

FX transactions are similar. These are quite large (global credit card transactions are about 8% of world GDP – about USD 3 trillion per annum) and possibly 10% of them are cross-border. We can assume these all fall into the non-FX banks category. Using various other sources, I have estimated the proportion of deals with each counterparty type that fall into each "price" category (retail; captive wholesale; competitive wholesale) have been estimated.

We can conduct a much simpler calculation for the non-financial sector (which is "trade" or "current account" industrial transactions and hedging). Table 2 shows the assumptions and calculations, and includes a summary (the total) from Table 1.

From this, we discover that I have estimated that the global income of the FX industry is some estimated USD 100 billion per annum, three-quarters of which is accounted for by a relatively small amount of retail turnover (USD 12 billion (= 141 × 8.5%) daily). The next bulk of the income comes from "intermediate cost" dealing (which has been termed "captive wholesale"), and most of this will accrue to the distributors and asset gatherers around the world, rather than FX dealing rooms. The direct income of FX dealing rooms is a relatively modest USD 10 billion or so (perhaps USD 15 billion – since they will get a share of the spreads from captive and retail business).

The very large income that accrues to retail FX providers is highly disaggregated, and will have very significant associated costs. These extend down to the costs of holding and transporting foreign notes all around the world, as well as the very large number of staff associated with the "foreign" desks of bank branches and *bureaux de change* around the world. A worldwide financial services business that turns over USD 75 billion could be expected to employ some 0.75 million staff or more.

As a "spot check" on the intermediate estimate, we can look at the net income breakdown in the financial statements of five of the largest global custodians – and they report a total of USD 1.3 billion net income from FX dealing. This represents net profit after costs, and on some assumptions about profitability (which will be high in this sector), this might translate to about USD 3 billion of gross income. Custodians represent only a small part of the "captive wholesale" market (it appears to be about 15% from just these top five), so my feeling is that the USD 22 billion global income estimate for this class looks about right.

The heart of the FX market, the FX dealing rooms, appear from this analysis to earn only about USD 15 billion income per annum. On the assumption that 40% of a dealing room's income is spent on staff, and the staff are considerably more expensive than the average bank staff (USD 100,000 per annum all up, versus USD 50,000 all up for normal bank staff), I estimate that this income could support, say 60,000 people.[23] This "feels" about right for the numbers in the world's FX dealing rooms (and the associated marketing and back-office staff), and is supported by recent research on City of London employment, which puts London employment in the FX market at 20,000 in 2001.[24] London holds about 30% market share of the global FX market.

CONSOLIDATION AND COMPETITION

There has been a considerable amount of consolidation in the FX market at the market-making level, and Table 3 shows how concentrated the ownership of FX market-making capacity has become.

While this survey is not definitive, it gives the right "flavour". It shows that the top ten banks listed control 63% of global FX volume, and the top three, 31%. All the top four banks have concluded

Table 3 Top foreign exchange banks

	% market share
UBS	11.5
Citigroup	9.9
Deutsche Bank	9.8
JP Morgan Chase	6.8
Goldman Sachs	5.6
Credit Suisse First Boston	4.2
HSBC	3.9
Morgan Stanley	3.9
Barclays Capital	3.9
ABN Amro	3.6

Source: Euromoney Forex Survey 2003

substantial mergers in the past few years, and this has contributed greatly to the consolidation of the FX market. The business needs of FX dealing rooms were not the reason for consolidation, but since the FX market-making industry has tremendous economies of scale, with high fixed costs and high marginal profitability, the consolidation of FX dealing would have been one of the positive aspects of the continuous merger trend.

Continuing consolidation will continue to reduce the reporting volume of interbank trading as a percentage of the total (and obviously, by deduction, increase the proportion of "customer volume"). The economics of the FX markets do not display obvious limits to the economies of scale, and so, if consolidation pressures continue in the parent banks, the FX market will become even more concentrated. We are not yet anywhere near the stranglehold that, for example, Microsoft has on personal computing operating systems, but it is not inconceivable that monopolistic behaviour from the survivors might emerge. Two factors, however, militate against this. The first is that the barriers to entry at the wholesale level are not high – capital, market-standard technology and people are all readily transferable. There is no legal protection or "embedded systems". The second is that FX is uniquely mobile. Competition can appear and disappear in response to the profitability of the business. Monopolistic behaviour is likely to be quickly spotted, and arbitraged away by new capital seeking supranormal returns.

MARKET HISTORY AND STRUCTURE

The bulk of the earnings of the wider FX market are highly disaggregated. In some niches, mainly in captive wholesale and systems-based retail, profitability can be very high.[25] However, many of these highly profitable areas are protected by high barriers to entry (credit cards being a good example), and the FX is often a subsidiary (and little regarded) activity within the main service.

Similar consolidation has been taking place in the *location* of FX dealing. There have been a number of studies analysing the key criteria that determine a location's attractiveness or otherwise. Time zone, a strong legal framework, political stability, a light but effective regulatory framework and a pool of skilled workers seem to be some of the most important. There is undoubtedly also a "critical mass" effect, which creates significant barriers to entry. The BIS survey provided comprehensive information in this area, and Figure 8 shows the market shares of turnover of the top ten countries. Some, for example the UK, are completely dominated by one city – London. Others, such as the US, do have FX dealing in more than one city.

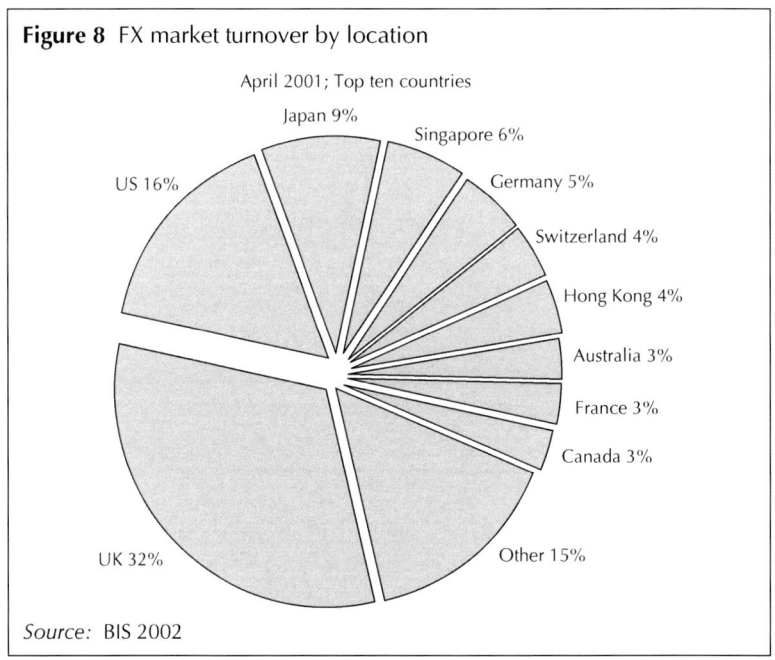

Figure 8 FX market turnover by location

April 2001; Top ten countries

- Japan 9%
- Singapore 6%
- US 16%
- Germany 5%
- Switzerland 4%
- Hong Kong 4%
- Australia 3%
- France 3%
- Canada 3%
- UK 32%
- Other 15%

Source: BIS 2002

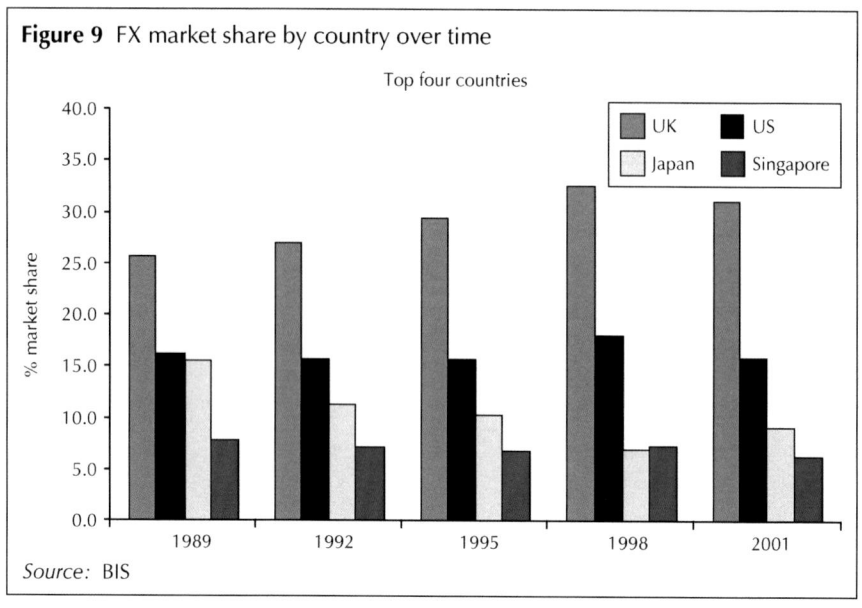

Figure 9 FX market share by country over time

Source: BIS

The UK (in practice London) is clearly dominant, and that dominance has been increasing over the past ten years or so. Figure 9 shows the change in the top four countries' market share over the past twelve years.

London's strengths have matched to the needs of the FX market – in particular: stability, a light regulatory touch, a strong legal framework and an international outlook. Despite a history of onerous controls on its own citizens in the FX market, and taxes and regulation on all participants in other markets within its jurisdiction, the UK government has behaved in an exemplary way in relation to the development of London as the global centre of the FX market.

RE-EMERGENCE OF CENTRAL BANKS

This chapter has spent some time describing the postwar Bretton Woods structure, which gave central banks a pre-eminent role in the international monetary system. Once the system collapsed, central banks lost both their role and their control of the FX market. The loss of role was quickly adjusted to; the loss of control was not. The history of the 30 years since then has been one of attempted regaining of control by the central banks, and repeated failures. Time and again, governments have targeted rates, bands,

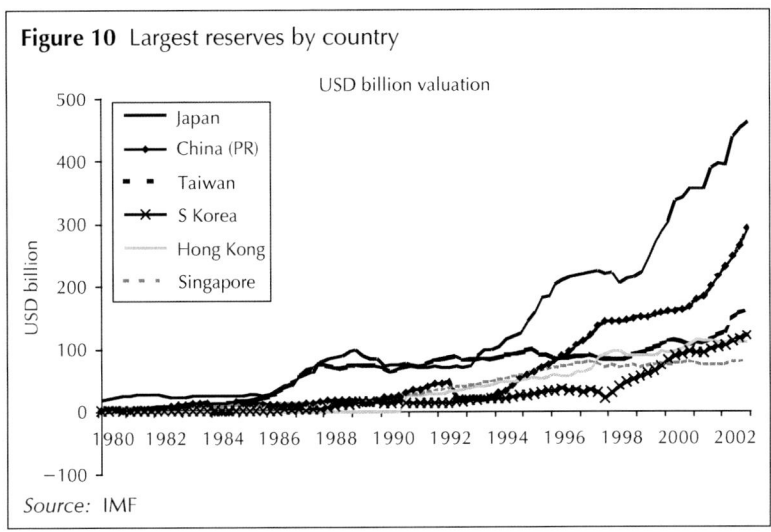

Figure 10 Largest reserves by country
Source: IMF

targets "smoothing" and many other names for regaining control of exchange rates. With one or two exceptions, all such attempts have at best been only temporarily successful, or most have failed quickly.

The failure of the US to arrest both the rise and the fall of the US dollar in the 1980s, the failure of European governments to maintain ERM in anything like a stable system and the failure of the Japanese government to control the wild gyrations of the yen over the past 15 years have led, although very slowly, to an acceptance by most central banks that intervention by them to control exchange rates is ineffective as a policy tool.

However, one very important exception to this rule has emerged over the past few years. Pacific Rim governments and central banks have for 20 years maintained policies to depress the value of their own currencies, in order to continue to stimulate exports in their "export-led" economies. However, recently (post-2000), the scale of this intervention by the Pacific Rim central banks has grown rapidly, along with the scale of the US balance of payments deficit. Figure 10 shows the scale of the accumulated reserves. China has accumulated some USD 300 billion of foreign currency reserves, accounting for some 25% of Chinese GDP – an astonishingly high number.

The pace of reserves acquisition activity by the Pacific Rim central banks has quickened in the past few years.

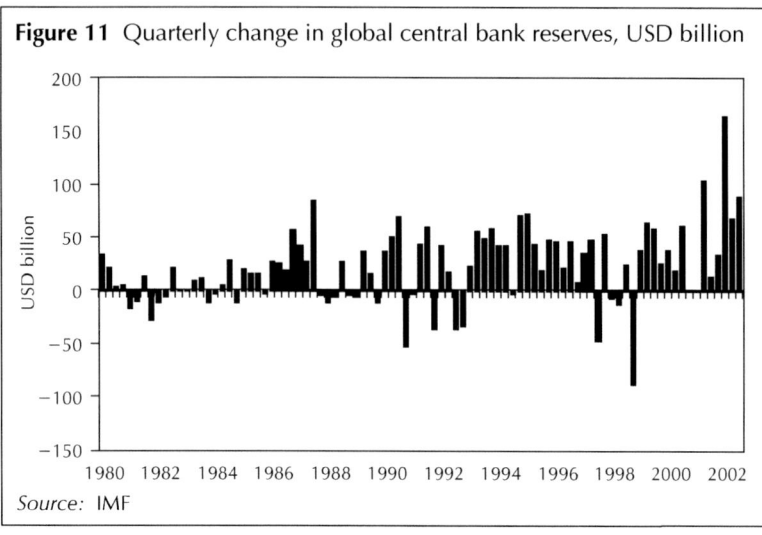

Figure 11 Quarterly change in global central bank reserves, USD billion

Source: IMF

Figure 11 shows the global quarterly rate of net acquisition of foreign currency reserves over the past 20 years. This trend – the acquisition of unprecedented reserves by a few export-led "surplus" economies – is part of the continuously changing nature of the FX market. The central banks' behaviour may be having a similar effect to the Bretton Woods in its heyday: preventing (or delaying) FX rates from operating their signalling role. Of course, in the nature of a failure like this, the structural problem does not go away – it gets bigger. Figure 12 shows the US balance of payments over the past 30 years. The US will ultimately have to bring its deficit under control, but the incentive to do so is in the hands of the governments and taxpayers of Japan and China.

CUSTOMERS

The FX market exists because it provides a service to customers, who pay for the service. This chapter has already devoted several pages to a discussion of how the payment is made by the customer to the market, and estimates of the scale of the payment. The following sections look at the types of customers in the FX market, and their differing aims and objectives, styles of behaviour and scale.

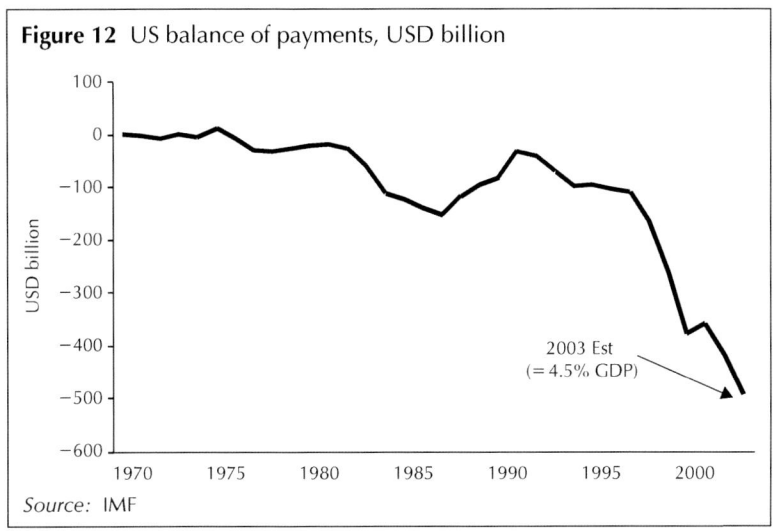

Figure 12 US balance of payments, USD billion
Source: IMF

ICCs – current account

Industrial and commercial companies (ICCs) are the traditional mainstay of the FX market.

Profit-seeking

There are a number of types of market behaviour subsumed within this category. Most obviously is the treasury department given leeway to take positions in forward currency contracts, derivatives, capital instruments or cash. These decisions could be model driven (technical, fundamental, option replication, hybrid); they could be the result of a "currency committee" deciding to extend or reduce coverage of key variables (import/export exposure); or they could be the discretionary undertaking of financial contracts or derivatives, which open, close or modify currency exposure.

This is a very large category of decision-making processes, but they are all characterised by a lack of systematic nature, by fundamentally differing perspectives (importer/exporter; US dollar-based/euro-based/yen-based/sterling-based), and almost universally by a lack of clear benchmark against which to measure success. They are also carried out by employees of ICCs with no general access to close or inside information on the FX market, and with fewer analytical resources than professionals in financial organisations.

Non-profit-seeking

In contrast to the above behaviour, which is profit-seeking, much of the day-to-day transactions of ICCs are simply automatic responses to contracts, deliveries, invoices or other underlying business events. A typical example of this category is where an importer takes delivery of some goods from a foreign supplier, and is presented with an invoice for payment of a foreign currency amount due on a particular day. Just prior to the payment date, the importer rings their bank, and undertakes a spot FX deal to buy the required amount of foreign currency. The importer is almost completely impervious to movements in the spot rate or the rate achieved. They have to do the deal, so they do.

The behaviour can apply to forward rates just as much to spot rates. On placing a firm fixed-price order for (say) a consignment of oil in the future, the customer may execute a forward contract to "lock-in" the cost in his home currency. The customer will have no leeway over whether or not to execute the deal: it will be done if the overall package of the foreign currency rate and the oil price at the time are acceptable.

ICCs – capital account (ships, aircraft, etc)

ICCs can also trade in capital goods, and make investment decisions that have currency implications. Large manufactured capital goods, sometimes worth hundreds of millions of US dollars each (ships, aircraft, power plants), can create "lumpy" needs for foreign exchange from both the exporter and importer. The FX deals that these transactions engender can take many forms, but will typically be a small number of very large FX deals.

The largest of all FX deals are generated by merger and acquisition (M&A) activity. Takeovers are frequently measured in billions of US dollars; sometimes tens of billions. These transactions often have a large equity element in them, but sometimes they can be largely or mainly cash; and, when these are cross-border transactions, the FX implications can be enormous. Each deal is different, but, where such a cross-border M&A deal does take place, it will generate very large customer volumes that have to be absorbed by the FX market.

Traders and merchants (oil, commodities)

This sector is very active in the FX market because of the nature of their business. Even quite modest merchants can conduct very large and frequent FX deals, as each supplier and customer contract is risk-matched in every aspect. The vast bulk of this volume is not profit-seeking: the answer from a merchant as to why they bought USD 100 million for sterling this morning will almost always be "because I was simultaneously selling a crude contract to a UK customer priced in sterling and covering it on the Rotterdam market", or similar. It will not be because they think the dollar will on balance go up.

There will be smaller net amounts of profit-seeking behaviour, say from the well-capitalised merchants, and this can be categorised in exactly the same way as the equivalent behaviour from the ICC sector.

Investment banks (proprietary trading and M&A)

Investment banks (as opposed to FX market-making banks) can behave in two, strikingly different ways. On the one hand, many investment banks have proprietary trading activities, and they will undoubtedly include currency as one of the "moving parts" in their hunt for returns around the world's market. They may also use the currency market as a risk-control instrument to ensure that deals in other instruments are fully matched.

In their role as advisers to ICC and government clients, investment banks are rarely principals to significant deals. However, they can frequently be asked to assist a customer in the execution of currency deals that arise from cross-border transactions. As mentioned above, these can be very large indeed, and the investment bank may be the determinant of the timing of these deals and the way in which they are executed.

Asset managers and currency overlay managers

This group is roughly homogeneous in structure, in that they manage on a more or less discretionary basis, the assets (and in this context cross-border assets) of the world's funded pension schemes. These are principally schemes located in the US, UK, Switzerland, Netherlands and Japan. From national estimates, these pension systems account for about 95% of the roughly USD 8.6 trillion of global funded DB pension assets.[26] From the same estimates, about USD 1.2 trillion of assets is held cross-border. This creates a pool of USD 1.2 trillion in the hands of this group of investment managers and currency overlay managers that can be moved across the exchanges, or hedged using forward contracts, either for profit or as a result of non-currency-led policy decisions.

The behaviour of this group in the FX markets is better documented than most of the customer groups in the FX market.

Most cross-border (or "international") fixed-income mandates are established with a fully hedged benchmark. This means that no economic exposure generally flows across currencies – when foreign bonds are purchased, the currency exposure is simultaneously sold forward. This sector (which is small compared with internationally held equities) is therefore characterised by small and selective profit-seeking bets, often more or less loosely based on the "forward rate bias" theory, or on opportunistic "plays".[27]

In international equity mandates, research indicates that between USD 80 billion and USD 130 billion of international equities have fully or partially hedged benchmarks or have active currency mandates associated with them. Of this total, probably around USD 80 billion have active currency management mandates. Active currency mandates will generate variable hedge ratios (generally but not universally between 0% and 100%), and these variations will be entirely profit-seeking.

Currency overlay managers, as distinct from investment managers, generally have more systematic or model-driven approaches. Investment managers (whose principal responsibility is to manage the underlying assets) tend to undertake more opportunistic "bets" on currency. Many (not all) currency overlay managers, but few investment managers, exploit a well-known inefficiency in the currency market – that of "trends". Without going into details, this exploitation tends to make the currency overlay sector as a whole a perverse trader just like option hedgers – they buy when currencies are going up and sell when currencies are going down. While this behaviour is destabilising, the effect on the market (if any) clearly depends on the relative scale involved. Other management styles tend to be more heterogeneous (and therefore harder to summarise), although the forward rate bias, technical indicators and fundamental forecasting all play a part.[28]

FX option hedgers

This is a little understood, but quite important, category. There is now a well-developed FX option market, and the technology and software exist for uncovered option-writers to hedge their resultant currency exposure in the cash (spot and forward) markets. This technology is now pretty standard, and it requires option writers to vary the proportion of their forward cover in a process called delta hedging. Any regulated bank that holds a balance of uncovered "delta" will be active in this category, not least because its regulator will demand it.

It is very difficult to categorise this behaviour into either the non-profit-seeking or profit-seeking pot. It is profit-seeking in that the bank involved will seek to make a profit out of the totality of the options book (ie, premiums charged) and the related hedge. However, the immediate behaviour in the market is largely mechanistic. This sector increases its delta as a currency strengthens and reduces it when a currency weakens; this means buying currencies as they go up, or having what an economist would describe as an "upward-sloping" or perverse demand curve. Such a demand curve is destabilising to markets in the short term.

At particular times, delta hedgers can become quite dominant in the market. That was true in 1985, when high currency volatility and a period of rapid growth and new technology in the FX option market meant that they generated large and destabilising FX volumes. This effect was self-correcting, as the high option premiums, and losses incurred by the delta hedgers, quickly removed both option demand and option writing capacity from the market. Exactly the same phenomenon was seen again in 1992 in the successful speculative attack on sterling. It is likely that the sum of the net sales of sterling by delta hedgers in the run-up to the ERM exit was much greater than the legendary USD 10 billion bet by George Soros (see below). Ironically, however, option writers over this period would have lost significant amounts of money (despite the fact that their hedges made money), as they would have sold options at low "implied volatilities", and hedged them in the very volatile subsequent market behaviour.[29] This is borne out by statements made by the major FX option-writing banks in the aftermath. There was also a similar period in October 1998 in the yen exchange rate crisis (see below).

Hedge funds

This is the only category whose involvement in the FX market is wholly profit-seeking. Such a fund may have an absolute return target, with very wide discretion as to the instruments and markets that the fund can invest in.

These players' entry into (and exit from) the FX market has developed into a pattern over the years, and two distinct styles can be distinguished. One is the attack on artificial prices maintained by central banks or their governments. These attacks can take place only when a rate is being defended, and they also tend to take place in a herd manner at particular times of stress. The most famous attack was by George Soros on the UK pound in September 1992. This was successful, and by repute Soros's quantum hedge fund made £1 billion out of the trade. The success of the attack was predicated on two key elements: weak political will and a large herd attack. It is likely that the weight of "speculative" attack was an order of magnitude larger than the USD 10 billion principal value that Soros reputedly put at risk. Much of this "herd behaviour" will have been essentially defensive in nature (see FX Option Hedgers and Asset Managers and Currency Overlay Managers above). It is worth noting that speculative attacks are not always successful. A sustained and large attack on HKD/USD parity at 7.80 was mounted in 1998, and the Hong Kong government, clearly demonstrating the will to defend this level, mounted a successful campaign of interest-rate rises together with some physical intervention to maintain the parity level. The cost to the unsuccessful attackers (which included a significant number of hedge funds) was high – a US/HK-adverse 1 month interest-rate differential, which rose to 11% per annum, paid by the attackers.

The other style is the "macro" style, which does not require defensive levels to attack. Hedge funds also tend to hunt in packs in this approach, but they usually have an "obvious" play, which becomes popular. The most notorious of these was the so-called "carry" trade of 1998 against the yen. In the popular language of the time, speculators were being "paid" to "short" the yen, since borrowing yen short-term cost about 0.5% per annum, and lending US dollars paid about 5.5%. This thinking, combined with a long period of yen weakness that had started in 1995 following a period of strength, led hedge funds to believe that there was a "free lunch".

For several months in 1998, the lunch did indeed appear to be free. Then, in October 1998, a rally in the yen prompted the hedge fund sector to reduce their short positions to stem mounting losses. This process rapidly fed off itself, pushing the yen sharply upwards, prompting more buying (in a vicious circle) to cover remaining short yen positions. The outcome was an exceptionally large movement in the JPY–USD exchange rate (around 11% depending on the time reference of consecutive days), the largest one-/two-day movement seen in any of the major traded currency rates in 30 years. This experience (which was very painful for the hedge funds and invalidated many of their risk models) largely removed the macro hedge funds from the FX markets, and there is little evidence of their return at the time of writing (2003).

Central banks

The behaviour of central banks has been discussed above, and they clearly remain a potent force in the market, even if not "in control".

Their behaviour can be categorised into four types:

1. Declared target exchange rate defence

This is the Hong Kong model, and the ERM prior to 1992–3. In this behaviour, the central bank has an absolute requirement to ensure that the spot exchange rate trades within more or less narrow bands. In earlier environments (say Bretton Woods 1948–71), this effort scarcely involved domestic interest rates – direct use of foreign exchange reserves was enough. However, with the scale of private capital stock and flows hugely outgunning the relatively modest official foreign exchange reserves, exchange-rate-defending central banks, particularly the successful ones, have marshalled domestic interest rates to the defensive armoury. This involves using domestic-monetary-policy muscle to raise domestic interest rates when the currency is under external attack. The downside of this policy is that unless euro-interest rates[30] are separated from domestic rates by exchange controls (as they were in France in 1982[31]), then the domestic economy is put through the mill for the sake of the defence of an arbitrary external exchange rate.

2. Strategic intervention

This is the behaviour of the Pacific Rim central banks discussed above. It is almost always designed to keep the domestic currency above its equilibrium rate. It is visible in large and growing foreign currency reserves, and in the structural external surpluses that these countries display.

3. Tactical intervention

Many OECD countries, while not maintaining a fixed-exchange-rate policy, have not abandoned their ability to intervene in their own and others' exchange rates to further economic or political policy. The timing, size and stated reason for intervention of this type is very widely varied, from a smoothing operation to calm the market (perhaps in the wake of an external shock), to an organised and concerted attempt to move the equilibrium market exchange rate or trend. Examples of this are numerous in recent history of the yen, and also in the failed attempt by the ECB to stem the fall of the euro in autumn 1999 through the psychologically important level of 1.00 USD/EUR.

4. Rejection of FX intervention

The UK has largely pursued this policy in the last 10 years, as has the US. Both governments regard the external value of the exchange rate as a matter for the markets.

The overriding common characteristic of the behaviour of central banks, whatever their policy framework, is that it is not profit-seeking. Generally, although not universally, it is designed to act in a "smoothing" capacity, and tends to buy weaker currencies and sell stronger currencies.

Credit card companies, tourism and retail banks

In all these categories, the ultimate customer is the small-scale retail consumer. Retail customers, however, do not have direct control over their FX deals, since they will have to accept very wide spreads within an "administrative system", rather than a "market-place". However, the gatherers of these retail deals will (after netting out matching but opposing deals) send the balance into the FX market in particular, defined ways. The key is that their processes are largely systematic, and that stable levels of FX deals will be brought to the market every day, regardless of the rate or of any other market activity. This, along with the larger volume ICC activity provides a platform of liquidity that is not found in other, purely investment oriented, markets.

Forwards, swaps, etc – instrument development

This chapter has deliberately not devoted much time to describing the various instruments that have evolved in the FX market beyond a brief description of the basic spot market and the forward market. The behaviour of these markets/instruments will be fully explored in later chapters.

These two instruments have been the mainstay of the FX market, and even today dominate its volume. The BIS calls these the "traditional" FX market.

There is one other type of instrument that deserves to be mentioned in the mainstream FX market: currency options. These contracts were "invented" in 1982, and have grown to be an important part of the armoury of both the customers and the FX market makers. Again, these will be explored in much more detail in later chapters.

The BIS mentions currency swaps as one other instrument in the FX market, but in practice, currency swaps originate in, and are largely confined to, the fixed-income market, and appear in the FX market only as the residual FX risk where an investment bank has not managed to match them.[32]

POSSIBLE FUTURE TRENDS

The FX market provides a clearing house for the world's currencies, and, while more than one tradable currency exists, it will always fulfil a vital function. While it is not a market in crisis, it is experiencing the pressure of changing customer needs and behaviour, of changing labour costs and technology, and this will continue to prompt changes in the market's structure.

Several trends have already emerged that are likely to continue; others may have reached maturity or "plateau". The following is a selection of my hostages to fortune:

❑ continued consolidation of the market-making banks at the centre of the market …

- ... which will lead to an increasing proportion of customer turnover in total market turnover (ie, reduced interbank turnover) ...
- ... which in turn will lead to headline FX turnover, static or falling, despite modest growth in customer turnover;
❑ downward pressure on headcount in the market-making banks;
❑ increasing use of electronic trading platforms, which may include electronic market making right at the centre of the market;
❑ increasing use of the CLS Bank or similar – central clearing systems for settlements in the FX market;
❑ no taxation of FX market turnover;
❑ competitive wholesale market spreads that will not narrow much more;
❑ no return to a fixed-exchange-rate environment; and
❑ statistical inefficiencies in the pattern of exchange rates that will not disappear, despite the weight of active management applied to them.

---

1 480 grains = 1 troy ounce; 12 troy ounces = 1 troy pound; 437.50 grains = 1 avoirdupois ounce; 16 avoirdupois ounces = 1 avoirdupois pound; 1 troy pound = 1.2152 avoirdupois pounds. Modern oz and pounds in the UK and US are avoirdupois, and 2.2046 avoirdupois pounds = 1 kilo.
2 1 SDR = 1 US dollar, 1945–71.
3 ±1% versus the USD meant ±2% (at the extreme) between non-USD currencies.
4 The use of the word "Euro" in this context is unrelated to the new euro currency. It was coined initially by American bankers in the 1960s, who realised that trading US dollar-denominated securities and foreign exchange in London circumvented the regulatory and tax hurdles erected at that time by the US government.
5 The Chicago Mercantile Exchange (CME) is one of the two big US futures exchanges (the other is the Chicago Board of Trade).
6 That is, ±4.5% at the extreme between non-USD currencies, or a 9% bandwidth.
7 In 1976 the floating-rate regime was made legitimate by the Jamaica Accord.
8 The EEC changed its name to EC (it dropped the "Economic") rather informally in the late 1970s and early 1980s, and changed to European Union (EU) with the Treaty of Maastricht in 1992.
9 France was the principal country attacked in the crisis. Other countries (particularly Italy) routinely devalued in realignments given the opportunity.
10 See BIS, 2002, "Triennial Central Bank Survey of Foreign Exchange and Derivatives Market Activity in 2001", March. This, and earlier survey results, are available for download on BIS's website at: http://www.bis.org/publ/rpfx02.htm.
11 Except the newly inaugurated CLS Bank. This plays no part in the deal-price-setting process, but is beginning to make inroads in centralising deal settlement. Consolidation of deal settlement is very attractive because it reduces banks' daylight risk. Daylight risk is the risk of delivering one currency to your counterparty before your counterparty has delivered the other currency to you.

12 There are regulators covering banks' solvency and behaviour in each jurisdiction, but no overarching FX market regulator.
13 There are international committees formed to try to standardise, for example, some of the legal aspects of FX trading, but their resulting codes or agreements are voluntary, and a "convenience" rather than essential to the market.
14 See Table 3.7 in Record, Neil, *Currency Overlay* (New York: John Wiley & Sons).
15 Although of course in the equity market there are commissions *and* bid–offer spreads.
16 The spread is twice the actual cost a deal. Suppose I ask a broker for the price to buy or sell Vodafone shares. He says 131p to sell, 132p to buy. The spread is $(132 - 131)/131.5 = 0.76\%$, but the "cost" of an individual deal is half of this – if I buy I spend 132 rather than the mid-price of 131.5.
17 There may be some local markets where taxes/levies are charged.
18 OECD = Organisation for Economic Co-operation and Development – the "rich nations" club.
19 The *retail sector* is largely self explanatory (travellers cheques; foreign cash; credit cards); the *competitive wholesale sector* is when the customer, say a corporate treasurer, calls a bank and undertakes a deal with the dealing room direct. The *captive wholesale sector* is where wholesale amounts are transacted by a third party that either does not have an interest in the transaction being competitive, or has a perverse incentive (makes money from the client from a less competitive deal). A well-documented example of the captive type is asset Custodian's FX transactions on behalf of pension and other investment funds (with the Custodian's own FX dealing room as counterparty!).
20 $E = \{A \times [(B \times 5\%) + (C \times 0.4\%) + (D \times 0.05\%)]/2\} \times 250$. The "2" term is because bid-offer spreads are the price for two deals, not one, and "250" is the number of business days in the year.
21 Same formula as Table 1.
22 Note that USD 208 billion is 43% of USD 490 billion, where 43% is the proportion of traditional FX turnover that is spot or outright, and USD 490 billion is the total customer (rather than interbank) turnover. Numbers may not exactly add because of rounding.
23 USD 100,000 per annum is the average for all grades of staff: FX sales people and market makers will earn significantly more; admin and back-office staff significantly less.
24 Lombard Street Research, 2003 Report on "Growth Prospects" for the Corporation of London.
25 An example of "systems-based retail" is cross-border credit card transactions.
26 Source: Watson Wyatt and OECD, September 00 (updated to December 02 with market valuation changes). Note that Germany and France have very small funded pension sectors.
27 The forward rate bias theory stipulates that the average mean appreciation of the low-interest currency in a currency pair is less than the full interest rate differential. It obviously applies vice versa to high-interest-rate currencies.
28 Technical trading is a long-established approach designed to capture movements generated by "market dynamics" (often the relative behaviour of differing horizon moving averages). I place Chartism (where the shape of time series price charts is seen to be important) as a subsection of technical trading. As with all active approaches, there is an underlying assumption that markets are not random-walk.
29 An "implied volatility" is the standard deviation of annualised changes in the underlying FX market that is implied by the Black–Scholes (or similar) option-pricing formula from the option premium traded in the option market. This rather complicated concept is very important in all option markets. Indeed many option traders will claim that they "trade implied volatilities".
30 "Euro" used in its old meaning here – not the single currency but the "black" or "uncontrolled" foreign market in domestic interest rates.
31 In 1982 (and again in 1983) the markets attacked the FRF/DEM parity in ERM. The French defended with intervention and domestic interest rate rises (to about 18%). However, interest rates in the "euro-franc" (uncontrolled francs owned offshore) rose to peak overnight

interest rates of 3,000%. The French lost the fight and devalued 8% (one day's worth of 3,000% interest rate differential!).
32 Currency swaps are long-term contracts to exchange bondlike payments in one currency with similar payments in another currency. They are to be carefully distinguished from FX swaps, which have no relation to currency swaps, and which are "time-shifting" deals.

2

The Electronic Revolution in Foreign Exchange

James van den Heule

Citigroup

In the past 10 years the foreign exchange market has seen some of its most significant changes. Single events such as the introduction of the euro have changed the course of history, whereas technology continually changes the shape of the market and has the greatest influence on how all banks and their customers trade their foreign exchange exposures. The foreign exchange market has always been at the forefront of technology, making use of the latest communication and electronic equipment. In the fast-moving FX market, the ability to transmit news, analysis, prices and information efficiently is vital to all of today's participants. Technology has changed the way banks interact with their customers and revolutionised the distribution and transparency of pricing so that all market participants have a clear and accurate view of the market.

In this chapter we will look at the changing face of the foreign exchange market and its evolution into an electronic age. We will examine each of the stages as the market adopted electronic distribution of information and prices all the way through to the multibank portals, straight-through-processing (STP) solutions, benchmarking, crossing and white labelling.

VOICE BROKERS TO ELECTRONIC BROKERING SERVICES
One of the most important themes to note about the use of technology in foreign exchange is the improvement of efficiency.

For many years the market was characterised by a long chain of manual processes all being brought together to deliver an exchange of currencies for the customer. In the life cycle of a trade, a client would call their sales representative at their bank to ask for a price. The sales person in turn would stand up and shout to a trader to find out a market level and the trader would listen to his broker on a squawk box to help determine his level.

This process was cumbersome and costly in the fast-moving FX markets. The time taken for each of the steps increases the risk of a market move. In addition, there was considerable scope for error as each of the verbally communicated pieces of information could be misheard on its way back to the client. The process was also expensive as each of the intermediaries needed to be compensated for the service they were providing. In each transaction these costs were loaded into the bid–offer spreads charged. The combination of the increased risk spreads and the payment to all of the intermediaries made a relatively simple transaction extremely costly.

In the late 1980s a revolutionary new idea was born within the top foreign exchange banks to provide a service that would facilitate trading between the interbank traders without the need to talk to brokers. This idea was to allow traders to input their bids and offers into an electronic dealing service. The best bid and best offer available at any one time would be displayed and could be hit by anyone with suitable credit for the counterparty displaying that price. The service updated in real time and for the first time traders had access to a uniform dealable price that was distributed to all participants simultaneously. Over the course of the next few years, EBS (Electronic Broker System) started to replace the voice brokers in price delivery between interbank counterparties. This was followed by the Reuters Dealing System that is now the main competitor to EBS. In fact, between them the two systems now account for approximately 85% of all interbank trading. Both systems have captured liquidity in certain currency pairs and for historic reasons they have maintained their respective dominance in particular pairs. For example, EBS is the preferred provider of pricing in EUR, JPY and CHF, whereas Reuters dealing is preferred for GBP, Nordic currencies and emerging markets.

As a result, the foreign exchange trading floors of today no longer ring with the sounds of voice brokers screaming their prices at traders. This has served to increase the flow of information and reduce the cost of transactions as one of the links in the chain has been removed for the major currencies.

THE DISTRIBUTION OF PRICE FROM TRADING TO SALES

Electronic price distribution sources such as Reuters and Telerate had been around for some years but these were initially intended to give market participants only an indicative level of the market. They relied on banks posting prices of where they believed the market to be. In quiet times this formed a very good market level but when times became volatile the lag could be extremely confusing, thus causing a poor level of transparency.

Over time, the methods of distributing prices electronically became more sophisticated. The next stage was for banks to start using this greater level of sophistication to distribute prices within their own organisations. The best way to extract value from this was if the prices were not only good for information and market indications but also if they could be used by the banks' dealers to transact with their customers without the need for calling a trader. For example, at the start of 1990 in Citibank there were over 30 traders in Europe trading USD/DEM alone. If we multiply this by the number of major currencies and by all other regions, you can see clearly the inefficiencies in providing prices to customers. Each of the dealing rooms maintained trading staff, sales staff and the expensive infrastructure required to support them.

As liquidity migrated to the interbank pricing sources such as EBS and the feeds became more reliable, it became clear that it was possible to create an electronic price in the major currencies that could be distributed across networks of dealing rooms and be disseminated to sales staff wherever they were located in the world. A number of banks sought to implement such a system that was to revolutionise delivery of pricing to sales teams. In the early 1990s Citibank used this technology to deliver spot, forward and swap prices electronically to most of the countries in its global network. This allowed for the trading function to be centralised in a number of key hubs such as London, New York, Tokyo and Singapore.

In each of the individual countries the banks maintained sales teams dedicated to the local market but they had removed the need for traders in the individual countries. This brought huge cost savings and served once again to increase the transparency in the market as the hubs pooled liquidity and benefited from economies of scale and the considerable netting accrued from bringing all of the deals together.

The process for a customer to transact an FX deal was now reduced to only two manual steps, as the price distribution from traders to sales groups had been automated for the majority of deals. These electronic prices, delivered initially over "dial-up"-based systems, also allowed for much greater efficiency in pricing certain types of transactions, including cross-currency deals, forward forwards and mismatches. The software was being refined all of the time, to give instantaneous pricing, compared with the many manual calculations that needed to be performed previously.

The electronic delivery of the pricing also allowed for one other cost saving and that was the booking of the deals into risk management systems for processing. Where manual tickets had been required previously, it was now possible to download all trade details, including cross-currency components, directly into the back office systems.

THE FIRST CUSTOMERS DEAL ELECTRONICALLY

The final major step in consolidating the foreign exchange price distribution chain outlined at the beginning of this chapter was to bridge the gap between the banks and their customers. Dial-up technology made it possible for a customer to connect with their foreign exchange bank by using a PC with modem. The first such system, called "currency trader", was introduced in 1990 by Citibank. This allowed request for quote trading on small ticket deals across all major currencies and a limited number of emerging market currencies. FXLink quickly superseded the product and this set the market standard for many years as the only comprehensive wholesale FX trading system.

The benefits of dealing electronically in this way were clearly seen by both banks and their customers. Both gained the efficiencies of having to input the deals only once, and the subsequent reduction in errors. In addition, it freed up dealers' valuable time to enable them to advise on more strategic foreign exchange issues and work on hedging strategies. In reality, only a few banks willing to make the considerable investment in development have adopted these systems.[1] The systems were also very costly to distribute, install and maintain because of the fact that software needed to be loaded onto customers' computers and that required dedicated lines for operation.

Early versions of rates engines and price feeds were also nowhere near as sophisticated as they are today. The price movements were not reflected with the split-second precision that we know today and there was no such thing as streaming dealable prices with split-second refreshes. Subsequently, deal limits were low and there was a limited amount of additional information available to the user. Take-up of these original dealing systems gradually picked up over the next five to seven years but never really captured a sizeable percentage of the foreign exchange markets' estimated USD 1.2 trillion of daily flow.

THE FIRST USE OF WEBSITES

The Internet was first used by banks to distribute research and analytical tools and as a way to receive feedback from their customers. We can all remember Monday mornings when we were bombarded with letters and research publications from economists from around the world. The paper usage alone by each bank was staggering and often going to outdated distribution lists at customers who may have changed jobs, moved on or simply moved offices.

E-mail and the Internet have allowed this process to be streamlined considerably as customers' preferences and latest contact information are kept online, and they can choose to receive exactly the research and articles that interest them. Most information sites from banks have the ability to sort and distribute, based on a set of rules updated by the clients, and in most cases this is transmitted via e-mail directly to their desktops. In addition, the analytical tools allow for this information to be stored and manipulated easily, helping with complex analysis of the markets.

The most powerful aspect of the web-distributed tools is that active participants can share the same information as the banks and can undertake their own studies of the data to analyse the market's expected moves. For example, the ability to chart market moves was originally the preserve of a limited group of specialist packages but with the development of modern websites it was possible to share this information with customers so that they could visualise analytical trends.

This sharing of information has also made it possible to price foreign exchange options online. The complex calculations involved in option pricing can now be shared so that strategies can be accessed simultaneously by customers and their banks. Modern websites will even allow for the pricing of complex structures, with many of the variables such as current spot, forward prices and volatilities automatically updated in real time.

It is also possible to carry out other complex calculations online, with the help of certain optimisation systems. These can help to provide the best possible course of action and hedging decisions, based on a given set of likely outcomes. Clearly, it is impossible to predict exactly how the market is going to behave but, based on expected values and the risk profile of an individual client, an optimal course of action can be taken.

Similar analysis can be undertaken using back-testing models to see how a particular strategy would have performed if run against historical data. The ability to store ever more granular tick data and market information has meant that very valuable databases are now available to run this type of analysis.

There is an ever-growing number of tools available online to help with analysis and pricing of the foreign exchange markets. The most important aspect of the Internet in this regard is to bring them all to the fingertips of all market participants so that they can share the very best possibility of predicting the course of action most appropriate for their business and risk profile.

THE INTERNET AGE OF TRADING

Following the distribution of information and analytics via the web, it was a logical step to migrate online pricing from the dial-up systems to the Internet. During the mid-1990s, Internet fever was starting to take over the world in the "dot com" boom. The revolutionary new force gripped all businesses and, country-by-country, the power of the Internet was becoming clear to everyone.

Following the distribution of Internet trading in the equity markets, the foreign exchange markets started to develop their own systems to deliver real-time pricing and trading capabilities to clients. As with every industry, millions of US dollars were sunk into systems and infrastructure within foreign exchange to provide a reliable source of pricing and dealing. Unfortunately, as with many of the other initiatives during the "dot com" boom, many of the attempts to provide systems were not successful or the take-up was low and they were soon outdated by the rapidly accelerating pace of technology.

In the early days of trading foreign exchange on the web, there were problems with speed and reliability of many of the services that made many of the systems much less useful than originally anticipated. Also, many people asked the question: what is the advantage of trading online? For many, it was still just as easy to pick up the telephone to transact a deal rather than logging on to a system and then having to enter a request manually. Early systems also had a number of restrictions, such as the amounts that could be traded. For example, early deal limits were often as low as USD 5 million for major currencies and USD 500,000 for exotics.

There was also an initial fear of the technology behind the systems, as companies were unsure of the risks of hacking and Internet fraud. Despite many millions being spent by the major banks to combat these issues, it took a while for many companies to adopt the Internet fully. Over time, banks adopted even more secure encrypting techniques and often employed teams of "ethical hackers" who were paid to expose weaknesses by trying to hack into the technology solutions. All of this work eventually helped to bring confidence to the market.

From 1997 onwards, a few of the major players such as Citibank and UBS started to build a successful online business. In the Citibank example, these developments came from the migration of knowledge and technology from its previous online business. Over eight years of prior experience arguably gave a good lead in the provision of these services because of already well-established rates engines and algorithms to ensure the most accurate dealing price at any time. The ability to deliver this via the web revolutionised the business and what was previously a slowly growing business exploded into double-digit growth year on year by the author's estimates.

At the same time as technology improved, it was becoming clear that the main advantage of online dealing was to deliver a platform that achieved STP. It was no longer good enough just to have a price available on a screen; it was also necessary to be able to link trading systems to treasury management systems and accounting systems. The top systems would allow for uploads of files for simultaneous dealing and return the completed trade details to the accounting systems and confirmation systems.

The best proprietary systems from the larger foreign exchange banks such as Citibank and Deutsche Bank captured substantial proportions of their banks' volumes. In some cases this accounted for up to half of the volumes flowing through the banks' books. These systems were also used to embed foreign exchange prices in other products and services within the banks, such as cash management and custody. The automation of these processes made the business much more efficient and able to handle much higher volumes.

Advances in technology have allowed banks to provide streamed dealable prices to their customers. This allows for one-click execution of deals or, in some cases, these prices are fed directly into the customers' systems to allow for automatic execution of the foreign exchange required to complete another type of transaction. For example, it is possible for online equity brokers to provide a local currency price to their customers and to transact the foreign exchange transaction simultaneously when the equity deal is closed.

THE MULTIBANK PORTALS

As the Internet boom matured, it was clear to many that the development of portals would lead to the greatest efficiencies in the marketplace. This was also true in the FX markets where the idea of bringing prices from many participants together would yield the best advances for customers looking for transparency and efficiency. The idea was to streamline the competitive process of dealing and thus reduce the need for customers to call two or three banks at the same time. Over time, many alliances between various banks emerged and these set about developing systems to deliver a multibank price to customers and a whole suite of other products and services to achieve the greatest level of STP possible.

All the portals are looking to expand their customer bases into other sectors, thus increasing competition between them. The daily volumes through these portals are estimated to have risen rapidly, from USD 7 billion per day in May 2002 to USD 14 billion per day by October 2002 according to one survey; and anecdotal evidence[2] suggests that volumes have continued to grow into 2003, with volumes expected to top USD 25 billion per day by the end of the year. However, in the same survey it is estimated that trading over multibank portals accounts for only 7% of the wholesale foreign exchange market. As a comparison, the April 2001 BIS Triennial foreign exchange survey estimated total daily average foreign exchange turnover at USD 1.2 trillion.

The multibank portals are viewed by many as pricing and connectivity utilities, with the banks picking up the vast majority of the transaction costs, as well as a significant proportion of the initial investment capital. All platforms face the challenge of making the pricing model more equitable to both parties and may seek to achieve this through product innovation and the addition of value-added services. A new development is end-user to end-user matching systems. These enable customers to post bids and offers anonymously, as well as to hit market prices. Banks provide liquidity by making prices and are able to take prices. This model is primarily attractive to hedge funds and professional foreign exchange trading entities.

There have already been some casualties in the multibank space and it is likely that there will be further consolidation in the future. Certain portals have found a niche market and a loyal following in certain countries. However, the strength of liquidity provision lies with the portal that has the greatest number of banks willing to provide prices.

The multibank portals have seen strong growth and have been the focus of the market's attention for a number of years. Multibank portals are able to offer STP and are advancing rapidly in providing new functionality for customers. Proprietary bank systems are being used to support pricing into the multibank portals but were not seen as competitive in their targeted market sector. However, in a recent report by the Bank of England Joint standing sub-committee in 2003, proprietary bank systems have been back in focus.[3] The larger banks are focusing upon targeting flows through prime brokerage, white labelling and liquidity-exchange models, and proprietary systems are central to these models.

Banks that have aggressively marketed their proprietary platforms reported to the committee that they saw much higher volumes across these platforms than through their participation in the multibank portals. It is the author's opinion that e-commerce volumes are growing.

Proprietary systems can also offer more tailored and integrated services and it may be argued the rates engines that power both the multibank and the proprietary systems are the same and all banks have honed their algorithms and sources to such an extent that many are almost identical to one another's. This erodes some of the value in the multibank business model and, when coupled with the lower marginal costs of a proprietary system, has meant that proprietary systems are still capturing the greater proportion of volumes.

STRAIGHT-THROUGH-PROCESSING – BENCHMARKING

The real advance from electronic delivery of pricing and technology is the ability to take advantage of STP. This became a key phrase in the second round of electronic delivery and it means eliminating manual processes in the lifecycle of a trade. Many of the early systems were criticised for helping banks to become more efficient but not really giving many advantages for their customers.

This was the problem of many of the bank's proprietary systems and the earlier versions of the multibank portals. These systems operated in isolation, with no connectivity to downstream systems on the customer's side. Over a short period in the late 1990s, it became very important to work on ways of delivering connectivity. Standards started to emerge that made it easier for systems to talk to one another. This also paved the way for more innovative solutions to make customers' processes cheaper.

Many foreign exchange deals are a secondary part of an underlying transaction. For example, foreign exchange may arise from an international equity or fixed-income transaction or from a corporation exporting goods. With the development of electronic delivery, it suddenly became possible to price the underlying transaction with an embedded foreign exchange rate. It became possible for buyers to see the true costs of transaction in their local currencies. The risk could automatically be taken care of in the market and the transaction details transmitted electronically to all settlement and confirmation systems. In the case of a corporation, the trade details could be sent directly to a treasury management system.

Systems that offered the best connectivity became the most successful in the market. For example, links via API's to systems such as UBS *TP trader* and Deutsche Bank's *Autobahn*. Another example of automated connectivity is the CitiFX benchmark and "Central Treasury" solutions that were designed specifically around investor and corporate processes. This system was designed to consolidate global foreign exchange requirements using a web-based interface that could be either manually loaded with trade details or linked directly to an accounting or treasury system. Once uploaded, the foreign exchange requirements could be sent to a central point (eg, central treasury) for netting and then the net flows communicated automatically to Citibank traders.

Once all of the trade requirements had been gathered, it was necessary to transact the netted deals automatically at an audited rate. It was important for customers to be comfortable that they were achieving the best possible market price. In order to achieve this, Citibank developed an algorithm to produce an audited snapshot of the market automatically, each hour. This snapshot sampled all market prices from the electronic brokers and data providers and chose the most appropriate weightings for each currency pair, dependent on market liquidity. After each fixing, all of the deals were rated with the benchmark mid price plus an agreed spread. These completed deals were returned to the customer on the web and could be downloaded directly into their treasury management system.

According to a report this has become one of the most popular methods for transacting operational foreign exchange flows and the volumes are still growing strongly.[4] It has the advantage of consolidating flows and achieving a level of market transparency unrivalled in other online products. This process was further refined in the last year by offering a fully integrated crossing service. "FXCross" was introduced by Instinet and Citigroup to provide anonymous matching of client foreign exchange requirements. Deals are matched and the residual unmatched amounts may be done at the benchmark fixing rates. The system greatly reduces transactions costs and slippage by matching flows, and it is completely transparent and anonymous. Analysis shows that transaction costs can be halved if deals are perfectly matched.[5]

The most important aspect of these systems is that they achieve efficiencies and reduce errors. Thousands of transactions can now be processed in seconds rather than hours.

CONSOLIDATION AND WHITE LABEL FX

Over the last year, the new buzzword in the electronic foreign exchange arena has been "white labelling". Unfortunately, many banks, when describing their own offerings, use this term loosely. We believe that many market participants and observers may be uncertain as to what "white label" really means. Some define the concept as outsourcing liquidity; others feel that it means outsourcing of client-facing FX technology to another bank.

We think it important to define "white labelling" as the outsourcing of liquidity in combination with a technology platform. A successful white label provider will have a suite of products and services covering both liquidity and technology from which a client-bank will be able to choose as they decide upon the strategic direction of their FX business. The full white label solution should service sales, trading and the end client.

Many banks have realised that the value for them is in their client relationships in their local market and trading in a limited set of currencies where they have a comparative advantage. Our experience is that the likely choice of currencies to outsource will be driven by geographical location. For example, Canadian, Australian and Scandinavian banks clearly have core competencies in their domestic currencies as driven by their client base and the quality and experience of their trading staff. The idea is to create a win–win situation where the white label provider gains increased flows and the partner bank receives an efficient technology solution and access to a much wider range of liquidity.

By offering the white label solution to a range of different banks in many markets, the costs of development and maintenance of the system are divided between them. This drastically reduces the costs. In addition, the economies of scale in development can be used to keep the system more up to date than otherwise possible. In the early days of online foreign exchange dealing online, many banks spent huge sums on technology development. There was a distinct fear that not having your own development team and your own system would leave you out of the market. The cumulative costs of this were incredible and with the pace of web technology development increasing rapidly, many of the initial offerings were rendered obsolete very quickly. The sunk costs also caused many to withdraw from the online trading arena or to cut their investments in favour of more traditional trading mechanisms.

Technology enables all of the major areas of foreign exchange to be wholly or partially outsourced to another bank. It is unlikely in many cases that a bank will totally outsource all areas of its FX business but in most cases it would take part of areas where it has no comparative advantage. The main areas for white labelling are in the following:

1. *FX sales.* Electronic price distribution now enables a partner bank to distribute prices electronically to all branches and sales staff globally. This removes the requirement for trading support in each of the branches and does away with the need for independent technology solutions in a cost-effective manner. Pricing can be switched between provision from the white label provider or from the partner bank, or a combination of both. For example, if the partner bank does not have a 24-hour trading operation this can now be serviced by the white label provider.
2. *FX trading.* Traders can now control the prices distributed to their customers and sales groups by using a white label system to price deals automatically but allowing the risk to flow into their trading books. In the event that the risk reaches a certain level, it is possible for the traders to lay off the risk to the market or to give it to the white label provider. It is also possible for traders to accept and administer market orders through such systems.
3. *Customers.* Foreign exchange white labelling is a very efficient way to give Internet trading access to clients. Customers can view rates online, manage positions, leave orders and confirm transactions. There are also many other efficiency gains to be achieved from using such systems that allow STP of trades and downloads to treasury systems.
4. *Post-trade.* Separate log-ins can be provided for real-time confirmations. Full segregation of duties can be provided to allow operations departments to confirm trades as soon as they have been

executed. This is an extremely efficient way to operate, compared with faxes and calls. The speed of confirmation is also much faster.

It is very early in the lifecycle of most white label initiatives. However, considerable growth is expected over the next few years. Some are concerned that this will lead to more concentrated liquidity and consolidation among the major players, whereas others believe that the efficiency gains will outweigh any negative impact.

White labelling will almost certainly cause consolidation in the market, to add to changes over the past decade caused by bank mergers, centralisation of trading operations and the introduction of the EUR. The growth of e-commerce in foreign exchange trading is accelerating this trend. High fixed technology costs, reduced spreads and margin erosion have meant that it has become necessary for banks to take better advantage of economies of scale. Over the past few years, interbank business between the top 10 liquidity providers has increased significantly. The number of banks able to provide liquidity in a full range of currencies is likely to continue falling.

E-commerce has also reduced the costs of processing trades, allowing banks to generate profits through trades of smaller and reducing values. Spreads are also tightening and banks need to see increased flows in order to maintain profitability. The cost of maintaining the technology required to run an efficient global business is now much higher, and the decreasing margins may make white-labelling models more attractive to many smaller and medium-sized banks, who are seen as customers by the top-tier banks, rather than competitors.

CONCLUSION

We have seen how new technologies are resulting in rapid changes in the way the foreign exchange markets operate. Greater automation through e-commerce is helping to reduce the processing costs of deals and changing the roles of traders and sales groups within banks. Increasingly, dealers at banks and their customers are processing a reduced number of trades and are expected to focus upon more strategic issues and relationship management, while traders are quoting fewer prices and instead managing flows, particularly around fixings.

The psychology of the foreign exchange markets is also changing. The increase in price transparency that e-commerce brings has reduced the aggressive trading style seen particularly in the late 1980s and early 1990s. Banks are communicating and cooperating more, particularly on infrastructure, technology and e-commerce standards. This has had a very positive effect on the service level and pricing available to all customers.

It is certain that e-commerce will play an increasingly important role in the FX markets and the percentage of transactions completed over electronic systems will continue to rise in the future.

1 For example, Citibank and Chase Manhattan.
2 Client knowledge quoted in *FX week* 2, 2003.
3 Foreign Exchange Joint Standing Committee e-commerce subgroup report 2003.
4 See "Changing The Way FX Is Transacted", *e-Forex*, August, 2001.
5 See Instinet 2003.

3

Risks and Rewards

Jessica James
Citigroup

This chapter describes the features of FX rates and the FX market that distinguish them from other instruments. On the way, we examine some popular assumptions and misconceptions about how the markets work.

WHY FX RATES ARE DIFFERENT

It is very easy to talk of trading as if all the different rates and instruments were very similar; as if switching from trading interest rates to equities or FX would be a trivial task. This is not so. It is rare for a trader to make a successful switch from one to the other, and where this does occur there is usually a fairly long acclimatisation period while the trader gets used to the new instrument. FX rates are often regarded as the "easy" option. They do not have the massive jumps that characterise equities, or the complex term structure of interest rates. The FX market does not trade many highly complex derivatives, in contrast to the fixed-income market. However, this simple picture is not quite accurate. FX rates are more subtly complex than they at first appear. In this section, we compare FX rates with other commonly traded instruments and look at similarities and differences.

FX rates versus interest rates

Interest rates in an established economy do not take just any value. We would be amazed, for example, to hear that rates in the USA had risen to 30%. We would be astounded to hear that interest rates anywhere had fallen to -10%. So there is a stable range of values, from about 2% to about 15%, to which interest rates are attracted. While it is not impossible for them to move away from this range, they experience a strong "pull" back towards it, which usually increases the further that they move away in an elastic fashion. This type of behaviour is known as *mean reversion*. Almost all reputable interest rate models will contain mean-reverting terms, although these can be complex; sometimes the model will have the interest rate mean-revert to a level that is itself mean-reverting to some constant rate (see James and Webber, 2000; "A chaotic model for interest rates", 2003).

FX rates, in contrast, do not mean revert. They have no preferred direction, and no range within which they are usually confined. Currently (late 2003) there are about 1,400,000 TRL (Turkish Lira) to the USD. No one would have invented a currency where the unit is this small; somehow it got there by progressive devaluation against the dollar, as can be seen in Figure 1. Note that there are a couple of data spikes in devaluation periods where a value for the TRL was hard to come by!

And yet, just because it is so low, there is no reason at all why it should not go lower. An FX rate can always go lower or higher,

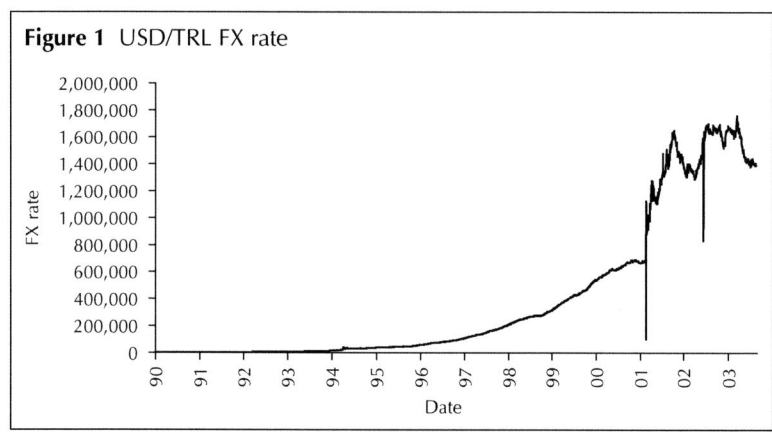

Figure 1 USD/TRL FX rate

with no "natural" level or barrier. Another, less extreme, example is the GBP. A few decades ago there were four dollars to the pound, a level considered to be stable. These days there are about 1.5 dollars to the pound, and this level is also considered to be stable. No one thinks that the rate will return to four. Thus we can see that an FX rate can be stable at any level. This has some implications for investors: while there is some justification in saying, "Interest rates are so high now, they just can't go much higher," there is no sense in applying the same sentiment to FX rates. In Figures 2 and 3, we see the difference between sample paths produced by a model with and without mean reversion – without mean reversion the rates

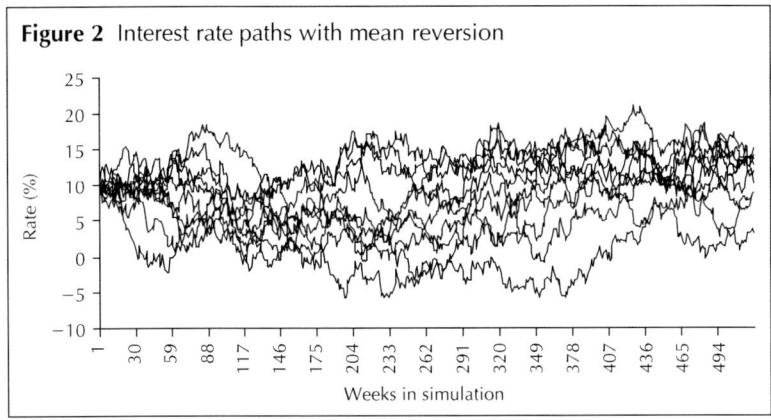

Figure 2 Interest rate paths with mean reversion

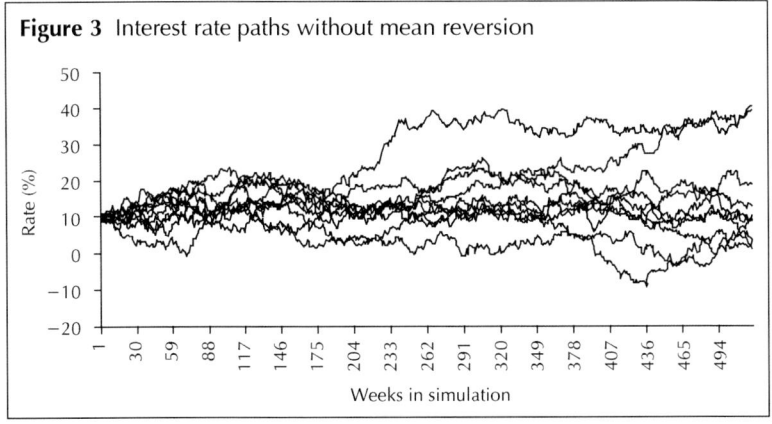

Figure 3 Interest rate paths without mean reversion

tend to move a lot further over time. The model used has the form

$$dr = \alpha(\mu - r)dt + \sigma dz$$

and is one of the simplest mean-reverting models. r is the rate, α is the coefficient of mean reversion, μ is the mean level to which the rate reverts, σ is the volatility, dt is the time step, and dz is drawn from a set of random numbers. In Figure 2, we have $\mu = 10\%$, $\alpha = 0.5$, and $\sigma = 5\%$. Figure 3 was produced with the same figures except that α, the mean reverting coefficient, was set to zero. Note that, because the model used was a very simple one, the rates can and do go below zero. More sophisticated models avoid this. (For a detailed discussion of this and other models see James, Webber, 2000; Rebonato, 1988.)

Another feature of interest rates is a "barrier" at or very slightly below zero, beyond which they do not go. It seems bizarre at first even to consider that rates might go negative – why on earth would one invest to lose money? Safer, surely, to keep it in a tin under the bed. But keeping millions of pounds under the bed is simply not practical (though fun to imagine), and so the equivalent in the markets would be to reinvest in some instrument believed to be safe. Depending upon one's point of view, this could be gold, or government bonds, or a different currency. All of these methods of "money storage" have some associated risk, and also there is a cost of transfer. These difficulties are sufficient just to make it possible for slightly negative interest rates to exist, though not for long. Negative rates have occurred, historically, in both Switzerland and Japan, for short periods of time. Negative FX rates, on the other hand, do not occur. There is no "zero" that an FX rate will ever actually pass through.

The last feature of interest rates that we will consider is hyperinflation (see James, Webber, 2000). This occurs when interest rates rise exponentially and is usually caused by governments "printing" money, though in ancient times hyperinflations were caused by devaluation of coinage. The exponential rise in interest rates is accompanied by rampant inflation in the economy. While no one denies that currencies can exhibit highly volatile behaviour, and move a long way in a very short time, they do not undergo classic hyperinflation behaviour such as that experienced by Germany

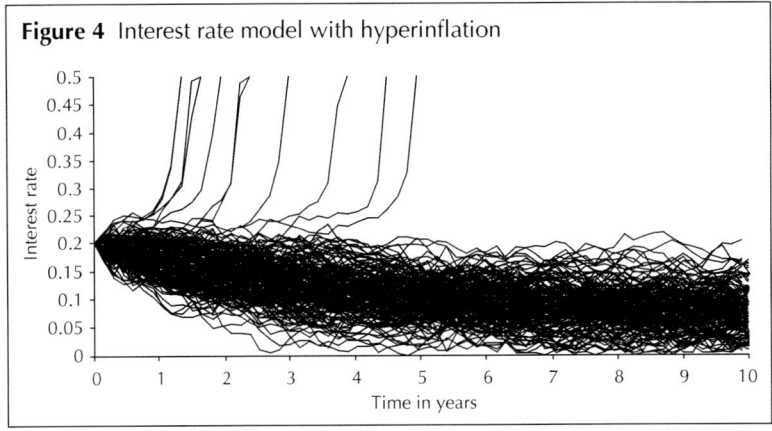

Figure 4 Interest rate model with hyperinflation

earlier this century. However, if a hyperinflation occurs in a country, its currency will show a huge decrease in value due purely to the hyperinflation itself. Figure 4 shows 100 sample paths of a model that includes hyperinflations – the occasional path shoots off to infinity. The model used has the form

$$dr = \left(De^{-\lambda_1 r} + Ee^{-\lambda_2 r} + F\right)dt + \sigma dz$$

where D, E, F, λ_1 and λ_2 are constants.

FX rates versus equity returns

Consider the issue of expected return. When an investor buys an equity, for example, she has a reasonable expectation that the equity will increase in value. A quick glance at the major equity indices over the last 20 years reveals that in general this is indeed the case – they show an exponential increase over a long timescale, though there is volatility in the shorter term. Thus, an investor expects an equity to increase in value, to compensate her for the risk of holding on to it.

A currency, in contrast, will probably give her just as much risk with no expectation of an increase in value. Equities are asymmetric: their value cannot fall below zero and they are expected to rise in value. Currencies are symmetric: there is no limit to how low one currency can go relative to another, and there is no expectation that they will either rise or fall. This is because, in a world where gold standards etc no longer exist, a currency is not a store of intrinsic value, but is simply a rate of exchange, and therefore it has no limit beyond which it cannot fall. Thus, an investor who expects an increase in value to compensate her for currency risk is in for an unpleasant surprise.

Data density and availability

In terms of data availability the FX market is relatively rich. Data are not quite as easily obtained as they would be for equity indices, but it is possible to purchase data for most of the major currencies at daily or higher frequencies. As FX markets are generally deep and liquid, high-frequency data are a rich source of information, with several rate changes per minute at peak times of day. Figure 5 shows how data density varies throughout the day for EUR/USD (DEM for pre-EMU times). When dealing in large amounts, it is always advisable to do it at times of high data density, when the largest number of dealers are in the market.

In Figure 5, the time is Chicago time, so 8:00 corresponds to 14:00 in the London day. The trading low on a global basis is after the close of the West Coast of America but before the opening of the Tokyo market, close to midnight London time. The units are minute changes per 10 minutes, so the graph does not show the very high data densities that can occur in the middle of the London day, as it has an upper limit of 11.

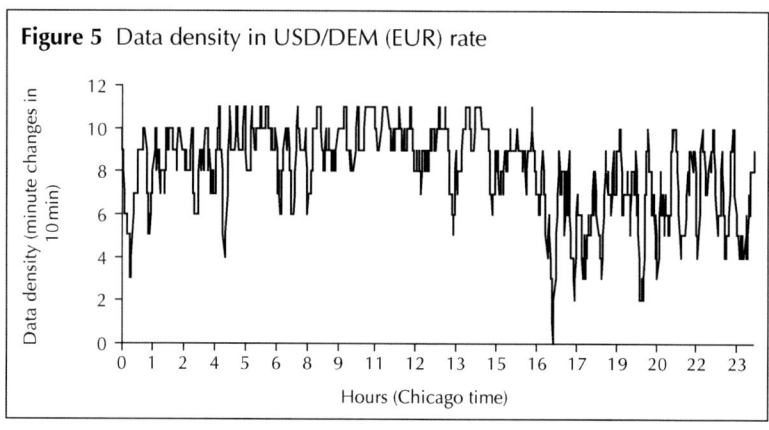

Figure 5 Data density in USD/DEM (EUR) rate

Other data associated with the FX rates are also available to a limited extent. In order to value FX options, one needs to know the implied volatility of the FX rate. This is basically is the traders' estimate of the standard deviation of FX returns in the future. As such it is not a directly traded quantity, though it may be inferred from option prices. Therefore it is difficult to collect, as it does not necessarily pass through the standard dealing systems. Implied volatility data are most available for equity indices, and are stored by various exchanges. These will sell the data on to customers for analysis. While FX-implied volatility data are not quite as easily obtained, there are various data companies who do store and sell them, and though the data's quality and quantity leave much to be desired, they does exist and may be purchased. Interest-rate-implied volatility data are far more difficult to get hold of and rare indeed is the bank that systematically stores them.

COMMON MISCONCEPTIONS

Like the rest of the markets, FX has its share of myths and legends. Here we look at some of the most popular and see what truth they contain.

Are FX rate moves predicted by forward FX rates?

One of the most common assumptions made in the FX markets is that the forward FX rate is a good predictor of the rate in the future. The forward FX rate is the current rate adjusted for interest rate effects, and it is worth briefly discussing how it is calculated. Taking USD and GBP as an example, we would like to arrange a rate today to convert from GBP to USD in six months' time. There are two ways to get from GBP now to USD in six months:

❑ convert now at FX rate 1, invest USD at US interest rate for 6 m;
❑ invest GBP now for 6 m, then convert at FX rate 2.

We assume that a competent banker never leaves his money uninvested ...

Setting the two to be equivalent will give you FX rate 2, the FX forward rate, as shown in Figure 6.

Of course, this is only the forward rate for a period of six months; there will be forward rates in the market for any period of time, and these rates, plotted as a function of time in the future, will

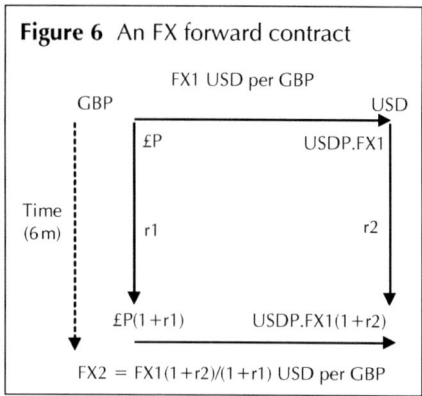

Figure 6 An FX forward contract

Table 1 Average prediction errors using forward rates

Currency pair	RMS error using forward as predictor (%)	RMS change in spot rate over one month (%)
USD/JPY	3.45	3.43
USD/CHF	3.22	3.19
USD/AUD	2.84	2.82
USD/CAD	1.60	1.59
EUR/USD	2.94	2.92
EUR/JPY	3.52	3.55
EUR/GBP	2.37	2.37
EUR/CHF	1.10	1.10
GBP/USD	2.56	2.61
GBP/JPY	3.83	3.84

map out a path that the spot rate could, if it chose, follow. Many people think that the spot rate will follow this course, or that it is the most likely one that the rate will follow. Is there any truth in this assertion?

In extreme cases, certainly there is some effect – we will discuss the example of USD/TRL shortly. However, for small interest-rate differentials like those found in Europe, it is not clear that the forward rate has any predictive power at all. In Table 1 we show the root-mean-squared (RMS) error resulting from the use of the one-month-forward rate as a predictor of the spot rate for a range of currencies. We used monthly data from a range of FX rates for the period January 1992 to September 2003. If f_t is the forward rate at time t and s_{t+1} is the spot rate one month later, then the RMS prediction error is defined as

$$\text{RMS error} = \sqrt{\frac{\sum_t \left((f_t - s_{t+1})/s_{t+1}\right)^2}{N}}$$

where N is the number of data samples used.

We also show the RMS move in the spot rate over one month for each currency pair. For all currencies, there is little difference between using the spot rate or the forward rate as predictors.

Is the direction of an FX move predicted by the forward FX rates?

While the previous section seems to offer evidence that spot FX rates are not, at least over a one-month horizon, predicted by the forward rates, it is sometimes argued that at least the direction of the next spot move is indicated by the forwards. If this were true, it would be possible to trade in the spot market according to the direction indicated by the forward rate, and make money. To examine whether this works, we used the same data set from January 1992 to September 2003. If the forward rate were higher than the spot rate, our simulated strategy bought, and sold if the forward predicted a lower rate. The

Table 2 Returns from spot trading strategy

Currency pair	Average return per deal from the spot trading strategy (%)
USD/JPY	−0.27
USD/CHF	−0.10
USD/AUD	−0.19
USD/CAD	−0.09
EUR/USD	−0.35
EUR/JPY	0.15
EUR/GBP	0.00
EUR/CHF	0.09
GBP/USD	0.07
GBP/JPY	0.07

position was held for one month. If the forward rates had predicted the direction of spot rate moves then this strategy should have returned a profit.

As we can see, in general the strategy lost money. The forward rate is not even a negative predictor of spot movements.

Interest rate differentials as currency drivers

It is commonly assumed that currencies are heavily influenced by interest-rate differentials. If one currency offers a higher rate of interest than another, the immediate temptation to the investor is to borrow in the low-interest one while simultaneously lending in the high-interest one. This will increase demand for the higher-interest-bearing currency at the expense of others, which will, all other factors being equal, drive the FX rate up so that the higher-interest-bearing currency is more valuable. It is this movement, in fact, that is predicted by the forward rates. However, this does not always happen, because the factors that can lead to high interest rates are often those that would give the investor less confidence in the currency. So, when the UK experienced the ERM crisis, and the UK government raised rates to very high levels in a very short time frame, the currency continued to weaken, because investors had no confidence in the currency and not even the high interest-rate levels could tempt them to buy it.

The medium- and long-term effects of higher interest rates can be opposite to the short-term ones. High interest rates are usually associated with high inflation. High inflation leads to high levels of seigniorage, where additional money supply is generated by the government to ensure that the total value of circulating money remains the same year on year. Thus, when seigniorage is high, the value of a fixed sum of money decreases. This means that high interest rates make investors wary of holding on to a currency for too long, as it will be likely to decrease in value. Thus, the assumption that interest-rate differentials drive FX rates is not a good one to make – the situation is usually far more complex.

The TRL is a good example of systematic devaluation of a currency where high interest rate differentials exist. For many years interest rates in Turkey have been very much higher than those in the rest of Europe. The forward FX rates have therefore consistently predicted devaluation of the currency. On the whole, this has

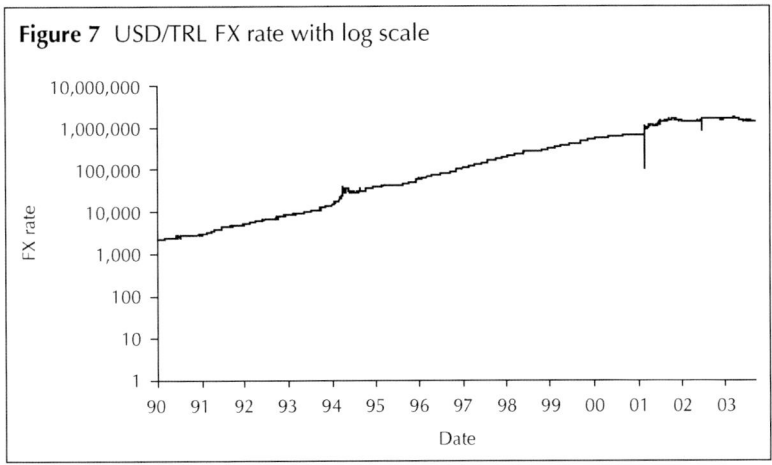

Figure 7 USD/TRL FX rate with log scale

happened, and the currency has become progressively weaker. If we look at Figure 7, which is just Figure 1 with the y-axis on a log scale, we can see that the plot is nearly a straight line, indicating that its percentage weakening per unit of time has been roughly constant.

However, the degree to which it has weakened has been consistently smaller than that predicted by the differential and forward rates. Over the past 15 years, betting that the TRL would not weaken as much as the forward rates predict would have, in general, been a good idea.

It is worth noting that one cannot separate the effects of interest-rate differentials and the forward rate. The former creates the latter. If interest rates are identical in two countries, then the forward FX rates are all the same as the spot rate and the forward points are zero. In practice they may be regarded separately.

Economic fundamentals as currency drivers

Various economists are fond of stating that economic fundamentals, like current-account balances, control currency rates. They are paid to forecast market rates using these techniques, so this is hardly surprising. In a world without volatility or speculative trading it might well be the case that economic drivers dominate currency movements. However, that world is not this one, and in fact economic fundamentals can disagree with currency rates over long periods of time, and to a highly significant degree. Purchasing power parity, a calculation based on a basket of goods that may be purchased by a unit of currency, gives an indication of the absolute value of currency. This can lie significantly out of line with actual exchange rates, for periods of up to five or six years. Eventually, trade arbitrage will act to bring the exchange rate back into line, but import duty and tax issues often extend the lifetime of the discrepancy. We can conclude that economic fundamentals have only a long-term effect upon currency rates, and in the short and medium term can often be irrelevant.

External controls

Governments often try to put constraints and controls upon currency movements, and claim that they will "keep a currency steady" within certain ranges. There are various ways of doing this, ranging from intervention in the market by the central banks to imposition of legal constraints. In the most strictly controlled cases, money is recognised as legal tender only if it resides within the country, and expatriate money is not recognised. This enables the government of the country to control exchange rates. A less coercive method would be for the central bank to intervene regularly in order to keep the currency "pegged" to another major currency, usually the USD. This method can work for some years, but if, for example, persistent inflation increases the money supply to the point where intervention will no longer work, catastrophic devaluations can result. A case in point was Mexico. The exchange rate was pegged to the USD for many years, but a series of collapses led to the abandonment of the policy.

There are three ways in which a government can control a currency without the imposition of legal constraints. The first is to buy the currency on the open market, creating a demand for it, which pushes up its cost. The second is to sell the foreign currency against which the currency is depreciating – this is usually the USD and large reserves of USD are needed for this strategy to be successful. The two strategies of course may be combined by selling USD for currency. As can be imagined, these strategies can work out to be rather expensive for the central bank involved!

The third way is to raise interest rates. This can create a temporary demand for the currency as it yields high returns, but can also erode confidence in the long-term value of the currency.

In general, external controls upon a currency work only in a limited way. The United Kingdom, with all the resources of the Bank of England, did not manage to keep the currency steady on Black Wednesday, when it raised interest rates to try to keep the currency within the band specified by the European Exchange Rate Mechanism. However, limited intervention is believed to be effective in damping down large currency movements.

Internal effects

"Internal" currency effects are those that come from things such as trader preference and human overreaction and feedback. A common assumption to make is that these effects are small and overwhelmed by economic effects. However, this is not true. While it may initially seem counterintuitive, the majority of short- and possibly even medium-term moves are largely driven by internal effects. For example, suppose a senior analyst perceives a "resistance" level. He expects the currency to rebound from this level, or at least not pass through it without hesitation. He publishes his opinions, and traders take note. Then, as the currency approaches the level in question, a number of traders will sell the currency because they assume it will go no higher, and there is no benefit to holding on to a long position. This selling action will by itself make the price go down, thus making the analyst's prediction somewhat self-fulfilling.

The vast majority of currency trades are made more for speculation than hedging or cash-transfer reasons, and thus many moves are driven by these so-called "technical" signals, which as well as levels include trends and channels and many other features.

The importance of this kind of internal effect may be illustrated by considering whole numbers. There is no earthly reason why currencies should, from a fundamental point of view, prefer a number that ends in a zero. Surely, for all reasonable purposes, 5.001 is the same as 5.000. However, human beings are the agents in the market, and humans like 5.000 much more than 5.001. To illustrate how powerful this human preference is, we can look at the distribution of rates in the market. If there were no preference for whole numbers, then the last digit of the rate could be any number from 0 to 9, with equal likelihood. If however there is a "preference" for whole numbers, then the rate will linger at levels that end in zero, and thus there will

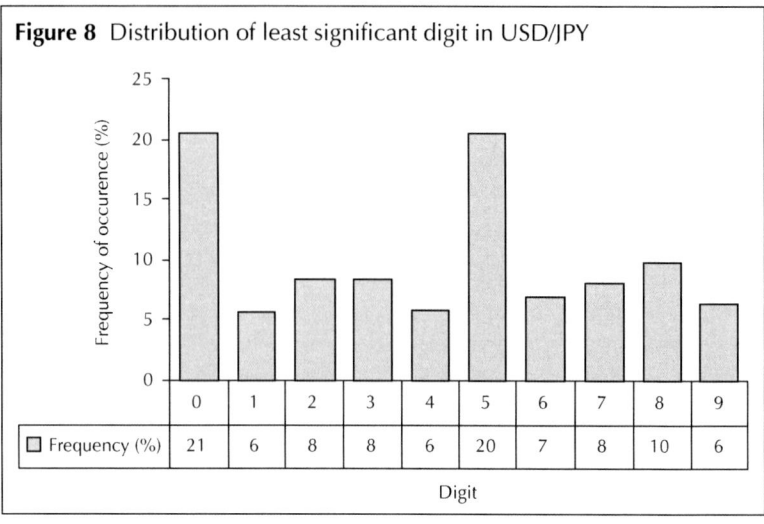

Figure 8 Distribution of least significant digit in USD/JPY

be a higher number of zeros than expected. This is exactly what we do find, as shown in Figure 8. The data for this graph was USD/JPY hourly closes, ie, the USD/JPY rate at the end of each hour of the day, and we used data from 2 January 1990 to 27 December 2003. As can be seen, there is a definite preference for rates ending in zero and five, while rates ending in 1 or 9 were relatively unpopular. There is no external economic reason for this preference; only human tendencies can account for it (see Attfield, James, 1999).

All in all, it is safe to say that there are a large number of underlying drivers of currency movements, and that it is difficult at any one time to tell which of the various candidates is dominant.

True cost of options

It is worth considering one last widely held assumption in the currency markets: that options are expensive because of their premium cost. The most common hedging alternatives to neutralise currency risk are options and forwards. A forward locks an investor into a future rate, giving her stability at the risk of losing out on positive currency movements. Forwards are zero-cost instruments, with the only outlay to the investor being the bid–offer spread. Options, on the other hand, have an immediate cost: the premium, which is something like 2% for a three-month option, depending upon volatility levels. They allow the investor to profit from positive currency moves, while guaranteeing protection on the downside.

What is needed, to discover if options truly are too expensive, is actually to track the value of bought options over the years. To do this we need a database containing implied volatilities, FX rates and interest rates, to calculate the premia of the various options. We can then find what they would have paid out (if anything) to their owners upon expiry, by tracking the progress of the FX rate. We performed an extensive simulation of this type, assuming that we bought a one month put and a one month at-the-money call option every day for the whole data period, and seeing what the payoff of each option would have been. We purchased both a put and a call and averaged the result to isolate the results from any overall directional bias, and no delta hedging was used. The results are presented in Table 3.

As can be seen, the "true cost", calculated as (premium–payoff), is on average close to zero. The average premium is about 1.17%, while the average "true cost" comes out to a tiny 0.06%. In three of the currencies, USD/JPY, GBP/JPY and NZD/USD, the average payoff is actually slightly larger than the average premium – and

Table 3

Currency	Average option premium (%)	Average option payoff (%)	True cost (premium–payoff) (%)
EUR/USD	1.27	1.20	0.07
USD/JPY	1.34	1.38	−0.05
EUR/JPY	1.37	1.37	0.00
GBP/USD	1.06	0.94	0.12
USD/CHF	1.34	1.34	0.00
EUR/GBP	0.95	0.92	0.03
EUR/CHF	0.53	0.44	0.09
GBP/CHF	1.06	1.02	0.04
CHF/JPY	1.50	1.45	0.05
GBP/JPY	1.42	1.50	−0.08
EUR/SEK	0.90	0.81	0.08
EUR/NOK	0.75	0.65	0.10
USD/SEK	1.23	1.13	0.11
USD/NOK	1.23	1.11	0.13
AUD/USD	1.16	1.09	0.06
USD/CAD	0.68	0.58	0.10
NZD/USD	1.35	1.36	−0.02

yet in all of these currencies the implied volatilities were systematically higher than the realised. Thus, on average, options have paid out an amount roughly equal to the value of the premium, and it can be concluded that they are good value for money.

Periodicities

It has often been suspected that some currencies exhibit periodic behaviour – for example, in USD/JPY, there is often an end-of-month settlement when Japanese companies need to square up accounts. If it were true, then it would be a useful and easily managed addition to a currency trading portfolio, as trade directions and amounts would be known well in advance. However, while some strategies claim to exploit just such a phenomenon, there has been little empirical investigation as to whether periodic strategies actually exist, or whether assiduous data mining has just thrown up an outlier.

In order to first establish whether there is any possibility of finding such a model, we used USD/JPY as a test bed. We looked at the results of buying and selling once per period, and also allowed the length of the actual period to vary. Thus we had three variables:

❑ period length;
❑ buy day; and
❑ sell day

which we wished to optimise to find the combination with the best information ratio.

The problem with optimising such a set of parameters is that the surface that we need to search has many local maxima and minima, and in general it is difficult to say that one has found the best combination of parameters. Accordingly, we decided to search the whole space, allowing the period to be up to 65 days long, and allowing the buy and sell days to have any values within this. Obviously, this leaves us with a pile of data to analyse, so, for each period length up to 65 days, we just recorded the buy and sell days that gave the best information ratios. We then selected the best of these 65 information ratios, and came up with the following:

❑ sell on Day 12;
❑ buy on Day 37; and
❑ period has 60 days.

Our data set started on 1 July 1988, so these numbers take Day 1 of the first period as that day, but obviously any other start date would have left us with the same period length and different start and end dates to pick up on the same trades.

The statistics on this optimised strategy are as follows:

❑ annual return on face: 12.0%;
❑ information ratio: 1.05.

The cumulative returns during the backtesting period are shown in Figure 9.

As can be seen, although there are some drawdowns, in general the returns are excellent. The trading strategy, if real, is a desirable addition to any portfolio.

But is it real? In order to determine if this is a genuine result or just a data "feature", we wish to know what kind of returns might be expected from such a strategy. We would expect that there are maybe one or two combinations of parameters that give very good results, and the rest give results that are essentially random, centred roughly on zero. However, to look at the whole spectrum of results would involve a huge number of records, so instead we just look at those information ratios obtained from a period of 65 days, with all possible variations of buy and sell days within the period. This provides more than 4,000 points, which is statistically adequate.

We find that the mean of the information ratios obtained for the distribution is zero, as expected, with a standard deviation of 0.20.

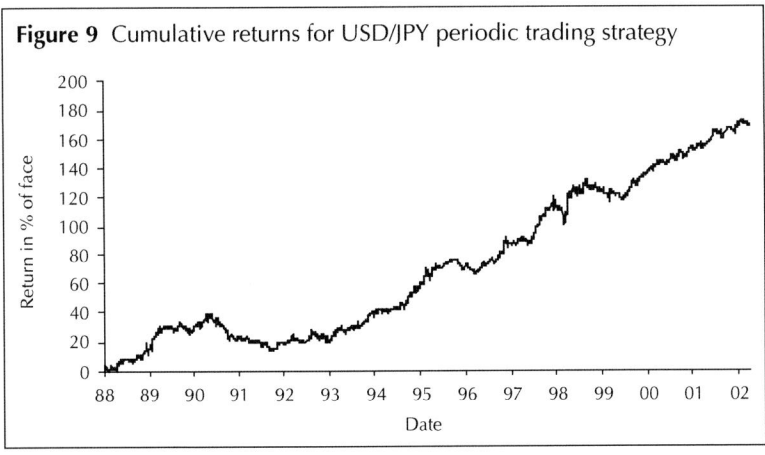

Figure 9 Cumulative returns for USD/JPY periodic trading strategy

This means that the information ratio of 1.05 is 5.1 standard deviations away from the mean, a result we would not expect to see with fewer than 31 million points in the distribution if the distribution is normal. Taking into consideration that the total number of strategies within the space is of the order of 200,000, we may say that this result is very significant and likely to be real.

The above analysis does make the assumption that the distribution of information ratios is normal. If it is fat-tailed instead, then the information ratio of 1.05 may still be just a data feature. Financial markets and trading strategies are not exactly famed for sticking to the normal distribution – in general they are pretty non-linear systems, which can have significant fat tails. Thus a more stringent test is needed to ascertain whether the strategy is tradable.

If our information ratio is way higher than the best one might reasonably get by looking at all possible variations of period and trading days with a randomly generated rate, then we may have some level of confidence that the strategy is real. However, normally generated random numbers will not duplicate a lot of the fat-tailed features of the FX rates, so instead we randomly reordered the daily returns of the actual USD/JPY series. Then we repeated the search of the whole strategy space, finding the very best information ratio for all combinations of period length and buy and sell days.

The first random reordering gave a best IR of 0.84, 4.2 deviations away from the mean. One would expect a result about this good from the randomisation, so we are confirmed in our optimism that the strategy is real. However, a second randomisation gave a best IR of 1.12, which rather blows the strategy out of the water. We must conclude that the distribution of information ratios expected from such a strategy is very fat-tailed, and the results we found are nothing but data mining. We do not expect that the trading strategy will have any future predictive power. Rather sad, really.

As USD/JPY was the most promising of the currency candidates, it is unlikely that a similarly exhaustive search will throw up any more useful results. Periodic trading models – though they may look impressive in backtesting – are best omitted from currency funds and overlay programmes (see James, 2003).

CURRENCIES AND CORRELATIONS
A natural hedge?
The assumption is sometimes made that currencies offset other risks, and that this correlation effect in some way compensates for currency risk. While a superficial examination of some data series may appear to indicate significant degrees of correlation or anti-correlation between currencies and other financial variables such as equities, a more in-depth study will show that such correlations are highly variable, can range from positive to negative and are not to be relied upon. Thus, currency risk cannot be said to be compensated in this way, either. We illustrate this variability in the next example with a look at currencies and equities.

Example: A look at currency and equity correlation
Why do investors worry about the correlation between equities and FX rates? For many people this is a relatively new problem, particularly in the USA. Here, many companies grow to a substantial size without ever needing to expand abroad. When overseas investment finally occurs, the exchange rate risk can come as something of a surprise. Consider a US-based company with exposure to the EAFE index.

As can be seen in Figure 10, changes in the FX rate are comparable to changes in the index. A US company could make a good and

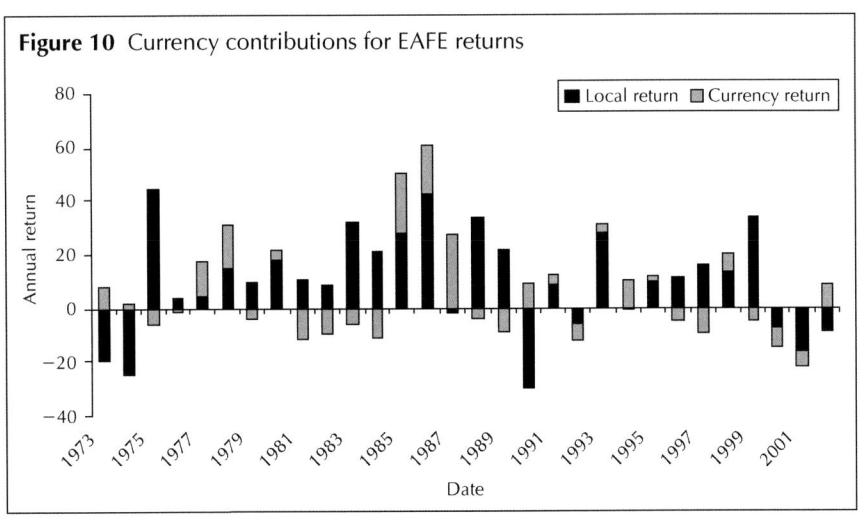

Figure 10 Currency contributions for EAFE returns

accurate judgement about the likely change in value of their equity exposure, but the FX rate changes can completely alter the situation. The FX effect is utterly variable, and, as can be seen, includes the following effects:

❑ turning a profit into a loss – 1982;
❑ reducing a profit – 1998;
❑ augmenting a profit – 1997; and
❑ worsening a loss – 2002.

The reason that the correlation between FX rates and equities is important is that an investor needs to know whether the FX rate is more likely to offset a loss than worsen it. If he can rely on the FX changes to offset losses because it is negatively correlated to the equity, then the FX effect is very desirable. However, if the two are positively correlated, then the FX effect will probably exacerbate any equity losses, and so eliminating it becomes a priority.

It is not uncommon, in the light of these concerns, to see figures published about the correlation between FX and equities. But the data that are available are sketchy and often incomplete. A point that is often missed is that it is not possible for FX rates to obey all the correlations that are assigned to them. Consider the FTSE and the DOW indices. These two equities are highly correlated with each other. It would be very difficult for the GBP/USD FX rate to have a very different correlation to the FTSE than to the DOW.

A common statement made by investors who are holding foreign equities is, "We don't hedge, because the FX rates are anticorrelated to the equities." However, what is anticorrelated? If the FX rate for the USD investor (ie, in USD terms) is anticorrelated to the FTSE, then the USD investor indeed will gain from the anticorrelation. But this will imply that the FX rate for the GPB investor (in GBP terms) will be correlated. So, one investor's protection is another's additional risk.

It is thus a good idea to be very careful of statements about correlation. Another reason for this can be seen in the Figure 11.

The graph shows the correlation between the one-day changes in the Nikkei index and the USD/JPY FX rate. However, correlations are usually quoted as a single figure, and this figure shows a line that varies over time. What is happening? What we have done

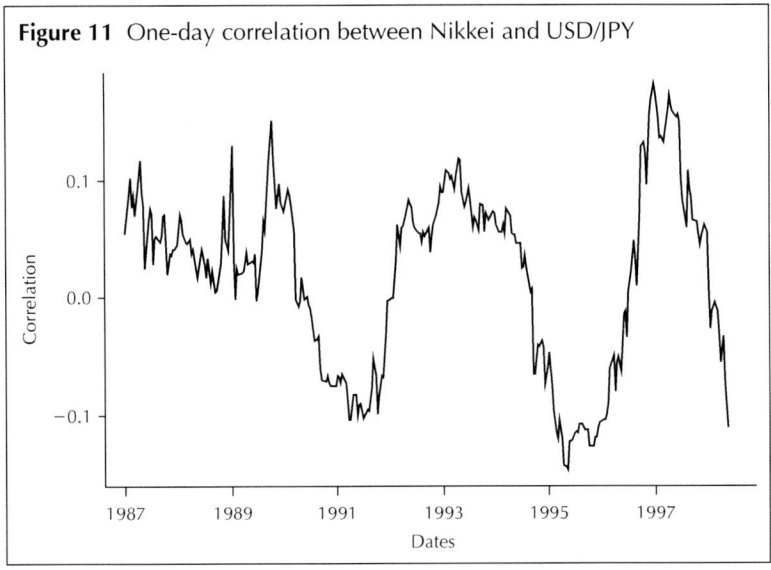

Figure 11 One-day correlation between Nikkei and USD/JPY

is use one year of data to produce each correlation number. Thus, the first number is created using data from (say) 1 January 1986 to 1 January 1987, and the second number is created using data from 2 January 1986 to 2 January 1987. There is, inevitably, a lot of overlap between successive data sets, but it does serve to illustrate how correlations do not stay constant over time.

Another effect that is not often discussed is the change of correlation with the time interval over which moves are made. Thus in Figure 11 we are looking at correlations between daily moves, a time interval of one day. We could also look at correlations between monthly moves, a time interval of about 21 business days, or longer. Figure 12 shows that time interval cannot be neglected when analysing correlations.

Looking at Figure 11 and Figure 12, we can see that the correlations are generally larger in magnitude for longer time intervals. The possible range of correlation values increases with time interval, but they are still highly variable and can be zero.

What is needed, obviously, is a way of looking at all the correlation properties of an FX rate and the relevant equity index. One excellent way of achieving this is by means of a correlation surface. On this type of graph, the time interval is plotted along one horizontal axis,

CURRENCY MANAGEMENT: OVERLAY AND ALPHA TRADING

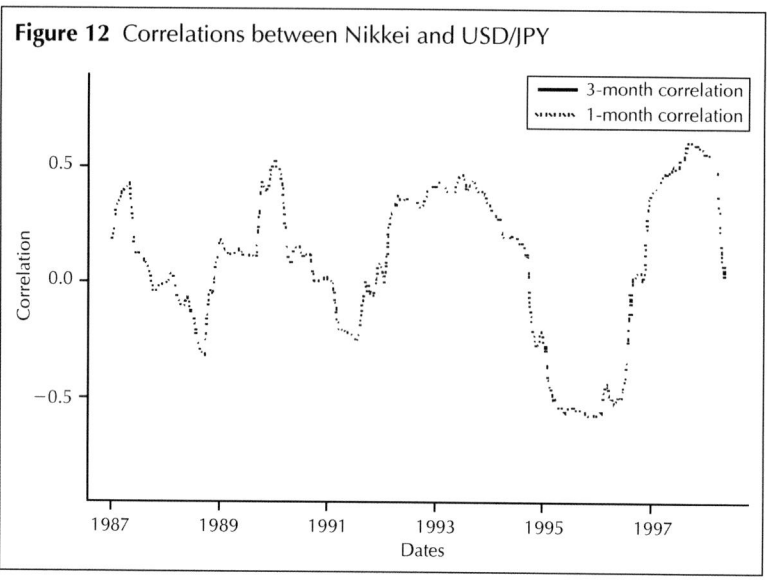

Figure 12 Correlations between Nikkei and USD/JPY

while the date goes along the other. The vertical axis represents the correlation values. The correlation surface for the changes in the Nikkei and the USD/JPY FX rate is shown in Figure 13. Note that the FX rate is from the USD investor's point of view.

This type of graph combines all available correlation information. The smaller range of correlations for smaller time intervals can be clearly seen, as can the large and significant changes in longer-term correlations. In effect, Figure 11 and Figure 12 are both "slices" through Figure 13. Why do longer time intervals seem to correspond to larger correlation values? This is simply because, as we move to longer time steps, we start to pick up joint trends in the equity and the FX rate. At very long time intervals the term "correlation" becomes less meaningful.

The correlation surface has one feature that seems consistent: the increase in the possible range of correlation values with time interval. However, it is not clear whether this range of values is skewed to the positive or negative side, or centred on zero. In Figure 14 we answer this question. This graph shows the average correlations vs time interval, compressing Figure 13 into a 2-D graph. It can be seen that while the range of correlation increases with time interval, the average is very close to zero for all time intervals.

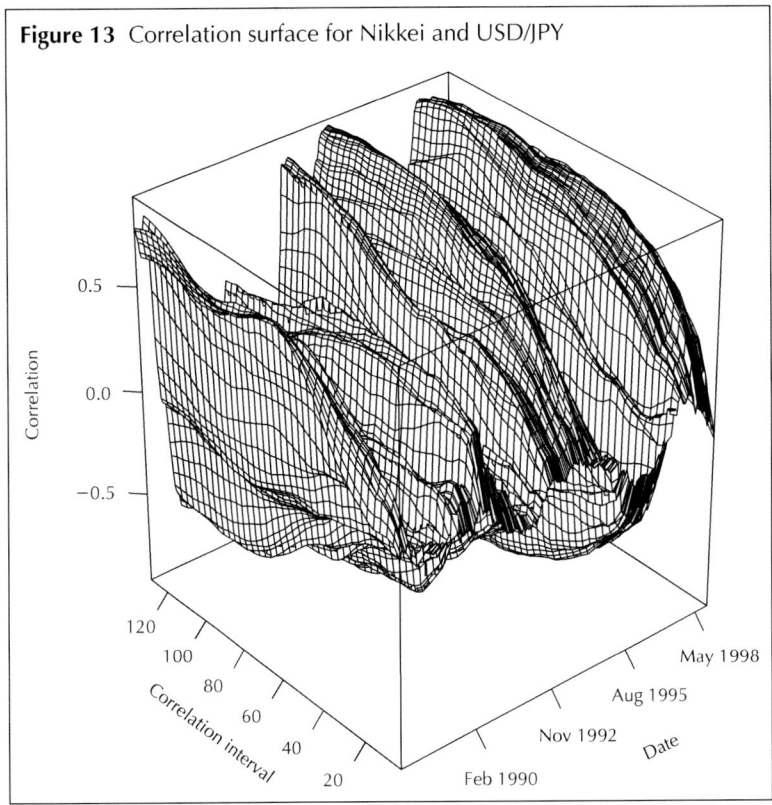

Figure 13 Correlation surface for Nikkei and USD/JPY

We can conclude that correlations between FX rates and equities are complex and unpredictable. Anyone who quotes a single number has obviously not looked into the issue in any depth. A single number is equivalent to picking a single point on the whole complex surface (see James, 1999).

More significantly, we can now confidently answer the question that a US-based investor might ask: "Should I leave my FX risk unhedged, in the hope of some protection from adverse equity moves?" The answer is no. While under some circumstances the FX risk may have a negative correlation to the equity move, it is entirely unpredictable, and is just as likely to exacerbate the losses entailed in such a move. Those very large short-term moves that hit equity investors very hard are unlikely to be mitigated by FX rates.

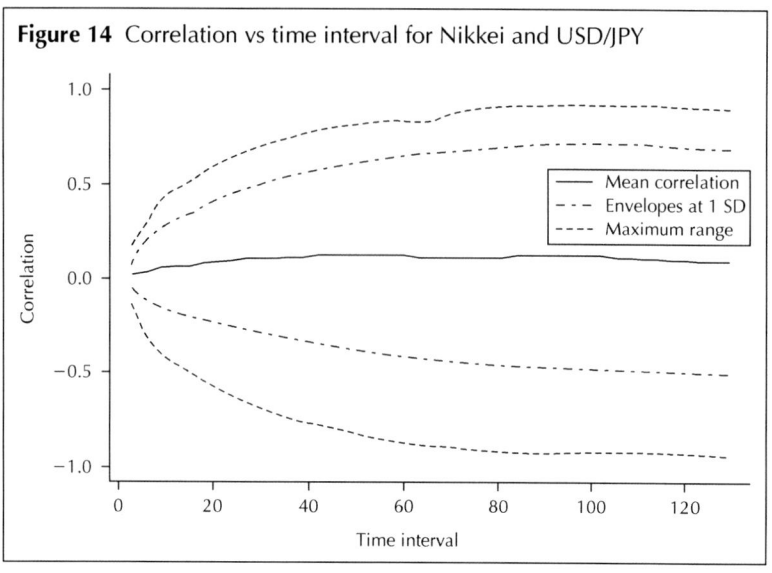

Figure 14 Correlation vs time interval for Nikkei and USD/JPY

CONCLUSION

FX rates are unique in the market with their own risks and rewards. It is all too easy to think that they are the "little brother" of interest rates, and are simpler and easier to model and trade. They have their own features and foibles, and should be regarded with respect and caution.

REFERENCES

James, J., and N. Webber, "A Chaotic Model for Interest Rates", 2003, *Quantitative Finance*, 3(1), p C8.

Attfield, C., and J. James, 1999, "In Praise of Forex Bar Data", *Risk*, September.

James, J., 1999, "Why Equities Hedging is Beneficial", *Investment and Pensions Europe*, September.

James, J., 2003, "Periodicities in Currency Trading Models", *Derivatives Week*, 12(6), February.

James, J., and N. Webber, 2000, *Interest Rate Modelling* (New York: John Wiley and Sons).

Rebonato, R., 1988, *Interest Rate Option Models* (New York: John Wiley and Sons).

4

Where Overlay Comes In

Arun Muralidhar

FX Concepts, Inc*

INTRODUCTION

In 1995, the author was asked by the treasurer of the World Bank to review the currency management arrangements for the staff retirement plan. He believes that his only real qualification to make such an assessment was that he had traded derivatives, but had no prior knowledge in either pension fund management or currency overlay for asset management. As a result, the author searched out a few overlay firms (there are not many more today) to get his education in this business.

His education, while valuable, was limited in the fact that (a) currency management was a relatively new business (FX Concepts' first client, for instance, initiated its programme only in 1987); (b) currency overlay managers had never managed pension funds and hence had a limited knowledge of the value of the overlay at the overall fund level; (c) there was a marketing dichotomy between "active managers" and "risk control" managers, without either side realising that all currency management is active management and provides risk control; and (d) an attempt was made by some of the managers to show clients that currency management was essential because without currency management there would be

---

*The author would like to thank his colleagues at FX Concepts, Inc and Ray King for helpful comments. Any errors are the author's own.

huge embarrassment risk from large negative performance outcomes – such a negative approach had marketing appeal in certain markets but conveyed a wrong view of what currency management was about.

The world is different today and clients are much more sophisticated than they were in 1995 (see Mashayekhi-Beschloss and Muralidhar, 1997) and clients have implemented many innovative programmes to improve the overall return-risk characteristics of currency overlay programmes and their overall pension funds. This chapter will briefly summarise two approaches to overlay – the first they will call the 20th-century view of currency management and the second they will call the 21st-century view of currency management. In the latter, it will demonstrate how different clients have created innovative versions of currency overlay, while tapping into the positive attributes of currency management. In closing, this chapter will demonstrate important aspects of strategies employed by managers and how they can give pension clients the maximum value for the risk allocated to this activity.

THE 20TH-CENTURY VIEW OF CURRENCY MANAGEMENT

Currency overlay was born with some innovative clients (for example, Kodak and General Motors) realising that investing abroad carried with it some unique challenges – most equity managers were held to unhedged international equity benchmarks and hence made little or no attempt to manage the "translation" risk of foreign currencies back into the base currency. For example, if the yen was going to be weak, equity managers would have an incentive to favour export-oriented companies in Japan, which would probably be a terrific equity trade, but the act of converting the client's base currency into yen to buy Japanese stocks would be a terrible currency transaction (since it would lead to lower returns in the base currency). Hence these clients realised that it was possible to hire managers with an expertise in only currency, which would not, in any way, intrude on the activities of the equity manager, to ensure that the currency composition of the international equity portfolio was managed. Prior to such a business's existence (and even many years after), there was a naïve view that if one had an unhedged international exposure it was synonymous with currencies being "unmanaged".

EVOLUTION OF THE INDUSTRY AND ITS IMPACT ON INVESTMENT STRATEGIES

The industry grew out of managing the translation risk with respect to international equity investments, and hence a number of biases began to creep into the investment strategies of managers as well as the "education" they imparted to clients. The first bias was that most pension plans looked at the currency management only as a risk management programme, and typically it pertained only to international equities. As a result, the early versions of the programme were such that currency managers were typically allowed to sell only foreign currencies in favour of base currencies (and were not allowed to enter into cross-hedges or trades where the two legs of the currency transaction did not include the base currency).

For simplicity, we will call this approach "selective hedge". This had many negative implications that we will explore later, but probably the most significant was that it caused most currency managers to build individual currency models for the major currency pairs (models for US dollar/French franc, US dollar/Japanese yen and so forth). As a result, the creation of the euro would have interesting implications for a number of strategies and optimal portfolio construction.

The second naïve focus on purely embarrassment risk allowed currency managers to exploit the fact that currency returns had fat tails – in other words, there was a reasonably high probability that currency returns could be very negative, thereby embarrassing the client. In such a situation, clients felt the pressure to implement a currency programme for fear of being accused of being negligent. Figure 1 demonstrates how unmanaged currency returns from international equity portfolios, for Canadian clients are fat-tailed (light bars). The case was made to clients that hiring currency managers would generate excess returns and make the return distribution more normal. However, if large negative returns were an issue for clients, active management is not the only solution – a simple 50% passive hedge ratio would eliminate these tail events as shown in Figure 1 (dark bars).

The third naïve recommendation came from the fact that the primary roots of the business were in trying to manage large negative events and profiting from positive movements. The ideal instrument for such a transaction would be for the client to purchase an

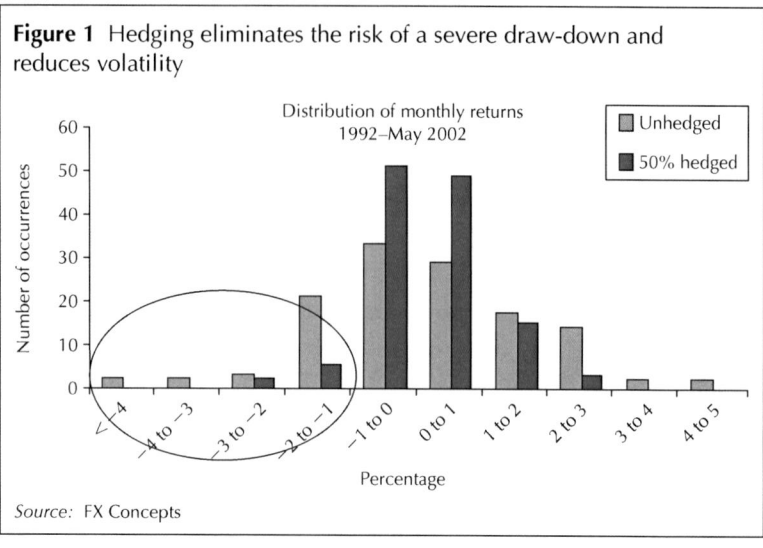

Figure 1 Hedging eliminates the risk of a severe draw-down and reduces volatility

Source: FX Concepts

option, but most managers realised early on that options are typically overpriced. Hence, the activities of most managers are in the form of creating options dynamically through the use of forward contracts. While most "active managers" would be loath to admit that they are "dynamically" creating options – as that is the reserve of the "options replicators" – there is nothing wrong with generating a call option profile, if the mean of the returns is higher than that of the benchmark – ie, the manager generates excess returns. The managers adopted three styles of management: *trend following*, *fundamental economic analysis* and *risk control* (a form of trend following with more focus on options replication than directional trading). Most clients early, on and even most managers, precluded the use of options in currency management programmes. However, by diversifying across managers, most clients diversified their risk of underperformance (Muralidhar and Tsumagari, 1999). Finally, most clients did not even bother to consider emerging market currencies, as most managers did not provide products to cover this market (see Muralidhar, 2001).

CURRENCY OVERLAY DELIVERED ON ITS PROMISE
In spite of these restrictions, currency managers had a reasonably strong performance over the first decade of their existence

(Strange, 1998; Baldridge, Meath and Myers, 2000; Hersey and Ogunc, 2000). Most consultants by the end of the first decade had come out in favour of active management as a means of generating positive returns. What is interesting is that these studies did not focus on the risk management aspects of currency overlay, even though the industry grew out of a risk management focus. Most of these studies explicitly or implicitly recognised that currency management had a higher calling. Some simple analyses demonstrated that active currency programmes, by effectively eliminating the large negative tail events, were able to change the distribution of returns not only to shift the mean (ie, add excess returns), but also eliminate the left tails (see Muralidhar, 2000). Further, by examining the positions of all currency managers, it was possible to show that even those managers who classified themselves as "risk control" were taking off-benchmark positions with embedded directional views (see Muralidhar and Pasquariello, 2001). In short, all managers, regardless of marketing label, were active managers, and, by virtue of dynamically creating options through the use of forward contracts, were providing risk control as well. Moreover, even though the data on these programmes ranged from as little as three years to as many as ten years, it was possible to have a high confidence that there was skill in these investment processes (Muralidhar, 1999).

THE EVOLVING VIEW ON CURRENCY MANAGEMENT AND THE COMING OF THE EURO
Don't be cross with cross-hedging
As clients had more experience with currency management they began to realise that programmes could be improved from the selective-hedge programmes. The first realisation was that the exclusion of cross-hedging as a strategy to be used by currency managers could actually lead to more risk in the portfolio. For example, if an equity manager allocated more to British equities with a corresponding underweight in Japanese stocks, they were also implicitly taking a view on the pound–yen relationship. Not allowing a currency manager to implement a cross-hedge ran the risk of leaving a position in the portfolio that could be detrimental to the performance of the fund. In addition, currency managers were clamouring for the possibility to diversify risk in a market

where, even prior to the creation of the euro, there were only 20 possible trades that could be implemented in selective-hedge programmes. Cross-hedging gave managers more possibilities and allowed them to generate higher information ratios (Muralidhar and Richmond, 1999).

Taking off the blinders – A portfolio view of currency management

The more important realisation was that just managing the currency risk in international equities with a view to lowering the risk from international equities and potentially raising returns was extremely naïve. Any activity made in the context of any part of a portfolio needs to be viewed from the perspective of what it provides to the total portfolio and not just to a microcosm. The realisation that active currency returns were uncorrelated with the returns of most asset classes (Muralidhar, 2000) – and, more important, because the lack of correlation with these assets would have a significant ability to lower asset-liability risks and lower potential contributions for a pension fund (Muralidhar, Prajogi and van der Wouden, 2000) – led to a much more refined view of the benefits of currency management. In effect, currency overlay could provide an uncorrelated source of alpha to the pension fund. Hence, limiting the contribution of such an alpha source to international equities (or worrying about whether it made one asset-class return more normal) would limit the overall benefit to a pension fund, especially in the 21st century, when many funds found that their risk to liabilities was increasing and potential contributions rising.

Europhobia, euphoria and adapting to the new world in currencies

The creation of the euro played a bad trick on currency managers. To begin with, currency managers had strong performance and information ratios, and this was managed with only 20 currencies (which, given cross-hedging, gave a fair opportunity set). A number of research studies highlighted earlier suggested that the alphas in currency management were approximately 150 bps annualised and information ratios ranged from 0.5 to 0.7. However, the arrival of the euro took 10 currencies off the table – this would be akin to an equity manager being told that the S&P500 was now suddenly just the S&P250!

Most currency managers reacted to this event by modifying their Deutschmark models with mixed results. However, the bigger problem for currency managers was that the markets were moving sideways more frequently and performance was becoming more lumpy (Muralidhar and Neelakandan, 2002b and 2003). Moreover, since currencies were moving sideways currency managers were struggling with another problem – building a strategy that was based on many individual currency-pair models required the manager to have a good sense of which currencies would be in motion or else the client's risk was being poorly allocated.

THE 21ST-CENTURY VIEW ON CURRENCY MANAGEMENT
The impetus to currency overlay management came from two fronts: first, a number of consultants verified that this activity was an alpha generator and that the industry as a whole had performed well; second, with mainstream markets starting to underperform, there came the recognition that even 150 bps of excess return (without any upfront funding) could be invaluable to improving the overall returns of the pension fund. Very quickly, the focus shifted from hedging exposures inherent in underlying equity exposures to a concept of budgeting risk to generate the highest possible uncorrelated return (uncorrelated to other asset classes).

The many virtues of currency management
The attractiveness of currency management was that (a) it was unfunded; (b) it was completely transparent; (c) it exploited a market inefficiency in that there were many nonprofit participants (unlike other asset classes where all participants are profit-oriented); (d) it was a very large market and hence could be exploited in size; (e) it was a pure cash-generation strategy; and (f) liquidity was not an issue as a programme could be terminated in as little as two days (Muralidhar, 2002).

Around this line of thinking, there are two schools of thought: (a) those clients who apply currency management to both international bond and equity allocations (increasingly clients are realising that most of the alpha from international bond investments can be attributed to currencies); and (b) those clients who realise that holding the base currency is an active currency decision and are willing to apply currency management to the entire portfolio. In the latter camp, one is likely to find innovative clients who realise that the absolute value of the fund needs to be protected. Hence, holding assets in the local currency may be detrimental to overall value and they want to reserve the right to sell the base currency as well. These mandates are implemented on either an unlevered or levered basis. Under this form of currency overlay, which we label "diversified currency overlay", discretion is given to managers to create optimal portfolios of currencies, with cross-hedging, net shorts and net longs permitted. Typically, restrictions, if any, are based on liquidity tiering, whereby the manager is constrained from allocating a large portion of the risk budget to illiquid currencies (see Muralidhar, O'Grady and Simotas, 2002). More sophisticated clients also tend to want managers who create portfolios dynamically (rather than on the basis of individual currency models) within a risk-budgeting framework. As one can see, within the space of a little more than a decade, the objectives – and thereby the focus of clients – have shifted, causing managers to evolve the strategies they offer.

ARE CURRENCY CLIENTS BEING SHORT-CHANGED?

As clients have begun to focus more on currency as a provider of a high return–risk ratio, the biggest challenge to managers continues to be the reduced opportunity set after the creation of the euro. Instruments and markets that currency managers had previously ignored are now vital to the success of the industry. As Figure 2 demonstrates, clients could have three types of objectives/desired mandates as shown on the vertical axis of the matrix: (a) standard overlay or selective hedge; (b) enhanced overlay or diversified currency overlay; and (c) leveraged versions of the diversified currency overlay. The sources of diversification are shown on the horizontal axis: (a) using forwards only in developed markets (current practice); (b) including options in developed markets; and (c) adding in emerging markets, which could provide as many as 22 additional currencies.

In the boxes of the matrix, we can see the number of managers, the alpha expectation and the expected information ratio. The chart shows that the industry is concentrated in the top left corner of the

Figure 2 Innovative ideas in currency management

	Developed markets (forwards)	Developed markets – options enhanced	Emerging markets (deliverable and non-deliverable forwards)
Standard overlay			
❑ No of managers	20	Fewer than 5	Fewer than 5
❑ Return expectations	1–1.5%	1.75–2.25%	2–3%
❑ Information ratio	0.4–0.5	0.6–0.8	0.8–1.0
Enhanced overlay			
❑ No of managers	10–15	Fewer than 5	Fewer than 5
❑ Return expectations	2–2.5%	2.5–3%	3.5–5%
❑ Information ratio	0.6–0.8	0.8–1.0	1–1.25
Leveraged products			
❑ No of managers	5–10	Fewer than 5	Fewer than 5
❑ Return expectations	10–15%	15–20%	20–25%
❑ Information ratio	0.6–0.8	0.8–1.0	1.00–1.25

matrix, and, while that is acceptable given the information ratios in other asset classes, clients would probably want to be in the bottom right corner (Muralidhar, 2002). In short, clients could be getting short-changed by managers only because there are simple rules that make money in currency markets and allow for decent information ratios – decent from the perspective of what other asset classes offer (Muralidhar and Neelakandan, 2003). However, as one moves to the bottom right corner, the choice of managers, already somewhat limited in this industry, is likely to get even worse.

INCREASING YOUR OPTIONS

Research has shown that options strategies can clearly benefit currency clients (see Huang, Srivastava and Raatz, 2001; Colchester and James, 2003; Muralidhar and Neelakandan, 2002a; Muralidhar and Neelakandan, 2002b, 2003) and this will be a new growth area. Already, one innovative client has implemented an options-only overlay on an existing overlay strategy with a fundamental and technical manager as a way of increasing the information ratio of the mandate, without increasing the risk budget and severely reducing the number of negative months. As more clients realise that mandates that exclude the use of options provide less than adequate diversification and potentially lumpy returns, the scope of the industry is likely to expand greatly.

APPLICATIONS TO OTHER INVESTMENT AREAS

While the industry grew up around managing the risk of pension funds, increasingly providers of products to this client base have begun to realise that leaving currency risk unmanaged is bad for business. If one wants to provide products on a truly global basis, then products need to be provided which protect the value regardless of base currency. We have seen interest from real estate funds and hedge funds that want to offer their investors the choice of currency in which they would like to receive their returns – ie, investment made independent of the base currency of the client with currency overlays implemented to protect the base currency value for the client (see Mehrzad and Muralidhar, 2001). More important, even hedge funds fund-of-funds have begun to realise that the absolute level of their returns is impacted by the fact that they are benchmarked to a cash index (eg, LIBOR) and when US dollar LIBOR declines, as it did in the early 2000–03 period, the absolute value of the returns of these funds-of-funds declined dramatically. One way for these funds-of-funds to extract more value from their cash allocations is to implement currency strategies on the cash component to allow them to increase the return without having to liquidate other investments, while benefiting dramatically from the lack of correlation with other strategies (Krishnamurthi and Muralidhar, 2003).

SUMMARY

The industry has evolved from naïve risk management of currency exposures that were left unmanaged by equity managers, with minimal alpha expectations, to one where mandates are sophisticated versions of those one would typically find in hedge fund funds-of-funds portfolios. Increasingly, the focus is on budgeting risk to managers that create optimised portfolios with limitations on individual currency allocations based on liquidity rather than underlying allocation of equity managers. Moreover, the recognition that uncorrelated alpha strategies are desirable from the point of view of overall portfolio construction means that the industry will grow exponentially. For it to do so, strategies will need to evolve to include instruments and markets previously underexploited, such as options and emerging markets, and the challenge will be for research staff to be at the cutting edge as the desire for high return–risk strategies increases in coming years.

BIBLIOGRAPHY

Baldridge, J., B. Meath, and H. Myers, 2000, "Capturing Alpha through Active Currency Overlay", Frank Russell Research Commentary, May.

Colchester, H., and J. James, 2003, "The Value of FX Options. Citigroup", *FX Advisory*, Issue 19, February.

Hersey, B., and K. Ogunc, 2000, "Designing Portable Alpha Engines", *Investments and Pensions Europe*, October.

Huang, T., V. Srivastava, and S. Raatz, 2001, "Portfolio Optimization with Options in the Foreign Exchange Market", *Derivatives Use, Trading and Regulation*, 7(1).

Litterman, R., et al, 2001, "The Green Zone … Assessing the Quality of Returns", *Journal of Performance Measurement*, 5(3), Spring.

Mashayekhi-Beschloss, A., and A. Muralidhar, 1997, "Managing Implementation Risks of Currency Overlay", *Journal of Pension Plan Investing*, 1(3), Winter.

Mehrzad, K., and A. Muralidhar, 2001, "Hedging Currency Risk in Hedge Fund Investments", *Hedge Fund News*, Issue 27.

Muralidhar, A., 1999, "Currency Overlay Performance: Luck or Skill?", *Investments and Pensions – Europe*, September.

Muralidhar, A., 2000, "Enhancing Performance through Currencies in a Risk-Controlled Way", *Global Pensions*, January.

Muralidhar, A., 2001, "Why Plan Sponsors Should Hedge Emerging Market Investments", unpublished FX Concepts Research Paper.

Muralidhar, A., 2002, "Currencies as a Perfect Long–Short Alternative Investment Strategy", *AIMA Newsletter*, Issue 51, April.

Muralidhar, A., 2003, "Are Currency Overlay Clients Getting 'Short Changed'?", unpublished FX Concepts Research Paper.

Muralidhar, A., and H. Neelakandan, 2002a, "Options to Enhance Currency Overlay Programs", *Investments and Pensions – Europe*, February.

Muralidhar, A., and H. Neelakandan, 2002b, "Don't Be Grumpy if Your Returns are Lumpy", *GT News*, September.

Muralidhar, A., and H. Neelakandan, 2003, "Unstrangle' Currency Performance by Straddling Different Strategies", *Investments and Pensions – Europe*, September.

Muralidhar, A., R. O'Grady, and P. Simotas, 2002, "Emerging Innovative Trends in Currency Management", *FX and MM*, Issue 3.

Muralidhar, A., and P. Pasquariello, 2001, "Views: Use and Abuse", *Journal of Asset Management*, 2(1), June.

Muralidhar, A., R. Prajogi, and R. J. P. van der Wouden, 2000, "An Asset–Liability Analysis of the Currency Decision for Pension Plans", *Derivatives Quarterly*, 7(2).

Muralidhar, A., and H. Richmond, 1999, "Action Stations", *Futures and OTC World*, Issue 336, April.

Muralidhar, A., and M. Tsumagari, 1999, "A Matter of Style", *Futures and OTC World*, Issue 336, April.

Strange, B., 1998, "Currency Overlay Managers Show Consistency", *Pensions and Investments*, 15 June.

5

The Case for Currency Management

Brian Strange

JPMorgan Fleming Investment Management

As investors worldwide continue to increase allocations to non-domestic assets, in both equity and fixed-income markets, they face a volatility of returns, which they often fail to consider adequately, because it is an inherited risk – an afterthought. Along with those stocks and bonds comes a hidden source of risk – the currencies in which they are denominated. If currencies rise, returns are boosted; if they fall, earnings are diminished. Those currency moves can be substantial in relation to the underlying investment return and they're not always a one-way bet. They can be substantially positive for a period of years, enhancing international investment returns and then turn equally negative, subtracting value. It is estimated that around 40% of the volatility of non-domestic equity assets arises from currency movements. The figure rises to 60–70% for offshore bonds.

History has shown that:

❑ in the short term, currency moves have been significant, in relation to underlying asset returns, leaving scope for active management;
❑ in the long term, currencies offer only risk and little return;

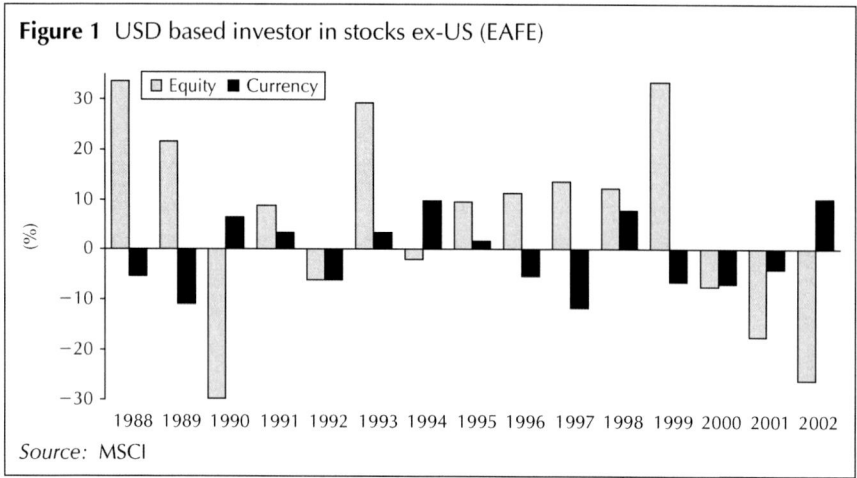

Figure 1 USD based investor in stocks ex-US (EAFE)
Source: MSCI

- currency risk is properly managed, first, by making a hedging benchmark decision; and
- currency managers on average have added value, suggesting that active management is more successful in this asset class compared with others.

CURRENCY MOVEMENTS CAN BE SIGNIFICANT

Figures 1, 2 and 3 show the experience since 1988 for international equity investors from various base currencies:

- a USD-based investor in the EAFE index;
- a GBP-based investor in the MSCI ex-UK equity index;
- a European EUR-based investor in the MSCI ex-Europe equity index.

Currency return is the difference between local market equity return and the total return back into base currency. Each figure details the local market return and the currency return. It is easy to see that in all cases:

- currency return is substantial when compared with investment returns; and
- currency moves can both enhance and diminish returns.

There is no clear pattern emerging of one strategy dominating another. In summary, the impact from each investor's perspective for the 15 years is as shown in Table 1.

THE CASE FOR CURRENCY MANAGEMENT

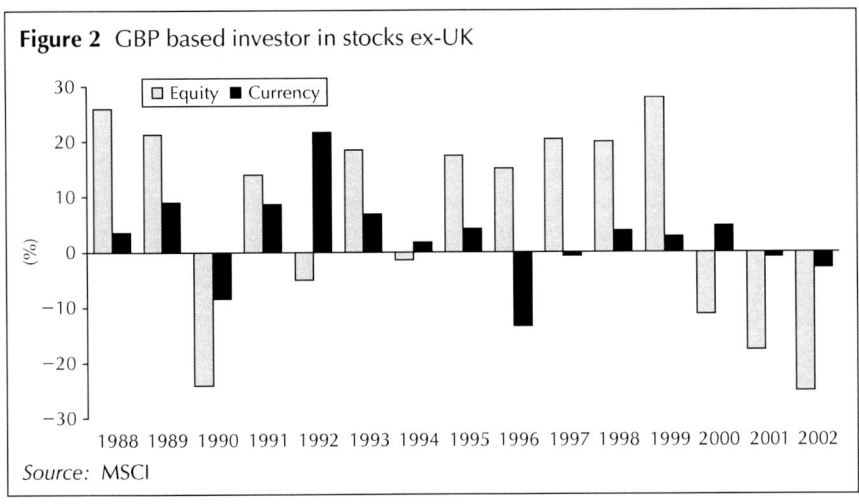

Figure 2 GBP based investor in stocks ex-UK
Source: MSCI

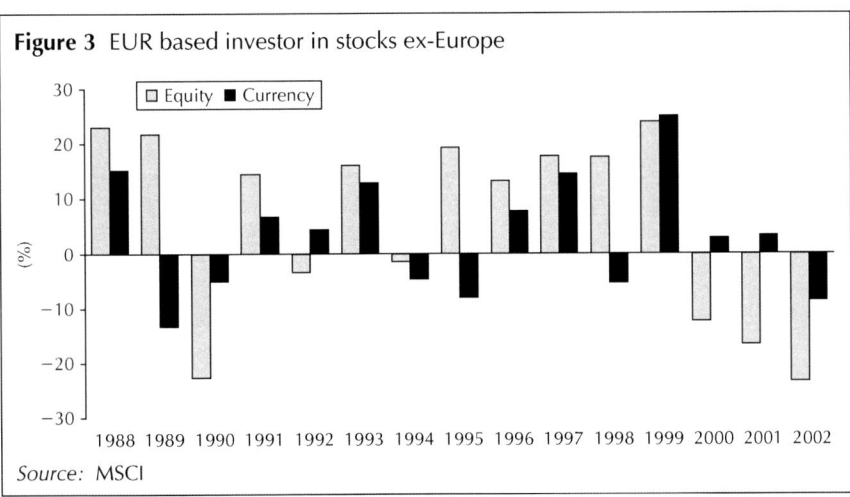

Figure 3 EUR based investor in stocks ex-Europe
Source: MSCI

Table 1 Summary of the return, between local return and currency

	Number of years		
Currency impact	USD investor	GBP investor	EUR investor
Enhanced returns	7	10	9
Detracted from returns	8	5	6

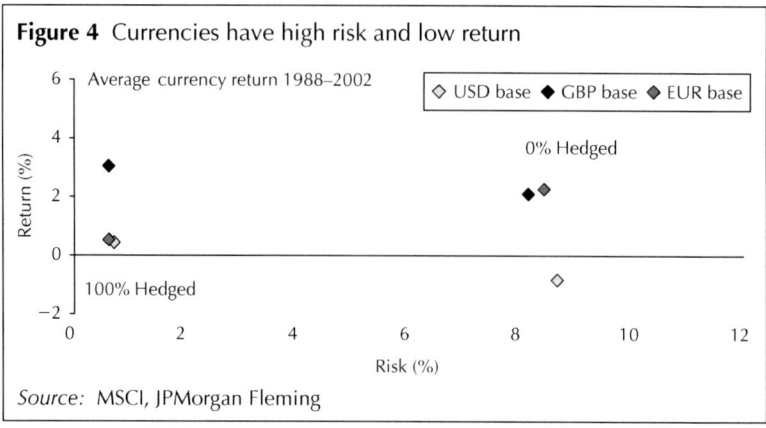

Figure 4 Currencies have high risk and low return

Source: MSCI, JPMorgan Fleming

CURRENCY IS AN UNREWARDED RISK

While Figures 1, 2 and 3 show a year-by-year picture, over the longer term it is clear that currencies are an unrewarded risk. Figure 4 details the average return and standard deviation of the currency component of world equity baskets ex-UK and ex-Europe and EAFE. It covers the same time period as the annual charts.

From all investor bases it is evident that currency is a relatively unrewarded risk. Both US and UK investors could have earned more by hedging all the time and taking no currency risk. Such was the power of forward premiums on currencies against the US dollar and against sterling. In essence, hedgers in each country earned the differential between their generally higher interest rates and the predominantly lower interest rates in other currencies, notably Europe and Japan. EUR-based investors fared slightly better on an unhedged basis than if they'd hedged. However, the enhanced return was rather slight in proportion to the incremental risk borne. The Sharpe ratio is an unimpressive 0.22.

What should an investor do? We'll consider one option briefly – raising strategic benchmark hedge ratios – and another in more detail – active currency management.

CHOOSING A BENCHMARK HEDGE RATIO

Most often when pension plans do asset allocation studies, they will use only unhedged return and risk assumptions for foreign assets, calculated back into their base currency. They then optimise

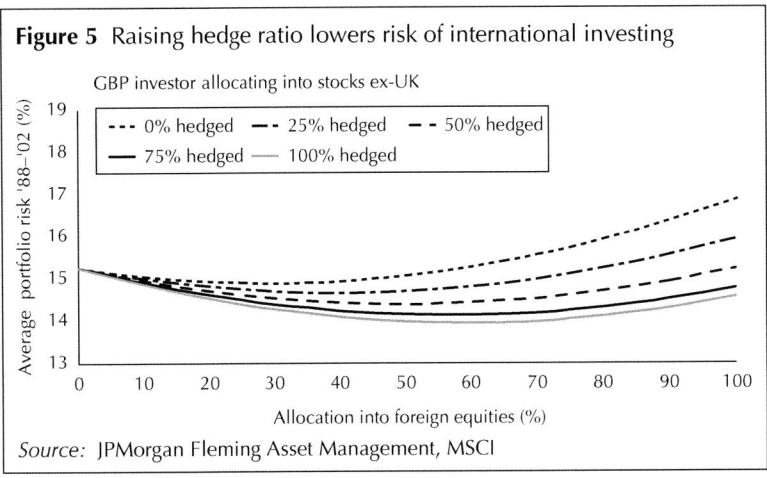

Figure 5 Raising hedge ratio lowers risk of international investing

for the asset classes delivering the most return for the risk taken – ie, the Sharpe ratio. If a slightly more detailed approach is taken, and foreign asset return/risk assumptions are broken out into those for hedged and unhedged assets, the optimisation exercise usually suggests higher hedge ratios as a policy benchmark. This comes as a result of the earlier observation that the difference in currency returns between unhedged and fully hedged is very slight, while the difference in risk is sizable.

From a portfolio perspective, it is interesting to note the difference in overall risk as increasing allocations are made to international assets. Figure 5 focuses on the experience of a GBP-based investor. While international investing provides portfolio diversification in the form of lower overall risk, it does so on an unhedged basis only up to a certain point. Once allocations extend beyond about 30%, portfolio risk tends to rise if foreign investments are unhedged. It is easy to see that as hedge ratios rise, greater portions can be invested in international assets without raising total portfolio risk levels. It can also be noticed that as the hedge ratio is raised, each successive level provides proportionately less risk reduction. Most of the job is done once the 50–75% hedged level is reached.

The implication of this is that other asset classes might produce better incremental returns for the incremental risk than currencies. After reducing portfolio risk by choosing higher hedge ratios, many plans opt for higher commitments to equities or other risky assets where there is a risk premium to be earned, although much discussion argues that the level of the equity premium is waning.

CONSIDERING ACTIVE MANAGEMENT

Once the strategic benchmark hedge ratio is established, active management should be considered. Several observations are worth exploring:

❑ currency markets offer several inefficiencies which active managers exploit;
❑ even fairly simple naïve trading rules can produce results; and
❑ the general industry track record of currency overlay managers has also been encouraging.

MARKET INEFFICIENCIES

Two market factors seem to stand out – the forward rate bias and the fact that exchange rates tend to trend. The Purchasing Power Parity theorem predicts that inflation differentials between countries will be made up for by appreciation/depreciation of exchange rates. While this may hold in the long run, shorter-term observances prove otherwise. Figure 6 details the change in exchange rates for a given

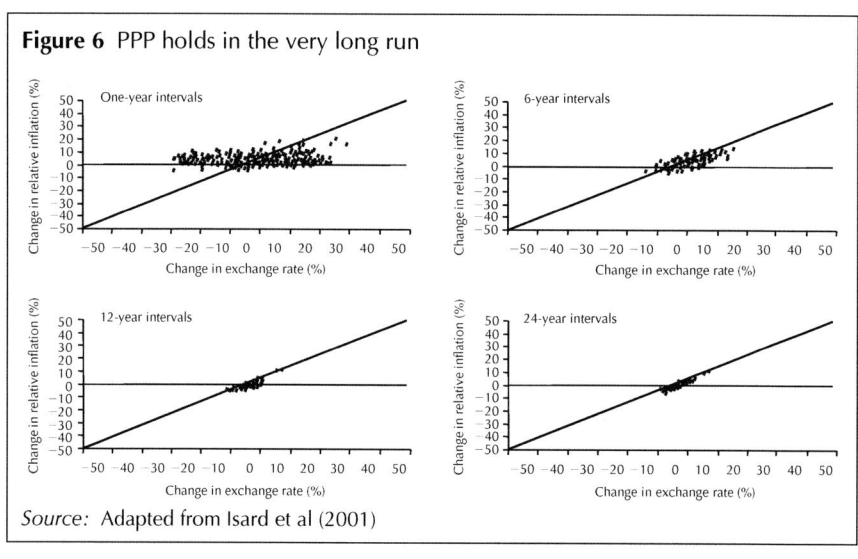

Figure 6 PPP holds in the very long run

Source: Adapted from Isard et al (2001)

THE CASE FOR CURRENCY MANAGEMENT

inflation differential. The fit doesn't even come close until much longer intervals are achieved.

Interest rates are, however, more tied-in to inflation rates and much more immediately. Interest rates also determine the forward prices of currencies for future delivery, with currencies having lower interest rates than the base currency offering premiums, and those with higher interest rates selling at discounts.

Several writers, focusing on the fact that, contrary to theory, forward rates were very poor predictors of future spot rates, observed a bias of forward rates consistently falling short of their theoretical target (see Fama, 1984 and Kritzman, 1993). If premiums suggest that currencies should rise, they never consistently rise to the forward rate; when discounts imply currencies falling, they fall short of the level suggested by the forward rate, this can be seen in Figure 7.

The conclusion was that the "forward rate has systematically and significantly overestimated the subsequent change in the spot rate. On balance, hedgers have suffered losses when they have sold forward contracts at discounts or purchased them at premiums, while they have reaped gains when they sold currency forward contracts at premiums and purchased them at discounts" (see Kritzman, 1993). A simple rule to capitalise on this would be to hedge whenever offered a premium and never hedge when it costs a discount.

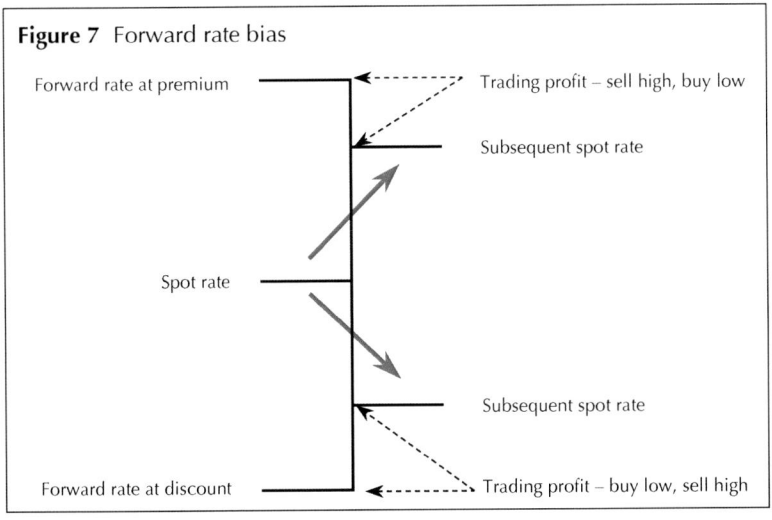

Figure 7 Forward rate bias

An AIMR publication focusing on currency risk management examined the behaviour of exchange rate prices and pointed out that currencies tended to exhibit persistent monthly trends (serial correlation, see Clarke and Kritzman, 1996). Thus, investors could profit by hedging less when positive trends existed, and more when they were negative. The trick, of course, is to identify the trend, and technical trading rules are the tool. In a recent study, Deutsche Bank demonstrated the effectiveness of moving average combinations. Figure 8 displays the results for optimised moving average combinations for a variety of currency pairs for the period from January 1986 to April 2002, put together by Deutsche Bank (see Rosenberg and Folkerts-Landau, 2002). All were profitable, with respectable Sharpe ratios indicating that good returns were produced with acceptable levels of risk. Other writers have also confirmed the effectiveness of technical rules (see Levich and Thomas, 1993 and Reinert, 2000).

If, as Roger Clarke and Mark Kritzman pointed out, serial correlation suggests that the probability is higher that currencies will rise this month if they did so last month, rather than revert to a mean (and vice versa), then a simple rule can be cobbled together to try to exploit this trending environment – whatever worked in the prior period should be pursued again. If hedging made money, then hedge again; if hedging lost money, then don't hedge. Success will depend upon spot rates moving in trends and overcoming the level of forward rates.

SIMPLE RULES CAN ADD VALUE

If the market observations are universal, then they should hold true, despite the currency base. So let's apply the rules for investors from all currency bases, to the exposures they hold in their world equity portfolios outside of their currency base. The object is to analyse the effectiveness as a substitute for an active management strategy, to see if value can be added. They'll be applied to the portfolio as a basket, and only at the beginning of each month. If a portfolio as a whole offers a premium, it will be hedged for the month. If the basket forward is at a discount, it will be left uncovered. If the portfolio rose in value last month due to currencies, it will be left uncovered this month. If the value fell last month, it will be hedged this month.

Figure 8 Trend identification rules work

Profit and losses from optimal moving-average trading rules (January 1986–April 2002)

	DEM	JPY	GBP	CAD	AUD	NZD	CHF
Optimal moving-average (days)	**1/32**	**8/59**	**1/19**	**14/199**	**1/16**	**10/17**	**1/57**
Average annual return (%)	5.0	9.2	5.8	1.9	3.5	5.2	8.6
Standard deviations of returns (%)	11.1	11.8	9.5	4.8	10.3	10.8	11.7
Sharpe ratio	0.45	0.78	0.61	0.40	0.34	0.48	0.78
Total recommended trades	342	81	452	35	218	165	217
Winning trades	91	37	126	13	61	58	57
Winning trade percentage (%)	27	46	28	37	28	35	26
Losing trades	251	44	326	22	157	107	160
Losing trade percentage (%)	73	54	72	63	72	65	74
Average profit on winning trades (%)	2.97	5.92	2.27	3.69	2.03	2.11	4.63
Average profit on losing trades (%)	−0.77	−1.72	−0.62	−1.03	−0.63	−0.84	−0.84
Ratio of profits/losses	3.86	3.44	3.66	3.58	3.22	2.51	5.51

Note: A Sharpe ratio measures the amount of return on an investment (less the return of a risk-free asset) per unit of risk, which is proxied by its standard deviation.
Source: Datastream and Deutsche Bank.

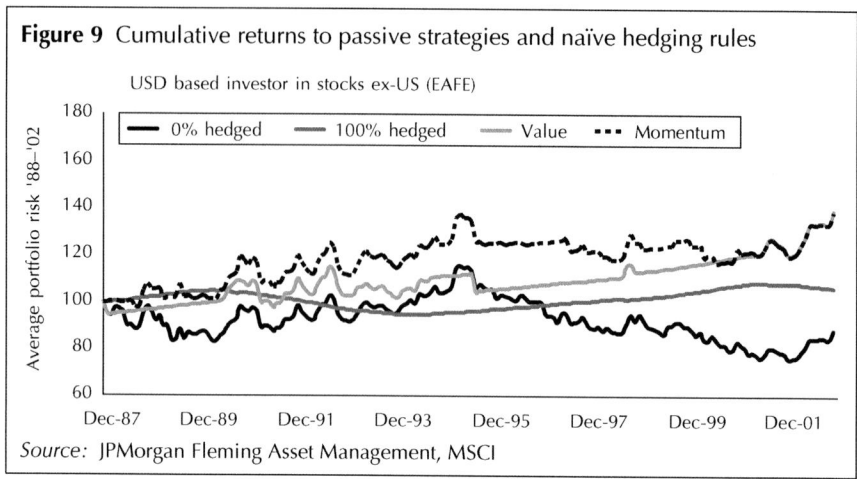

Figure 9 Cumulative returns to passive strategies and naïve hedging rules

Source: JPMorgan Fleming Asset Management, MSCI

Table 2 Summary of figures 9–11

	Rank of cumulative returns		
Strategy	**USD investor**	**GBP investor**	**EUR investor**
Passive unhedged	4	4	2
Passive fully hedged	3	1	4
Value	2	2	3
Momentum	1	3	1

The strategies will be referred to as "Value" and "Momentum", respectively. Two other sets of writers have confirmed similar approaches. The Differential Forward strategy examined by Acar and Maitra (2000) is a counterpart to the Value, and the AFX basket of moving averages spelled out by Lequeux and Acar (1998) mimics the idea behind Momentum, identifying trends when they exist.

Each strategy is ranked for its ending cumulative value for each investor base, although, throughout the time period, there was considerable changing of places. At least one of the naïve strategies placed in the top half for each investor, and the other one was the in the next rank down. (See Table 2.)

Figures 9, 10 and 11 detail the progress of each strategy from the various investor bases. Generally, the unhedged approach was the more volatile, eventually losing money for the US investor, gaining

THE CASE FOR CURRENCY MANAGEMENT

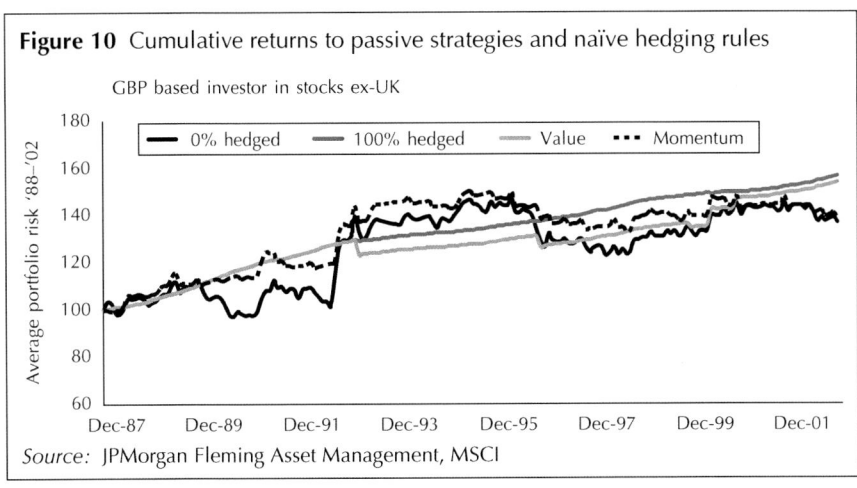

Figure 10 Cumulative returns to passive strategies and naïve hedging rules

Source: JPMorgan Fleming Asset Management, MSCI

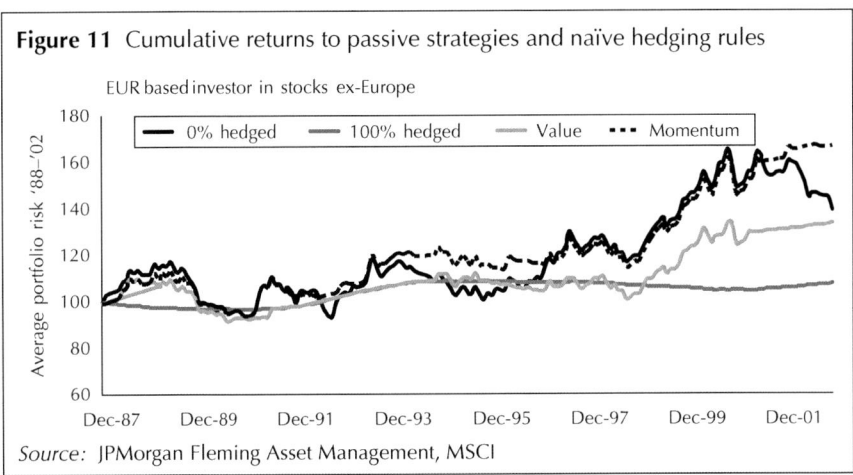

Figure 11 Cumulative returns to passive strategies and naïve hedging rules

Source: JPMorgan Fleming Asset Management, MSCI

for the UK one, and mostly flat until the very end for those with a European base.

Passively hedging was generally a flat, smooth ride for US and European investors. For a UK base, passive 100% hedging led nearly the entire time period. Such is the power of the long-term accumulation of premiums from forward contracts. Sometimes spot movements overcame the forward pricing, while at others it lagged, but in the long term it won out. The "Value" approach looks almost identical to the passively hedged approach for the

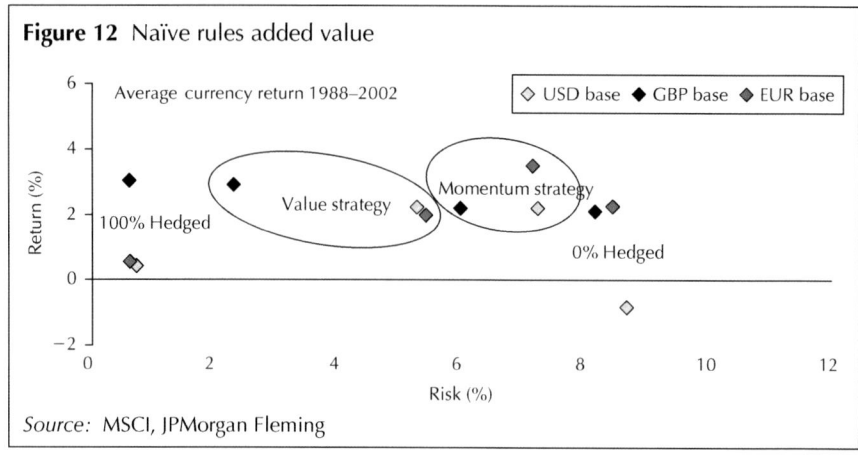

Figure 12 Naïve rules added value

Source: MSCI, JPMorgan Fleming

very good reason that most currencies had lower interest rates than sterling, thus offering a premium in the forward market. The opposite is true for the EUR investor, since discounts generally dictate an unhedged approach under the Value strategy. For the USD base, it changes places several times.

The average risk and return calculations for the active strategies are shown in Figure 12 and indicate that value has been added relative to doing nothing. Returns have been enhanced and risk has been reduced, generally falling between the two passive approaches.

The good news is that active strategies (as represented by the Value and Momentum approaches) didn't destroy diversification, a frequent concern of portfolio investors. The correlation coefficients for the monthly returns for each strategy, compared with the local return of stocks and bonds, ranged between +0.11 and −0.25 for the entire period.

CURRENCY OVERLAY MANAGERS HAVE ADDED VALUE

After seeing that inefficiencies persist in foreign exchange markets, and that simple rules can be structured to exploit them, the question of just how actual managers have done might be raised. The first survey of currency overlay manager performance was completed and published in 1998 (see Strange, 1998). Fourteen managers participated, submitting quarterly data for both account returns and the relevant benchmark returns for 152 accounts

THE CASE FOR CURRENCY MANAGEMENT

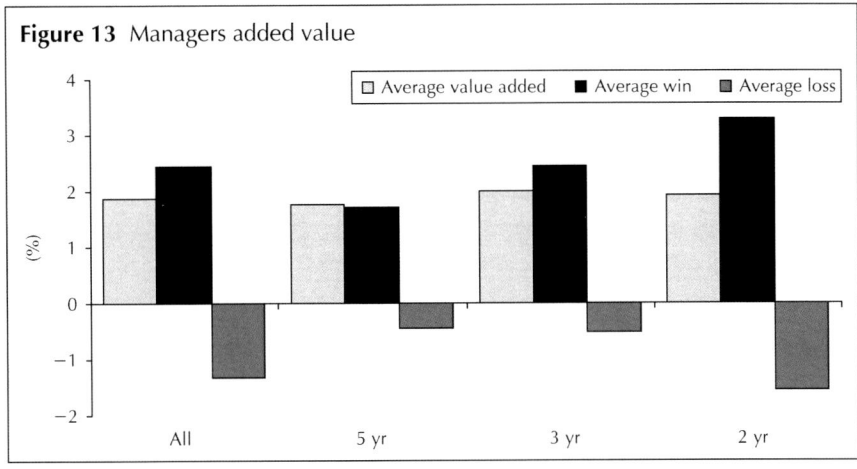

Figure 13 Managers added value

from inception (the earliest was 1989) until the end of 1997, or the termination date, if the account had been discontinued (32 accounts had been). This avoided biasing the results by having only the surviving accounts in the study. The respondents covered roughly USD 40 billion of mandates from a variety of currency bases (though largely USD based) with an average life in excess of three years. The results were assembled for all accounts submitted, and for those in existence for the prior five, three and two years respectively.

Figures 13 and 14 reveal that managers added value averaging near 2% per annum and that 80% of the accounts showed value added on a cumulative basis (the "success ratio"). The information ratios were reported in excess of 0.5, comparing favourably with active management in other asset classes. Furthermore, active managers generally reduced risk (Figure 15), with account returns showing smaller standard deviations than those for the benchmark returns.

Excess returns were explained to be dependent upon several factors:

❑ benchmarks – whether they were polar (0% or 100% hedged) or mixed (somewhere in between);
❑ the direction of currencies relative to the base currency of the portfolio; and
❑ whether mandates were restrictive or permissive.

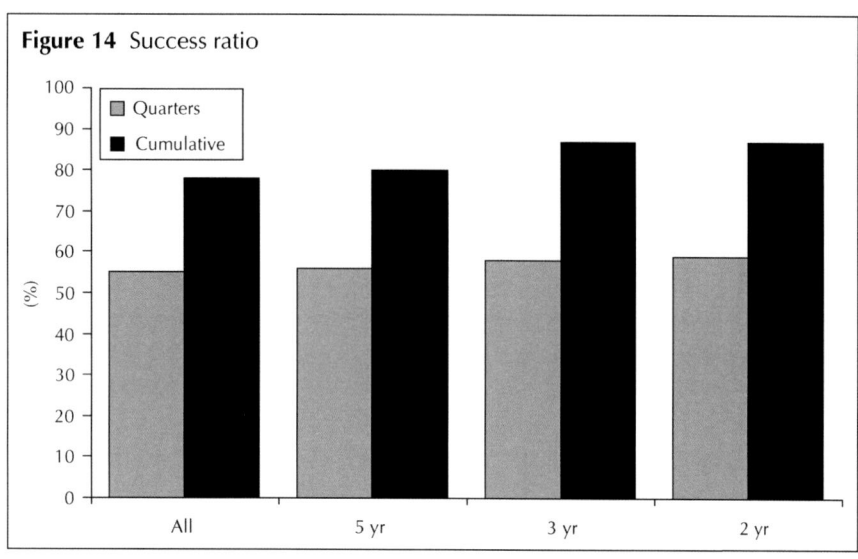

Figure 14 Success ratio

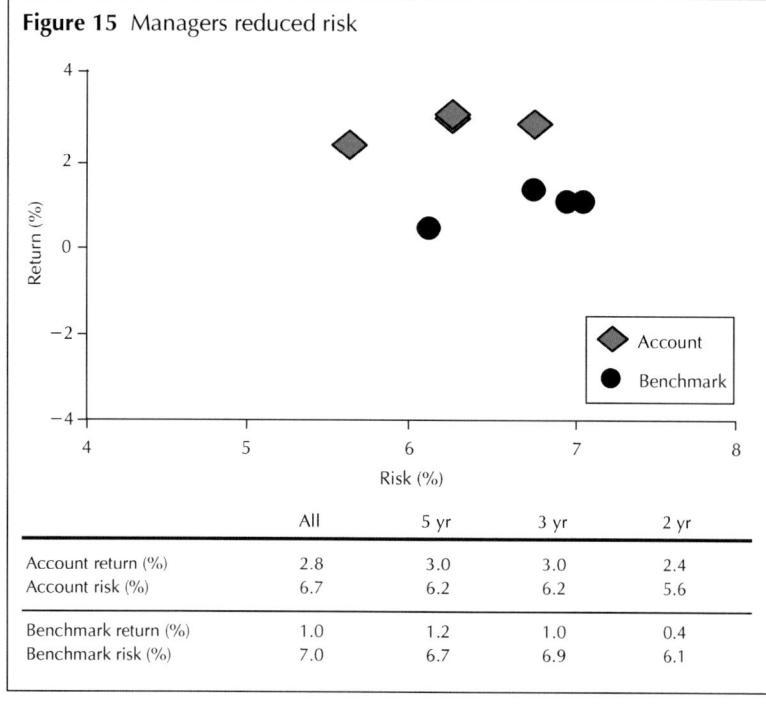

Figure 15 Managers reduced risk

	All	5 yr	3 yr	2 yr
Account return (%)	2.8	3.0	3.0	2.4
Account risk (%)	6.7	6.2	6.2	5.6
Benchmark return (%)	1.0	1.2	1.0	0.4
Benchmark risk (%)	7.0	6.7	6.9	6.1

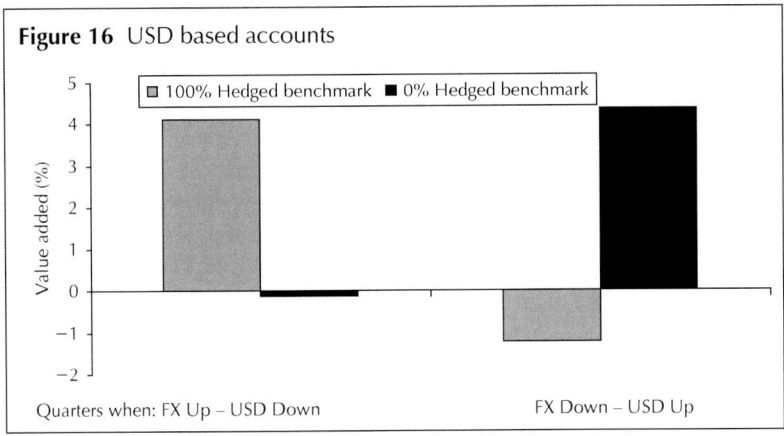

Figure 16 USD based accounts

In all time frames, excess performance for accounts with mixed benchmark hedge ratios exhibited less volatility. Managers were more consistent in adding value. It was tougher for accounts with polar benchmarks, depending upon which way currencies moved relative to the base currency. Focus on Figure 16. For USD-based accounts it was easier to outperform fully hedged benchmarks in quarters when currencies were rising relative to the US dollar. All managers had to do was to get somewhat unhedged when they were rising. However, the converse is also true. The unhedged benchmark accounts showed underperformance. During quarters when currencies fell relative to the US dollar, the results are also reversed.

Lastly, managers who could do more than simply hedge back to the base currency, in amounts equal to the portfolio exposures, more consistently added excess return, though on a risk-adjusted basis they were reasonably comparable to the more restrictive mandates. Contrary to the notion that taking positions in currencies unrelated to the underlying portfolio increases investment risk, results show greater diversification and less risk when managers have the freedom to make more currency decisions. This is intuitive, since a 15-stock portfolio has less risk than a 3-stock portfolio.

Other investment-consulting firms subsequently confirmed this initial canvas. Frank Russell published *Capturing Alpha Through Active Currency Overlay* in May of 2000 (see Baldridge et al, 2000).

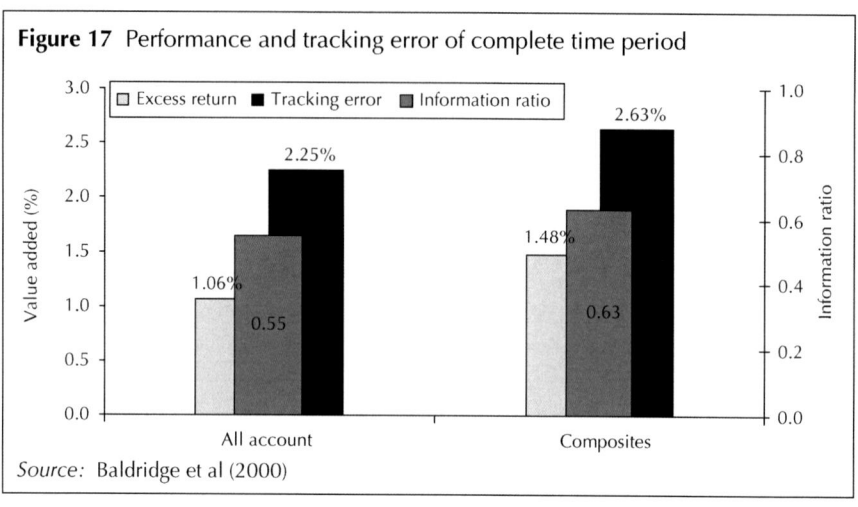

Figure 17 Performance and tracking error of complete time period

Source: Baldridge et al (2000)

For this study, the number of reporting managers rose to 18, the amount of overlay represented in excess of USD 85 billion and the number of accounts increased to 241, 75 of which had been discontinued. The same methodology was used as in the earlier study (see Strange, 1998) with the exception that monthly data was reported, providing 10,041 account months for the sample, which extended to mid-1999. As in Strange, account date was consolidated in two ways:

❏ all account basis – where the manager with more accounts for a longer period influences the average to a greater degree;
❏ manager composite basis – where an average of all accounts for each manager is calculated and then these composites are further averaged, giving each manager an equal say in the results.

Figure 17 confirms that either way it is calculated, managers added value and produced respectable information ratios confirming the results in Strange. Also corroborating the earlier work are the results exhibited in Figure 18. Since the majority of the USD-based accounts were of a more recent vintage prior to the mid-1999 cut-off date, and foreign currencies were persistently falling against the US dollar from mid-1995, one could expect that it was easier for managers to outperform unhedged benchmarks

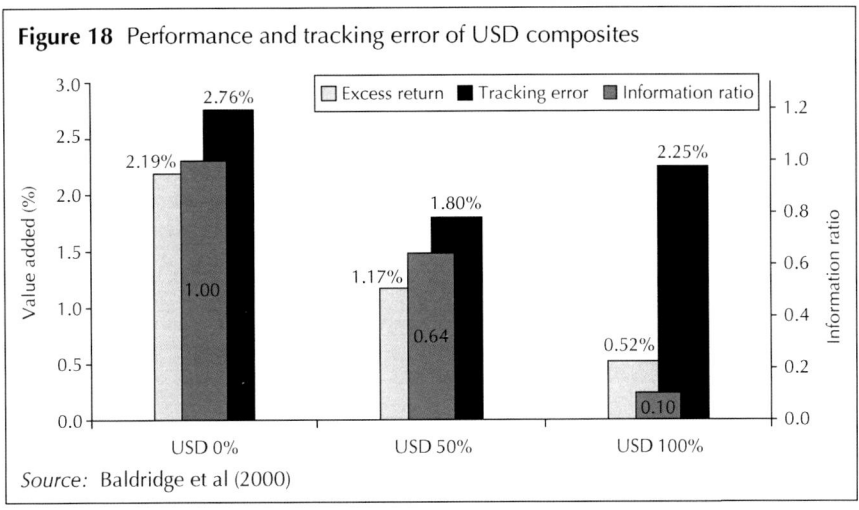

Figure 18 Performance and tracking error of USD composites

Source: Baldridge et al (2000)

by doing some hedging. The following results clearly show that this was the case:

❑ excess performance was greatest against unhedged benchmarks;
❑ however, it was more consistent against mid-point benchmarks – lower risk but with equivalent risk-adjusted return;
❑ fully hedged benchmarks were tough to outperform in a largely downward currency market.

Russell/Mellon – CAPS continues to follow currency managers and track their performance. Although it has gathered data at one time or another from 29 managers for as many as 514 accounts, its current universe comprises 149 accounts from 20 managers, representing USD 54 billion of overlay mandates. The results continue to show:

❑ positive excess performance above 1%;
❑ respectable information ratios;
❑ more consistent (lower tracking error) performance against mid-point benchmarks. (See Table 3.)

Watson Wyatt Worldwide also published a study and continues to collect data from managers (see Hersey and Minnick, 2000). One interesting aspect of its work is its analysis showing that portfolio risk falls when employing more than one manager, confirming multi-manager diversification as a fact.

Table 3

	All	Composites USD-based vs 0% hedged benchmark	USD-based vs 50% hedged benchmark	USD-based vs 100% hedged benchmark
Excess return	1.12	1.44	0.83	1.05
Tracking error	2.34	2.56	1.9	2.49
Information ratio	0.27	0.69	0.43	0.27

MORE INVESTORS SHOULD CONSIDER ACTIVE CURRENCY OVERLAY MANAGEMENT

In conclusion, we've seen, from period to period, that currency movements can be substantial and not always helpful, irrespective of the currency base. We've also seen that despite presenting more risk, unmanaged currencies don't offer a reward in the long term. A more proper use of an investor risk budget would be to set a higher-than-zero hedge ratio, and substituting risk from assets offering a risk premium or from active management strategies.

Market inefficiencies seem to offer opportunity for active management such that even simple rules, when consistently applied, produce better results in the long run than passive strategies and do not compromise asset diversification.

Finally, several independent studies have confirmed that, as a whole, active currency overlay managers have done their jobs, adding return and reducing risk. Yet, despite the evidence, it remains a mystery that few investors, particularly European, have chosen to implement currency overlay programmes. It is too often easy to neglect currency impacts because of the extra analysis required. Yet it is important enough that all aspects should be considered carefully and not simply accepted by default.

BIBLIOGRAPHY

Acar, E., and B. Maitra, 2000, "Hedging Using Forward Rate Bias", *Risk*, February.

Baldridge, J. et al, 2000, *Capturing Alpha Through Active Currency Overlay* (New York: Russell Research Commentary).

Clarke, R., and M. Kritzman, 1996, *Currency Management: Concepts & Practices* (Pennsylvania: AIMR).

Fama, E. F., 1984, "Forward and Spot Exchange Rates", *Journal of Monetary Economics* 14, pp. 319–338.

Hersey, B., and J. Minnick, 2000, "Active Managers Generating Positive Returns Over Benchmarks", Global Pensions, February.

Isard, P. et al, 2001, "Methodology for Current Account and Exchange Rate Assessments", IMF Occasional Paper.

Kritzman, M., 1993, "The Optimal Currency Hedging Policy with Biased Forward Rates", *Journal of Portfolio Management*, Summer.

Lequeux, P., and E. Acar, 1998, "A Dynamic Index for Managed Currencies Funds Using CME Currency Contracts", *European Journal of Finance* 4.

Levich, R., and L. Thomas, 1993, "The Significance of Technical Trading-Rule Profits in the Foreign Exchange Market: A Bootstrap Approach", *Journal of International Money and Finance*, October.

Reinert, T., 2000, "Practical Active Currency Management for Global Equity Portfolios", *Journal of Portfolio Management*, Summer.

Rosenber, M., and D. Folkerts-Landau, 2002, "The Deutsche Bank Guide to Exchange-Rate Determination", Deutsche Bank, May.

Strange, B., 1998, "Currency Overlay Managers Show Consistency", *Pensions & Investments*, June 15.

Part 2

Currency Risk and Hedging

6
FX Risk

Jessica James
Citigroup

WHAT IS CURRENCY (OR FX) RISK?

The word "risk" is at once crystal clear and murkily ambiguous. We all feel that we know instinctively what it means, but would be hard put to define it in a quantitative sense. This is partly because, like many terms within specialist disciplines, it was a word in general use that has been absorbed into a subject for a more precise application. Examples in physics are "force" and "energy" – they are simultaneously technical definitions and general concepts. However, unlike "force" and "energy", the term "risk" has never been unequivocally associated with one mathematical definition. In the financial world, risk is used both specifically and technically, and will often occur with several meanings in the same document. Thus calling this chapter "FX Risk" means that we have to address a variety of issues.

It is safe to say that, in the financial world, risk is always concerned with the possibility of there being less money around than would be desirable. Within this extremely broad definition, let us look at some of the general situations where currency risk is deemed to arise:

❑ where a currency deal has been done that goes against the investor or trader;
❑ where an overseas investment is held without hedging and currency moves reduce its value in the home currency;

- where a company has cashflows in a foreign currency (for example, a German car manufacturer that has substantial sales in the USA) and currency moves reduce the value of incoming cashflows or increase the value of outgoings in the home currency;
- where a hedge such as a forward contract is purchased, which loses money, cancelling gains in the currency;
- where a hedge such as an option is purchased, at a cost, which then proves to be unnecessary as subsequent currency moves are in the investor's favour; and
- where the FX component of a portfolio increases the volatility of the portfolio.

The list could be added to indefinitely but these are some of the situations where currency risk can be said to exist. However, knowing where to find it is not the same as measuring it. What are the metrics which will tell us how "big" a certain piece of currency risk is? Unfortunately, there are many of these, and people think of new definitions all the time. We can give a selection of the most popular:

- volatility (standard deviation of percentage returns);
- maximum drawdown (a drawdown is a period of loss);
- maximum monthly (or daily, yearly, etc) drawdown;
- a VAR figure (see next section);
- a loss with a certain probability (eg, there is a 1% chance that losses will exceed USD 1,000,000 in the next year) – this is related to VAR; and
- some kind of currency "exposure" – there are different definitions of this and they will be discussed later.

For those concerned with trading strategies there are also:

- the traditional *Sharpe's ratio* (the profit in cash divided by the volatility over the complete period, also known as *information ratio*);
- the *downside Sharpe's ratio* is identical to the Sharpe's ratio, except that only downward movements are considered when calculating the volatility;
- the *window Sharpe's ratio* calculates an averaged Sharpe's ratio over shorter, consecutive periods of time;

- the *scrolling window* method looks at every possible holding period of that length, and tells you what percentage of these periods resulted in a loss;
- the *maximum drawdown* is the biggest cash loss made during the time period covered by the data;
- the *maximum drawdown time* gives the length of the longest drawdown period in days; if the data were the performance of a fund, this would be the longest time an investor could go before the initial investment made was recovered;
- the *mountain lake* method takes both the duration and the depth of a drawdown into account to find the worst drawdown period by calculating the area (duration x depth) of each such period; and
- the *slope factor* is the slope of a straight line which has been fitted to the data using the method of least squares, with the starting point fixed to be the starting point of the series, divided by the standard error on that slope; thus, series score highly if they are (a) linear and (b) profitable.

Risk measures basically break down into two kinds: the volatility type, which relate to the likely range of currency movements in the future; and the loss type, which relate to the likely loss in the future. It is perhaps a little counterintuitive to use volatility as a risk measure, since a high volatility indicates a high risk of positive moves as well as a high risk of negative ones. Additionally, it is truly valid to use volatility in this way only if one accepts the assumption that markets are largely explained by random moves – an assumption that this book is hardly in agreement with. However, for various reasons, including the fact that volatility is used in option pricing, that it is mathematically and computationally reasonably tractable, and that it has always been done that way, it is very common to find volatility used as a risk measure.

RISKS FOR HEDGERS VS RISKS FOR TRADERS

There have always been traders and speculators who wanted to "punt" on the currency markets, but in recent years the degree of global connectivity has meant that companies have more and more business overseas, with profits and outgoings that are not in their home currency. The latter are the hedgers – those to whom currency risk is a source of anxiety and who would ideally like to see it disappear. The former regard currency risk as an opportunity for profit, and might be out of a job if all currencies were merged.

The risks for "hedgers" – though the name implies currency exposure rather than a particular hedging strategy – are very different from those that apply to traders. A trader's chief worry is that he will lose money, plain and simple. The worries of a hedger are more complex. For a start, the hedger may decide that his "strategy" is not to hedge. This may be because he believes that hedging is too expensive, or that it is ineffective, or that he does not have the expertise to implement a strategy correctly. However, it can be argued that not hedging is in itself a form of speculating – the only way to eliminate currency risk entirely is to hedge with forward contracts. However, hedging with forwards introduces another risk, that of losing out on currency gains. A forward hedge provides almost equal and opposite cashflows to that of the hedged underlying currency exposure. Thus, if I have an overseas asset whose value does not change in its local currency, but whose value to me in my home currency depreciates by 10% due to weakening of the local vs the home currency, a forward hedge would provide me with exactly that 10% to make up the difference.

This makes forwards sound attractive, but the opposite situation is markedly less pleasant. If the value of the asset appreciated by 10% due to currency movements, then the investor will be pretty sick to think that he has to pay out 10% to fund the losing hedge. A forward is a double-edged sword, which will cost the investor money as often as it saves his bacon. Moreover, a losing forward hedge must be paid out in cash – it is not just a theoretical loss of asset value that is not crystallised until the asset is sold.

The next stage on in complexity in the hedging process is the purchase of options. These do not have the very large potential for losses that a forward hedge involves, because the maximum loss is the upfront option premium, but they do have the risk that the currency will move in such a way as to ensure that they do not recover any of the premium outlay.

There are a large number of more and more complex combinations of forward and option strategies available, but the trade-off between locking in a possible loss and paying a premium is hard to avoid.

The last risk for the hedger is encountered when the hedger decides to implement a dynamic strategy, where trading models are used to decide when a hedge is appropriate, and when it is better to lift the hedge. This type of strategy holds the promise of an option-like return profile, with limited losses but unlimited gains, but does not provide guarantees. The risk for the hedger with this approach is that the strategy that he or she chooses does not work!

The situation is simpler for a trader. He or she needs to devise a strategy that will make money in the FX markets by judging when the market is rising or falling. In the last decade or so the market has changed in that it has become more and more possible to take complex positions whose sensitivity to underlying rate moves may be very high indeed, and, instead of simply having a view on which rate is going up or down, one may devise strategies that will monetise views on implied volatility levels and other market parameters. Thus, there are more ways to make money, if the trader chooses to become familiar with some complex techniques. However, the current FX market, as opposed to that which existed 30 years ago, is a very much tougher place for the average trader. This is because the bid–offer spread, where the trader will buy for less than he will sell, has shrunk dramatically: it is now of order one or two points, when it used to be forty or fifty in the 1960s. A point is the last digit in a rate, so if the GPB/USD rate was 1.6543, one point would be 0.0001 GBP per USD. The reader can see that, even if the trade size is a million dollars, the profit made from the bid–offer spread will not be very great. So the modern FX trader is more reliant than ever upon good trading strategies.

New philosophies in the FX world mean that there are other ways for the trader to improve his profitability. Increasingly, institutions that provide FX to the investor are trying to provide more than just a competitive bid–offer spread, since they have competed with each other to the point that further spread reduction would not make a deal worth the cost of the phone call to the trader! So other services, such as research and market advice, are being offered to investors who have good relationships with FX institutions, to make them more attractive to trade with.

Risks of margin trading

Margin trading is not new, but is worth a mention, because it is very easy to take on large risks with only a little initial outlay. It is also a relatively easy way for newcomers to enter the FX markets. The traditional venue for margin trading is futures and options exchanges, which have operated a margining system for many years. The trader may believe that GBP will rise versus USD – for example, the GBP/USD rate might be 1.650, and he believes that it will go to 1.700. So he will go to the exchange and buy a future contract on the value of the exchange rate. Futures are very similar to forwards, the difference being that they start and end on fixed dates to facilitate trading. The exchange sells contracts in lots of fixed face amounts such as £100,000. To enter into a contract, the trader needs to put up a "margin" amount, which can be very much smaller than the face amount – for a single contract, the margin could be something like £5,000. Every day at the same time, the exchange checks the value of the contract, and, if it has lost more money than the margin amount, the trader will be required to post more margin – probably another £5,000.

The risk arises when one considers that in a single day FX moves can be very large. In September 1992, the GBP/USD rate moved from 1.87 to 1.78 USD per GBP. If one had bought 100,000 GBP for 187,000 USD (when the rate was 1.87), then a move to 1.78 would mean that the 100,000 GBP was worth only 178,000 USD – a loss of USD 9,000 or £5,056. Thus in a single day the whole margin amount was exceeded. This can be even more of a problem in the volatile equity markets, when losses of 30% or even 50% of the value of the index can occur in a single day, leaving the trader with a debt far greater than his margin amount.

There is a temptation to regard the margin amount as some kind of invested capital. This can lead to unrealistically optimistic estimates of what "can" be lost. It is important to realise that with margin trading the entire amount of the margin can be lost, very quickly indeed, and that it is possible for losses to greatly exceed the margin amount.

EXPOSURE DEFINITIONS AND CALCULATIONS

"Exposure" is another word that, like "risk", has several definitions in the markets. When an investor is "exposed" to a market rate, he or she is vulnerable to losses in the event of certain moves that it is possible that the rate may make. Probably no one would argue with this definition, but defining exposure more precisely is probably done differently in every bank. However, there is some degree of consensus as to the "best way" of measuring exposure, and it is this that we will describe.

Exposure is usually a concept that is used when one has several deals combined into a portfolio, and one wishes to quantify the risks on the portfolio by somehow aggregating the risks of the deals. It is used for FX products and all other market instruments. Market rate exposure is often combined with likelihood of default of a counterparty to produce a kind of counterparty exposure or credit risk. While it is not the purpose of this book to go into detail about credit risk, we will mention it here to illustrate the exposure methodologies used.

In the simplest terms, the exposure of a deal is a measure of the market risk of the deal. It depends upon the possible range of future values of the deal. Thus, a deal that has a very high sensitivity to movements in underlying rates, such as some option or barrier products, will have a higher exposure for the same notional amount than a simple swap.

There are three reasons for the measurement of exposure.

- ❏ A portfolio measure to determine overall risk on a portfolio, and perhaps to allocate capital to cushion possible future losses.
- ❏ To find exposures on a deal-by-deal basis, to discover which deals or sections of the portfolio are the riskiest. These can then be hedged or monitored.
- ❏ To be able to decide whether to take on a deal using risk criteria. Frequently, a total amount or exposure (credit line) is allocated to each customer, based or credit grounds, and then the exposures of each deal done with that customer gradually eat up this exposure. Once the credit line is all used up, no more deals may be done with the customer.

Calculating deal and portfolio exposures

So, how is deal and portfolio exposure calculated? There are a variety of very simple and rather crude methods, such as multiplying the face amount of the deal by a fixed percentage, which varies with deal type, and then calling the resulting figure the exposure, but these are generally regarded as inferior methods to using exposure curves. An exposure curve is a simple concept: it is

Table 1 Appropriate models for different market rates

Underlying rate	Model
FX	Lognormal model
Equity index	Lognormal + trend
Interest rate	2-factor model, which includes mean reversion
Commodity	Lognormal + trend

just the range of possible future values of a deal. We can simulate the possible future market rates, using a good model, and thus calculate the exposure curve. Usually we will do this at a two standard deviation level, or 95%, so we can say "the most extreme value of the deal at a point in the future is less than X with a 95% probability".

To calculate the market risk or exposure curve of a deal, we first consider the underlying rates upon which the deal depends. These may be interest rates, FX rates, equity indices, bond prices or others. The first step in the exposure calculation process should be to simulate these rates out to the desired horizon – say a date in 10 years time to obtain a good range of values.

Let us consider the interest rate simulation first. The simulation will start at today's value of interest rates, so that the particular rate which we are interested in will have a value of, say, 5%. The simulation will then allow this rate to vary over time. Initially, it will not go far from the 5% value but after 10 years it will have a fair range of possible values. If the path density is represented by darker shading, we should end up with a picture like Figure 1.

In Figure 1 the greatest path density lies along the 5% line, illustrating that there was no drift or trend in the simulation. Thus, the interest rates in this calculation do not follow the path predicted by forward interest rates. Whether they do or not does not make a lot of difference, because the drift implied by the forward rates is small compared with the spread of rates; but, if the same simulation is to be used for valuation purposes, it will need to follow the forwards. The fact that in reality rates are no more likely to follow the forward path than any other makes little difference to exposure calculations.

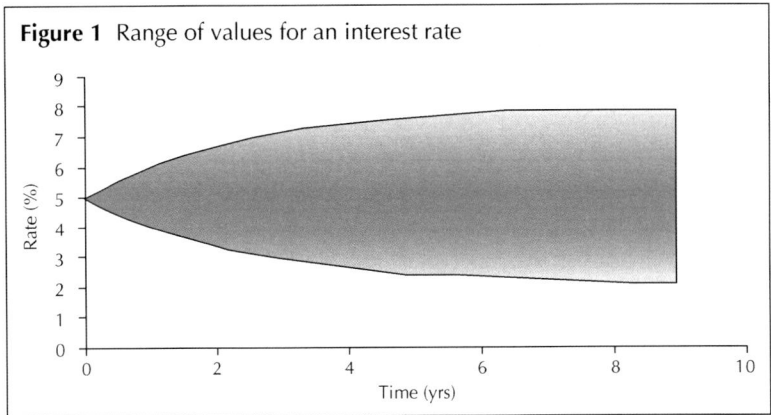

Figure 1 Range of values for an interest rate

FX rates should be simulated in a similar way, but the process will of course be rather simpler as FX models tend to be simpler than interest rate ones. The result of the simulation will be similar to Figure 1, but the spread will be larger, because the FX rates have no mean reversion embedded into them. Equities and commodities can be simulated like FX rates, but possibly with a drift term allowed to account for inflation.

The next step, now that the underlying rates are simulated, is to use them to produce simulations of the instruments in the portfolio. To produce a simulated price path for an instrument, it is necessary to have values for all the underlying rates that are used to value the instrument. While these data are certainly available for most currencies, things get a little more difficult once one considers instruments such as options. To value an FX option correctly at the start of its life, it is necessary to have values for the implied at-the-money volatility. To value it later on in life, however, you will need the relevant out-of-the-money volatility as well. Thus the implied volatility and volatility smile will need to be some of the underlying rates that are simulated. Implied volatilities may be modelled as mean reverting processes, but the smile is difficult to model, partly because there is little historical data available. A parabolic smile is often used.

At every time step, the instrument that you wish to model should be valued, using the underlying rates. This will result in a price path for the instrument, from which exposure may be calculated. The exposure is calculated by almost as many methods as there are institutions, but the general consensus of the definition of the exposure of

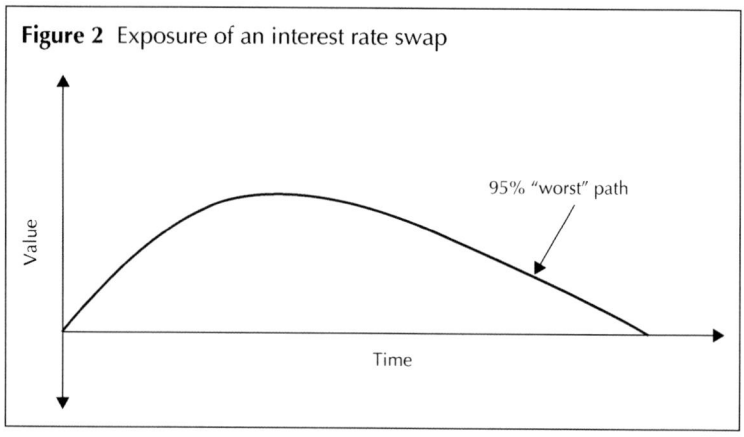

Figure 2 Exposure of an interest rate swap

an instrument or deal is the worst anticipated future values at a 95% confidence level, as illustrated in Figure 2 for an interest rate swap (IRS). This is sometimes referred to as the "95% worst path", but this is not strictly true, because it would be very unusual to have a random path perfectly follow the 95th percentile. The 95% line is generated from the composite distribution produced by many paths.

Although it is common practice to say that the peak of the resulting exposure profile is the "exposure", in fact it is much better to use the whole exposure profile in the subsequent process of aggregation.

Exposure aggregation

Let us start by giving an example of the worst way to aggregate the exposures of different deals so that you end up with an overall portfolio exposure. This would be to just add the peaks of the exposure profiles to get the final number. Now, not only is this an attempt to combine different things, for a ten-year exposure number should not be added to a three-year, but also it is a ludicrously conservative way to go about the process. Exposure profiles of each deal should instead be bucketed into quarterly or six-monthly values, and these values added together, to generate an overall exposure profile, as illustrated in Figure 3.

If necessary to have an overall "market risk" number for the portfolio, then the peak of the composite exposure profile may be taken. None of these aggregation methods would be necessary if a full simulation approach was taken, but, as discussed before, this approach is not always possible.

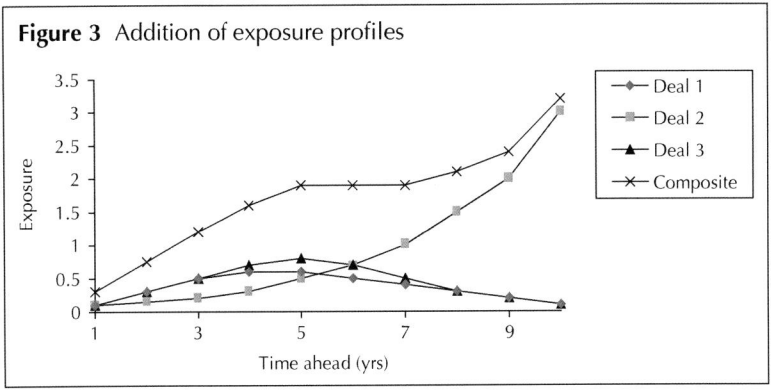

Figure 3 Addition of exposure profiles

Other features of a good exposure aggregation process include:

❑ allowing different exposures to the same counterparty to be netted. This means that, if there is a legal netting agreement in place, deals in the same instrument but opposite ways round may be offset. Thus, if a counterparty buys a five-year USD interest rate swap from me in a notional amount of 10 MM USD, and later sells me 3 MM of the same swap, I can consider that I only have a 7 MM USD swap to include in exposure calculations. Similarly, deals in similar instruments but different maturities should be allowed to net over the appropriate part of their lifetimes. It is important, however, that this approach be taken *only* when there is a legal netting agreement in place, otherwise, in a default event, those deals which the defaulting entity owes money on may be reneged upon while those which result in money being paid to the entity may be rigourously enforced!

❑ allowing natural offset between all deals in the portfolio. This means that if one deal will have a high exposure if a rate moves up, and another will have a high exposure if the same rate moves down, then in the aggregation process it is not allowed for both deals to have a high exposure at the same time. This can be rather complex to implement but is very useful as it can significantly reduce overall exposure. After all, not even in the most volatile markets can a rate go up and down at the same time!

❑ allowing historical correlations between rates to be taken into account. This is a little more of a heroic assumption, because correlations may not stay constant and the biggest failures of risk management in recent times have been concerned with incorrect estimation of correlations. However, to omit correlations completely from the process would be rather unrealistic and they should be included at conservative levels.

Tiered exposure limits

This means that there is no single maximum exposure number that is the credit line for each customer, but instead an allowed exposure "profile" that may be tiered according to maturity. Thus, there might be more exposure allocated in the three-year bucket than in the ten-year bucket, and deals will be allowed accordingly. Thus it might happen that, while all line was used up in the three-year area, there might still be some "room" for ten-year exposure to be added. In practice longer maturities tend to get used up first.

What-if capability

This can make a huge difference for day-to-day risk management of the portfolio. A what-if or query capability means that marketers or traders can query the effect of adding a particular deal to the portfolio, and see what effect it will have on the exposure profile with that counterparty. This means that the "front-line" people can participate in the day-to-day risk management of the portfolio, and, for example, do hedging trades to free up more exposure with a given counterparty. Of course, while freeing up exposure or credit line is good for a marketer, because it allows him or her to do more deals with the counterparty, it is also good for the risk manager, because it is hedging the portfolio and reducing market risk.

Counterparty credit classes

In order to facilitate the credit line or exposure allocation process, counterparties are generally divided into "credit classes", according to the perceived credit quality of the counterparty. They are probably, in most institutions, closely related to ratings from agencies like Moody's or Fitch, but may be slightly different to reflect the relationship of the counterparty with the institution. For example, an American company would probably have a higher internal rating for an American company as opposed to European ones, while the rating agencies try to be impartial. Credit classes will play an important part in determining the amount of credit line available for the counterparty.

Use of default-likelihood matrices

This is the next stage in the risk management process. In order to get a good idea of the true risk of loss, once the exposure for single counterparties and for the portfolio is calculated, each counterparty can have their exposure multiplied by a factor designed to indicate the risk of loss. This factor is usually dependent upon the credit class of the counterparty. It may be a single number, which is crude, or a series of numbers differing by maturity, which would be better and more realistic. Care must be taken with the confidence on the final risk-of-loss figure. A useful equation to remember is

$$1 - C_{TOTAL} = (1 - C_{MARKET})(1 - C_{DEFAULT})$$

where the Cs are confidence limits. The expression is true only when market and default risk may be assumed to be uncorrelated, which is a pretty heroic assumption, but it does provide a useful approximation. Thus, from the equation, it is easy to see that if one has a 95% confidence exposure number, and if one has also generated 95% confidence default numbers, then the confidence limit for the final risk-of-loss number will be 99.75%. This is fine as long as this is what was wanted in the first place! However, a common mistake to make is to assume that two 90% numbers give another 90% number – which is wrong.

Under the right circumstances, it may be possible to use rating agency default probabilities as credit-class factors. The advantage with this approach is that rating agencies are very experienced and the probabilities are likely to be reasonably accurate. The disadvantage is that the rating agency default-likelihood numbers are mean values rather than taken at any confidence limit. To use a confidence limit on the rating agency numbers you would need to have a probability distribution of the likelihood of default – which is not impossible, but it is probably better to use the mean values if the calculation can be arranged that way.

A point that is essential to grasp is that improving calculation methods inevitably reduces the portfolio exposure. Crude exposure addition methods inevitably result in overestimates of the total exposure, because any uncertainty results in conservative approximations. There is no doubt that accurate exposure calculations take time and effort, but for many institutions they will yield unexpected benefits.

VALUE-AT-RISK (VAR) METHODS

In recent years VAR techniques have grown hugely in popularity. This is overwhelmingly due to the simplicity of the VAR approach – what other technique allows the risk of a deal, portfolio or even institution to be encapsulated in a single number? The ease of the approach can be derived from its origins. It was devised to allow traders to quantify the risk of their books at the end of the day, and judge whether they had more or less risk than on previous days. Thus it is hardly surprising that such a tool, when uprooted from the trading book and applied to a vast number of other risk classes, sometimes turns out to be inappropriate.

For FX purposes, VAR is useful and appropriate when considering the risks of a portfolio of deals over the short term. It is less useful, but just as much used, when analysing FX risks of institutions whose risks are highly complex and may depend upon accounting rules as much as market movements.

A VAR number is a loss figure that has a given probability of occurring. Thus there is no single VAR number for a portfolio – the statement "My VAR is USD 1,000,000" is meaningless without both a confidence limit and a timeframe. Valid examples of VAR numbers are:

❏ USD 1 million at 95% for the next year (ie, there is a 5% chance that in the next year the portfolio will lose USD 1 million); and
❏ USD 5 million at 99% for the next month (ie, there is a 1% chance that in the next month the portfolio will lose USD 5 million).

Different types of VAR

VAR may be divided into many different types but for convenience we introduce three major divisions here, bearing in mind that other taxonomies exist. They are:

❏ variance–covariance VAR;
❏ historical VAR; and
❏ simulation VAR.

Variance–covariance VAR is the most venerable and the original VAR method. It is also the easiest, and, unsurprisingly, the most inadequate. Let us consider a portfolio of instruments – they could be FX deals or other types. To do a variance–covariance VAR calculation, we need a historical time series of the value of the instruments in the portfolio. To obtain this it may be necessary to take a time series of underlying rates first – for example, to calculate a time series of FX option values, one needs FX rates, FX-implied volatilities and interest rates. Once the time series of the instrument values has been obtained, it is easy to produce a variance–covariance matrix from the time series. This is a simple mathematical operation that many software packages will do automatically. On a spreadsheet it will be a square grid of numbers with the variances down the diagonal, and the covariances filling in the body of the matrix. For two series X and Y, the covariance σ is given by

$$\sigma_{XY} = \frac{1}{n}\sum_{j=1}^{n}\left(x_j - \mu_x\right)\left(y_j - \mu_y\right)$$

When the two series X and Y are the same, the covariance becomes the variance.

Once a matrix has been built, all other information from the time series is effectively thrown away. This is the point at which variance–covariance VAR becomes less than adequate for the majority of financial data series, because only normally distributed data are adequately analysed in this manner. Using only the variance–covariance matrix effectively ignores all the information in the data series about fat tails or other abnormal features, and it is these very features that introduce the majority of risks to currency portfolios.

Once the matrix has been built, the standard deviation σ_P of the portfolio may be calculated. This is given by

$$\sigma_P = \left[\sum_{i}^{n}\sum_{j}^{n} w_i w_j \sigma_{ij}\right]^{\frac{1}{2}}$$

where σ_{ij} is of course the covariance.

This method of calculating VAR is easy and quick, and does not require much computing power. However, it does assume that the data series are normally distributed, which can be very misleading if true distribution is not normal. Most market portfolios are of course not normal and tend to be fat-tailed or skewed. Another problem with this approach is that non-linear or path-dependent instruments such as options or barrier products cannot be properly included. The payoff of an option is so very far from any kind of normal distribution that attempting to include it without special treatment would lead to a set of meaningless results.

Historical VAR methods are an improvement upon the traditional variance–covariance approach. The beginning of the process is similar to the variance–covariance method: one takes a set of historical series of instrument prices. However, these series are then combined to create a similar historical series of the portfolio values. It is then easy to produce a distribution of the portfolio values, or returns, that will reflect actual events rather than a normal distribution.

Stress testing is a related process, except that the historical series of portfolio values is created using artificially generated underlying moves. It is useful to the risk manager who is trying to understand what effect simultaneous currency crises might have upon his portfolio. Essentially, he can imagine some very high-risk market scenarios, generate them in the underlying rate series, and see how his portfolio suffers. The drawback to this process is that he has no idea how likely any of the scenarios truly are, and thus the distribution of portfolio values will be highly dependent upon his subjective opinion.

Historical VAR gives a realistic distribution of portfolio values, because skew or fat tails are included if they were there originally. In this respect it is a great improvement upon the variance–covariance technique. Additionally, non-linear and path-dependent instruments may also be relatively easily included, as long as sufficient valuation data are available. However, by its nature it suffers under the assumption that "past is prologue", ie, that all the information needed to understand the future is contained in the past data. In fact, markets are unpredictable animals and tend to do the unexpected. Another slight disadvantage to historical VAR methods is that they are rather more sensitive to missing/poor-quality data than variance–covariance VAR.

The last VAR type in our scheme of things is simulation VAR. This is often known as the Rolls-Royce of VAR methods: it is expensive to implement, but one is usually very happy with it. As with variance–covariance and historical VAR, one initially obtains a historical series of underlying market rates. It is then necessary to select a set of market models to use for the simulation, and this selection process is critical to the function of the method. The models will all have one or more floating parameters, which are there to allow them to be fitted to actual market data. The models are fitted to the historical data series, and then may be used to produce future rate paths. The portfolio is valued along these various different rate paths, and once more a distribution may be created from these values.

The immediate advantage of this method is that much more data are available. The historical VAR method has only the single history to draw upon; in a simulation there will be thousands. It has all the advantages of historical VAR in that it can handle non-linear and path-dependent instruments, but does not rely on the single historical path for its data. If correctly implemented, there is no doubt that simulation VAR is the superior method, but unfortunately it is heavily dependent upon the quality of the models used to produce the rate paths. Poor-quality models tend to give misleading results, leading to risk of over- or underestimates. Another issue that needs to be addressed with simulation VAR is that of calculation time – it may take some hours to run simulations over a large portfolio, so it is not always suitable for daily VAR calculations.

Problems with VAR

VAR is very useful as a relative risk measure. For a trader, it is useful to know what his VAR is at the end of the day, relative to the VAR of the previous day. Decreases or increases in VAR are usually useful indicators of risk changes. However, particularly with simpler VAR types, it would be rather credulous to assume that the absolute VAR figures are actually correct. In reality they can be rather far off the mark and it is wise to use other estimates of risk in conjunction with VAR. For a complex portfolio, it is much better to have a picture of a distribution than a single VAR number. A VAR number is in effect just a "slice" through the tail of a distribution, and it is obviously much more informative to look at the entire distribution.

A major difficulty with VAR is that adding a deal to a portfolio usually necessitates a whole new portfolio VAR calculation. Initially this proved a major obstacle to implementation of good VAR systems, but the development of more sophisticated techniques alleviated these problems.

A more fundamental problem with the whole VAR approach is revealed once the question of tail risk is considered. One would hope that any decent measure of risk would rank risks correctly – that is, would be able to say which of any pair of portfolios or deals was the more risky. Unfortunately, the traditional VAR approach does this only if the tails are monotonic – that is, without lumps (see Figure 4). If the tails of the distribution are not monotonic, then traditional VAR methods can make incorrect risk assessments. Unfortunately, these "lumpy" tails are very characteristic of volatile or data-sparse markets – as an example, the most extreme move in the USD/JPY rate was from about 118 to 112 in one day. This was about 5% of the underlying rate. However, there is no move in the data series of 4% or 3%. This type of data is utterly typical of the financial markets.

Finally, VAR techniques can fall into trouble when attempting to extrapolate beyond existing data sets. If one only has 1,000 daily data points, and wants to know the largest likely daily move in the next 10 years (about 2,500 business days), then one has no option

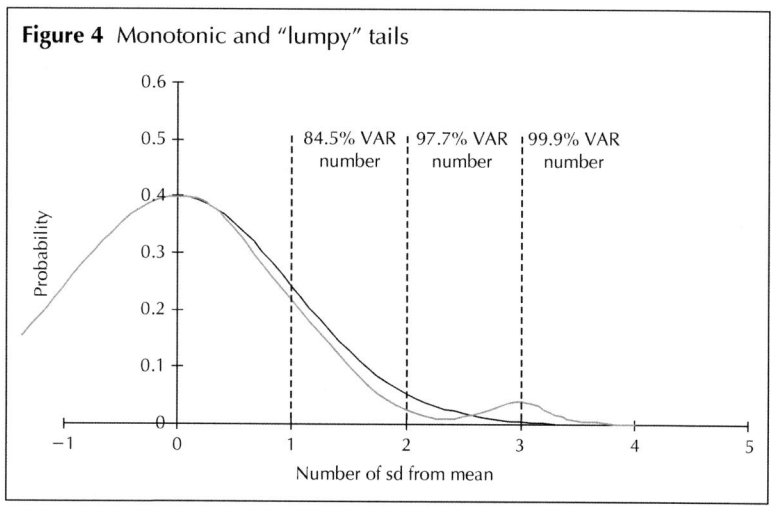

Figure 4 Monotonic and "lumpy" tails

but to try to extend the tail of the data distribution until the 1-in-2,500 point is reached. However, to do this, one needs to assume a form for the tail, and for this one needs a distribution or tail model. There are good tail models available, but they have not been widely used until recently. The default distribution that is still often used tends to be the normal distribution, which is completely inadequate for the type of extremes encountered in financial data. The discovery that *extreme value theory* (EVT) is applicable to financial data means that there is a good and realistic tail model that may be used for extreme moves.

In the next sections we will look at various ways of overcoming some of the problems with traditional VAR techniques.

Using EVT as a risk or VAR measure

It is worth explaining some of the rationale behind using EVT in financial markets, since it is a branch of mathematics originally devised for the study of natural phenomena such as hurricanes and earthquakes (see Embrechts, 1997). Before EVT became available for financiers, the normal distribution was often used to fit data for risk purposes. Normal distributions are found everywhere in nature: for example, the height of people in a room, or the sizes of stones on a beach. It is natural to try to apply these findings to financial markets, and to a certain extent this works: the Black–Scholes valuation model, which is universally used in the FX markets, assumes a normal distribution of price changes. However, true financial distributions of returns tend to be leptokurtotic, which means that they are both more sharply peaked and have longer tails. We can see this effect easily looking at Figure 5, which is of the S&P equity index returns. We have selected the S&P because it shows some of the most extreme moves ever experience in financial history, but, as will be seen later, FX markets can be similarly volatile.

We can see that normal distributions underestimate the probability of very small and very large moves. The small moves are not really at issue, but problems can arise when looking to estimate the probability of a large loss. For example, the worst day for the S&P showed a 23% loss. This has a probability, given by the normal distribution, of 6.7×10^{-131}. It is 24 standard deviations away from the mean, and the normal distribution would not have

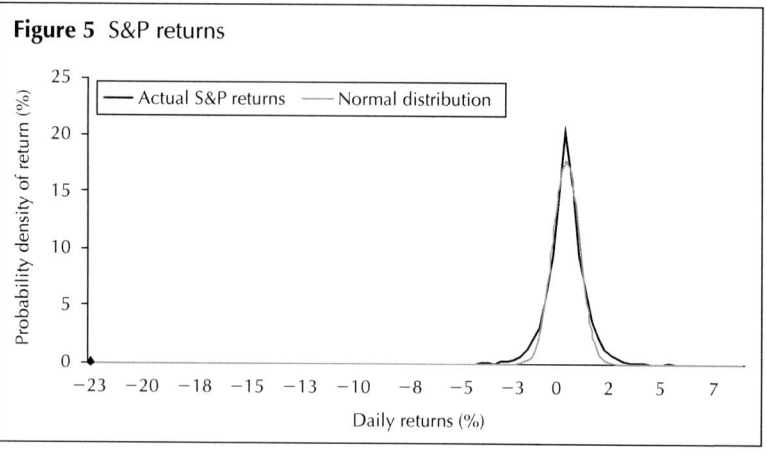

Figure 5 S&P returns

predicted the 23% move to happen in the ages of several universes! However, it happened, and the prudent trader or risk manager would like to have a better handle on predicting the future likelihood of similar or greater moves. The normal or lognormal distributions are clearly inadequate, but there are a myriad other distributions to choose from. We need to find a "best" distribution for all occasions.

Most commonly utilised distributions resemble the normal distribution in the central peak range, due to a piece of mathematics called the *central limit theorem*. Similarly, in the extreme tail, distributions converge to the generalised Pareto distribution (GPD). The GPD is the natural approximation to the unknown distribution above sufficiently high thresholds – ie, it is the best fit for the far tail. This is true for a large class of distributions, in which we would expect financial data to fall. Thus, as long as there are some points in the extreme tail region, we will should able to fit them to the GPD.

The GPD is given by

$$G_{\xi,\beta}(x) = 1 - \left(1 + \frac{\xi x}{\beta}\right)^{-1/\xi}$$

where x are the data points, and the parameters ξ and β are fitted to the data.

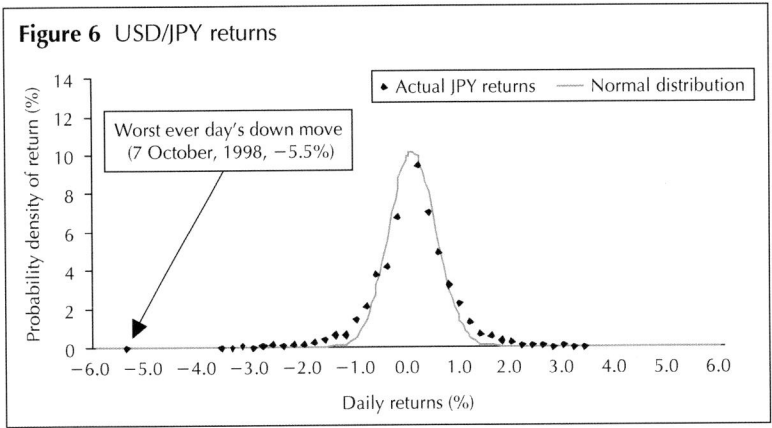

Figure 6 USD/JPY returns

One question remains: where does the true tail "start"? The strictly correct method of finding the start point is as follows:

1. take just a few tail points, fit, and note the parameters x and b;
2. include a few more points from further into the distribution and repeat.

The parameters will initially change, then enter a "region of stability", then change again. The stable values should indicate where the tail begins, while the second set of changes indicates that the dataset is starting to include points that are not in the true tail region. In fact, finding the point at which the normal distribution starts to be a poor fit will often accomplish the same thing.

Example of risk analysis for USD/JPY daily moves

To illustrate the process of using EVT to analyse FX risk, we can consider the USD/JPY rate. In Figure 6, it can be seen that it has the lumpy, data-sparse tail so characteristic of financial data.

To test the power of EVT in VAR techniques, we wish to use it to calculate the likelihood of such a move, without the benefit of hindsight. Thus we truncated the dataset so that it stopped on 6 October, the day before the largest ever move. We wanted to model the tail of the distribution of percentage changes. The changes are graphed in Figure 7.

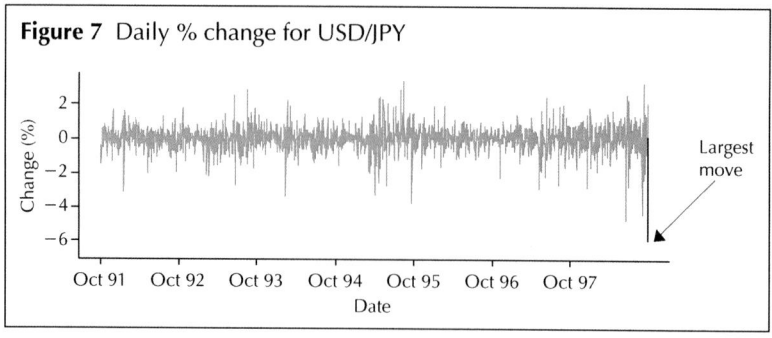

Figure 7 Daily % change for USD/JPY

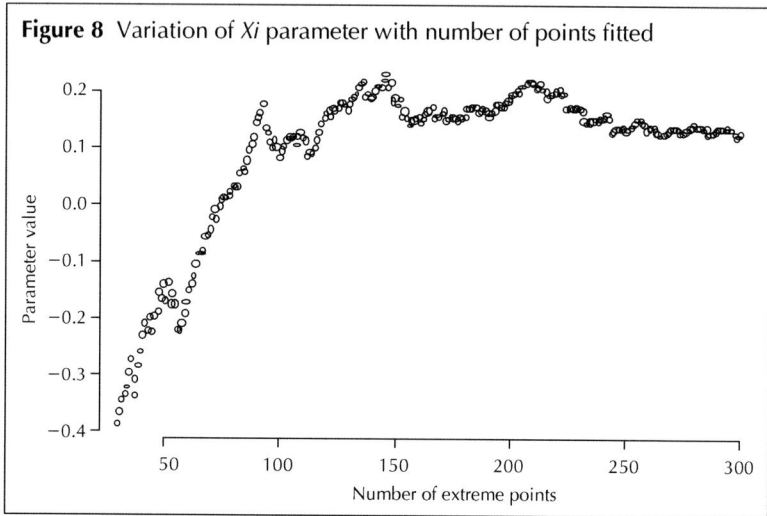

Figure 8 Variation of Xi parameter with number of points fitted

Using only the information available before the date, can we say that such a move was likely? The first stage is to select those data points that belong in the far tail. As described above, we looked at the parameters ξ and β and found a region where they were reasonably stable, as shown in Figures 8 and 9.

Then, using the number of points that we had determined lay in the "tail" – ie, the most extreme 80 or so – we fitted the tail to the GPD. Figure 10 shows the fit, together with the fit that would be obtained using the normal distribution.

The most obvious feature to note is the very poor fit of the normal distribution compared with the GPD, but it should also be

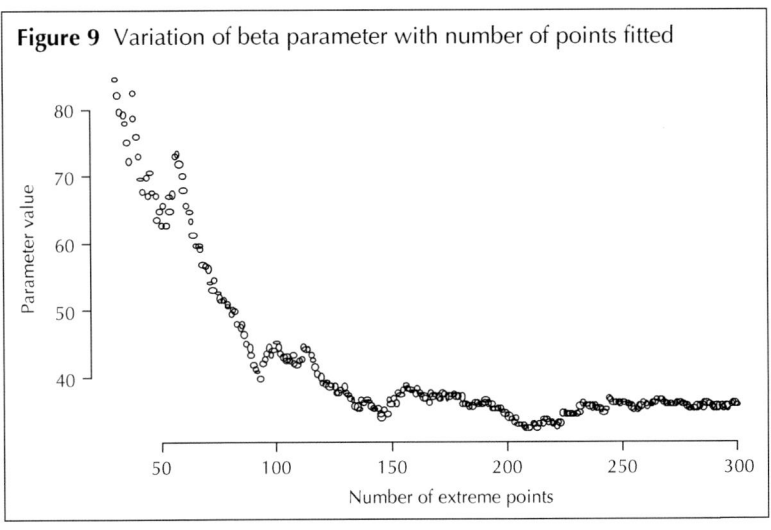

Figure 9 Variation of beta parameter with number of points fitted

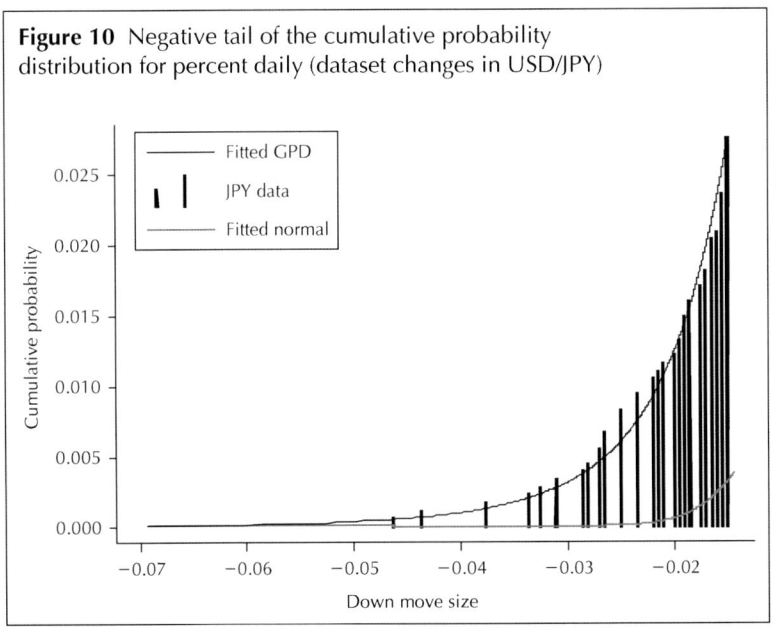

Figure 10 Negative tail of the cumulative probability distribution for percent daily (dataset changes in USD/JPY)

noted that the very worst point (5.5% loss) is not included, because the data set stops the day before it occurred. Thus, we are now in a position to evaluate the likelihood of such a loss before it actually occurred. The likelihood of a 5.5% down move given by the normal

145

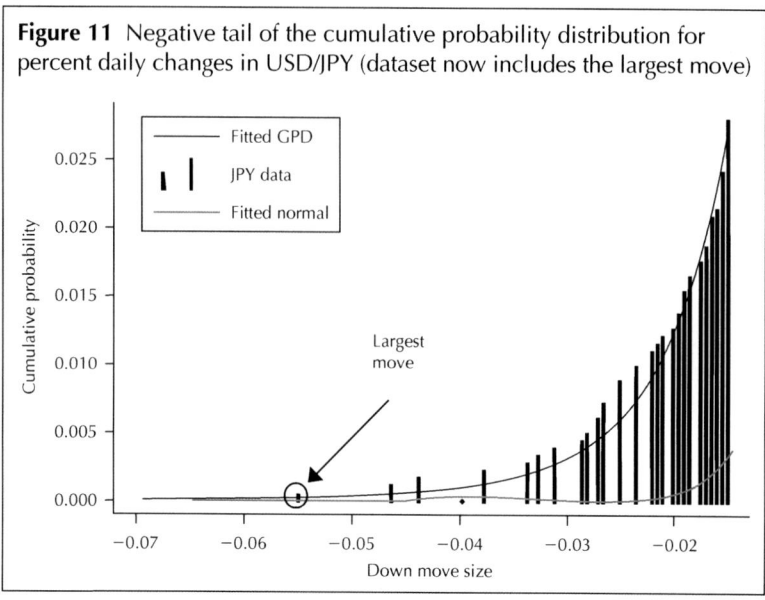

Figure 11 Negative tail of the cumulative probability distribution for percent daily changes in USD/JPY (dataset now includes the largest move)

distribution is 4.11×10^{-15}, which is roughly once every 10,000,000 years! The GPD fit, on the other hand, gives the 5.5% move a 1-in-5,000 chance of happening, roughly once every 19 years – a much more realistic risk estimate, and one that is consistent with history.

To illustrate this improved fit, we home in on the USD/JPY loss tail in Figure 11. We can see that the GPD fits the JPY data very well, even for the largest ever daily down move of −5.5%.

The GPD will not be much use for everyday risk analysis if all we can do with it is calculate the probability of very large moves. We also need to be able to use it in less extreme situations. A good example of such a situation is a move of 2% or more in USD/JPY. A move of this size in a day is an important event, but it happens frequently enough that market makers cannot afford to ignore the possibility that it might happen. How often would we expect this kind of move to occur?

In Table 2 we show how likely different moves are in USD/JPY. The first column tells us how likely the moves are as calculated by the normal distribution. The second uses the GPD to get a better estimate. The third shows us how often the moves actually do occur. For clarity the figures are approximated to familiar timescales.

Table 2 Probability of different move sizes, calculated using different methods

Size of move	Probability from normal distribution	Probability using GPD	Actual number of moves
0.5%	Once every 2–3 days	Once every 2–3 days	Once every 2–3 days
1%	Once every 1–2 weeks	Once every 1–2 weeks	Once every 1–2 weeks
2%	Once every 9 months	Once every 2–3 months	Once every 2–3 months
3%	Once every 140 years	Once every year	Once every year
5%	Once every 10 million years	Once every 7 years	Once in the 10-year dataset

The results for a 2% move and a 3% move are particularly interesting. The normal distribution gives a very unrealistic picture for risks which are frequent enough to need precautionary measures.

HOW A COMPANY MIGHT ACQUIRE FX RISK/EXPOSURE

In general, companies start small, in one country, and grow until they begin to export and establish branches in other regions. It would be rare to have a company that started off with multiple FX exposures, though the exceptions are of course those companies formed specifically for export. A classic case would be an American manufacturer that begins to export to Europe. Initially it will have started small in the USA, gradually capturing market share and growing. At a certain stage it will decide that it is advantageous to export. The obvious markets will be Canada and Europe.

The export business, if successful, will produce a revenue stream for the company. However, this revenue will be in foreign currency. At first there won't be much of a problem with this, and the incomings will be exchanged for USD as soon as they arrive. However, after a short while, the company will need to anticipate the overseas demand and the income stream, and this is where the problems begin. If the CAD or the EUR strengthen against the USD, all is well and good, because the manufacturer will receive more USD than he planned for. If, however, the foreign currencies fall vs the USD, then the USD income will be less than anticipated. These gains or losses will have nothing to do with the rest of the business, which may prosper and thrive throughout, but they can be considerable. FX moves of over 30% in the year are not very unusual, even in supposedly stable currencies, and a company will acquire this kind of income volatility simply by exporting. As a company expands and develops overseas branches and manufacturing capability, the FX risk may become more subtle but does not disappear. It often becomes an internal problem where the profits from an overseas subsidiary need to be repatriated to the home company.

Once this type of FX exposure has been acquired, the company may think that the "safest" thing to do is not to hedge, to avoid all financial derivatives. This is tempting but wrong. To do nothing, under these circumstances, is to speculate. There are various hedging choices available to the prudent company, but sitting tight and trying to pretend that FX risk will go away if you ignore it has not to date been a successful strategy.

Hidden exposures

It is reasonably obvious how FX risk has been acquired in the previous example, but it can worm its way into the balance sheet in more insidious ways. If a company has fixed assets or investments overseas then it will have to report the value of these in its balance sheet. If they vary with the FX rate, there will be an undesirably volatile item in the balance sheet. This volatility can, depending upon local accounting rules, be hedged away, but this hedging can create its own problems. Consider the case where a forward hedge is used to hedge the value of overseas fixed assets such as buildings. If the value of the buildings appreciates, then the hedge will lose money. However, the increase in the value of the building is not available as cash with which pay the losing hedge. This cash needs to be obtained from elsewhere – and it may be very painful to find it.

RETURN ON CAPITAL AS A RISK MEASURE

Everyone is familiar with the idea of return on capital (ROC). When capital is being used, for example, to buy shares, then calculating the return is a simple business. Once more complex products such as FX and derivatives are considered, however, the situation is more complex. The amount of capital that is "invested" in a derivatives portfolio is that amount considered necessary to support the market and credit risks.

To understand how to calculate the amount of capital that needs to be allocated to support these risks, we can consider a hedged FX portfolio. Such a portfolio is immune to market risk, unless a default occurs on one of the deals. Let us assume, somewhat simplistically, that all the deals are in matched pairs, hedging each other with a small but safe profit margin in between. At the time that the deal and its hedge were put on, both had a market value of roughly zero. However, as time goes on, an FX deal may radically change its value. Thus, if one half of a matched pair of deals is suddenly eliminated by a default, the holder of the portfolio is still obliged to maintain the opposing cashflows, which may be very expensive to do. Market risk enters via default risk.

The risk of loss depends upon (1) the probability of default (credit risk) and (2) the loss in the event of default (market risk).

For the manager of an FX portfolio, the capital question is critical. It is obviously necessary to allocate sufficient capital to the portfolio to absorb losses when they do occur, but allocating too much capital will mean that investors receive a poor ROC. Thus calculation of the "right" amount of capital is extremely important. It is worth noting that any poor calculations lead to overcapitalisation, as approximations must always err on the conservative side.

In the youth of the FX industry, deal spreads were wide, and only crude calculations were necessary to show that a given deal was generating a satisfactory return. However, in the current mature market, deal spreads are much tighter. Only the most accurate calculations will now suffice to give investors an idea of the true ROC of a deal. Moreover, a single FX deal at market spreads will never give an adequate ROC. This is unconnected with fixed costs such as communications and computers. Unless the deal is considered in the context of a large portfolio, the capital necessary to support the risk is always unreasonably large. Once the deal is considered as being added to a large portfolio, however, it becomes possible to look at the incremental capital needed, which will be added to the capital already allocated to the portfolio. This is inevitably very much less than that needed to support the deal on its own, due to the netting and diversification effects within the portfolio.

Market and credit risk calculations

How would we go about calculating the amount of capital which we need to allocate? We want to combine the market and credit risk distributions to find the "expected" or average loss due to default on a single deal, and allocate that much capital to the deal. However, what if the average loss in any one year is USD 1,000,000, but there is a 30% chance that there will be a loss of USD 10,000,000? Obviously, unless we know very accurately what the expected loss will be, we need to allocate additional capital to cover our uncertainty. This additional capital (sometimes called economic capital) will depend upon the loss distribution obtained from combining the market and default risks.

The market risk distribution is similar to the normal distribution, but with fatter tails. The default risk distribution is skewed, with non-zero probabilities of very high losses, shown in Figure 12 (**a**). The combination of the two has the worst of both worlds, as illustrated in Figure 12 (**b**), which also shows the relationship of economic capital (unexpected loss) to the risk of loss distribution. Several standard deviations of the risk of loss distribution are used to determine the amount of capital allocated to the portfolio, depending upon the safety level desired. For example, if the safety level desired was 99.97% (equivalent to an AA rating), capital equal to about 3.5 standard deviations would be necessary, assuming that the risk of loss distribution is normal. In fact, more (6–7) may be needed due to the fat tails. A safety level of 99.97% means that in any one year there is only a 0.03% chance that losses will exceed the total capital held.

How is this calculation done in practice? While a Monte Carlo simulation would be ideal, lack of default data and computing power means that it is not an automatic choice for all but very large institutions. In practice, market risks are calculated separately and then multiplied by a factor dependent upon the credit status of the counterparty.

Figure 12 Market and default risk distributions

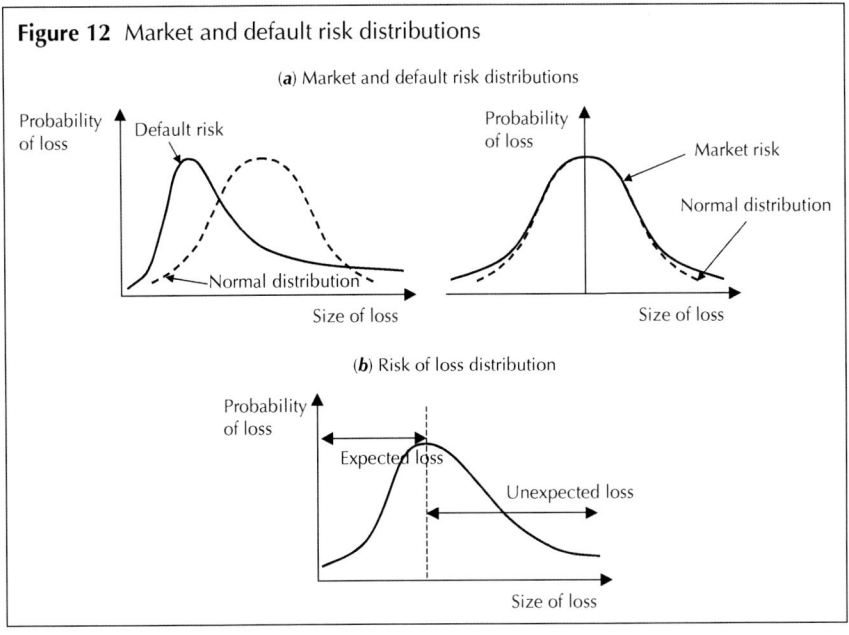

CONCLUSION

FX risk is similar to but subtly different from other market risk types. It can enter a business unannounced, and can be both large and unexpected. The fat tails so apparent in the equity market are clearly evident in FX. The key to understanding and living with FX risk is forethought. It may be managed and reduced as long as sufficient thought and analysis goes before.

REFERENCE

Embrechts, P., 1997, "Extremal Values in Insurance and Finance" (Springer-Verlag).

7
Traditional Hedging Methods

Chris Attfield
PaR Asset Management LLP

INTRODUCTION

The previous chapter looked at some of the ways in which a company may gain exposure to FX risk, meaning that its financials are subject to variability due to movements in one or more foreign exchange rates. This chapter examines various traditional methods of protecting oneself against these uncertainties.

We look first at a number of reasons why a company or fund manager may feel it necessary to hedge, touching on a variety of definitions of "risk" and also hedging philosophy: what hedging can and cannot be expected to do. If an entity does decide to hedge, it is immediately confronted by a host of new questions, including choice of instrument, tenor and hedging methodology. This chapter also covers hedging with forwards and options, including some simple option strategies. Judgemental hedging is the modification of one's hedging strategy to express a market view and we will look at how such a strategy might be implemented and what the pitfalls can be.

It is assumed that the reader is moderately familiar with the concept of forward and option contracts. Further information on arbitrage pricing of forwards, Black–Scholes and put/call parity may be found in Hull (2002), and a more practical approach to options focused on exchange-based trading in Natenberg (1994). We will be focusing on the practical application of these instruments for hedging, and the risk trade-offs that each may bring.

HEDGING INSTRUMENTS
Forward contracts

Foreign exchange is conventionally traded "for value spot": that is, the deal that is struck today will result in physical delivery of currency to and from the counterparties' nominated accounts on a date which is generally two business days in the future, called the "spot date" (a few trivial exceptions to this apply, for example in the CAD, for which "spot" is defined as one business day). The roots of this are in history, when arranging the transfer of funds could take up to 48 hours and so dealing for immediate delivery was not practicable. Nowadays, electronic fund transfer does allow near-instantaneous transfer, but the convention has been maintained.

For a hedger, dealing for value spot is not ideal. Physical delivery of cash is administratively expensive (especially if individual exposures are covered on an *ad hoc* basis, which would result in many cash transactions to be settled), and pre-supposes that the funds to settle the transaction will be available in advance, which will probably not be the case. However, the foreign exchange forward market gives the market participant a way to adjust the delivery date of their deal away from the spot date, so that no exchange of funds takes place until the appropriate date, for example the date on which a foreign currency cashflow must be repatriated.

The pricing of forwards through "cash and carry" arbitrage has been covered in Chapter 3. Dealing forward is done as an adjustment to the underlying spot market; a deal is agreed for value spot, and then an FX swap (not to be confused with the longer-dated cross-currency swap) is performed which adjusts the spot price for the interest rate differential between the two currencies to give the correct arbitrage-free forward price. The swap transaction effectively sells the currency bought for value spot, and buys it back on some date in the future.

For example, on 1 January a US-based company, ABC Corp., may wish to hedge a cashflow of EUR 10 million which it will receive on 1 April. It would therefore firstly do a spot deal to sell EUR and buy USD in EUR 10 million. This, by itself, would give it the obligation to deliver EUR 10 million on 3 January (two business days' time: the spot date) in return for receiving an appropriate amount of USD. Say the spot rate it agreed for this transaction was

0.8500 EUR/USD, which means that for every EUR it sells it will receive 85 US cents. The USD amount it would receive for the spot transaction would therefore be USD 8.5 million.

However, ABC Corp. will not receive its EUR until 1 April! It therefore enters into a forward swap to sell and buy EUR spot to 1 April. This means that it sells the EUR versus the USD for value spot (effectively cancelling the spot transaction) while simultaneously agreeing to buy it back for value 1 April. Because of the interest rate differential, the price agreed for 1 April will be slightly different from the spot price; the forward swap will be quoted as the difference between these two prices (this difference is called the "forward points"). In our example, let us assume the forward swap agreed was quoted as −30 points. EUR/USD is quoted to four decimal places, so this implies that the correction to be applied to move the delivery date from 3 January to 1 April is −0.0030. The all-in, or "forward outright" rate, that ABC Corp. has obtained to repatriate its EUR cashflow to USD on 1 April is therefore 0.8500 − 0.0030 = 0.8470, and the USD amount that it has guaranteed in exchange for this EUR amount is USD 8.47 million.

Options

An option contract is one that gives the buyer an element of choice. A price for some underlying commodity is agreed for a point in the future but, depending on some condition or combination of conditions, the buyer may choose not to accept that price, but deal at a different and more favourable one, typically the prevailing spot market price. In its simplest form, an option gives the buyer the right, but not the obligation, to trade at the agreed price (the strike price) at an agreed date in the future, termed the expiry date.

One of the most important distinctions in option contracts is between a call option (giving the right to go long the underlying exchange rate or security) and a put option (which gives the right to go short). In contrast, the buyer of a forward contract is *ipso facto* long the underlying market. The buyer of a call option becomes long the underlying (ie, they will make money as the price rises), but so will the seller of a put option; this is because the opposite side of the right to sell is the obligation to buy. The length of time the option has to live before expiry is its tenor. In foreign exchange, options are peculiar in that any option to buy one currency is *ipso facto* an option to sell the currency it is being traded against; every call option is thus also a put, and it is important to specify the contract unambiguously, as conventions between market participants vary as one crosses the Atlantic!

If it is to the buyer's advantage to take the strike price rather than the current market spot price when the option expires, the buyer *exercises* the option, and the option is said to be "in-the-money" (ITM). In fact, any option for which the strike is more attractive than the prevailing market price is termed ITM, and one for which this is not true is "out-of-the-money" (OTM). Options are very commonly struck at the forward price when the contract is initially traded, and are then termed "at-the-money-forward" (ATM or ATMF). An ITM option is said to have intrinsic value, which is equal to the difference between the market and strike price; however, an OTM option need not be worthless, as there is the possibility that the market will move in its favour and it will be ITM at expiry. This "probability value" is called *time value*. Before expiry, options may have both time and intrinsic value, but at expiry only the intrinsic (if any) remains. (See Figure 1.)

For a hedger dealing options with a bank to hedge foreign exchange risk, the contracts will nearly always be exercisable at expiry. These options are termed European-style options, and differ from American-style options which can be exercised at any time prior to expiry. American-style is most common in exchange-traded contracts where only certain delivery dates are available. In contrast, with an "over-the-counter" (OTC) option traded direct with a bank, the contract details are customisable, largely removing the need for early exercise. As early exercise only gives you the intrinsic value of the option rather than realising the total value, it is usually best avoided.

To return to our example, if ABC Corp. were to hedge with an option rather than a forward to cover its EUR 10 million receivable, it would buy a EUR put/USD call option (ie, an option to sell EUR and buy USD), which expires on 30 March, two business days before the cashflow is due (in order that delivery may take place on the correct date of 1 April). It strikes the option at-the-money-forward (ATMF), so the strike price is the same as the forward price in the previous section of 0.8470. On 30 March, if the spot market

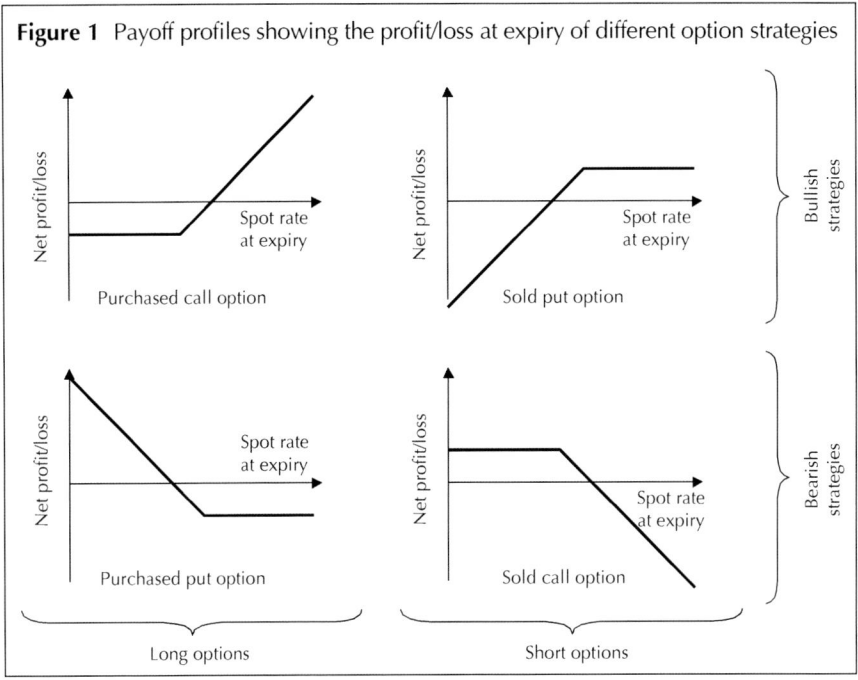

Figure 1 Payoff profiles showing the profit/loss at expiry of different option strategies

price is greater than 0.8470 then it is in ABC Corp.'s best interest to let the option contract expire worthless, and sell its EUR in the spot market – for which the spot date is 1 April. Alternatively, if the market has fallen such that the spot price is below 0.8470, it would exercise the option, as it gives it the right to deal at a better price than the prevailing market.

The market-standard model used for option pricing is a modification of the Black–Scholes model that allows both "asset" and "pricing" currency to have continuously compounding interest (in practice, the continuous rates will be derived from annually compounding money market rates, usually termed "deposit rates"). The model is so universal that FX option prices are regularly quoted by option traders as the volatility implied through the model. The Black–Scholes formula (as given in Hull, 2002) for the price of a call c or put p is:

$$c = FN(d_1) - XN(d_2)$$
$$p = XN(-d_2) - FN(-d_1)$$

where:

$$d_1 = \frac{\ln\left(\frac{F}{X}\right) + \frac{\sigma^2 t}{2}}{\sigma\sqrt{t}}$$

$$d_2 = \frac{\ln\left(\frac{F}{X}\right) - \frac{\sigma^2 t}{2}}{\sigma\sqrt{t}} = d_1 - \sigma\sqrt{t}$$

and:
- F = Forward
- X = Strike
- σ = Volatility

Note: Prices are calculated as Future Values.

The value σ here is the most important element in the equation. It is the only element that is unique to the options market: the other inputs either have secondary markets of their own (spot, forward, interest rates) or are part of the option specification (call/put, tenor, strike). What Black and Scholes realised is that option traders are not so much trying to guess the correct price for an option as making an estimation of how volatile the underlying market will be during its life. The volatility input to the Black–Scholes model should be understood in this light: not as a measure of historical market volatility, but as an estimation of future volatility. This is termed an *implied volatility* as it can be implied from the option price.

The relationship of an option price to implied volatility is important; as the market becomes more volatile, the potential payoff of an option increases, but the minimum payoff is still zero. The value of the option therefore increases as the implied volatility increases; for ATMF options, there is a direct proportionality between σ and option premium.

WHY HEDGE?

Non-transferable risk

Before considering hedging, a company must be sure that the risk it has cannot simply be passed on. If that company is a price-setter in its market, it may be able to dictate the price of its end product, and is thus free to vary it in line with the market pressures it feels.

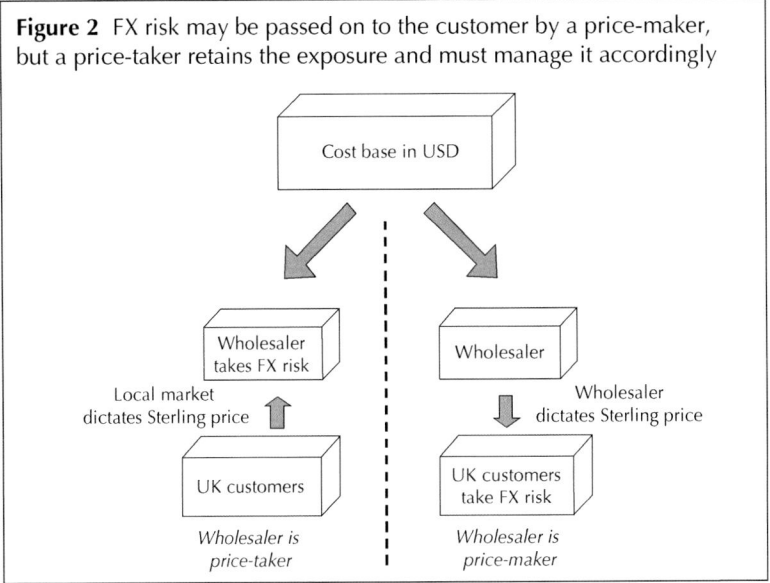

Figure 2 FX risk may be passed on to the customer by a price-maker, but a price-taker retains the exposure and must manage it accordingly

Alternatively, if a company is selling into a more competitive market, but the conventions of that market are that the prices will vary according to market forces that affect all participants, the impact of that market on any of those participants is minimised.

For example, if all producers of instant coffee varied their prices to the wholesaler according to the price of coffee on the world market, variability in the price of coffee would have little direct effect on one supplier's earnings. If the price was allowed to vary as the market price of coffee varied, the market risk is effectively passed on to the wholesaler and thence to the consumer. Hedging is only necessary to the extent to which this is not possible, and the risk must be borne by the company itself (see Figure 2).

The same is true in the foreign exchange risk. If a US company is importing goods into the UK, it will have much less need for hedging if the price can be fixed in USD and allowed to vary in GBP. This is much more likely to be true if most of its direct competitors are also US based and suffer the same problem. If, however, the competition is indigenous, it may have to fix its prices in GBP and itself bear the risk that USD strengthens against GBP.

There is an obvious limit to which this is true. It is all very well saying that you can pass the risk on to your consumers, but markets are not infinitely elastic, and there may come a point at which you price yourself out of the market, especially if selling non-essential goods. This second-order effect would come into play in the event of a severe FX move, causing your sales volumes to fall and offsetting the price increases you had hoped to foist upon your customer base. In such a situation, all that can be done is to drop the price to a more reasonable level, thus wearing the market movement yourself.

The worst-case scenario here is if a company is a price-taker in a very competitive market. Here, demand may dictate that favourable moves are passed through to the customer, whereas the ability to pass on adverse moves immediately is restricted. The company is in effect granting the customer an option on the market in question, but does not receive any compensation for this one-sided risk.

Competitive hedging

A company that offers the same goods as its competitors, but for more money, is in trouble. Competitive hedging acknowledges that a company's performance is largely relative to those in the same field as itself, and that deviation from the behaviour of the competition may have benefits but also dangers.

If you choose to hedge forward, effectively locking in an FX rate you see as particularly favourable, then you may be very well placed to undercut the opposition when rates move against you in the future. However, if you have a policy of always hedging forward when none of your competitors does, it is likely that there will come a time in which rates move sharply in your favour, and also in theirs. They will be able to undercut you, forcing you to fund the cost of your losing hedging yourself. If you had run unhedged like everybody else, a disadvantageous move would be felt by all equally, placing no one in a comparatively worse position. Your benchmark here is not the consumer of your products, but deviation from your peers.

What if there is no consensus amongst the competition? This can lead to a thorny problem. If your direct competitors are Company A that always hedges forward, and Company B that always runs unhedged, you are potentially in a no-win situation. If you decide to run fully hedged and rates move in your favour, Company B has a decisive advantage over you. On the other hand, if you elect to run unhedged and rates move against you, Company A will be able to undercut you. Not an enviable position!

Economic and accounting hedges

Hedging is traditionally thought of in economic terms. If a company prices its goods assuming a certain rate of exchange, but the foreign currency revenues are repatriated at a different rate, then this is an economic loss to the company. However, this is not the only risk the company runs due to its foreign earnings.

The company may have the freedom to alter its prices several times a year, depending on its ability to act as a price-maker. This will limit the length of time in which it is exposed to the chance that FX rates move against it, making its earnings worth less in its local currency. A publicly owned company will typically also have to make some representation to its shareholders about forecast earnings for that financial year. If the company's performance does not match up to these forecasts, it may be forced to issue a profits warning to its investors. The stock market in general, and stock analysts in particular, can take a very dim view of profit warnings, and this can have serious repercussions on the company itself in the form of a plunging stock price, downgraded ratings and even ultimately the departure of the board members seen to be responsible for this underperformance. Clearly this "Wall Street risk", or accounting risk, is every bit as real as the economic risk on which we might conventionally focus.

Hedging accounting risk can be difficult. It is typically longer-dated than the economic risk of holding prices at a given level and may not receive favourable accounting treatment, as the underlying is more abstract than the firm commitments beloved of accounting standards such as FAS 133 in the US. This can cause companies to be wary of putting hedges into place to protect their earnings forecasts, and leaves them in a situation where they may have to make conservative estimates to try to protect themselves.

TRADITIONAL HEDGING: CONSERVATIVE PRICING AND FORWARDS
Hedging without hedging

If a business decides that it is either unable or unwilling to take out contracts to hedge itself against foreign exchange risk, it can

CURRENCY MANAGEMENT: OVERLAY AND ALPHA TRADING

still address the situation in other ways. The most elegant way to do this will be to spread the corporate cost base across the countries in which it does business, in the same ratio as the expected earnings and/or assets it possesses in those regions. For example, if goods are to be sold in Germany, then locating the production facilities in Germany ensures that the cost base will also be in EUR along with the revenues. If EUR debt is used to finance the operation, then the net result should be an offset of the assets and liabilities, with only the repatriation of profits requiring hedging. Using natural offsets in this way is an effective tool to reduce the need for hedging.

Alternatively, a company may be able to control the FX risk on the prices it quotes. These prices may be either externally quoted to that company's clients, or an internally guaranteed rate that is set by the treasury of a company acting as "internal bank" to its international subsidiaries. The way this can be done is to be conservative in how the rates used to set prices or earnings forecasts are set.

The forward price for an exchange rate may be thought of as the centre point of the distribution of possible future rates (in fact, this is exactly what is assumed by most pricing models). It therefore follows that there is a more-or-less 50:50 chance that the actual market rate at a given point in the future will be greater or less than this value. The fact that FX rates are lognormally distributed distorts this picture slightly, as the distribution is asymmetrical, with unlimited possibility of movement to the upside but limited possibility on the downside. Still, the 50:50 rule is a good approximation, and is widely assumed to be the case.

A company wishing to make conservative prices in a foreign currency can do so in the following manner. Suppose a UK-based company is exporting to Euro-land, and the EUR/GBP exchange rate for a three-month forward contract is 0.6500. The risk for our exporter is that, if it does not hedge, the market will weaken, and the EUR it receives will be worth less than GBP 0.6500 when it comes to repatriate its earnings. It therefore decides to base the EUR price it charges upon a EUR/GBP rate of 0.6300. This "pads" the price and ensures that it will not have made a loss on the assumed GBP profits, provided that the market is above 0.6300 in three months' time. The probability that this will happen is clearly less than 50:50, so it has moved the odds in its favour.

TRADITIONAL HEDGING METHODS

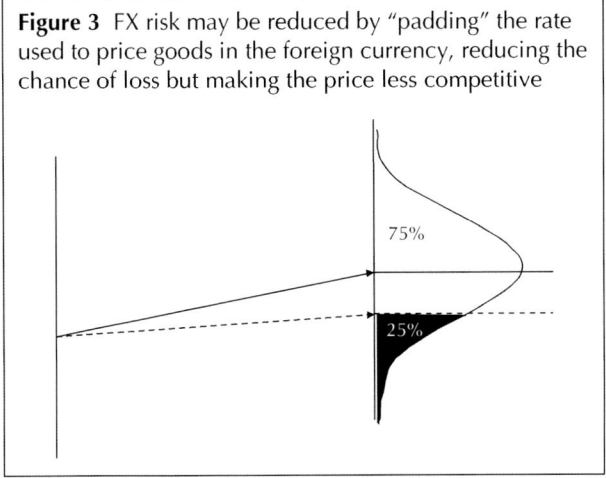

Figure 3 FX risk may be reduced by "padding" the rate used to price goods in the foreign currency, reducing the chance of loss but making the price less competitive

How far is it appropriate to move the rate? This obviously depends on the amount of certainty the company wishes to have that its profit margins will not be eroded. The drawback is that, as the level of protection increases, the price inevitably becomes less competitive, as it is based on an artificially inflated FX rate. The trade-off here is between aggressive pricing and level of protection, and in order to choose the correct levels, it is important to be able to measure what level of protection is being provided. This can be done by calculating the distribution of rates in the future, and using this to calculate an estimate of the percentage chance that the market movement will eliminate the advantage from the padded FX rate. This is shown in Figure 3. A lognormal distribution is calculated using the forward rate as the mean, and with the standard deviation taken from observed historical spot market moves.

A variation of the above methodology is to use option implied volatilities as a base for the calculation of the forward distribution, rather than figures derived from past spot moves. While less conventional, this has the advantage that option volatilities are forward looking, and represent the true level of risk priced into the market. For sophisticated users, information about future directional risk from the implied volatility smile can also be used in the same methodology.

Forward hedging

This is the most basic way of hedging with a traded instrument. Given the knowledge that a certain amount of foreign currency must be bought or sold on a given date in the future, a forward contract allows a price to be locked in for that transaction. Once entered into, a forward is a legal obligation: even if the underlying cashflow does not materialise, the contract obliges the party to make the exchange at the agreed rate. Forwards may be traded out of, if this is the case, but the obvious risk is that the market has moved against the party, and a net loss is realised.

Forward hedging is therefore appropriate only for hedging exposures that have a high degree of certainty. This poses problems, for example, if a company must hedge its earnings from sales abroad, but the actual sales figures cannot be known in advance. Selling the foreign currency for the entire forecast amount will work out well if those figures are realised, but if the sales forecast/targets were optimistic, an overhedge situation may well occur. This gives the company exposure in the opposite direction to its natural exposure – and is potentially embarrassing to the corporate treasurer who must explain to the board why a market movement in its favour has cost the company money!

A probabilistic approach may be of help here. By analysis of the company's past sales volumes, a measure of the historical volatility of sales can be made, and forecasts or the historical trend can be used to project an expectation line out into the future. Volatility cones are a tool that can be valuable in determining this, as shown in Figure 4. The "cones" represent a level which sales may be expected to meet or exceed with a given level of probability. They are calculated by taking the mean μ at a time t in the future, and the volatility σ, which is estimated from the historical volatility as above. A lognormal formula can be used to avoid negative sales forecasts. These cones show the sales volume which one can have a given level of certainty will not be breached at a given point in the future. With sufficiently high confidence, for example 90%, it is then possible to forward hedge and be reasonably sure than an overhedge situation will not occur.

As discussed above, the forward price is chiefly determined by the current rate of exchange trading for value "spot" (generally two business days), with a small adjustment to allow for the interest

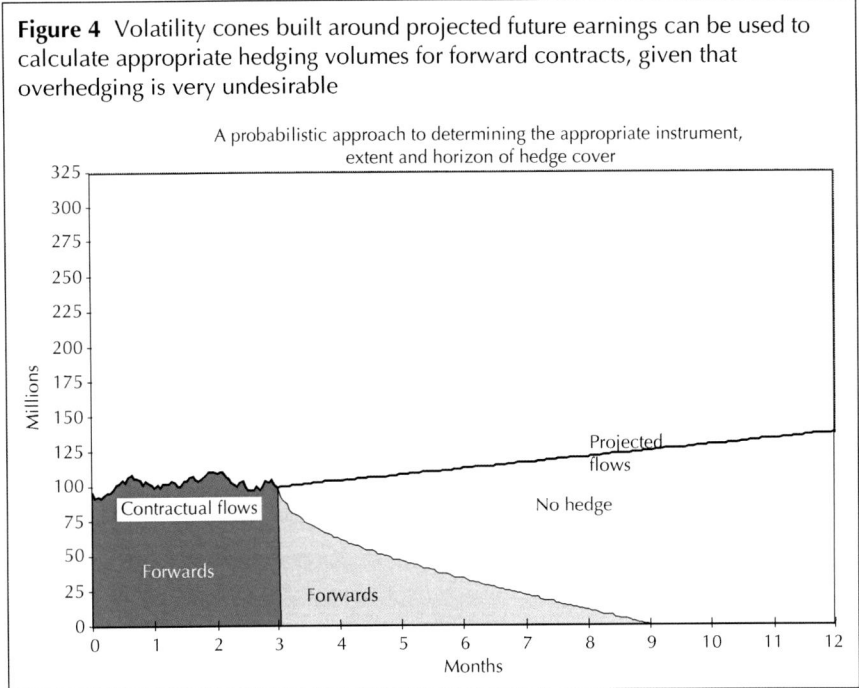

Figure 4 Volatility cones built around projected future earnings can be used to calculate appropriate hedging volumes for forward contracts, given that overhedging is very undesirable

rate differential between the two currencies, which will get larger as the tenor of the forward increases. Forward hedging therefore chiefly consists in locking in the currently available spot rate, and then making adjustments to that rate to alter the times at which the currency will be delivered during the hedging period.

There are various ways that this can be achieved. For an example, let us take a US company that wishes to hedge its foreign earnings for the coming calendar year. The company's budgeting exercise is carried out one quarter in advance, and the budget FX rate is therefore set at the start of October for that hedging period. As this rate is the one which will be used both to set prices for its products in that foreign currency, and also to forecast the USD value of the earnings it makes in that currency for the purpose of making profit forecasts to Wall Street, the company desires to lock in that rate for the entire hedging period. The company's foreign earnings will be translated back into USD on a monthly basis, and for this example we ignore any accounting considerations and offsetting foreign expenses the company may have.

The simplest, and most common way to do this is with a strip of forwards. Conceptually this involves hedging forward the amount of earnings forecast to the end of each month in the hedging period. The strip would therefore contain 12 forwards for value at the end of January, February, ... December, with the amounts reflecting the foreign currency earnings forecasts. In practice, it is not necessary to implement this by doing 12 forward outright trades; one trade for value spot is done, selling the foreign currency and buying USD. The value dates are then adjusted by a series of 12 FX swaps, which buy the foreign currency for value spot and sell it for the desired end-of-month date – effectively shifting the value date of a proportion of that spot trade out to that point. Forward outright trades are commonly split out in this way, reflecting the fact that the trades are being done by different desks in the bank, and that risks of the two portions are very different, with the FX spot market being much more volatile than the forward market.

The strip, then, allows a company to sell its foreign receivables at regular intervals and receive a known amount of USD for them, the rate of which is in agreement with the budget rate set before the start of the year. The **stack** of forwards is very similar, the idea being to limit the number of transactions involved in hedging by only hedging to a few value dates, possibly only the end-of-year date. As the dates come for the foreign receivables to be converted, the relevant amount of the stacked hedge is swapped forward, and delivery is taken as usual. The advantage of this is that it allows for unknown seasonal variation to be accommodated easily: the only thing that must be decided in advance is the total receivable amount for the year. The drawback is that this does not allow the exact rate to be known in advance, as the swaps forward occur at the prevailing forward market rates, which have not been locked in (although the spot component of the hedge was fixed at inception – see Figure 5).

Another variation on this theme is the *par forward*. This is essentially the same as the strip, but here all the forwards are done at the same rate, irrespective of their maturity. This does not mean that the trade is mispriced: although the rates of the individual legs of this trade will not equal the market forward for that value date, the rate at which they are traded is calculated so that favourable rates of some of the trades cancel out with unfavourable rates on the

TRADITIONAL HEDGING METHODS

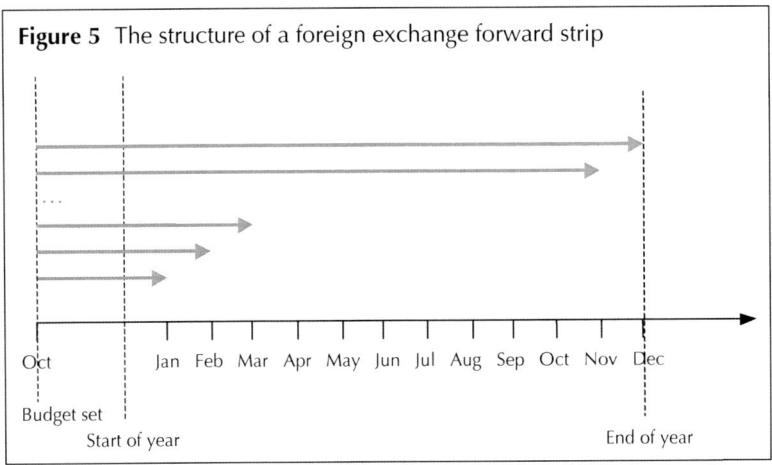

Figure 5 The structure of a foreign exchange forward strip

other trades, and the whole structure is fairly priced, having zero expected return. This is done for the customer's convenience: the bank has some extra credit implications which arise from the fact that the trades done at worse-than-market rates are funding those done at better-than-market rates. In a situation where the customer takes delivery of the trades priced favourably to itself but then goes bankrupt, the bank's loss is greater than if all the forwards had been individually priced at fair market value.

TRADITIONAL HEDGING: OPTIONS
Simple option hedges

As explained above, a foreign exchange option is conceptually even more basic than a forward contract. Whereas a forward gives the buyer both the right and the obligation to make/take delivery of a given currency at a set date in the future, an option contract removes the obligation part from the equation, leaving only the right to do so for the buyer (the seller, conversely, forfeits this right and is obliged to deliver if the buyer so chooses). An option can therefore be looked at as half of a forward: the buyer receives the upside half ("reward") and the seller assumes the downside ("risk").

The advantages to a hedger of purchasing an option are obvious. Forward hedging carries the risk that the hedges will make a loss due to the market moving against them, making their use

167

impractical for uncertain flows and running the risk of putting the company in an uncompetitive position. Options remove these problems, as the owner is free to walk away from any contract that carries an agreed price (the *strike* of the option) that looks less attractive than the rate currently available in the spot market at expiry.

As one might expect, the best of both worlds comes with a price tag attached. For the right to walk away from a losing contract, the buyer must pay a premium, unlike forward contracts where the strike price is set such that no payment is required by either party. This is possible because forwards have a symmetrical risk/reward: the upside can be made to equal the downside. With an option payoff, there is no downside, so the value to the buyer must be positive. Option pricing models offer a way of calculating what this value is, in order that the correct price may be charged up-front.

Whether option premiums are indeed fairly priced has always been a contentious issue amongst option users, not surprisingly. On the one hand, the pricing model universally used to value these contracts (a variation on the famous Black–Scholes model as stated above) is simple, and its approximations well known and allowed for by the options market, which is itself highly liquid for the major currencies. On the other hand, corporate and institutional hedgers tend to be on the buy side, as selling options is perceived with some justification as being a high-risk strategy with an undesirable pattern of returns for a hedger. With the banks mostly on the sell side, suspicion that supply and demand will inflate option premiums is never far away.

Research performed by the author with Dr Jessica James while at Bank One clarified this question. Although it can easily be seen that levels of market volatility are implied from option prices (the implied volatility that is widely used and quoted by currency option traders), it is also well known that the Black–Scholes formula underestimates the probability that large moves will occur in either direction. This *leptokurtosis* ("fat-tails") has the effect of increasing the value of simple purchased options, which would be expected to inflate the value of the implied volatility. The question is whether the market overcompensates for this effect. Our results, for hedgers of USD versus DEM on both sides of the Atlantic, are shown in Table 1.

TRADITIONAL HEDGING METHODS

Table 1 Average premiums and payoffs for USD/DEM call and put options

	Average	Average	True cost of
12m ATMF			
Calls	(4.39%)	4.14%	(0.25%)
Puts	(4.39%)	4.58%	0.19%
Average	(4.39%)	4.36%	(0.03%)
6m ATMF			
Calls	(3.20%)	3.18%	(0.02%)
Puts	(3.20%)	3.46%	0.26%
Average	(3.20%)	3.32%	0.12%
3m ATMF			
Calls	(2.25%)	2.24%	(0.01%)
Puts	(2.25%)	2.44%	0.20%
Average	(2.25%)	2.34%	0.09%

These results suggest that the market gets it right on average, although any particular option may still be over- or underpriced. This analysis does not include the effects of the bid/offer spread, which will always be to the detriment of buyers, but is known and quantified at the time of purchase.

Option structures

Simple options give the hedger a new dimension in risk control, as they confer the ability to reshape their risk profile in ways that would otherwise be impossible. However, even greater flexibility can be obtained by the combination of options into option structures. These structures give the hedger the ability to express a directional or technical view in very precise terms, shaping their profit/loss to take advantage of perceived resistance/support levels as well as risk limits and premium constraints.

One of the most common desires among option users is to avoid paying premium. Although this can be done by borrowing money, another and much more elegant solution is to offset the premium of a purchased ("protective") option with the premium received for selling a "financing" option with a different strike. A simple example of this is the zero-premium collar, which in foreign exchange is usually termed a "range forward" (although option traders commonly refer to the hedge structure as a "risk reversal"; a profusion

CURRENCY MANAGEMENT: OVERLAY AND ALPHA TRADING

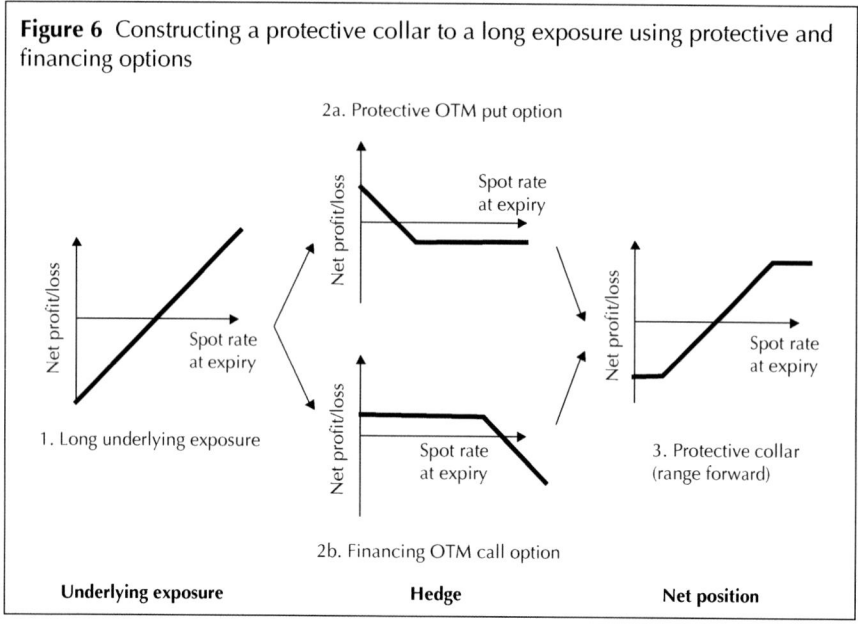

Figure 6 Constructing a protective collar to a long exposure using protective and financing options

of names is a common feature of hedging structures of this kind!). In this structure, an underlying exposure has worst-case protection provided by a purchased option struck at worse than the forward rate. This makes the option premium smaller than the corresponding ATM option, and allows that premium to be fully offset by the sale of an OTM option of the opposite type (put/call). If the market at expiry is between the two strikes, both options expire worthless and the exposure must be covered in the spot market. The effect is thus to provide both a worst case and a best case for the exchange rate, in between which the exposure floats with the underlying market. An example of how this sort of trade is structured is shown in Figure 6.

Exotic options

Exotic options build on the foundations of vanilla (non-exotic) options, but add extra elements of conditionality to the payout or different ways of calculating the payout. For a hedger, the chief use of exotic options is to reduce premium cost by setting additional constraints in line with a view that they hold.

Average rate options (AROs, also called Asian options) are often referred to as "slightly exotic" as they differ from vanilla European options only in that their final payout is determined by the average of a series of spot observations before the expiry point, rather than just by the spot at expiry alone (a vanilla European option is thus a special case of an ARO). They cost less than European options for the simple reason that the average of spot is less volatile than the spot rate itself and, as discussed above, lower volatility leads to lower option premiums. The price of the option is lowered by increasing the frequency of observation and by starting the averaging earlier in the option's life (the observations are taken from an agreed fixing rate). AROs can be useful to firms that have many irregular flows that are repatriated continually throughout the hedging period, and also for those wishing to hedge accounting exposure for which the benchmark is set at the average spot rate.

Barrier options are options which pay out as European options, but with an additional reference level (the barrier) which must either be touched for the option to pay out (a knock-in option), or which must never be touched during the option's life for a payout to be made (a knock-out option). Market convention is that if the barrier is hit as the option moves into the money, it is a "knock up" option, and a "knock down" if the barrier is in the OTM direction; each of these being defined relative to spot, as the barrier may be hit at any time, not just at expiry. Options are hence classified as, for example, "up and in" or "down and out", depending on the position of the barrier and the effect it has.

If a hedger has a view on a resistance level in the market, which they do not believe will be breached in the life of the option, then they may take advantage of this perceived level by placing a barrier safely on the other side of the level, and thus reducing the option premium that must be paid. Obviously, this level must be reasonably close to the market (as measured by the probability of its being hit, taking into account the implied volatility and the market forward rate) for there to be any worthwhile reduction in cost! This underlines the fact that, in order for any of these sophisticated strategies to be profitable, the view on which they are based must be correct. If your view does not differ in any way from the market's, all strategies have an expected value of zero.

Other types of exotic option include: digital options, which offer a known payout if a condition is met, much in the same way as a bet at the bookmaker's, and lookback options, which offer the opportunity to buy/sell at the best price seen in a given period, in return for a substantial premium. These are not commonly in use by the hedger with conventional market exposures, as they are either poor matches for their underlying exposures, very expensive, or a combination of the two.

THE LIMITATIONS OF TRADITIONAL HEDGING

Traditional hedging methods as described above can all be valuable tools to cover the market risks incurred by international businesses or asset managers. The problem with these often comes from the choice and implementation of hedging strategy.

Problems in implementation

Firstly, a strategy may be chosen to take into account a certain macroeconomic view of the treasurer or board members, but then left in place after that view is no longer relevant. For instance, a UK asset manager may choose to leave themselves unhedged because of a view that GBP depreciates over time. This may have been appropriate for a period in the 1980s, but conditions change, and having a fully unhedged benchmark is a very aggressive way of stating the view that this will continue. Making decisions about a hedge strategy based on historical correlations between equities and FX rates is also suspect, given the unstable and statistical nature of correlations; given that they only apply to an "average" case, the offsetting move you need might not be there in the specific year you were relying on it!

Secondly, hedging strategy decisions are usually made at board level. This is appropriate for large-scale policy, but hedging is often employed with a particular market view in place – a borderline speculative practice sometimes called "hedge-ulation". Doing this can amount to "trading by committee", which is rarely a rewarding activity.

Systematic problems of traditional hedging

The second point underlies the real limitation of traditional, passive hedging. Hedging reshapes the market risk profile of an entity, but it is often expected that a correctly implemented hedge should earn a return, in the shape of either income or competitive advantage. Something which was designed solely as a risk control measure thus becomes viewed as a speculative investment.

It is easy to see why this confusion arises. Traders take market risk, acquiring positions in order to generate returns. Hedgers also take market positions; the only difference is that the risk is pre-existent in the latter case, and the hedger traditionally seeks to mitigate that risk rather than add to it. With the instruments at their disposal, a hedger is able to offset all market risk in their portfolio or balance sheet; the decision to do anything but that is therefore tantamount to taking a market position. This places the partial hedger in the same position as the trader: they voluntarily take (or retain) risk, and should therefore be expected to make a return from it.

The problem with this is that passive hedging strategies are typically designed only to mitigate risk, not to generate return. The problems of trading by committee or view-based hedging both have their root in the fact that the hedge is being asked to do both things. The only thing that will generate return in the zero-expected return world of FX is correct market positioning and timing, and passive strategies are not good for that.

It is not unreasonable to ask that risk to which your business is exposed be compensated by incremental return, but in order to do that it is necessary to bring trading discipline to the hedging process. The process of managing currency exposure in order to generate returns is called *active management*, and will be addressed in later chapters.

BIBLIOGRAPHY

Hull, J. C., 2002, *Options, Futures, and Other Derivative Securities*.

Natenberg, S., 1994, *Option Volatility and Pricing*.

8

Active versus Passive Hedging

Henrik H. Pedersen*

CitiFX Risk Advisory Group

OVERVIEW

Once a currency manager has decided that they want to do something about the uncompensated portfolio risk arising from currency in their international portfolio, the next question that arises is "how" the manager should proceed. This decision is often based on the fundamental beliefs of the fund manager as to how currency markets operate and how important they are for the manager. Naturally these beliefs will vary from individual to individual and from manager to manager. As in all decision making processes involving human beings, these beliefs can be engraved in cultural norms, traditions or political factors. This means that presented with exactly the same analysis, two different people might come out with totally different interpretations of what it means to them, and what it requires of them in terms of actions.

Because of this paradigm there can be no right answer. Therefore the purpose of this chapter is to create awareness of the different possibilities available to the current or would be currency manager. To this effect, the chapter will attempt to provide an objective

---

*Henrik Pedersen is vice president of the CitiFX Risk Advisory Group in London, where he develops financial products, proprietary trading models and hedging strategies for institutional investors. The views expressed are the author's own and are not necessarily shared by Citigroup or any of its affiliates.

outline of the considerations, opportunities, costs and benefits associated with the hedge decision. The intention is to do this as factually as possible. This means that the reader will be presented with a number of considerations that this author believes is in line with best practise throughout the industry.

The purpose of this approach is to enable informed decision-making based on what is right for each individual manager. Hopefully, the considerations outlined in this chapter will support the trend towards smarter currency management that is already taking place across the industry. This trend is mainly driven by the wish to ensure that the chosen hedge strategy is aligned closely to the objectives of the fund and its beneficiaries, than to what might be current (or past) industry practises.

In order to make this evaluation the chapter has been structured as follows:

First, it outlines a currency management framework that can be used to clarify the objectives related to currency management, and therefore facilitate the selection of appropriate strategy and to ensure a common language or terminology. This will enable a proper evaluation of the pros and cons of each of the different currency management efforts described.

Having defined the framework, it will evaluate the passive vs active currency management choice. This part has been separated into two main sections. The first section analyses the passive management choice, the second the active choice. After a brief introduction of the general characteristics of each methodology, it will proceed to discuss the management objectives typically associated with each choice.

Throughout this chapter the illustrations made are prepared using a EUR-based investor who is investing internationally (MSCI world or USA). This is done in order to be able to compare the results within a consistent framework. While any other base currency examples might not have provided the same conclusion, they would have been equally illustrative in terms of comparing the active versus passive hedge decision. Most of the illustrations are based on equity examples. However, as there will be some variation in results depending on whether the portfolio is overwhelmingly bond or equity, a comparison between the two asset classes is made at the end of this chapter.

Following on from that, the consequences of having made this selection will be discussed. This will be evaluated based on the portfolio impact caused by the hedge strategy and also the management considerations related to each option. This should hopefully facilitate an objective choice of "how" for each manager and where applicable it will follow with a proposal of best practice. In the last section there will also be a brief introduction to the notion of passive hedging with the use of options. This part will try to place this product in the traditional toolbox of spot and forward hedging. The intention of this section is primarily intended as food for thought related to the general hedging decision going forward. Finally, this will lead to an evaluation of the overall merits of each type of strategy, hopefully to facilitate the decision-making process.

THE CURRENCY MANAGEMENT FRAMEWORK

Before discussing the virtues of active versus passive currency managment, it is important that we talk the same language in relation to currency management. Passive hedging, for example, means different things to different people. For some it means simply benchmark replication. In that case the manager will simply do exactly the same type of hedging as the standard benchmark that has been selected for the portfolio (for example, a hedged MSCI index will typically use monthly currency hedges to calculate returns). For others, the term "passive" will instead involve a separate evaluation as to what type of hedge process and (fixed) hedge ratio it would be appropriate to apply to the portfolio. For this type of manager, passive hedge considerations will also typically involve decisions around the particular level of risk that is acceptable for the manager.

The same can be the case for active management. For those new to the currency markets, the word "active" might imply associations with casino-style gambling. The classic stereotype is of a privileged few, trading huge amounts of money based on an insider network that provides superior access to market information. While this is perhaps an image nourished by Hollywood in films such as *Wall Street* and *Dealers*, it is very far from the practises followed by most market participants. This will be illustrated by some simple examples of the risk–reward that can be provided by active management. This will demonstrate that a controlled active

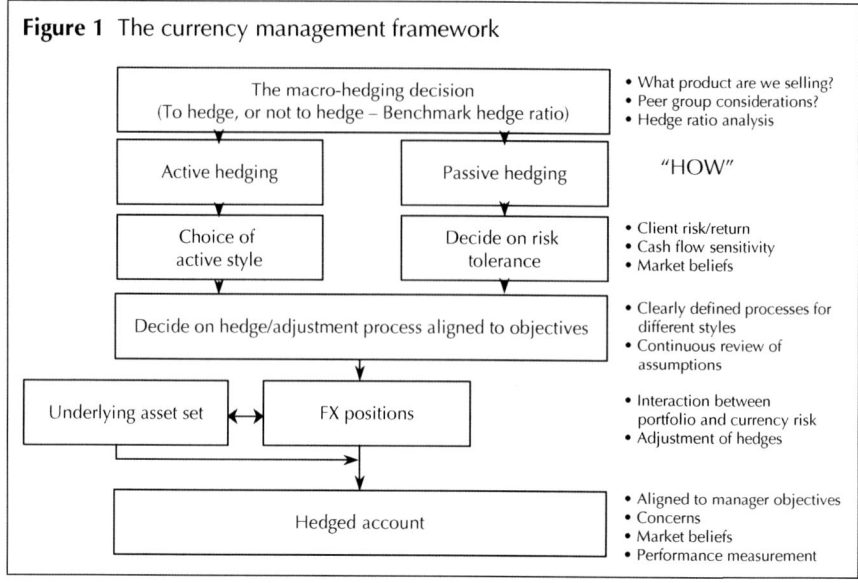

Figure 1 The currency management framework

approach can be a very prudent way of implementing hedge decisions and managing currency risks.

In this chapter, currency management will generally be referred to as a hedging decision. In other words it assumes that a proactive decision has been made as to whether to hedge or not to hedge. In order to clarify this statement, a currency-management framework is being introduced. The intention of the framework is to provide a common language and clear reference point for this chapter's discussion. In other words, it should ensure that the terminology used be consistent with this framework. The framework has been illustrated in Figure 1. It will hopefully help clarify the various examples and references made when evaluating hedging decisions going forward.

The framework describes the decision-making process in chronological order in terms of the decisions a fund manager needs to take when deciding on a currency overlay strategy. The first decision is the macro-hedging decision. Here the manager makes the fundamental decision on whether to do something about currency or not: ie, do we want a hedged or unhedged benchmark? It is an important point that within this framework, a decision to not hedge *is not a passive decision*. Instead, it says something about the product the manager is selling to your client. Is it a product with or without foreign-exchange risk? It is as simple as that.

Before objecting to this statement, please try to put this into a private context. Put yourself in the place of an individual who has to make up his or her mind whether or not to take out car insurance.[1] If you decide to insure the car, you will then proceed to determine the best cover available in your given price bracket. If you decide not to take out insurance, you are instead taking a calculated risk that your car will not be stolen at any time in the next 10 years. This might be a good idea if the value of the car is £500, but how about a brand-new BMW X5? Also, note that the default position, if you can't make up your mind right now, is to remain uninsured. Not making a decision does not mean that you have not taken a choice. Your exposure to theft or accident remains uninsured.

For an international investment portfolio it is essentially the same. If it is an investment product with foreign-exchange risk (unhedged benchmark) the client should expect a possibility of loss even though the underlying bond or stock markets go up. If it is a product without foreign-exchange risk this will not be the case.[2] As in our car example, there may indeed be currency exposures that are deemed too expensive to hedge. The Turkish lire at an 80% interest rate is a good example of that. Nevertheless, the little story illustrates that the choice is related to the investment product we sell.

The macro-hedging decision therefore includes a decision about some appropriate hedge ratio. This hedge ratio may differ depending on the underlying assets that the manager is considering for hedging. In addition to this it would typically involve a wide range of considerations (the free-lunch argument, portfolio optimisation, the notion of least regret, time horizon, sensitivity to and funding of mismatch in cashflows) to name just a few.[3,4] Even though all these factors are a consequence of the macro-hedging decision, they may still influence decisions on how the hedge process is managed. Where it is critical to the understanding of the hedge process, these influences will be mentioned. Otherwise they will not be evaluated in exhaustive detail in this chapter.

For our purpose, it is only in the case where we have decided to hedge all or part of our portfolio, that it really becomes relevant to discuss "how" we are going to do this.[5] This is similar to the point when we are about to select the right insurance

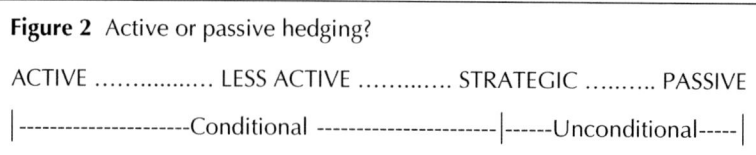

Figure 2 Active or passive hedging?

policy. This is where the passive or active choices need to be considered. In reality, the line between the active and passive characterisation is much more blurred than first meets the eye. For example, one could say that there are different degrees of activeness. Also, in truth, there are some passive investment processes that are active in nature. Figure 2 illustrates the soft line in the terminology and the borderline case between the active and passive choice of hedging.

In all cases it is about how you hedge. In the extreme case the passive manager will never change their hedge ratio no matter what happens in the market place. In practise, however, some may claim that they are passive, but do actually have "strategic" considerations. Strategic hedging can be defined as either infrequent changes in the percentage of the portfolio hedge, or as the use of alternative "passive methods". An example of such a method is the replacement of a forward hedge with an option hedge in order to reflect certain expected changes to market dynamics. The portfolio effect of choosing such a hedge will be discussed in more detail in the last part of this chapter.

Another important distinction from Figure 2 is the degree of activeness that is applied. Some might see frequent hedging adjustments as "speculative", whereas less frequent adjustment are generally considered "prudent". If you are nodding to this statement, you will probably agree that this can be a very loaded issue. Unfortunately, decisions based on emotional standards can cloud the decision-making process. This again may lead to a rejection of what might be appropriate hedging strategies. To be really prudent, an objective judgement should be delivered only when based on the "after-transaction-cost value-added" provided by each different methodology.

For simplicity we will here simply define an active strategy as one that is conditional of the investment environment, and a passive hedge as one that is unconditional. An example of a conditional strategy would be one that hedges only if the forward points are in your favour. The unconditional strategy on the other hand will not reflect this. Going forward, it will be assumed that an affirmative macro-hedging decision has been made. In effect this means that we can now proceed to look at the "how". How do I hedge my portfolio, now that I have decided to reduce the impact from currency fluctuations?

Only when we have considered this shall we be able to choose a currency-management strategy that will provide us with a hedged account aligned to our market beliefs and concerns. Within the framework, only the influences coming from the underlying portfolio volatility will be discussed. This means that the influences from the specific asset type (bonds/equities) on selecting a suitable hedging strategy will be covered. This will focus only on the initial strategic choice and the consequences of it. The actual selection of active styles, model building and practical implementation is discussed in more detail in other chapters of this book.

PASSIVE HEDGING STRATEGIES

Passive management of currency risk is a frequently encountered method of currency risk management across the investment industry. The reasons for selecting a passive hedge strategy can differ from manager to manager. However, the most frequently cited reasons are:

1. lack of resources to manage currency risk actively;
2. a belief that currency risk does not matter or that currency management is not a priority in the investment process; and
3. that the plan sponsor does not believe in the existence of currency market inefficiencies.

Whatever the reason, any of these beliefs will lead the manager to select some appropriate passive hedge ratio given the objectives of the fund. Ideally, this will be a result of an appropriate macro-hedging evaluation as described earlier. For ease of discussion, this passive section of the chapter will primarily consider fully hedged portfolios (100% hedge ratio).

This is partly because it can be shown that portfolio risk will tend to be the lowest for fully hedged portfolios.[6] In addition, by considering only the full hedge, we are able to consider the greatest portfolio influences created by this choice. Finally, it provides a common reference point to the comparisons and objectives of this kind of strategy. Nevertheless, the concepts explained are equally applicable to partly hedged portfolios, or for benchmark hedging of active currency-overlay mandates.

Objectives for the passive manager

Passive management is unconditional. This means that in principle the strategy does not change with the environment, interest-rate differentials, market volatility, etc. This is a key feature because it can provide some sense of stability and control to ensure that "nothing goes wrong". As we will see, the downside of this is that a passive strategy designed for a certain environment may not suit another. It is therefore important that the manager be very clear about the objectives and reasons for selecting a passive hedge programme. It also means that the utmost care should be taken when designing such a programme.

Hedging impacts the risk–reward characteristics of your portfolio. It should, because this is the intention. Again it is outside the scope of this chapter to evaluate the "best" benchmark hedge ratio but no matter the choice of hedge ratio, the prime objective will always be to reduce the level of uncompensated currency risk in the portfolio. In addition to this there are many other important factors that need to be considered.

An illustration of this consideration can be found in Figure 3. Portfolio risk is measured as the standard deviation of monthly

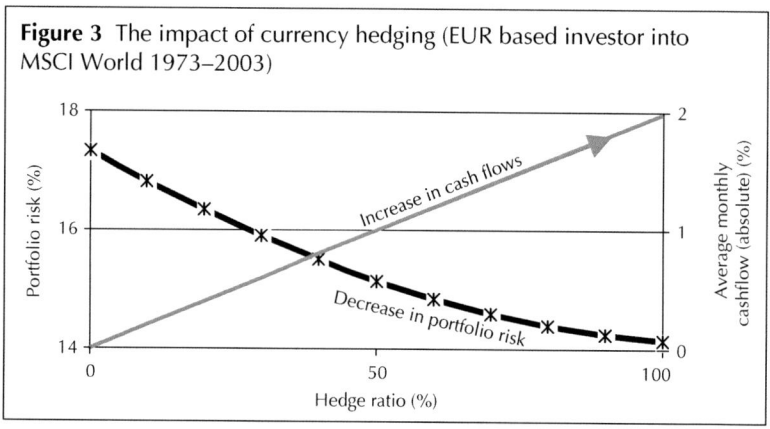

Figure 3 The impact of currency hedging (EUR based investor into MSCI World 1973–2003)

portfolio returns given a chosen hedge ratio (left scale). The average monthly cashflow is calculated as the average absolute value of the profit or loss deriving from the settlement of forward hedges as a percentage of the total portfolio value. The calculation is based on one-month-forward hedges and excludes transaction costs.

The chart shows that, while currency hedging will almost always reduce overall portfolio risk, the short-term cashflows and increased portfolio transaction costs are the price to pay for taking an affirmative macro-hedge decision. Also note that there seems to be an asymmetry, in that the cashflow impact increases proportional to the increase in hedge ratio, whereas the incremental risk reduction from currency hedging is greater when we increase the hedge ratio from, say, 10% to 20% than when we increase it from 90% to 100%. This is due to the diversification effect provided by the unhedged part of the portfolio. Whereas it can generally not compete with the hedged portfolio element in terms of risk reduction, its impact increases the smaller it gets.

In effect one could consider the hedge and the no-hedge as two competing assets for inclusion in the portfolio. The unhedged asset is generally the less attractive of the two but, because of its diversification effects, it may still be optimal to hold small values of the asset in the portfolio. From a hedging point of view, Figure 3 also helps to explain why, say, an 80% portfolio hedge may be a more attractive trade-off in terms of overall portfolio considerations than a 100% hedge.

In addition to this, the portfolio might impact the effectiveness of our currency hedges. For this reason it is important to select a passive strategy that will minimise this impact while at the same time meet the objective of eliminating unwanted risk from the portfolio. This means that we will need to articulate an investment process that can deliver on these goals. The next section will illustrate why the choice of process can significantly impact on portfolio performance.

The real cost of hedging

If we consider only the reduction in overall portfolio risk, then passive hedging might seem to be a "free lunch". However, as most practitioners are aware, there is no such thing. Figure 3 illustrates that one of the biggest impacts on a portfolio can come from the need to settle forward contracts before the assets of the fund are realised. This issue arises because the realised gain/loss from the hedge settlement is only matched by a similar unrealised change in the value of the underlying asset.

In the particular event that the hedge has lost money, the manager will be required to obtain funding to cover this mismatch. This cash needs to come from somewhere and the most obvious place is the portfolio itself. This means that the manager might have to liquidate some assets (or reinvest if the hedges have made money). This buying and selling can interfere with the manager's investment objectives and can also be costly.

Figure 4 illustrates the cashflow effect in more detail. It shows the observed cashflows for a fictive international portfolio as a percentage of the underlying portfolio value. The observation period is 1990–2003 and the analysis assumes that hedges are settled every three months. The base currency is the euro. The frequency of a certain cashflow occurring is measured as a percentage (of total occurrences) on the left scale. The corresponding cumulative frequency is illustrated on the right scale. The bars illustrate quarterly cashflows, while the cumulative probability is illustrated with the dotted line.

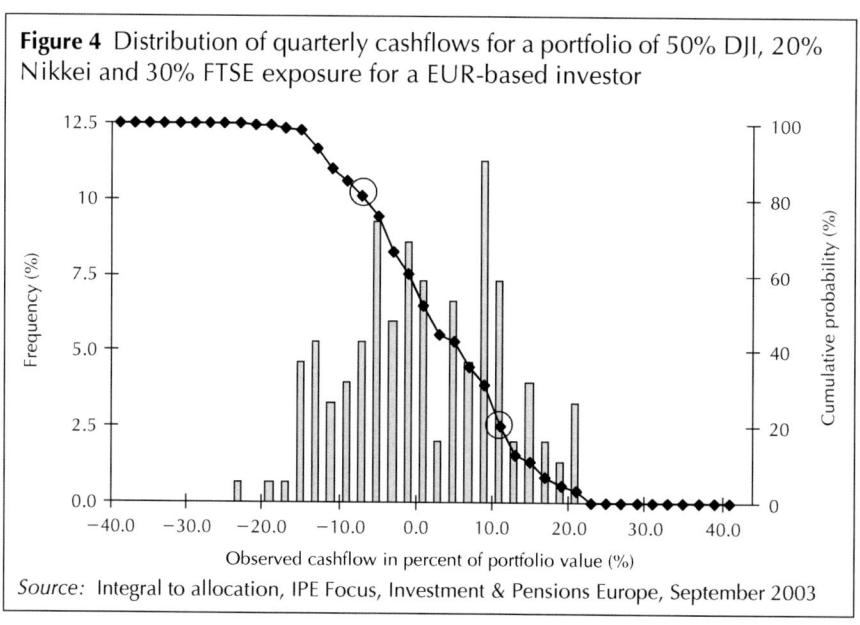

Figure 4 Distribution of quarterly cashflows for a portfolio of 50% DJI, 20% Nikkei and 30% FTSE exposure for a EUR-based investor

Source: Integral to allocation, IPE Focus, Investment & Pensions Europe, September 2003

The two circles show the point where we observe 20% of the lowest and highest observations. They appear around the 10% mark of portfolio value. This means that the cashflow effect would have required a sale or reinvestment of more than 10% of the notional portfolio for 40% of the quarterly hedge settlements for the period analysed. Needless to say, such liquidity swings can impact the investment process significantly. The next section will attempt to quantify this effect on a more general basis. This will allow the passive manager to minimise the costs associated with this phenomenon.

In addition to the impact from cashflows, there will also be other hedging costs involved. In transaction terms these are related to the bid–offer spread paid when rolling hedges and when adjusting forward hedges to the value of the underlying asset. These adjustments are necessary because of the fluctuations in portfolio value driven by market volatility or from payments to or from the portfolio. These items will be analysed in more detail below.

In addition to this there will be a significant impact to the portfolio from the interest-rate differentials that may exist between the base currency and the international currencies in the portfolio. The net difference is the base currency interest rate minus the weighted average of the non-domestic interest rates. It is the nature of humans that we would probably prefer to get paid for hedging. However, in many cases it can still make sense to hedge even at a cost. Acar and Maitra (2000) discuss a rational framework for setting currency hedge policy in more detail.

Needless to say, it can become an uncomfortable experience to discover that changes in global interest rates suddenly mean that you are now paying to hedge where the decision was previously based on a premium. This has been experienced by most US-based investors since October 2001, when the short-term USD interest rate suddenly meant that hedging came at a cost after five years of additional receipts.

Designing an optimal passive strategy

I will briefly cover the notion that an optimal passive strategy does exist once the manager has selected the macro-hedge ratio that they want to track. This is possible because of the unconditional nature of the passive hedge strategy. As we saw earlier, it means that any action taken within a passive framework is independent of what happens in currency or interest markets (except for portfolio fluctuations). The benefit of this is that it becomes possible to evaluate any potential process that the manager may consider to implement. This again means that it is possible to identify the most appropriate process, given portfolio characteristics and management objectives.

The framework is described in more detail by Pedersen (2002, 2003) but in essence the optimal passive hedge strategy can be determined if we have approximate values for:

- portfolio volatility;
- currency volatility;
- currency transaction cost;
- portfolio (asset) transaction costs; and
- interest-rate differentials between base and portfolio currencies.

Essentially, the optimisation process is considered against two individual criteria. Apart from the initial portfolio hedge, future hedge decisions are typically driven by the need to adjust hedges to asset fluctuation in the fund. These fluctuations can create a mismatch between the required and the actual hedge ratio. In effect this means that unless the portfolio hedges are adjusted the portfolio is subject to currency risk because we will have hedged either too much (assets fell) or too little (assets rose).

This is called the *currency hedge rebalancing strategy* and is comparable to the portfolio adjustments carried out to match portfolio components to their benchmark weight. It can be shown that a trade-off exists that is independent of portfolio risk, currency risk and currency transaction costs. The first hedge criterion is therefore the desire to eliminate currency risk while at the same time reducing the transaction cost related to the *initiation* of the hedge decisions.

An example of a typical rebalancing analysis is shown in Figure 5. It illustrates the empirical trade-off between hedge efficiency and currency related transaction costs available to an EUR-based investor investing in MSCI world for the period 1990–2002.

The chart shows the tracking error (here measured as the standard deviation of the performance impact) for a given rebalancing strategy. The different strategies analysed are fixed frequency (periodic), asset trigger (percentage change in asset) and a combination of the two. For each different hedge process the performance

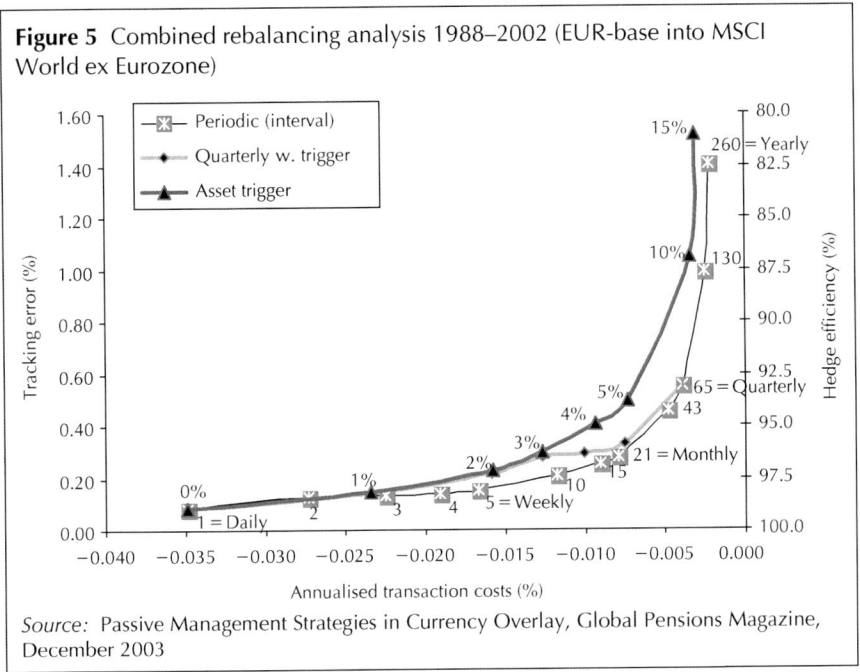

Figure 5 Combined rebalancing analysis 1988–2002 (EUR-base into MSCI World ex Eurozone)

Source: Passive Management Strategies in Currency Overlay, Global Pensions Magazine, December 2003

impact on the portfolio from being over- (or under-) hedged was calculated. In addition to this the corresponding annualised transaction cost (based on a bid–offer spread of 0.05%) was derived.

The numbers indicate the days in-between hedge adjustment (for percentage numbers it is the different asset trigger levels) so that "1" = daily and "65" = quarterly. We see that the maximum expected transaction cost of around 3.5 bps per annum comes with daily rebalancing ("1"). Decreasing the frequency (or increasing the trigger) will rapidly reduce costs towards zero. From this example it is visually apparent that we can reduce our rebalancing strategy to weekly without a significant increase in tracking error.

After that point the cost savings largely disappear and the portfolio is exposed to significant currency fluctuations. We also see that it is possible to find a periodic strategy with a better trade-off than the other available processes (the line is always lowest). The weekly rebalancing strategy is therefore the optimal hedge adjustment strategy available to the passive manager.[7]

On the right axis the tracking error has been translated into a hedge efficiency measure. The measure illustrates the effective hedge ratio produced by the rebalancing strategy. For example, using a quarterly rebalancing process will produce 0.6% tracking error corresponding to an equity portfolio that is hedged only 93%. In line with previous considerations, we also see that it is in practice not possible to design a viable hedge strategy that will eliminate all currency risk. The weekly rebalancing strategy recommended above would have provided the manager with a 99% effective hedge at around 1.5 bps in annualised transaction cost.

The second criterion is the desire to eliminate the portfolio-related transaction cost *caused* by the hedge programme and the need to settle forward contracts periodically. It can equally be shown that this impact is directly related to the choice of forward roll tenor (ie, the length of the forward contracts initiated with the purpose of hedging the currency risk). Because interest-rate differential may vary over time, the constant factors in this evaluation are the cost of selling/ buying assets (to fund/invest cashflows generated by the need to settle currency hedges) and the cost of rolling the forward book.

Table 1 illustrates this trade-off for fictive bond and equity portfolios where the cost of selling/buying the underlying asset is 0.10% and 0.50% respectively. Generic results are shown for all possible hedge tenors from one week to ten years. The first row explains the cashflows that we would on average expect as a consequence of currency fluctuations for a G3 currency pair (9% volatility). The results are based on a large number of simulations with return characteristics in line with EUR/USD. The maximum and the worst 10% of outcomes are listed separately for each simulation period.

The average outcome of the simulations is compared with the MSCI world portfolio that was analysed previously. We see that the simulations were representative and they enable us to calculate the annualised portfolio transaction costs generated by the asset turnover. These cost are shown in the second row of results for two types of asset.

In the third row is the cost related to maintaining the portfolio hedge itself. This cost was derived from the bid–offer spread quoted in the forward market in September 2003 for EUR/USD forwards. These spreads vary across different tenors primarily as a function of time, liquidity and credit risk. We see that, despite the fact that spreads are tighter for the very short tenors, the best tenor from an annualised cost perspective is three to six months.

Table 1 Summary results of hedge tenor analysis

Summary results	1wk	1mth	3mth	6mth	9mth	1y	2y	3y	5y	10y
Cash flows										
Maximum	6.32%	9.61%	17.97%	24.68%	30.99%	30.07%	48.63%	49.16%	70.22%	64.57%
10% CFaR	2.11%	4.34%	8.06%	10.90%	13.48%	15.96%	21.32%	25.33%	30.06%	34.37%
Average	**1.01%**	**2.17%**	**3.86%**	**5.15%**	**6.45%**	**7.31%**	**10.73%**	**12.44%**	**14.64%**	**16.75%**
Empirical*	0.91%	1.90%	3.50%	5.03%		6.92%				
Asset turnover					Annualised portfolio transaction costs (average)					
Equities (0.5%)	**0.26%**	**0.14%**	**0.08%**	**0.05%**	**0.04%**	**0.04%**	**0.03%**	**0.02%**	**0.01%**	**0.01%**
Bonds (0.1%)	**0.05%**	**0.03%**	**0.02%**	**0.01%**	**0.01%**	**0.01%**	**0.01%**	**0.00%**	**0.00%**	**0.00%**
Hedge roll cost			Annualised roll cost in percent of notional (EUR/USD assuming constant spreads)							
Bid–offer spread	0.00%	0.00%	0.00%	0.00%	0.01%	0.01%	0.06%	0.13%	0.36%	1.07%
Annualised	**0.02%**	**0.02%**	**0.01%**	**0.01%**	**0.01%**	**0.01%**	**0.03%**	**0.04%**	**0.07%**	**0.07%**
Total portfolio Tcost				Annualised total portfolio transaction costs (average)						
Equity portfolio	**0.285%**	**0.157%**	**0.086%**	**0.060%**	**0.055%**	**0.050%**	**0.058%**	**0.063%**	**0.086%**	**0.080%**
Bond portfolio	**0.076%**	**0.044%**	**0.024%**	**0.019%**	**0.021%**	**0.021%**	**0.037%**	**0.046%**	**0.075%**	**0.073%**

*EUR-Based Investor into MSCI World (ex Eurozone).
Source: Passsive Management Strategies in Currency Overlay, Global Pensions Magazine, December 2003

In the final row we add the two types of hedge-related transaction costs together. We see that a long-hedge tenor of six to twelve months is optimal. This of course assumes that credit lines are not an issue. For the equity portfolio the cost would here be around 5 bps per annum. This means that, with a weekly rebalancing strategy, the total annual cost of maintaining a 100% hedged equity portfolio is around 7 bps and provides the manager with a 98% efficient currency hedge.

Pros and cons

The key benefit from an evaluation of the passive hedge process is that it immediately increases the understanding of the dynamics associated with currency hedging. Yet more importantly, it also allows us to quantify the actual costs associated with managing currency risk. In most cases this will enable us to improve the processes already in place. In addition it may also enable us to change our perception of currency management. Such an evaluation can also benefit an active currency manager. This is because even an active manager will need a benchmark on which to evaluate their performance. In most cases such a performance benchmark will be a passive hedge and so most of the considerations suggested in this chapter should ideally be carried out as a general process for benchmark management. The annualised portfolio-related transaction cost for a fully hedged equity manager will be around 5–10 bps, which is not prohibitive.

In addition to this, the pros of passive strategies are as follows.

❑ They are unconditional, and do not require any currency management skills.
❑ Once an appropriate process has been designed, the manager can allocate uncompensated risk from foreign-exchange movements into another asset class where the manager thinks a competitive advantage exists.

The cons of passive strategies are that even though portfolio hedge generally reduces risk, as illustrated in Figure 3, one is using a static framework for a dynamic world. Let us be direct here: once you have chosen to implement a passive hedge programme there is no regret! The objective of a passive hedge programme is to eliminate unwanted currency risk. In exchange for this one gives up the possibility of participating in advantageous market moves (one important exception to this rule is to hedge using options, as will be discussed later).

Also, this can have serious implications for the manager sensitive to short-term reporting requirements. Additionally, it may disrupt the investment process, particularly in periods where the hedge is "not working" and cashflows require significant portfolio liquidations.

ACTIVE HEDGING STRATEGIES

Active currency management is a frequently occurring management strategy particularly among the more competitive segments of the money-management industry. Here an active currency strategy will often be an integral part of the perceived value added from the product offering. The value-added intention is an important feature of any active strategy proposal. However, no value added comes for free and certain risk-management capabilities are required before it can be considered safe to proceed along this route. This is because the effects of an active strategy need to be monitored, and safeguards need to be put in place to ensure that the actual management style is aligned to the guidelines, and objectives, decided by the plan sponsor.

If these capabilities are not in place, there is a choice of outsourcing the process to one or more professional companies that exist in the market today. There are currently a large number of providers offering a wide range of management styles to their clients. Many of these have been in the market for many years and therefore can document the value-added that they have produced.

Alternatively, the manager may decide to build his/her own in-house capabilities or even decide on a combination of the two. As always, there is no "right" answer to the most appropriate route. It will be easier for some companies to build in-house capabilities than for others, or they may already exist. In cases where it will take a long time to build the appropriate capabilities internally, the most appropriate route will be to outsource first in order to accelerate the organisational learning process before building a proprietary setup.

There are plenty of examples of time and opportunity wasted, waiting for an internal set-up to be established, where an acceptable value-added solution could have been implemented sooner by a professional third party. Where time is money, this delay may have been costly for the beneficiaries of the fund.

Why consider an active hedge process?

In essence, an active strategy is conditional upon certain market factors that the manager believes will impact the currency environment. These beliefs can be based on empirical evidence of certain observed market relationships or aligned expectations about these kinds of relationships in the future. These considerations are integral to the active process design and are covered elsewhere in this book. Essentially, what it means is that the manager has elected to consider the influence of certain market factors before determining the appropriate hedge ratio to apply to the portfolio.

Advocates of active currency management have a couple of very powerful arguments to support their case. Importantly, they are both integral to the "no regret" feature of the passive hedge discussion that we mentioned previously. If the manager wants to be able to "regret" a hedge decision and thereby give him/herself the possibility of changing it, he or she by our definition becomes active. Essentially the debate should therefore not be about passive versus active but of no regret versus regret. Returning to our car insurance example, it is comparable to changing cover midterm, or removing it entirely because the value of the car has fallen to a point where it is no longer economically viable to insure. We will consider the following two key arguments in more detail:

1. there is no universal hedge ratio; and
2. empirical analysis indicates that currency markets are not efficient.

(1) There is no universal hedge ratio that will always be the best portfolio hedge. While many consultants or portfolio advisers still herald the idea that an optimal hedge ratio exists, the validity of this argument really depends on the context in which it is considered. It is, for example, 100% correct that if you look back on past data, an optimal hedge ratio can be found. An optimal hedge ratio is typically referring to the specific degree of portfolio hedge that would have provided you with the best risk-adjusted returns for the period in question.

Take, for example, our EUR-based investor into MSCI world from our past examples. The best possible information ratio (return divided by the standard deviation of the returns) is found for a portfolio that is 100% hedged. However, if we look at Figure 6 we see that this "composite" number actually covers significant periods where

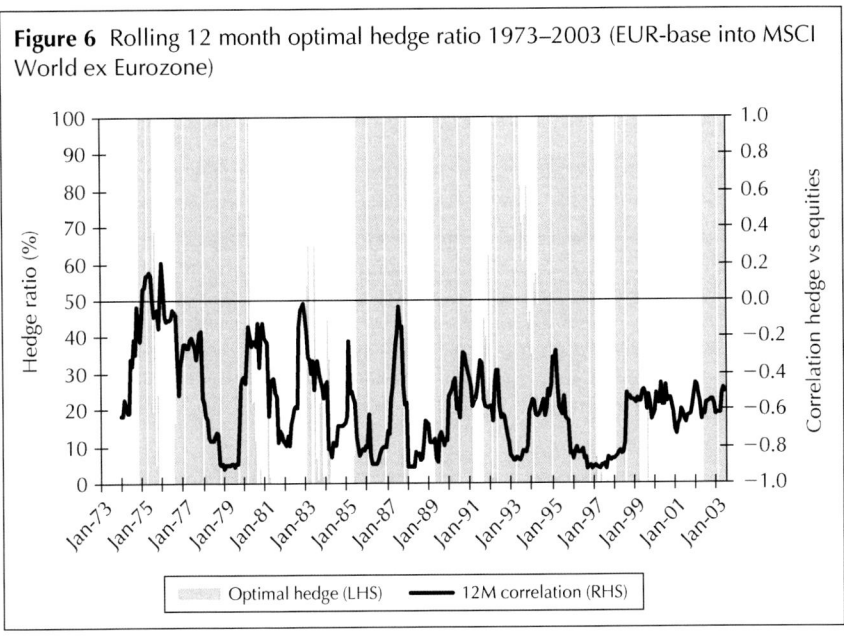

Figure 6 Rolling 12 month optimal hedge ratio 1973–2003 (EUR-base into MSCI World ex Eurozone)

the information ratio would have been highest for an unhedged portfolio. For this particular data series this corresponds to about 40% of the period (or 12 of the 30 years). Also note that there are very few "magic numbers" such as 50% or 83% hedge ratios occurring in Figure 6. Indeed, it does happen but in general terms we see that the optimal hedge ratio would have been either zero or 100%.

An often-used argument for applying a certain hedge ratio is that the correlation between asset and currency is consistently either high or low. To examine this further, 12-month rolling correlations between asset and hedge book returns are also illustrated. We observe that it is mainly "not consistent" and has little impact on whether a given hedge ratio should be chosen over another. The reason for this is that it is essentially the underlying currency move that determines what would have been the optimal hedge ratio. For example, we observe that during the US dollar rally that ended in 2001 the best portfolio would have been – yes – unhedged. Whereas, in the recent US dollar down trend, the best strategy was to hedge the US dollar.

This analysis provides a clear illustration of the fact that a certain hedge ratio is better for certain times than others. As such this should really be one of the prime motivations for choosing an active hedge strategy. It also explains why there have been particular "hedge ratio flavours" promoted over different time periods in the past.[8] Again, it is not the intention to discuss this in more detail, just to underline that this is the best and often overlooked way to convince oneself that active management can be appropriate.

(2) The second and more frequently used argument is that empirical analysis shows that active management can add alpha over passive alternatives (Baldridge, Meath and Myers, 2000; Levich, 1993; Lee, 1995; to mention but a few). In summary these analyses show evidence of:

❏ trending behaviour, particularly for US dollar-based currency pairs;
❏ forward rate bias (Kritzman, 1993; VanderLinden, Jiang and Hu, 2002);
❏ mean reversion (fundamental argument): when currencies are significantly out of line with real effective exchange rates some corrective adjustment will eventually occur; and
❏ active currency managers generally adding value (Baldridge, Meath and Myers, 2000).

These opportunities may exist because some currency market participants have motives that are not profit-motivated. For example, Banerjee (1992) concluded that investors act irrationally and do not trade independently of each other. Central bank intervention may also reject the profit-motive assumption of FX market participants (Szakmary and Mathur, 1997; LeBaron, 1999). Other examples are tourists and corporate treasuries, who also have different motives for transacting.

Essentially, the individual fund manager may believe this evidence or not. However, let us for a moment buy into this idea. In that case the final barrier before electing a conditional hedge programme becomes the availability of resources, and to ensure that these additional returns can provide a significant improvement to the competitive position of each specific manager. One can argue that, with the rise of fund supermarkets, the importance of relative peer performance should matter more and more, particularly for the rational investor.

That said, it is also reality that in some markets there is not yet free competition, and a rational choice may therefore not be easily available. In these markets you may find managers who are not directly rewarded (or accountable) for optimising the future returns available to the final beneficiary. In these cases there is probably little immediate incentive to engage in this kind of activity.

Objectives for the active manager

As discussed previously, the objective of an active management strategy is essentially to add value to the fund. However, as we shall see, an active strategy can also be successful in reducing the overall level of risk portfolio. In addition to this, the ability to change hedges so that they are aligned to the environment can bring other benefits. The most important additional benefit is the ability to position oneself in accordance with the interest-rate environment so that overall hedge costs are reduced. In addition, the attempt to create additional alpha for the portfolio can also correspondingly reduce the negative cashflow impact from the hedge decision.

Active management can be measured both on the relative and absolute portfolio level. The absolute consideration will suit both a generally passive asset manager (such as a tracker fund) as well as active managers concerned with overall portfolio volatility. The relative argument is likely to have the most clout with those managers already employing specialist fund managers to actively make asset allocation decisions and/or stock-bond-picking decisions. Where this is the case, it should be a natural extension of this principle to also apply this concept to currency. After all, currency moves can be responsible for a significant part of portfolio returns.

Empirical studies indicate that 85–150 bps would have been consistently available to the manager in the past. For some this might not be significant enough to warrant the resources required to enter into active management. However, for most general-purpose equity funds an additional 3–5% in revenue over the last three to five years would most likely have been a welcome addition to the metrics.

Active management styles

Active management can be separated into different "styles" according to what the manager is trying to achieve. As before, this choice should ideally be aligned with the fundamental beliefs of the currency manager. If not, the attempt is likely to be short-lived because of lack of buy-in. This is only natural: after all, if you don't believe in the chosen style, why should anybody else?

The good news is that there are many different management "styles" available to choose from.

First, the manager needs to decide to what extent his or her management context should be *discretionary* or *systematic*.

A *discretionary* trader will typically base their hedge decision on a combination of factors. These could be fundamental analysis, technical analysis and market psychology. The intention from this is to capture profits from short- to medium-term price trends while maintaining stable hedge ratios in ranging markets. The benefit of this is that the management style can be adapted to those exhibited in the market at any point in time. The downside to this method is that the trader might him/herself become embedded in the market psychology of greed and fear. This means that, while opportunistic, it is also subject to lack of predictability and inconsistent trading.

A *systematic* trader might consider the same factors (as the discretionary trader) but might have designed a system to generate trading signals based on certain predefined changes from these. It is the strict application of these buy and sell signals that is the most important part of a systematic investment process. This is because, if applied as intended, it removes judgement from the implementation of trades. The good thing about a systematic approach is that – if properly explained – you know what you get, and it ensures that the investment process is 100% rational.

This means that one knows at all times why a certain hedge ratio has been applied to the portfolio. The downside is that the signals will typically have been designed from market history and there is no guarantee that past relationships will endure in the future. A good piece of advice is to avoid black-box models where the output and resulting hedge recommendations are not clearly understood. This is because you will eventually end up in a situation where your hedge position is losing money and someone will want to know why it is that you have it on. Obviously, most of us would like to understand the hedge signals that are produced, even though we have given away the discretion to the system. In effect, this is a requirement in order to appropriately manage risk and to maintain a systematic trading system. If the manager is not aware at any time exactly why they have hedged their portfolio or not, it is very likely that someone will one day pull the plug.

The most frequently used methods for systematic trading are:

1. trend identification;
2. interest differentials;
3. fundamental methods;
4. option replication; and
5. a combination, or derivative, of any of the above.

The particular merits of each of these strategies are discussed in more depth in later chapters of this book. However, the next part of this section will give a brief introduction to a few of these strategies and illustrate the individual performance characteristics. These characteristics will be evaluated in the context of absolute portfolio impact (hedged account including underlying assets). The strategies used to illustrate the impact from choosing an active strategy are as follows.

❏ sixty-five day moving average of spot rate. If base currency is stronger than MA, hedge 100%; if weaker, then leave portfolio unhedged.
❏ carry, hedge only if the three-month base currency interest rate is higher than the investment currency.
❏ PPP/Modified BigMac Index. Hedge only if base currency is more than 5% overvalued compared with the BigMac Index.[9] Or else leave exposure unhedged.

These cover the basic strategies 1–3 stated above. Option replication has not been considered, as purchased put options will be evaluated in the last part of this chapter. As before, they have been expressed only on a USD investment for an EUR-based investor. It is important to stress that the outcome of active hedge strategies such as those investigated here is linked to the currency pair to which they have been applied. This means that there are certain currency pairs where this type of active management may not be suitable. Extensive analysis should therefore be carried out before deciding on how to go about this.

It is necessary to evaluate internal capabilities. To manage this risk oneself is not the only option available. An increasing number of managers elect to outsource this type of issue to a number of professional currency managers. This in principle corresponds to outsourcing a specialist equity or bond mandate to a third party. Typically, consultants such as Watson-Wyatt generally recommend that a number of different strategies be used in order to diversify the value-added by benefiting from different management styles.

Portfolio impact

While the general perception is that active management increases overall portfolio risk, this is not necessarily the case. Figures 7a and 7b show the risk–reward diagram for two distinct periods for EUR/USD. In 1995–2000 the USD generally went up and, being unhedged, was generally profitable. This is illustrated by the macro-hedge curve in Figure 7a. We see that, although the 100% hedge would have provided the manager with the lowest-risk portfolio, it would also have led to a significantly lower annual performance. Figure 8b illustrates the period 2001–3, where the US dollar was generally weak. We see that the roles are here reversed with the full hedge now not only providing us with the least risky portfolio but also with the highest returns.

It is, however, the active strategy labels that provide us with the biggest insights from this analysis. In the 1995–2000 period the risk reward for the PPP and carry strategy closely mimics that of the unhedged benchmark. The moving-average strategy comes in around a 30% hedged benchmark. But note that in all three cases

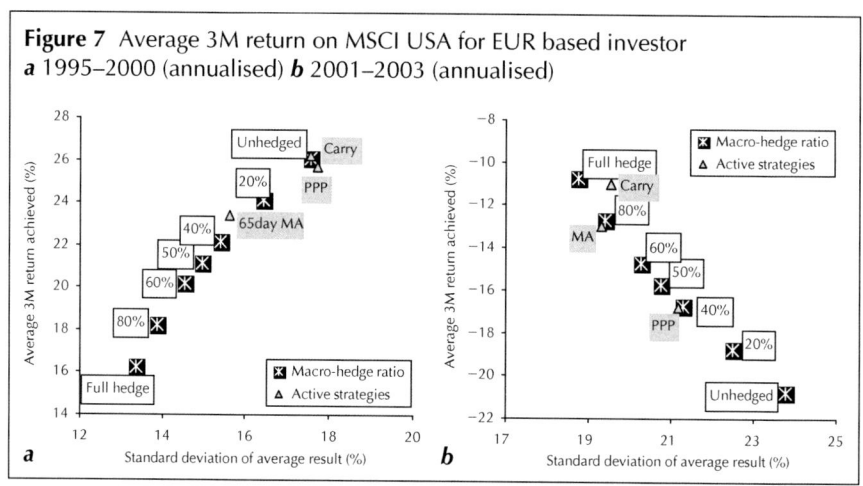

Figure 7 Average 3M return on MSCI USA for EUR based investor *a* 1995–2000 (annualised) *b* 2001–2003 (annualised)

we are at the "right" place in the chart from a performance point of view. If we turn to the 2001–3 period, we see that the results are similar. This time, both the carry and moving-average strategies come in between 80% and 100% hedged benchmark, which would have provided the maximum portfolio return. The PPP strategy would have performed less well but still mimics a 40% hedge. Based on this, we can conclude that an actively hedged portfolio would have tended to position the hedge towards the "best end" of the risk–reward spectrum.

Pros and cons

Based on the above considerations, it becomes clear that the main advantages are that active management can provide the manager with a much more flexible framework on which to base their hedge decision. It should be stressed that the portfolio impacts illustrated above might not be repeated in the future. In fact for shorter time horizons it is probable that active strategies might even underperform. This underlines the cons of active management. Because it is a conditional strategy it is also to some degree unpredictable.

This means that, just as there was no optimal hedge ratio for the passive manager, there may not be one single active strategy that will always provide value in the future. The PPP/BigMac strategy was an example of that. In addition to this, it does take time and resources to manage a strategy that is variable in nature. Most importantly, it requires a deep understanding that markets can go up as well as down and that some patience may be required before one can harvest the fruits of this kind of strategy. In addition to this, the manager will still experience some cashflows and probably increased portfolio transaction costs from pursuing such a strategy. Active hedging is not the remedy for all evils, although we would expect the cash flow impact to be reduced somewhat.

HEDGING USING OPTIONS – AN INTERESTING ALTERNATIVE

Options have so far not been considered, but it is in fact the only product available that allows someone to be passive with regret! This author believes that is appropriate to consider briefly this alternative solution to currency hedging. The first consideration to make is whether a currency hedge using options is passive or active. If we again use the insurance context we can describe this hedge as an option to take out the car insurance only if our car is stolen. In simple terms, we save the monthly instalments but have to pay some upfront premium equal to the probability that we will make use of the insurance.

In effect, this means that, if our base currency falls, we have what corresponds to a forward hedge at expiry. The rate at which we can buy our base currency is the difference between the hedge rate and the premium paid for the protection. In case the base currency falls, we will not make use of the hedge. The beauty of this payoff is that we do not need to adjust our hedges based on what we expect will happen in the market. But, nevertheless, the hedge is in effect conditional on what actually did happen. We can choose to describe the payout as follows.

Payout at hedge maturity:

❑ if spot above option hedge rate: spot rate minus premium;
❑ if spot rate below option hedge rate: hedge rate minus premium.

Based on this, we see that a put option can be considered as a forward hedge (the put-option strike price minus the option premium). This will be the worst hedging rate that we will ever get and is similar in concept to the passive hedge described at the beginning of this chapter. From Figure 2 we deduce that the most appropriate description is that option hedging is unconditional at initiation. It simply replaces a forward hedge in the portfolio. However, since it does involve an assessment of the benefit of regret versus the cost of taking out the insurance, it is probably best categorised as a strategic hedge. A comparison of all strategies is made in Figure 8.

Figure 8 compares the average annualised return from applying three-month option hedges to a portfolio consisting of MSCI US for an EUR-based investor. The three put-option strategies included are the 50-delta or ATMF option (this means that the strike price is set at the forward rate), and 10- and 30-delta put options. The comparison was made for the full period 1995 to 2003, which is analysed separately in Figures 7a and 7b. The comparison is made with the overall portfolio impact of applying a series of passive hedge ratios (including the no-hedge option) as well the three active strategies discussed in the previous section.

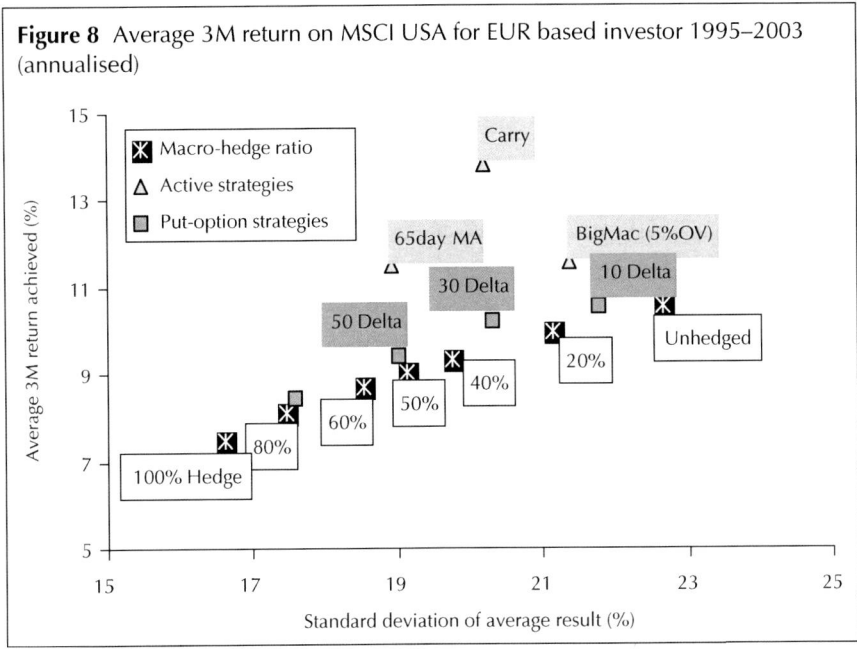

Figure 8 Average 3M return on MSCI USA for EUR based investor 1995–2003 (annualised)

In this case we see that option hedging could have provided a small return improvement on the passive strategy for similar amounts of portfolio risk. For example, one would have been better off purchasing 10-delta US dollar puts than doing nothing. On the surface, options therefore look like a much better alternative than straightforward hedging. However, this observation comes with a big word of caution, since the results are dependent on the period we analysed. In truth, if we consider that the insurance company is right in assessing the probability that your car is stolen over the long run, you would expect that the efficient frontier of the straightforward option strategies would be identical to that of the various macro hedges.

It is, however, important to note that, from a fund beneficiary or money manager's point of view, they may be much less concerned with "good volatility" (currency hedges make money) than with "bad volatility" (currency hedges lose money) and so, if we consider portfolio drawdowns, then option hedging should provide you with some significant advantages. Figures 9a and 9b illustrate this example in more detail.

MAKING THE RIGHT HEDGING DECISION

First, as previously discussed, not making a hedging choice is not the same as being passive. While it may be convenient not to take this decision, the result is a default choice of "no hedge". In most cases this means an exposure to the maximum potential portfolio risk. As mentioned before, there is in itself nothing wrong with making a zero hedge decision simply because in some instances – such as an emerging market portfolio with exorbitant hedging costs – it simply does not make sense to hedge all the time. Ideally, this choice should be based on some form of sound analysis and an awareness of the impact that "not doing anything" may have, at some unexpected point in the future.

History is littered with examples where such a policy proved extremely expensive, such as the Black Wednesday (sterling's exit from the ERM in 1992), the Asian crisis, Brazil, Turkey, USD/JPY in October 1998, the recent EUR rally and so on. The hedge decision should be made based on the beliefs of the fund in question. The key reason for this is that if it isn't the currency hedging process might become political. This would typically mean random changes in portfolio hedging processes based on short-term consideration, and the results of such a process will always be inferior.

The first piece of advice is therefore to appropriately make an evaluation based on the interest of the different stakeholders linked with the fund. This includes both fund managers and potential currency managers, and also the beneficiaries of the fund. Make sure that all information and empirical information is available and that the consequences of a certain option is perfectly understood. One way of doing this might be to submit your current policy to a number of worst-case scenarios and see if you like what you see.

Also, make sure that fact and objectives, as opposed to perceptions, drive the discussion. For example, if the purpose of the currency-management process is to achieve the lowest possible level of portfolio risk, then the 100% hedge decision is the only right decision that the manager should take (risk reduction is the primary utility).

So far there has been no evaluation as to whether the underlying asset type in any way influences the decision of how the portfolio is hedged. This is because within the currency framework it ideally relates to the macro-hedging decision. However, as mentioned at the beginning, there is some spillover effect between the two disciplines, and, in order to correct for this omission, the final charts of this chapter compare the different strategies that have been evaluated, *seen in the context* of a bond/equity manager's perspective.

In order to capture as many of the key issues as possible relating to choice of hedge strategy, the comparisons are made by portfolio-level information ratio and the resulting cashflows (cost) of the strategy. This provides a unique insight into the issues discussed and ensures that the interlinking factors of risk/return and cashflows are evaluated on the same basis and should hopefully provide some insights into the remaining part of the puzzle.

Figure 9a shows the portfolio output for a European bond investor into a US. As expected, we see that a 100% hedged strategy provides the biggest cashflow at risk (worst 10% of outcomes). We also see that in passive terms an 80% hedge ratio would have provided the best portfolio information ratio but still significant cashflow risks. We also see that on average only the carry strategy would have provided a significant improvement on both information ratio and cashflow at risk, which are now less than 2% of the nominal portfolio value.

In essence, this is not that surprising, because bond market allocation is often driven by yield considerations. Put options all reduce the impact from negative cashflows significantly and seem to perform better than the passive portfolio hedges for small hedge ratios. Also don't forget that you would not have known in advance that the 80% hedge ratio would have been the best. That said, it is

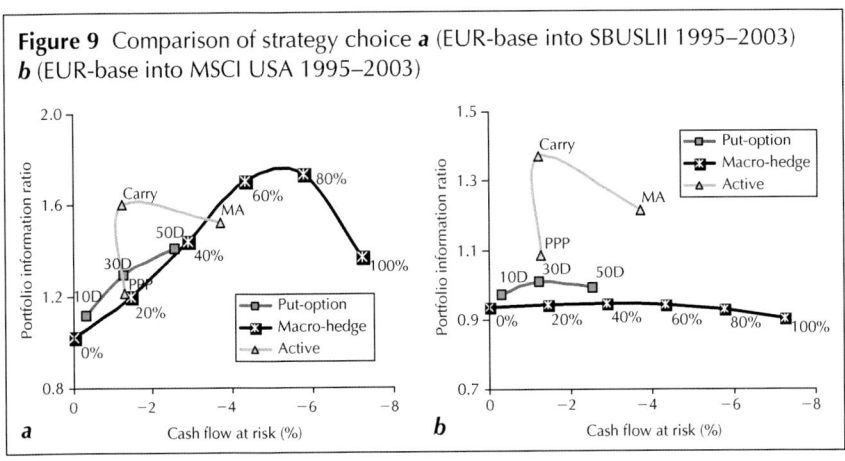

Figure 9 Comparison of strategy choice **a** (EUR-base into SBUSLII 1995–2003) **b** (EUR-base into MSCI USA 1995–2003)

not an unusual feature of international bond portfolios to provide the best risk-adjusted returns when portfolio hedge ratios are high.

This is in line with the conclusions drawn in Acar and Pedersen (2000) and means that the value-added from active strategies can come in exchange for higher portfolio risk. In the end what matters here is the utility function of the bond investor in question. If there are no negative cashflow concerns, then a passive hedge is probably most suited. However, if they are a concern, then options or active strategies might be more optimal.

Figure 9b shows the similar strategies applied to the MSCI US portfolio analysed earlier. We see that the considerations are here very different. The degree of currency hedging did not have a significant impact on the portfolio information ratio. This is because currencies are generally less correlated with equity than bond markets. However, the choice made a significant difference to cashflow at risk for the portfolio. As the information ratio is similar across the various passive strategies, the prime utility becomes the sensitivity to cashflows versus overall portfolio risk.

This is also the case for choice of active or alternative strategy. We see that in the case of this particular equity portfolio all of the simple active strategies described would have provided the manager with a higher information ratio and lower potential negative cashflows than any of the passive strategies. Additionally we see that the purchase of a put option would have provided a similar to slightly higher information ratio but with significantly less cashflow risk than the mandates with a 50% or higher hedge ratio. The choice is yours!

SUMMARY

This chapter set out to discuss the active versus the passive hedge proposition. In order to facilitate this discussion a currency decision framework was introduced. It links the passive or active choice to how the manager is intending to implement an affirmative macro-hedge decision. It also illustrates how once a fund manager has decided to "do something" about unwanted currency they immediately face another choice.

This choice relates to "how" this currency hedge should be managed. In addition to this, an appropriate terminology for the active versus passive discussion was identified. This defined the main distinguishing features such as the conditionality of the process and the opportunity of regret.

Following from this, the passive hedge decision was discussed in more detail. The primary reasons for considering this type of strategy were discussed. This involved a discussion of the passive hedge process required both for the passive manager and any other type of passive benchmark management. It showed that the process needed to be designed carefully to reflect manager objective fully.

The active hedging decision was then evaluated based on the different types of management style available to the manager and the primary reasons for choosing this particular route. In order to evaluate the portfolio impact of implementing such a strategy, three simple strategies were constructed and tested on an equity portfolio. The analysis demonstrated how an active strategy can provide a more optimal reflection of the market environment and help make flexible decisions about portfolio hedging.

In the final part of the chapter we investigated an alternative approach to passive hedging and hopefully provided some food for thought as well as putting some perceptions to rest. This led to a final evaluation of the primary factors that should ideally influence the decision-making process. This evaluation included asset class, risk-adjusted portfolio returns and the risk of experiencing large negative cashflows that could force disruptive asset liquidation.

In conclusion, this author will repeat his main argument that the final decision should be based on an informed set of beliefs. This means two things: first, these beliefs having been determined, there is awareness that some hedge decisions are more appropriate than others; second, it becomes possible to make a rational decision based on the facts and sensitivities that you have identified as important for your particular portfolio, and the final beneficiaries of the fund.

Good luck with the decision making!

---

1 Normally the "insurance example" is appropriately used to describe the payoff associated with the purchase of option: ie, the insurance premium is the upfront premium that over the long run will cover the insurance company for the payouts it will have to make to policyholders (before profits). In this case I ask you to consider the decisions as to whether putting and insurance "hedge" on or not. In this case the premium could correspond to the forward points of your hedge, and you know that, no matter what happens, the monetary value of your car is guaranteed. For example if we were paid for insuring our cars, most people

would not hesitate (equal to when forward points are in your favour). If the costs are prohibitive relative to the value of the car, it is most likely that you will refrain, or get less efficient cover. The most frequent objection against hedging is in the case where the forward points are against you. So the example is still appropriate to describe the decision-making process regarding whether to hedge or not.

2   Except for cases with unreasonably high hedging costs.
3   Perold and Schulman (1988) argue that currency hedging is a free lunch. They note that, since currencies are volatile and have long-term zero-expected return, then hedging will reduce portfolio volatility without affecting overall returns.
4   Notion of least regret is derived from game theory and investigates decision making under uncertainty. If the goal is to minimise the magnitude of the worst possible outcome. In terms of currency hedging this would suggest a 50% hedge ratio.
5   There is only one exception to this. It is possible to have active management based on an unhedged benchmark; however, in that case the macro hedging decision included the option to hedge.
6   Although a few expectations can be identified, most empirical studies suggest that the choice of hedging can often be distilled to a traditional risk–reward trade-off, where fully hedged portfolio generally displays less variance than partly or unhedged portfolios. Abken and Shrikhande (1997) provides a comprehensive overview of both the literature and influences.
7   It can be shown that this recommendation is universal and applicable across all developed countries and indices. See Pedersen (2002).
8   Academic literature about the "correct" hedging policy for international portfolios has spanned the spectrum from full hedging (Perold and Schulman, 1988) to no hedging at all (Froot, 1993).
9   Published in *The Economist* every April since 1986.

REFERENCES

Abken, P. A., and M. M. Shrikhande, 1997, "The Role of Currency Derivatives in Internationally Diversified Portfolios", *Economic Review* (Federal Reserve Bank of Atlanta), Third Quarter, 82(3), pp. 34–60.

Acar, E., and H. Pedersen, 2000, "Currency Strategies for an Active Portfolio Manager", *Foreign Exchange and Money Markets*, pp. 52–5, July.

Baldridge, J., B. Meath, and H. Myers, 2000, "Capturing Alpha through Active Currency Overlay", *Russell Research Commentary*, Frank Russell Company, May 2001.

Froot, K., 1993, "Currency Hedging over Long Horizons", National Bureau of Economic Research Working Paper 4355, May.

Kritzman, M., 1993, "The Optimal Currency Hedging Policy with Biased Forward Rates", *Journal of Portfolio Management*, Summer.

LeBaron, B., 1999, "Technical Trading Rule Profitability and Foreign Exchange Intervention", *Journal of International Economics*, 49, pp. 125–43.

Lee, C. I., and I. Mathur, 1995, "Trading Rule Profits in European Currency Spot Cross Rates", *Journal of Banking and Finance*, 20, pp. 949–62.

Levich, R. M., and L. R. Thomas, 1993, "The Significance of Technical Trading-Rule Profits in the Foreign Exchange Market: A Bootstrap Approach", *Journal of International Money and Finance*, 12, pp. 451–74.

Maitra, B., and E. Acar, 2000, "Optimal Portfolio Selection and the Impact of Currency Hedging", *Journal of Performance Measurement*, 5(2), pp. 45–53, Winter.

Perold, A. F., and E. Schulman, 1988, "The Free Lunch in Currency Hedging: Implications for Investment Policy and Performance Standards", *Financial Analysts Journal*, 44(3), pp. 45–50, May/June.

Pedersen, H., 2002, "Eliminating Risk", *Global Pensions Magazine*, July.

Pedersen, H., 2003, "Passive Management Strategies in Currency Overlay", *Global Pensions Magazine*, "Currency Overlay Issue", December.

Szakmary, A. C., and I. Mathur, 1997, "Central Bank Intervention and Trading Rule Profits in Foreign Exchange Markets", *Journal of International Money and Finance*, pp. 513–35.

VanderLinden, D., C. Jiang, and M. Hu, 2002, "Conditional Hedging and Portfolio Performance", *Financial Analysts Journal*, pp. 72–84 July/August.

9

A Framework to Determine a Currency Hedge Ratio for an International Portfolio

Eric Busay[*]

Fixed Income Unit, CalPERS

The following chapter considers the role that currency plays as a diversifier in an international portfolio, on a portfolio wide basis. It does not make the case that currency is an asset class; rather that currency is a choice that is removable. Hence currency overlay can be considered at the asset allocation level, principally considering currency correlations to asset classes as a means to determine the passive hedge ratio for the entire portfolio of assets.

WHAT IS CURRENCY OVERLAY?

Currency is an integral part of the international equation. Literature suggests that in the long-run the expected (spot) return is zero. Therefore currency is not a "buy and hold" investment but a risk exposure. For the USD-based investor, expressed in an equation

$$\begin{aligned}&\textit{International asset returns in USD} \\ &= \textit{local asset return} \pm \textit{currency impact} \end{aligned} \quad (1)$$

where currency impact is the variation of the local currency to USD.

---

[*]So many individuals have helped with this chapter. My colleagues at CalPERS were of great assistance; Mark Anson, Curtis Ishii and Warren Trepeta all have read early drafts and offered helpful suggestions. Most recently, Chi Yin helped tremendously with compiling data and helping me make sense of it. External professionals such as Bill Sharpe, George Chow, Ron Liesching, Arun Muralidhar, and Emmanuel Acar were others who offered encouragement, inspiration and support. Any mistakes in this chapter are my sole responsibility.

CalPERS has defined the following:

Hedge, hedging – taking an investment position that counterbalances the risk of another position. Hedging is the offsetting risk: diversification is the spreading of risk.

The only difference between exchanging currencies in the spot market and exchanging currencies in the forward market is the timing of the settlement. Each currency can earn a return based on local interest rates. Interest rate parity (IRP) shows that there is a relationship between the spot and forward exchange rates and the domestic and foreign interest rate in the countries represented by the exchange rates.

Mathematically, the IRP equation is:

$$Forward\ (DC/FC) = spot(DC/FC) \times [(1 + r_{domestic})/(1 + r_{foreign})] \quad (2)$$

where: DC = domestic currency, FC = foreign currency, $r_{domestic}$ = domestic interest rate, $r_{foreign}$ = foreign interest rate.

Therefore, the forward rate is considered an unbiased predictor of future spot rates. This assumption tends not to be true in practice. Analysis of actual FX data suggests that in fact the spot rate tends to perform better than the forward as an unbiased predictor. However, in this chapter, we are not focusing on extracting alpha but rather on passive management and thus using the forward-as-predictor assumption.

Under this assumption, a passive hedge can be constructed. A consideration of the passive hedge is a starting point. Therefore:

$$Currency\ hedge\ cost = (forward\ (DC/FC)) - transactions\ costs. \quad (3)$$

If currency is eliminated (hedged), the equation becomes:

$$\begin{aligned}&International\ asset\ returns\ in\ USD \\ &= local\ asset\ return \pm currency\ hedge\ costs \quad (4)\end{aligned}$$

where: *currency hedge costs is the interest rate differential of the local currency to USD, transaction costs of execution and the cash flow costs associated with hedging.*

Equation (3) lies at the heart of passive currency overlay. The risk associated with currency can be removed at a cost, which usually includes transactions costs (often small but negative) and forward costs – the associated interest rate differential can be positive or negative, depending on the relative interest rates in the domestic and foreign country. In this case, currency has a return, whether positive or negative, based on Equation (3), less transactions costs.

Therefore, according to Equation (4), a 100% hedge removes the currency risk from international investing. This is the removal of currency volatility from returns. This can be accomplished passively and is the basis of passive currency overlay.

Active currency overlay assumes a return beyond hedging costs. It assumes that alpha exists in currency selection. However, active currency overlay is not a focus of this chapter.

WHAT IS A HEDGE RATIO?

As shown previously in Equation (4), currency is a choice in international investing, in that all or part of the currency portion of the investment is removable, or in other words hedgeable. This is the hedged percentage or hedge ratio.

To clarify the preceding: a first and second order decision is made.

First order – do you want currency or not? It is the author's opinion that this choice is based on a set of beliefs, such as the following;

❑ that currency adds risk without return, therefore hedge 100%.
❑ that local asset return cannot be separated from the asset, therefore hedge 0%.

If one has another belief about currency risk in some way offsetting or diversifying asset risk, choose a different benchmark hedge ratio.

The passive approach is just like indexing. One passively hedges 100%, or a predetermined percentage. Once the decision to hedge is made, automatic (passive) rules can be followed, as Equations (1)–(4).

Second order – does one *actively* make the decision, for whatever reason (primarily correlation, in this chapter), do you want to vary from the benchmark hedge ratio? The act of making a decision is *not* passive, even if the program execution is passive.

In a multi-manager scenario the hedge ratio (% of cover) can be separated from the *benchmark* decision one sets for one's managers (even if internal management is included). For example, say one has

211

a USD 1 billion portfolio in an international asset and one's goal is 50% cover. One could give currency managers a 100% benchmark on 50% of the assets – namely an expected market neutral hedge of USD 500 million. Alternatively, one could give managers a 50/50 benchmark on 100% of the assets – namely an expected market neutral hedge of USD 500 million. There are many ways to get to a particular hedge ratio and some may well be purely definitional.

The central point of this chapter is to develop a framework for a hedge ratio for an entire portfolio, not just one international asset. It is based upon the belief that a unit of foreign currency affects the returns of an unhedged international portfolio uniformly, regardless of the asset held. In other words, a 10% appreciation of a non-domestic currency will raise the value of any asset by 10%, *ceteris paribus*. Most international investors look at only one asset class. Therefore the hedge ratio for an asset class and the portfolio are one and the same. However, if an international investor looks at multiple asset classes, very little consideration is given to the decision of looking at currency overlay on an asset class by asset class basis or a portfolio-wide basis. This is due in part to the lack of attention to considering currency overlay at an asset allocation level.

AN ASSET ALLOCATION FRAMEWORK

Let us start by defining a standard framework for maximising an investor's utility function, following the examples of Grinold and Kahn (2000), Jorion (2000), Sharpe (1990), and Anson (1999: 2002) and describe an investor's static utility function as:

$$E(U_i) = E(R_p) - A_i \sigma^2(R_p) \qquad (5)$$

where:

$E(U_i)$ *is the expected utility of the i-th investor;*
$E(R_p) = \Sigma_i w_i E(R_i)$ *is the expected return of the portfolio;*
$\sigma^2(R_p) = \Sigma_i \Sigma_j w_i w_j \sigma_{ij}$ *is the variance of the portfolio returns;*
A_i *is a measure of relative risk aversion for the i-th investor;*
w_i *and* w_j *are the portfolio weights of the i-th and j-th asset classes; and*
σ_{ij} *is the covariance of returns associated with the i-th and j-th asset classes.*

In words, the above may be thought of as:

$$\text{Investor utility} = \text{Expected return} - \text{Risk aversion} \qquad (5a)$$

The expected utility in Equation (5) may be viewed as the expected return on the investor's portfolio minus a risk penalty. The risk penalty is equal to the risk of the portfolio multiplied by the investor's relative risk aversion. Consequently, the expected utility is a risk-adjusted expected rate of return for the portfolio, where the risk adjustment depends on the level of the investor's risk aversion. The reader should note that there is no time element associated with this model.

An advantage of defining expected utility as a risk-adjusted return is that the absolute risk aversion of the investor decreases with the expected return. From Equation (5a) investor utility rises as expected returns rise and risk aversion is constant. That is, absolute risk aversion declines as an investor earns a higher return on the portfolio. Absolute risk aversion is measured as:

$$-U''(R)/U'(R)$$

If we define the variance of the portfolio as

$$\sigma^2(R_p) = E(R_p^2) - [E(R_p)]^2$$

then

$$U'(R) = 1 + 2A_i E(R_p) \quad and \quad U''(R) = 2A_i$$

therefore

$$-U''(R)/U'(R) = -2A_i/[1 + 2A_i E(R_p)]$$

For a risk-averse investor, A_{ii} is positive, as is $E(R_p)$. Consequently, the minus sign before the last equation makes the value of absolute risk aversion negative. This means that the absolute risk aversion decreases as $E(R_p)$ increases.

Whether we call Equation (5) the expected utility or the risk-adjusted return, solving this function requires quadratic programming. This is because solving for $E(U)$ involves both squared terms (the individual asset variances) as well as multiplicative terms (the covariances of the various asset classes). The important point to realise is that quadratic solutions recognise that the risk of the portfolio depends upon the interactions among the asset classes.

To simplify our analysis, we use Equation (5) to consider only three asset classes: domestic equity, international equity and international hedged equity. We denote the weights allocated to these three asset classes as w_d, w_i, and w_h, respectively. We also denote the expected return to these three asset classes as μ_d, μ_i, and μ_h, respectively.

The objective of Equation (5) is to select w_d, w_i, and w_h so as to maximise an investor's utility. However, depending on how currency hedging is used in the investment process, the weights of these three asset classes will vary.

To solve the utility maximisation Equation, we program an optimisation as follows:

$$Maximise\ E(U) = E(R_p) - A_i \sigma^2(R_p)$$

Subject to the constraints $\Sigma w_i = 1$, and $0 \leq w_i \leq 1$, where A_i represents the risk aversion of the *i-th* investor. Generally, this is a relative scale where $A_i = 0, 1, 2, 3 \ldots$ for different levels of relative risk aversion.

We define two different investment processes. The first is where the currency hedging decision is made at the strategic asset allocation decision. The second is where the currency hedging decision is made after the asset allocation decision. Grinold and Meese (2000) call this the "one-step vs two-step" asset allocation procedure.

To demonstrate the unintended biases that may arise with currency hedging, we solve the equation for the weight committed to domestic assets, w_d in two different fashions. In the first example, we solve Equation (4) without including currency hedging in the strategic asset allocation decision. This means that we solve for the portfolio weights allocated to domestic equity and international equity. In other words, we initially set $w_h = 0$, and solve for w_i and w_d, where:

$$w_i = 1 - w_d$$

We take the first order conditions of Equation (4) with respect to w_d and w_I:

$$\partial E(U)/\partial w_d = \mu_d - 2A w_d \sigma_d^2 - 2A w_i \sigma_{id} = 0 \qquad (6)$$

$$\partial E(U)/\partial w_i = \mu_i - 2Aw_i\sigma_i^2 - 2Aw_d\sigma_{id} = 0 \quad (7)$$

recalling that we can set $w_i = 1 - w_d$, we can solve for the value of w_d:

$$w_{d1} = (\mu_d - \mu_i)/2A(\sigma_i^2 + \sigma_d^2 - 2\sigma_{id})$$
$$+ (\sigma_i^2 - \sigma_{id})/(\sigma_i^2 + \sigma_d^2 - \sigma s_{id}) \quad (8)$$

We use the notation w_{d1} to indicate the allocation to domestic equity when currency hedging is not included at the strategic asset allocation level. Equation (7) looks a bit complicated. However, it depends only on the expected returns of the domestic and international unhedged equity returns, the variance of the two asset classes, and the covariance between their returns.

In our second example, we include the currency hedging decision at that asset allocation level. We now set $w_h > 0$, and $w_i = 1 - w_d - w_h$. We use the notation w_{d2} to indicate the solution for domestic assets when currency hedging is included as part of the strategic asset allocation decision.

Following the same first order conditions as in Equations (6) and (7), the solution for w_{d2} is now:

$$w_{d2} = (\mu_d - \mu_i)/2A(\sigma_i^2 + \sigma_d^2 - 2\sigma_{id}) + (\sigma_i^2 - \sigma_{id})/(\sigma_i^2 + \sigma_d^2 - 2\sigma_{id})$$
$$+ w_h(\sigma_{id} - \sigma_{hd} - \sigma_i^2 + \sigma_{ih})/(\sigma_i^2 + \sigma_d^2 - 2\sigma_{id}) \quad (9)$$

Subtracting (9) from (8) leaves:

$$w_{d1} - w_{d2} = w_h(-\sigma_{id} + \sigma_{hd} + \sigma_i^2 - \sigma_{ih})/(\sigma_i^2 + \sigma_d^2 - 2\sigma_{id}) \quad (10)$$

Equation (10) is the amount of the bias towards domestic assets when currency hedging is not considered as part of the strategic asset allocation decision. We maintain that this bias is positive. That is, there is an unintended bias towards committing a larger weight in the portfolio to domestic equity when currency hedging is part of a tactical decision, as opposed to a strategic decision.

Consider the denominator in Equation (10). We can introduce a time element and define σ_{idt}, the covariance of the returns to domestic and international unhedged equity at a specific point in time, as:

$$\sigma_{idt} = r_{idt} \times \sigma_{it} \times \sigma_{dt}$$

where:

r_{idt} is the correlation coefficient between the returns to domestic and international unhedged equity at a specific point in time.

σ_{it} and σ_{dt} are the square roots of σ_{it}^2 and σ_{dt}^2.

It will always be the case that $\sigma_i^2 + \sigma_{dt}^2 \geq 2\sigma_{idt}$. In fact, the only time that the equality, $\sigma_{it}^2 + \sigma_{dt}^2 = 2\sigma_{idt}$, will hold is when the returns to domestic and international unhedged equity are perfectly correlated, that is $r_{idt} = 1$. Otherwise, the denominator in Equation (10) is always positive.

Note also, that the closer the correlation coefficient is to one, the smaller will be the value of the denominator, $\sigma_{it}^2 + \sigma_{dt}^2 - 2\sigma_{idt}$, and the greater will be the bias. This makes sense, because (to extent that the bias is positive) the closer the correlation coefficient is to one, the lower will be the diversification benefits from international investing, and the greater will be the commitment to domestic equity.

Therefore, to prove a positive bias towards holding more domestic equity, it only remains to prove that the numerator, $w_h(-\sigma_{id} + \sigma_{hd} + \sigma_i^2 - \sigma_{ih})$ in Equation (10) is positive. By definition, w_h is positive, because the investor has decided to hedge a portion of their portfolio, where w_h is computed as part of the strategic asset allocation.

The value of w_h can be determined from the first order conditions of Equation (5) as:

$$w_h = (\mu_i - \mu_c - c)/2A(\sigma_h^2 - \sigma_{ih}) - \sigma_{id}/(\sigma_h^2 - \sigma_{ih}) \\ + w_d(\sigma_{ih} - \sigma_{id})/(\sigma_h^2 - \sigma_{ih}) \qquad (11)$$

where:

$$E(R_h) = \mu_i - \mu_c - c$$

μ_i is the expected return to international unhedged equity;
μ_c is the expected return to the currency exposure;
c is the cost of currency hedging.

If we define $w_i = 1 - w_{d2} - w_h$, then, with Equations (6) and (9), we have three equations to solve for three unknown variables, and solutions for w_i, w_{d2}, and w_h can be found.

It is the term $(-\sigma_{id} + \sigma_{hd} + \sigma_i^2 - \sigma_{ih})$ that must be computed to determine if its value is positive. A positive bias to domestic equity will result if

$$\sigma_{hd} + \sigma_i^2 > \sigma_{id} + \sigma_{ih} \qquad (12)$$

Equation (12) states that there will be a positive bias towards domestic equity if the covariance of domestic and hedged international equity plus the variance of the international unhedged equity is greater than the sum of the covariance for international unhedged equity and domestic equity, and the covariance of international equity and hedged equity. If the inequality in Equation (12) is reversed, the bias will be negative. That is, the domestic equity allocation will be biased downwards.

The bias in Equation (10) exists independent of an investor's risk preferences. In Equation (5) we specify A_i as an investor's measure of risk aversion. This conclusion occurs because when we take the difference of Equations (8) and (9), the risk aversion term falls out. Therefore, a positive bias can exist both for a very low risk-adverse investor as well as for a high risk-adverse investor. The bias will exist regardless of the nature of an investor's risk preferences but the relative size of an investor's risk aversion will affect the size of the bias.

Equation (10) is also independent of the expected returns associated with the different asset classes. Therefore, a higher or lower expected return for domestic equities compared with foreign assets will not affect the bias. In fact, a positive bias for domestic equity class can exist even if an investor's return expectations for domestic equity is *lower* than that for foreign assets.

Equation (10) is, however, affected by the variances of the individual asset classes as well as the covariance of returns between the asset classes. Therefore, the bias does depend upon how the different asset classes interact. This is especially important for currency.

The expected utility in Equation (5) may be viewed as the expected return on the investor's portfolio minus a risk penalty. The risk penalty is equal to the risk of the portfolio multiplied by the investor's relative risk aversion. Risk aversion now includes:

1. keep funded ratio at target;
2. minimise contribution rate and its volatility;
3. perform relative to peers and benchmark.

These issues, all other things being equal, should increase risk aversion but should not change the validity of the model.

This implies that what is really being sought is a portfolio with high returns, low standard deviation *and* low tracking error, relative to the risk averse factors.

Modifying Equation (5):

$$E(U_i) = E(R_p) - A_i\sigma^2(R_p) - B_{it}\sigma^2(R_{p-b}) \qquad (13)$$

where:

$E(U_i)$ is the expected utility of the i-th investor;
$E(R_p) = \Sigma_i w_i E(R_i)$ is the expected return of the portfolio;
$\sigma^2(R_p) = \Sigma_i \Sigma_j w_i w_j \sigma_{ij}$ is the variance of the portfolio returns;
$\sigma^2(R_{p-b}) = \Sigma_i \Sigma_j w_i w_j \sigma_{ij} - \Sigma_{ib} \Sigma_{jb} w_{ib} w_{jb} \sigma_{ibjb}$ is the variance of the portfolio returns relative to benchmark;
A_i is a measure of relative risk aversion for the i-th investor; at a specific time;
B_{it} is a measure of tracking error relative to the benchmark (risk averse) factors for the i-th investor;
w_i and w_j are the portfolio weights of the i-th and j-th asset classes; and
σ_{ij} is the covariance of returns associated with the i-th and j-th asset classes.

Benchmark risk may be defined to include tracking error and/or include risk adverse factors. In words, the above may be thought of as:

$$\text{Investor utility} = \text{Expected return} - \text{Risk aversion} \pm \text{Tracking error} \qquad (13a)$$

or

$$\text{Investor utility} = \text{Expected return} - \text{Risk aversion} \pm \text{Risk budget} \qquad (13b)$$

Equation (13) may be a more complete representation of what may bring one to an optimal hedge ratio, at a specific time, due to changing market conditions. Furthermore, it may be updated periodically as tracking error estimates change.

Equation (13) represents the expected utility of the i-th investor equalling the expected return of the portfolio *less* relative risk aversion *less* tracking error. Equation (13) has many inputs, among them the variation of the covariance of returns between asset classes. The covariance of currency to asset class elevates currency to the asset allocation level, even if currency has a zero expected return. This avoids the currency as an asset class argument. Currency is a choice that is removable, partially removable or not to be removed at all.

SOME PRACTICAL ISSUES

Table 1 and Figure 1 are provided to highlight the instability of correlations. It is interesting to ask the question: are the correlations telling us something, especially if the primary goal is to reduce risk? Clearly, the low and especially the negative correlations make

Table 1 Correlations: 12-month rolling equity: USD

	Local equity: USD	SPX: USD
Minimum	−0.8494	−0.5718
Maximum	0.5780	0.6497
Average	−0.2837	−0.0370

Source: CalPERS, SSB Period: 01/86 to 09/03
Note: Local equity is CalPERS' customised developed markets, excluding the US. The USD is the US dollar as represented by the US Trade Weighted Major Currency Dollar.

Figure 1 Correlation of monthly returns based on 12-month rolling correlations

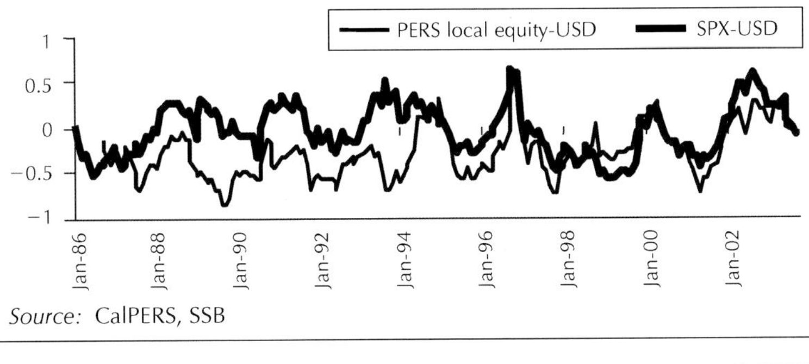

Source: CalPERS, SSB

currencies attractive, at least on the surface, as a diversifier. This implies a changing hedge ratio. The question is, which correlation, over what period?

Another issue is how to extract local returns. If one has local returns, how does one collect these returns and amalgamate them? The combination (weighting) issue requires a common factor, namely a currency to translate different local currency returns into a single return. *Ceteris paribus*, the weights will be affected should the USD move in a less than uniform fashion against all currencies in the index. Weighting is an issue for local equity returns because the index provider is constructing a dynamic market cap index. The dynamic market cap issue was lessened by assuming fixed weights for the different components – ie, this is equivalent to assuming the USD is moving uniformly against all currencies in the index all of the time. Therefore it is impossible to exclude all aspects of currency movements in local return. However, using the previous day's exchange rate minimises this effect.

Table 2 shows the local international equity returns and local international bond returns correlation to the S&P.

There are choices to be made with respect to arithmetic or logarithmic returns, time horizons used, length of correlation period (ie, three-month rolling, one-year rolling, etc). Each of these decisions regarding input will impact the optimal hedge ratio. Figures 3 and 4 illustrate these issues.

Notice that Figures 3 and 4 show correlations to hedged international equities. That adds another choice to the mix. So, what are the correlations to be used? That is yet to be determined and is not a topic to be covered in this chapter. The critical issue is that inputs change to Equation (13). The point is to indicate that the component $B_i\sigma^2(R_{p-b})$ of Equation (13) is variable, especially with respect to currency.

Table 2 Correlations: 12-month rolling international: S&P

	Local equity: S&P	Local bonds: S&P
Minimum	−0.4295	−0.6422
Maximum	0.9571	0.5818
Average	0.5546	−0.0150

Source: CalPERS, SSB   Period: 01/86 to 09/03

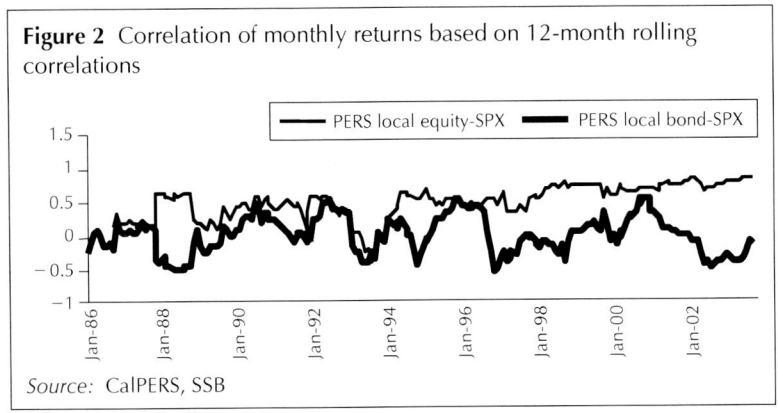

Figure 2 Correlation of monthly returns based on 12-month rolling correlations

Source: CalPERS, SSB

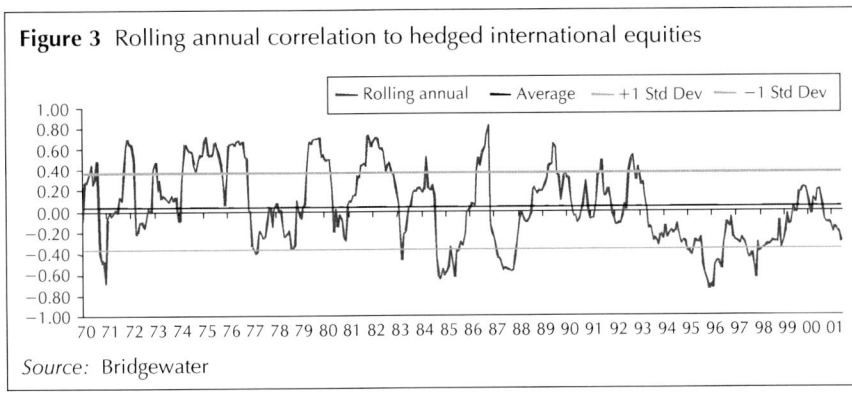

Figure 3 Rolling annual correlation to hedged international equities

Source: Bridgewater

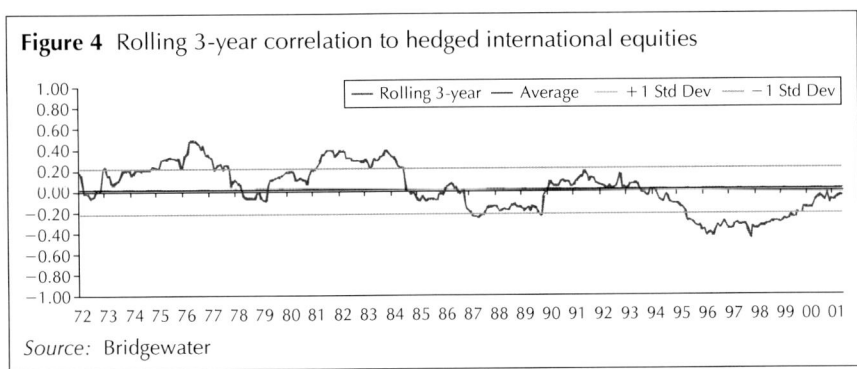

Figure 4 Rolling 3-year correlation to hedged international equities

Source: Bridgewater

What this implies for the model is that the inputs provide *an optimal hedge ratio based on the inputs for a period of time* not *the optimal hedge ratio for all time*. This hedge ratio is dynamic. It changes as correlations and other factors change. There is no right answer, just choices to be made. Correlations based on three-month rolling periods are going to change more dramatically than one-, three- or five-year rolling periods. However, correlations are not the only thing to change. Interest rate differentials (Equation (5)) are dynamic also.

There is no reason to expect that an asset class by asset class currency overlay program would arrive at the same hedge ratio as a portfolio-wide approach – unless each asset class assumes a passive 100% hedge and the model optimises in such a fashion that the currency as a diversifier in the portfolio is simply not worth the tracking error.

HOW TO HEDGE AN ASSET CLASS AS A STAND ALONE

So what is different if an international asset class is not considered at the asset allocation level? The international asset class amount or percentage of the whole portfolio is taken as a given. A hedge ratio is determined arbitrarily or with respect to the tracking error it will add to the asset class. However, if one assumes the return to currency is zero, then one should be at a 100% hedge ratio, as currency adds risk but not return. If one assumes a degree of offset between currency and asset, then the hedge ratio should vary accordingly.

A further consideration is the cashflows associated with the hedge. The concept is similar to a wealth versus income consideration. The asset value fluctuations are not regularly monetised but held and the international asset value fluctuations are analogous to an increase or decrease in wealth. The currency overlay fluctuations are regularly rolled and monetised. This is analogous to an increase or decrease in income, namely cashflow. There is a mismatch between the asset being hedged and the instruments used to implement the hedge, which can be overcome by selling or buying the amount of the international asset to match the cashflow, although this involves additional transactions costs.

This methodology would be preferred to the portfolio-wide approach by the manager of the international asset class if he were held to a hedged benchmark. However, this problem could be solved by changing the benchmark to local currency returns or producing a synthetic 100% hedge ratio currency overlay for this international asset class and aggregating the actual hedge ratio to the portfolio as a whole.

CONCLUSION

Anson (2002) states:

> "The bias towards domestic assets in the asset allocation process is independent of an investor's risk preferences and return expectations (but not their respective size) regarding each asset class. This revelation means that this bias is a structural bias; it arises simply because of the way we construct the asset allocation decision. Therefore, it should be correctable.
>
> Unfortunately, many institutions consider currency hedging to be a tactical rather than strategic decision. One reason is that this bias is *latent*. It is not obvious to the institution that it is unintentionally constructing an upward bias to the domestic allocation.
>
> A second reason is the nature of international investing. For example, institutions hire international equity managers first to find undervalued companies and second, to diversify the investment portfolio. In this context, the currency hedging decision comes in third. This tends to be true of other assets as well, except for global fixed income. This point relates back to currency hedging is often an afterthought, when it should be a primary consideration."

In cases where one hedges the international asset by international asset rather than the portfolio-wide scenario, several problems can be inferred:

1. The returns of the international asset class will affect the bias of a hedge ratio. If the returns are low, the bias will be to eliminate tracking error caused by currency. Where the returns are high, this is less of a concern.
2. Cross-correlations of all assets in the portfolio to currency are not considered.
3. The hedge ratio for the individual portfolio is not optimal for the portfolio-wide hedge ratio.
4. The hedge ratio will be higher, probably incurring additional cost, at least transaction cost.

As stated earlier: the pursuit of an optimal hedge ratio on an entire portfolio at the asset allocation level implies a passive hedge, not active management. Varying the hedge ratio is desirable to account for changes in currency correlations to other asset classes. The element of tracking risk relative to some notional benchmark or collection of constraints may be a way to deal with volatility in correlation between asset classes and currency to asset classes. This is the point of Equation (13). Perhaps the tracking error component could help handle some of the unstable element of correlation. The very nature of unstable currency correlation may suggest some form of active management. The hedge ratio decision remains the biggest decision. However, varying the hedge ratio because of shifts in correlation of currency to other asset classes may be possible (and even preferred?). Using Equation (13) may be the basis for periodic revisiting and revising of the passive hedge ratio, although this might be easier in theory than practice. Optimisation is often a backward-looking exercise and attempting to make it more forward-looking may prove challenging. If one can solve the problem of forward-looking correlations to asset classes, then varying the hedge ratio on a passive portfolio should be a viable active strategy. If the model developed in this chapter is found to have merit, periodic re-calibration of the passive hedge ratio may be a most effective currency strategy.

It is important to note that this approach is different from the "two-step" asset allocation process utilising unhedged international assets versus hedged international assets. (See Grinold and Meese, 2000.) This "two-step" asset allocation process still considers international assets as whole, just with or without the currency component. This chapter suggests that currencies should be treated separately because currency *is* separable. To recall the equation:

$$\textit{International asset returns in USD}$$
$$= \textit{local asset return} \pm \textit{currency impact}$$

The currency impact means variation to an unhedged international portfolio. If this is redefined as:

$$\textit{International asset returns in USD}$$
$$= \textit{local asset return} \pm \textit{currency hedge costs}$$

this implies that we can trade the currency impact for currency hedge costs. One could utilise the "two-step" approach to determine the underlying international asset allocation, then determine the currency hedge. This may then become a "three-step" process.

If alpha exists for currency, then the expected return is not zero. This implies that an active element may be pursued *beyond* the adjustment of the hedge ratio. The two strategies, dynamic hedge ratio adjustment and alpha, may be pursued separately or concurrently. Just pursuing an active alpha strategy in currency does not consider other issues relevant to the entire portfolio, such as currency correlations to other asset classes or how those correlations may be shifting.

Also note that the case for currency as an asset class has *not* been made. Currency is a separable decision that has diversification benefits. Whether currency is or is not an asset class is not a question that should affect this analysis, except if it were proven that currency was an asset class, the expected return would be an additional input.

The model suggests (1) start with a passive approach of a 100% hedge (2) remain passive but see if it makes sense to move away from a 100% hedge. This transforms a purely passive approach into one with an active element. It is distinguished from existing active strategies, which take their cue from the market (ie, technical, fundamental, option replication, etc) to an approach that starts with the portfolio and considers the role currency can play. There is input from the market but it is a longer term input, somewhere between strategic and tactical. The time horizon considered is crucial, allowing one to consider a dynamic element of changing correlations to recalibrate the passive hedge ratio with a primary objective to reduce risk. Since almost nothing comes for free, the model incorporates the concept of allowing for a risk budget to accomplish this end.

BIBLIOGRAPHY

Abele, L. et al, 1999, *Currency Management Handbook* (San Francisco: Barclays Global Investors).

Anson, M., 1999, "Maximizing Expected Utility with Commodity Futures", *Journal of Portfolio Management* 25(4), pp. 86–94, Summer.

Anson, M., 2002, "Asset Allocation, Currency Hedging and Latent Biases", *Journal of Investment Consulting* 5(1), July, pp. 20–27.

Binny, J., 2001, *The Risk and Reward of Currency Overlay* (London: Gartmore Global Partners), pp. 1–16.

Chow, G., 1995, "Portfolio Selection Based on Return, Risk and Relative Performance", *Financial Analysts Journal*, March/April, pp. 54–60.

Dales, A. and R. Meese, 2001, *Strategic Currency Hedging* (San Francisco: Barclays Global Investors).

Desbois, L., 2000, *FX Risk Management Analytics* (New York: Citibank).

Desbois, L. and T. Huang, 2000, *Charting the Course of Optimal FX Policies* (Citibank).

Gartmore Global Partners, 2000a, *Currency Risk Management*.

Gartmore Global Partners, 2000b, *Does Currency Overlay Reduce the Diversification Benefits of International Investing?*.

Grinold, R. and R. Kahn, 2000, *Active Portfolio Management* (New York: McGraw-Hill).

Grinold, R. and R. Meese, 2000, "Strategic Asset Allocation and International Investing", *Investment Insights*, Barclays Global Investors, August.

Jorion, P., 2000, "Risk Management Lessons Learned from Long Term Capital Management", European Financial Management (September 2000), pp. 277–300.

Lebov, L., 1998, *Developing and Implementing a Currency Risk Management Policy* (New York: Citibank).

Liesching, R., 2001, *Currency: Turning Risk into Return* (London: Pareto Partners).

Liesching-Layard, R., 1999, *The Role of Currency Overlay Managers* (London: Association for Investment Management and Research), pp. 50–57.

Muralidhar, A. S., 2001, *Innovations in Pension Fund Management* (Stanford: Stanford University Press).

Nesbitt, S. L., 1991, "Currency Hedging Rules for Plan Sponsors", *Financial Analysts Journal*, March/April, pp. 73–81.

Sharpe, W., 1990, "Asset Allocation", in J. Maginn and D. Tuttle (eds), *Managing Investment Portfolios: A Dynamic Process* (New York: Warren, Gorham and Lamber).

Part 3

Designing and Implementing a Trading Strategy

10

Trading for Profit

Jessica James

Citigroup

TRADING FOR PROFIT – IS IT POSSIBLE?

As someone in the finance industry, I am often asked questions about all things monetary at parties – much, I imagine, as a doctor is asked about everybody's different ailments. And what I am asked most often, when folk hear that I am involved in the foreign exchange area, is "What will the pound do this year? Will it rise or fall?" Usually the question arises because somebody is thinking of going on holiday and wonders how far their currency will stretch.

To this I have to reply, occasioning no little disappointment, "If I knew that, I would have retired rich by now." There may be those rare and fortunate individuals who know when a currency will move and where it will move to. But in general it isn't that easy: many a highly intelligent person has found that trying to make their fortune in the FX markets can be an expensive failure. A true story from my pre-financial days serves to illustrate the point. While I was pursuing my PhD at the Clarendon Laboratory in Oxford, one of my fellow researchers was convinced that he had found the secrets of the markets and would run simulations and test runs all night on the spare time of the university computers. He looked for repeated patterns and sequences of up and down moves, reasoning that this type of pattern could be spotted before its end and exploited to make money. His rate of return from this strategy was highly variable: when I first knew him he was in profit; by the time I departed the lab he had given up in disgust, having lost enough money to convince him that this research was not going anywhere. With all his training, and all the computing resources of Oxford University at his disposal, he had failed.

Why it really can be done

This doesn't mean, however, that all such attempts are doomed to failure! Where my friend went wrong was by having little practical knowledge of how markets work, and basically by trying the oldest idea in the book. Every amateur trader in the world will look for the type of patterns that he was pouncing on. Even if they are repeated, as soon as there is enough information about them out there, literally hundreds of traders will try to trade them, which will effectively move the markets in such a way that the patterns rapidly disappear. There are better ways to try to make money on the trading floor.

Why do we think that it is possible? The most reliable information about this comes from the various currency overlay programmes currently extant in the financial world. Overlay companies manage FX exposures for their customers, effectively using their market knowledge and modelling ability to obtain enough information about future market movements that they can correctly judge whether it is necessary to hedge or not. If there is no way that the FX markets can be successfully modelled and predicted, then overlay companies will be quite unable to do their jobs.

Such does not appear to be the case. Currency overlay is a product that has grown in popularity over the last 10 years, and there are now enough providers of the product to enable some statistics to be gathered about the success or otherwise of these programs. It would appear that, although there are differences in performance between different overlay providers, almost all of them add value for their clients and make more money than they lose. While this could have been a lucky coincidence right at the start of the decade, it has now continued long enough, and been repeated by enough different companies, to appear to be beyond doubt.

1998 survey

As evidence we offer the Tables 1–5, published by Brian Strange (1998). Eleven overlay firms were surveyed to provide these figures, which was most of the market in 1998. In total they were running 152 different overlay programmes. Ninety-four of the 152 accounts were over two years old at the time of the survey, and 24 were over five years old.

Table 1 Overall figures

Number of firms examined	11
Number of programmes	152
Number positive	121
Ratio positive	80%

Table 2 Annual averages

Average profit	0.61%
Average loss	−0.33%
Win/loss ratio	1.9

Table 3 Quarterly figures

Account quarters	1,783
Number of positive quarters	1,077
"Success ratio"	60%

Table 4 Added value

Average added value if +ve	2.4%
Average loss if −ve	−1.3%
SD of added value	3.5%

Table 5 Return/risk ratios

Account return/risk ratio	0.21
Benchmark return/risk ratio	0.07

In 2002 Frank Russell, the pension consultants, pursued a similar investigation and assessment.

2002 survey

Russell used monthly returns from December 1988 to June 2002 of all active currency overlay accounts/managers. Obviously, for

Table 6 Results for 0% hedge ratio programs

	2001	2000	1999	1998	1997	1996
Max, %	5.12	6.23	4.40	5.38	10.56	16.45
25th percentile, %	2.12	3.21	1.62	1.32	7.22	5.27
75th percentile, %	−0.38	−0.10	0.03	−1.55	2.88	2.24
Min, %	−0.88	1.28	−0.98	−2.37	−0.89	0.73
Mean, %	**0.88**	**1.10**	**0.98**	**0.11**	**4.90**	**4.39**

Table 7 Results for 50% hedge ratio programs

	2001	2000	1999	1998	1997	1996
Max, %	2.12	3.67	0.66	2.76	3.37	5.81
25th percentitle, %	0.47	1.77	0.18	0.23	3.24	2.72
75th percentile, %	−1.14	−0.46	−0.59	−0.69	0.83	1.15
Min, %	−1.49	−1.38	−1.18	−1.58	−0.13	0.36
Mean, %	**−0.10**	**0.67**	**0.08**	**−0.08**	**1.82**	**2.18**

those that had not been in existence for the whole period, there were fewer data points. They divided them by hedge ratio, roughly separating the active from the more passive strategies. The results, in percentages of assets under management, are given in Tables 6 and 7.

As can be seen, there are good years and bad years, but overall results have been good, particularly for 0% hedge ratio programs.

Why it's hard

However, none of this is to say that it is easy to make money from the FX markets. In some markets, the generation of some kind of income is relatively straightforward – in the equity markets, on average shares are expected to increase in value by at least the rate of inflation and probably more. Just holding a fairly diverse portfolio of equity products will probably generate a profit, unless one is unlucky.

Similarly, investors in fixed-income products have a reasonably simple job to do. They may choose what credit quality of bonds they buy. The poorer-credit-quality bonds, issued by smaller and relatively risky companies, will pay them a higher rate of interest. This compensates them for the greater degree of risk that the company will default and pay them nothing. While one might think that on average the rate of defaults will mean that they make the same amount of money as they would if they invested in a "safer" company, in fact this is not the case. A simple strategy, over the years, of buying a fairly diverse set of risky bonds would have made more money than a similar strategy that invested only in "safe" bonds.

In contrast, there is no such simple strategy available to the FX trader. Rates can go up or down and there is no safe general strategy that will make money. Even very long-term trends can reverse unexpectedly, for no reason that is readily apparent at the time, and indicators like interest differentials and relative purchasing power have been found to be notoriously inaccurate. It is often referred to as an "uncompensated risk" – holding an unhedged FX position exposes one to uncertainty but no expectation of gain.

Overoptimisation is a trap that has snared many a budding FX trader. If a strategy has been devised by testing on past data, then one needs to have a reasonable expectation that it will continue in the future before putting money on it. However, if it critically depends upon precise values of many different parameters, and performs poorly for parameter values that are not these particular optimised ones, then one can have very little expectation of any returns in the future. In all probability one has just discovered a data glitch that fortuitously looks good in backtesting but has no predictive power whatsoever. However, to deliberately use a non-optimal parameter seems crazy! The solution is to ensure that all parameter values may be varied through a reasonable range without seriously damaging the strategy returns, and that there are not too many parameters or rules in the first place. So we are looking for a simple, profitable, as yet undiscovered strategy. No wonder it is a challenge.

The job gets even more difficult when one realises that it's not just making money that is important: it is making *enough* money. For a strategy to be a success it has to make more money than one could get by salting away the relevant amount of capital in a deposit account. In the finance world the equivalent of the deposit account is probably government bonds. So, for a UK investor, the measure of whether a strategy works is whether it gives a better rate of return than purchasing gilts, which mature over the same period that the strategy runs. This is a little unfair, as the effective rate of interest on gilts varies with the interest-rate environment, but nevertheless it is the target to beat.

TRADING STRATEGY ISSUES
Margin trading and return on capital

The one thing that saves the FX trading strategy's bacon on the returns issue is that the phrase "relevant amount of capital", which has been so glibly used in the above paragraph, does not necessarily mean the whole face amount of the trades. A cash FX deal – like changing money before a holiday at the airport – does involve the whole face amount. One is required to hand over cash or account details, and receives cash in exchange. The whole amount is involved and tied up in the transaction.

In contrast, the whole face amount of an FX deal is rarely actually tied up on the trading floor. Spot FX trades done within the day are usually netted out at the end of it, so buying a currency at one rate, and later in the day selling it back for a profit or a loss will only show up at the end of the day as that profit or loss. If it is desired to hold a spot FX trade position for longer than a day, it is usual to do a forward trade instead. Forward trades consist of agreeing to exchange one currency for another at an agreed future date, at a rate that is just the current rate adjusted for interest-rate effects in the two currencies.

At the time when a forward trade is done, no money changes hands. It is all settled at the end of the deal. Essentially, an agreement has been made to exchange one currency for another at a certain rate fixed at the time of the deal. If, when the end date arrives, the current spot rate in the market is not precisely equal to that fixed rate, then there will be a guaranteed profit or loss to be made by making the agreed exchange and doing the relevant spot deal at the same time. What actually happens is that this guaranteed profit or loss is calculated and paid, and at no point do the actual face amounts change hands. So, although the deal may have been done with a face amount of "50 million dollars", at no time was there anything like this amount of money actually tied up or at risk. This kind of trading, where the face amounts are never truly exchanged, is referred to as "margin trading" from the way it is carried out at exchanges. The investor who is dealing with the exchange is asked to post "margin" amounts, to prevent a build-up of debt between inception of the deal and the final payment, and these margin amounts are usually just a few per cent of the face value of the deal.

So the FX strategist is saved from having to beat the percentage returns obtained from investing the face amount of the trade in a government bond. Instead, the returns he makes will be calculated on some different capital amount. But what?

The amount of capital that is "tied up" in an FX trading strategy should be the amount that is "at risk" – in other words, whatever amount the strategy might lose. This amount should be available to cover losses and thus in some way "set aside". The question is, how should this amount be calculated before the strategy begins? In order to do this calculation, it is essential that there be some way of estimating the profit and loss swings that the strategy will undergo, whether by simulating the strategy using past data, or, if this is not possible, by using what past data are available on the performance of this type of strategy. For example, if the "strategy" is to allow a team of good traders to trade a set of currencies to make money, then data may be available on the previous performance of that team or similar teams. If the strategy is rule-based and takes buy and sell signals from previous currency movements and other market rates, then it should be possible to use historical data to calculate the profit and loss (P/L) swings that the strategy would have undergone, had it been traded, in the last 10 years or so, or whatever past period for which there is data available. A judgement must inevitably be made as to what period of time is used, as there is little sense in going back too far to when the markets had little resemblance to their current form, but 10 years is often taken as appropriate.

Assuming, then, that we have some way of estimating previous profits and losses, what kind of estimate can we make of the amount of capital that is at risk, which might be lost? We assume implicitly here that the strategy has losses as well as profits, because an FX strategy that never makes a wrong trade (a) is unbelievable and (b) would have a capital at risk of zero dollars.

There are various different ways of making estimates of this capital, the more common of which are listed below.

- Largest ever drawdown over any time period.
- Largest drawdown over a fixed time period, like 1 month or six months.

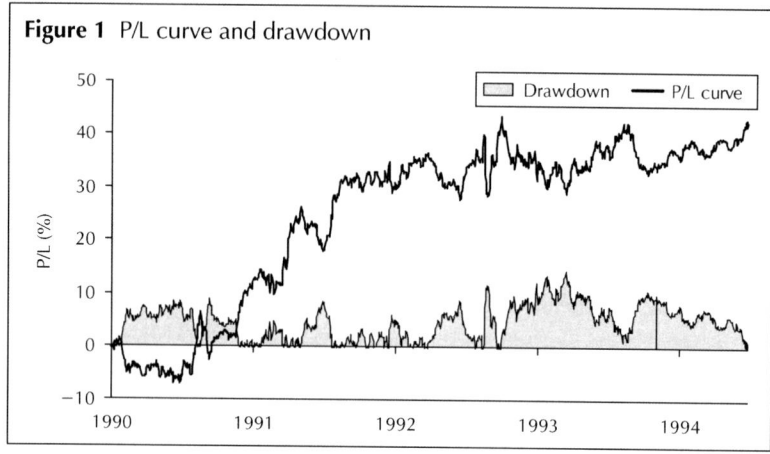

Figure 1 P/L curve and drawdown

- Two times the standard deviation of moves over a given time period, such as one or three months. It is not sensible to use periods very much longer or shorter than this – using daily moves will give too small a capital amount, which will be "hit" very quickly, and longer moves will start to incorporate the actual positive profit accrued over the testing period, and this will incorrectly lead to an excessively large risk number.
- Two times the largest ever drawdown, or the largest drawdown over a given time period.

The word "drawdown" refers to a period of loss during which there may have been small reversals, but not enough to bring the P/L above its last high, as illustrated in Figure 1.

In Figure 1, for simplicity's sake, the returns are given as a percentage of face amount.

Once the capital assigned to the trading strategy is known, then the "return on capital" may be calculated, and fairly compared to the returns from other asset classes. However, the percentage return on face amount is often used as a useful figure because it is unambiguous. A few examples of returns based on different capital amounts are given in Figure 2 – we use the P/L curve above to base them on.

As can be seen in Figure 2, the returns look much more attractive when smaller capital amounts are used. Thus it is important, for comparison purposes, to be able to see the return on the face

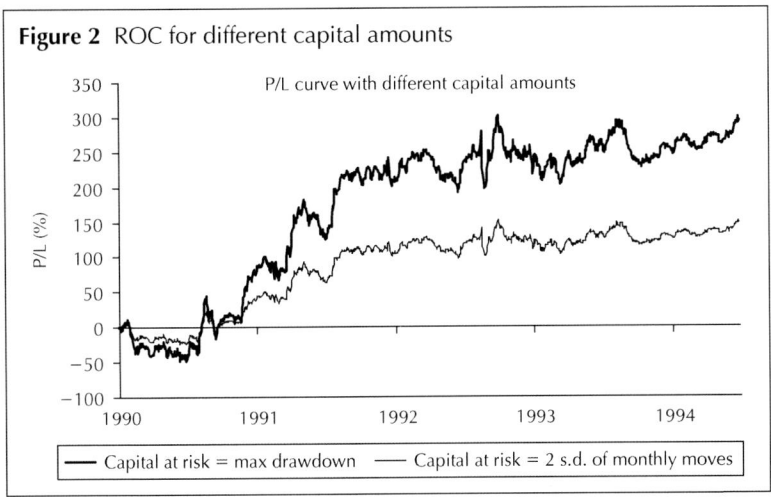

Figure 2 ROC for different capital amounts

amount of a strategy or model – it may not be representative of the return on risk capital, but it is the same for every model.

What not to do

So, now that it seems reasonable that trading for profit in the FX markets is feasible, it is worth pointing out a few ideas that have been tried and tested many times, and that, for various reasons, don't really work.

❑ precise pattern matching;
❑ trading using the forward rates as predictors;
❑ very fast trading strategies; and
❑ complex FX derivative strategies.

First on the list is precise pattern matching. It's just no good looking for repeating patterns of ups and downs. There is no reason for such patterns to repeat, and, in any case, a zillion investors around the world are looking for the same thing. Summary: it doesn't work, and, even if it did, someone else would get there first.

Next we have the issue of trading using the forward rates as good predictors. As is discussed in detail elsewhere, the forward rates do not in general convey any information about future FX rates. Only in some extreme interest-rate regimes is there any information in the forwards – and even in this case the forwards may be predicting a devaluation years in advance. In all cases one is better off on average betting that the forwards are wrong. This is in itself a reasonably successful strategy, as mentioned elsewhere in this book.

Very fast trading strategies are animals to treat with caution, though some do work. Slippage and dealing costs become critical here, as the moves that the strategy is attempting to capitalise from are small. It hardly matters for a slow trading system whether one slips a little on every deal, obtaining a slightly worse price than that which was wanted, because the moves that one is attempting to make money from are large. For a very fast trading system with a deal every hour or more, the slippage will be hugely more important. Similarly, bid–offer costs become a larger part of the expected profit from each deal and so a strategy that shows profitable simulated returns where a certain bid–offer spread is assumed may suffer badly when actually traded if this spread was even slightly too small.

Complex FX derivative strategies do have applications, but not many. FX options are a liquid market instrument and may well be used in successful strategies, but more structured and less liquid instruments like knockouts and barriers tend to be expensive and very difficult to resell. The occasional strategy that works using complex derivatives is usually for a very specific hedging or income-smoothing purpose.

What to be careful of

Under this heading we include all the ideas that might well work but that we believe should be treated with caution. These are:

❑ neural nets;
❑ genetic algorithms; and
❑ economic data.

Neural nets have a very mixed reputation. Some folk claim to have been made rich by using such systems. Others curse them with many curses. More common than either of these reactions is the statement, "Well, it worked for a while, but then it stopped and we didn't know why". This last is very characteristic of neural net systems. To understand why, we can explain a little of how they work. A neural net takes a variety of inputs, feeds them all into a "black box", and produces an output. For example, the output might be "up" or "down", indicating the direction of the next market move. In order to learn what outputs are appropriate to different inputs, the net must be "trained" on original data. The huge number of internal variables in the net are adjusted by the training until the outputs match the actual outputs. Then, when data that it has not been trained on are fed into it, the outputs will hopefully be correct if the training data were appropriate and sufficiently extensive.

The problem with neural nets is that they are good interpolators but not very good extrapolators. Thus, if they are trained on a range of inputs from 1 to 10, for example, they will know what to do with 8.5 but not with 20. Similarly, in the markets, nets can be spectacularly successful when market activity is broadly similar to the training set, but go horribly wrong as soon as the nature of the markets changes. And, as the markets change continually, there will inevitably come a time when the net starts to get it wrong. Unfortunately, the only way to tell that the net isn't working is, well, to see that it is not working. In other words, you don't know it's going wrong until it has lost more money than it was supposed to. Which is a rather expensive way to find out.

Of course, there are some ways that in part get around this problem, like continual updating of the training set, or frequent testing on recent data. However, a system that relies so completely upon the future being similar to the past is always going to be difficult to use in an environment like the markets, which are continually changing.

Genetic algorithms have basically the same problem as neural nets. They work by "breeding" or combining different strategy features so that only the fittest survive – the fittest being those that make the most money. As with neural nets, they must be calibrated using past data, and thus will have problems in changing environments.

Economic data-based strategies are very different. There is no doubt that economic figures like the Non Farm Payrolls in the USA or the RPI index in the UK have a significant impact on the FX markets – traders wait avidly for the figures to be published and many a blip in the FX rates can be traced to an unexpected figure hitting the marketplace early in the London afternoon. However, creating a trading strategy using this type of data is not easy. Some of the problems encountered most frequently are listed below.

- *Economic data are often "revised"*. Figures such as the non-farm payrolls are often revised and changed from their initial estimates. The market will respond to the initial estimate but also to the revision, which is not on a fixed date.
- *Historical series of economic data are difficult to interpret.* Is it the initial or the revised version that one is seeing? This type of information is often impossible to obtain when one is trying to make sense of a series of economic data.
- *Economic data tend to change their nature over time.* The figures in an economic data series are taken from a vast number of sources, and it is not possible for them to remain constant in nature for ever. Series that were highly coupled and correlated in the past can diverge in the future. For example, money supply was taken to be a strong indication of how much was available in the economy for spending. To reduce spending and thus inflation, it was argued, reduce the money supply. This was utterly confounded by the growth in credit usage, and the money supply became decoupled from inflation in the UK.
- *The market response to economic figures is often immediate and difficult to take advantage of.* It may be a simple matter to say "a higher than expected non-farm payrolls figure in the US means that the dollar will strengthen", but trying to take advantage of this figure will be difficult, as everyone will be doing the same thing at the same time. It becomes the case that one ends up needing to predict what the data will be, rather than predicting the response of the markets to the data – which is a whole different ballgame. Predicting the non-farm payrolls figure or similar is a constant obsession with economists, distinguished by its lack of success. It turns out to be a bit of a dead end for the FX modeller.
- *FX rates can remain "out of line" for some years.* While economic imbalances do affect FX rates, they do not do so quickly. For example, the purchasing power parity (PPP) approach argues that, as the values of goods vary with the exchange rate, that arbitrage trading, or sourcing goods from cheaper countries, will bring rates back into line. However, this idea is stalled somewhat

by transport costs and import duty, and legal issues, and so it is quite possible for large imbalances to exist for a number of years before they are brought back into line.

All in all, while economic data certainly impact the FX markets, using them as inputs for a trading strategy is not as easy as it might seem.

Some good ideas
"Human" market features
The tendency of humans to jump onto bandwagons is well known. In the FX markets, this results in the acceleration of both down and up moves, giving the typical high volatility seen today. In the equity markets, it creates bubbles and crashes. Other features, such as the tendency of rates to "stick" at values ending with a five or a zero, can only be attributed to human preference for this type of number. The great thing about this type of feature is that it isn't going to go away in a hurry – the markets will have humans participating in them for a long time to come.

Technical trading
This is the science (perhaps it should rather be called an art) of drawing lines on charts of financial data and using them to predict further moves. Apart from lines, features like "double tops" etc are identified. We discuss technical trading in more detail later in the chapter, but for now we can confine ourselves to the observation that, if enough market participants believe that a certain feature like a resistance level exists, then their subsequent actions will cause it to exist, regardless of whether it had an independent life to start with. Technical traders are surprisingly successful, and technical "signals" are regarded as very important. It's a bit like hanging a horseshoe on your door even if you are not superstitious, just because somebody has told you that it works even if you don't believe in it!

Signals from other markets
There is no doubt that FX rates affect each other, and also no doubt that other rates like interest rates and equities influence and are influenced by FX rates. It is possible to use this fact to create trading

strategies, though it is not as simple as it might appear. This is a situation where neural nets and genetic algorithms may have a role to play, as they can reconcile the various inputs with ease. If it is desired to avoid this type of black-box approach, however, then there are a number of things that are worth looking out for.

Finding the "dominant" FX pair in a group can yield good results. Usually the dollar will tend to dominate major markets, and so a general "dollar weakening/strengthening" will show up in several currencies. This is not always the case, however – for example, the euro takes on the dominant role when currencies like the Polish zloty or Czech koruna are considered. Also, the dominant currency can change. The euro has replaced the dollar in some cases.

Using technical signals from one FX rate to predict changes in another is also a viable technique. If a major currency (eg, EUR/USD) is about to hit a "support" level and the trader is pretty convinced that it will bounce off, then other currencies such as GBP/USD will be affected. A canny trader might choose to make money in auxiliary markets, where there are fewer participants watching every move.

Option volatility holds a surprising amount of information about FX rates. Using the level of vol as an indicator of different environments where different model types will do well is a very successful strategy. In general, trend, carry and fundamental models do less well at times of high volatility.

Interest rates and equities can also influence FX rates, but not necessarily in a trivial manner. One might think that a rise in interest rates would boost the currency as folk scrambled to buy it for its additional returns. However, the rise might be due to rapid inflation and unstable economic conditions, which would trigger a sell-off of the currency. It is difficult to develop trading models that may be backtested on historical data that use this type of signal, but a good trader with full access to newsfeeds and market information can make good use of them.

Is the FX market random?

One of the fundamental dichotomies of the financial markets is the question of valuation versus trading. Valuation of deals involves use of models, and all valuation models include a stochastic component, which essentially states that one can know the distribution of future rates (such as their mean and standard deviation) but not their actual path. Trading, on the other hand, assumes that there are identifiable patterns within the market that the traders may pick out and make money from (ie, that the market is in some way deterministic). Somehow, both activities are supposed to generate revenue for the bank!

Is it possible to tell which approach is true? Not really, is the answer. One imagines that it ought to be possible to do some kind of statistical test upon a historical rate series, and sum up with the answer, "Yes, it fits this model with a random component; but no, it does not fit this deterministic one." Unfortunately, statistical analysis of financial rates does not give answers that are anything like as clear-cut. There is never enough data to give a good degree of statistical certainty, and one ends up with something like a mild preference for one model over another, but that preference may well be reversed if data from a different time period are used.

There is no doubt that some random models are very successful – the Black-Scholes model, for example, is universally used to value simple option structures. So it would be very difficult to argue that models with a random component are "wrong". However, it is also generally believed that trading makes money. Most traders are expected to turn in a profit over the course of a year. Part of this comes from the bid–offer spread, but in general a good trader will make more money than could be accounted for by spread alone. Moreover, there are some deterministic trading models that have been making money for 10 years or so and show no sign of slowing down.

A fair compromise between the two modelling extremes is to state that market data series have both random and deterministic characteristics, and that different models are appropriate for different purposes. A point in favour of this compromise may be made by using both random and deterministic models to generate financial data series. Some of the more complex deterministic models can be used to produce data series that are almost impossible to distinguish from random, no matter what techniques are used. Figure 3 is a series formed by the deterministic function given in the graph, but to look at it one would initially guess it was randomly generated (see Johnson, 2000).

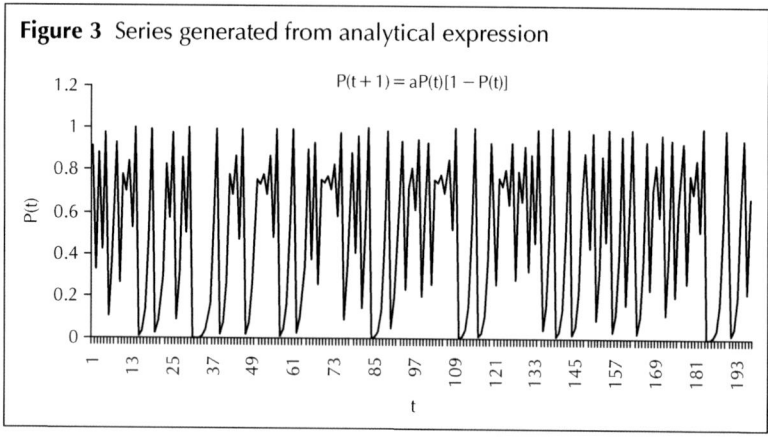

Figure 3 Series generated from analytical expression $P(t+1) = aP(t)[1 - P(t)]$

THE MAJOR AND FEATURES OF TRADING MODELS

Although trading models can differ widely with regard to their origins, once they have been turned into working models used on a trading desk it is possible to identify a number of common features.

Model metrics

Once you have a series of trading model returns, either backtested or actually traded, you may wish to judge it, to place it somewhere between "truly awful, let someone else trade it" and "guess I can retire in a year, then". To do this effectively, and to usefully compare one model with another, one needs a set of metrics, quantities which represent features of the models, which may then be ranked and used in turn to rank the models.

What model features should one measure and compare? Return is important, as is maximum loss, but perhaps the most useful thing to measure is the smoothness of return. There are a large number of measures of the smoothness of a return profile – information ratio, mountain lake, return/drawdown ratio, etc. But all of them are different ways of saying "straight line good, wriggly line bad". When it comes to looking at the returns, smoothness and small drawdowns are highly desirable. A model that in simulation makes money in the end but suffers a number of large drawdowns on the way is one to treat with caution. In Table 8 are a few rough figures that give a feel for the kind of metrics to use and the values that they should take in a decent model. All are given in percentages of

Table 8 Model metric and working ranges

Metric	Working model range	Comments
Annualised return	5–25%	Any better than this and you should check your simulation! If it's true you don't need to read this book.
Maximum drawdown	4–20%	The 20% is high but some high-risk managers will tolerate it as part of a portfolio.
Information ratio	1.0–2.0	1.0 is fine, 2.0 is superb.
Percentage of years which make a loss	0–20%	It's quite possible to have no loss-making years in simulation, and should be aimed for.
Maximum drawdown period	<2 years	Any more than this and you need very deep pockets indeed!
% profitable months	30–80%	Take care with those in the lower part of this spectrum, and understand them well.
Best month	6–25%	Greater than this and one becomes suspicious.
Worst month	4–20%	The 20% is high but some high-risk managers will tolerate it as part of a portfolio.

the face amount. The information ratio is defined as annualised return divided by annualised risk.

Use of stop losses

However good a system, there is going to come a time when a trade goes wrong. Either the market has changed and the model has stopped working quite so well, or this is a period when the model is adjusting from one mode to another (from ranging to trending, for example) or a number of other reasons. When this happens some kind of stop loss is invaluable. Setting a stop loss usually is as simple as saying that, once a trade has lost a certain amount of money, it will be stopped out or reversed, which both locks in the existing loss and prevents further loss. After the stop loss has been executed, the currency may move such that the original loss would have been reduced or even turned into a profit, but the fact that the stop loss has been executed prevents this move from being realised. The loss is locked in and will stay on the books. Of course, a currency move that would have worsened the loss is similarly ineffective – and it is this type of move that stop losses guard against.

On average, stop losses will actually damage the overall return of a trading system. The reason for this is that some of the trades that are stopped out would in fact have gone on to make a profit. However, a stop loss at the right level can prevent moves that would mean the demise of the company, without a large negative impact upon performance.

Percentage of profitable trades

This does sound like a no-brainer, but in fact there is a little more to it than meets the eye. The simple assumption is that, if more than 50% of trades make a profit, then the system is viable. However, this is neglecting the fact that some trades may make more than others! Some successful systems have a large number of trades that are swiftly stopped out at a small loss, with a smaller number of trades that make a large profit. These systems are usually those that specialise in spotting large, long-term trends. When they have successfully detected one of these and a trade has been put on that is making money, the trade will be left on for some time, taking advantage of the trend. Once the market starts behaving in a choppier fashion, making smaller ranging movements, the trade should be taken off. During the "choppier" periods, the system well may trade quite frequently and make some losses. So it is possible to have a working system in which losing trades are more frequent than winning trades.

However, this proportion of losing to winning needs to be reasonable. Avoid like the plague a system with only 5% winning trades! The fact that it has made a profit when tested on historical data is probably due to data quirks. In general, a system should have at least 30% of its trades making a profit.

Predefined cutout levels

It is rather optimistic to assume that your models will never get to the stage at which you have to say, "I don't like this – perhaps it doesn't work any more." If there are no preset criteria that, when met, give the definitive signal that the model has stopped working, it is all too easy to run an outdated, losing model for too long. The criteria could be as simple as a single exceedance of the largest drawdown in the backtesting data, or could be more complex, involving the time over which a drawdown is observed or the ratio of down days to up days. But, whatever the criteria are, they need to be in place before trading starts.

Volatility cutouts

A very large number of different models perform poorly during periods of high volatility. A few, of course, like those involving option selling, are at their best during these periods, but it is fair to say that most models that involve buying and selling over the short to medium term are degraded by the high-volatility periods in their return series.

The solution is almost embarrassingly simple – cut out of trading at times of high market volatility. The level at which one cuts out can be varied according to the model details, and to how much time one wishes the strategy to be "down", but in general introducing a vol cutout will effect an improvement over a range of strategy types. We give some examples later in the chapter.

Another way of handling the poor performance of some models at times of high vol is to switch to a different model at these periods, possibly one involving options.

Plateau optimisation

When two or more variable parameters are involved in backtesting a model, a dilemma arises. There will always be a "best" set of values for these parameters, which make returns look smooth and high, with low drawdown periods. Now, not to use this "best" parameter set in actual trading seems like the action of a madman – or at lease the action of a philanthropist anxious to swiftly distribute his or her wealth away from him or herself! But to use overoptimised parameters is also a recipe for swift wealth redistribution. What is the best thing to do?

By looking at the parameter "surface" one may become aware of the "plateaux" or regions of stability, where returns and information ratios are similar for a range of parameter values. As an example, consider the differential forward or carry model. In this model, currencies are bought and sold according to which has the higher

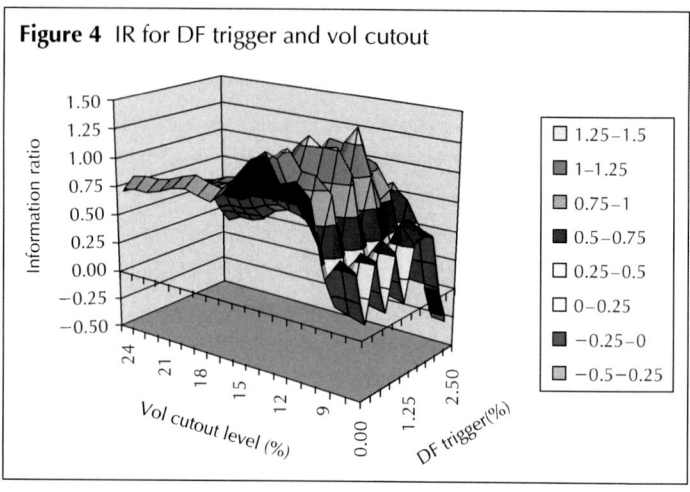

Figure 4 IR for DF trigger and vol cutout

interest rate, so that one is investing in the higher yield and borrowing in the lower. A trigger may be introduced, so that the interest rates in question have to have a difference of at least the trigger level before a trade can be recommended. The trigger level becomes one optimisable variable.

We then introduce a volatility cutout, whereby trading is suspended when volatility is above a certain "cutout level". This becomes the second variable.

In Figures 4 and 5, we now plot the information ratio versus the vol cutout level and the trigger level, in two different graphical forms. The first attempts to plot the information ratio (IR) as the height of a surface, with trigger and vol cutout as the x and y axes. The second has the same colours and information but is of the heat map type, and is possibly easier to read.

It can be seen that the strategy does well between 2% and 0% trigger levels, with a vol cutout between 10% and 15%. This is the "plateau". Within this large region of parameter space the strategy delivers good returns, in which one may have some confidence for the future. Finding the best point on the plateau is not a dangerous thing to do!

In contrast, had there been a tall narrow peak away from the plateau, it should be ignored in favour of the region with greater stability. Narrow sharp peaks are generally caused by data quirks.

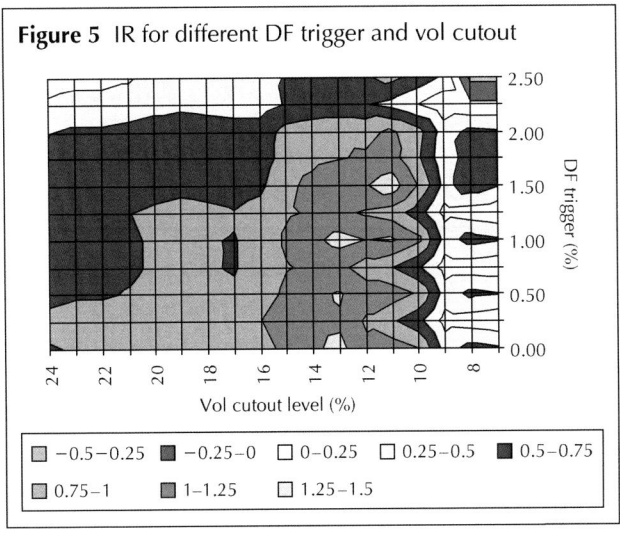

Figure 5 IR for different DF trigger and vol cutout

CARRY OR DIFFERENTIAL FORWARD
Model theory

The example above of plateau optimisation utilises this robust and useful model. The carry model has been successfully used over the last decade for medium- and long-term positions, though it is not suitable for short-term trading. The theoretical basis for the model is simple: essentially, it assumes that the forward points have no predictive power and thus may be taken advantage of. When one calculates an FX rate for a date in the future, it is arrived at by assuming that one can get there by investing one currency for the period and then exchanging at the end, or by exchanging now and investing the other currency for the period. Equating the two processes gives a value for the forward FX rate, and any other value can be "arbitraged" by one or other of the processes. Thus, the forward rate is merely today's rate adjusted for interest-rate effects, and as such never pretended to be a "prediction" of the future.

This has never stopped market participants from looking upon the forward rate as some kind of market prediction. It's not, and it never has been. The arguments that are put forward to support this view are that the country with the higher interest rate will have to issue more money in the future (a process known as seigniorage) and this will lead to a devaluation of the amount indicated by the forwards. While over the very long term, about 20 years, this may be a good argument, over the shorter term the opposite is more likely to be the case. Higher interest rates will attract investors, thus making the currency more attractive and driving the price up. For currencies with interest-rate differentials that are not very large, which includes all the major traded currencies, there is absolutely no connection with the forward rate and the rate in the future.

Thus, if one bets against the forward, buying the currency if the forward is lower than spot and selling if it is above, one might expect to make money over a period of time. This is indeed the case – the market moves mean in any month the noise is larger than the signal but over a period of years the strategy does indeed perform well. An interesting question that often arises is, does one make the expected amount of money, ie, the forward points, overall? The answer is that, for one-, two- or three-month rates, one makes slightly more – possibly due to the fact that higher interest-bearing currencies are often attractive in the short term.

Another question that naturally arises is, which interest rate? Due to the nature of interest-rate yield curves, usually if one part of a curve in one currency is above the same part in another currency, the rest of the curves will follow suit, but it is quite possible for them to "cross" at some point. In this situation one usually looks at shorter-term rates of less than a year. The actual trades are usually done over this timescale as well.

Model variations
Trigger

The main variation on the carry strategy is when to indicate a trade. In the simplest form the model is always in the market, indicating trades for even very small interest-rate differentials. In this form the only time when no trade would be indicated would be when the two interest rates were exactly the same – which happens a vanishingly small percentage of the time. Variants concentrate on waiting until the actual value of the differential meets a certain trigger value, which can be a constant, or can vary with circumstances. There is some value in this, in some currencies, but in general not as much as one might think. Table 9 shows results for different currencies and different trigger levels.

Table 9 Effect of trigger levels on Differential Forward strategy

Currency	USD/JPY	USD/CHF	AUD/USD	USD/CAD	EUR/USD	EUR/JPY	EUR/GBP	EUR/CHF	GBP/USD	GBP/JPY	GBP/CHF	CHF/JPY
						0% trigger						
Information ratio	0.49	0.19	0.64	0.72	0.71	0.22	0.22	0.19	0.18	0.30	0.27	0.16
Annualised return, %	5.66	2.15	5.85	3.97	7.23	2.68	1.69	0.71	1.57	3.86	2.28	1.96
			1% trigger			2%		1% trigger		3%	1% trigger	
Information ratio	0.40	0.45	0.52	0.49	0.66	0.24	0.36	0.36	0.10	0.43	0.43	0.29
Annualised return, %	4.29	4.69	3.18	1.80	6.20	2.90	2.41	1.29	0.76	5.24	3.48	3.24
			2% trigger			3%		2% trigger		4%	2% trigger	
Information ratio	0.51	0.41	0.55	0.09	0.48	0.15	0.70	0.62	−0.03	0.41	0.45	0.37
Annualised return, %	5.11	3.81	2.55	0.20	3.68	1.52	4.03	1.25	−0.20	4.62	3.42	3.00

Note that in Table 9 there are some crosses where the 1% and 2% triggers had little effect, and so larger values were used.

In general, the positive returns of the strategy are apparent. A number of currencies show healthy returns. However, there is not really any consistent improvement gained by applying triggers. On average the intermediate trigger levels effect a small improvement in both information ratio and annual returns, but this is not true for the currencies whose returns were good at the 0% trigger. One may perhaps say that in general a small trigger level improves the poorer performing currencies.

Overall, the trigger effect is not really good enough to justify its frequent use in the markets. Of course, this is only the simple trigger – a more complex version would possibly give a trade signal when the interest differential was significantly larger than recent levels.

Currency pair

Another variation on the carry theme is to select a basket of currencies and select a number with very high or very low interest-rate levels. One then pursues the differential forward strategy between these currency pairs, effectively borrowing in the low-interest-rate ones and lending in the high-interest-rate ones. This can work well, but it's worth noting that one has to place some constraints on the strategy or one ends up long an awful lot of emerging market currencies, and short an awful lot of JPY!

Volatility cutouts

The differential forward strategy responds well to volatility cutouts. The best volatility to use seems to be the one-, three- or six-month at-the-money option volatility – most strategies are insensitive as to which of these is actually used. The implied option volatility in all cases works better than the realised volatility, though it is more difficult to obtain – though historical vol can also be successfully used. In Figure 6 and Figure 7, we can see the effect of different levels of cutout on various currency pairs, for a 0% trigger differential forward strategy. The volatility used for the cutout signal was the 1m ATM option volatility.

The form of the graphs benefits from some explanation. At high cutout levels such as 30%, the cutout is rarely or never implemented.

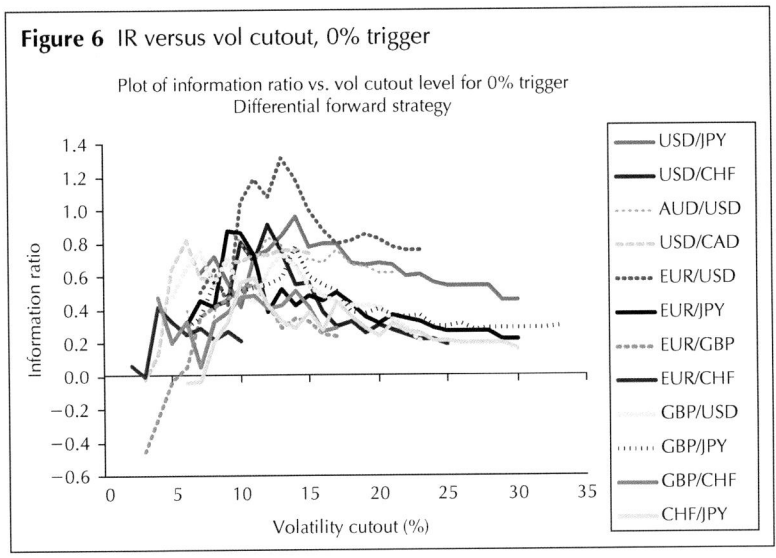

Figure 6 IR versus vol cutout, 0% trigger

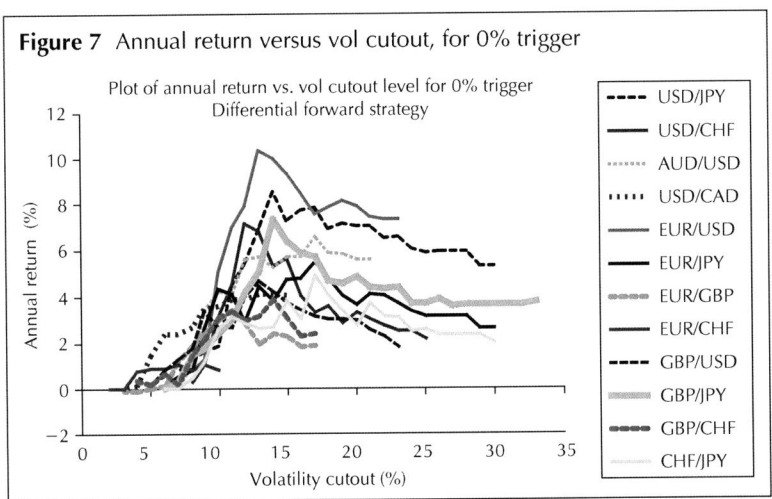

Figure 7 Annual return versus vol cutout, for 0% trigger

At very low levels close to zero, it will be almost continually implemented, so there will be close to no trading – hence the alignment of all the annual returns with zero at zero vol cutout level. But intermediate between the two there is an unambiguous tendency for returns and information ratios to rise as the cutout is implemented. There can be little doubt that on average the

Table 10 Effect of volatility cutout on 0% trigger Differential Forward strategy

Currency	USD/JPY	USD/CHF	AUD/USD	USD/CAD	EUR/USD	EUR/JPY	EUR/GBP	EUR/CHF	GBP/USD	GBP/JPY	GBP/CHF	CHF/JPY
					0% trigger, no volatility cutout							
Information ratio	0.49	0.19	0.64	0.72	0.71	0.22	0.22	0.19	0.18	0.30	0.27	0.16
Annualised return, %	5.66	2.15	5.85	3.97	7.23	2.68	1.69	0.71	1.57	3.86	2.28	1.96
					0% trigger, 12% volatility cutout							
Information ratio	0.75	0.91	0.84	0.73	1.08	0.38	0.43	0.19	0.63	0.56	0.40	0.42
Annualised return, %	5.49	7.35	5.77	4.00	8.09	2.95	2.85	0.71	4.06	4.27	2.97	2.89

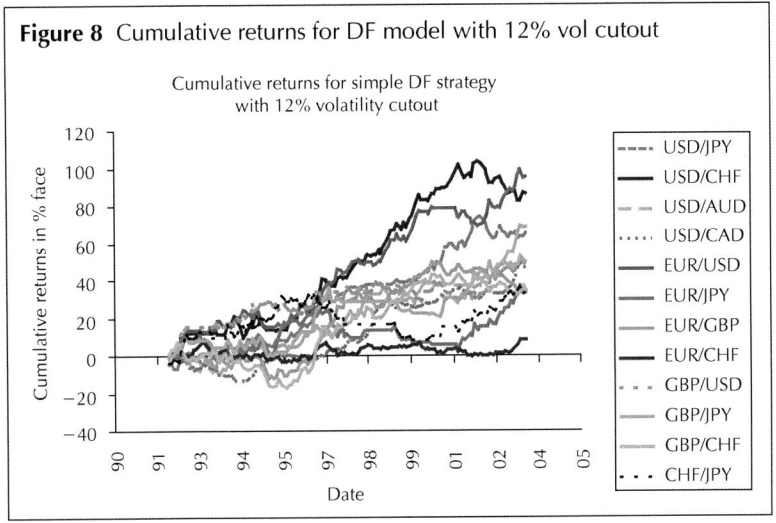

Figure 8 Cumulative returns for DF model with 12% vol cutout

introduction of a volatility cutout is beneficial to the differential forward strategy.

Table 10 shows the annual returns and information ratio for no vol cutout, and a cutout at 12%. As can be seen there is a near universal improvement. The graph in Figure 8 shows the cumulative returns with 12% cutout.

Returns are positive and at attractive levels for some currencies. This is a satisfactory result for a simple robust strategy with a single variable parameter (level of cutout). Almost certainly a more sophisticated cutout mechanism would improve results further.

TREND MODELS
Introduction
"The trend is your friend", as they say on the trading floor. Long-term economic pressures mean that trending behaviour is common in the currency world – and, unlike other market instruments, such as interest rates and equities, FX rates have no natural barriers or limits. Currency trends can last a long time.

Thus, trend-following trading strategies are a useful addition to any currency portfolio. However, not all currencies trend. Some, such as USD/CAD, are the exchange rate between two very strongly linked economies, and the pressures and differences that lead to trends are absent in these currency pairs.

The simplest trend-following strategies use moving averages. The variations that these can exhibit are many. They can use one, two or even three moving averages, which may be simple rate averages, or exponential averages, or even GARCH-based numbers. The trading rules can also be complex, with different weights applied to portfolio components according to how many of the moving averages are above or below the rate at the time. However, models that have a great many floating parameters are easily "overoptimised" until the backtested returns are merely fitting data quirks. Such strategies seldom survive the test of actual trading. If a currency pair cannot be traded successfully with a simple trend-following strategy, it is unlikely to be realistically improved by adding levels of complexity to the same technique.

We sought to establish which currencies "trend" or not by looking at the results of the simplest possible trend-following strategy – that of a single moving average. By buying when the rate was above a simple arithmetic moving average, and selling when it was below, we obtained a P/L curve for the trading strategy since the start of the data set, in 1988. We looked at every length of moving average strategy from 5 to 130 days, and found some interesting results. We use USD/JPY and USD/CAD as opposite examples.

Figure 9 plots the information ratio and annual return of the simple moving average strategy as a function of the number of days in the moving average, for both USD/JPY and USD/CAD.

As can be seen, the behaviour of the two currencies is utterly different. USD/JPY makes money and has a positive IR for any length of moving average, while USD/CAD stubbornly refuses to rise above zero under any circumstances. It is not difficult to draw the conclusion that USD/JPY trends and USD/CAD does not. In fact, so strong is the trending behaviour of the JPY that similar all-encompassing positive results are obtained for most of its crosses.

When one looks at the graphs in Figure 9, it seems reasonable to use the average IR over all moving-average lengths as a metric for the degree of trend-following behaviour that exists in a currency. Obviously, this precise figure will vary somewhat according to the range of moving-average strategies that are tested, but it should be possible to see which currencies "trend" and which do not. Table 11 gives the average IR for a number of different major currencies and crosses. Trading costs were included for all currencies.

TRADING FOR PROFIT

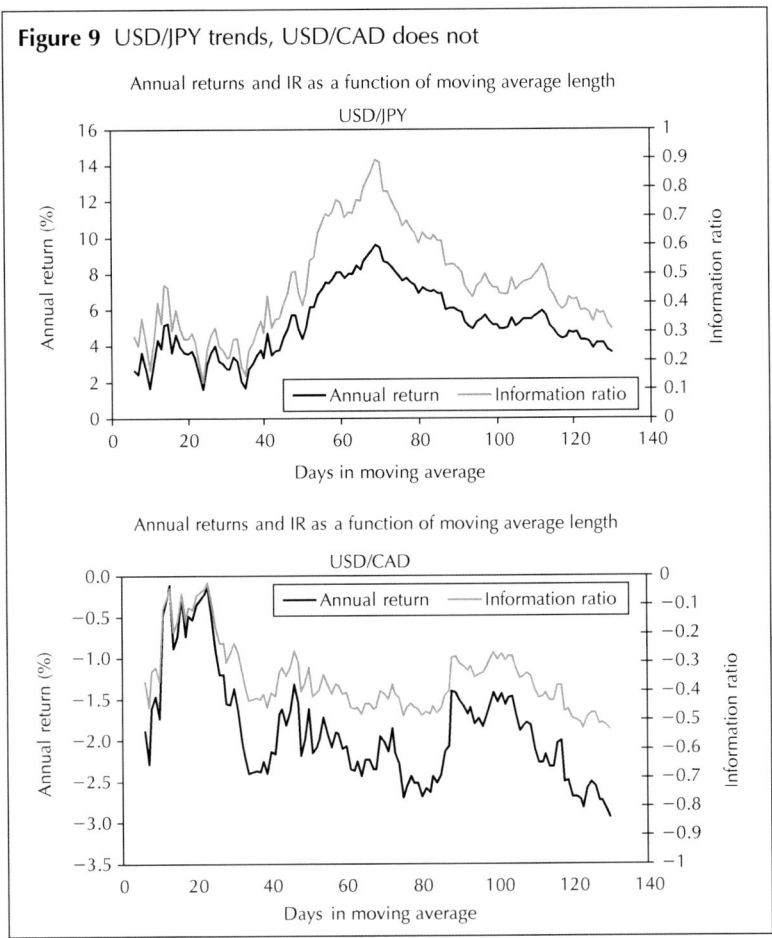

Figure 9 USD/JPY trends, USD/CAD does not

Table 11 Average information ratio over all trend following strategies from 5 day moving average to 130 day moving average

Currency	Average IR for trend-following strategies	Currency	Average IR for trend-following strategies
USD/JPY	0.46	GBP/USD	−0.01
USD/CHF	0.21	GBP/JPY	0.22
USD/AUD	−0.13	GBP/CHF	−0.06
USD/CAD	−0.34	CHF/JPY	0.41
EUR/USD	0.24	USD/SEK	0.16
EUR/JPY	0.38	USD/NOK	0.15
EUR/GBP	0.23	EUR/NOK	−0.10
EUR/CHF	0.00	EUR/SEK	0.00

257

Table 12 Annual returns for different lengths of moving average

Days in MA strategy	20	40	60	80	100
USD/JPY, %	3.43	3.19	7.81	6.71	4.98
USD/CHF, %	0.20	3.37	5.54	4.19	3.09
AUD/USD, %	0.03	−2.33	−1.60	−1.52	−0.56
USD/CAD, %	−0.35	−2.05	−1.98	−2.63	−1.51
EUR/USD, %	2.62	3.26	3.27	2.70	3.40
EUR/JPY, %	5.12	3.44	5.02	5.20	4.15
EUR/GBP, %	0.19	2.96	1.62	3.32	2.53
EUR/CHF, %	−0.33	−0.42	−0.08	0.09	−0.02
GBP/USD, %	2.49	−0.79	−0.95	0.78	−0.63
GBP/JPY, %	1.35	1.46	2.91	4.32	2.68
GBP/CHF, %	−3.22	−1.18	−1.41	−0.30	1.33
CHF/JPY, %	2.49	2.53	4.07	6.23	6.67
Average, %	**1.17**	**1.12**	**2.02**	**2.27**	**2.01**

It is very clear that the JPY crosses and a few others exhibit trending behaviour, while others, such as USD/CAD and USD/AUD, are not trend followers at all on this timescale.

It doesn't matter which trend!

We tested out the stability of the strategy with respect to the number of days in the moving average, finding that in fact there is a large range of moving averages that deliver reasonable returns for the portfolio. Table 12 shows the annual returns for the various currencies, and for the portfolio as a whole, as a function of the number of days in the moving-average strategy.

As can be seen in Figure 10, the strategy is astonishingly stable over a very wide range of moving averages. There is obviously an ideal region around 80 days, with an annual portfolio return of 4.31%, but strategies with moving averages of 60 or 100 days deliver returns of 3.98% and 3.60% respectively.

The information ratios are obviously also of interest, though they will follow the annual returns closely. They are shown in Table 13.

Once more, the best lies around 80 days, but again there are good results across the board.

It is interesting to find the "best" moving average – obviously this is an optimisation, but only of a single parameter. Accordingly we repeated the analysis with finer granularity, creating returns

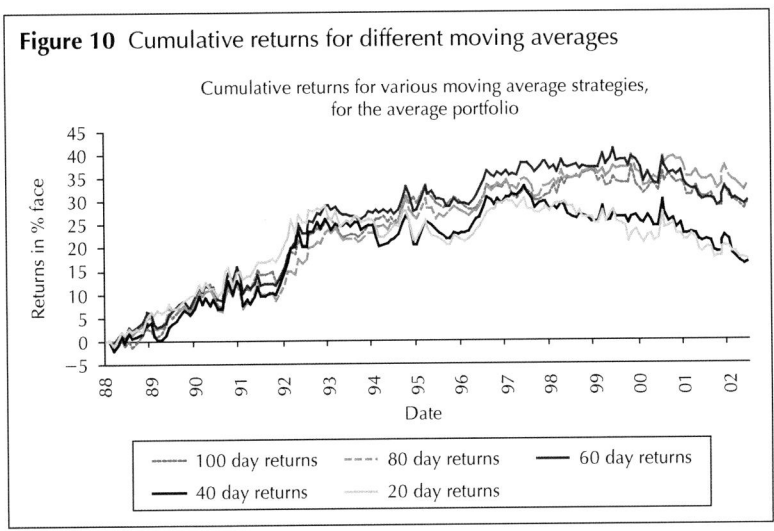

Figure 10 Cumulative returns for different moving averages

Table 13 Information ratios for different lengths of moving average

Days in MA strategy	20	40	60	80	100
USD/JPY	0.28	0.26	0.73	0.60	0.45
USD/CHF	0.02	0.27	0.45	0.35	0.28
AUD/USD	0.00	−0.25	−0.18	−0.16	−0.06
USD/CAD	−0.07	−0.39	−0.38	−0.49	−0.29
EUR/USD	0.25	0.28	0.28	0.23	0.33
EUR/JPY	0.45	0.29	0.42	0.46	0.34
EUR/GBP	0.02	0.38	0.20	0.45	0.34
EUR/CHF	−0.07	−0.10	−0.02	0.02	0.00
GBP/USD	0.25	−0.07	−0.09	0.08	−0.06
GBP/JPY	0.10	0.12	0.23	0.36	0.22
GBP/CHF	−0.34	−0.13	−0.15	−0.04	0.16
CHF/JPY	0.20	0.21	0.34	0.57	0.60
Average	**0.23**	**0.21**	**0.40**	**0.46**	**0.43**

and information ratios for moving averages between 20 and 100 days with "steps" of 5 days. The results are more suitable for graphical than textual display! The graphs in Figures 11–12 reveal the optimal region.

As can be seen in Figure 13, the "best" moving average strategy for the portfolio is about 70 days, with an annual return of 2.88% an information ratio of 0.591, but there is great stability around that

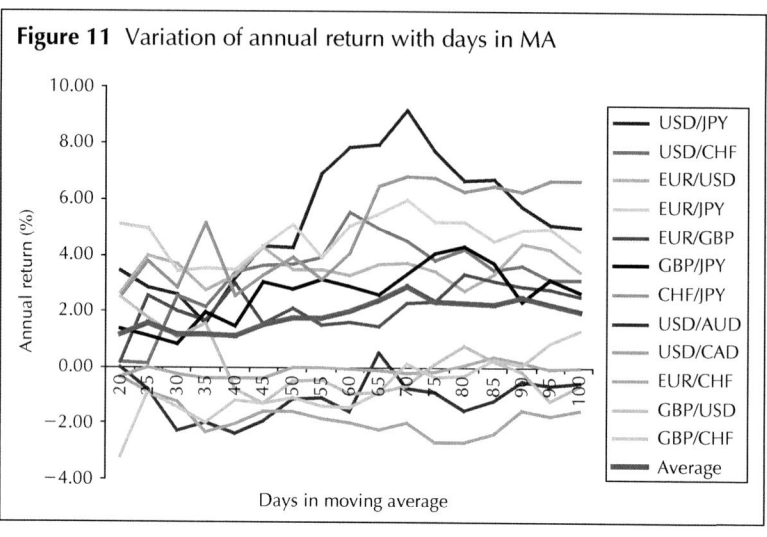

Figure 11 Variation of annual return with days in MA

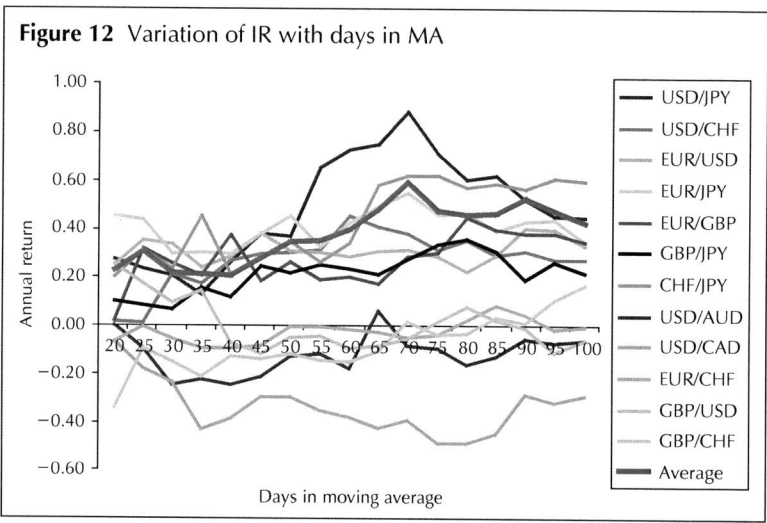

Figure 12 Variation of IR with days in MA

region. The graph shows the cumulative monthly return for this "best" strategy. Since 1999, it is worth noting, the longer moving averages, from 60 upwards, have outperformed the shorter ones, whereas earlier periods are roughly equal.

Trading costs were included, and our data set began in 1988 for most currencies.

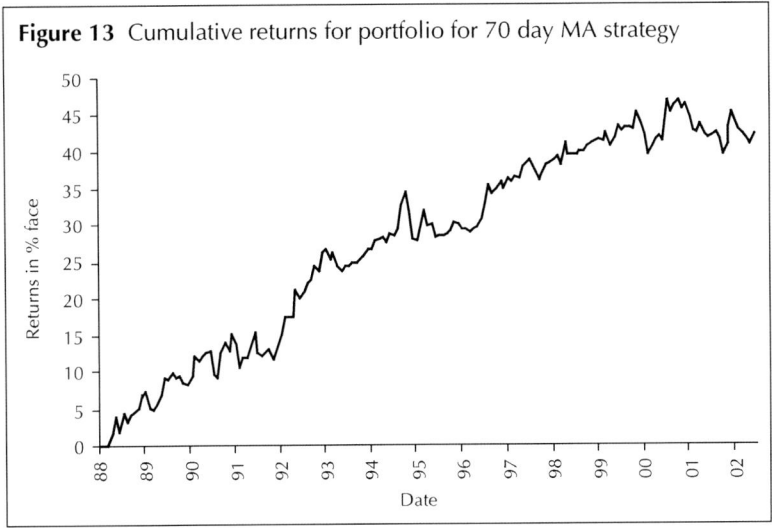

Figure 13 Cumulative returns for portfolio for 70 day MA strategy

Single MA versus multiple MA

Strategies with multiple moving averages are popular in the FX modelling world. This is for several reasons.

(1) As a trend establishes itself, the moving averages will gradually cross over the actual rate and each other, the shorter followed by the longer, until all of them lie below the actual rate. There is thus the possibility to "fade in" and gradually take increasing positions as the trend becomes stronger.
(2) By optimising the fade levels and the numbers of days in the moving averages, backtested returns can be greatly improved over simpler models.
(3) For advisory rather than strict model-following approaches, there are a number of different-strength signals for trends.

While (1) has some merits, (2) has to be regarded with caution because overoptimisation is very easy to achieve with this method. In general, if a currency is not tradable with a simple single moving average, then "improving" its backtested performance by optimising additional moving averages is unlikely to improve returns in the future. On the other hand, a currency that already works reasonably well with a single MA might have some robust improvements from the introduction of another. Some kind of plateau optimisation should be performed to reduce the chances of overoptimisation.

Collapse of multiple moving averages with cost introduction
An interesting fact about moving-average systems, which is little known, is that the introduction of trading costs can often lead to the best two moving averages actually being the same: because trading costs penalise frequent trading, at some cost level it is better to have just one moving average, no matter the improvements that having two or more have created in a zero-cost framework. Thus, when one optimises to find the best two, they turn out to be the same.

The question is, at what level of costs does this occur? In fact, for most currencies, this will happen at or just above normal trading costs. It is worth being very careful about costs with trend-following systems.

For fade-in and fade-out systems this problem is somewhat alleviated.

Effect of volatility cutout

Volatility cutouts in trend-following models do work but do not have any consistent effect on those currencies that are poor trend followers in general. Thus we selected a number of currencies with "good", single moving-average results, and applied a volatility cutout at the 85th percentile of historical levels of volatility. For further investigations of this effect see Huang (2002), Acar (2001) and Green (2001).

Thus, whenever the historical volatility of the FX rate, calculated as the standard deviation of the previous 21 business days, was above the 85th percentile of its range, the face amount of that currency was reduced to zero. When the volatility moved below the 85th percentile, the face amount was adjusted to its original level. This means that the total face amount of the strategy varied with the number of currencies that were disqualified due to high volatility.

The improvements due to the volatility adjustment are in Table 14, together with the 85% volatility cutout levels for each currency. As can be seen, the IR is considerably improved for the volatility-adjusted strategy.

In Figure 14 and Figure 15, we can see the cumulative returns and frequency distributions of the strategy with and without volatility adjustment.

Table 14 Effect of volatility cutout on trend following strategy

Currency	No volatility adjustment		With volatility adjustment		
	Annual return, %	Information ratio	Annual return, %	Information ratio	Volatility cutout level, %
USD/JPY	9.49	0.88	8.78	0.88	14.57
USD/CHF	5.43	0.45	6.85	0.63	14.66
EUR/USD	4.59	0.44	4.47	0.50	13.98
EUR/JPY	6.14	0.59	8.34	0.92	15.75
EUR/GBP	3.23	0.40	3.37	0.54	10.02
GBP/JPY	5.32	0.47	5.51	0.56	15.35
CHF/JPY	6.53	0.60	7.48	0.72	15.88
USD/SEK	6.36	0.56	7.45	0.82	13.90
USD/SGD	7.57	0.82	5.28	0.73	8.52
Average	**5.57**	**1.07**	**5.70**	**1.48**	–

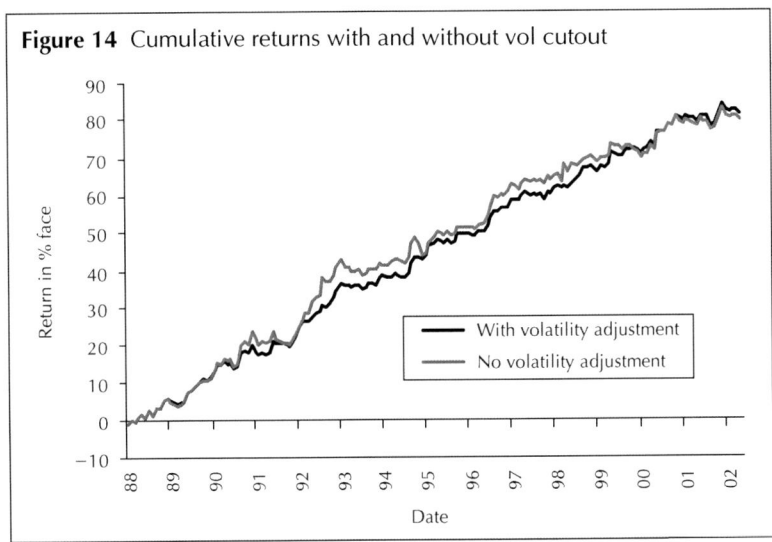

Figure 14 Cumulative returns with and without vol cutout

It can be clearly seen that the volatility adjustment reduces the standard deviation of returns, shifts the peak of the returns distribution in the positive direction, and cuts short the loss tail. This comes at the expense of sacrificing a few of the very best monthly returns, but overall the effect is very pleasing, reflecting the improvement to the information ratio.

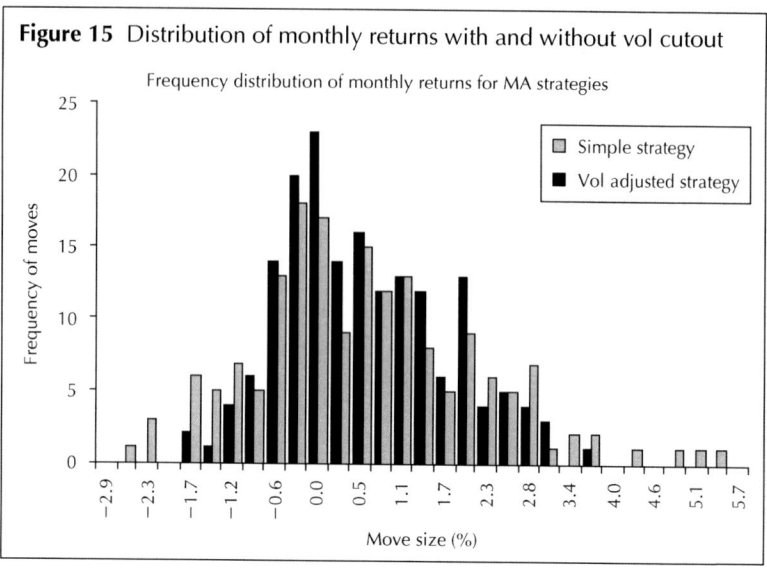

Figure 15 Distribution of monthly returns with and without vol cutout

Effect of stop loss

As in the DF strategy, in general, stop losses are detrimental to strategy performance. Obviously, there are circumstances where stops are essential but in general they should be kept at a wide level so as to have minimal impact upon performance. In Table 15 we illustrate the effect of stop losses on the 70-day moving-average strategy, for various currencies.

As can be seen, there is a consistent worsening of returns and IR as the stop loss decreases – ie, as it is used more often. There are a few exceptions for a wide stop loss but the narrower 2% stop degrades every positive return apart from that of EUR/GBP.

RANGE MODELS

These are the models that we will spend the least time on, as they are the most difficult and least successful, in general. As a generic example we present the following model, a simple range buy-and-sell strategy. In Figure 16 its functionality is illustrated. A range has a number of days (n days) to become established – n is a variable that may be optimised. Then, after it is established, there is a lookback period of m days, during which the strategy identifies a high and a low. The strategy then trades between these levels, selling as

Table 15 Effect of stop loss on 70 day moving average strategy

Currency	USD/JPY	USD/CHF	AUD/USD	USD/CAD	EUR/USD	EUR/JPY	EUR/GBP	EUR/CHF	GBP/USD	GBP/JPY	GBP/CHF	CHF/JPY
					70 day MA, no stop loss							
Information ratio	0.737	0.371	−0.147	−0.174	0.423	0.438	0.383	−0.087	−0.158	0.285	0.056	0.385
Annualised return, %	7.72	3.90	−1.37	−1.01	4.23	5.09	3.00	−0.35	−1.38	3.70	0.50	4.49
					70 day MA, 4% stop loss							
Information ratio	0.609	0.345	−0.257	−0.169	0.477	0.445	0.412	−0.087	−0.229	0.260	0.118	0.302
Annualised return, %	6.57	3.53	−2.37	−0.97	4.52	5.03	3.17	−0.35	−2.00	3.11	1.00	3.57
					70 day MA, 2% stop loss							
Information ratio	0.487	0.165	−0.088	−0.090	0.322	0.360	0.463	−0.074	−0.144	0.236	0.031	0.247
Annualised return, %	5.09	1.59	−0.70	−0.49	2.90	3.70	3.36	−0.29	−1.16	2.50	0.25	2.71

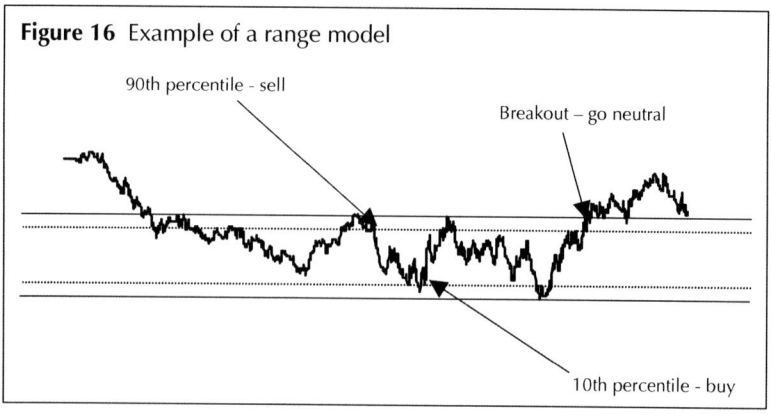

Figure 16 Example of a range model

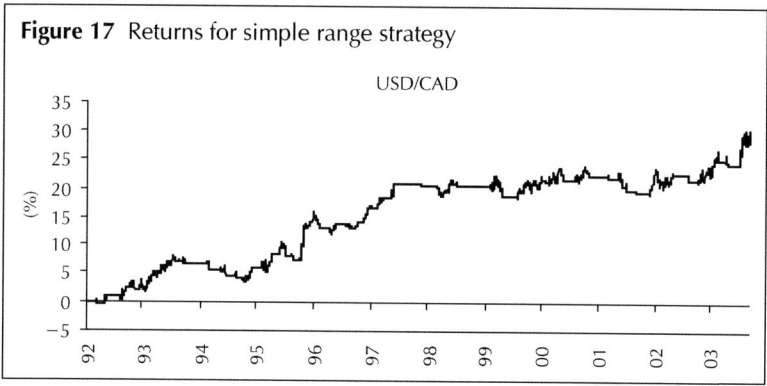

Figure 17 Returns for simple range strategy

it goes down through the 90th percentile and buying as it rises through the 10th percentile of the range. As it breaks out of the range it goes neutral and waits for a new range to establish. Thus n and m are both optimisable variables.

This strategy performs reasonably well for ranging currencies like USD/CAD as shown in Figure 17. Below we chart the returns for a lookback period of 30 days and an establishment period of 5 days for this currency.

The IR of this strategy is 0.74 and the annual return is 2.56 – not high but reasonably smooth.

However, for USD/JPY there is no stable region of returns and the same holds true for many other currencies. The difficulties attendant upon defining a "range" and how to trade it are far greater than those involved with trends. If one believes strongly that a currency is trading in a narrow range, often the best strategy would be to sell an option!

SYSTEMATIC OPTION-SELLING STRATEGIES

For a number of years one has been able to find references to "option-selling programmes" as alpha-generating vehicles. These strategies promise to deliver steady returns, presumably on the basis that options are on average overpriced and thus selling them will make money, albeit with a certain amount of risk.

However, in the FX world, vanilla options are often fairly priced, in that their average payout over history has been close to their premium (see James and Colchester, 2003). This statement holds for many of the major currencies for a wide variety of liquid option tenors, and thus the opportunity for generating alpha by selling FX options would seem to be limited.

This is not quite the whole story, though. A closer look at the actual data reveals that for some currencies there is a small but steady overpricing of options, and, while this is not large for liquid at the money forward structures, it becomes more significant for out-of-the-money products. It is possible to discern this feature only if one has access to detailed historical option data series; fortunately, such a database is maintained at Citigroup.

Straddle/strangle writing strategies

A natural way to exploit persistent over- or underpricing of options is with the use of straddles and strangles. A straddle is the simultaneous purchase or sale of an at-the-money put and call, which must have identical amounts and maturities. A strangle is the same structure but both the put and the call will be out of the money by some amount. The use of straddles and strangles minimises the effects of any overall trend that would skew the results. We thus decided to use systematic straddle and strangle writing to monetise any persistent mispricing in the options market. To smooth results and collect as much data as possible, we would ideally like to sell straddles every day. However, in the real world, this would be a very time- and capital-intensive strategy to pursue, and thus

Table 16 Information ratios and annual returns for weekly option selling strategies

Currency	Information ratio			Average annual return, %		
	ATMF	25 delta	10 delta	ATMF	25 delta	10 delta
USD/JPY	0.01	0.09	0.24	0.11	0.43	0.69
USD/CHF	0.09	0.19	0.58	0.59	0.75	1.19
USD/AUD	0.41	0.68	1.50	1.54	1.84	1.95
USD/CAD	0.98	1.30	1.60	2.17	2.01	1.23
EUR/USD	0.39	0.50	0.76	2.01	1.81	1.35
EUR/JPY	0.03	0.15	0.28	0.18	0.67	0.73
EUR/GBP	0.21	0.23	0.21	0.82	0.73	0.48
EUR/CHF	1.33	1.79	1.94	2.28	2.18	1.26
GBP/USD	0.71	0.70	0.48	3.16	2.42	1.13
GBP/JPY	−0.17	−0.17	−0.23	−1.41	−1.13	−1.14
GBP/CHF	−0.01	−0.07	−0.18	−0.02	−0.28	−0.60
CHF/JPY	−0.08	−0.04	0.04	−0.41	−0.14	0.12
USD/SEK	0.27	0.25	0.34	1.47	1.03	0.77
USD/NOK	0.83	0.82	0.67	4.03	2.84	1.28
EUR/NOK	0.80	1.13	0.97	1.10	1.18	0.64
EUR/SEK	0.97	1.23	1.70	2.84	2.53	1.48

we decided on a weekly strategy as being both feasible to trade and likely to yield interesting results.

Using the historical option database, we simulated the effect of simultaneously, once a week, selling both a one month put and a one month call in a variety of currencies. Trading costs were included, and the options were all held to expiry.

Results

The results of the simulation are very interesting. While the majority of at-the-money options are, as previously found, fairly priced on average, there is a significant subset where a steady alpha generation is possible, which is often improved by moving to 25 delta or 10 delta structures. Table 16 shows the annual return and information ratio for the various currencies and deltas.

It can be seen that the currencies show a wide range of behaviour, with some, such as EUR/CHF, giving smooth returns with a high information ratio, while others have unpredictable or negative returns. The following graphs show the cumulative returns resulting from the strategies over the data period.

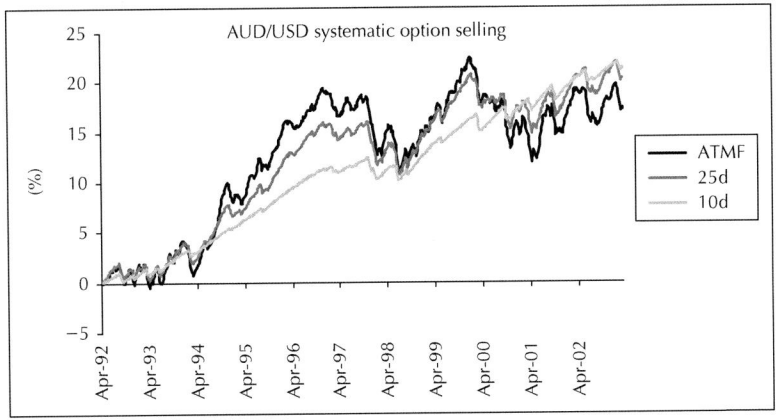

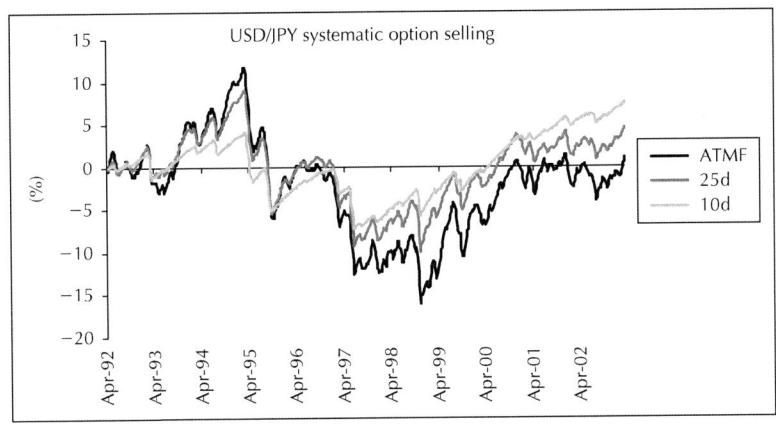

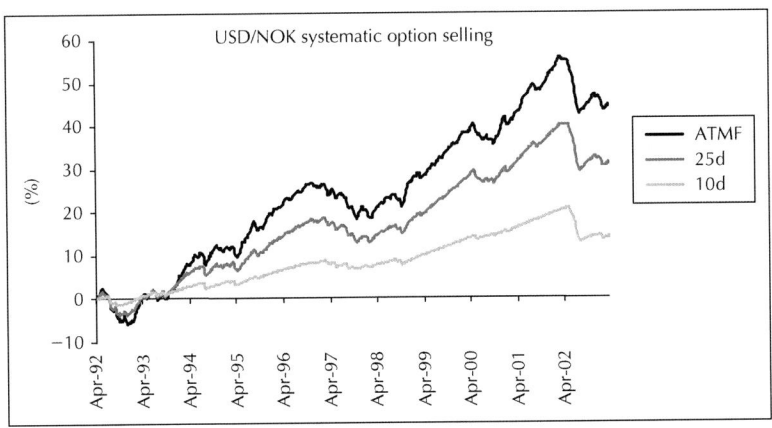

CURRENCY MANAGEMENT: OVERLAY AND ALPHA TRADING

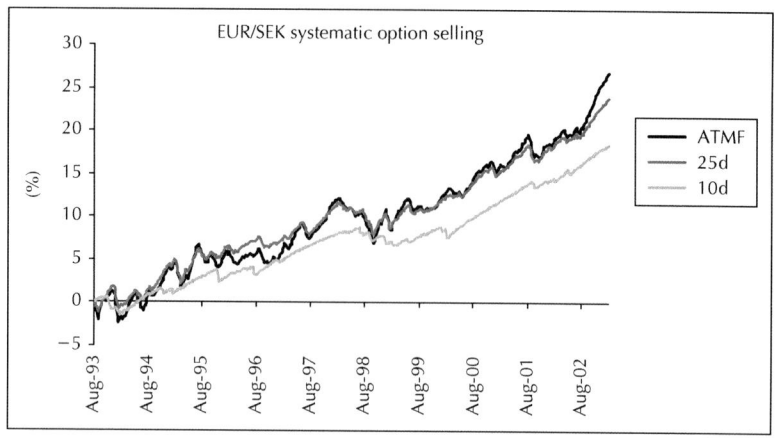

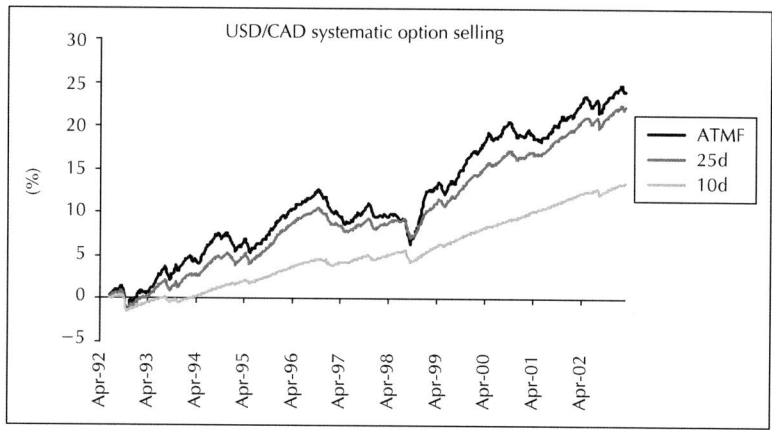

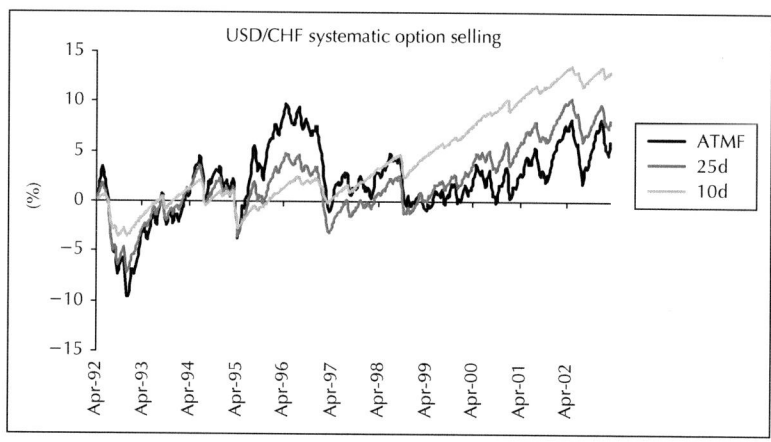

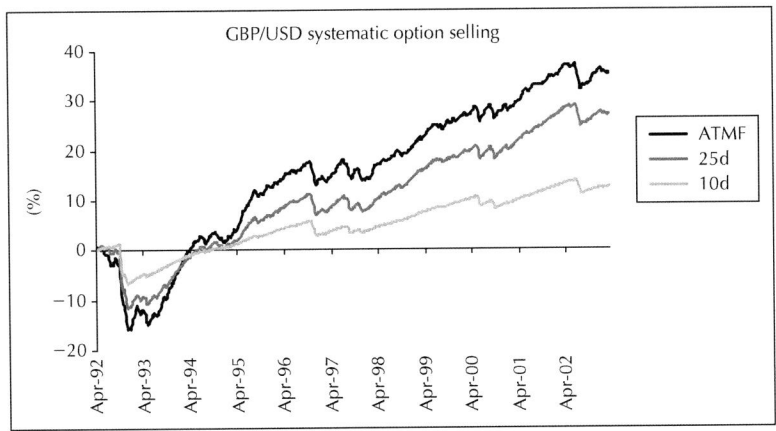

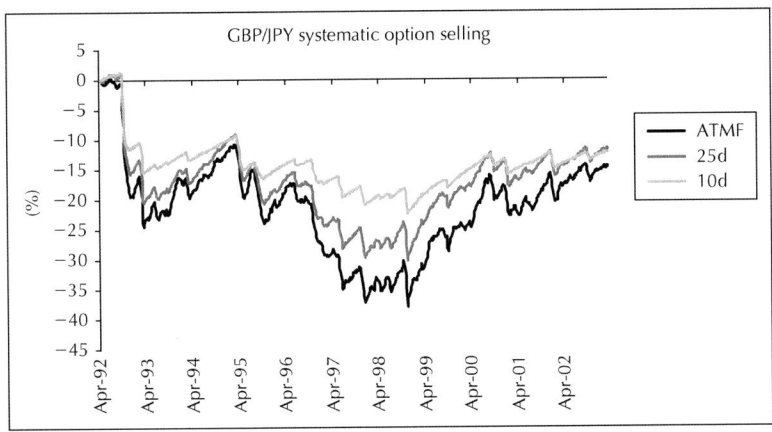

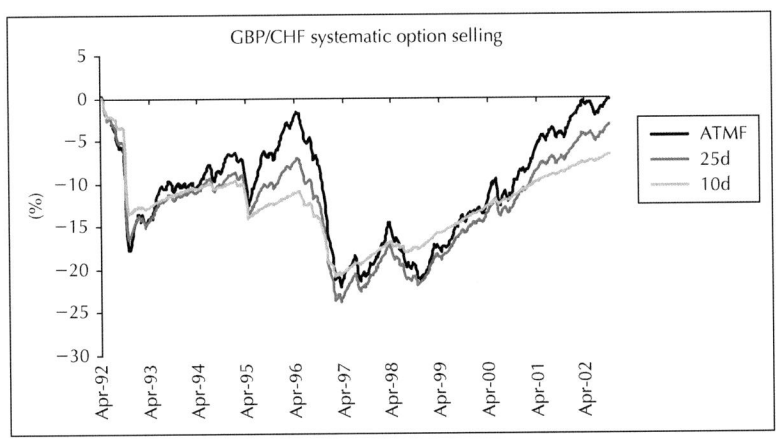

CURRENCY MANAGEMENT: OVERLAY AND ALPHA TRADING

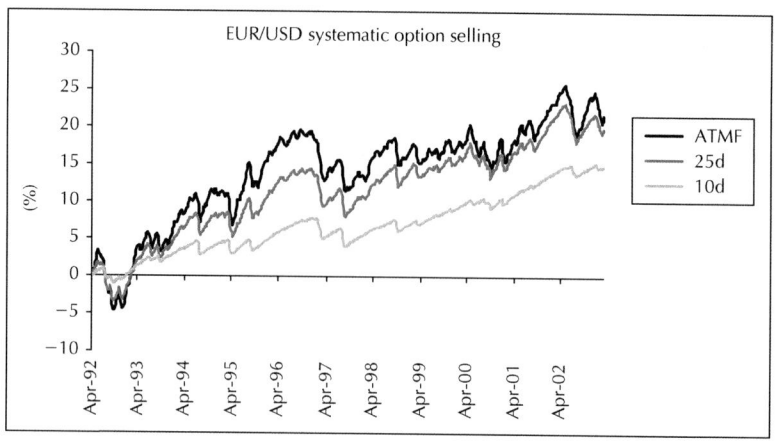

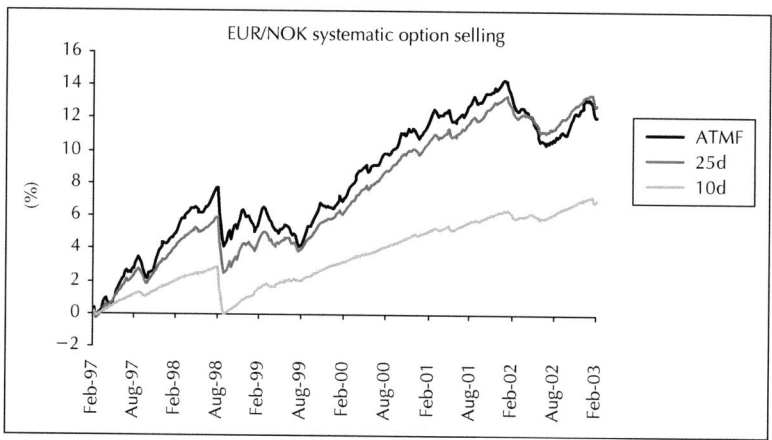

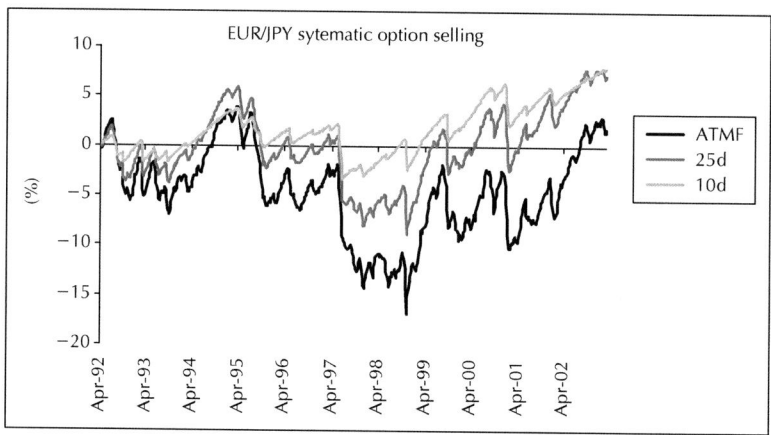

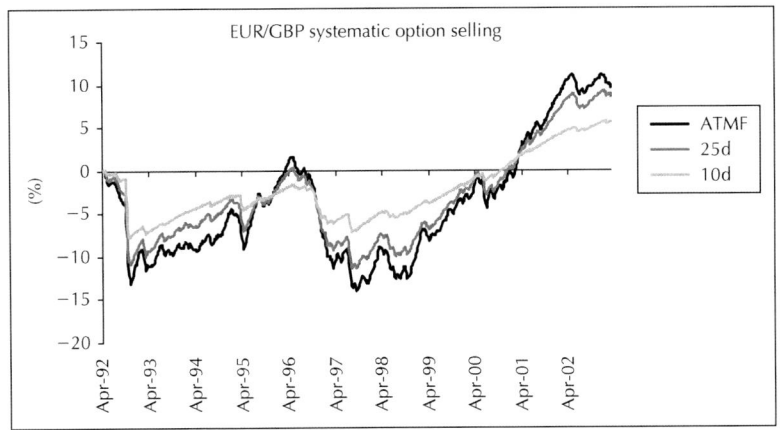

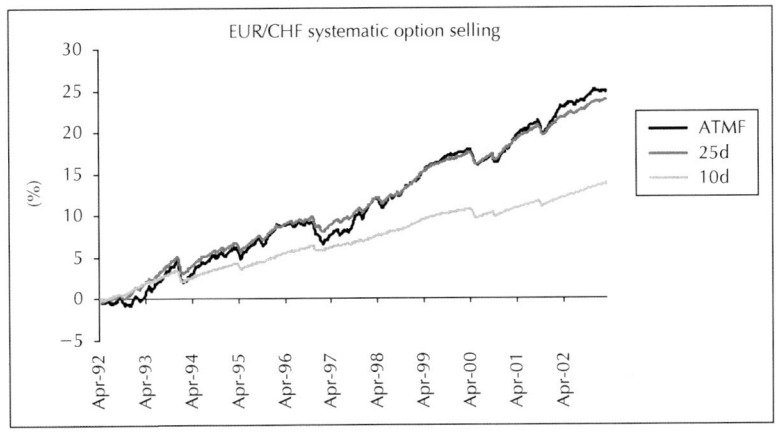

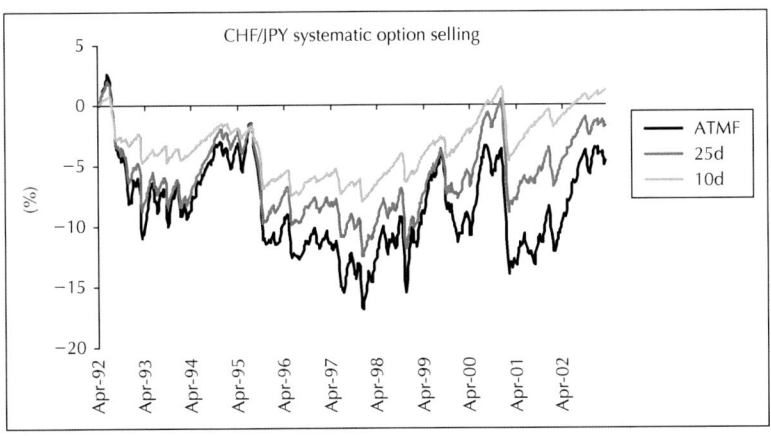

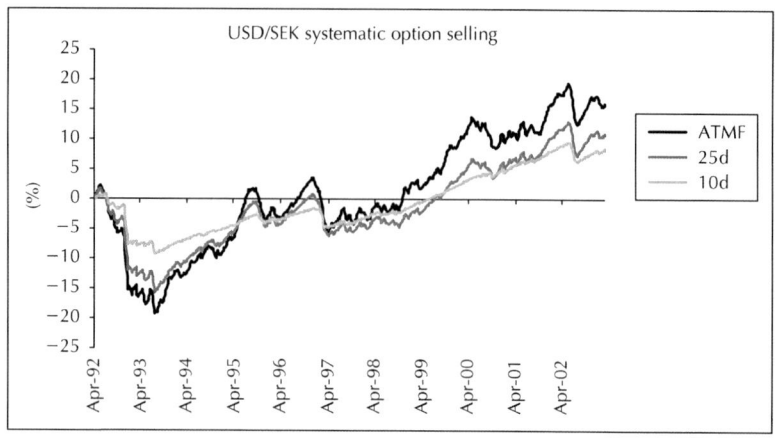

Averaging the viable strategies

It is fairly easy to see that those currencies in which viable option-selling strategies exist are AUD/USD, USD/NOK, EUR/SEK, USD/CHF, USD/CAD, GBP/USD, EUR/USD, EUR/NOK and EUR/CHF. Although different delta options can improve or degrade the IR for a given currency, one can say that it is the currencies that "work" or not, rather than a particular level of moneyness. In general the 10 delta options provide the smoothest returns but this is not always the case. Figure 18 shows the results of combining the returns of the strategies for these currencies, in each case selecting the delta that gave the smoothest returns.

The information ratio for the average strategy is a satisfactory 1.36; if one truncates the data set and looks only at post-92 data, after the ERM crisis, the information ratio soars to 1.86. For a trading strategy with all costs included, this is a very respectable figure indeed. However, it is worth looking at the absolute annual returns, which are only 1.94%. This is a strategy that would need considerable leverage to implement, which could in itself affect the market rates.

We can say that option selling strategies do seem to work consistently in certain currencies, while others show no such mispricing characteristics. A combination strategy, averaging all the viable currency returns, has an excellent information ratio, but in fact this combination strategy is not such a good performer as some of the star single currencies such as EUR/CHF. This is due to the high level of correlation between the returns of all the viable strategies – most

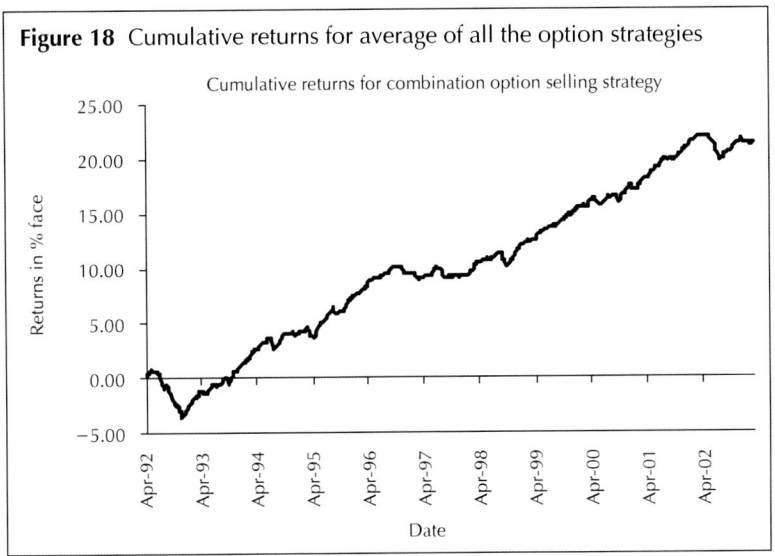

Figure 18 Cumulative returns for average of all the option strategies

of them show a dip in 1992 and 1998–9. However, if an investor was interested in trading the strategies to generate alpha, he or she would be advised to use several currencies to spread the load over the market a little: due to the levels of leverage that would be required, utilising just a single currency might have an adverse effect upon the options market.

CONCLUSION

This chapter has surely only scratched the surface of the myriad trading strategies and methods that exist in the FX market. But it is enough to show that, if one is careful and very wary, and sceptical and rigorous, there is money to be made. Avoiding overoptimisation and data mining is critical; and a healthy dollop of common sense is essential, but the FX market does have opportunities and patterns that may be exploited.

REFERENCES

Acar, E., 2001, "Volatility-Adjusted Exposures", *Currency Issues for Asset Managers*, 10, October.

Green, H. G., 2001, "Combining Performance and Market Volatility in Portfolio Allocations", AIMA Newsletter, April.

Huang, T., 2002, "Dynamic Adjustment to CitiFX Overlay Models", *Currency Issues for Asset Managers*, 16, October.

James, J., and H. Colchester, 2003, "Defining Forex Option Value", *Risk*, January.

Johnson, Neil, 2000, Clarendon Lab, Internal Research Material.

Strange, B., 1998, *Pensions & Investments*, 15 June.

11
Trading Models
James Binny
ABN AMRO

OVERVIEW

The objective of this chapter is to give a summary of the various techniques that are used to manage currency, whether that management is from a perspective of risk management or return generation. It is not intended to be a chapter on the economic theory of exchange rates, rather a summary of techniques used by successful currency management specialists. It is not possible to delve into the full details of each one – whole volumes have been written on individual techniques in the past. However, there is hopefully sufficient information to compare and contrast the different styles and techniques.

The techniques described are used by both currency overlay managers and currency managers running leveraged alpha funds (such as hedge funds and CTAs). In terms of technique employed the differences between these investors are small, although the difference in leverage can be considerable.

The aim of the models described in this chapter is to forecast the future behaviour of an exchange rate, so as to make active management possible. Therefore these models can be loosely described as trading models – or investment processes, as overlay managers would prefer to call them. Most tend to focus on forecasting the direction of currency moves rather than precise currency levels. This is because the objective is to decide whether to be long or short of individual currencies for clients, as opposed to publishing forecasts of future rates for clients (as bank strategists are frequently required to).

As with any form of portfolio management, there are many opinions as to the best techniques and processes to use when managing foreign exchange, including the following:

- that currencies have a fair value, which the market will ultimately revert to, despite shorter-term misvaluation.
- that the focus should be on other external factors that drive foreign exchange markets, perhaps even driving the market away from fair value – for instance looking at relative economic growth rates or what is happening in equity and interest rate markets.
- that such valuation and forecasting techniques are a waste of time, but that the price series of the exchange rates hold information, which can be exploited through technical analysis and other trend-following processes.
- some focus on how to make money from non-directional strategies, such as trading volatility through the options market.
- some do not attempt to forecast exchange rate direction – focusing instead on forecasting and managing the risk of foreign currency exposures.
- others – mostly those not directly involved in the foreign exchange market – believe that it is not possible to manage exchange rates. For this group the model assumed is, whether implicitly or explicitly, a random walk.

We assume that currency markets do not move in a random walk and so it is possible to manage currency exposures actively – taking as our evidence surveys such as that by Brian Strange (1998), now of JP Morgan Fleming Asset Management, and the consultants Frank Russell, which demonstrate that currency overlay managers have generally added value historically. Such analyses are described in greater detail in other chapters – and so are not explored here.

The reality is that, as with the management of any asset or exposure, there are a variety of techniques that can be used to exploit the various inefficiencies that exist. At different times and in different circumstances it is likely that they will all be successful. The aim of this chapter is to describe and categorise those techniques. There are various ways in which trading models can be categorised, not just the sources of alpha described above. For the purposes of this chapter, we can identify four dimensions over which currency trading models can be organised:

1. time horizon;
2. degree of judgement employed;
3. modelling technique; and
4. source of alpha.

It is important for someone selecting currency managers – such as a pension fund selecting a combination of currency overlay managers, or a fund-of-funds manager selecting a series of currency CTAs or currency hedge funds – to understand where individual currency managers fit on the four dimensions. This can be visualised as a hypercube with four dimensions (if hypercubes can be visualised!), which can be split down into series of smaller constituent hypercubes. The objective of the manager selection is to populate as many of the smaller hypercubes as possible.

Probably the most important and obvious dimension where diversification should be maximised is that of source of alpha – which inefficiency is being exploited – and that is the one to which we give the most attention. However, first of all we should address the preceding three dimensions.

DIMENSION 1: TIME HORIZON

The breakdown here is fairly straightforward and obvious. We would identify four horizons:

- long-term
- medium-term
- short-term
- very short-term

The trouble is that these time horizons mean different things to different participants. To paraphrase a characterisation described by Eric Busay from CalPERS at a recent ABN AMRO conference regarding the difference between the time horizon of a pension fund and a bank spot trader.

For a pension fund with many active members (so a long time to maturity) or an endowment plan, the following definitions would apply:

- the long term is the plan's investment time horizon – this could be 25 years.

- the medium term is the likely job tenure of the member of the pension plan staff. Over this time horizon the person's job would be considered a success or failure: perhaps five years.
- the short term is the frequency with which the quarterly (or possibly monthly) investment report is received from the investment manager.
- the very short term is for those pension funds that receive daily valuations from their custodian – most would regard such daily returns as "noise".

At the other end of the extreme is a bank spot trader:

- the very short term is the time between quoting a price for a client and receiving their response.
- the short term is the time until the trader can execute an offsetting trade in the interdealer market (taking out the bid–offer spread).
- the medium term is when they miss the bid, the market runs away from him and they hold the position for the next half-hour, until the market comes back to a better level.
- the long term is when the market doesn't come back and the trader has to hold the position overnight!

The above is a caricature, but it is clear that, when defining the time-horizon dimension, we must be careful to define what we mean. It is possible for a client and manager to be speaking at cross-purposes due to a different understanding of the time horizons. For the purposes of this chapter we use the following definitions, which are those of a typical currency overlay manager:

- the long term is measured in years;
- the medium term is measured in months;
- the short term is measured in days and weeks; and
- the very short term is measured in hours.

For a currency overlay manager it is difficult to take long-term positions as defined above. This is because the manager feels that, by the time the forecast is achieved, the client may well have sacked the overlay manager for underperformance (whether that feeling is justified or not). However, modelling over such a time horizon can be useful to help adjust the benchmark of the mandate tactically. Separately, this is the time horizon over which managers would hope that their appointment would be judged a success or failure.

The medium term is the time horizon over which the currency overlay managers report back to the underlying client. Therefore, such a time period is crucial to the overlay manager, as the measurement period. Some positions will certainly be taken for longer periods, with the aim of maintaining them for several months. However, the manager will usually have half an eye on the monthly return.

The short term is the time period over which a typical currency overlay manager will adjust positions so as to achieve the medium-term aims. It should be noted that the typical currency overlay manager will trade more frequently than a typical equity portfolio manager, who is more likely to hold positions for longer. This is possible because transaction costs are substantially lower in foreign exchange. That said, a typical overlay client (such as a pension fund) is likely to be alarmed if turnover rose to the level of short-term proprietary trader.

The very short term is the period over which the manager will seek to "time" the short-term decisions – this timing is frequently achieved by the trading desk of an investment manager, rather than the investment managers themselves, who are typically less in tune with the minute-by-minute flows in the market.

The above definitions are generalisations across the currency overlay industry, but different managers focus on different time horizons. CTAs and currency hedge funds tend to feel less constrained by the concerns over turnover and some do focus on shorter time horizons. As a result, it should be possible to populate all four nodes when selecting managers – although there is probably the greatest concentration of managers in the short-term and medium-term areas.

On the whole, as models move from the long to the short term, the techniques used for forecasting the currency's behaviour move from being more fundamentally based to being more time-series-based. Some managers try to provide some diversification across time horizons: for instance evaluating a long-term equilibrium value for the currency, but timing the decision to take a position (to reflect that valuation) by using short-term technical measures.

These different techniques are discussed in greater detail in Dimension 4: Source of Alpha.

DIMENSION 2: DEGREE OF JUDGEMENT EMPLOYED

Currency managers vary in the degree to which human judgement is utilised – or, conversely, the degree to which the investment process is systematic. There are a few managers who are purely systematic "black-box" managers and some who are purely judgemental (or discretionary). However, most managers sit on the continuum in between. Four points on that continuum are defined below:

- ❏ pure discretionary;
- ❏ flexible decision support;
- ❏ systematic investment process; and
- ❏ pure black-box.

A pure discretionary manager relies on a variety of factors – whether fundamental, political or technical – to predict future exchange rate movements. The factors are not set in stone, nor defined in advance, and vary according to the drivers of the market at any particular time. However, we are assuming in this chapter that such managers still have a rational reason for taking positions – rather than pure "gut feel".

A manager with flexible decision support has a series of predefined models, which can be implemented as and when the manager feels each is appropriate.

A systematic investment process is predefined. The process is relatively transparent so that the managers can understand, explain and monitor what is driving the decisions, but ultimately most (but not all) of the positions recommended by the model are implemented in the market. Frequently the investment managers add some value through trying to time the implementation of model decisions over the short and very short term and perhaps by adjusting level of risk taken by the process, according to level of conviction.

Pure black-box systems are implemented with the minimum of human contact. Such processes are frequently, although not exclusively, self-regulating and calibrating, using processes such as neural networks and genetic algorithms and other forms of "artificial intelligence".

The advantages of more systematic processes are:

❑ they give a degree of consistency in the way in which positions and risk are analysed and taken.
❑ a systematic process removes emotion and so gives greater discipline – a model will not hold onto a losing position just because it does not want to appear wrong, as an undisciplined human trader might; also a model will not become nervous of a position and remove it when the rationale for the position still exists.
❑ it is possible to demonstrate, describe and attribute how a process has been successful historically and how it will operate in the future.

There is clearly an implicit assumption that the structure of the market defined by the model will be sustainable in the future. However, there are also some advantages in not being constrained within the straitjacket of a rigid investment process.

❑ financial series are usually assumed to be non-stationary – that is, the degree of influence of individual factors, as well as the behaviour of the exchange rate itself, varies through time.
❑ also, there is sometimes a need to take into account exogenous factors, not included in the model, that nonetheless have a temporary impact on the market: for instance, war, terrorist activity or manipulation of the exchange rate by a central bank.

The flexibility of a less systematic process can help to address such problems. In addition, perhaps, the emotion and "gut feel" that is inherently part of the judgement can be useful occasionally in dysfunctional markets – even if it is only to reduce risk.

For a pure discretionary manager there is a potential marketing problem: it is hard to explain how the returns are generated when the process is constantly changing and so will be different in the future. All the manager can do is point to historic success and describe past positions and rationale – however, such marketing is constrained in most countries by such statements as, "Past performance is not necessarily indicative of future returns." For a pension fund (or fund-of-funds manager) with fiduciary duties, it is harder to justify hiring such managers without being able to describe an "investment process", and there is a clear "key-person risk". However, as part of a portfolio of currency managers, the flexibility of a discretionary manager may be a useful diversifier, particularly in times of market dislocation.

DIMENSION 3: MODELLING TECHNIQUE

Where some degree of systematisation is utilised, there are various modelling techniques that can be used. For models using a series of input variables, the most obvious econometric technique to use is regression – with ordinary least squares (OLS) being the most established and easiest to estimate (although there are many other, more sophisticated, regression methods). This will result in a forecast being calculated as follows:

$$\text{Forecast} = A + Bx_1 + Cx_2 + Dx_3 + \ldots$$

where A, B, C, D ... are coefficients and x_1, x_2, x_3 ... are the explanatory variables used to create the forecast. Various search and analytic techniques exist to calculate the coefficients; the objective of OLS regression estimation is to find values of the constants so as to minimise the squares of errors in the forecast historically. Having established these constants, then today's values of the explanatory variables can be input and so a forecast extracted.

Two problems arise with such traditional techniques. The first is *stationarity*. A reasonably long set of data is required to estimate the coefficients in the models and the coefficients tend to be fairly stable (one would worry if they were not) – evolving only slowly as new data become available. This is potentially a problem for two reasons:

❏ in the long term, while there is room for debate on the issue, the dynamics of the market evolve as new players enter and leave the market and existing players learn how to play the game better.
❏ in the short and medium terms, the influence of individual variables waxes and wanes as market participants (particularly the shorter-term players) focus on different factors.

Second comes *non-linearity*. As is evident from the regression equation shown above, the constants A, B, C and so on are not only assumed to remain constant through time (stationarity), but are also assumed to remain constant for different levels of variables. However, such linear assumptions are not necessarily valid – for instance, the US current account deficit did not appear to have much influence on the US dollar over recent years – until it reached more critical levels (perhaps 5% of GDP).

To an extent, the above problems can be resolved by allowing some judgement in the implementation of the models – as discussed in Dimension 2. However, there are also systematic techniques that seek to solve these problems.

One way to deal with the varying influence of different variables is to use regime-switching techniques. Using these techniques, it is possible to have two (or more) models – a different model for each regime. A further model needs to be estimated in order to indicate the prevailing regime – to perform the "switching". One popular type of variable for indicating the switch is the prevailing level of risk aversion among market participants. For instance, during risk-*seeking* times, investors favour high-interest-rate currencies; during risk-*avoiding* times, investors return to low-interest-rate currencies. The problem with estimating such models is the amount of data required to create statistically significant models: this is because there are so many coefficients and models that need estimating.

There are various advanced techniques for dealing with non-linearity and non-stationarity. They are often known as *non-parametric processes*, as they do not impose a structure on a market and then try to find the parameters of that structure – rather they allow the data "to do the talking". Such techniques tend to fall in the "artificial intelligence" category, including:

❏ *Neural networks*. These mirror the behaviour of the human brain and consist of a series of parallel (or pseudo-parallel) processes that interact with each other, feeding information forwards and backwards between themselves so as to adjust the sensitivity of the model to the inputs and adjust the processing of those inputs.
❏ *Genetic algorithms*. These mirror Darwinian evolution, whereby unsuccessful strategies are allowed to "die", while successful strategies are allowed to combine with one another and grow. Through this form of natural selection the investment strategies should become stronger.

- ❏ *K-nearest neighbours*. This concept is used to recognise patterns in the times series or input variables. Past patterns are codified and stored. The current set of data is then compared with history; similar patterns are extracted from that history and so used to predict what will happen next.
- ❏ *Expert systems* that create rules to explain how an "expert" thinks, of the type, "If X happens, followed by Y, then buy dollars". (In order to create rule-based systems, it is necessary to interview or observe such an expert so that the rule set can be created, although it is possible for expert systems to be created through "learning" from past data.)

The processing and estimation of the advanced techniques above can be a little opaque: it can be difficult to understand and direct what is going on within the process, just as it is hard to understand exactly the mechanism of how a human brain is processing and analysing data. Therefore such processes tend to be used as pure black boxes.

Two sets of techniques that have not been included here are technical trading models and risk modelling (or dynamic hedging), which are discussed in "Dimension 4: Source of Alpha". Both rely more on the time series of the exchange rate itself than on external variables.

There is always a danger, when estimating models, of "data-mining", whereby a model learns the history too effectively, merely fitting the past with no thought as to whether it will represent the future. Data-mining occurs when models are "overoptimised" with variables and coefficients fitted to produce fantastic historic simulations, but are not necessarily of any use going forwards. This danger is particularly acute with more opaque systems such as neural networks or other black-box techniques.

Of course there is no point creating a systematic process that does not make money historically, so there is a difficult balance to be achieved. At this point, maximising the extraction of information from data while minimising overfitting is where model development becomes as much an art as a science and the full skill and experience of the researcher is required.

DIMENSION 4: SOURCE OF ALPHA

What are the possible ways of making returns from currency management? Figure 1 shows a "taxonomy of currency managers",

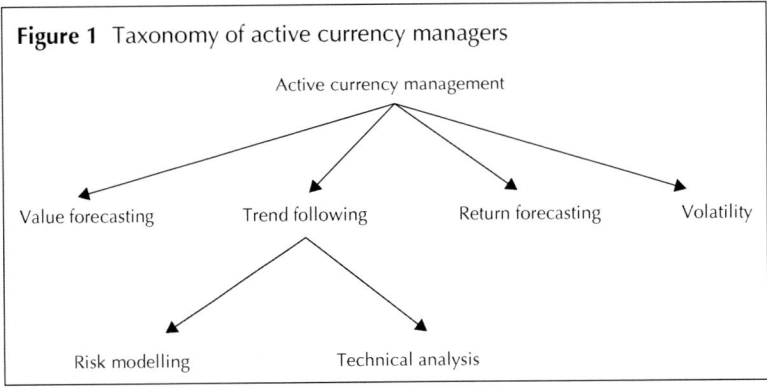

Figure 1 Taxonomy of active currency managers

the nodes of which will be explained on the following pages. The objective of the taxonomy is to group together trading models that seek to exploit similar sources of excess return and so have correlated returns.

First, "value forecasting". This type of assessment can be found in economics textbooks – usually related to "purchasing-power parity" (PPP) and its variations. Essentially, PPP states that goods purchased in one currency should cost the same in another currency – if they don't, then the currency should move to correct the price difference. As a result, a theoretical fair value – or equilibrium level – can be computed, which the exchange rate is assumed to revert towards.

The most popularly known variant of the theory is the Big Mac index, published annually in *The Economist*. In this analysis *The Economist* compares the price of the McDonald's Big Mac in different currencies, the theory being that the product is the same wherever it is purchased and so should cost the same. The analysis is slightly tongue-in-cheek and, by the compilers' own admission, ignores several important factors, but it has proved surprisingly accurate: for instance, it signalled that the dollar was significantly overvalued in April 2002, and the dollar fell sharply in the months following. Dori Levanoni and Max Darnell showed in a First Quadrant research paper (1999) that it is possible to add value using the Big Mac index as the only input to an investment process.

As an example of a very basic form of PPP, Figure 2 shows how the dollar has evolved against the euro (using Deutschemark prior

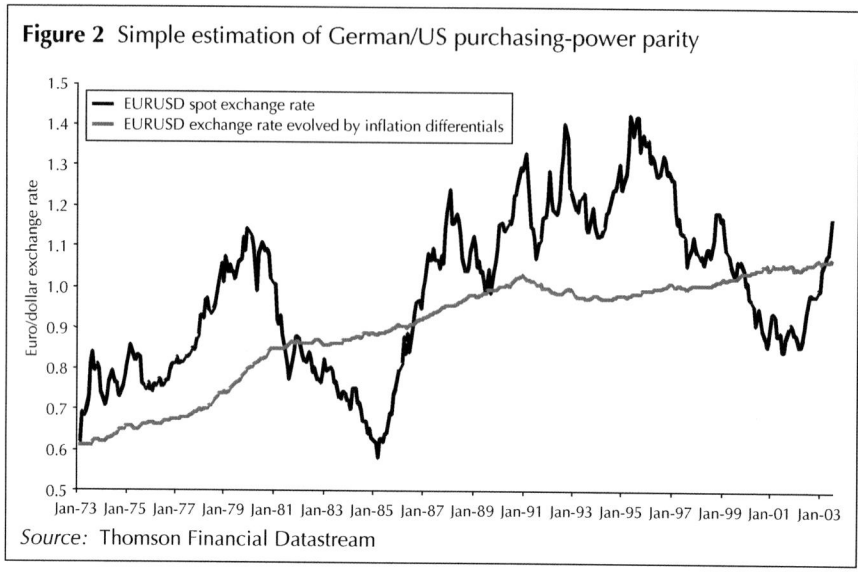

Figure 2 Simple estimation of German/US purchasing-power parity

Source: Thomson Financial Datastream

to 1999) since 1973 and how it would have evolved if it merely reflected the differentials between Germany and US CPI. This is clearly a very basic form of PPP and starting-point-dependent. However, it is evident that the two lines cross several times and that the drift in direction is the same (ie, strengthening euro/ Deutschmark together with lower German inflation – with a cumulative difference of over 75%), indicating that the exchange rate does revert to the expected level. However, it is also evident that there are significant deviations that can last for sustained periods.

It is certainly possible to refine PPP: for instance, adjusting for productivity differentials as well as inflation differentials. An alternative method of calculating equilibrium levels is to calculate the fundamental equilibrium exchange rate (FEER) that is consistent with internal and external macroeconomic balance – that is full employment and low inflation together with a sustainable current account balance. The calculation of FEERs has been described by John Williamson (1994).

As Figure 2 shows, ultimately currencies do usually move to equilibrium levels. The problem is that such moves can wait a long time to occur and patience is required if portfolios are positioned to benefit from such "value management". For instance, many commentators insisted that the euro was undervalued during 2000 and 2001; it was not until 2002, however, that such analysis began to be reflected in the market, as the euro rose back through parity against the US dollar. Froot and Rogoff (1994) examined the empirical evidence for PPP, showing that a typical half-life of deviations from fair value was about four years (implying that it takes four years for half of the over/undervaluation to be reversed).

The next type of return source on the taxonomy diagram is "trend following". Sometimes the moves in currency markets seem to take on a life of their own and the easiest way to make money is merely to follow the trend – spawning such phrases as "the trend is your friend". While there is some evidence that the degree of trending is less than it used to be (see Binny, 1998), it is still a successful way of making money from exchange rate moves.

Do trends exist? Early academic analysis found it hard to dismiss the hypothesis of a random walk for exchange rates. The existence of trends was denied, as exchange rates were shown to have low levels of serial correlation and trend-following processes were viewed as somehow intellectually inferior. However, over the last 10 to 15 years, there have been a series of studies showing that trend-following strategies can make money. For instance, a paper by Levich and Thomas (1999) concluded that simple trend-following processes could add value.

The third source of alpha from the taxonomy is return forecasting. Such forecasts focus on the factors that drive currencies using factors other than the price series themselves. To an extent one might expect such strategies to be grouped with the value style, as that also uses more fundamental data. However, the objective of the taxonomy was to group together styles or sources of return that are correlated – and return forecasting is not necessarily correlated with value management. Quite often the forces driving exchange rates, which are picked up by return forecaster over the short to medium term, can actually be driving exchange rates away from fair value.

One very well-known anomaly that such strategies seek to exploit is known as the "forward-rate bias", which was described in a paper by Mark Kritzman (1999). This involves buying high-interest-rate currencies and selling low-interest-rate currencies in the forward market – benefiting from the "carry". Historically, this has achieved remarkably stable returns.

The forward-rate bias should work even if the spot exchange rate behaved as a random walk. This is because the price of a forward is set according to short-term interest rates – it is not a forecast of the future path of the exchange rate. (If this were not the case, it would be possible to borrow in one currency, transfer the money into the other currency at the spot exchange rate, place a deposit in that currency and eliminate currency risk in the forward foreign exchange market – but locking in the interest rate differential.) As a result, it is possible to buy high-interest-rate currencies at a discount in the forward market and so, if the spot exchange rate remains stable, profit as time advances and maturity nears, and the original forward date becomes the spot date.

There are many other inputs that return forecasting models use, such as relative economic growth rates and what is happening in equity and bond markets. In addition, a source of information can be the foreign exchange market itself (and its derivatives): for instance, there has been an increasing interest in recent years in looking at market flows and investor positioning data as a guide to future direction.

The last source of alpha does not seek to benefit directly from forecasting the directions of foreign exchange rates. Rather, it focuses on another moment of FX returns: volatility. This can be traded through the options market. It is possible to trade volatility in a variety of ways, which, as with all sources of alpha, can be more or less systematic. For example:

❏ trading the implied volatility of options against the actual volatility that is experienced: by buying an option if implied volatility is too low (so options too cheap) and delta-hedging (to eliminate directional risk), or by selling an option and delta-hedging, if implied volatility is too high.
❏ trading different strike prices and expiries in the same currency pair against each other.
❏ trading exotic options against vanilla options.

The main advantage of such non-directional strategies is that there is not necessarily any correlation with other, more directional, strategies.

In the taxonomy we have broken "trend following" down further into "risk modelling" and "technical analysis". At first glance, it may not seem obvious that these two sorts of managers should be grouped together, as different reasoning drives their currency positions. However, the reasons for their similarity should become apparent as their operation is described.

Technical managers examine the time-series of the rate being forecast, for the most part trying to exploit trends to create profits. Originally, most technical analysis was based on the visual analysis of charts of prices. The invention and ubiquitous presence of the personal computer, however, has made it possible for more systematic trading rules to be created using the same time-series data. Although clearly related, it is still possible to separate technical analysis into the two camps: the first can loosely be described as pattern recognition; the second is based on mathematical formulae of the time series.

Pattern recognition assumes that the market has a memory and that price patterns that have existed in the past will be replicated in the future – identifying channels, lines of support and resistance, and patterns such as "head and shoulders" to signal reversals of trend. Most pattern recognition tends to be based on traditional chartist techniques, interpreted by skilled and experienced experts. It has also been more formalised in techniques such as Elliot waves and Fibonacci and Gann analysis – but these still, in my experience, require a fair amount of skill in interpretation.

Some techniques have been used to recognise patterns automatically such as K-nearest neighbours and expert systems. As described in "Dimension 3: Modelling Technique", when using K-nearest neighbours, the current pattern, or series of patterns, is codified and then compared with periods in history to see where similar patterns occurred previously. Expert systems are rule based attempts to replicate the logic of an "expert", who must be interviewed, or observed, in order to distil that logic.

The second form of technical analysis, using mathematical formulae, has become increasingly complex as the power of personal computers has increased and data availability has increased. This has enabled everyone, from nuclear physics PhDs to bored traders, to start developing trading systems using price data. However, the basic task behind most systems is to capture trends while avoiding losing money from other environments. One of the most simple of these techniques is a moving-average strategy, which is used as an illustration with euro/dollar in 2002 on the following page.

CURRENCY MANAGEMENT: OVERLAY AND ALPHA TRADING

A simple moving average strategy works as follows.

- ❏ calculate the average of the last N days' prices.
- ❏ calculate a shorter-term average over the last n days.
- ❏ compare the long-term average with the short-term average.
- ❏ if the short-term average is above the long-term average, then buy.
- ❏ alternatively, if the short-term average is below the long-term one, then sell.

This will work if and when the current price has moved above (below) the moving average, it continues to rise (fall). Therefore, this is a very simple trend-following strategy. Figures 3 and 4 show how the strategy would have performed for euro/dollar in the second quarter of 2002 – using N as 40, and n as 5 – when there was a clear trend. Figure 3 shows how the spot, two moving averages and position (+/− 100%) evolved; figure 4 shows the cumulative profit generated. As the euro rose, so the short-term moving average moved above the longer one and so a long position was taken. The move continued strongly for the rest of the quarter – clearly a successful strategy: the trend was captured effectively.

However, such a process can detract value under other environments. Moving-average strategies suffer from two environments in particular: when a market becomes overextended and snaps back, and, worse, during a period of range-trading ("whipsaw" market). Figures 5 and 6 show a classic "whipsaw" market: the quarter following on from the last example (the third quarter of 2002). In this case, more value is detracted during this period than was added in the previous quarter as the process buys high and sells low.

Therefore two simple filter rules are added to the simulation.

First of all, a filter rule to deal with the issue of extremes: in the simulation, the position is set to neutral if the spot exchange rate exceeds the 40-day moving average by more than six daily standard deviations.

The second filter rule attempts to avoid the whipsaw environments by moving to a neutral position if the direction of the 40-day moving average is not in the same direction as the position. The results are shown in Figure 7. The difficult period, while not eliminated is substantially reduced.

If we look over the entire 2002 (the results can be seen in Figure 8) the information ratio has risen from 0.51 with the simple strategy, to

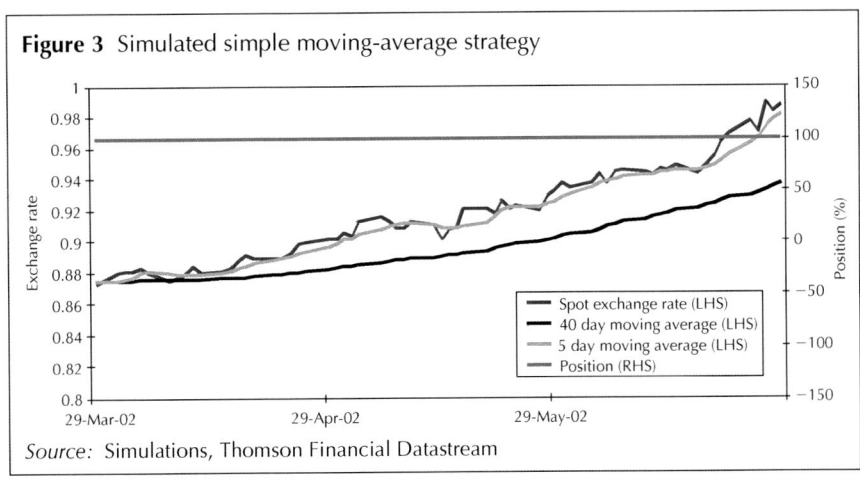

Figure 3 Simulated simple moving-average strategy

Source: Simulations, Thomson Financial Datastream

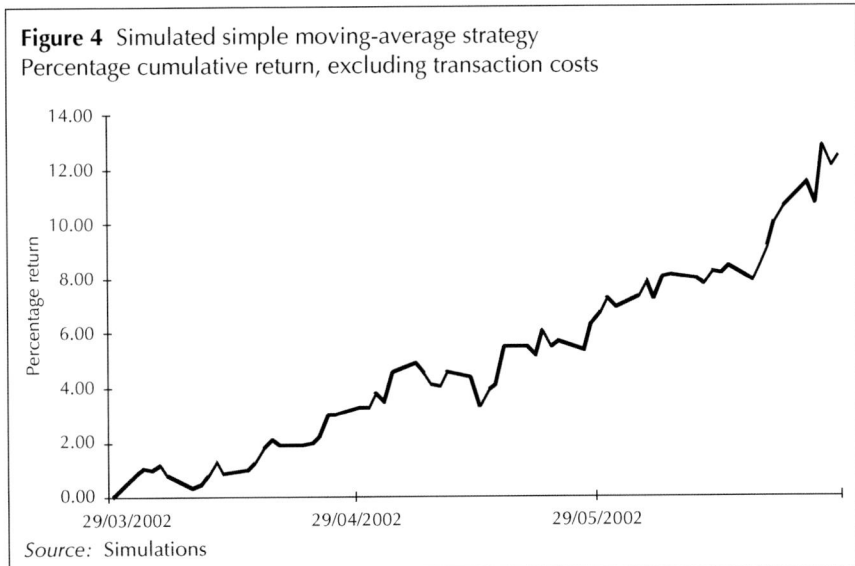

Figure 4 Simulated simple moving-average strategy
Percentage cumulative return, excluding transaction costs

Source: Simulations

0.63 with the avoidance of extreme moves, and 0.92 with the whipsaw filter added as well – a very respectable information ratio for most currency managers, especially if just trading a single currency pair! This simple moving-average and filter strategy is clearly very naive. However, it is probably impossible to eliminate all whipsaw trading – merely minimise the impact.

As discussed earlier, data-mining is always a danger of which a developer of trading models should be aware. This is particularly

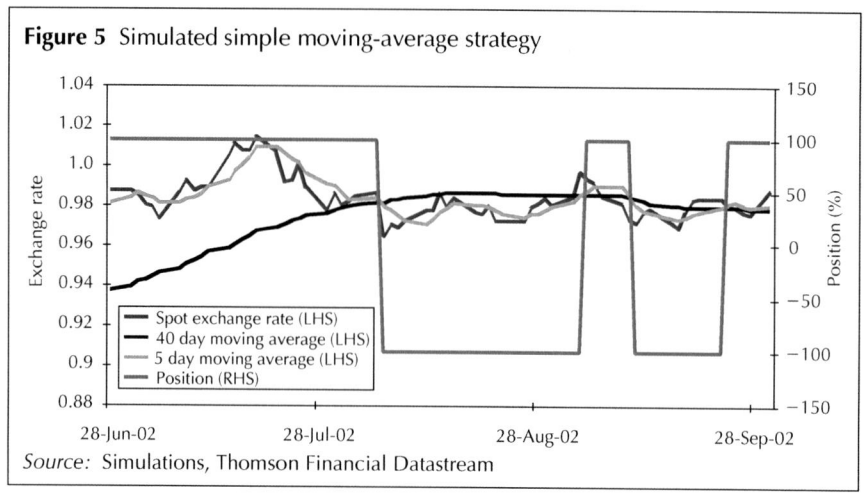

Figure 5 Simulated simple moving-average strategy

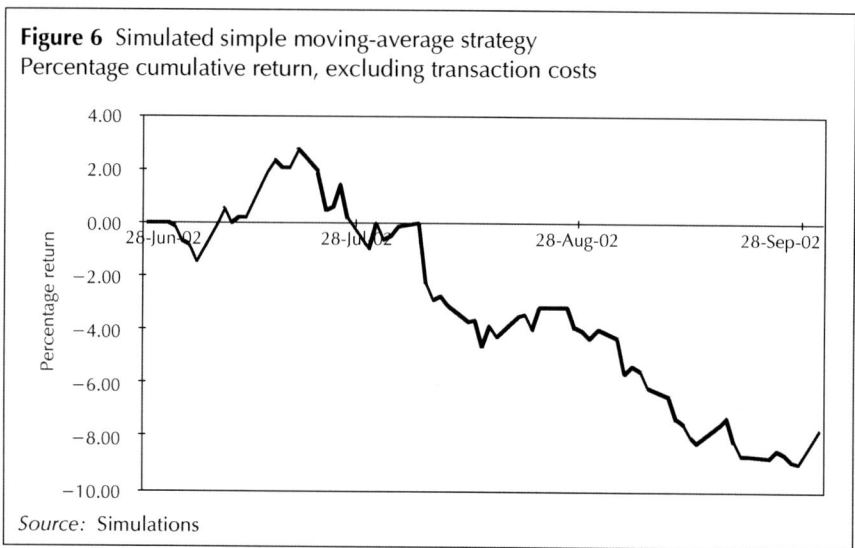

Figure 6 Simulated simple moving-average strategy
Percentage cumulative return, excluding transaction costs

true with technical trading rules. It is easy to overoptimise such trading rules so that they make money in historical simulations, but are ineffective going forward. With the bored trader mentioned earlier, finessing trading rules on their PC, this is potentially an issue. However, it is also a danger with the PhD who is creating sophisticated trading rules using the latest techniques adapted from nuclear physics but with little knowledge of the underlying market or trading experience. One advantage that the trader has is

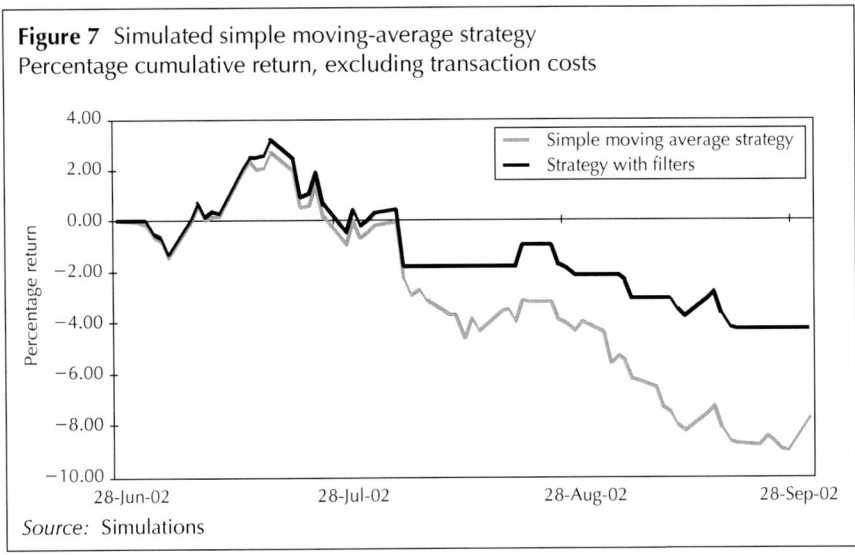

Figure 7 Simulated simple moving-average strategy
Percentage cumulative return, excluding transaction costs

Source: Simulations

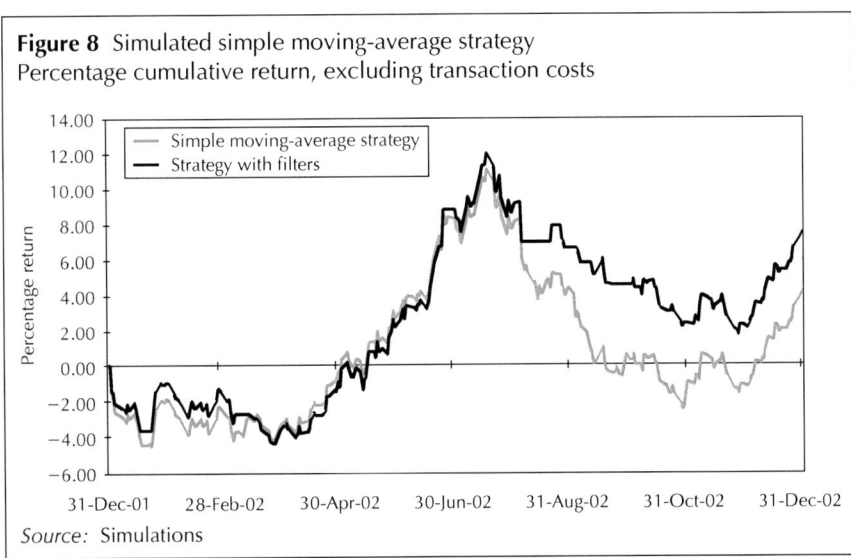

Figure 8 Simulated simple moving-average strategy
Percentage cumulative return, excluding transaction costs

Source: Simulations

that, with time, they will gain experience as it becomes apparent that the overoptimised rules frequently lose money and impact their profit and loss. Perhaps the ideal combination is an experienced trader who also has a PhD in nuclear physics!

It would be easy to argue that the rules described for euro/dollar were previously overoptimised over too short a time period,

CURRENCY MANAGEMENT: OVERLAY AND ALPHA TRADING

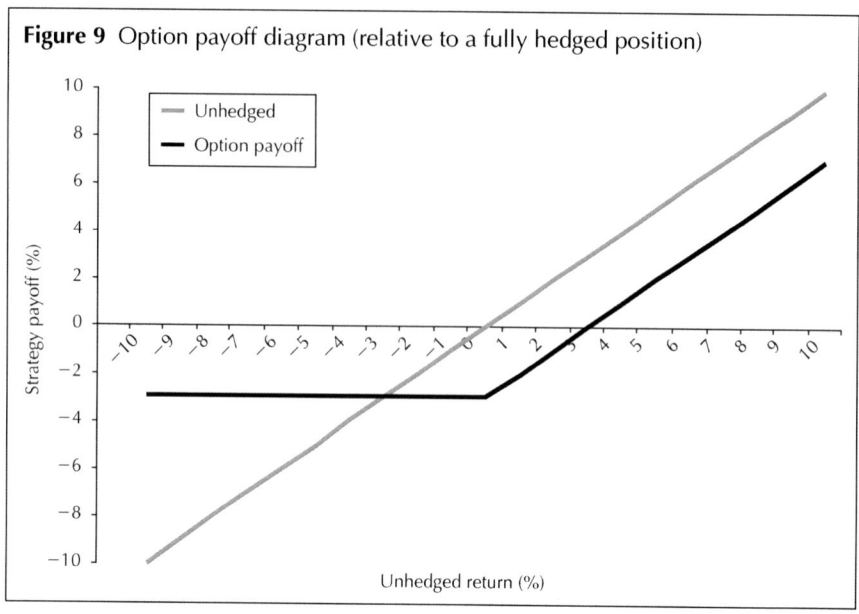

Figure 9 Option payoff diagram (relative to a fully hedged position)

and there should be a caution against using them directly. They were a useful illustration, however, that such processes benefit from trends while suffering from other environments.

The other type of trend-following process that was in the taxonomy was risk modelling. This is a very popular technique used in currency overlay and is also known as dynamic hedging. There are now many variations of the process, used by various different overlay providers. However, most risk-modelling processes have their beginnings in option replication – even if the processes have been subsequently considerably enhanced. The original rationale for such a process was not so much driven by a desire to generate return directly: the objective was, rather, to manage the risk implicit in currency exposures; risk for this purpose is described as downside risk relative to a benchmark.

The objective of simple risk modelling is to limit the downside (relative to a benchmark) when the exchange moves in the wrong direction, while participating in the upside when the exchange rate moves in the right direction. This generates a "dogleg" payoff similar to that of an option. The option payoff diagram is displayed in Figure 9. This shows that, when the unhedged return is positive (right hand side), a significant amount of upside is captured; when the unhedged return is negative, then the downside is limited (the strategy merely loses the cost of purchasing the option). Figure 9 also shows the return that would be gained from a simple unhedged strategy.

Although the original rationale was to control risk, the process can still add value. To understand why, consider two consecutive periods where a foreign currency first falls 10% and then rises 10%. Assume that base interest rates remain 1% below foreign interest rates, giving a fully hedged return of −1%. Assume that the risk model is working with a fully hedged benchmark (so aiming to limit the amount that can be lost due to currency) with a "floor" (worst-case underperformance) of −3%. As we can see from Figure 9, the returns from an efficiently replicated option (adjusting for the fully hedged cost) would be as follows:

Period 1:

- unhedged currency return: −10%,
- fully hedged currency return: −1%
- risk model return: −4%

Period 2:

- unhedged currency rises: +10%
- fully hedged return: −1%
- risk model return: +6%

Therefore the combined return over the total period:

- unhedged return: (1 − 10%) * (1 + 10%) = −1.00%
- fully hedged return: (1 − 1%) * (1 − 1%) = −1.99%
- risk model return: (1 − 4%) * (1 + 6%) = +1.76%

In this simplistic example, the risk model has outperformed not only the fully hedged benchmark, but also the unhedged position. Therefore, at its simplest, by aiming to protect investors from the adverse effects of large currency moves while benefiting from the large positive moves, risk modelling adds value.

The above example was effectively replicating a fully hedged position combined with buying a call option on the foreign currency – that is, participating when foreign currencies rise (the option matures in-the-money), while providing a floor when they fall (the underperformance caused by the cost of the option). However, when risk modelling is used to generate return as well as minimise risks, it is necessary to make profits when foreign currencies fall as well as when they rise. Therefore, the synthetic call position needs to be combined with a synthetic put, so that profits can be made whatever the direction of movement in foreign exchange – effectively creating a synthetic straddle.

An investor makes money from holding a long-option position if the payoff from the option exceeds the premium paid for the option. Similarly, the simple example of risk modelling worked because there was a significant move in the exchange rate – the move was sufficient to compensate the investor for the cost of the synthetic option. This is one of the rationales for using risk modelling: the moves that a client needs to be protected or benefit from are the "big moves". For example, the dollar falling over the last year or the euro falling subsequent to its launch in 1999. Such "big moves" are also the medium-term trends that many technical managers are looking for, so the two styles tend to be correlated. To examine further why the styles are correlated, consider how the process is implemented.

Most risk models are implemented using forwards rather than physical options, using variations on delta hedging to replicate the payoff. This reflects one of the insights of the original Black–Scholes pricing formula – the fact that an option can be replicated using linear instruments. This is achieved by calculating what the delta of an option (with a strike price set so as to achieve the desired minimum return) would be. The delta is the sensitivity of the value of the option to moves in the market. For instance, if trying to replicate a call option on foreign currencies:

❑ to match the delta of the (theoretical) option, buy enough foreign currency so as to give the portfolio the same sensitivity as the option – for instance for a USD 100 million foreign currency exposure, with a desired delta of 40%, buy USD 40 million of the foreign currency.
❑ as the foreign currency rises, the option would become more in-the-money and as it becomes more in-the-money, so the delta rises; similarly, as the foreign currency rises, the delta hedger must buy more foreign currency so as to increase its sensitivity (to match the delta).

❏ conversely, as the foreign currency falls, the delta of the option would fall; therefore the delta hedger must decrease the sensitivity to the foreign currency by selling it.

It is necessary to have some "trading rules", to indicate how frequently to trade – the theoretical option's delta will change for every small move in the market, but it is not possible for the delta hedger to trade continuously. However, the same basic fact will remain: as the foreign currency rises, the delta hedger will buy foreign currency; as the foreign currency falls, the delta hedger will sell. This is clearly a trend-following strategy and therefore correlated with technical analysis.

We have enumerated four main classes of extracting value from the foreign exchange rate market: value forecasting, trend following, return forecasting and volatility forecasting. Over the fullness of time all individual styles should add value. However, over the short term, there will inevitably be times when individual styles underperform. It makes sense for an investor who is starting currency overlay, or a fund of currency hedge funds, to employ a selection of managers with different styles in order to exploit all the opportunities – for instance, don't employ two trend followers and assume that manager diversification has been achieved!

SUMMARY

It is possible to categorise currency trading models (or investment processes) along the four dimensions of a hypercube: time horizon, degree of judgement, modelling technique and, most importantly, source of alpha. Within each dimension there are a variety of possible nodes. Ideally, when combining managers, as many nodes on each dimension should be populated as possible (whether by multiple managers or by a single manager), thereby occupying as many of the constituent hypercubes as possible.

REFERENCES

Baldridge, J., B. Meath, and H. Myers, 2000, "Capturing Alpha Through Active Currency Overlay", Russell Research Commentary, May.

Binny, J., 1998, "Evolution of the Foreign Exchange", IFE Conference Papers, October.

Froot, K. A., and K. Rogoff, 1994, "Perspectives on PPP and Long-Run Real Exchange Rates", NBER Working Paper (4952).

Kritzman, M., 1999, "The Forward Rate Bias", AIMR Conference Proceedings.

Levanoni, D., and M. Darnell, 1999, "Purchasing Power Parity: Even the Big Mac Index Works!", First Quadrant Research Paper, October.

Levich, R., and L. Thomas, 1999, "The Significance of Technical Trading-Rule Profits in the Foreign Exchange Markets: A Bootstrap Approach", *Journal of International Money and Finance*, October.

Strange, B., 1998, "Currency Overlay Managers Show Consistency", *Pensions and Investment*, June 15.

Williamson, J., 1994, "Estimating Equilibrium Exchange Rates", Institute for International Economics, September.

12

Model Building and Testing

Gerben J. de Zwart

Robeco Quantitative Research

INTRODUCTION

When building a trading model one will be confronted with a wide variety of problems and pitfalls. The purpose of this chapter is not to provide a perfect trading model but to present a method that could be used for building and testing a model in the search for the ideal currency-trading model. To this effect this author will first present some fundamental questions that should be answered before building a model in the section entitled *Research Set-up*. The following section addresses the data characteristics that are relevant for model building and performance evaluation. Under *Testing FX Trading Models* we discuss the set-up of a trading model test. We conclude the chapter with a case study that illustrates the foregoing theory.

It is important to realise that currency modelling is different from the modelling of other pricing processes in finance such as stock selection or asset allocation. The reason for this is that currency prices are always relative prices: the purchasing power of one currency is denominated in another currency. This implies that a single currency has many prices. The euro (EUR), for instance has a price in Great Britain pounds (GBP), EUR/GBP, but also in US dollars (USD), EUR/USD, or in Chinese yuan (CNY), EUR/CNY, etc. It is therefore impossible to speak about *the* value of the euro or to buy/sell *the* euro.

The author would like to thank Sible Andela for his help in the empirical analyses and Patrick Houweling, Olaf Penninga, Ernesto Sanichar and David Uljee for their helpful comments and suggestions.

RESEARCH SET-UP

Several fundamental questions need to be answered at the start of the model-building process. The aim of this section is to present four issues that should be taken into account at the start:

- What does a trading model predict?
- What is the optimal trading frequency?
- What is the base currency?
- Which trading strategy could we use?

Focus on returns

An important question is: what should the trading model predict? Modelling the future spot level of the exchange rate seems to be the obvious answer. Unfortunately, the spot rate time series does not follow a stationary process. Broadly speaking, this means that the mean, volatility or autocorrelations are not constant over time. A stationary series tends to return to its mean and the variability of the series does not alter as we move through time.

The non-stationarity of the spot rate can be formally tested (see Baillie and Bollerslev, 1989), or intuitively illustrated: the average spot rate of the EUR/USD for the 1998–2002 period (0.989) is obviously different from the average spot rate for the 1993–7 period (1.238).[1] The standard regression modelling techniques are capable of dealing only with stationary time series. The distribution of conventional test statistics may not be well behaved for a non-stationary time series. In the case that we would have used the spot rates there are two potential problems. Firstly, the model would be sensitive for structural changes that fall outside the scope of the model. Secondly, there is a risk that the statistics suggest a good fit although in reality there is no relation (spurious relations). We conclude that it is problematic to predict non-stationary spot rates.

Modelling exchange-rate returns overcomes the problem of the non-stationarity of the spot rates. In general, the exchange-rate returns show more signs of stationarity and are therefore useful for modelling.

Investment horizon and trading frequency

The next issue is the selection of the optimal trading frequency. The currency market seems to be characterised by trends on each desired time horizon, just like fractals. This is illustrated in Figure 1, which shows the shape of the EUR/USD spot rate for three different data frequencies: 24 hours for the one-minute basis (1,440 observations), 48 hours for the five-minute basis (576 observations) and 1 year for the daily basis (260 observations).

The most important objective in the selection of the trading frequency is a maximisation of the profit. An important restriction in this optimisation process is the organisation of the trading desk and the investment horizon of the organisation. A high trading frequency requires a sophisticated trading desk that is capable of doing a trade immediately after a new buy or sell signal. Specialised currency overlay managers, hedge fund managers and investment banks are generally capable of employing a high trading frequency. This trading frequency is in line with their relatively short-term investment horizon. Asset managers and institutional investors generally have a longer investment horizon, making their investment process less equipped for very fast execution of trades.

The trading frequency also depends on the data employed to model the currency market. Technical indicators are available for each trading frequency. The trading frequency of macroeconomic trading models will be lower, owing to the fact that these data are available only on, at best, a monthly basis. This makes macroeconomic data a less useful tool for high-frequency traders.

In practice, a lot of hedge funds update their models every 30 minutes. This does not imply that they trade every 30 minutes; they have the opportunity to trade. Generally, institutional investors update their models daily or weekly. The update frequency of currency overlay managers depends on their investment style.

The optimal trading frequency should be a profitable frequency that is more or less in line with the investment horizon and process of the investor.

Base currency
Every investor is based in a certain market and currency. Therefore the concept of the base currency is an important issue. The base currency is the currency used as a basis for all calculations in the portfolio. For example, a US investor has the USD as his base currency and a German investor has the EUR as his base currency.

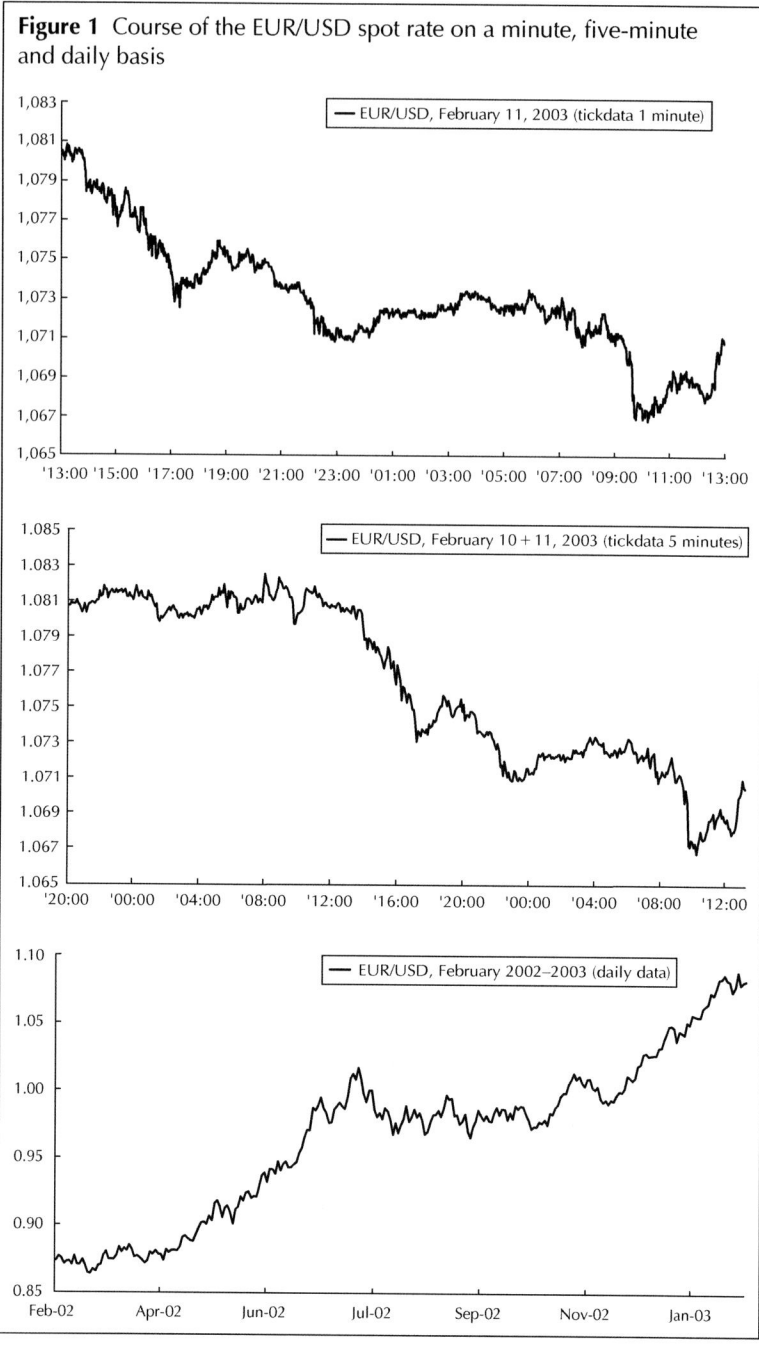

Figure 1 Course of the EUR/USD spot rate on a minute, five-minute and daily basis

As already mentioned in the introduction, a currency price is always a relative price: the purchasing power of one currency is denominated in another currency. Most investors watch closely the movements of all currencies relative to their base currency and use models to predict the return. The consequence is that the currency portfolio of two worldwide investors with different base currencies differs. For example, a US investor is interested in the USD/JPY, USD/EUR and the USD/GBP, while a German investor is interested in the EUR/JPY, EUR/USD and the EUR/GBP.

The EUR/JPY is called a *currency cross* for the US investor. A currency cross is the implied exchange rate between two currencies that is derived from the two exchange rates with the base currency. For instance, the EUR/JPY spot rate is equal to the USD/JPY spot rate divided by the USD/EUR spot rate. This shows that the portfolios of the German and the US investor are not as independent as suggested. The high liquidity of the currency market ensures that crosses are fairly priced. Most investors do not invest in crosses, although we remark that a position in two currency pairs can be an unnoticed position in a cross. For instance, a short position in the EUR/JPY and a long position in the EUR/USD is a short position in the USD/JPY. With the concept of this example, it is also possible to create a synthetic position in a cross in the case that an investor is allowed to invest in the currency pairs only with his base currency.

A special group of participants in the currency-exchange market are the central banks. Most central banks are extremely interested in the general movement of their own currency. To measure the movement of their currency in a single measure, they have developed trade-weighted or effective exchange-rate indices. These indices measure the average value of the currency against a basket of other currencies relative to a base year. Obviously, the used weights in the average are important for the final value of the exchange rate. As an overall measure, effective exchange rates provide a good measure of the competitive position of a country and could be a guide as to what extent a currency may be overvalued. Trade-weighted indices are considered a useful information source but not as an investment vehicle.

Just as currency portfolios can differ for different base currencies, the returns can also differ. When the euro was introduced in 1999, it was valued at 1.18 USD. By a year it had depreciated 14.4% against the USD to 1.01. During the same year the dollar appreciated 16.8% from 0.847 to 0.990. This single observation illustrates the asymmetry in exchange-rate returns and is a feature of Siegel's paradox. This paradox is well described in Kritzman (2000).

Siegel's paradox refers to the mathematical fact that the expectation of the reciprocal of an exchange rate is greater than the reciprocal of the expectation of the exchange rate, or in a formula:

$$E\left(\frac{1}{S}\right) > \frac{1}{E(S)}$$

with spot rate S and expectation E.

This equation implies that an increase in the exchange rate is in the perspective of the domestic investor a smaller decrease in the perspective of the foreign investor. This is a generalisation of the asymmetric feature of foreign-exchange rates. The common way of avoiding Siegel's paradox is to define all exchange rates in logarithms, s_t. By definition it holds that:

$$s_t = \log(S_t) = -\log\left(\frac{1}{S_t}\right).$$

An intensive discussion of the calculation of the returns is presented in the next paragraph.

Trading model

The final issue is the selection of the trading model. Several empirical studies have found that fundamental models tend to perform poorly, particularly over short-term periods. See, for example, Meese and Rogoff (1983) or Frankel and Rose (1995). Due to the fact that most investors are evaluated over relatively short time frames, many market participants favour shorter-term forecasting models. We discuss five forecasting approaches that can be used as a trading model: trend-following models, interest-rate differential, risk appetite, position data and flows, and volatility.

Trend-following models are the most commonly used models to forecast the currency-exchange market. Trend-following models generate currency forecasts by extrapolating past sequences of currency market movements into the future. They all have in common that they seek to identify the direction in which a trend is heading. The moving-average trading rule is an example of a trend-following strategy and will be discussed in the case study of this chapter. For a good long-term performance track record, prolonged exchange-rate upswings and downswings must occur frequently to overcome the losses generated when currency movements are not highly trended. Several papers conclude that it is possible to make significant profits with trend-following models (see, among others, Levich and Thomas, 1993; LeBaron, 1999; Sullivan, Timmerman and White, 1999). Pedersen and De Zwart (2003) give an explanation for the good performance of trend-following models.

The interest-rate differential strategy or forward-rate bias is also a model commonly used. The concept of the strategy is that investors benefit from overweighting currencies that trade at a forward discount and underweighting currencies that trade at a forward premium. The same strategy is to buy the highest-yielding currencies in the developed world and to sell the lowest-yielding currencies. Fama (1984), Baz, Breedon, Naik and Peress (2001) and Ilmanen and Sayood (2002) all report a good performance for the forward-rate bias models.

The risk-appetite model is a strategy that is based on the assumption that currency values could be affected by shifts in investors' overall appetite to take on risky positions. During periods of high risk aversion, investors tend to reduce their exposure to risky investments and during periods of low risk aversion investors tend to increase their exposure to risky investments. Certain currencies are more vulnerable than others during risk-averse periods. Countries that run large current-account deficits or have a high short-term interest rate might see their currencies weaken if capital is withdrawn during a period of high risk aversion. Examples of risk-aversion indicators are the high-yield bond spread or the emerging-markets bond spread. Several authors have analysed the risk-appetite model (see, among others, Persaud, 1996; Brousseau and Scacciavillani, 1999; Misina, 2003).

A model that became popular in the late nineties is one that uses institutional investor position and transaction (fund flow) data.

The rationale behind this model is that the currency markets are more and more driven by financial transactions and no longer by physical goods. A way to measure the influence of these financial transactions is to follow fund flows or position data. In general these data are difficult to obtain. A commonly used public data source is the weekly report of the breakdown of the positioning by type of trader for currency futures contracts by the Commodity Futures Trading Commission. These publications are also known as the International Monetary Market (IMM) positions. Furthermore, a lot of investment banks publish a fund flow indicator and sometimes an international mergers and acquisitions index. A point of attention is that flow data are very often a good indicator to explain currency moves but not always a good forecasting tool. The EUR/USD move in 1999 and 2000 could be explained well with the help of flows. Until now, academic papers about position and flow data are scarce. Froot and Ramadorai (2002) show a weak relationship between daily currency flows and excess returns. Evans and Lyons (2002) find that interdealer order flows explain a large part of the daily exchange-rate changes.

Although we focus on the forecasting of currency returns in this chapter, we want to mention that recently quite some attention is given to volatility trading in currency markets. Volatility trading is interesting because it can add value to other trading models. In periods without a clear trend it can become the alpha generating vehicle. The concept of volatility trading is to identify periods where options are over- or undervalued and to implement an option strategy to profit from the over- or underpricing. For instance, the selling or buying of a straddle, the simultaneous purchase or sale of at-the-money put and call options with identical notional and maturities. The use of straddles minimises the effect of an overall trend that would skew the result. Knauf (2003) reported that option selling strategies do seem to work in certain currencies.

Independent of the trading model, the physical transactions take place in individual currency pairs independent of whether a cross-sectional or bilateral model is used for the trade idea. Most practitioners use a bilateral trading model. This means that the trading model is designed to give trading advice for a certain currency pair, eg, EUR/USD. The output of the model is a buy or sell signal for the trading currency (EUR) and an opposite signal for the pricing currency (USD). The trend-following model is a good example of the bilateral model; the other models in this paragraph are mostly converted into a bilateral model. A less commonly used trading model is the cross-sectional model. In a cross-sectional model all currencies are ranked from the most attractive to the least attractive, like a stock-selection model that ranks all individual stocks. The most attractive currencies are bought and the least attractive are sold. A good example of a cross-sectional model is the forward-rate bias model. In a cross-sectional model an investor could always have an active position.

FX DATA CHARACTERISTICS
Currency data collection

Currency data are widely available. Well-known providers are Reuters, Bloomberg and Datastream. These providers are able to deliver the data with different frequencies up to a frequency of several ticks per minute (Reuters and Bloomberg). The providers offer a wide variety of data, including the necessary interest rates, eg, the euro rates, for the backtest of a trade model.

Currency data for most of the G10 currencies are available from 1974. The data before that period are not representative for the current floating exchange rate system, because of the fixed currency rates of the Bretton Woods System before 1974. In December 1971 the Smithsonian Agreement superseded the Bretton Woods system and in 1973 the 10% devaluation of the US dollar was the start of the current floating-exchange-rate system.

At the start of a model test, the question is what data history is representative for the future. Or, stated otherwise, is the past currency market behaviour consistent with the future behaviour for a currency pair? There are two ways to determine the subsets for which a currency pair has the same structure.

A simple method is to use the history books. Several historical events have had a large impact on the currency markets. Some of these events cause a structural break in the history of a currency pair, others not. The influence differs for each currency. A major event was the second oil shock in 1978/9. The huge increase in the oil price was caused by the fall from power of Iran's shah and caused a significant decline in global economic activity. Another major event was the Plaza accord on 22 September 1985. The accord stated an orderly appreciation of the main non-dollar currencies, which meant a serious major devaluation of the USD. This accord impacted all USD currency pairs and has a very positive impact on the performance of trend-following models. Another important event was the European Monetary System (EMS) crisis on 16 September 1992. The EMS was designed to stabilise exchange rates for the members. In 1992 the UK pound and the Italian lira had become overvalued, and on 16 September 1992 (Black Wednesday) both currencies were forced to devalue and to fall out of the EMS. Due to the EMS crisis, the history of the pound before September 1992 is not representative for the period after September 1992. A more recent event was the introduction of the euro on 1 January 1999. The introduction of the euro implies that there is only a limited available history for this currency. A commonly used proxy for the history of the euro is the Deutschmark, because the policy of the European Central Bank is in line with the policy of the Bundes Bank, as mentioned by Malliares (2002). Furthermore, the mark has been one of the most reliable and important European currencies and the mark was also the core currency in the EMS.

Another way to determine the subsets for which a currency pair has the same structure is a statistical structural-break analysis. This analysis should detect structural breaks that may have destroyed past regularities. All structural-break analyses start with an initial hypothesis that will be tested. A structural break in volatility levels could be tested with the help of the modified Levene test, which is also known as the Brown-Forsythe test, a break in the skewness could be tested with the help of D'Agostino's test for skewness and Kurtosis could be evaluated with the Anscombe-Glynn test for kurtosis.

Relevant currency data characteristics

To be able to test the trading models we need to know more about the empirical distribution of currency returns. Table 1 depicts the descriptive statistics for the daily log returns of the three most important currency pairs over the period 1975–2002. We employ the 1975–2002 data because we do not have a clear indication of a structural break for these currency pairs.

Table 1 shows that the characteristics of each individual currency are different. The Jarque-Bera test is a test for normality. One important resemblance is the three high Jarque-Bera statistics, which are highly significant, suggesting that the log returns are not normally distributed for all currency pairs. This is mainly caused by the so-called fat tails (kurtosis) of the distribution. For instance the −7.05% return of the USD/JPY was due to the sudden appreciation of the yen in October 1998 because hedge funds and other yen borrowers closed out yen carry trades. As an illustration of the fat tails, Figure 2 depicts the daily log returns for the EUR/USD and a three-standard-deviation band. According to the normal

Table 1 Data characteristics of the EUR/USD, USD/JPY and GBP/USD over the period 1975–2002

Statistic	EUR/USD	USD/JPY	GBP/USD
Mean	0.003%	−0.013%	−0.006%
Maximum	4.01%	4.85%	4.67%
Minimum	−5.25%	−7.05%	−3.87%
Standard deviation	0.66%	0.66%	0.60%
Skewness	0.05	−0.60	−0.04
Kurtosis	5.73	9.09	6.80
Jarque-Bera	2226	11502	4330

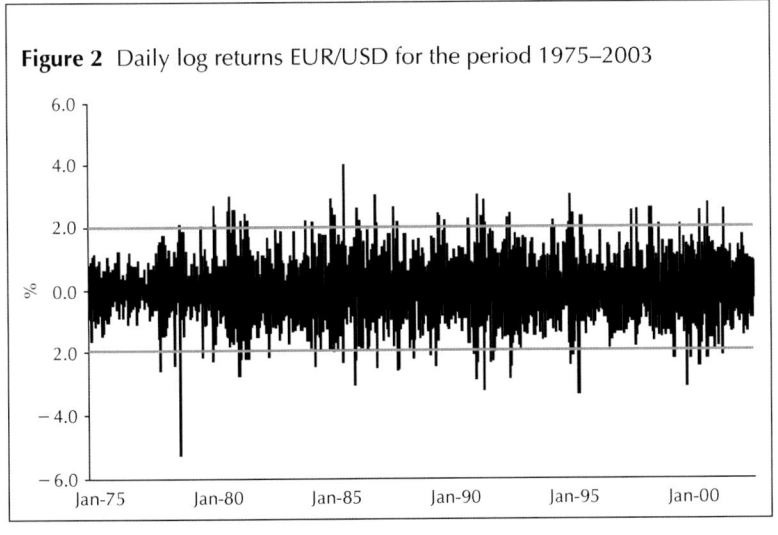

Figure 2 Daily log returns EUR/USD for the period 1975–2003

distribution one could expect 0.26% of all observations to be outside this three-standard-deviation range. Figure 2 shows that there are 55 observations above the three-standard-deviations line and 43 observations below the minus-three-standard-deviation line. This corresponds to 1.3% of all observations.

The currency markets are also notorious for their volatility clustering or volatility persistence. This means that large changes in return series tend to be followed by more large changes, and small changes tend to be followed by more small changes as can be observed in Figure 2. In either case the sign of the change from one period to the next is more difficult to predict. The volatility persistence has some forecasting power, ie, the current volatility will be comparable to the volatility of tomorrow.

TESTING FX TRADING MODELS

The quality of a trading model can be tested with statistical models or with trading strategies. A statistical model estimates the future return with the help of a statistical model, for instance a linear-regression model, a time-series model, a Bayesian model or a neural network. The model specification is important for a statistical-model approach. The modelling complexity is often very high and the model is a black box for most users. The trading-strategy approach involves the backtest of an investment strategy based on the trading model. We prefer to test a trading model with the last approach because in our experience, simple rules remain the most efficient and give the user the best insight and confidence in the model. This section gives an overview of the set-up of the trading strategy and the most important performance evaluation criteria.

Trading set-up

Most trading models give a directional signal for a currency pair. This signal could, for example, vary between a strong buy $(++)$, buy $(+)$, neutral (0), sell $(-)$ or strong sell $(--)$. The source of the signal could be a single trading model, as discussed in the section on trading models above, or a combination of models. For an optimal trade implementation of the signals there are four features that need to be set: timing the entry, defining the stop-loss, timing the exit and timing the re-entry.

The easy part of the trading set up is the timing of the entry of a trade. It seems logical to start a trade after a signal change. The exit of a trade is more difficult. The obvious way to exit a trade is after a signal change. However, it is also possible to exit each trade after a certain time period, eg, one week. By introducing a stop-loss level the possibility is created to exit a trade before a signal change or certain time period because the trade is loss-making. The use of a stop-loss rule could reduce the loss. A commonly used stop-loss rule is to set stops as a percentage of the entry level with the help of the historical volatility of the exchange rate:

$$S_{stop\ level} = (1 - \lambda \sigma_t) S_{entry\ level} \quad \text{for a long position}$$
$$S_{stop\ level} = (1 + \lambda \sigma_t) S_{entry\ level} \quad \text{for a short position}$$

In this context σ_t is the spot rate volatility and λ is a multiplier for the volatility. The stop-loss rule could be made more complex by moving the stop level to lock in profits. A problem of a stop-loss rule is that it is possible to exit a position while the trend is still intact. Therefore we need a re-entry rule to re-enter the old trade after an exit of a trade. A good re-entry rule enables a model to profit from long trends. An example of a re-entry rule is to re-enter the trade if the current spot rate is higher than the last stop level of the spot rate for a long trade or if the current spot rate is lower than the last stop level for a short trade.

Stop-loss and re-entry rules make the trade modelling more complex and therefore more sensitive to data mining. A good strategy should work with only the entry timing and exit timing. A stop-loss and re-entry rule in general reduces profits in back-tests, though it may be needed for other reasons. In general, a stop-loss rule will increase the number of trades.

Performance calculation

The evaluation of a trading model is based on its performance. This section deals with the determination of the returns.

The payoff for an active position is the daily return on the spot rate adjusted for the interest differential between the currency pairs. The interest adjusted return, R_t, depends on the current spot rate, S_t, and the past forward rate, F_{t-1}, and is defined as follows:

$$R_t = \frac{S_t}{F_{t-1}} - 1, \quad \text{with } F_{t-1} = S_{t-1} \frac{1 + \text{Interest}_{t-1}^{\text{pricingcurrency}}}{1 + \text{Interest}_{t-1}^{\text{tradingcurrency}}}.$$

We prefer to calculate the statistics on the log daily interest adjusted returns, r_t:

$$r_t = \ln(S_t) - \ln(S_{t-1}) + \ln\left(1 + \text{Interest}_{t-1}^{\text{pricingcurrency}}\right) \\ - \ln\left(1 + \text{Interest}_{t-1}^{\text{tradingcurrency}}\right)$$

Transaction costs are an important factor in the calculation of the returns of a trading model. We prefer to explicitly incorporate the transaction cost in the calculation of the returns. There is an ongoing debate about the approximation of the cost. Neely, Weller and Dittmar (1997) discuss the use and size of transaction costs. They conclude that transaction costs used in academic papers have declined over time. This is consistent with the decline of the actual cost in practice. The academic consensus on the issue of transaction cost agrees on 0.05% round-trip transaction cost to be realistic in a backtest (see, among others, Levich and Thomas, 1993, or LeBaron, 1999). On top of the execution cost one should consider the slippage and market impact cost. Slippage cost is the cost originating from a triggered trade where the trader does not have enough time to execute at the recommended entry point. Market impact represents the change in the currency's price caused by the execution of the trade. The slippage and market impact will be different for each individual organisation. The slippage mainly depends on the structure of the investment process and the market impact depends on the volume of the transactions.

Performance evaluation

The performance of a trading model is evaluated with the use of several criteria: average annual return, turnover, success ratio, information ratio and t-value. It is useful to evaluate the performance with the help of different statistics because each statistic provides different information about the quality of the trading model.

The average annual return gives an indication of the profitability of the trading model. A high average return is desirable but additional statistics are needed to identify whether the high return is driven by additional risk taking or a good trading model. Furthermore, the average return can be influenced by outliers in the returns.

The average turnover of a trading model is defined as the average number of position switches per year. The turnover is important because each position switch involves transaction costs.

The success ratio is the ratio of the number of signals that result in a positive returns and the total number of signals. A high success ratio (>50%) implies that the frequency of profitable trades is higher than the frequency of negative trades. This statistic adds value to the average annual return because the success ratio is not influenced by outliers. As a rule of thumb, a success ratio higher than 70% indicates an error in the model-building process or an over-optimised model.

The information ratio is a statistic that can be regarded as the average return adjusted for risk or the average return per unit of risk. If $\hat{r}_t$ is the empirical average annualised return and $\hat{\sigma}_t$ is the empirical annualised volatility of the trading model, then the information ratio is defined as:

$$\text{IR} = \frac{\hat{r}_t}{\hat{\sigma}_t}.$$

A positive information ratio indicates an outperformance and a negative information ratio indicates an underperformance. In practice an information ratio above 0.5 is considered good and above 1.0 as excellent. The information ratio is a commonly used measure. Another frequently used measure is the Sharpe ratio. This measure is very similar to the information ratio. The only difference is that the Sharpe ratio is based on excess returns. Excess returns are returns in excess of the risk-free cash rate. The information ratio is a measure for the outperformance of a strategy relative to a benchmark. The outperformance is defined as the return in excess of the benchmark return. Coincidentally, currency returns are already the returns above cash, so that the information ratio is equal to the Sharpe ratio for currency returns.

The information ratio could also be interpreted as a measure for the probability of loss if we assume that the underlying returns are realisations of a normally distributed stochastic variable.[2]

The t-value gives an indication whether the average return is significantly different from zero. If we assume that the returns of the trading model are normally distributed, $N(\mu, \sigma^2)$, then we are able to test the null hypothesis, H_0: $\mu = 0$, against the alternative hypothesis, H_1: $\mu \neq 0$. If $\hat{r}_t$ is the empirical average annualised return, $\hat{\sigma}_t$ is the empirical annualised volatility of the trading model and N is the number of years in the backtesting period, then the t-statistic is defined as:

$$t = \frac{\hat{r}_t}{\hat{\sigma}_t} \sqrt{N} = \text{IR} * \sqrt{N}$$

The null-hypothesis will be rejected if the t-value is big enough. We will reject the null-hypothesis on a 5% significance level if $t > 1.96$. We prefer a two-sided test but there is an ongoing debate about whether this t-test should be used as a one- or two-sided test. Pillemer (1991) gives a good overview of this discussion.

The definition of the t-value shows that there is a direct relation between the information ratio and the t-value. With the help of a little algebra we could calculate that we need an information ratio of 1.13 for a three-year period to have a performance that is significantly different from zero. For a five-year period we need an information ratio of 0.88 to have a performance that is significantly different from zero.

Risk of data mining
The above sections give us the tools to calculate and evaluate the performance of a trading strategy. A problem in the model-building process is overfitting, also known as overoptimisation, data snooping or data mining. This means that although a trading model has a good performance, this performance is not based on a sound model but is enhanced by optimising the degrees of

freedom in the model-building process to fit the model to the data or by testing a lot of different trading models. Although a 100% remedy for overfitting does not exist, we are able to moderate this problem: (1) by reporting the results from all tested trading models; (2) by utilising as long as available data series; (3) by analysing the robustness of the model across various non-overlapping subperiods or across different currency pairs that are not used in the model-selection process (in-sample model building versus out-of-sample testing). These three remedies will be discussed in more detail in the case study. There have been several academic studies to correct the performance of a trading model for overfitting. The White reality check is a result of this discussion (see Sullivan, Timmerman and White, 1999; White, 2000).

CASE STUDY: A TREND-FOLLOWING MODEL FOR EUR/USD

In contrast to the current popularity of trend-following models, the 1970s and 1980s were characterised by a meagre number of publications on this topic, due to the firm belief in the efficient-market hypothesis. A study of Brock, Lakonishok and Lebaron (1992) led to a renewed interest for the testing of trend-following models. In this case study we build a trend-following model as an illustration of the above sections. The simplest trend-following strategies use moving averages. We will select the parameter settings for a double-moving-average trading model for the EUR/USD with the help of Reuters data for the period 1976–2002. The 1975 data are used to generate the first signal and we take into account 0.05% transaction cost.

The moving average, MA(m, t), on time t is the average of the spot rates over the previous m time units, including the current one. The double-moving-average trading model, also known as moving-average crossover model, is based on the behaviour of two moving averages, MA(m_1, t) and MA(m_2, t) with $m_1 < m_2$. A crossover occurs if the sign of the difference between the two MAs changes. Buy and sell signals are generated by the crossovers between the slow-moving average, MA(m_2, t), and the fast-moving average, MA(m_1, t):

$$\begin{cases} 1 \text{ (buy)} & \text{if } MA(m_1, t) - MA(m_2, t) > 0 \\ -1 \text{ (sell)} & \text{if } MA(m_1, t) - MA(m_2, t) < 0 \\ \text{maintain position} & \text{if } MA(m_1, t) - MA(m_2, t) = 0 \end{cases}$$

Table 2 Statistics for the best model based on information ratio, return and success ratio

	Strategy (M_1/M_2)	Average return (%)	Turnover	Success ratio (%)	Information ratio	t-value
Highest information ratio	20/65	7.3	3.5	52.0	0.68	3.6
Highest return	20/65	7.3	3.5	52.0	0.68	3.6
Highest success ratio	24/115	5.0	2.6	52.7	0.47	2.4

Using the daily EUR/USD exchange rate series we assess the profitability of the crossover model, depending on the length of the moving averages. We vary the length of the short-term moving average from 1 to 25 days and the length of the long-term moving averages from 30 to 150 days with steps of 5 days (30, 35, etc). In total we test 625 combinations. Table 2 summarises the obtained results for the strategies with the highest average return, the highest success ratio or information ratio.

As can be seen, the 20/65 parameter setting is the best model setting for two of the three criteria. The performance of the 20/65 model looks good on all the criteria. The t-value indicates that the performance of the model is significantly different from zero. Figure 3 gives a graphical overview of the performance (information ratio) of all the tested models. The arrow in Figure 3 marks the 20/65 model.

The black areas in Figure 3 can be identified with the best available parameter settings because the models in these areas have the highest information ratio. We conclude from Figure 3 that all models are capable to give a positive performance. Despite the good results, the selection of the best model does not guarantee a good performance over sub-samples or for other currencies.

To minimise data-mining we calculate the same statistics for three sub-samples: 1976–84, 1985–93 and 1994–2002. Figure 4 depicts the same grid-graph as in Figure 3 for the three sub-samples.

We can conclude from Figure 4 that the performance of the 20/65 model is relatively good for all three sub-periods, although

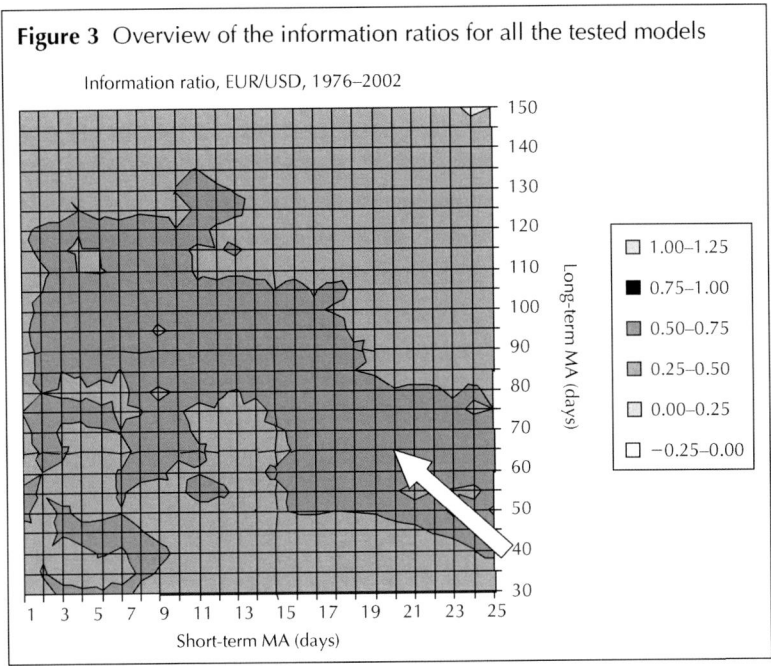

Figure 3 Overview of the information ratios for all the tested models

the 20/65 model is not the best model for the 1974–84 period. We also see that the performance of the double-moving-average model deteriorates in time: the 1976–84 graph shows more black areas than the 1994–2002 graph. Furthermore, the parameter settings with the best performance change in time. For the 1976–84 period we prefer a short momentum of 1 to 10 days in contrast with the preference of 15 to 25 days for the 1994–2002 period.

A final check of the robustness of the 20/65 model is to calculate the performance of the model for a different currency pair: USD/JPY, which was not used in the model-selection process. The result is depicted in Figure 5 and Table 3. Figure 5 both depicts the grid-graph for the USD/JPY as well as the cumulative outperformance for the 20/65 model for the EUR/USD and USD/JPY.

We conclude from Figure 5 and Table 3 that a 20/65 double moving average trading model could be a useful model to catch the trends for EUR/USD because the performance is good for all three sub-periods and also for the USD/JPY.

To make the performance of the 20/65 model for the EUR/USD more robust, it would be worth the effort to combine

Figure 4 Overview of the information ratios for all the tested models over three sub-periods

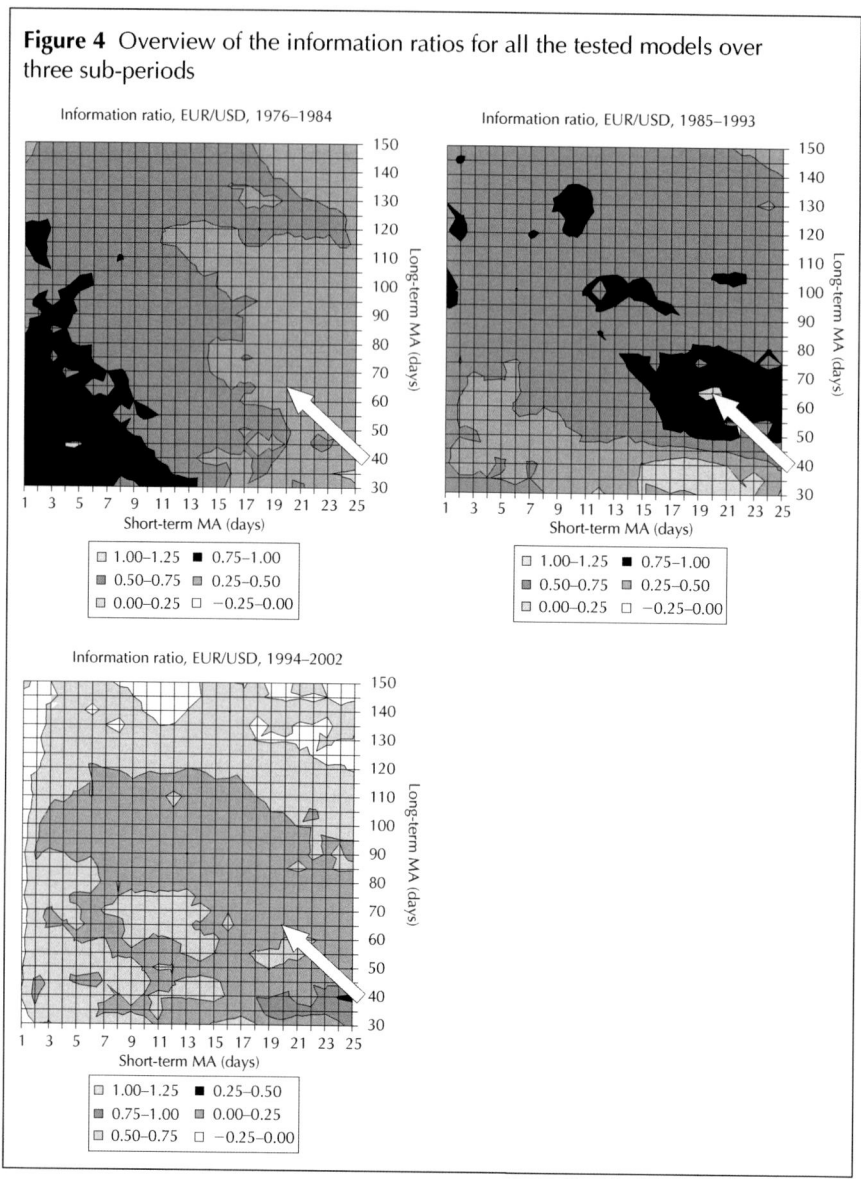

this trend-following model with other trading models such as the interest-rate differential, risk appetite, position data and flows, and volatility models. The general thought behind the combination of trading models is to diversify over different models. Notice that different currencies have different trend characteristics (see James, 2003).

MODEL BUILDING AND TESTING

Figure 5 Overview of the information ratios for the USD/JPY and the cumulative outperformance of the 20/65 model

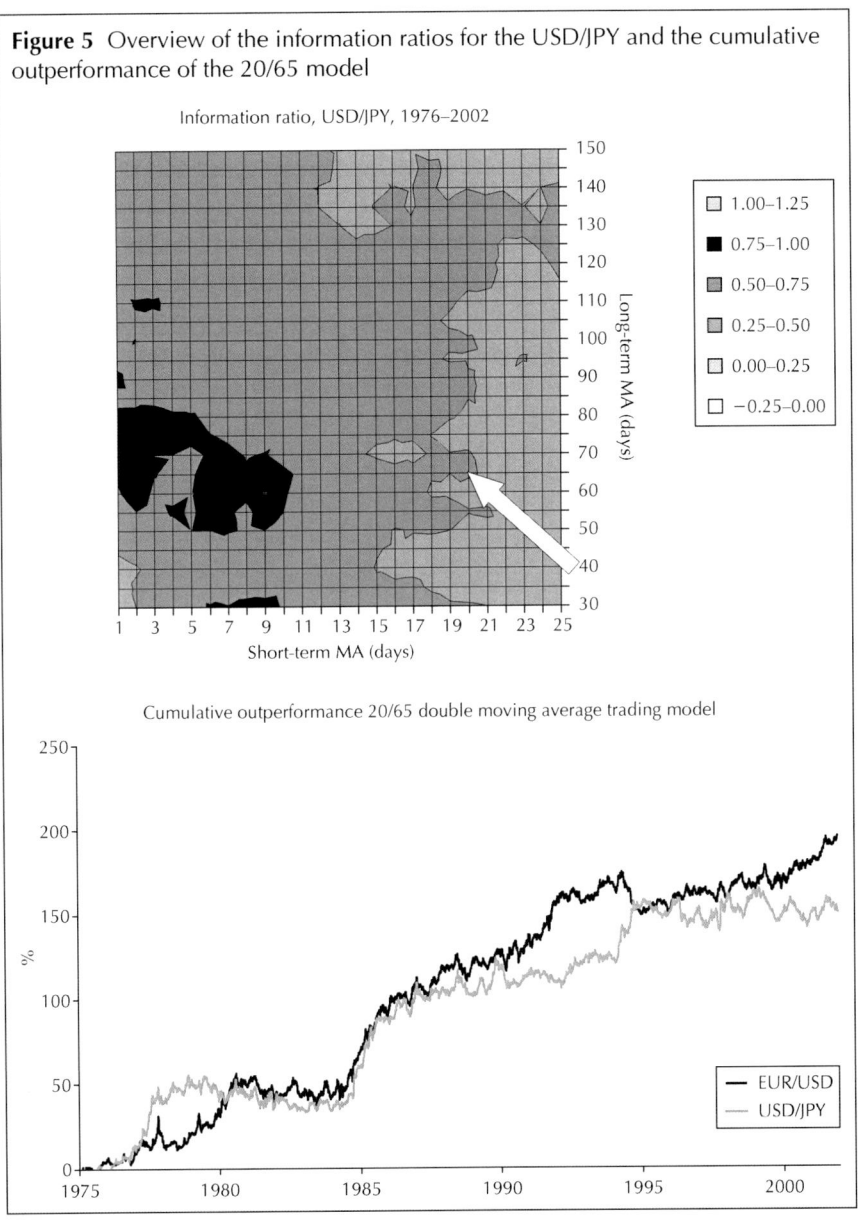

This case study illustrated the process of model-building and testing. A lot of choices have been made in the case study: for instance, the data period used, the definition of the trading set-up, an emphasis on the information ratio in the selection of the model.

Table 3 Statistics for the 20/65 model for different sub-samples and the USD/JPY

	Average return (%)	Turnover	Success ratio (%)	Information ratio	t-value
EUR/USD 1976–2002	7.3	3.5	52.0	0.68	3.6
EUR/USD 1976–1984	4.8	3.5	51.5	0.50	2.6
EUR/USD 1985–1993	12.8	3.5	53.0	1.08	5.6
EUR/USD 1994–2002	4.2	3.8	51.5	0.40	2.1
USD/JPY 1976–2002	5.6	3.7	51.6	0.52	2.7

Furthermore, it is obvious that the risk of data mining was imminent due to the 625 different combinations that are tested. Although all choices have a solid basis, this illustrates that model-building and testing is an art combined with science.

1   The Deutschmark is used as a proxy for the euro.
2   If the returns are realisations of a normally distributed stochastic variable, $N(\hat{r}, \hat{\sigma}^2)$ then the probability of a loss for the next day is defined as:

$$P(\text{loss}) = P(r_t < 0) = P\left(\frac{r_t - \hat{r}}{\hat{\sigma}} < -\frac{\hat{r}}{\hat{\sigma}}\right) = \Phi\left(-\frac{\hat{r}}{\hat{\sigma}}\right) = \Phi\left(-\frac{\text{IR}}{\sqrt{260}}\right)$$

Since the cumulative normal distribution, Φ, is monotone increasing, the higher the information ratio the lower the probability of loss.

REFERENCES

Baillie, R., and T. Bollerslev, 1989, "The Message in Daily Exchange Rates: A Conditional Variance Tale", *Journal of Business Statistics*, 7, pp. 297–306.

Baz, J., F. Breedon, V. Naik and J. Peress, 2001, "Optimal Portfolios of Foreign Currencies", *Journal of Portfolio Management*, pp. 102–11, Autumn.

Brock, W. A., J. Lakonishok, and J. LeBaron, 1992, "Simple Technical Trading Rules and the Stochastic Properties of Stock Returns", *Journal of Finance*, 47, pp. 1731–64.

Brousseau, V., and F. Scacciavillani, 1999, "A Global Hazard Index for the World Foreign Exchange Markets", European Central Bank, Working Paper series No 1, May.

Evans, M. D. D., and R. Lyons, 2002, "Order Flow and Exchange Rate Dynamics", *Journal of Political Economy*, 110, pp. 170–80.

Fama, E., 1984, "Forward and Spot Exchange Rates", *Journal of Monetary Economics*, 14, pp. 319–38.

Frankel, J. A., and A. K. Rose, 1995, "A Survey of Empirical Research on Nominal Exchange Rates", in G. M. Grossman, K. Rogoff (eds), *Handbook of International Economics*, Vol. 3 (North-Holland, Amsterdam).

Froot, K. A., and T. Ramdorai, 2002, "Currency Returns, Institutional Investor Flows, and Exchange Rate Fundamentals", NBER Working Paper 9080.

Ilmanen, A., and R. Sayood, 2002, "Quantitative Forecasting Models and Active Diversification for International Bonds", *Journal of Fixed Income*, pp. 40–51, December.

James, J., 2003, "Trend Following and Option Writing – A Surprising Portfolio", *Quantitative Finance*, 3(5), pp. C97–C100.

Knauf, S., 2003, "Making Money from FX Volatility", *Quantitative Finance*, 3(3), p. C48–C51, June.

Kritzman, M. P., 2000, *Puzzles of Finance* (New York: John Wiley & Sons).

LeBaron, B., 1999, "Technical Trading Rule Profitability and Foreign Exchange Intervention", *Journal of International Economics*, 49, pp. 125–43.

Levich, R. M., and L. R. Thomas, 1993, "The Significance of Technical Trading-Rule Profits in the Foreign Exchange Market: A Bootstrap Approach", *Journal of International Money and Finance*, 12, pp. 451–74.

Malliares, A. G., 2002, "Global Monetary Instability: The Role of the IMF, the EU and NAFTA", North American Economics and Finance Association Presidential Address.

Meese, R., and K. Rogoff, 1993, "Empirical Exchange Rate Models of the Seventies: Do they fit out-of-sample?", *Journal of International Economics*, 14, pp. 3–24.

Misina, M., 2003, "What does the Risk-Appetite Index Measure?", Working Paper 2003-23, Bank of Canada.

Neely, C. J., P. Weller and R. Ditmarr, 1997, "Is Technical Analysis in the Foreign Exchange Market Profitable? A Generic Programming Approach", *Journal of Financial and Quantitative Analysis*, 32, pp. 405–26.

Pedersen, H., and G. De Zwart, 2003, "Uncovering the Trend-Following Strategy", Working Paper.

Persaud, A. D., 1996, "Investors Changing Appetite for Risk", JP Morgan Global FX research.

Pillemer, D. B., 1991, "One- versus Two Tailed Hypothesis Tests in Contemporary Educational Research", *Educational Researcher*, Vol. 20, No. 9, pp. 13–17

Sullivan, R., A. Timmerman, and H. White, 1999, "Data-Snooping, Technical Trading Rule Performance, and the Bootstrap", *Journal of Finance*, 54, pp. 1647–91.

White, H., 2000, "A Reality Check for Data Snooping", *Econometrica*, 68, pp. 1097–1126.

13

Implementing Currency Management

Ron Liesching

Pareto

CURRENCY MANAGEMENT BACKGROUND

Currency management has transitioned into a mainstream activity for funds around the world. Five years ago, currency management was mainly undertaken by large funds with high (typically 20% or above) international allocations, or by "early adopters" looking for incremental return. Now every large fund has identified currency as a major source of investment risk, and potential return. Institutional currency management comes in three basic flavours. First, there is classic currency overlay hedging. Second, there are hybrid programmes that go beyond strict hedging. Third, there is currency management as a pure alpha activity. This last activity is unconnected to any pre-existing currency exposure the fund already has. Classic overlay is by far the largest of these activities for institutional investors. It now has over a decade of successful application in funds around the world.

Currency overlay management has also broadened in its scope of application in recent years. Originally, currency overlay was only applied to the hedging of currency exposure created by international equity investment. Today, currency overlay is applied to many assets. For example, it is now employed on global bond portfolios, to hedge private equity investments and to "port" USD hedge fund returns for non-USD investors. Understanding currency management takes time and is complex. However, finding currency managers is not: There are relatively few institutional currency managers. Surveys of currency assets hedged, or of currency management performance, typically list some 20 currency managers. There is a marked concentration of assets within the managers: only six firms manage over USD 5 billion.[1] These six firms account for nearly 80% of the total. There are four reasons for this concentration. First, as in any form of active management, firms who add most value dominate new business flow and so grow to be biggest. Second, currency management mandates can be very large. At our own firm, the average mandate is 400 million USD, while the median programme size is 200 million USD. The reason for the large size of mandates is that funds *have* to develop a currency policy when the currency exposure is large, either as a percentage of assets or in size alone. With large mandates, funds undertake extensive due diligence on depth of resources, infrastructure, backup, disaster recovery etc. Few firms can afford to have such resources in place. Third, only a few firms have long-run track records from multiple currency bases. Fewer still provide independently audited, AIMR/GIPS-compliant, performance numbers. Fourth, there is a shortage of experts with deep currency management experience. This is the reason for the surprisingly high level of movement of currency experts between the firms. However, there are many firms (equity managers, global bond managers and independent firms) who are currently trying to develop currency management capability. So the manager roster will expand in the coming years.

CURRENCY MANAGEMENT EXPERIENCE IS CONCENTRATED

Live currency management experience has been concentrated among a few currency management firms, and relatively few funds.[2] As a result, there is limited information available on practical implementation aspects of currency management. In contrast, there are literally hundreds of articles and books on currency theory, on how theorists *believe* that currencies should behave, policy should be set and currency exposure should be managed.

Many academic recommendations on currency are simply dangerous, and most are ill informed. Most have never actually managed currency. As the currency market is the largest and most liquid market in the world, it is best to draw on actual experience in this activity.

A key point is the massive structural change in the currency market. The most obvious recent change was the arrival of the EUR. A larger development is the change in *use* of currency. Historically, the primary use of currency was to finance exports and imports of goods and services. International portfolio investments were minimal 20 years ago. Today, it is shifts in international portfolio investments which totally dominate foreign exchange. These structural changes render textbook theories of currency determination irrelevant. Currency movements have become larger, and more unstable, over the last two decades. At the same time, economic fundamentals have become much less volatile and, in the case of interest rates and inflation rates, have converged.[3]

Large currency moves are a double-edged sword: when a major currency rises, or falls, by 20% it alters the domestic economic conditions. This leads to more beneficial diversification of asset returns between countries for global investors. However, the currency moves constitute a major risk. This risk is unrewarded, *unless* it is actively managed. That is why active overlay is needed.

WHY FUNDS HAVE TO IMPLEMENT CURRENCY MANAGEMENT

All funds have reduced their long-term return assumptions for equities and bonds. Bond yields are low, and equity valuations remain high by historic norms. Hence, it is inconceivable that future equity and bond returns will be anywhere close to the returns of the last 15 years. However, the average size of currency moves remains high. Figure 1 shows the absolute size of 12-month moves in hedged international equity returns from a USD base. It also shows the absolute size of the currency translation impact.

When a fund invests internationally the *capital* is given to the equity manager. The currency is an *exposure*. When equities are invested passively, there is no currency management. Bottom-up equity managers have no basis on which to take currency positions. So they do no currency hedging. A few top-down equity managers intermittently engage in currency hedging. Because most equity managers are given, eg, an unhedged EAFE benchmark, few take large currency positions because of their own business risk. Individual international equity managers rarely hedge more than a

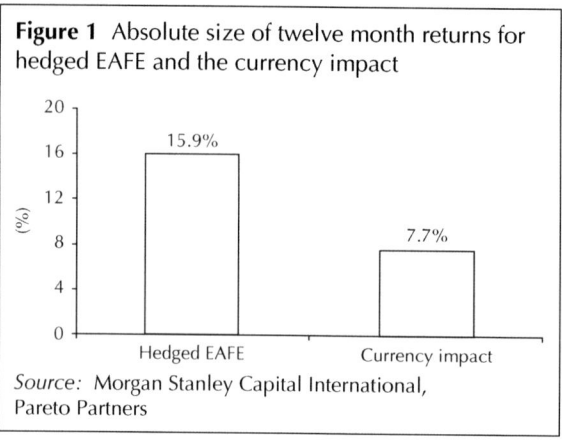

Figure 1 Absolute size of twelve month returns for hedged EAFE and the currency impact

Source: Morgan Stanley Capital International, Pareto Partners

quarter of their total currency exposure. So when several international equity managers are hired, the aggregate currency hedging is minimal. Performance attribution by investment consultants showed no evidence of active currency management skill by equity managers.[4]

DOES CURRENCY WASH OUT? NO!

Historically, equity managers – and many academics – argued that in the "long run" the currency impact would wash out. If you are a long-term investor and it washes out, the argument went, then you should not hedge currency because of the hedging cost.[5]

There are two reasons why this is totally wrong. First, there is no evidence that currency returns do wash out in the long run. The fixed exchange rate system stopped in December 1971 with the Smithsonian agreement.[6] The JPY was then 361 against the USD. Not long enough? GBP was 4.50 against the USD in 1945. If you are reincarnated, you may recall that GBP was at 7.70 to the USD 150 years ago. There is no statistically significant evidence whatsoever for any reversion either in nominal, or indeed "real", exchange rates.[7] Second, long-run analysis of exchange rates is truly irrelevant. *Short-run* currency loss can be massive: for a USD fund investing in an EAFE-like portfolio, from April 1995 to end January 2002, currency caused a 48.8% loss relative to being fully hedged.[8] Most USD-based funds did not even measure this unmanaged currency loss separately. The central point: no fund would *ever* consider taking unmanaged currency exposure by itself. Why should a fund take a massive unmanaged, and unrewarded, currency risk? It is simply a side-effect of international investing.

MECHANICS OF OVERLAY

In an overlay on international equity the first question is: which exposures will be managed? The data on the international holdings can be accessed electronically from the global custodian. There are four choices of what exposure should be actively managed:

Actual holdings

The most common form of overlay is for the currency manager actively to hedge the actual currency exposures created by the equity managers. Monthly audited data can be obtained electronically from the custodian. Many custodians can provide higher frequency reports (weekly or daily estimates). It is also quite common for funds to make significant injections (or withdrawals) into international. The currency manager's administrative team will see this if daily reports are available from the custodians. However, funds usually warn the manager in advance of the date of the allocation shifts. The currency manager is also notified of any large intra-month allocation shifts.

Handling underlying equity manager currency hedging

The arrival of the EUR massively reduced European "country" impacts on equity returns. The growing importance of global sectors, and increased use of international style investing, has increased the use of bottom-up international equity selection. Thus, in most cases, international equity managers do not hedge currency. However, some equity managers with a top-down process wish to retain currency hedging authority.

Some funds permit equity managers to hedge currency on a "no excuses" basis (ie, the manager claiming underperformance could have been avoided if currency hedging were permitted). There are then two alternatives. One approach is for the overlay manager to hedge the net currency exposure after any "underlay" manager hedging. This is the norm. Another is to measure the equity manager as a separate currency manager. We have seen this happen only once and in this case the programme was terminated.

Overlay on the benchmark

It is common for funds to start currency overlay first on their passive international equity investment. This is because no one is even monitoring the currency exposure. The capital is being invested passively, to harvest the equity return premium with no active risk. So adding a very large unmanaged currency risk on top makes little sense from an active risk budgeting perspective.

If the overlay programme is on the benchmark, then the manager only needs to know the asset size. We have also seen a few funds run overlay on the benchmark even when the actual exposures differ from this. This is either because the differences are small (and accurate information is difficult to obtain), or a few sponsors argue that active benchmark relative currency deviations are the equity managers' risk.

Neutralise equity managers' implicit currency positions, and actively hedge the benchmark

Bottom-up equity managers seek the most attractive equities, irrespective of country, currency or sector. So the resulting currency exposure is a pure, unplanned side-effect of *equity* selections. A decade ago, equity managers were often totally out of Japanese equities on a bottom-up valuation basis. As a side-effect, they had zero JPY exposure. As the JPY rose dramatically in some periods, the plan sponsor found that the portfolio returns were below the index as a result.[9] The equity manager would argue that they were right to be out of Japanese stocks, and that currency would "wash out in the long run". Meanwhile, the fund was getting way below a passive return. In addition, the currency exposure that was used was totally different from the exposure used in the asset allocation study.

For this reason, some plan sponsors specify in the overlay mandate that the currency manager should first passively neutralise the equity manager's benchmark relative currency deviations, and then actively hedge the benchmark (of course, the currency manager combines the two transactions into one net transaction[10]). This approach is used by fewer funds. It is generally used if the underlying managers are very aggressive in their implicit currency allocations, when the exposure is very large, and/or the plan sponsor has a tight performance attribution system.

CURRENCY BENCHMARK

This is one of the most contentious and vexed questions in currency management. To start with basics: a benchmark serves two purposes. First, it is the neutral position for the fund. It reflects the position that the fund would hold if there were no active management in place. Second, it is a passively implementable alternative, against which an active management can be measured. Most discussions over the currency benchmark are highly confused. There are a lot of papers on this topic. Many come to diametrically opposed conclusions. The primary reason for this is that currency returns are not related to any other returns in a stable way.[11] The second reason is that currency is an *exposure*, not an investment.

The conventional approach is to employ the mean/variance framework to determine the "optimal" currency benchmark. To deal with the fact that currency is an exposure, in these exercises currency return is tacked onto capital invested (ie, it is introduced implicitly as international equities *hedged* and *unhedged*). This is a first defect.[12] Second, because of the instability of currency relationships, the purported "optimal" currency hedge ratio fluctuates dramatically depending on the time period, and time frequency, analysed.[13] To avoid this problem, and come up with one "simple answer", other authors have suggested universal hedge ratios.[14] An alternative is a 50% benchmark position as being a "no view" or "minimum regret" position.[15]

Many currency managers argue that a 50% hedged benchmark is best, as it provides *them* with the opportunity to add value in all environments. With a polar benchmark (ie, either an unhedged or fully hedged benchmark) the overlay manager can only be able to add value in half the years. There is the very obvious point that benchmarks should be set to meet *fund* goals, not to make managers happy.

A 50% currency benchmark is appropriate for many funds. Indeed, some two-thirds of the US funds we deal with have this benchmark. However, the argument that it provides the maximum value added is false. With a polar benchmark, when value can be added there is a 100% active hedging range to be exploited (versus only a 50% active range for a 50% benchmark). So, although value can only be added half the time, when it can be added, the potential value added is twice as large.

Forget about theories, and manager claims: look at the real long-term numbers. Consider the multi-manager currency programme at CalPERS.[16] This programme commenced in July 1992, it covers 4.5 billion USD, and has a polar, fully hedged, benchmark. This means that in the years when the USD was strong it was *impossible* for the active managers to beat the benchmark. The average underperformance was 140 bps per annum. When the dollar fell, much greater value could be added: average value added was 240 bps per annum. This outcome compares favourably with the seven-year 60 bps per annum average value added over a 50% benchmark reported in the Russell Mellon currency performance survey[17] of *surviving* currency managers.

HOW CURRENCY BENCHMARKS ARE *REALLY* SET

The real way that currency benchmarks are set depends on revealed preference: funds have many conflicting issues that they must consider in setting a currency benchmark. The two main issues are the trade-off between wanting to control risk, and wanting to enhance return. However, many other factors are also very important. Not least is the issue of cashflow: consider a 50% hedged benchmark. The USD falls 20% against the foreign currencies, and the manager hedges 25%. As a result, the benchmark shows a 10% rise, versus the 20%, paper, currency translation gain on the overseas equities. However, having any hedge in place causes cash loss when the foreign currencies rise. While the manager outperformance is a spectacular 5% versus the benchmark, there is a cash outflow of 5% of international assets (offset by the larger paper translation gain on the international equities). Large cash outflows can become unsustainable if they lead to forced liquidation of the underlying investment assets. A major benefit of successful active currency overlay is that it truly reduces the regret of passive currency exposure. Overlay managers rarely capture all the gain. They rarely avoid all the loss. However, risk-controlled approaches definitely minimise the maximum worst-case outcome (technically this meets the "minimax" objective).

Other real-world issues are important: consider if a fund is planning to double (or in two cases almost *triple*), their international equity allocation in one step. The fund staff do not want to see an immediate massive underperformance relative to the domestic equity market from unmanaged base currency strength. In this case the fund may *start*[18] the currency overlay with a more heavily hedged benchmark. This reduces potential regret attendant on the *de facto* timing of their major jump in international allocation (in both cases of the near-tripling of international, the funds started with a more fully hedged benchmark, subsequently migrating to an unhedged benchmark).

In summary: there is no one simple answer that is the best currency benchmark for all funds. Just make sure that you have fully discussed the different considerations in advance within your fund as the choice is made.

LINES AND CAPITAL AT RISK

Currency overlay is very attractive because it dramatically reduces a fund's pre-existing currency risk. The international equity allocation can be doubled, with the same level of longer-term funding shortfall risk, once active currency overlay is employed. This is the reason why most large funds increase their active currency overlay programmes over time.[19] In addition, the value added in active overlay, relative to the active risk taken, is much higher than is seen eg, in a Core US Bond mandate. For example, in the Russell/Mellon currency management survey, the seven-year universe numbers show the average risk taken was 2.6% per annum, while the value added was 83 bps per annum.

A major reason for the current high level of interest in currency management is that it does not require upfront capital investment. So, successful active currency management adds pure incremental return to the fund. As individual programmes can be billions of US dollars, this is significant value added. However this is not "money for nothing". Theory and common sense tell us that it should be impossible to make money without investing capital, particularly in the world's largest and most liquid financial market. Fees on overlay are 25 bps, and much less on large programmes. If the value added is 100 bps per annum, and it required no capital, then the manager would do it for their own account. The capital required for overlay is *contingent capital*. The only reason that the banks will set up dealing lines in the name of the fund (the currency manager is appointed as the agent of the fund) is because the bank knows that the fund will meet any losses that occur.

This is a very important point that has two serious implications for implementing overlay programmes. First, it means that the fund is also exposed to the banks' credit rating.[20] Hence, currency overlay managers tightly monitor the exposure to banks, and have an active process for credit evaluation of the bank counterparties. There have not been problems of which we are aware with the major currency management firms in this regard. However, there have been problems with smaller firms in their dealings with banks.

ACTIVE CURRENCY RETURNS MUST BE MEASURED RELATIVE TO FUND CAPITAL AT RISK

Second, the correct way to evaluate active currency management returns is to measure the US dollar return relative to the US dollars of fund capital placed at risk. This is very clear if we consider currency speculation. Suppose a manager is hired to take currency positions simply to generate profit. Say four banks each set up line room of 400 million USD for the fund (this means that they will each permit gross currency positions up to 400 million USD). If the manager generates a trading profit in the year of 5 million USD, what is this amount as a *percentage return on capital*? Should we divide the 5 million USD by the total available line room (of 600 million USD) or by 100 million USD or by the average size of the position that the manager took during the year?

The only meaningful way truly to evaluate active currency returns is to measure return relative to the fund's capital placed at risk. Currency is an *exposure*, it is a long/short position. In this sense it is just like a long/short equity position. The capital at risk is an estimate of how much of the fund capital must, in potentiality, be held to support the activity. We can calculate this by looking at the worst-case outcomes. Consider the two distributors of currency returns shown in Figure 2. One manager takes a 3% tracking error and seeks a 1.5% per annum return. However, currency returns are not normally distributed, so for example one-year losses of 6% have been seen in mandates of this type. Contrast that with the risk-controlling style which takes a 2% downside tracking error, and returns 1% per annum.

If we simply look at short-run (three-year) returns of the managers, then the highest (and of course lowest) returns will usually

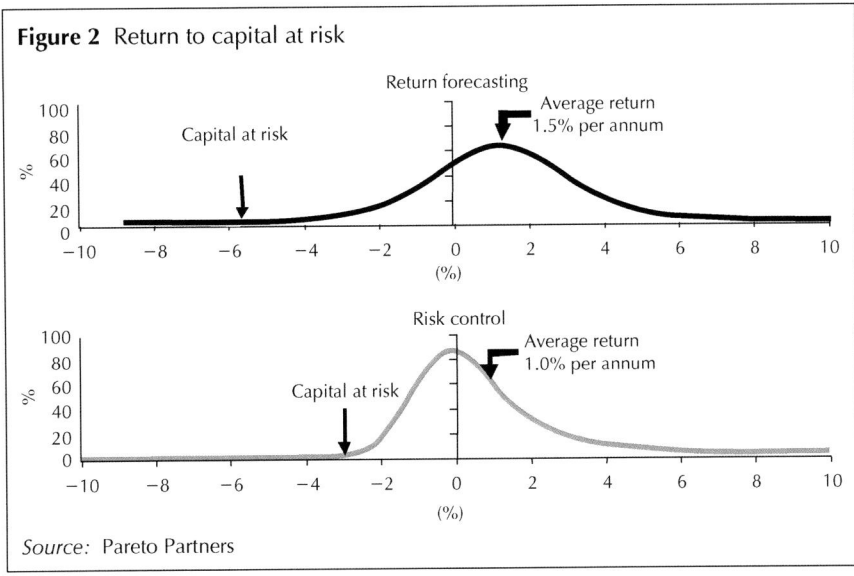

Figure 2 Return to capital at risk

Source: Pareto Partners

be from the high-risk approaches. However, long-term return relative to the capital placed at risk is higher with the lower-risk approaches. Hence, a low-risk currency overlay approach means that higher risk can be spent elsewhere in the fund. When high-risk currency management programmes are terminated, funds generally increase the size of the low-risk approach – and simultaneously take more risk elsewhere within the fund in other activities. We have seen many funds build their alternative programme.

THE THREE TYPES OF CURRENCY MANAGEMENT

There are three basic types of currency management. The first is strict currency overlay hedging. The second are hybrid approaches, which go beyond strict hedging. There are several different variants of hybrid currency programme. This may, for example, permit the manager to sell up to 20% of a currency even if it is only a small percentage of international holdings (eg, the size of AUD investment is usually only 4% for a US fund). Alternatively, the hedge range may be expanded to permit, for example, net purchase of foreign currency. Third, there is currency as a pure alpha source. This is currency speculation: new currency risk is created in order to generate return. Although the term "speculation" has a bad connotation, this is a perfectly valid activity. However, it is important to remember that this *increases* pre-existing currency risk. Currency as a pure alpha approach is not hedging. Conceptually it belongs in the alternative asset category. We will discuss these three activities in more detail.

Origin of the definition of "hedging"

It is useful to review what hedging is, and how the definition of "hedging" arose. In the late 1970s, active currency management grew very rapidly. The largest demand was for corporate hedging of the currency exposure created by their overseas operations. In the US, in particular, the introduction of the accounting standard FASB 8 forced corporations with overseas exposures to hedge currency actively.[21] If they did not do so, there were huge P&L implications. In the late 1970s, there were extreme divergences in interest rates between different countries. Furthermore, many of the currencies appeared to be massively out of line with their fundamental value. As a result, currency return forecasters saw opportunities to exploit the interest differentials: if interest rates were low and the fundamentals poor, then the currency would be sold to exploit the "forward rate bias" (bear in mind that in that period the annual interest differential might exceed 10%. As currency volatility was lower than today, trying to exploit the purported "forward rate bias" seemed much safer then than it does today). Unfortunately, the low-interest-rate CHF rose explosively, while the JPY in one period plummeted unexpectedly.

This caused *massive* currency hedging losses at corporations around the world who had, for example, been borrowing "cheap" CHF to invest in high interest rates in, for example, USD, AUD, CAD etc. Worse still, many of the positions were taken in currencies in which the corporations did not have any operations or exposure. The currency positions were taken simply to make money. There were widespread currency losses and disillusionment with these return forecasting approaches.[22] The lack of underlying exposure also meant that the currency losses could not obtain favourable tax treatment. This is what led to the accounting definition of "strict hedging". That definition is:

❏ hedging is the systematic reduction of pre-existing and unmanaged currency risk;

- only net sale of foreign currency is permitted; and
- net sale is permitted only up to the size of the underlying exposure.

Hybrid programmes

Now note that this is only one definition of "hedging". Some currency managers argue forcefully that *increasing* currency risk by cross-rate positions is hedging. They define "hedging" as the expectation that the cross-rate positions they take will add value, and reduce the variance of return of the total fund. There is nothing wrong with this definition. An overlay programme which permits overhedging, or cross-rate positioning (with net purchase of a foreign currency), can be viewed as a combination of a strict overlay hedging programme plus a set of speculative currency positions simply to enhance returns. The only reason for seeking to expand the opportunity set via a hybrid mandate is to capture more return. Thus the manager can break down the risk taken, and the value added, into the returns on strict hedging and on the pure alpha component.

Note that some return forecasting currency managers request authority to take cross-rate positions as a matter of course. This is because they produce indicators to forecast currency returns.[23] It may be the case that their indicators produce very weak signals for, for example, EUR against USD. For a USD-based client, the EUR is 40% of the exposure. Hence, in order to add value, the currency manager may request that the mandate includes, for example, permission to purchase a smaller currency (such as the NOK), where their signals are stronger and have historically added greater value.

Currency management as a pure alpha source

There has been a rapid rise in interest in currency as a pure alpha activity over the last two years. This interest comes from three areas. First, there are institutions who have run successful currency overlay, and now wish to employ currency as a portable alpha source. Second, there are funds who are under acute pressure to enhance returns, and see active currency management as a pure return enhancer that requires no upfront funding. Third, there is interest from hedge fund of funds, they see currency as a form of scaleable macro strategy.

337

Institutional investors usually run currency alpha programmes on an unfunded (and thus notionally unlevered) basis: a notional programme size is established. The currency manager operates as in an overlay capacity, but without the hedging (ie, risk reduction) goal – and the constraints this imposes. In the hedge fund construction, the currency manager is given actual capital by the investor. Based on this capital, dealing lines are set up with banks (ie, the counterparty is no longer the institutional investor; it is the fund in which the capital is placed). Banks will provide lines of up to 20 times the capital. The manager will target a certain level of return. This will translate into an average leverage amount.

To give some illustrative calculations: in currency overlay an information ratio of 0.3 to 0.5 is achievable. Without the constraints of hedging, the information ratio might rise to 0.6 to 1.0. (Note that, because of noise, actual track records range from severely negative to well over 1. Generally, the higher track records are on smaller accounts and involve positions in smaller currencies). If the manager is aiming for a 15% rate of return, then the average leverage of the capital will probably be close to five times. However, the currency manager actively manages the exposure level.

Note that currency as an alpha activity has been around as a separate activity for decades. There are usually around 40–50 managers in this activity. These managers charge the classic hedge fund fees of 100–200 bps per annum plus 20% of profits. Some currency overlay managers have always offered such currency alpha products. Most of the small firms who have offered currency alpha product are unlikely to be hired directly by institutions (as they would not pass institutional due diligence screens). However, they are often present in hedge fund of fund pools in the "global macro" sub-category.

Unfortunately, there are no independent audits of returns or products offered. Usually, a manager is an adviser to a fund. Many such funds close down. There is horrendous survival bias. A firm closes and another starts with the same trading personnel. Most of these smaller firms would not make it through normal institutional due diligence screening. The largest survey at such strategies covers 47 managers.[24] In total, they manage 6 billion USD before leverage.

CONFLICTS OF INTEREST

There have been problems in some currency programmes with conflicts of interest. These can all be addressed by appropriate due diligence and documentation. A first point to note is that currency is a dual-capacity market: banks who make markets in currency also take large proprietary positions for their own account. In addition, they advise clients on currency positioning, and some also often offer currency management services. The dual-capacity role in currency is vital for efficient market functioning. However, as banks pride themselves on making money by "seeing the client order flow" it is important to understand where potential conflicts may occur.

An egregious (but sadly not one-off) problem is when a manager (or affiliated entity) received commissions, or fees, on foreign exchange transactions. To be clear: the currency market is a net market. There are no commissions paid. If monies are paid to the manager it is because the rate is an off-market rate and has been loaded against the client with a hidden cost. Neither the manager nor affiliate should *ever* receive any commissions for trading volume. These commissions can be disguised as per transaction processing fees. This has occurred mainly at small firms.

Conflicts can be more subtle. Suppose the currency trader(s) are not just doing currency management. In a multi-product firm they may, for example, be handling the foreign exchange associated with buying equities. In one case, profitable currency overlay trades were allocated into a different equity client's account. Proper, independently audited record-keeping can eliminate this.

Currency forecasting firms face another problem. If they change their view on a currency outlook, then they must trade immediately for all their clients (otherwise the last client to be traded will be disadvantaged). Most of these firms bundle together all their clients' trades into one single transaction. For example, if a firm has 20 clients and changes its view on the JPY, then it may sell, say, 10% of the total client exposure in transactions with a bank. This trade then has to be equitably allocated out across client accounts. It becomes more difficult because of two factors. First, some clients can be much larger than others. Individual currency programmes can much exceed 1 billion USD, or be as small as 30 million USD. How is the trade allocated?

Second, many firms are rapidly building up their currency alpha activities. Here, the fees are often five times higher than currency overlay *and* the manager receives 20% of any profits. Usually these are a smaller size than overlay programmes. If a manager is going to alter the JPY hedge on a 2 billion USD overlay programme, how should the trade on a 50 million USD currency alpha programme be handled? The answer for these firms is a scrupulously clear policy, and to maintain independently auditable, real-time record-keeping.

This issue first surfaced several years ago when some forecasting firms became so big that their trading began to impact on the market. Of course, the banks they dealt with knew they would be trading for all their clients. This meant that the banks would also position the same way. (It is impossible to measure front running in the currency market, as it is dual capacity.) Unless this is properly addressed, it can lead to a hidden adverse move in the exchange rate for the client, and potential inequity between clients.

DUE DILIGENCE ON INFRASTRUCTURE

The currency market is the world's largest financial market. The market participants are the most highly capitalised financial firms, with the most sophisticated systems and expert staff. This is a market which trades 24 hours a day. Dramatic short run moves do occur, such as the 7½% rise in JPY/USD in two hours in October 1998. Or the 4½% rise in the USD against the DEM when the Gorbachev coup occurred at the worst possible dealing time (late on US Sunday night) in August 1991. Funds want to ensure that there is a proper infrastructure in place in the currency management firm. Note that currency is not like equities: currency turnover is over 10 times the turnover of all the global equity markets combined, and that covers 35,000 equities. In the currency market, the top six currencies account for 87% of all trading.[25] This is one of the reasons why there have often been disappointments when equity managers try to manage currency actively.

Even five years ago, when we discussed with funds about having an onsite power generation, secure offsite record keeping, a hot backup trading location, detailed disaster recovery procedures etc, there was frank disinterest. Nowadays, funds are acutely aware of the importance of proper infrastructure. In a recent case, a fund lost money on a currency overlay programme when the founder died, and there was no backup. This was not a manager problem; it was a due diligence deficiency. At the other extreme, we have had monetary authorities and corporations send teams of three to five staff for a full day, just to review infrastructure and risk controls. Due diligence review can certainly take more than eight hours. A *very* brief checklist of the issues is:

- ❏ people – critical staff in key areas, research, trading, administration etc should be backed up;
- ❏ systems – the computer systems should be backed up with off-site records;
- ❏ record keeping – dealing lines should be taped and a real-time log kept of all transactions;
- ❏ location – a fully operational backup trading location is needed;
- ❏ disaster recovery – there should be a fully documented and tested disaster recovery plan;
- ❏ liquidity – the trading team should be dedicated, and have sufficient experience;
- ❏ STP – automation of every aspect from front to back office settlement and reconciliation;
- ❏ conflicts – ensuring that all potential areas are clearly identified and addressed; and
- ❏ compliance – having properly qualified compliance staff with independent reporting.

CASH SETTLEMENT

Institutional currency management programmes employ the spot and forward currency market. Some currency managers also make use of currency options. These markets are used because they are the largest markets, with the lowest trading costs. Settlements occur based on the maturity of the contracts that the manager employs. Maturities range from monthly out to one year.[26] When maturity of the contract approaches, the manager closes out the contract to deliver foreign currency. Simultaneously, the position is re-established with a new contract. On the settlement date, the foreign currency transactions offset. This leaves a net USD payment (for a USD-based programme) to be either sent to, or received from, the fund. This is referred to as "rolling" the hedge.

As the maturity date approaches, the manager will have an estimate of the settlement amount. The actual cash amount is fixed once the contract is rolled. This will be sufficiently long before actual settlement so the coordination of the cash transfer can proceed smoothly. Most funds handle the cash inflows and outflows via their short-term cash investment fund. The currency manager coordinates this process so that it operates seamlessly. However, note that this is not a costless process. If there are large exchange rate moves, then there can be large cash inflows or outflows. Hence, investment, or disinvestments, from other assets must occur. So there is this hidden transaction cost of investing and disinvesting the currency gains and losses in the international asset class.

Cash management can be an issue when the exposure is closely tied to an asset class. Take, for example, currency overlay on global bonds, or a hedge fund pool. If the overlay makes a large profit, the investor will want to have this invested as soon as possible. If there is a loss, then cash must be raised. Given lock-up periods in some hedge fund strategies, cash management is an issue. Hence, the mechanics of cash management must be addressed in advance, in order to minimise the impact on the underlying active managers.

Managing cash has never been an issue in conventional international equity overlay programmes, as far as we are aware. However, if the overlay is on a private equity investment the question is: where does the cash come from? While there is a notional rise in the base currency value of the assets, actual cash is needed to settle the forward transaction. In an illiquid asset class like this, there has to be a financing available.

Note a couple of observations. First, cashflow management is even worse on passive currency hedging (indeed, it is the very large negative cashflows, when the base currency falls, that often trigger funds to move to active currency management). Second, the size of prospective cashflows depends on the benchmark selected, as discussed earlier. The more hedged the benchmark is, the higher will be the potential worst-case cashflow. When this is an issue, it is quite common for programmes to start with an unhedged benchmark. With a risk-controlled style, there is then a highly certain worst-case cashflow outcome.

CURRENCY MANAGEMENT ON GLOBAL BONDS

Currency overlay started on international equity programmes. This was because either the currency risk was not being managed at all, or it was being managed ineffectively. In contrast, it was generally believed that global bond managers had currency management expertise: Because they relied on a top-down macroanalysis, they claimed that this gave them value-added insights into currency trends. In fact, disappointment with bond managers managing currency came early on: in 1988 Illinois teachers started a currency overlay programme on equities. They did not consider those of us who were just offering currency overlay, as our track records were then short. They requested that global bond managers report their long-term currency management track record. Two bond managers were hired to manage the overlay. They both claimed 2% per annum value added (a common claim of currency return forecasters at that time). Fatally, they both used the same fundamental approach. Because their models differed in estimating the "fair value" of currencies, they took offsetting positions. Two years later, the programme was terminated. Both firms did build significant currency overlay client bases in the United States a decade ago. However, subsequent poor performance, staff departures and ownership changes meant they lost all their clients and they both exited the business.

More recently, there has been an upsurge in interest in hiring currency overlay for global bond programmes. Obviously, this is being done for two reasons: First, currency managers have proven ability to add value in active currency management. Second, it is superior to manage currency risk separately from bonds. The starting point is to observe that there are four potential sources of active value added in global bonds:

- *Market selection.* This is selecting which country has the most attractive bond outlook.
- *Yield curve positioning.* This is taking duration and yield curve shape positions relative to the benchmark.
- *Credit risk.* This is selecting non-government bonds to pick up yield.
- *Currency.* This is the currencies which are perceived as being attractive relative to the benchmark.

Historically, there were much higher yields in some countries (eg, in Australia, Canada or Denmark). In addition, interest rate cycles were very different between countries. This meant that there was a very high *available return* both to market selection and to yield curve positioning.[27] Today, bond yields have fallen dramatically; bond yields have almost converged except for Japan. Worse still, there is currently a high correlation in the economic/monetary policy stance. This means that available return to market selection and yield curve positioning is much reduced. Even if you correctly forecast the future, the returns per unit of active risk are much lower than a decade ago. Credit returns have been positive, but are small and negatively correlated with yield levels. This makes currency the key component in determining active global bond returns. This is just an arithmetic fact. Unfortunately, until recently, global bond managers' conventional style of currency management was still a classic fundamental style.[28] This worked well for positioning between tightly linked currencies in Europe before the EUR was created, for example in forecasting the trend in, say, ITL versus DEM. So, global bond managers showed spectacular value added as convergence occurred within Europe prior to the creation of the EUR. Unfortunately, the arrival of the EUR eliminated *both* the intra-European market selection *and* currency alpha sources.

Worse still, currency market structure has evolved dramatically over the last decade. Rather than fundamentals driving currencies, currency movements are now much larger than fundamental changes. So the causality is reversed: a rising EUR bears down on EUR inflation, rather than low inflation causing a future EUR rise.[29] The bottom line is that most global bond managers got the EUR wrong when it was created in 1999. The fundamental value models claimed it would rise from 1 to the fair value of 1.10 to 1.15. But it fell to near 0.80.

Large investors often employ multiple (from three to over 10) global bond managers. There was no diversification in their currency bets; they all went overweight. The funds then requested proper performance attribution of returns. They were surprised to find that many bond managers were good *bond* managers, but poor *currency* managers. As there are only three major currency pairs, from any given base there are only two large bets to take, for example the position on JPY and EUR will dominate returns for a

USD-based investor. So, if you have five bond managers all taking currency positions, based on the same information set, a period of major disappointment is guaranteed.

Next is the interesting, and controversial, result that currency is better managed separately from bonds. Note that this is true even if both activities are carried out within the same global bond firm.[30] Historically, economists used to argue that domestic monetary policy would create a tight, and forecastable, relationship between currency and bonds. For example, it used to be argued that if there was economic overheating with a loose monetary policy, then both the currency and bond market should be vulnerable. As in the US currently, this correlation can occur, but there is no stable relationship.

The currency market is also massively larger in turnover than the bond market. So causality is more likely to go from the currency market *into* the bond market, than the other way round. We are already seeing this "reverse" causality even within the US bond market: the US mortgage market is now larger than the US Governments. So the dramatic 130 bps backup in 10-year US yields within June 2003 was primarily caused by US mortgage participants hedging convexity (as the duration of the mortgage index shot up from one year to four years within that month). Returns in the currency market do not have a stable correlation with any other returns. That is why currency should be separately managed. Appointing a separate currency overlay manager for global bonds is a much more recent activity than equity overlay. However, the top four currency firms also manage global bonds: within these firms we have always used separate currency overlay on our own global bond portfolios. The issues are complex. Hence it is the larger funds with resources to analyse this issue who first moved ahead to appoint separate currency management. It is like the situation in *equity* overlay at the start of the 1990s.

ADVICE ON IMPLEMENTING CURRENCY PROGRAMMES

Successful currency programmes run for decades. Unsuccessful programmes cause losses, but more importantly absorb a lot of management time. The scarcest resource in any fund is the corporate governance budget. Hence it is best to spend the time to set up an active currency programme properly. It was common for large funds to spend well over a year studying currency management, before putting an active currency programme in place. Nowadays there is much more information available and there are long-term audited track records. Hence, programmes can be put in place more quickly. Nonetheless, it is best to spend time in programme design. There are five strong pieces of advice on implementing a currency management programme.

1. Develop a consensus within the fund on the reasons for doing active currency management, and realistic expectations for this activity.
2. If there is an oversight board, then do educational sessions on what currency hedging is. Explain that unmanaged currency is an unrewarded risk. Explain the cashflow issues of hedging. Explain the innately episodic nature of currency returns.
3. Do proper due diligence on the currency managers. Both large and small firms have provided disappointments. Proper due diligence would have eliminated many of the more painful outcomes.
4. Specify the mandate clearly in a way that reflects the desired goals, and to avoid unexpected outcomes.
5. Start your programme taking less active risk than you hope to deploy eventually. Currency crises can occur at any time. It is simple to increase the risk in a successful currency management programme, by extending the size or scope of a mandate. It is difficult to deal with rapid unexpected loss in a large new programme in a new activity.

Historically, currency management was seen as a niche activity reserved only for the very large funds with high international allocations. Today, all funds are under pressure to enhance returns. Active currency management is central in two ways. First, the largest single action any fund can take to enhance returns relative to the total active risk budget is not to invest in hedge funds (which are this decade's private equity), but to raise the non-domestic allocation. In large economies, the optimal international equity allocation for a fund is near 30%. For small open economics, the international allocation should be higher. Second, active currency management controls an unrewarded risk, and can add pure incremental return. So active currency management is central to modern institutional fund management. Unlike many other activities, actively managing the existing currency risk created by international investing is ultimately not optional: you can't leave home safely without it!

1 Source: *Investments and Pensions Europe* (2003).
2 Adding the number of clients in the survey gives a total of 420 overlay programmes. As some funds hire multiple managers, the total number of funds employing overlay is still a tiny fraction of the number of funds employing international equity managers. Over a decade after it started, currency management is still in its infancy.
3 An early paper on this is Goodhart (1988).
4 Note that several equity firms are currently developing active currency management capability.
5 See, eg, Froot (1993).
6 Free floating of exchange rates commenced in June 1973.
7 See, eg, Kilian and Zha (1999).
8 Data sources: Pareto Partners and Morgan Stanley Capital International.
9 In that period, the Japanese market, and thus the JPY, had close to a 40% weight in the EAFE benchmark.
10 Performance attribution becomes slightly more complex: the active currency manager is evaluated only on the active currency management component.
11 Technically this is referred to as "non stationarity".
12 Currency cannot be entered by itself into conventional mean variance, because it is an *exposure*: there is no denominator of capital to enter currency by itself.
13 See, eg, Abken and Shrikande (1997) and Busay (2003).
14 See, eg, Black (1989) and Adler and Prasador (1995).
15 See Gardner (1994).
16 Source: calpers.ca.gov/whatshap/calendar/board/invest/200212/item06a.doc. Note that, in the decade of this programme, the USD was strong for six years.
17 Source: Currency Overlay Manager Profile, Q2/ 2003, Russell/Mellon Analytical Services.
18 Roughly a quarter of funds change their currency benchmark over time. Usually this is after three to five years of programme success, and is in the context of a broader asset review.
19 Increased funding from existing clients is the largest source of business growth for successful currency managers.
20 Note that no major bank has ever failed on a foreign exchange transaction. Nonetheless, the credit positions must be monitored rigorously.
21 FASB 8 was updated by FASB 52 in 1981, and by FASB 133 in 1998.
22 See, eg, Levich (1983).
23 These are a combination of fundamental, capital flow, technical signals and judgement.
24 Source: Parker Global Strategies.
25 Source: Bank for International Settlements (2001).
26 Use of beyond-one-year forwards is unusual in active currency management, because they expose a fund to significant differential interest rate risk, use up a different credit line allocation and have higher transaction costs.
27 Available return is measured, after the fact, by looking at the returns which would have been achieved if the manager a) had perfect forecasts, b) had a given active risk budget, and c) had realistic turnover constraints. This then enables the plan sponsor to determine whether the return was a good, or bad, outcome in the environment.
28 In contrast, fundamental *currency* managers moved away from classic fundamental currency models after the performance disappointments of 1994, and more recently 1999.

29 The statistical test for causality is called the "Granger–Sims" test. Nowadays this test shows that an exchange rate move causes, eg, future inflation to change, rather than inflation causing future exchange rate changes. So, a rise in the EUR will cause a lower inflation in the EUR area in 2004.

30 For proof, see Chapter 15, this book and Abberley (2003).

BIBLIOGRAPHY

Abberley, P., 2003, "Currency in the Global Bond Portfolio: To Integrate or Not?", Institutional Investor Institute Consultants round table, ABN AMRO, September.

Abken, P., and M. Shrikande, 1997, "The Role of Currency Derivatives in Internationally Diversified Portfolios", Federal Reserve Bank of Atlanta Economic Review, Third Quarter.

Adler, M., and B. Prasador, 1995, "On Universal Currency Hedges", in R. Aggarwal and D. C. Schirm (eds), *Global Portfolio Diversification*, pp. 81–104 (San Diego, California: Academic Press Inc.).

Bank for International Settlements, 2001, Tri-Annual Foreign Exchange Survey. Bank for International Settlements (www.bis.org/tubl/rpfx02t.pdf).

Black, F., 1989, "Universal Hedging: Optimizing Currency Risk and Reward in International Equity Portfolios", *Financial Analysts Journal*, July–August.

Busay, E., 2003, "Currency Overlay: Fund-Wide or Asset-by-Asset Approach?", June.

Froot, K., 1993, "Currency Hedging Over Long Horizons", National Bureau of Economic Research, Working Paper 4355.

Gardner, G., 1994, *Managing Currency Risk in US Pension Plans* (Frank Russell).

Goodhart, C., 1988, 'The Foreign Exchange Market: A Random Walk with a Dragging Anchor', *Economica*, 55, pp. 437–60.

Kilian, L., and T. Zha, 1999, "Quantifying the Half-Life of Deviations from PPP: The Role of Economic Priors", Atlanta Federal Reserve Board, Working Paper, pp. 99–21.

Levich, R., 1983, "Currency Forecasters Lose their Way", *Euromoney*, August.

Currency Overlay Manager Profile, Q2/2003 (Russell/Mellon Analytical Services).

Investments and Pensions Europe, 2003, September.

Part 4

Case Studies

14

Bringing FX Prime Brokerage to Currency Overlay

Philip Simotas
FX Concepts

In this chapter, we will report on how the currency overlay industry is missing out on an important tool that can help reduce the implementation headaches that plan sponsors frequently face when implementing a currency overlay programme.

INTRODUCTION
While foreign exchange prime brokerage is becoming increasingly popular in the absolute-return world, it has been largely bypassed in the currency overlay industry. Why currency overlay practitioners (plan sponsors as well as managers) have yet to embrace FX prime brokerage is something of a mystery. As one of the early pioneers in currency overlay and FX prime brokerage, FX Concepts has found it to be an invaluable tool to reduce implementation hurdles and risks for clients. Specifically, prime brokerage not only reduces a client's legal costs, but also the settlement and credit risks associated with a currency overlay programme.

OVERCOMING MISCONCEPTIONS AND MARKET CULTURE
FX prime brokerage has become standard operating procedure for CTAs and leveraged currency managers. For CTAs, adopting prime brokerage is a natural, since the concept is similar to clearing their futures trading through a single FCM. But the concept of clearing interbank FX contracts through a prime broker has not

gained traction in currency overlay as a result of several misconceptions, two of which are:

- *Myth 1:* FX prime brokers duplicate a service that is performed already by a plan sponsor's custodian. Why do I need an FX prime broker to clear my trades if my custodian can already do that for me?
- *Myth 2:* Clearing through a single entity will increase my risk as opposed to "spreading it out" across a lot of different counterparties.

To us, this demonstrates a lack of understanding as to how the prime brokerage process works. Clearly, part of the problem is that the people who are responsible for marketing prime brokerage are not necessarily fully conversant with the issues that pension funds face. We will try to bridge the gap in this chapter.

CURRENCY OVERLAY BEFORE PRIME BROKERAGE

We first started employing FX prime brokerage in 1994, having developed the framework with AIG Trading Corp. Prior to adapting this new clearing facility, currency overlay implementation was very time-consuming and fraught with all kinds of back-office-related risks.

Because currency overlay runs under a managed account framework, all our clients come equipped with their own sets of banking relations. While we tried to establish FX lines with the same banks for all of our clients so that we could trade their accounts in a single block, this was not always possible. As we gained more and more clients, keeping track of which clients had lines with which banks became increasingly complex. So did the process of establishing FX lines at each bank. This was a very time-consuming and expensive process. Each bank had its own documentation, which had to be reviewed by the plan sponsor or its custodian.

This also led to inefficiencies in the front office. Inefficient execution resulted as the best price provider was often not an approved counterparty. Figure 1 shows how the managed account framework required for currency overlay can lead to inefficient execution, as not all pension funds maintain identical banking relationships. In addition, traders needed to split transactions and effect multiple trades for the same strategy.

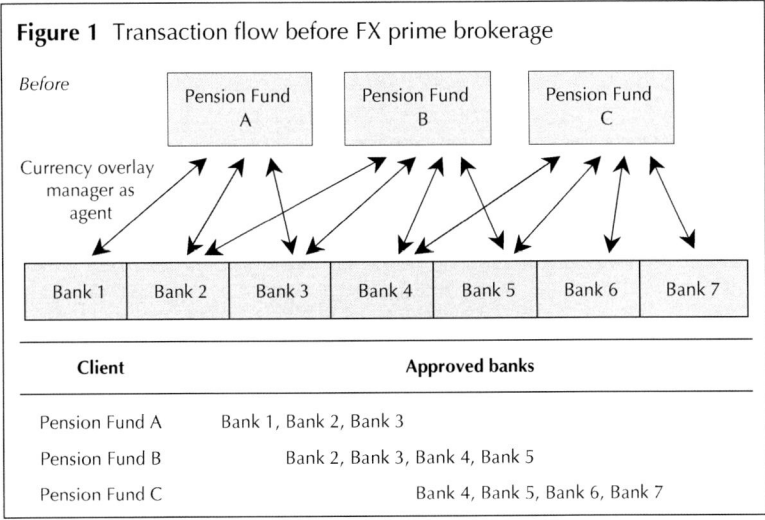

Figure 1 Transaction flow before FX prime brokerage

Client	Approved banks
Pension Fund A	Bank 1, Bank 2, Bank 3
Pension Fund B	Bank 2, Bank 3, Bank 4, Bank 5
Pension Fund C	Bank 4, Bank 5, Bank 6, Bank 7

Once we were up and running, there was the issue of settlements. Foreign exchange forward contracts that were opened with one bank were frequently closed with another dealer. On settlement day, we then had the responsibility of ensuring that the plan sponsor's custodian delivered the right currency balances to and from the various dealers with whom we had outstanding settlements. This could be across as many as 10 to 15 different banks. Any slip-up, and the next few days were spent making good on deliveries and resolving any resulting interest costs. The unseen credit risk to our clients arose if their respective counterparties were unable to make a delivery. As a by-product of our being in the currency overlay business, we were necessarily in the back-office business and clients were bearing the risk.

THE BASICS OF FX PRIME BROKERAGE

In 1994, FX Concepts announced a foreign exchange trading and clearing facility with AIG International, which allowed us to greatly improve foreign exchange execution and clearing for our clients' accounts. This facility also enabled our clients to minimise the credit exposure in the foreign exchange markets by allowing them to house their currency positions at one of the foremost financial institutions in the world. Figure 2 shows how, under prime brokerage, FX Concepts is able to trade on behalf of our clients, a

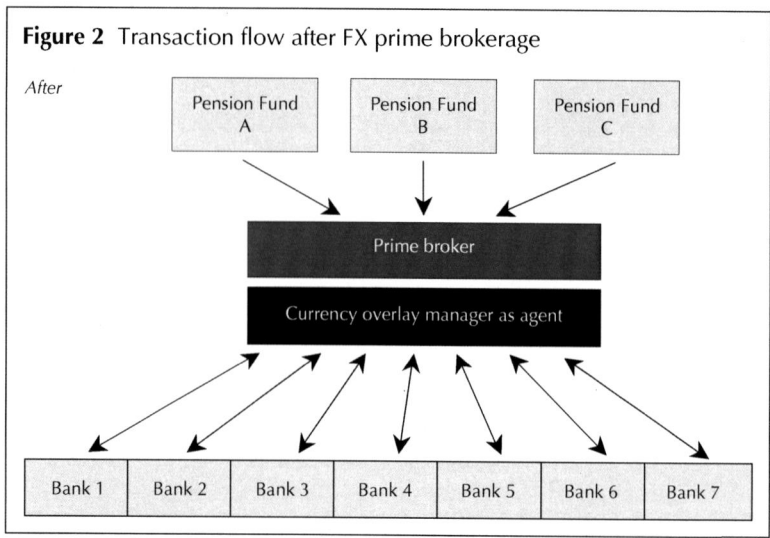

Figure 2 Transaction flow after FX prime brokerage

number of institutions – clients are thereby assured of obtaining the best execution while simultaneously reducing settlement and clearing risks.

We now employ prime brokerage for all of our clients (both currency overlay and absolute return) through facilities with both AIG and Deutsche Bank. They benefit our clients in several important ways. Our clients have only to maintain one trading facility, review one set of legal documents, monitor one counterparty credit and have their custodian/back-office deal with one institution. At the same time, we are able to trade on our clients' behalf with 15 to 20 major market-making institutions. Under prime brokerage, FX Concepts is able to trade on behalf of its clients with the prime broker directly and in the name of the prime broker with other institutions – our clients are thereby assured of obtaining the best execution under all market conditions, 24 hours a day.

THE BENEFITS OF PRIME BROKERAGE

FX prime brokerage presents a number of important benefits for our clients.

❑ Best execution is greatly enhanced by virtue of having a large number of banking counterparties available at any time. This flexibility increases our ability to alter our execution

strategies to obtain the maximum advantage for all our clients under all market conditions.
- Reduction of risk for the majority of our clients will be possible because all client positions will be with the prime broker. For those clients with multiple bank relationships, large currency settlement exposures are almost entirely eliminated since all transactions are settled with one institution on a net basis.
- Transaction processing becomes standardised and automated, leading to clear audit trails and enhanced controls.
- Legal documentation is necessary for only one account.
- It allows the manager to execute all client accounts as single-bloc trades, thereby ensuring identical performance across all accounts.
- Prime brokerage provides the client with an independent audit. This is very important, as not all custodians are familiar with FX contracts and often do the related accounting only once a month.

Furthermore, it allows the currency overlay manager to outsource the back-office element of his operation and to focus on its core competence, which is managing currency risk. Ultimately, prime brokerage has allowed us to manage a larger asset base with the same number of people as the efficiency of our operation has improved.

SETTLEMENT RISK REDUCTION – THE DETAILS

Prime brokerage greatly reduces settlement risk for those currency overlay clients who currently maintain credit lines for foreign exchange trading at more than one financial institution. When the overlay manager liquidates a client position, which was initiated with a different bank, the client is responsible for the delivery and settlement of currency balances on value day for both contracts.

For example, if FX Concepts, on behalf of a customer, buys €20 million from one bank and later closes that position by selling €20 million with a different bank, the customer bears the full responsibility of the euro and US dollar payments from one bank to another. By dealing through a prime brokerage relationship, this responsibility and the accompanying risk are eliminated. Designated banks under the prime brokerage facility will now recognise only transactions with the prime broker. The customer is relieved of any obligation should one bank make an error in delivery or fail completely. Our clients' only risk is for the net position with the prime broker, as all trades are in and out with the clearer. In the above example, the only exposure would be the net US dollar amount from the two trades. (The euro balances net to zero.)

This facility allows our customers to maintain all the benefits of trading with multiple counterparties, namely liquidity and flexibility of execution, while eliminating a potentially enormous exposure in the form of settlement risk. The resulting dollar settlements to or from the prime broker will be small relative to the bulk amounts traded.

CONCLUSION

As plan sponsors frequently struggle with the complexities surrounding currency overlay, prime brokerage can help to streamline many of the implementation issues. The benefits to clients (pension funds, institutional funds and so on) employing currency overlay managers are numerous and should not be ignored. The reduction in settlement risks, clearing risks, credit risks and legal costs – coupled with the enhancement in execution and audit procedures – is a benefit that extends above and beyond what might be provided by custodians. Currency overlay managers need to do a better job of communicating the potential benefits from a prime brokerage arrangement to their clients as well. Finally, helping to remove some of the hurdles in enacting a currency overlay and improving manager efficiency will help to grow the overlay market as well.

15

Currency Risk versus Return in Global Bond Portfolios: A Policy, not a Benchmark Issue

Charles Dolan

Pareto

INTRODUCTION

Currency in global bonds is an opportunity to diversify sources of return, even if many see it as a vexing issue for pension funds.[1] What frames global bonds as an issue instead of an opportunity is that there is no position that leaves a fund safe from regret. While global bonds are not alone in this regard, the depth of currency markets and the separability of currency returns present an opportunity to be exposed to the upside of currency returns while limiting downside.

LACK OF A "SAFE" POSITION

Because hiring an external manager for an asset class requires choosing a measurement benchmark, currency is often viewed primarily as a benchmark choice (eg, hedged, unhedged, 50/50, etc). However, it may not be helpful to view the currency issue through the sequential choices of benchmark (eg, hedged versus unhedged), active versus passive, and risk budget (ie, amount of active risk).

When choosing a benchmark, a desirable choice is one where holding the benchmark would only result in missed opportunities and not in negative returns from currency. Holding either the hedged or the unhedged benchmark in global bonds can result in regular exposure to scenarios of extreme regret. Holding the hedged benchmark in the face of large, negative, short-rate differentials can

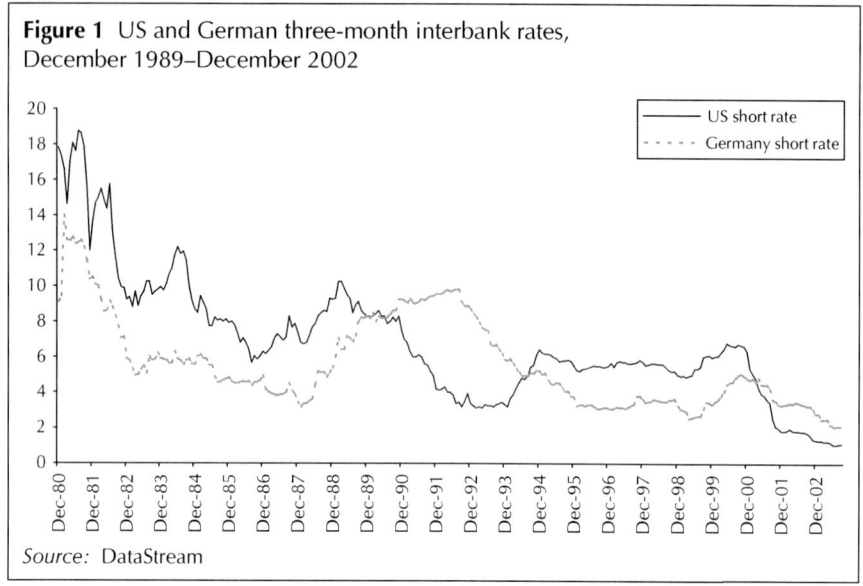

Figure 1 US and German three-month interbank rates, December 1989–December 2002

Source: DataStream

significantly erode the yield of the bond portfolios. Holding the unhedged benchmark in volatile currency environments can result in returns that are dominated by currency instead of bonds.

By choosing a benchmark for a global bond manager, a fund establishes a risk-free position for the manager, but not necessarily for the fund. Because global macroeconomic differences can persist for years at a time, leaving currency exposure at the benchmark is almost certain to expose the fund to regret.

Figure 1 above shows that extreme divergence among short-rates is the norm rather than the exception. A static hedged position in European bonds from 1991 to 1993 had hedging costs that would have probably outweighed any advantages reaped from allocating to global bonds from the perspective of a USD investor – including active management outperformance. From the perspective of a DEM (or EUR) investor, the difference is even more marked as, for most of the period (1980–90 and 1994–2000), hedging cost worked against the yield of the non-domestic bond exposure.

Similarly, holding the unhedged benchmark exposes a fund to extreme volatility relative to the asset that brings the fundamental return. Figure 2 shows the relative volatility of German currency,

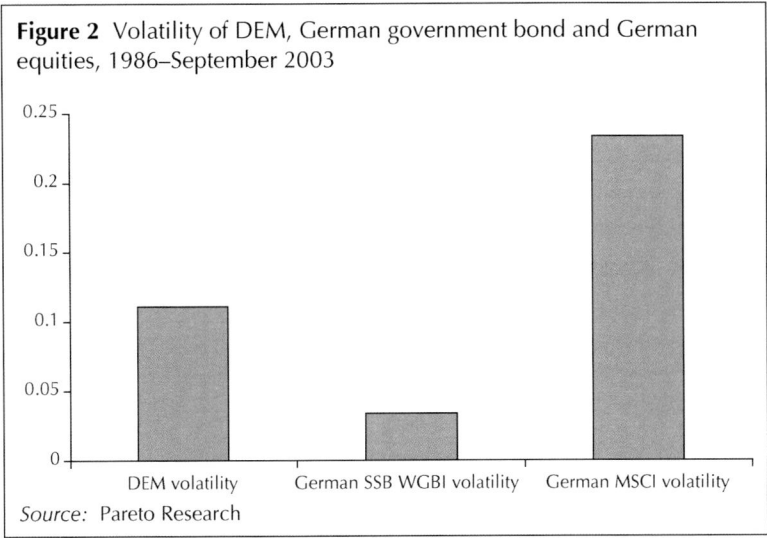

Figure 2 Volatility of DEM, German government bond and German equities, 1986–September 2003

Source: Pareto Research

bonds and equities from a USD base. Again, if a manager holds the benchmark position, a fund will frequently find itself in the position where the currency component of return dominates the bond returns.

In global bonds, the volatility and cost of hedging relative to the long-term return of the asset class negate the safe haven status of any static benchmark.

Because the potential hedging costs and volatility of currency are so much larger relative to bonds than they are relative to equities, the benchmark cannot be viewed as an isolated choice from which small, modest, active positions will be taken. More appropriately, currency should be viewed as establishing a policy for global bonds.

RE-FRAMING THE PROBLEM AS A POLICY DECISION

The definition of "investment policy" used here is the conjoint decisions on benchmark, active risk budget and risk control. Although increasing the number of dimensions makes the trade-off more complicated, the combined influence of currency and bonds outlined above makes it clear that a satisfying sequential decision is not possible, let alone optimal.

The experiments described below make the case that combining risk control with active management of currency in bonds enhances returns even when the information edge in currency is minimal compared with that in bonds. Using synthetic history, strong prior assumptions are embedded about the quality and style of the forecasting process to demonstrate the need for combining risk control with active positioning of currency in global bonds.

In the approach used below, a relatively small number of paths are used to compare specific policy combinations over the length of a full market cycle. As used here, synthetic history is distinguished from Monte Carlo by two modelling assumptions:

1. Strong prior assumptions on the forecasting process are used because standard assumptions of normality and serial independence are even more powerfully breached in forecasting processes than they are in asset returns.
2. A relatively small number of paths are used so that there is no temptation to read too much into a particular modelling of a forecasting or return-generating process.

The style of analysis used here (ie, a small number of paths) allows the examination of only a small part of the conceptual space spanned by benchmarks, risk budgets and risk control regimes. Here, the benchmark used is the hedged benchmark because, ultimately, global returns are almost always brought back to a base currency. Although a hedged benchmark does not always allow a manager to outperform in currency over a market cycle, the final policy configuration explored later (under Policy Decision II) does allow judgement of a currency manager's skill while maintaining a hedged benchmark. The return objective for all the experiments is 2–3% per annum.

In addition, a comparison is made between taking some currency risk and taking more currency risk. As with many trade-off decisions, examining the edges of the design space illuminates particular trade-offs, and here the starting point is the assumption of some active currency risk in the global bond portfolio. Additionally, the emphasis will be placed on the difference that the choice of risk control makes in choosing a policy combination.

EXPERIMENTAL SETUP

The volatility and correlation data needed for setting up Monte Carlo return series were drawn from monthly currency and bond returns for the US, Germany and the UK. Along with the exchange rates, three points on the yield curve were used: three-month, five-year and 10-year. Monthly data from 1992–99 were used to drive a multivariate-normal random walk process.

While standard assumptions were used in generating the return series, more specific assumptions were used in creating synthetic history forecasts. For 10-year bonds, a value investment strategy was assumed and the synthetic forecasts were generated such that there was a relatively low chance of poor forecasting ability over a five-year market cycle.

For short-term interest rates and foreign exchange, it was assumed that the forecasting process captured some portion of the underlying causal processes; however, factors that are not modelled result in forecasts that can be wrong for extended periods of time. In addition, the currency forecasts are assumed to be only half as accurate as the bond and short-rate forecasts.

Figures 3–5 show the distribution of five-year correlation measures for the three different types of forecasts. As described above, Figure 3 shows that there is a relatively low chance (1 in 20) of going through a five-year period where value in bonds is not

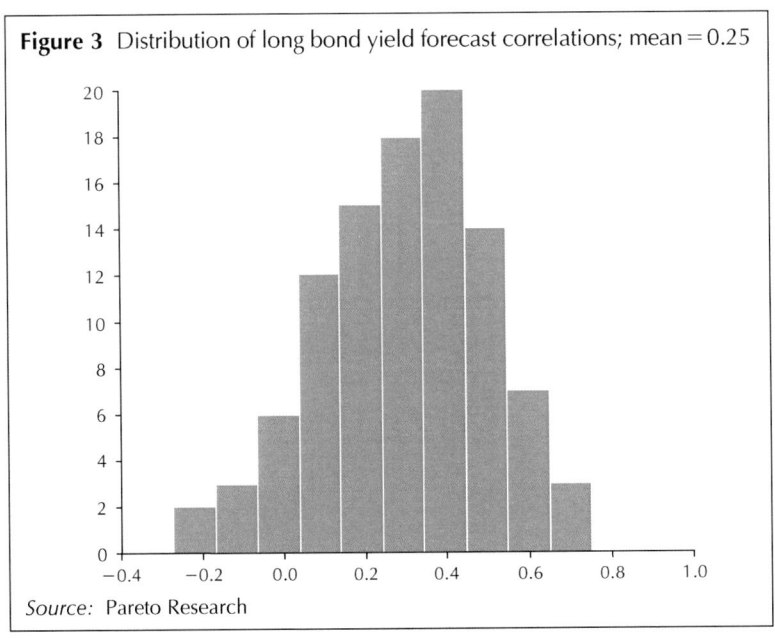

Figure 3 Distribution of long bond yield forecast correlations; mean = 0.25

Source: Pareto Research

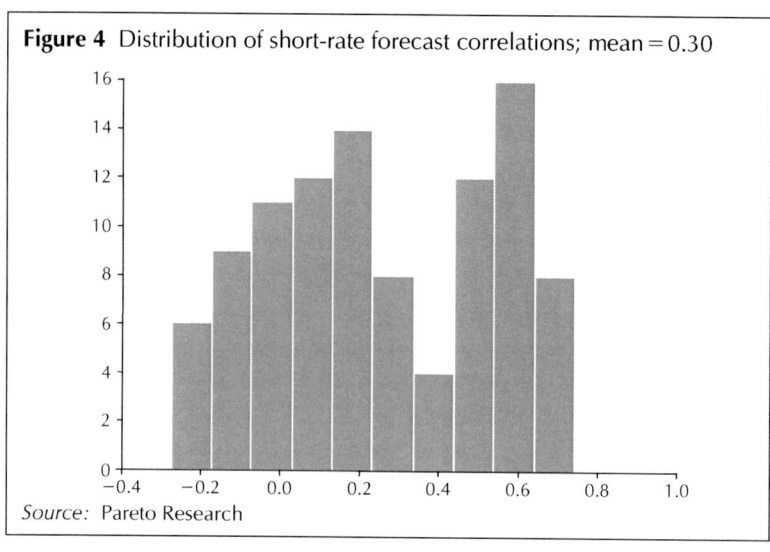

Figure 4 Distribution of short-rate forecast correlations; mean = 0.30

Source: Pareto Research

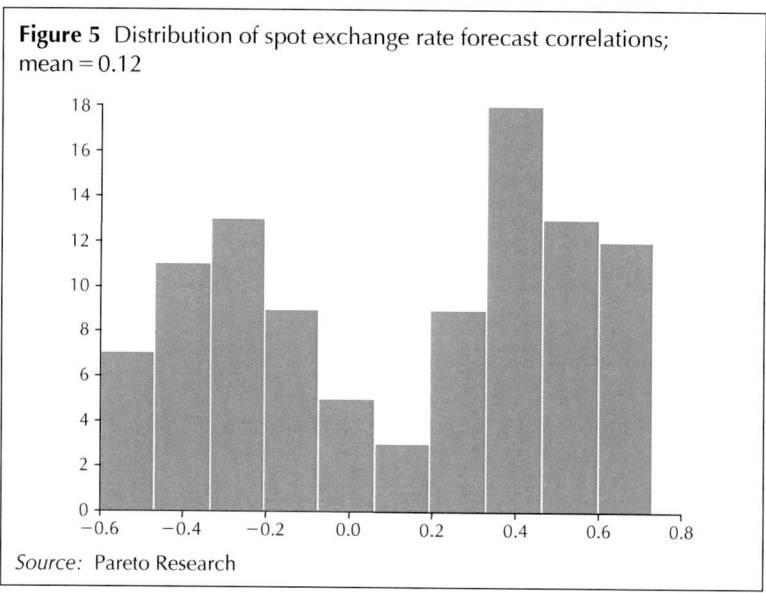

Figure 5 Distribution of spot exchange rate forecast correlations; mean = 0.12

Source: Pareto Research

rewarded. However, Figures 4 and 5 show that there are essentially two regimes for forecasts not based on value: (1) a regime where the forecasts are correct; and (2) a regime where the forecasts are wrong. To test the robustness of a policy that includes significant currency risk, the currency forecasting process has been modelled such that there is a 40% chance that the currency forecast will be poor in any given five-year market cycle.

POLICY DECISION I: HOW MUCH FX RISK TO TAKE RELATIVE TO FORECASTS

As described above, the first experiment illuminates the decision on whether to change a policy from the position of having significant active currency risk in a portfolio and addresses the question of whether there should be more active risk. In a tracking error-based optimisation framework, to achieve a 2–3% value-added objective, a portfolio might be run at an *ex ante* tracking error of 3% relative to the benchmark. In addition, either bond or currency might be allowed to have a sub-tracking error of three-quarters of the total or 2.25% per annum.[2] The policy choice drawn out by this experiment is whether the use of downside risk control *per se* changes the decision of whether to include more currency risk in the portfolio.[3]

Table 1 summarises the results of 25 synthetic history draws of five years each. The three configurations are: the starting configuration; more currency risk without protection; and more currency risk with protection. Currency protection is modelled by assuming that fairly priced one-month puts are purchased each month at 1% out-of-the-money.

Table 1 Adding more currency risk to a global bond portfolio with and without protection

	(1) High risk, 75% currency risk limit, 75% bond risk limit	(2) High risk, 100% currency risk limit, 75% bond risk limit	(3) High risk, 100% currency risk limit, 75% bond risk limit, purchased protection
Average return	2.58%	2.59%	3.64%
Standard deviation	2.83%	2.97%	2.59%
Information ratio	0.91	0.875	1.40
Difference t-statistic		−2.29	5.59

Source: Pareto Research

Here, the premium for a one-month, fairly priced put is determined using the Merton model, based on underlying volatility used to generate the currency returns.[4] Therefore the cost of the protection, while fair, will probably understate the cost to the portfolio using options purchased in the market.

The last line of Table 1 gives the t-statistic on a difference of means test between the first column (the starting assumption) and configurations that allow more currency risk with and without protection. All the differences are significant even with only 25 draws, and the case is clear: given significant currency risk, more currency risk should only be taken with protection.[5]

POLICY DECISION II: SHOULD THERE BE SYSTEMATIC FX RISK IN THE PORTFOLIO?

Starting from the position of significant currency risk in the portfolio, the next experiment attempts to determine under what circumstance the portfolio should have systematic currency risk.[6] "Systematic currency risk" is defined here as a bias towards foreign currency exposure, regardless of outlook, even when the ultimate currency benchmark is hedged. The introduction of systematic currency risk is accomplished by optimising against an unhedged benchmark, even though the measurement benchmark is the hedged benchmark.

Optimising against the unhedged benchmark means that the *ex ante* tracking error will be measured against a different benchmark than the *ex post* tracking error. The different optimisation and measurement benchmarks will necessarily mean a higher *ex post* tracking error, but not necessarily a worse information ratio.

The decision on policy in this section introduces a new alternative: cheap currency protection. Although no rational person buys expensive insurance over cheap insurance, the inclusion of cheap currency protection demonstrates that the belief in the efficacy of a practice can, and should, influence policy choices.

Cheap protection is modelled, as in the previous section, with one-month, 1% out-of-the-money puts. However, the options are priced at two-thirds of the underlying volatility used to generate the currency returns. Comparing Sections I-2 and II-2 of Table 2, the availability of cheap protection makes the use of significant amounts of active currency risk more compelling, even before including systematic foreign currency risk.

Table 2 Adding systematic currency to a global bond portfolio

	(1) High risk, 100% currency risk limit, 75% bond risk limit	(2) High risk, 100% currency risk limit, 75% bond risk limit, purchased protection	(3) High risk, 100% active currency risk limit, 75% bond risk limit, purchased protection, systematic foreign currency risk
Fixed price protection (I)			
Average return	2.59%	3.64%	9.09%
Standard deviation	2.97%	2.59%	7.00%
Information ratio	0.875	1.40	1.27
Difference t-statistic		5.59	1.47
Difference t-statistic vs (2)			−3.15
Chief protection (II)			
Average return		3.73%	10.20%
Standard deviation		2.51%	7.08%
Information ratio		1.49	1.41
Difference t-statistic		11.45	8.89
Difference t-statistic vs (2)			−0.97

Source: Pareto Research

A murkier picture arises when considering the use of systematic currency risk in global bond portfolios. A comparison of Sections I-1 and I-3 of Table 2 shows an increase in both risk (from 2.97 to 7.00) and return (from 2.59 to 9.09) and an increase in information ratio (from 0.875 to 1.27). However, the t-statistic on the differences of the information ratios (1.47) shows that including systematic currency risk is not significantly better than leaving extra currency risk out of the portfolio.[7]

In addition, with fairly priced protection, the alternative of simply adding more risk relative to the measurement benchmark dominates the inclusion of systematic foreign currency risk as shown by the t-statistic (−3.15) for the differences in information ratios between Sections I-2 and I-3.

Section II of Table 2 gives a different picture for the case where protection can be had at two-thirds of the fair cost. When there is cheap protection available, inclusion of systematic currency risk statistically dominates the alternative of leaving the extra currency risk out of the portfolio. In addition, there is no significant difference in information ratio between Sections II-2 and II-3: merely a very large difference in the mean and volatility of the portfolio returns.

The large difference in the magnitude of the returns in Sections I-2 and I-3 shows that, for high-return objectives, there must be systematic currency risk. In addition, a comparison of Sections I-3 and II-3 shows that accepting and protecting any systematic currency risk is only rewarded if the cost of protection, eg, an option premium, is below the fair cost. If the cost of protection is equal to a fairly priced option, then the extra systematic currency risk only adds volatility.

CONCLUSION

Looking at the currency decision as a policy decision and not a benchmark decision sidesteps many of the issues of benchmark selection in global bonds. If the policy decision is viewed as conjoint decisions on benchmark, active risk budget and risk control, and suitable risk control regimes are available, a policy can be established that statistically dominates the benchmark.

This chapter has used short-sample synthetic history to illustrate some policy trade-offs on the inclusion of various types of foreign currency risk in global bond portfolios. There is an unambiguous case for including vigorous foreign currency risk for high-return (>2%) objectives when protection is used.

If a particular active currency hedging strategy adds value, then another policy alternative is available: inclusion of systematic currency risk. For very high-return (>5%) objectives in global bond portfolios, the inclusion of systematic currency risk with protection is a viable alternative to managing strictly relative to a hedged benchmark.

In addition, the policy of including systematic currency risk in a portfolio gives a reference point for assessing manager skill in selecting currency exposures (other than allowing short foreign currency). If the portfolio is understood to hold some level of foreign currency risk as a matter of policy, then the manager should not systematically underperform the unhedged benchmark, even if the hedged benchmark is strong over a market cycle.

1 In this chapter "global bonds" is meant to refer to either an investment mandate that includes both domestic and international bonds or only international bonds. None of the arguments presented rely on the inclusion of domestic bonds in the benchmark or the portfolio.
2 In the experiments described here, all *ex ante* tracking and sub-tracking error constraints are implemented using quadratic constraints on the trailing covariance matrix.
3 Even in the face of the well-known shortcomings of mean variance (Michaud, 1989) and tracking error-based optimisation (Roll, 1992), the results reported here are robust enough to hold under a variety of portfolio construction techniques.
4 See Kolb (1997) for a treatment of pricing currency options.
5 The noticeably lower absolute t-statistic on differences for configurations (2) versus (3) in Table 1 can be interpreted to indicate that, for high-return objectives, a large amount of active currency risk is inevitable in global bond portfolios.
6 Because all configurations presented here are against the hedged benchmark, the term "systematic currency risk" is used to connote accepting foreign exchange risk in the same manner as equity market investors accept market risk in addition to company specific risk.
7 However, given that the t-statistic is positive, giving the manager the ability to access both sides of the benchmark is indicated if there is protection in place.

BIBLIOGRAPHY

Kolb, R. W., 1997, *Futures, Options, and Swaps* (Oxford: Blackwell).

Michaud, R., 1989, "The Markowitz Optimization Enigma: Is 'Optimized' Optimal?", *Financial Analysts' Journal*, **45(1)**, pp. 31–42.

Roll, R., 1992, "A Mean/Variance Analysis of Tracking Error", *Journal of Portfolio Management*, **18(4)**, pp. 13–22.

# Index

20th-Century View of Currency Management 90
21th-Century View of Currency Management 90

A
A chaotic model for interest rates (2003) 66
ABC Corp 154–7
ABN AMRO 32, 279
Acar (2001) 262
Acar and Maitra (2000) 110, 185
Acar and Pedersen (2000) 204
Active
  Currency Overlay 115, 118, 211, 231, 332, 333
  Hedging Strategies 191
AIMR 108, 326
Anscombe-Glynn test 310
Anson (2002) 223
ARO *see* Average rate options
Artificial intelligence 282, 285
Asset Allocation Framework 212
at-the-money-forward 156
ATMF 156, 158, 169, 200, 268
Attfield, James (1999) 78
Average rate options 171

B
Baldridge *et al* (2000) 115
Baldridge, Meath and Myers (2000) 93, 194
Banerjee (1992) 194
Bank for International Settlements 21

Barclays Capital 32
Basics of FX Prime Brokerage 353
Baz, Breedon, Naik and Peress (2001) 307
Benchmark Hedge Ratio 104, 106, 182, 211
BigMac Index 197
Binny (1998) 289
BIS
  data 28
  survey 21, 27, 33
  Triennial 57
BIS *see* Bank for International Settlements
Black Wednesday 77, 202, 310
Black-box
  models 196
  techniques 286
Black–Scholes
  formula 157, 168
  model 157, 158, 168, 243
Bretton Woods
  Philosophy and Purpose 6
  1948–71 43
  system 9, 10, 17, 309
Brian Strange (1998) 230, 278
Brock, Lakonishok and Lebaron (1992) 317
Brousseau and Scacciavillani (1999) 307
Bundes Bank 310

C
Capturing Alpha Through Active Currency Overlay 115

369

cashflow
  management 342
  risks 203, 204
central limit theorem 142
Chicago Mercantile Exchange (CME) 15, 24
Choppier fashion 246
Choppier periods 246
Citibank 51, 52, 55, 59
Citigroup 32, 59, 175, 267
Clarke and Kritzman (1996) 108
CME *see* Chicago Mercantile Exchange
Colchester and James (2003) 97
Commodity Futures Trading Commission 308
Credit Suisse First Boston 32
critical mass effect 33
CTAs 277, 279, 281, 351
Currency Hedge Ratio 209, 331
currency hedge rebalancing strategy 186
Currency Management
  Background 325
  experience 326
  framework 176–8
  on Global Bonds 343
Currency Overlay
  before Prime Brokerage 352
  Delivered on its Promise 92
  Management 95, 118, 325
  managers 39, 40, 42, 89, 106, 112, 118, 277–9, 281, 303, 334, 338, 356
currency risk 70, 78, 83, 94, 98, 102, 104, 108, 121, 123–6, 181, 182, 186, 188, 190, 211, 290, 329, 330, 333, 335–7, 343, 347, 355, 357, 360, 363–6

D
D'Agostino's test 310
day-to-day risk management 134
Deutsche Bank 32, 108, 109, 354
Dittmar (1997) 314
Dublin Summit of 1996 19

E
E-commerce 58, 62, 63
EAFE 83, 102, 104, 327
EBS *see* Electronic Broker Services
ECB 20, 44
EEC 16
Electronic Broker Services 50, 51
Embrechts (1997) 141
equity
  indices 69–71, 130
  Markets 13, 21, 25, 54, 128, 151, 232, 241, 333, 340
ERM 17, 18, 20, 35, 41, 43, 74, 202, 274
EU Treaties 20
Euromoney Forex Survey 32
European
  Central Bank (ECB) 20
  Commission 20
  Economic Community (EEC) 16
  Exchange Rate Mechanism 77
  Monetary System (EMS) 17, 310
  Single Currency 20
  Snake 15
Europhobia 94
europhoria 94
EVT *see* extreme value theory
Exchange
  Controls 7, 9, 10, 14, 19, 23, 24, 43
  Rate Mechanism (ERM) 17
Exotic options 170, 290
extreme value theory 141, 143

F
Fama (1984) 107, 307
FCM 351
FEER *see* fundamental equilibrium exchange rate
foreign currency
  cashflow 154
  exposure 298, 364
  revenues 161
  risk 364–6
foreign exchange risk 156, 159, 161, 179
Franc Fort policy 18
Frankel and Rose (1995) 306

Froot and Rogoff (1994) 289
FTSE 84, 184
fundamental economic analysis 92
fundamental equilibrium exchange rate 288

G
Genetic algorithms 238, 239, 242, 282, 285
Global
  Bond Portfolios 325, 345, 357, 365, 366
  Pensions Magazine 189
Goldman Sachs 32
Green (2001) 262
Grinold and Meese (2000) 214, 224
Growth of e-commerce 62

H
hedge
  currency 328, 329, 336
  funds 27, 29, 42, 43, 57, 98, 277, 279, 281, 299, 303, 311, 346
  ratio 91, 105, 118, 177, 179–83, 186, 188, 192–4, 196, 199, 203, 204, 209, 211, 212, 218, 220, 222–5, 232
Hersey and Minnick (2000) 117
Hersey and Ogunc (2000) 93
HSBC 32
Huang (2002) 262
Huang, Srivastava and Raatz (2001) 97

I
IBRD *see* International Bank for Reconstruction and Development
ICC *see* industrial and commercial company
Ilmanen and Sayood (2002) 307
IMF 6, 7, 9, 10
IMM *see* International Monetary Market
in-the-money 156, 297, 298
Income
  Flows 24
  volatility 148

industrial and commercial company 18, 37
institutional investors 175, 303, 325, 338
interest rate parity 210
interest rate swap (IRS) 132
International Bank for Reconstruction and Development 6
International Monetary Fund (IMF) 6
International Monetary Market 6, 308
Internet Age of Trading 54
IRP *see* interest rate parity
ITM *see* in-the-money

J
James (1999) 87
James (2003) 82, 320
James and Colchester (2003) 267
James, Webber (2000) 66
Jarque-Bera test 311
John Williamson (1994) 288
JP Morgan
  Chase 32
  Fleming Asset Management 278

K
K-nearest neighbours 286, 291
Knauf (2003) 308
knock-in option 171
knock-out option 171
Krishnamurthi and Muralidhar (2003) 98
Kritzman (1993) 107, 194
Kritzman (2000) 306

L
Le Baron (1999) 194, 307, 314
Lee (1995) 194
leptokurtosis 168
Lequeux and Acar (1998) 110
Levich (1993) 194
Levich and Thomas (1993) 108, 289, 307, 314
LIBOR 98
London's Financial Times 16

M
Maastricht Treaty 19, 20
macro-hedge ratio 185
macro-hedging decision 178, 179, 181, 202
Malliares (2002) 310
Mark Kritzman (1999) 289
market
 behaviour 37, 41, 309
 liquidity 21, 59
 risks 29, 129, 130, 132, 134, 149–51, 159, 172, 173
Mashayekhi-Beschloss and Muralidhar (1997) 90
Mechanics of Overlay 329
Meese and Rogoff (1983) 306
Mehrzad and Muralidhar (2001) 98
merger and acquisition (M&A) 38
Misina (2003) 307
Modern Market Structure 22
Monte Carlo simulation 150
Morgan Stanley Capital International 328
Mountain lake method 125
multibank
 portals accounts 57
 price 56
 space 57
Muralidhar and Neelakandan (2002 and 2003) 95
Muralidhar and Neelakandan (2002a) 97
Muralidhar and Neelakandan (2002b, 2003) 97
Muralidhar and Pasquariello (2001) 93
Muralidhar and Richmond (1999) 94
Muralidhar and Tsumagari (1999) 92
Muralidhar (1999) 93
Muralidhar (2000) 93, 94
Muralidhar (2001) 92
Muralidhar (2002) 95, 97
Muralidhar, O'Grady and Simotas (2002) 96
Muralidhar, Prajogi and van der Wouden (2000) 94

N
NASDAQ 21
neural networks 282, 285, 286, 312
New single European currency 19

O
OLS *see* ordinary least squares
ordinary least squares 284
OTC *see* over-the-counter
OTM 156, 170, 171
over-the-counter 156
Oxford University 230

P
Pareto
 Partners 328, 335
 Research 359, 363, 365
parity level 8, 42
Passive Hedging Strategies 173, 181
Passsive Management Strategies 189
Pedersen (2002, 2003) 186
Pedersen and De Zwart (2003) 307
Persaud (1996) 307
PPP 197–9, 287–9
purchasing power parity 240, 287
purchasing power parity theorem 106

Q
quadratic
 programming 213
 solutions 213

R
Re-Emergence of Central Banks 34
Reinert (2000) 108
return on capital (ROC) 148, 149
Reuters Dealing System 50
reverse causality 345
risk control 89, 92, 93, 169, 173, 359, 360, 363, 366

Risks for Hedgers vs Risks for Traders 125
RMS *see* root-mean-squared
ROC *see* return on capital
root-mean-squared 72, 73
Rosenberg and Folkerts-Landau (2002) 108

S
S&P250 95
S&P500 95
SDR 10
SDRs *see* Special Drawing Rights
Settlement Risk Reduction 355
Sharpe's ratio 124
Siegel's paradox 306
slope factor 125
Smithsonian Agreement 309, 328
Special Drawing Rights 6
SPX 219
Squawk box 50
SSB 219, 220
stable hedge ratios 196
standard regression modelling techniques 302
STP 56–8, 61, 341
straight through processing (STP) 49
Strange (1998) 93, 112, 116
Sullivan, Timmerman and White (1999) 307, 317
Swedish krone devaluation 18
systematic currency risk 364–6
Szakmary and Mathur (1997) 194

T
Three Types of Currency Management 335
Tiered exposure limits 134
time
  horizon 179, 225, 279–81, 299, 303
  zone 33
Trading
  for Profit 229, 237
  Models 82, 126, 175, 242–4, 277–9, 286, 287, 293, 299, 301, 303, 308, 310, 312, 317, 320
  Strategy Issues 234
trend following 92, 289, 290, 299

U
UBS 32
UK institutional investors 10
US
  current account deficit 285
  Federal Reserve Bank 6
Utility maximisation Equation 214

V
Value-At-Risk (VAR) 136
VanderLinden, Jiang and Hu (2002) 194
VAR
  number 136, 139
  techniques 136, 140, 141, 143
viable
  active strategy 224
  hedge strategy 188
  option-selling strategies 274
volatile equity markets 128

W
Wall Street 161, 165, 177
Weekly rebalancing strategy 187, 188, 190
Whipsaw
  filter 293
  market 292
White (2000) 317
World Bank 6, 89

Y
yawning culture gap 16

Z
zero JPY exposure 330
zero-cost
  framework 262
  instruments 78
zillion investors 237

CATTLE ANNIE
✫ AND ✫
LITTLE BRITCHES

by Robert Ward

CATTLE ANNIE AND LITTLE BRITCHES
SHEDDING SKIN

CATTLE ANNIE ☆ AND ☆ LITTLE BRITCHES

By ROBERT WARD

WILLIAM MORROW AND COMPANY, INC.
New York   1978

Copyright © 1977 by Robert Ward

All rights reserved. No part of this book may be reproduced or utilized in any form or by any means, electronic or mechanical, including photocopying, recording or by any information storage and retrieval system, without permission in writing from the Publisher. Inquiries should be addressed to William Morrow and Company, Inc., 105 Madison Ave., New York, N. Y. 10016.

Printed in the United States of America.

1 2 3 4 5 6 7 8 9 10

Library of Congress Cataloging in Publication Data

Ward, Robert (date)
    Cattle Annie and Little Britches.

    I. Title.
PZ4.W2549Cat 1978   [PS3573.A735]   813'.5'4   77-241
ISBN 0-688-03252-4

BOOK DESIGN   **CARL WEISS**

FOR

MY MOTHER

AND

MY FATHER

AND FOR

ROBIN FINN

AUTHOR'S NOTE

Cattle Annie and Little Britches is a novel, that is an act of the imagination, which is based on a framework of historical fact. "Annie," "Britches," the "Doolin-Dalton Gang" and their nemesis, "Big Bill Tilghman," were of course all real people, but they're also legend, which is one of the things they set out to be. This legend inspires in each of us a fantasy of the Old West, which is like a dream of America, a dream that instructs us about our own rootlessness, ambitions and desire for both adventure and community. This novel is my personal interpretation of our oldest romantic legends, ones which, despite all our progress, live on in the hearts of most Americans.

CHAPTER

I

THE RACE, OKLAHOMA, 1895

THE DAMNED DUST WAS FLYING IN GREAT SWIRLS UP IN MY FACE, causing me to choke and gag, but I kept right on after Annie. I was trying powerful hard to feel all excited and tingly about meeting *them,* but the truth of the matter was I was getting pretty wore out. Chasing Annie (as I was prone to do, me not being the ideal horsewoman) is a tiring proposition. First off, she gets hunched real low, and second off, she knows how to make her bones just flow with the horse . . . something any good rider can do. . . . They say you can learn it, but here's one cowgirl who never could. I still bounce around like a dude even to this day.

I'll say one thing though; she was beautiful up there in front of you, all flowing away, her black hair streaming in the night wind, and her red scarf trailing behind her. She looked like some kind of magical fairy princess swooping out of the clouds (though in this case the clouds was horsedust). Not that I'd have ever told her that. She didn't like fairy tales, considered them sissyfied. Her idea of a good girl's yarn was *Bat Masterson Meets Dead Eye Dick*. She was always reading that stuff.

But first things first. Like I say, I was trying to catch up with her, and she finally slows down a bit, turns her sassy head, gives me that cockbrowed look, and says: "Are you coming along, girl, or do I leave you here in the dust?"

"I'm coming," I say, my voice sounding like a frog with the whoop.

Annie smiled then, and I had to laugh myself (though jes once I woulda loved to beat her somewheres).

"It's right over yonder," she said, pointing across the field of blue flowers, toward the barn, which was lit up like some great big surprise.

"Jes like it always is," I said in my cynical voice, though I didn't feel all that hard inside.

"But tonight is different," Annie said.

Her eyes got big as moons then, and she bit her lower lip. Sometimes when she was real excited she looked jes like the little girl of fifteen she was. It always surprised me, because I thought of her as older. How old I couldn't say, but the way she talked and held herself made you forget she was jesta kid.

"Every night is gonna be different," I said, sounding like a mortician (though my heart was thumping).

"No, Jennie. Tonight they're gonna be there. Come on. I can hear the fiddles playing."

She looked down at her big six-gun strapped to her leg. The truth is the gun came almost down to her knee, but there wasn't no doubt she could use it. Target practice was Annie's big passion.

"Let's go, girl," she said.

With that she turned and left me standing there coughing, gagging and eating her dust.

"I'll catch you, Annie. Look out, cause I'm a-coming."

I dug my heels into Jake's sides, and he sprung across the blue field toward her. Even though I knew she was gonna beat me, I couldn't help but get caught up in it all. I mean what if they *were* there? The Doolin-Dalton Gang! Annie had been reading me stories about that bunch for a month and a half, all those good novels by Ned Buntline. Whenever we had a break at Morgan's Hash House, she would get out the books, and start in acting out the Gang's latest adventures. God she was a great reader, and now here I was cutting through the night, the wind blowing my hair back, my horse snorting and heading toward the square dance (the fiddles and guitars were soaring all around). Even though I like to think I'm kind of level-headed, I have to admit it was damn intoxicatin. The Doolin-Dalton Gang, right here in our own little barn dance! And Annie sailing across the lake of flowers ahead of me . . . she looked so beautiful there in the saddle . . . why it just *had* to be so . . . we *would* meet them, and we would *dance* with them . . . with Bill Doolin, Bill Dalton, Bittercreek Newcomb, that big handsome half-breed I'd half fallen for just from the pictures in Ned Buntline's books . . .

Oh, how I wanted it to happen. By the time we got to the barn, I guess I was as excited as Annie. My flesh was tingling and even the sweat on my forehead felt good.

Annie dismounted from her horse, Rex, in one quick swoop. Then as we tied up the nags, she tapped me on the back and pressed the cold gun barrel into my back.

"Stick 'em up, pardner," she said. "This here's a robbery!"

"Annie," I said. "Put that thing back in your saddle bag."

She smiled and pushed her dark hair back from her face. Her teeth shone in the night, and she held herself tensed, like a cocky little rooster.

"If guns is good enough for the Doolin-Dalton Gang, they're good enough for me."

"There's just one problem," I said.

"What's that?"

"You ain't them."

"Hell, girl . . ."

But she saw I was right.

"Oh, all right," she said. "I'll put it back. I wouldn't want to terrify the good citizens."

"Thata girl," I said, sounding just like her mother, though she was a year older than me.

She turned and just before sticking the gun in her bag, she got the drop on Rex.

"Gotcha," she said, aiming the gun at Rex's bloodshot eye. He was real unimpressed though, just snorted a bit, and nuzzled against the barrel. I guess with all the sweat dropping off of him, the cold steel felt kinda nice.

"Come on," I said, rolling my eyes and trying to act as unexcited as Rex. "Wouldn't want to miss the Gang! Though I don't see no horses, or hear no commotion."

"They're not here yet," Annie said, turning and taking my arm in her strong little grip.

"But they're gonna be here, Jennie. Oh yes. Tonight *is* the night."

"Sure, sure," I said, hoping like hell I was wrong in my doubting.

We walked around the side of the barn and stared inside at the dancers, the bright party lanterns hanging from the ceiling, and the band. "Turkey in the Straw" was whirling away, and in spite of everything I felt my heart soar, and my breath got taken away.

Annie turned and smiled at me.

"Shall we dance, my dear?" she said.

"By all means, my lady," I replied.

And so we strolled inside.

CHAPTER *II*

THE DANCE

"Check out them geezers playing up there," Annie said, pointing to the bandstand.

"Have you ever seen a sadder assed looking group? That fiddler looks like he was born in a storm cellar and let out jes to scare the pigs!"

Which, Lord knows, was the truth. This dude was an *old* seventy, and he had an Adam's apple that popped up and down like there was a little man with strings somewhere inside of his balding red-faced head. Still and all, when it came to hitting the notes, he had the knack, that's for certain. He could make that old fiddle stand up and talk. They were sounding pretty darned good, in spite of their looks. Which is more than I can say for the so-called young men in the audience.

"Check them," I said, turning to the far side of the room, where five of the sorriest-looking creatures in God's creation were sitting all lined up, and staring at us as if we had just descended from the heavenly choir. Once they saw Annie's black almond eyes boring into them, they began to snicker, and shoved one of their kind, a kid dressed in blue overalls and a pair of boots that were guaranteed to fracture your feet.

"Come on, Billy Joe, get out there. You ask them girls to dance, Billy Joe. Come on now!"

Poor Billy Joe didn't look like no Romeo. He was resisting with all his puny weight, trying like hell to get back in the wallflower line.

Annie gave one short snort of disgust and led me across the room, where we spied a couple of empty chairs. Meanwhile the old geezers up on the bandstand were ripping into a reel, and the farmers and their tired, skinny wives were kicking up their heels.

"Well," Annie said, slumping down in her chair, "it won't be long now."

"Right," I said. "Right, right, right."

Annie turned to me and gave me that big hopeful smile, the one she knew I couldn't resist. She was right there. Even when I knew *she* knew I was gonna get caught up in her enthusiastic foolishness, well I still went for it. A cynic is jes waiting for an optimist to show her the way.

"But what makes you really think they are gonna come?" I said.

"I told you," she said, fixing her shirt collar. "I got the news from C.J., and he heard it from Elwood. You know Elwood always keeps up with the outlaw gangs. Anyway, they are supposed to be here tonight. On their way back from Bartlesville. I think they hit a bank down there."

"Great," I said. "We get to meet 'em with a posse on their tail."

Annie smiled, as if I was a natural-born moron.

"You ever hear of any posse catch Bill Doolin?" she said. "The Doolin-Daltons specialize in losing posses."

"Speaking of losing people," I said, "we oughta specialize in losing this lizard creeping around the wall toward us."

Annie followed my finger to the opposite side of the room.

Sure enough, old Billy Joe was creeping toward us, as if he were advancing on a couple of wild stallions, or a nest of snakes.

"This ought to be good. Look at the rest of them rubes."

I looked over at the other young men. A homelier lot you couldn't hope to find this side of a medicine show. Joshing and punching each other, they found the pathetic advances of their pal to be the funniest thing short of a hanging.

Now the poor soul was on our side of the room, moving forward toward us, like he had a bunch of rusty joints. His arms was stuck out straight, and his hair was standing up on his head, like some ghosts were hovering in front of his bloodshot eyes.

"Hi," he said, giving a grin with his big yellow corn teeth.

Before we could think of a suitable reply, he tripped over a bench and sprawled head first on the floor.

"I'm Billy Joe Jeever," he said, looking up and taking the splinters out of his nose.

"Charmed, I'm sure," Annie said, bowing from the waist.

The other lads on the opposite side of the room thought their friend's disaster the funniest thing since sin. They began pounding one another on their backs, and screaming at him. A real chorus of woe.

"Chick Chick Chick. . . . Look at lovvvvver boy!"

Billy Joe scrambled to his feet, and took off across the room after them, but they all headed out into the starry night, screaming, hooting and generally acting as if they had never heard of "civility" (one of them fancy new words Mrs. Patterson taught me).

"Well this *is* a good time," I said, starting to feel kind of bad for real. We had come all the way from Guthrie, a ride of some thirty miles, through some real rough country in the piney woods. Worse, we had to get back tomorrow morning to sling hash again for Old Man Morgan. I could already see his great red nose all lit up and the words shooting out of his mouth like Injuns' arrows.

"You girls stay out late? Well, that's too bad. It ain't no fault of mine. You keep slinging that hash. Keep those dishes in the air. One in the air at all times. You think I'm running a resort for your benefit?"

A nicer man you couldn't hope to find.

"Hell, Annie," I said, staring at the riffraff. "This is no fun at all. Those Dalton boys are jes passing this place by."

But Annie was never one to quit. She set her jaw, crossed her arms and legs and shook her head.

"They'll be here," she said, waving her arms and smiling. "And when they do come . . . it's going to change everything. Ain't you tired of Guthrie? God it's like an old age home. Don't you want some adventure?. Riding the purple plains . . . running down vast shipments of gold on speeding trains? . . . Fighting off posses and stealing out of town in the dead of night?"

"That ain't the point," I said, trying not to get swept away by Annie's poetry. "That ain't it at all. The point is that we are here and the Doolin-Daltons are more than likely on their way to Tulsa, or to their hideout up in Ingalls. And what if they'd come here. Let's say they do. How are we gonna talk to them? Us talking to . . . living legends?"

"*Living* legends is right," Annie said, smiling as happy as the sun. "They're *living,* and they're gonna show us how! Listen to this a minute."

I knew what was coming. Annie's latest outlaw book. But I didn't discourage her none. Hell, I'd rather listen to her reading than watch these duffers kick each other in the shins.

She brought the book out of her back pocket and opened it up. It was always a pleasure to watch Annie right before she started reading. She'd lick her index finger and flip through the pages. Then her tongue would come out and wet her lips, and sometimes she'd bite her lower lip, and her eyes would get all big. A more enthusiastic reader you couldn't find outside of a traveling theater troupe, which by the way was another of her life's great ambitions. To be an actress . . . oh, this girl always thought big.

"Now listen, Jennie. Here. It's right here," she said, clearing her throat. " 'Wild Bill Doolin, the toughest and smartest of the dying breed of outlaws, has a face like a huge, friendly walrus . . . but don't be fooled by this gentle fatherly countenance.' "

"What's a countenance?" I said, playing dumb.

"And this," Annie said, ignoring my crack (she was real good at getting deaf when she wanted to make a point). " 'His partner is the handsome, dashing Bill Dalton, the sole surviving member of the murderous Dalton Gang, who were wiped out on October fifth, 1892, while attempting to stage the most daring twin bank robbery in all of recorded history at their hometown in Coffeyville, Kansas.' "

I slumped over on Annie's shoulder, and started making snoring noises, but she was hot now and no amount of joshing was going to keep her from getting where she wanted to go.

"They woulda made it too, in Coffeyville," Annie said, "if it hadn't been for a time-lock safe."

"What's that?" I said, getting interested in spite of myself.

"I'm not exactly sure," Annie said, turning to me, and talking loud over the music. "I think it's some kinda new invention. You lock the safe at twelve o'clock, and it stays locked until twelve o'clock the next day. You jes can't open it before then. And what happened was that the Daltons robbed the bank across the street, and then stood around waiting for the lock safe to open. By the time it did, the people in the town had gone and gotten their friends and a whole hell of a lot of guns. When the Gang came out back, they just got blasted away. Bill Dalton was the only one to survive!"

"Gee," I said, sounding jes like a kid.

Annie smiled and raised her eyebrows.

"Listen to this one, Miss Jennie Stevens," she said. "You'll find this passage particularly interesting: 'And Bittercreek Newcomb, a rugged brawling saloon fighter . . . but quite a ladies' man.' "

"Yes, yes," I said, getting very very interested now. "Where are these lads? Tell me more."

"They'll be here," Annie said. "They're gonna come soon."

If it had been in one of Annie's books it woulda seemed kind of corny, but the truth is that not five minutes after Annie's reading of Ned Buntline to me, we began to hear a tremendous kind of thumping noise outside the window, which was directly behind us. There was no doubt about what it was. If you have never heard a huge mob of cowboys coming up toward you, you have missed one of the great sounds in the world, but if you have never looked out a window and seen them coming toward you, a thundering herd of them, waving their hats, and yelling, "Yaw Yaw," with the big yellow moon behind them, the horses' nostrils open as they get closer and closer, and the dust rising around them like steam from a sulphur bath . . . well, it's enough to take away your breath and stop your heart.

"God," I said. "God, look at 'em!"

For once Annie had nothing at all to say. She was just sitting there, her legs straddling the chair, and her mouth falling open. Then both of us pressed our noses up against the dusty window and looked closer at the Gang.

And what a sight they were!

First off his horse came Bill Doolin. A huge man, with a black moustache, and a belly which swayed over his belt like a sack of meal, he clenched his teeth together and used his right hand to prop up his left arm which was tied in a blue-and-white kerchief.

"Doolin's been shot," I heard someone say, so I turned around and behind me was half the barn dance, all lined up and pressing in on us. Only the fiddler and the banjo man were still playing. When I looked out again, I saw Bill Dalton taking off his big white hat, slicking back his hair and dusting off his wide leather chaps. He was a younger man than I had thought, from hearing

Annie's description in the books. In fact, the closer I pressed my nose on the glass, the younger he seemed to get. His hair was long and brown and greased straight back, his face was lean, and he was clean-shaven. I looked over at Annie and she turned to me and rolled her eyes.

"He's mine," she whispered. "Oh yes."

Behind Dalton was Bittercreek Newcomb, and I could feel my own breath being sucked out of my chest. He was a big strong man, with a face that was dark and all angles. I saw him look in the window, and our eyes seemed to meet, and I felt as though I were being pulled right through the glass towards him. It was a strange and troubling feeling, and I dropped my eyes, but it made no difference. He was still looking at me. I knew it, and I wanted him to, but I was afraid.

When I looked back up, I saw the other members of the Gang, but I wasn't clear who they were, so I asked Annie.

"That big one . . . the one with the scar is Dan Clifton and the little guy there with the silver coins in his belt is Dick Whisper. . . . He got shot in the throat once up in Kansas City and he can only talk in a whisper . . . and the one next to him is Little Bill Raidler . . . that one, smoking the cigar."

I felt suspended in a cloudy dream. Though I heard their names, I still didn't have them all placed; the window made the difference. It was as though I was seeing them through some kind of fishbowl, and I felt that even though they were right outside, only inches away, I'd still never meet 'em. Imagine how I felt, then, when I realized that Doolin and Dalton had come around front and were already in the door.

"God, he's beautiful," I heard Annie say.

She had turned from the window and was staring at Bill Dalton like he was a big juicy steak. Her eyes lit up and her teeth were clenched together. We watched as some of the old-timers, a man with a pocket watch and another guy with red lumps on his head, came up to Bill Doolin and hugged him tightly (taking care not to hurt his busted-up arm).

"Bill Doolin," the old guy said, his voice cracking with emotion, "we heard you was coming. How's the arm?"

Doolin nodded, gave the man a big warm grin, then reached his hurt arm across his body and quickly drew his gun.

"Works jes fine," he said.

The old guy about had a conniption fit, kept slapping his hand on his leg, like he had seen the Maker himself.

Meanwhile much the same kind of homecoming was being given to Dalton, who smiled and pumped hands with people just like he was running for sheriff.

"Let me get over to this punch bowl," I heard him say. "We been riding all afternoon and evening and I don't mind telling you I've worked up one hell of a thirst!"

While Doolin made his way across the room, I turned and saw Bittercreek coming through the door. He was powerfully built, with wide shoulders and a very narrow waist that you just wanted to squeeze. He turned and looked right at me, and I felt as though I was going to fall backwards right through the glass.

Before anything melodramatic like that happened, he was mobbed by a couple of older girls and I felt something hot spearing through me. Damn, if he wasn't a beautiful sight, just the ladies' man Ned Buntline had made him out to be.

Pretty soon the rest of the Gang came in and the music began to play again, while the outlaws gathered around the punch bowl, talking and laughing. Only Annie and I and a couple of the other younger kids stood in the back.

"Now what?" I said to Annie.

She smiled and put her hand on my wrist.

"I thought you didn't care if they came or not, Jennie dear?"

"Will you shut up and do something," I said. "You're the leader. Now lead on."

"My pleasure," she said.

With that Annie began to move up toward the crowd of men and women who were surrounding the Doolin-Daltons. The crowd was three deep and I didn't put much stock in Annie getting through, but I hadn't counted on her ability to squirm. When you get right down to it, there ain't no better squirmer in the Southwest than Annie McDougal.

CHAPTER

III

ANNIE GIVES ADVICE

She sort of elbowed her way in between an old guy leaning on a cane (almost knocking him over in the process) and then came to what looked like an immovable object, one of them cow-wide farmers, who seemed to cover the whole side of the room. But by tapping him on the shoulder she got him to turn around and stare down at the poor old limp duffer. As soon as he was staring Annie had disappeared into the mob and I guess she was practically right on top of the goddamned living legends. Well, that was my signal. In those days I wasn't especially brave, but I sure couldn't miss this! (Secretly, I think a small hunk of me wanted to see Miss Annie McDougal make an ass out of herself!) So here I went, right behind the trail she had squirmed and like a pack rat I kind of followed through the opening, and somehow I found myself (heart beating like a big bass drum) standing right up there next to her. And her standing right next to the man himself, none other than the Romeo of the West, Big Bill Dalton. He was turned away from her, but when she got within two inches of him, she gave a loud cough, and he turned around fast, just like a snake with fire in his eyes. (Excuse my purple prose, but you got to remember the only books I read until we got put in with Mrs. Louella Patterson was Ned Buntline's. And truth be told, I still am entranced by the majestic sweep of his florid pen.)

"Hey," he said, startled, "you shouldn't be sneaking up on people, you know?"

Annie put her hands on her hips and stared up into his eyes, with plenty of smoke in her own.

"I wasn't sneaking up on nobody!" she said, jes like she might trip him up and pin him to the floor.

Dalton looked a little taken aback then.

"Oh," was all he could muster up.

"I was jes happening to be getting some punch, that's all," Annie said, flip as you please. "You boys think you *own* the punch bowl?"

With that, Dalton kind of recouped and turned and looked at his pals. He had one eyebrow cocked, and he twisted his mouth around in a look that said, "What in the hell do we have here?"

Then, in a voice that sounded as polite as some kid from one of them fancy Eastern schools (like Pine Manor, but for boys), he said: "No ma'am . . . could I *please* get you some punch?"

The whole Gang showed their yellow teeth on that one, and I felt shaky, cause I thought Annie was going to be set back badly. But I should have known better.

She jes smiled her winning grin and with complete seriousness (jes like she wasn't aware he was joshing her—oh, she could be clever) said: "Yes, thank you, Mr. Dalton, sir. I'm very much obliged."

Well that stopped him cold again, and this time when he looked down at her it was with a little bit less playfulness. In fact, if I read him right, there was jes the beginning of a little anger in his eye.

Whatever he felt, he turned politely, picked up a glass and punch dipper, and made a great show of filling Annie's cup to the brim. Then, with that same real smooth style, he handed it to her and gave a little bow at the waist. Which Annie immediately answered with a curtsy. Dalton turned around, gave a short little smile, and then turned as if for him this affair had come to an end. I looked at Annie and shrugged my shoulders. She had tried after all, and I wasn't going to josh her much. But I shouldn't have counted her out yet. When our eyes met, I could see she was making one of her connections. That's how she has always worked. You couldn't call her really a brain or nothing but she works on what Mrs. Patterson called "poetic inspiration."

So a second later, she was tapping Mr. Bill Dalton, King of the Badmen, on his back, just like it was a door.

He turned around and she started smiling at him again.

"Excuse me, Mr. Dalton, sir. But my friend, Jennie, would *also* like some punch."

I held my breath, thinking that the Outlaw King might just fly off the handle a little. But he rose to the occasion like a real gentleman.

"Really?" he said, sounding like some kind of English lord or something. "Would she now? I'd be delighted to get your friend punch. Without a doubt!"

With that he turned and got me some punch. It was long about then that I noticed all them badasses were staring right at me. Dynamite Dick, and that shifty eyed looking little gila-monstered face, Bill Raidler, and Dick Whisper, no stage star himself, and Old Man Doolin, whose eyes were sagging and red, half-shut, and then Bittercreek, whose eyes held a different look, bright and frightening. All this attention made me go soft in the head, mushy in the knees and tingly all over. The silence seemed to last for an hour. Then Annie spoke up, as sure and straight as a bullet.

"You see, Mr. Dalton," she said. "I been following you boys' careers. I been waiting to meet you. And I'm right proud too! My name's Annie McDougal."

Dalton smiled then, a warm and friendly smile, and offered Annie his huge calloused hand.

"Bill Dalton," he said. "Who's your friend?"

I felt like running out of the room, but Annie reached around and tugged my sleeve a little, pulling me forward.

"This is my best friend, Jennie Stevens," Annie said.

Dalton's face was as friendly as a jack-o'-lantern.

"Hello, Jennie," he said. "These are my friends. Mr. Bittercreek Newcomb and Mr. Bill Doolin and Mr. Dick Whisper . . ."

When he heard his name announced, Dick Whisper moved up to the front of the group and offered his hand to me. I shook it, and he hissed something, but I couldn't make it out.

"What'd you say?" I asked him, and then the whole Gang started roaring, slapping their backs and making a hell of a fuss.

When all the commotion stopped, Mr. Dick Whisper started with that confounded hissing again.

"Pleased to meet you girls," he wheezed. "You certainly are pretty."

That comment made me blush and caused the boys to nod their heads, and say, "Oh ho, Oh ho," jes like those punks on the other side of the room might have done. I woulda thought big-time outlaws woulda had more savoir faire, and stuff of that nature, but it weren't so at all.

When they had stopped elbowing and hitting one another like a pack of barnheads, Annie spoke up: "I'm real sorry you got shot, Mr. Doolin, sir," she says in the sweetest little voice you could ever hope to hear.

Old Doolin sat down on his bench and nodded at her. When

he talked his eyes twinkled though, and his big walrus moustache seemed to float independent of his face.

"Thank you fer your concern, honey," he said in a gruff but kindly old voice. "But getting holes put in you is jes one of the hazards of my chosen profession."

That brought about laughs from all of us, and I could feel something stirring in me for the old-timer. He had real class, there was no doubt about it.

After the laughter died down, everyone sort of stared at one another, as if they were waiting for somebody to pick up the thread, but the thread had plumb ran out, and so the Gang slowly turned toward one another, and me and Annie seemed to be left out in the cold again. But Dalton hadn't forgotten us. He turned back around and said in a voice almost as tired and decent as Doolin's: "It was a real pleasure meeting you girls, but we're all tired. . . . We jes got in, you know, and it's been a hell of a day."

Annie nodded, and I was sure that was the end of it, but once again she was just warming up.

"Oh sure, Bill," she said, assuming a first-name basis right off the bat (something a Pine Manor girl would never do, heaven help me!). "But there was something I wanted to ask you about."

Dalton looked as strained as a constipated cow.

"Yes?" he said, jes a little coldly.

Annie nodded her head, squinched up her mouth, pulled up a chair, threw one leg over it like she was getting ready to swap mules with somebody, and started in talking: "Now, I couldn't help hearing what you boys was jes saying. . . . I mean you held up the National Bank of Bartlesville, and you got a couple thousand dollars, right? That's not bad . . . I mean you coulda done better, but all in all it's not bad. Now what I wanted to ask you about . . ."

Dalton rolled his eyes a little and began to shift his weight from one foot to another, like he had jes sat on a spur.

"Yes," Dalton said, "I was wondering about that."

I felt my stomach drop about a foot below my bootheels.

But Annie was going right ahead with it jes like she was invited to speak her piece.

"What I wanted to know was why in the hell did you take the straight route out of town, when you coulda gone round the other way . . . up by Okesa . . . and come outta there clean, just by using the Old Choctaw Pass."

As they say in the bad novels, you coulda heard a pin drop (also a feather—this was a *quiet* silence, believe you me).

Dalton turns around his head in such a jerky way, he looks like he's been hit by a stone. His eyes pop out a bit, and he stares at Doolin, the old bear, who strokes his chin and his moustache. The other boys had the hardest looks since rocks, and I could feel my temperature rising in my forehead.

"The Old Choctaw Pass," he says. "And what the hell is that?"

"You don't know?" said Annie. "Me and Jennie here take it all the time. You sure you never heard of it?"

I felt like I was gonna die. What the hell was Annie talking about? I had never heard of the damned pass!

After what seemed about a year of silence, Dalton looks at Annie, raises his eyebrow, and then looks over at Bittercreek (who is still staring at me—and it made me powerful uncomfortable and excited at the one and the same time), and then, finally, he opens his mouth and starts to laugh. He looks back at Doolin, who is *really* starting to roar. His mouth is thrown open, so as you could see some of his old rotten teeth, and he is throwing his head back, and giving out this bear's roar, and I'm watching Annie sinking lower and lower, jes like the floor was quicksand, and then Doolin's clapping Dalton on the back, and I'm feeling a little bit angry. So what if she has made a mistake . . . it was only cause she idolized them so much, and I feel like butting the sumbitch Doolin in his fat stomach, though I know if I did, I'd be looking like a piece of meat after the fork's been stuck in it a few times. So I jes stand there, and take Annie's arm, which is trembling and vibrating, and then Doolin speaks: "Well I'll be damned! Did you hear that? Did you?"

Now the whole place starts to laugh. The old woman behind me is roaring and shaking her fat stomach jes like she is some kind of fun house doll, them new kind they got that laugh and shake so you want to scream if they don't stop. And the little old guy with her who looks like he's been growed in a weed patch . . . well he's cackling. And all at Annie's expense. Then old Doolin, who is close to tears, starts holding his good arm up and swearing.

"Oh Christ, my arm. My arm. I can't believe my arm. It hurts from laughing. It hurts bad, but you know what else, Dalton? You know what else?"

And Dalton is shaking his handsome head and saying: "Yeah, Bill, I know what else."

And Annie is stepping forward and saying, "Well I wish to hell someone would tell me what else!"

And Doolin stops laughing and looks all relieved like he jes got rid of a powerful load of worry. "You're *right!*" he says (and you coulda blowed me over). "You are a hundred and ten percent right. We went out the wrong way. And it took a little damned girl to tell us."

The whole place stopped on that one and only Dalton and Doolin kept laughing. Then, slowly, like she was jes catching onto the joke, Annie laughed a little, and I did too.

"You are dead right," says Dalton. "Hell, I plumb forgot about the . . . what was it?"

"The Old Choctaw Pass," said Annie weakly.

"Yeah," said Dalton, rolling his eyes a little. "The Old Choctaw Pass!"

Dalton then bowed from the waist jes like he was some kinda prince I'd read about in the fairy books.

"Listen," he said, "anyone as smart as you should be able to dance a reel! May I *have* the honor?"

And Annie curtsied. I couldn't believe my eyes or ears. But I didn't have time to gawk, because away comes that half-breed Bittercreek and he was asking *me* to dance and there we were, the four of us circling the dance floor, while the whole crowd watched and "oohed" and "ahhed." I could feel Bittercreek's strong hands on my back, and I could feel his lean body pressing into mine, and even though I was only fourteen years old, there is some things a girl knows about without having to learn it from no book. (We weren't never no angels, anyway.) I'd like to paint a picture of what happened then . . . me dancing with Bitter and Annie circling the floor with Dalton, but I can't really remember how it looked (me being in the limelight, I didn't get to enjoy watching it). All I can tell you is how I felt. I felt like the whole darn barn was one of those new things you see in carnivals . . . a carousel . . . but that this carousel was different, because each time it went around it lifted another foot off the ground, and soon the whole barn was spinning through the blue starry night and I imagined the moon looking over at us and smiling, and the stars whizzing by, like diamonds, and I never wanted it to stop. Never, never, never. I had forgotten all about my fears, about who the Doolin-Daltons were. I guess I felt jes like a character in one of Annie's books . . . and though I'm not the kinda person who gets swept off her feet very often . . . well, I *was* that night, and that was the beginning of the whole damned crazy thing.

CHAPTER

IV

ONE IN THE AIR!

"One in the air, girls!" said Old Man Morgan while wiping his runny nose with his white coat sleeve.

My head was a-pounding and my neck was drowning in sweat. The water came running off the end of my nose like it was in some kind of race with the drops that come off my underarms and run down my blouse.

I was moving my hands in and out of the sink as fast as I could, hitting the damn fried egg with the old lye soap and rubbing till my wrists was aching. But it still weren't enough for Old Man Morgan and I cursed the day I ever took the job.

"One in the air, you two!" he said, baring his teeth and nodding his head like a buzzard about to pounce. "I got the lunch crowd in here and we got to have plates. Then when you get that done, you and Annie got to double up and waitress! So make it quick!"

On my right Annie stopped drying and stacking and wiped her steaming brow off with the dirty dish towel.

"Hey, now, Morgan," she said. "We already done our bit this morning. We served everybody we are supposed to. If I remember correctly we was supposed to get these dishes out, then we was supposed to git the rest of the day off."

Well that was all old Morgan needed. He put his fat hands on his hips and opened up his mouth. He looked like a mule ready to hit the apple tree.

"You two will do what I tell you!" he said. "I pay you good money, you understand? Where the hell else are two girls your age gonna get any jobs? And that means you leave here when I say you leave here. You understand, Annie?"

"Do I unnerstand?" Annie said in a bass voice which sounded exactly like Morgan's. "Do I unnerstand?"

"That's right," said Morgan. Now he was really hot and I was afraid he was gonna start threatening us with the broom like he had done before. "One in the air at all times. You better because I'm dead serious about it. I wanna see one dish in the sink and one in the air, ready to hit the racks. Then you two git yourselves cleaned up and git yourselves out there and smile pretty for them customers."

I felt like I was gonna burst for sheer exhaustion. And my head wouldn't stop spinning from last night. I kept thinking of that big brute Bittercreek and his handsome smile. And I kept feeling the knocking at my skull from all the sour mash we drunk out back of the barn.

"You still standing there?" Morgan said. "What in the hell did I jes tell you?"

Now Annie put her hands on her hips.

"I believe you told us that we are to keep one in the air at all times. Isn't that right, Jennie?"

"That's what the man said," I said.

"Yeah," said Annie, picking up about five plates. "I believe you then asked if we understood the concept of 'one in the air at all times.' "

"That is right," I said, feeling my head start spinning and my heart pick up a little.

"Well, I'll tell you what, Morgue, old pal," said Annie. "I understand the concept of 'one in the air' better than you could ever know. In fact I already got one in the air down real good."

Now Morgue squinched up his eyes a little and rubbed his hands on the side of his apron.

"Now wait a minute, Annie," he said.

"For example," said Annie, sliding one plate off her stack of five. "Here is your basic 'one in the air.'"

She held the plate out in front of her nose then she opened her fingers and let the plate smash to the floor.

"Goddamn it, Jesus," said Morgan.

I began thinking about all the hours we worked at this damned job and how damned little Morgan had paid us. In a second I had "one in the air" too.

"You two are gonna git it," Morgan said.

He took a step toward us, but Annie already had grabbed about thirty plates and handed them to me. In a second she was back at the shelf.

"Now from 'one in the air,'" she said, "we are gonna jump directly to 'four in the air.' Like so!"

She threw four blue plates in the air and I did likewise.

Morgan stopped in his tracks. In horror he watched the plates sail through the air and hit the sink and smash in a million pieces.

"You brats," he said. "You no-good brats!"

"How about twenty in the air," I screamed, feeling the chills through my body. Oh, how I wanted to be out of there, away from that slavedriver and my grandmother and the whole damned town!

With that I tossed all my remaining plates in the air.

A second later Morgan was coming toward us, but he slipped on the plate chips and fell on his back.

"You two bums," he said. "A couple of girl hooligan bums!"

Now Annie was steaming. She backed away from Morgan and reached for the salad tray.

"Hey," she said. "How about a salad? We already waited on everybody and cleaned the dishes. Maybe you'd like us to make the salad too. Here, lemme peel you some lettuce!"

So saying, she hit old Mr. Morgan with a head of lettuce.

"You two," he said. "I'm gonna call the law! I am gonna have you both put in jail. Get you on the work farm and we'll see how tough you are."

"How bout some tomatoes?" I said, taking aim and letting fly with a big red ripe one. It hit Mr. Morgan on one of the big bumps he had on his forehead, and the juice and seeds ran down his face.

"Want an onion?" Annie screamed and let a big one rip.

"How bout a radish?" I yelled. "A handful of 'em!"

Then we were by the door screaming and laughing and flinging the vegetables at the old sourpuss.

"You'll be sorry," he said. "I'm getting the law. I'm not kidding. I'm getting the law on you both!"

He tried to get back up, but Annie hit him with a chicken and he fell back, groaning. We were out the door in two minutes and it wasn't long after that we were packed up, had gotten our horses and Fred, our mule, and were on our way out of town.

CHAPTER

V

CODE OF THE WEST

THE SUN WAS GLOWING DOWN OVER US JUST LIKE IT WAS A BIG happy balloon. But a balloon that gave off heat, and a kind of heat that seemed to light me from inside out. Oh it was hot all right, as Annie and my mule, Fred, and I trotted slowly up the dusty winding road, but I was so excited with jes the adventure and the possibility of it all . . . that, heck, I didn't mind the heat at all. I felt all warm and happy inside, and when you feel that way, it don't seem to matter much what's going on in the real world. As far as I was concerned that day, every scrubby pine tree we come to looked like it belonged on a painting in a lawyer's office, and every little dandelion looked like it was a great big beautiful sunflower, and the sounds of the birds . . . something I always enjoyed anyway . . . well, this day they sounded like they had created a special song jes for Annie and me.

Thinking back on my mood that day, I guess I was already caught up in it all . . . but the interesting thing is that I never let on to any of it, because part of me felt so afraid of the glory of it all. I mean, jes what *were* the two of us, and our good old mule, Fred, doing clanking through the dustlands heading for the outlaws' ranch? It was the craziest idea in the world, and what made it even loonier is that Annie looked even happier than I was. And she wasn't hiding the fact one inch. Her black hair was tossing in the breeze and her red-and-white-checkered shirt was flapping behind her, and she was smiling at every squirrel, rabbit or lizard we happened to see, jes like she was some kinda queen and this was her own little plot of ground (called a "doochy" or something like that in fairy books). Every two seconds or so, I give Fred a tug, and all our pots and pans and belongings start in rattling against one another, and the sun is glancing off of them . . . and even *they* looked good. It wasn't at all usual for me to feel this way, and I tried as best I could to resist it a little now . . . jes to keep us in the proper frame of mind (which I kept reminding myself should be scared).

"Ah, listen, Annie," I said, as I bounced along on Jake.

But Annie wasn't in the listening mood. Jes as soon as I get my objection started in, she starts in singing:

> "Oh, I'm leaving old Guthrie behind.
> I'm leaving old Guthrie behind.
> They can have their stoveses . . .
> And their old kitchen clothes . . .
> Cause I'm leavin old Guthrie behind!"

When she gets done singing this pretty ballad, she looks over at me and smiles that smile of hers that says, "Ain't I the one," and I purposely made my face get a little long.

"What's a matter, girl," she says, pretending she's a little put out. "You don't like my singing?"

"You sound like a rooster with the cholera," I say, trying not to laugh.

"I guess I do at that," Annie says. "A singer I ain't. But that's not why you're looking so long-faced. What's a matter, honey, you missing old Morgan's Hash House already?"

With that I could not hide my smile any longer and pretty soon both of us were laughing and even old Fred give out with a hee-haw that sounds like he's enjoying the hell out of hisself.

"Missing Morgan's Hash House already?" Annie says, shaking her head. "Well, I know it's tough to leave, kid. They always treated us so good there."

"They treated us like mule dung, and you know it," I said. "And I been wanting to leave there ever since . . . since my folks died. As you well know, Annie McDougal, my long face ain't got nothing to do with us leaving. . . . It's jes the *way* we left that gets me."

I thought my objection might sober us both up a little (my God, I kept thinking, we are heading into real trouble!), but it didn't bring Annie off her high horse even a little bit.

"So you didn't like the way we left?" she says. "That's it, is it? Well what part of the way we left bothered you? Cause, personally, I kinda liked it. All of it!"

"Well," I says, "it's jes that there ain't no going back. My grandmother would jes as soon have us put on a work farm. I can hear her now saying, 'It's fer yer own good, honey.' "

"Real worried, huh?" said Annie, winking at me.

"Yes, I am," I said, tugging on my saddlehorn. "I mean, we have burned our bridges behind us and we ain't at all sure there are gonna be any new ones up ahead."

"Why's that?" asked Annie, as affable as you please.

"Well, look. Why should these guys take us in? They might not even remember us from last night."

Annie looked as calm as a cloud.

"Oh they'll remember us all right," she said. "And they will take us in too. They got to!"

37

"How come?"

"Cause of the Code of the West, stupid. Ain't you even half-educated?"

"I ain't ever heard of any such thing," I said, sitting up straight.

"Well," says Annie. "if you would have read Ned Buntline, you'd know. Ain't you ever heard of how Billy the Kid was sick and almost gone, lost in a terrible snowstorm, and he came upon Jesse James's hideout, and Jesse's girl, Flo, bandaged him and made mad, passionate love to him?"

"No," I says, not believing a word of it, but hoping that it's true all the same.

"It's the straight stuff," Annie says. "If an outlaw is sick or in trouble and he comes across the lair of another outlaw . . . then according to the Code of the West, the one outlaw has got to take the other one in."

We rode on in silence for a few minutes after that. The sun was coming down on us jes like it wanted to make us pay for busting up Morgan's Hash House, and I got to wondering what my folks would say . . . that is, if they was still alive. (I lost them in a tornado in 1893, when I was jes a kid of eleven, and my granny, Flo, took me in, but she is not right in the head and don't hardly know who I am. Annie's dad died and she lives with her mother, who is the town tart and don't see much of her.) It was strange thinking about it. I guess it's usual for kids who run away from home to feel all weepy and think about how folks are gonna miss 'em, and maybe even feel a little remorseful for pulling up stakes without so much as a "by your leave." But in this case neither one of us had anyone pining away for us, and while I shoulda felt better about the facts, the truth is thinking on them only made me feel more miserable than I already was. Even though the sun was blazing and the birds were darting to and fro like darning needles flashing, and the air smelled fine (though dusty), I was already thinking how it was gonna be in the evening when we were out here in Nature all alone. Nature don't seem half so grand when you're out stuck in it in the dark. Of course, I wasn't totally alone . . . I was with Annie, and in them days, I believed she could do anything, even fight off a bear if one happened to take a liking to us as dinner . . . and I suppose I shoulda felt better about the Code of the West, but then I got a thought that sent a chill all through me.

"Annie," I says. "This here Code of the West? You say every outlaw has to honor it with every other outlaw?"

"That's right," Annie says, smiling just as happy as you please.

"Well, I was thinking about it. What if the Doolin-Dalton Gang doesn't believe in the Code? I mean what if they don't think the Code applies to fifteen-year-old girls?"

Annie doesn't hesitate. She starts in shaking her head and smacking her lips as if I am the living end.

"Didn't you go out riding with Bittercreek Newcomb last night?" she says.

"Well sorta. We had some sour mash and a wrestling match!"

"Right. And didn't I talk to Bill Dalton and go out back with him?"

That was a stopper for sure.

"Go out back with him?" I said, pulling up my horse. "You did that?"

"I surely did," Annie said, getting this dreamy look on her face. "And he kissed me . . . twice . . . and told me I was the prettiest girl he had seen in his whole life."

"You didn't tell me that," I said. "I mean that's terrific."

"Right," said Annie, jes like I hadn't said a word.

"And then what?"

"And then he told me that you and I should come out and pay these boys a visit. And that's what we're gonna do. We're gonna stay for a while, and then move on. Or maybe we'll jes stay for a while, and then a while longer."

"How long's the Code of the West good for?" I said, as we

come up toward a big dark green hill with a pass the size of a skinny tree.

"Don't worry about a thing, honey," she says then, getting that dreamy tone again. "Cattle Annie has this outlawin business under total control."

"Yeah," I said, sounding as weak as a fly.

"Hey," Annie says, reaching over and touching my hand. "This morning when I suggested we come out here you was all for it. Don't you remember what we decided? How we was going nowhere in Guthrie. . . . How we wanted to go West . . . see the world. How we was going to stay with the Gang? Don't you remember how excited we was? Hell, you were more up for this than me. Now what's happpening? You going chicken on me?"

"Not on your life," I said, feeling all hot and flustered, and moving Jake and Fred in single line behind Annie.

She turned around and smiled at me and I felt a little ashamed.

"This is gonna work out jes fine," she said. "Them boys are gonna be crazy about us. You wait and see."

"OK," I said, smiling and trying to act like I wasn't shaking. "Yessir, I can hardly wait to get there."

"In the lair of the desperados," Annie said. "The adventuresome girls went boldly forth, with nary a twitch of remorse or fear in their lithe young limbs."

"Jesus," I said.

"He won't help you now, honey," Annie said, sitting straight and fearless. "It's all up to you and me. That's for sure!"

I gave a good yank on Fred and we followed Annie through the dark and narrow pass.

CHAPTER

VI

TARGET PRACTICE

AFTER WE CAME OUT OF THE PASS, THERE WAS A BIG HILL covered with the most beautiful blooming dogwood trees I ever seen. Even though I was still so jumpy I could hardly talk, I felt thrilled by the fantastic red flowers all around me. It was jes like we had left one world and was entering another. . . . A gorgeous world where the trees looked jes like spun sugar. Naturally I didn't say none of this to Annie, because she hated it when I got poetic and stuff like that. Still, in her own way, Annie loved Nature too and she rode her horse up the hill to the trees as happy as a loon.

"Ain't it wonderful up here," she said. "C'mon . . . it's jes like magic."

I gave Fred a yank, and we went plodding up the hill, the tin pans playing a musical tune as they clanked together. The leaves was so beautiful, and the trees was so strange, that I felt like I was on another planet . . . way out in the sky somewheres.

It was jes about then that Annie saw something curling above one of the dogwoods, and I got the shivers again.

"Look," she said. "Do you see that?"

I looked up and there it was. Sure enough, it was smoke and it seemed to be coming from jes the other side of the hill.

"This is it," Annie said. "They said it was jes the other side of the place where the dogwood trees was. I can't believe it. We found it."

Like a rabbit she was riding her horse to the very top of the hill, and I followed her as fast as Fred would allow.

A few minutes later, both our hearts was thumping as we looked down on a ranch house nestled in between some trees. The sun was hot on our backs, but down below there was lots of shade, because the house was pretty well covered round with pines and oaks and creepy crawlers, yellow, pink and blue.

"Is this the place for sure?" I said.

"I think so," Annie whispered.

"What do you mean you *think* so?" I whispered.

"What are we whispering for?" Annie said. "There ain't nobody around here for a hundred yards."

"You sure they told you it was all right to come out here?" I said again, in a whisper that wasn't meant to be one but wouldn't come out no other way.

"Hell yes," Annie said. "They told me jes about where the place was . . . and like that . . ."

I slapped my hand to my sweaty forehead.

"God!" I said. "You mean you got us all the way out here . . ."

"Wait!" Annie said, putting her hand over my mouth. "Look!"

I waited (having no choice—Annie was a strong girl) and I looked, and suddenly, from out the front door of the little ranch house, come the Doolin-Dalton Gang. I guess from the excitement, and the strange feeling I was having about that Bittercreek, I was expecting something real special . . . maybe something like in your basic "knight in shining armor" fairy book. At any rate, I wasn't expecting what I got . . . which was as sadassed and draggletailed a crew as I have ever laid eyes on. First come Bill Doolin, with an old white nightshirt hanging off of him and his arm dangling back and forth like a broken chicken wing. Then comes Bittercreek, rubbing his eyes, and staring at the afternoon like it was a posse out to get him. Behind him is Dick Whisper, Bill Raidler and Dan Clifton, as drunk a bunch of hombres as you'd care to lay eyes on. They were passing the bottle around and throwing it in the general direction of their mouths, but mostly hitting their chins. In addition they was kicking at one another like they was old yeller dogs on their way to Texas, and generally looking like hell in a handbasket. Finally, at the end of this feeble procession comes Bill Dalton. He's got on a pair of overalls and no shirt, and looked like some kinda God compared to the rest of that ragtag band. Annie started in with her sighs and her coos and her "oohs" and "ahs," jes like she ain't even seen the others. Boy it made me mad, and I wanted to say something mean, but before I could get the words out, Annie was hitting me on the arm like she seen something special that I hadn't.

"Look at them, Jennie," she said. "Look at them, boy. It's history in the making, I'll say."

I looked down at "history in the making."

What I saw, however, ain't likely to make it into many history books. The Gang moseyed down by the seedy-looking old barn with the roof half caved in and stood in a line and drew their guns from their holsters. Dan Clifton was filling up his chambers with bullets when Bill Raidler sneaked up behind him and crouched down on his hands and knees. That little water rat Dick Whisper came around in front of Dan and gave him a shove, sending Dan over Raidler's back.

"What in the hell are they doing?"

Annie looked real serious at me, her eyes squinching up like she was fathoming the deep meaning of it all. "It's some sort of strategy. . . . Maybe it's 'falling' practice."

About that time Dan Clifton got up and kicked Bill Raidler in the shins and shouted "asshole" at the top of his lungs. Raidler was hopping around jes like he was some kind of Civil War vet who had been visited by a mini-ball.

"It don't *look* like 'falling' practice," I said.

But Annie wasn't reacting to my joke. Instead, she watched everything, straining forward and looking like a hawk at Bill Dalton, who is walking through the shadows toward the fencepost. There he grabbed some kinda rope, and up popped what looked like four cardboard men.

Annie was besides herself now and moved down the hill a little to a nook of rocks where we could get a better view.

"Look," she said. "C'mon . . . they're about to have target practice."

I grabbed Rex, Jake, and stubborn old Fred, and made my way behind her. I'd like to be able to say I'd retained my cool and real sophisticated viewpoint . . . what Mrs. Patterson calls "critical detachment." But, in fact, my heart was pumping so fast, my lungs couldn't keep up, and I felt as light as a leaf.

A minute or two later I was leaning over a big gray boulder, staring down at the Gang, who was lining up real smart. (Well fairly smart, considering their general conditions.) Big Bill Doolin stood off to the side a bit and raised his arm jes like he was a cavalry commander. Maybe that's when I first got the bug. Jes watching him there, his one arm busted, but his other arm standing straight up . . . I started to realize what Annie had known all along. These boys *was* special, and Big Bill in his own way was the most special of them all. He looked grand out there and I felt all warm inside watching him, full of excitement and admiration.

"All right, boys," he said, his deep voice booming out over the landscape. "We're gonna shoot to kill. Dalton, you go first."

Bill Dalton stepped forward and Annie scrambled down through a crack in the rocks to a cluster of trees. We wasn't really more than a couple hundred yards away now.

"Right, Bill," Dalton shouted out.

He then commenced to shoot down all four targets, one at a time.

I pulled the horses and Fred around the rocks and came up besides Annie.

"Did you see that?" Annie said, so excited she looked like she would pop. "Did you? He hit everyone of 'em down."

"I saw it," I said.

"Bittercreek next," shouted Dalton.

Bitter stepped forward and aimed his gun and I felt myself gettin all knotted up inside. I didn't want him to miss none. But miss he did, on the very first target, and Little Bill Raidler started in laughing at him.

"Shucks," I said. "I was hoping . . ."

But before I could get very sad about it, Bittercreek turned to Bill Raidler and shot his hat off his head.

With that Raidler started to draw his gun and I heard a voice say: "You better not harm a hair on his head, Bill Raidler, or I'll blow your punk ass off."

Annie turned to me and ran her hands through my golden locks.

"Why, Jennie, honey," she said. "I didn't know you talked like a tramp."

"I couldn't help it," I said. "If he harms him, I'll . . ."

But nothing come of it. Raidler stopped drawing his gun and Bitter turned around and shot down the rest of the targets, without missing a one.

Next it was Dick Whisper's turn, and I was content to watch, but Annie grabbed her pinto and patted me on the back.

"Well it's now or never," she said. "Let's go."
"With all them guns out smoking?" I said.
Annie smiled and patted her own holster.
"You seem to forget that I am a desperado myself."
"Desperate, yes!" I said.

With that Annie got on Rex and I got on Jake (grabbing Fred), and we started down the hill toward the Gang. No sooner had we gone a few yards, though, when Fred hit a rock and stumbled a bit and his pots and pans start clanging like a goddamned one-mule band. (And they talk about the "sure-footed mules." Hell, Fred was clumsier than a pet pig, Orville, I used to own.)

I turned around to see what was the matter when I started to hear shouting and screaming from down below. When I looked back around I saw it was Bill Raidler shading his eyes and seeing something coming toward him. He started in shouting warnings at the rest of the boys.

"Watch it," he screamed. "It's Indians or Pinkertons. . . . I don't know *what* the hell it is."

I saw Bittercreek and Whisper dive behind a fencepost and I started to call out to Annie, who was now a good twenty feet ahead of me, coming into a clearing just above the ranch.

"Look out!" I yelled. "Annie, look out!"

There was a strange sound like the cracking of a big twig by a giant's foot, and then I see some bark on a tree near me just come flying off.

"They're shooting, Annie!" I yelled. "Watch out!"

But I wasn't scared. Not for myself. All I thought of was, "Annie's closer. She'll get shot if I don't do something." What it was I did was drop Fred's reins and gallop toward Annie. (I know, I know. What the hell sense did *that* make? But in times of crisis, you got to give me some credit for thinking of my friend.) Unfortunately, I didn't do neither of us much good Cause instead of Annie, it was me that felt something rip off the top of my head. I fell backwards off the horse, and then I remember seeing a blue sky, and a bird flying, and a couple of green tree limbs, and suddenly I was out cold. The next thing I remember is a whole deep well of nothing, and then a terrible strangling feeling, like someone was shoving a pillow over my head. I fought to breathe, but it was no use. I figured I was, as Ned Buntline would say, "heading for the Last Roundup!"

CHAPTER

VII

THE GANG FEELS GLUM

THERE WAS A TERRIBLE PAIN IN MY HEAD, WHICH FELT LIKE some little blacksmith was in there pounding horseshoes on my ears, but that wasn't the bad part. The bad part was the smothering, and as I got half-awake again, I thought to myself, "So this is what it's like. As you die you jes start smothering!" That made me real panicky. Not dying, but smothering. In fact, one part of me was hoping I'd die real quick so I could stop smothering. It was about then that I regained my senses enough to notice that this here smothering stuff was not the result of big bullet holes but was due to Annie's breasts. That is, the kid had me all bundled up in her bosoms and was crying out, "Jennie, oh, Jennie. Oh Jennie," jes like I was already up in the Big Cattle Drive.

I squirmed and shook free a bit, took one hell of a breath of that good clean air and said, "I believe I am shot in the head and on top of that you are smothering whatever life I got left."

That brough her around a bit and she seemed so glad that I wasn't dead that she broke down in tears of joy (which naturally ran down my nose, and just about drowned me. I'll tell you, getting shot ain't half so bad as folks grieving over you.).

"Annie, Annie," I heard in the background. And then "Jennie, Jennie." I knew them voices already, and the latter was none other than Bittercreek, who snatched me out of Annie's arms and took his turn smothering me. I got my head clear this time, though, and I didn't mind it half so much. But jes when I was getting accustomed to being made over, I felt something sticky coming down my head, and I got scared all over again. The little blacksmith was pounding hell out of my brains and it occurred to me that I may well be hurt real bad.

"Whoa, whoa," I cried out, as mournful as I could muster up.

"Jennie, honey," said Bittercreek. "What are you doing here?"

I cocked an eye and looked at Annie, who turned away and began right in on Dalton.

"A fine greeting for the two of us," she yowled. "Some big bad cowboys you are. Shooting a bunch of poor helpless girls."

"Never mind that," said Doolin, coming up and looking down at me with the kindest and saddest face I ever have seen.

"Bittercreek, get that girl down to the ranch house and fix her up."

Bitter put his big, calloused hands on my head, pulled my hair back, and wiped off the blood with his own neckerchief.

"Ain't too bad, ma'am," he said. "We're powerful sorry."

"Whoa, whoa," I said, feeling dizzy, foolish and kinda happy to be in Bittercreek's strong arms. A coupla minutes later we started down the hill toward the house.

I was propped up in bed with two big pillows behind me. On my head was a bandage Bittercreek had fashioned. He was hardly no real doctor, and the damned thing kept slipping over on my right eye. Sitting on my temple was an ice pack, but since it kept slipping off, Annie was sitting besides me and holding it on. In front of the bed, lined up against the wall, was the whole Gang. They had real sheepish expressions on their faces, jes like they were a bunch a little boys who had been caught in the molasses cookies, and if I hadn't been in such excruciating pain, I woulda laughed. Instead I made feeble noises like I was a helpless little robin who'd been felled by a wicked stone.

After a couple of my helpless groans, Bill Doolin stepped forward. His hands was folded at his sides and he cleared his throat a coupla times, though I didn't notice no signs of a cold.

"Uh . . . ah . . . we ah."

"Whoa," I moaned, half-acting, half-dying.

"Well, what it is we wanted to say . . ." Doolin said, rubbing his finger around his collar (though it was loose as could be). "What I wanted to say is that *we* ah . . . we are *outlaws,* that's for sure. But we don't shoot girls."

I shot a look at Annie, who nodded her head and looked back at Doolin like she was staring at Old Man Morgan.

"Women!" she said. "You don't shoot women!"

I expected that might get a rise out of him, but he was all humility.

"Right," he said. "Yeah, right. *Women.*"

Annie smiled a little there and I could barely resist laughing myself.

The rest of the Gang looked about as uncomfortable as Doolin. Raidler twitched back and forth on his toes like a bird in search of dinner, and Dick Whisper began taking these deep breaths, and Bittercreek jes stared down at his shoes.

"Well, you see," said Doolin again. "We, uh, hope you are feeling better, Miss Jennie."

I nodded and sniffled a little on that one.

"I'm not much of a doc," Doolin said. "But I seen more'n my share a gunshot wounds, and I'd say that in a day or so you'll be all right."

I sniffled a little, not letting on whether I believed him or not, and Annie moved the ice pack around on my head a bit, as if to relieve the pain. (It did help some at that.)

"My head," I said, in a voice that sounded like it come right out of the tomb. "I'm sorry I'm acting like a sissy, Mr. Doolin, sir, but this is my first time for getting shot!"

The Gang really began clearing their throats on that one. Sounded like the whole bunch of 'em had the pneumonia.

Little Dick Whisper steps forward and looks at Doolin like he's got this tremendous pain in his gut.

"Uh, Bill," he says, in the damnedest whisper I ever have heard. "Uh, Bill, can we leave now?"

Doolin turned and shot Whisper a look that woulda knocked me to my knees.

"No, damn it."

"Why not, Bill?" says Whisper, whispering up a storm.

"You know why not, damn it," Doolin roared. "Now do what you came for!"

Well old Dick Whisper starts in a-shuffling and looking at the ceiling, as if he's hunting for divine guidance.

"I'm real sorry, Miss. I hope it wasn't me who plugged you," he gasped.

Real quick like, as if to get the misery over as fast as possible, Bill Raidler stepped up.

"Me too, Miss. I'm terrible sorry."

Dan Clifton is next and he has a look like he's got to go to the outhouse. I ain't ever seen such agony.

"Real sorry. Terrible," he mumbles and drops his head.

Then Bittercreek moved to the foot of the bed. In his face was a longing like I never seen in my life, and it made me tingle all over but especially in my wound.

"I don't know what to say, Jennie," he said.

Annie gives me a look and says: "Hmmm."

She had a way with "Hmmm." Everybody jumped back a little.

"All right now, boys," Doolin said, stroking his big ole walrus moustache. "Time you boys got out and git your stuff together, and then git to sleep. We got work to do tomorrow."

As the Gang shuffled out, Bill Dalton and Doolin and Bitter moved up alongside the bed.

"I didn't say nothing yet," Dalton said. "I'm real sorry, too. But I was wondering . . . jes what *were* you all doing out there?"

Annie looked up at Dalton and had the biggest moony eyes I ever seen.

"You don't know, Bill?" she says.

Dalton gives Doolin a look and Doolin shakes his head.

"You all have your mule there. So we assumed you was moving. But what about your folks?"

"We ain't got no folks, Mr. Doolin," Annie said. "Jennie's folks was killed in a tornado. I hardly ever see my mom—she's too busy plying her trade."

"Oh," Dalton said.

"Oh," Doolin said.

"We worked in Morgan's Hash House, jes like we said last night. But we're sick of that, and now we're on our way to California. That's a long shot from here. And now that Jennie's shot up, we're liable to never get there."

Doolin's face lit up real hopeful.

"Well it's jes a day's ride back to town. You could go back there . . . after a day's rest."

I held my head and began to moan a little. These were my extra special whining, dying and bleeding moans.

"Oh my pooooooor head," I sighed. "It's pounding. On and off. On and off."

One little bit of that, and Bittercreek came bounding round the bed like he's going to swoop me up and carry me away.

"You'll be all right, Miss Jennie," he says. "Really."

"You're so sweet, Bittercreek," I said, meaning every painful word of it.

"But *you* ain't!" Annie says to Dalton and Doolin, drooping the ice pack on my shoulder and getting up out of her chair.

"So you want us to go back to town, huh? Back to the Hash House? You'd shoot a poor defenseless girl like Jennie and then kick her out?"

Dalton put up his hand and shook his head.

"Now wait a minute," he said. "Nobody said anything about . . ."

"I thought you boys was gentlemen," said Annie. "I thought you had some class, and here you go plugging girls. Boy!"

I moaned a little, this time not faking it. All that screaming was really getting the old anvil pounding in my head.

"Now wait a damned minute," Dalton said, staring down at Annie. "It was an accident. You wouldn't hold that against us!"

"Oh no," Annie said, walking around to the foot of the bed and then turning real sudden like (it made for some real drama, I'll say). "Not the shooting. But the way you're trying to get rid of us. . . . What's a matter, you boys afraid of women?"

"Hell no," said Dalton, smacking his fist on the bedpost and making the whole damned bed vibrate (as well as my head!).

Annie folded her arms and stood on her tiptoes.

"Say, why not let us stay a while," she said. "We can cook and sew and we can clean up, too. Take care of the horses . . ."

Dalton looked at Doolin and Doolin at Dalton and a more confused exchange you couldn't imagine.

"Hell no," said Doolin. "That's out. No way. No way."

Dalton took a softer approach, but it was the same verdict.

"Annie," he said. "We're outlaws. You don't want to git . . . mixed up with any outlaws. I mean . . . hell . . ."

Bittercreek looked down at me then, as if to say he didn't feel that way. Then he edged in between the rest of them and tenderly put the ice pack on my temple. Doolin saw him making this move and gave both him and me a stern look.

"Who said anything about getting mixed up with anybody?" Annie said. "I mean Jennie is hurting. We jes *can't* travel. And it's your damned trigger-happy faults. The least you can do is let us stay for a week!"

With her arms folded there and her chin out, Annie was a menacing little rooster and I felt a thrill shooting through me. It was a far cry from the Hash House, where we was the ones who took order after order from that poison-food, slime-slinging Morgan.

Well, Dalton looked at Doolin and Doolin looked down and stroked his moustache like he was figuring some way to git around the brute facts, but you could jes see the way he let the air out of his old, sagging stomach, that Annie's got him over a barrel. I guess I felt warm and good about him then, too. He may have been a badman but he had a big heart.

"She's right, Bill," Dalton said, in a soft voice.

"Goddamn it," Doolin said, putting his hands in his old black waistcoat. "You girls are . . ."

"They can help, Bill," Bittercreek said, gently rubbing the ice over my head in a way that made me almost forget how rotten I felt. "I'll take care of Jennie."

"I'll jes bet you will!" Doolin boomed, shaking his head and letting out one more of his long sighs. "Damn it, I suppose you have to stay till Jennie's head gets well. But no longer. You understand?"

Annie couldn't hold back no longer. She smiled and lit up the whole room, then ran over and gave Mr. Bill Doolin a big hug. Doolin started to clasp his own arms around her back, but stopped short. He looked pretty funny with his hands sticking straight out behind Annie like some kinda old, heavy scarecrow, and I felt like kissing him on his old head.

"That's a good sport, Mr. Doolin," Annie said. "You're as much of a gentleman as they say you are."

"As *who* says I am?" Doolin says, looking put out.

"As *these* say," said Annie, reaching in her pocket and pulling out her trusty Ned Buntline book.

She held it up so all of us could see.

The title of the book was *The Amazing Exploits of the Doolin-Dalton Gang*. The cover showed the Gang robbing a bank, with men and women hiding behind horses and doors and a sheriff clutching his bleeding stomach as he fell toward the dusty street.

Around the borders of the book were cameo pictures of each member of the Gang and each cameo was bordered by a lariat.

"Well look at that, will you," said Bill Doolin, with a great measure of delight in his voice.

He took the book from Annie and showed it to Dalton, who eagerly stuck his face in it. Even Bittercreek dropped the ice bag on my shoulder and peeked at the book.

"I've never seen this," said Doolin, laughing.

"Me neither," said Bill Dalton. "Damn, they painted our pictures real good."

"Got 'em off the wanted posters," said Bittercreek. "Lemme see. Look at that. That's me all right."

Annie came round to the bed. It sure was getting crowded.

"You boys is legends in your own time," Annie said.

Dalton smiled and slapped his hand around Annie's shoulder.

"If this don't beat all?" he said. "When they hang us they can put out another edition . . . with more pictures."

"That's a hell of a thing to say," I said, looking at the boys and shivering a little. It just occurred to me that they did shoot folks.

But the shiver melted when Annie looked at me and nodded her head. She was so damned happy that we could stay for a while and the boys was so damned happy about the book and I was so damned happy about getting away from that hash house and double happy about Bittercreek and Doolin and Dalton . . . well, it jes wasn't in me to feel scared, or even to worry about what was right and wrong. I looked up again at Annie and she winked at me. Maybe I shouldn't have, but I was only too glad to wink back.

CHAPTER
VIII
EXPLORATIONS

DURING THE NEXT COUPLE OF DAYS, THE LITTLE MAN WITH the anvil must have tired hisself out, cause my head began to perk up a bit. Not that I was entirely well. There was moments when I'd be standing in the kitchen watching the coffee brew and all of a sudden I'd start in feeling like the center of the earth had fallen through and I was heading down some long dark tunnel into pure blackness. The first time it happened I was by myself and it was a right scary sensation. I grabbed onto what looked like the edge of the cutting block, but my hand hit something squishy and I had a terrible feeling that what it was I was holding onto was my brains, all mushed up from the bullet. I gave out a scream and slumped onto the floor. A second later I felt some old big horny hands picking me up and heard Annie's voice saying, "You'll be all right now, Jennie. Set her down in that chair over there." Which they did, my head ringing and my stomach fluttering and my thoughts as black as the eyes which were boring in on me.

"You are all right now, Jennie," said a voice, and then my eyes began to focus a little and I realized I was staring at Bittercreek.

"I feel so funny," I said. "I can't tell you how strange. . . . There's something horrible in my hands. . . . I thought . . ."

Suddenly I began to whimper and I felt right disgraced by such un-cowgirllike behavior. But, thinking back on it, I guess it was at that moment that I realized I had been shot in the head and just barely missed going to the Big Roundup. Up till then I had been so much caught up in the games me and Annie was playing with the Gang that I hadn't had time to really speculate what would have happened if that bullet had moved about an inch over to the left.

"There *is* something horrible on your hands," Annie said, gently picking up my limp left one. "It's the most horrible-looking mess of grits I have ever seen. It's a miracle this Gang hasn't died from its own cooking. Looking at this mess of burned-up muck, I'd say you had a lot more to worry about in your own kitchen than you did from the Pinkertons."

Bittercreek laughed heartily at that one and I even managed a small yuck myself. Leave it to Annie to get through the bad stuff with a good crack. In a second I had regained my senses and my morbid thoughts of a moment ago felt like they belonged to someone else.

"Well," said Annie, "I got to go outside for a while. I got an important engagement."

"Oh, is that right?" I said, smiling at her as she sashayed across the kitchen floor, her nose up in the air as if she was the Royal Blood herself, getting all ready to receive Sir Francis Drake.

"I, ah, must go outside where I will meet with the terrible outlaw Mr. Bill Dalton. Sir Wild Bill is going to instruct me in the ways of throwing the Bowie knife."

So saying, Annie waved her arm dramatically and swayed her bottom from the room. Both Bittercreek and I laughed and then I felt a lid of silence descending on us. I'm a little ashamed of it now (considering that Mrs. Patterson is teaching us "to be independent women who do not kowtow to the bestial proclivities of the male sex"), but seeing Bitter there staring at me, and me knowing he wanted to say something and me wanting him to say something, but neither one of us able to say a damned thing for fear it would be dumb or dull . . . well, I figured I just might be able to help our relationship along a little by feeling a little faint on my own. So, with a small flourish of sighs and gasps, I sort of lurched forward and let him catch me with his big hands.

"Miss Jennie," he said so quietly, with so much tenderness that it took my breath away. "Let me help you to the bedroom. You have to rest and take care of yourself . . ."

"Oh yes, Bitter," I said. "I believe that scalp wound was a little deeper than you or I suspected. Oh . . ."

So saying this, I felt the little man work on me, only this time not in my head but somewhere around my heart. The truth was I don't enjoy such trickery . . . but I did enjoy his big hands wrapped around my waist and almost touching my breasts. Together we made our way out the kitchen, through the dining room, where I leaned on the old oaken table, and then through the little hallway to the back bedroom, where the sun was shining great yellow splendor on my green and red quilt.

"Let me help you down here," he said. "God, I'm powerful sorry about all this. I mean it for sure. . . . I never shot no girls before. In fact, I haven't shot anybody much for quite a while now."

"You haven't?" I said, feeling a trifle disappointed that we had made it to the bed, since that meant his big, strong arms were no longer encircling my waist.

"No," said Bitter. "We don't enjoy shooting people. . . . Well, *I* don't. My feeling is that a robbery should be like some kind of a . . . craft . . . you know? I mean like making a table or building a barn. You don't go building a barn by just tacking a bunch of wood together. Not if you want it to last. Likeways,

59

you don't go out and hold up a bank by just riding in and blasting folks. A really good robbery should happen . . . like a smoke signal. Here one minute, all beautiful and perfect, and then . . . poof, it's gone. . . . Nothing to it."

"Like a smoke signal?" I said. "Why that's a really novel notion. I mean can you see an old bank up there in the sky and the robbers all made out of smoke, and then, whoof, it's gone?"

"Sure," said Bittercreek. "I can see it right now. Outside there. Look."

He smiled and turned his handsome Injun profile at me and I knew he was showing off and delighting in it too. (Regardless of what Mrs. Patterson has to say about matters like these, there are fewer realer pleasures in the world than a man and a woman strutting around for one another.)

"Indian see smoke robbery in sky," he said. "Injun see bank of smoke and robbers of smoke and . . . agh . . . Indian see very bad sign."

By now I had forgotten all about the pain in my temple and I was laughing up a storm.

"What does Indian see?" I said.

"Indian see . . . money made of smoke. Very bad. Bad sign. Injun make whole vision go away."

Bittercreek waved his arms around and the cloud he had been looking at passed over the house, just like he had vanquished it.

"You are quite a character, Bitter," I said. "I really like you a lot."

He smiled at me then and sat down on the edge of the bed, and the heart-anvil started pumping, and I felt all the blood rushing to my face and I started thinking, "Oh, please don't let me blush. I don't want to look like a damned little girl who is afraid of the big bad Indian outlaw." But I might as well have been asking for mountains in Kansas, cause I could tell from his smile that my face was as red as a turnip.

"White girl's face make light like sun," he said.

"Aw heck," I retorted.

Then I reached up and put my arms around him and pulled him down on top of me and he made a little noise like the wind was knocked out of him. To tell you the truth, I think he was damned surprised.

A second later he was starting to wriggle under the covers with me and I felt so good all over, warm and safe, and tremendously excited. The blood was pumping through my arms and legs and I could feel my stomach muscles quiver . . . and then he was kissing me hard on the mouth and rolling on top of me . . . and I suppose I should have said, "Whoa now," "Hold on there," "Wait a minute," or some such ladylike lie like that, but I was feeling so good, just like a flower had bursted forth in my breasts and I was all over him and then I felt something down in between my legs. I knew that I was going to be changed by all this, completely, utterly changed, and a white fear kinda swept through me, but the fear itself kept changing shapes in me and in a second it had been turned into a kind of ecstasy . . . and he was mumbling, "Jennie. Jennie," and I wasn't mumbling nothing cause I was too busy feeling him move on top of me and besides my mouth was full with his ear, and . . . well, like Mrs. Patterson says, "A lady should be both modest and aggressive," so just let me say that I aggressively, but modestly, threw myself into it and was filled up with Bittercreek, with myself, and with love. . . . Oh, such sweet loving. The likes of which I suppose I might never have again.

Later in the afternoon Bitter kissed me sweetly and told me, "You are somebody special. Regardless of what you have heard about me, I want you to know, you are somebody special . . . indeed."

Being a woman of great reserve and style, I coolly and calculatingly told him I was "Totally yours. In love with you forever." Also I meant every last syllable of it . . . (and perhaps still do, no matter what's happened since). Ah, just lying there with him, watching the clouds outside and hearing the sounds of the pigs running by and the braying of Fred when he wanted his water and the dust motes circling over us in the air . . . it was just like time itself had stopped and we had been moved to that cloud outside the window, where everything was full of peace and clover. . . . I was perfectly content to lie there with him, making love, and talking for days, weeks if he wanted. . . . But after what must have been about an hour, he said he had some chores to do about the ranch, and in a second we had kissed and he was gone.

Alone, lying there, I thought about myself. About the fact that I wasn't a virgin no more. About how he hadn't bothered to ask whether I was or not . . . about whether I had been any good. Certainly I had been enthusiastic, but there must be a million little tricks of loving that I didn't know, and a man like Bitter . . . well, he maybe had seen them all and perhaps I was just a kid who had been taken advantage of. . . . Maybe he didn't even really like me. No, I was sure he did. But what if he didn't? Well, it went on like that for a while, but then I thought of what he had told me and I just made up my mind that it was the truth. Not that I still didn't have my doubts, but in those early days I had a great ability to believe in people. If I had second thoughts, they were easily laid to rest. I didn't think much about it, of course, but now thinking back on it, I used to believe you knew a person right away . . . and all the talking you did didn't really make that much difference. It was something deeper than words . . . a feeling in the gut that this one was good, and this one was a lying yellow dog who would make off with your saddle in the dead of night, and even though things have come to pass which makes me wonder about such simple feelings, I still believe that such stuff is the true way of going about in this confusing world. Only now, it's harder for me to smell 'em out than it used to be. . . .

Anyways, I spent much of that afternoon lying in my bed in rhapsody, thinking how sweet Bitter could be . . . when into the room comes Annie. What a sight she was, too. Her red-and-white-checked shirt was covered with hay, and her hair looked like the head of a scarecrow, and she was grinning ear to ear.

"Well?" I said. "And jes how many knives did you throw?"

Annie smiled and batted her eyelashes a little.

"Well, it started out being about knife throwing," she said, sitting down on the edge of my still very warm bed. "It really did. And Bill is one hell of a thrower too. He throws over the shoulder and he throws 'em behind the back and he throws 'em underneath the legs . . ."

"Yes, I would imagine especially well from there," I said.

Now it was Annie's turn to blush. In lotsa ways we was a whole lot like regular girls.

"Well, then he tells me he wants to show me a trick throw he does. It involves a target he has set up in the barn, see?"

"Yes," I said, shaking my head real proper and playing the role of the schoolmarm to perfection.

"So he takes me in the barn and do you know what that ogre does then?"

"No," I said, popping my eyes way open like a stagecoach driver who is looking down the barrel of a forty-four. "What happens next?"

"Why," says Annie, getting up and wandering around my bed like she is a rancher whose water rights have just been cut off. "The rascal tricks me into lying down on the hay."

"No," says I. "How on earth did he do that?"

"It was ingenious," says Annie, peering at me with her big black eyes from the end of the bed. "He tells me that he is going to throw his knife at a target on the ceiling, see? So naturally it'll be more to my comfort if I am lying down on the ground, so's I don't strain my lovely neck."

"Sounds logical to me," I said.

"Don't it?" said Annie. "Well, I no sooner had fallen on the hay, spreading myself out like a tent . . . and watching for the target on the ceiling then the rat says the trick is too easy to do standing up, so he will lie down besides me, and do it from a lying position."

"Well, that's the first truth that man has told yet," I said, loving every minute of it.

"And then," says Annie, feigning a cracked voice, and throwing her hands on her face. "The filthy varmint laid down next to me, threw the knife directly into the bull's-eye he had painted on the ceiling, and before I could say, 'Nice shot,' he had started nuzzling up to me and saying, 'What if the knife came down on top of us?' and terrible things like that."

"Terrible," I said, holding my face. "Tell me no more."

"Don't worry," said Annie. "I ain't gonna."

She was smiling like a banker then, her face all angles with the fading sunlight playing off her rosy cheeks. What I remember most about her, though, was her eyes. Lit up and full of mischief, her eyes was just like a second face. An older and stranger face. One which I loved, but didn't pretend to know. And yet, like always, one that made me forget faster than it made me doubt.

CHAPTER IX

THE HORSE

IT WAS ABOUT TEN O'CLOCK IN THE MORNING AND MY HEAD was feeling pretty good. I guess there was jes no way we was gonna be able to tell them otherwise. Now we stood with Doolin, Dalton, Bitter and Dan Clifton on the front porch. I was feeling pretty low and didn't even want to look at Bitter.

"Well," said Bill Doolin, stroking his old moustache and staring down on the porch like he was hunting for something.

Then he didn't say nothing else for quite a while.

"Well," he started again. "You see it's like this. We like both you girls. Hell, I'd be a liar if I didn't say that since you two come out here everybody has felt a lot better. I mean . . . well . . ."

There was another silence. I tried looking out at the trees and the little brown hill and the birds, but it didn't do no good at all. It was as bad as looking at Bitter. Hell, it was already more of a home than I'd ever known with my grandmother. I thought of her sitting on the front porch reading the Bible in that long, drawn voice, and I wanted to cry. I couldn't go back there, no matter what. And besides that there was Old Man Morgan to deal with. By now we was probably up on wanted posters.

"Look," said Dalton. "It ain't nothing personal. We would all like you gals to stay. But we talked it over and you got to go. I mean, it ain't right . . . girls joining a gang."

"Women!" Annie said. I could see the tears about to come from her eyes, but her mouth was set grim like.

"It ain't nothing personal?" she said. "You tell us to go on back there, kick us out like we was carrying the plague or something, and then tell us it ain't nothing personal! Well pardon me if I take it personal as hell!"

"Now," said Doolin, "that ain't no way for a girl to talk. You two ought to git back to town and marry up with some nice young—"

"Forget that!" said Annie. "We can't go back. We already told you what we did with Morgan. He deserved it, too, the rat. He's been working us into the ground!"

"Yeah," I said. "We ain't got nowhere else to go."

Bill Doolin showed us his old scarred palms.

"I know," he said. "But that ain't our fault. Listen—like I said, we like you gals. You brighten up the whole place. But we are thinking of you. You can't go on being outlaws. . . . I mean you are jes kids!"

"Kids!" said Annie. "How old was you when you robbed your first bank, Bill Dalton?"

Dalton looked over at Doolin and shrugged his broad shoulders.

"Fourteen," he said.

"Fourteen!" Annie said. "Well I am already fifteen and Jennie is only a year younger. We want to get started before we have to retire."

The Gang got quite a laugh out of that. And Annie didn't lose any time pressing her advantage.

"Listen," she said. "We'll cook and clean and take care of things for you. And meanwhile you can show us how to outlaw proper like. Cause there is one thing you have to understand right from the start. We are gonna be outlaws whether you help us or not. You see? So you might look at it like this. If you help us to be proper outlaws our chances of surviving and becoming real good at it is increased. If you don't help us, well, we are liable to go out into the big cruel world without no experience, which you could have given us, and get ourselves blasted out of the saddles. Then think how you'll feel? You'll have the death of two young girls on your conscience. At night you'll wake up all drenched in guilty sweat, and you'll say, 'I coulda taught them girls to outlaw right good, but I was too selfish to do it and now they are goners.' Think how you'll feel then!"

I had never heard such a lot of malarkey in my life. But judging from the reaction of the Gang, it sounded pretty darn convincing. For Bill Doolin began studying the porch real good again and Bill Dalton stared at Annie as if he had seen the light.

"Listen," said Dalton. "You ain't gonna be no outlaw. You can't even ride right!"

"Who the hell says?" said Annie, sticking out her pretty chin.

"I say," said Dalton, smiling. "I say you can't beat me in a race."

"You call it," Annie said. "I can already ride as good as any of you!"

"What about Jennie?" said Doolin.

"She can't ride real fast today but she is jes as good as me when her head don't hurt," Annie lied. "I'll tell you what. Bill and I will have a race. If he wins, we will leave. Not another word out of us. If I win, we stay and you teach us the fine art of outlawin."

"Now wait a minute," Bill Doolin said gruffly. "There is more to it than that!"

"I don't know," said Bittercreek, shooting a look at me. "I

think the girls have something here. If they can really ride, then that's half of it. Let's give 'em a chance."

"No more said about it," said Annie, walking off the porch toward Rex. "You jes tell us where we are racing to."

"But . . ." Bill Doolin said.

It weren't no use though. The rest of the Gang was already half off the porch.

"All right," said Bill Doolin, as he lined up even with Annie and Dalton, who were sitting atop their horses.

"You two got to race down to yonder oak tree where Dick Whisper is sitting. Then back here. Then off over there where Dan Clifton is waiting. Around that tree and over those rocks, and then back. The reason I'm sending you there is to see how good you can move in tough terrain. When you are outlawin you don't go down no good roads."

"I got it," Annie said, cockily.

"You better," said Raidler, taking a sip from a jug of rye. "Cause you are gonna git wiped up!"

"All right," said Doolin. "You go when I drop this handkerchief. Get on your mark, get set, and GO!"

The handkerchief fluttered from his hand and Bill Dalton and Annie was off across the pasture, heading toward the first tree. Oh she never rode better, keeping low and light and making her whole body at one with Rex. I took a look over at Doolin and his mouth just dropped. Them boys was likely to learn something.

"She's ahead," I screamed, as they came to the oak.

"Whip her, Bill," Raidler yelled. "Git her . . ."

"Yippppeeeeee!" screamed Bittercreek.

"Come on, Bill," screamed Doolin. "Yowwwwwwwwwwww!"

Then they was coming at us, pounding and straining, and Dalton managed to catch up with Annie, and when they hit the starting line they was dead even.

"I gotcha," Annie grunted as they made the turn for the rocks. "I gotcha, Dalton!"

"Like hell," he said.

Then they was off toward Dan Clifton and the rocks. Even all the way, and I seen Dan waving at 'em and looking like he was so excited he was going to explode like his dynamite.

"She's ahead again," I screamed.

And she was. They turned from the tree and headed into the rocky area. Annie made the turn and started up the hill for the last leg back to the starting line with Dalton just a pace behind her.

"Yippppppieeeeeee, Annie," Bitter yelled.

Doolin shot him a look, then smiled. "Damn," he said, "that girl *can* ride!"

It was then that Rex slipped. I don't know what happened exactly, but suddenly he and Annie went down and we was all rushing toward them.

Dalton reached her first and pulled her up. She was crying and swearing and looking down at her precious horse. He tried to get up but gave out with a terrible cry of pain and fell back on the rocks.

"He just tripped on them damned things," she said, the tears coming down her face. "I had that race. . . . Oh, God, he looks hurt."

Bill Doolin was looking down at the horse while Dan and Bitter held his head. I still remember his wild red eyes and the terrible snorts of pain he let out into the air.

"Ain't there anything we can do for him?" I said.

"Yes," said Bill Doolin finally. "There is one thing. You can shoot him!"

Annie looked at me and burst into tears and I joined her and held her in my arms.

"I'll do it," said Bitter.

"I'll help," said Dalton. "They have had enough for one day."

But Doolin crossed his big arms and stood his ground. He took out his old revolver and got Dan Clifton's from him.

"All right," he said. "It's like this. You can ride. You got spunk. But you got to be able to shoot. Killing a horse ain't nothing compared to killing a man. Not that we want to, but sometimes that's the way the cards fall. This ought to give you a good idea of what it's like. Shoot that horse, and you can stay."

"That's cruel," I heard myself say. "It's cruel."

I looked at Bitter, but he was looking at Rex, who sounded so pathetic I thought I would faint.

"Here," said Doolin, handing me one gun and Annie the other.

"Shoot him right below the head there," said Doolin. He sounded cold, but looked a little sad himself.

"Two shots there and then one in the head to make sure."

"Goddamn, Bill," said Bitter.

But Annie moved away from me and cocked her pistol. She sniffed a bit and shook her shoulders like she was passing a chill.

"I don't know," I said. I tried cocking the gun, then could feel something happening in my stomach and my legs turned to rubber.

"I jes don't know . . ."

"You are an outlaw!" Annie said to me, her voice as hard as the steel handle of the gun.

I grit my teeth and moved in front of Rex. His eye looked up at us and held our reflection. He made a terrible sick noise like a baby that had been caught by Indians.

"When I say 'now,'" Annie said, aiming the gun at him.

"All right," I said timidly.

We aimed our guns and I heard, "*Now*," and as Rex made one last effort to get up, I pulled the trigger.

He had moved and the bullets didn't hit him right. Mine went through his jaw, taking off part of it, and revealing his huge bloody teeth. Annie's hit the chest, but off center.

"Again," said Dalton. "Fast!"

And so we fired again. This time through the heart and Rex quivered and then was still.

"Now through the head," said Annie.

I cocked the gun again and aimed it at his head. I felt strangely quiet, silent, as if I were alone in a field of snow. I heard the gun go off and saw his head splinter, and I felt cold but in control of myself, terribly in control.

"Oh, God, that was awful," Annie said.

She turned away from her horse's body and went over in the rocks and began to retch. Dalton went over to her and I saw him hold her shoulders as she bent down.

Then I noticed that Bitter was beside me.

"Are you all right?" he said, holding me.

I stood there, staring at Rex's mangled corpse. I felt as if I were taking flight from the world. A strange and delicious sickness flowed through my veins.

"I feel fine," I said, sounding like a voice from the grave.

"Congratulations," said Bill Doolin. "You are in the Gang."

CHAPTER

X

BREAKFAST BEFORE BULLETS

THE GANG SAT AROUND THE LONG OAK TABLE, WHILE OUT IN the kitchen Annie and I cooked up a feast. I was so excited about what was going to happen that morning that I could barely think about the eggs, coffee and rolls. Annie moved around the kitchen like a snake, slithering from the stove to the table, everywhere at once and talking up a storm.

"God, I wish we could go," she said. "We would be great in a stickup. I just know we would."

"Well we can't, miss," I said, once again taking the role of the sensible down-to-earth one, when I wanted to be along in the stage holdup as much as anybody in the house.

"I know. I know," said Annie. "Come on, take those rolls out of there before the whole damned batch of 'em looks like coals."

I grabbed the rolls and held them high above my head. They smelled as sweet as dogwood and I carried them through the kitchen doors with a flourish.

Not that nobody noticed. The Gang was still hunched the same way they'd been for an hour. Dick Whisper, Raidler and Bittercreek sat on one side of the long table and Dalton and Dan Clifton on the other. At the head of the table Bill Doolin squatted, looking at once mean, powerful, tired and kinda funny.

"Breakfast is served," I said, plopping the pan of rolls down in the center of the table.

Behind me Annie brought in the eggs and sausages, and as soon as it hit the table the Gang began to scoop it on the plates. I don't know what I'd expected, but I guess I'd hoped that our outlaws would somehow be different eaters than the trashy businessmen at Morgan's Hash House, but it weren't so. When it comes to breakfast, I guess, the good and the bad are equal pigs.

After bringing in the coffee, Annie and I sat down and started to eat, but even the good smell of the food couldn't stop my heart from pumping and my knees from clattering together.

"Everybody eat their fill," said Doolin. "You can't hold up a stage on an empty stomach."

"That's right, Bill," said Dick Whisper in a hiss. "Pass the biscuits please, Dan."

Dan Clifton rolled his eyes, squinched up his big oatmeal face like Dick Whisper and hissed back at him: "OK, Dick. Here they are."

The joke got quite a rise out of the Gang. Raidler hooted and banged his paws on the table. His evil little coyote eyes blazed like two campfires.

Dick Whisper rubbed his nose and made his mouth look like a trout's snout, and hissed: "You shouldn't make fun of me, Dan. If you keep it up, I'll blow off your kneecaps."

This threat caused the Gang to guffaw again and Dan Clifton didn't even stop swiggling his coffee.

"Eat, don't talk, boys," Doolin said, looking and sounding like an old buffalo. "We got a good ride ahead of us. Also, I might add, Annie and Jennie, this is the first good food this Gang's had for quite a spell."

"Here, here," said Bittercreek, raising his mug.

Then the whole Gang joined him and Annie and I sat there blushing and feeling as happy as loons.

"Say," said Annie after the toast, "where are you boys going, anyway?"

"Towards Ponca City," Doolin said, while half a piece of toast hung out of his mouth. "There's a stage coming from St. Louis. Should be mighty fine."

Right after he said it, Doolin looked at Annie with a grumpy stare like she had gotten some information out of him he hadn't wanted to part with.

Annie smiled back at him extra large, and Doolin stared down at his plate, as if the eggs was staring back at him.

"This sure does taste good," said Bill Dalton, smiling at Annie.

Dalton was only trying to help, but him saying that only made the ensuing (new word learned just today) silence even more devastating.

A second later Doolin looked up at Annie and she smiled even wider. I thought, if he looks up again, he is gonna make her crack her lips.

A second later Doolin looked up again and there was Annie smiling like the man in the moon.

"Damn it, Annie," Doolin said, "what the hell are you gawking at?"

"Well nothing, Mr. Doolin. I was jes watching you eat."

Doolin got a real worried look on his face at that one.

"Well, what the hell for?" he said, real irritated like.

But Annie was still all smiles.

"Well you see, Mister Doolin. It jes reminded me of a scene in the book *The Amazing Exploits of the Doolin-Dalton Gang.* Listen to this . . ."

Annie reached behind her and whipped out the book but Bill Doolin held up his hand.

"Now hold on, wait a damned minute here. We got no time for stuff like that right now. We got to eat and get on with our work, right, boys?"

Doolin looked down at the table, and a sorrier bunch of outlaws you would never hope to see. Raidler stared at his fork like it was going to do him some damage. Whisper whispered, "Sheet," Bittercreek looked sadly at Dan Clifton, and Dalton opened his mouth, started to say something and then flapped his hands like he was a fish on the bank.

As for Annie, she just shrugged and sat the book down next to her plate and continued to gobble up her eggs.

Meanwhile, Doolin smiled as if he had finished off that little mess and started to eat again. His food, however, only got about halfway to his moustache when he looked up and shook his head.

"All hell," he said. "What does that damned book say, anyway?"

He reached over toward Annie to get the book, but she snatched it from him and held it up over her head.

"No, Bill," she said, "I think you are dead right. It's like Ned Buntline says here in the book. We don't want to break your 'iron-clad discipline and almost Oriental-like concentration.' "

Doolin's mouth dropped open like a trap door.

"Does it say that?" he gulped.

Annie smiled again, as pretty as you please, and nodded.

"Sure," she said, dropping the book to eye level. "Right here on page 101. Listen to this: 'Every morning before a major robbery, the Doolin-Dalton Gang has a huge breakfast. As Big Bill Doolin eats, however, his mind is not on grits or gravy, but, like a razor-sharp sword, he is cutting through the thickets of problems the Gang will face. How to minimize the opposition? Who will take care of the stagecoach guards? How will the Gang escape? Unlike most bad hombres, Bill Doolin is a thinking man's bandit. In over two years on their many fabulous raids . . . the Doolin-Daltons have not lost a single man.' "

Now it was Doolin's turn to smile.

"Does it say that?" he said. "Really? The 'thinking man's bandit?' That's good. Lemme see that!"

Annie gave Doolin the book and he read on in his lovable old bass.

" 'Only one problem remains for the outrageous Doolin-Daltons and that is the Pinkerton detective Big Bill Tilghman. Bigger and possibly even smarter than the aging Doolin, Tilghman has sworn a blood oath to catch and hang the entire Gang. "I won't rest until those outlaws are swinging at the end of a rope," Big Bill Tilghman declares.' "

Doolin made a face like he had just discovered a bad smell and slammed the book down hard.

"Aging, huh? Hell! Tilghman is only two years younger than me. That's enough of this book stuff. Let's go out there and git that stage!"

Suddenly breakfast was over and the Gang was everywhere at once. Annie and I sort of sat in the middle of it all, both of us wide-eyed with excitement. Up till then the only time we had seen them with guns was the day I had got grazed and they sure didn't look like much then. But now . . . in action, they was as cool and tense a bunch of outlaws as ever existed in Annie's books. In one corner of the room, Dick Whisper was filling his guns full of silver shining bullets and checking his buckskin around his leg. In another corner Doolin and Dalton filled their shotguns and buttoned up their windbreakers. Near me I saw Bittercreek like I was in a dream, and he couldn't see me. . . . He was putting his knife into its sheath and staring out the window at his pinto horse, his eyes little slits. The boy was all business, I'll say. And behind me Dan Clifton checked his dynamite, while Bill Raidler practiced his fast draw. You could hear the sound of the leather singing as he whipped out his guns.

Then, just as suddenly, the Gang was tramping out of the house and were mounting their horses, while me and Annie stood alone on the porch. I looked up at Bittercreek and felt something painful inside of me, and I fought hard to keep the tears from coming.

"You boys get home tonight," Annie said, with a little crack in her voice. "We'll have biscuits waiting for you."

Bitter stared down at me and winked, and I winked back, but by this time the tears were starting to come. Damn, I didn't want to cry and I cursed myself for being a kid.

"All right," said Bill Doolin, raising his arm. "Let's go."

The horses turned and snorted their breath out into the frosty air, and Bitter waved goodbye to me, just as Dalton did to Annie, and then they were heading out of the gate at a gallop and I felt the thrill down to my toes.

"God, they are beautiful!" I said, wiping back the tears.

"Ain't they?" Annie said, looking at me out of the corner of her eye.

"I think my headache's all gone."

"It is?" said Annie, as we watched the Gang disappear over the piney hills.

"Yes," I said, "and I been laid up for two days. I sure would love to take a ride!"

"You would?" said Annie. "You would?"

"I would," I said. "I would."

"Get Jake," Annie said. "I'll borrow Blackie here."

Then she was jumping on me and placing her warm cheek next to mine. "We are gonna take a ride! Whoppppppppie!"

I hugged her tightly for a second and then I was off the porch and running past Fred to get our mounts.

CHAPTER XI

WE RUN INTO SHIT

In ten minutes our mounts and us was working up a powerful lot of sweat, and even so I could feel a kind of chill running all the way down my back. It was like I was riding right into a kind of foggy dream and I almost had to pinch myself so's I could be sure all this was real. (Come to think of it, that's what the whole damned thing was like—a long, color-filled dream . . . and the wilder it got, the easier it was to just sort of banish my thoughts and get soaked by the whole crazy wave of it.)

Up in front of me a pace or two, Annie was leaning into the sun, and a prettier sight I could not imagine. The pine trees all around her, the sun just above her head like a stage light and her red ribbon flowing behind her, God she looked terrific. We went up a couple pretty good sized hills, then paused for a second to get our bearings and I got an idea: "Hey," I said. "If the men are going over near Ponca City, then maybe we could save a little time by following them up the Old Choctaw Pass."

Annie looked at me as if I were a Mexican dishwasher.

"The Old Choctaw Pass?" she said. "What the hell is that?"

I sighed a little and jiggled around in my saddle. "Don't you remember when we met the boys, you said they woulda got out of Bartlesville easier if they hada taken the Old Choctaw Pass, and Bill Dalton said you was exactly right!"

Annie's happy face got a strange look on it, as if she were talking to a schoolteacher!

"The Old Choctaw Pass," she said. "Is what they call in the theater 'a bit of business.'"

"A what?" I said, wiping off my brow and feeling like I was once again being taken for a very large sucker.

"A bit of business," Annie said. "I mean to say, there ain't no Old Choctaw Pass. Now let's get going and catch up with the boys. I reckon they are somewhere over by Redrock."

She kicked her heels into Blackie and was heading off down the mountain, and then I was left to come up behind her.

"Hey," I said, catching up and more than a little pissed off at her for being so damned sneaky and me for being so damned dumb. "If there ain't no Old Choctaw Pass, then how come Dalton said you was right and Doolin and him gave that great big horselaugh?"

Annie was laughing now and when I stared at her I began to feel strange, like I had no idea just who my best friend was. That kind of thing has happened a lot more since, but in them days I wasn't accustomed to it. I always figured I knew Annie, and she knew me. Now I guess I know that all anybody knows about somebody else is just a fragment of a puzzle. That's scary to me . . . a lot scarier than holding up banks.

To this last question of mine Annie didn't say nothing, so I got irritated and began to yell at her.

"Listen here," I said, as we rode along across a field of blue flowers. "I want to know about this. . . . I'm no damned dummy, and if you got me here, we got to be partners. . . . Right?"

Annie began to laugh a little now, a high sort of mocking laugh, and I felt very damned mad . . . almost mad enough to jump right over and knock her off her horse.

"Listen, Jennie," she said finally. "I'm not sure why they went for that. Maybe they don't know that there ain't no Old Choctaw Pass and they was afraid to say so in front of their friends . . ."

"What?" I said.

Annie stopped and smiled a different way at me, warm and friendly.

"I mean," said Annie, "I figured it this way. If they knew I was making it up, they might like us for just having the guts to come right in there after 'em. And if they didn't know, they'd more than likely never admit it . . . so they would assume I was right. Then there's a third possibility—that they knew I was lying and was just grateful for the lie because it enabled us to get to know one another. . . . There, dope, I got all the possibilities mapped out for you. Pick any one you want. But do it yourself. We got a goddamned robbery to attend, and if we don't hurry up, all the good shit, like the shooting and killing and the horses screaming and the stagecoach overturning, is gonna be gone."

Now she was smiling in full blossom. The teeth all white and the black eyes blazing, she shook her head at me in a way I could never resist.

"Let's go!" I said. "But you are a hell of a rascal!"

"Yippppppie!" Annie screamed. "We're gonna go get 'em, hoss!"

She pulled Blackie up on his two hind legs, and then they soared forward, leaving me behind in a cloud of dust. I kicked Jake in the ribs, and bounced along behind.

After about two more miles we was well into the dustlands and all around us was scrubby trees, mangy grass, yellow flowers and the darting tails of blue jays.

"They said they was gonna be not far from here!" Annie said. I started to talk but Annie motioned that I whisper.

"How do you know?" I said.

"Overheard Doolin and Dalton on the porch last night," Annie said. "They is gonna be up in the rocks somewhere around here . . . on Redrock Pass I think . . . Said there was a little woods around there, and I know just where it is. Down below them is gonna be the stage. This should be a real duckshoot."

"You don't mean they are gonna kill people, do you?" I said, going all clammy around the knees.

"No, not exactly anyway," Annie said. "Not unless the idiots try to protect the stage, which is highly unlikely. . . . Be real quiet now. . . . We can't let 'em know we are here. . . . What we're gonna do is merely watch the whole thing. This time."

"Yeah," I said. "We'll watch."

We moved on a little further. The woods were as quiet as the bottom of a lake, the only sounds being the snapping of twigs. In the distance I could see some more bright red flowers and I thought the blossoms felt just like the inside of my breast. To use the parlance of the Old West, I was "aflame with excitement."

Suddenly, from behind one of the evergreens, I saw something move. I pulled Jake up dead still and motioned to Annie. She pulled up along side of me.

"Something up ahead," I said. "Maybe it's them. We better stop here."

Annie raised her black eyebrows and rolled her eyes.

"You crazy?" she said. "You can't see nothing here. We gotta get around 'em . . . flank 'em a little. Where the hell did you see something anyway?"

I let Jake go a couple of feet further, then moved toward the left, through the thick underbrush. Suddenly we was in a little clearing where we could see in front of us just fine. And what we saw felt just like a Injun's knife tearing through my scalp. Because there in front of us was a gang of men all right, but they wasn't our Doolin-Daltons. No, this was a mean-looking group of people who looked like they had just escaped from the Guthrie Orphans' Home. Big skinny-looking boys with hair like straw and clothes that come right off the scarecrow. One kid had a shirt with so many holes in it, he looked like the grim reaper hisself . . . and another lad was wearing an old Confederate jacket with the epaulets hanging off it. They all sat on their horses with their heads hung down like they was real sorry about being there, and back and forth behind them rode a tall, fat man with a huge black moustache and a ten-gallon cowboy hat that looked big as a poker table. Next to the big man was what appeared to be an Indian. He had one mocassin and a broken green feather, which hung from his ear like a cheap necklace dangles from a farmer's wife. These two was whispering instructions to the band of men, who despite their rough-cut appearance was all brandishing rifles, which looked like them new Winchester models Annie was always buzzing about.

"There must be forty of 'em," Annie said.

"Leastways twenty-five," I said. "But where are *our* boys?"

Annie got off her horse and climbed up a rock and looked across the little valley.

In a second she had scrambled back down and was biting her lower lip.

"I got it," she said. "Our boys is up there, across the road."

"What road?" I said.

"The road down in front of those boys. . . . They are Pinkertons. They know our boys is up there and they are waiting for 'em to come down out of the rocks. Then they are gonna nail 'em."

"But they will get wiped out by our boys in the rocks," I said.

"No," said Annie. "We ain't gonna have anybody on the rocks. . . . The stage is gonna come up here . . . and jes try to drive straight on through. . . . The Doolins will have to come down to chase it. . . . Then they are gonna be ambushed from over here. . . . And he'll probably send some of these boys around the other side . . . too. Oh Jesus, we got to do something!"

"But what?" I said, feeling for all the world like I was gonna pee myself. Oh, I wondered if they would have that in the Ned Buntline books. Cowgirl pees herself at first robbery.

"We got to get around the back of these guys . . . and get down on the road, and warn 'em . . ."

"What?" I said. "Listen, I thought we come to watch. We could fire off some guns jes as well."

Annie made her mouth into a clown's lips and shook her head.

"Yeah," she said. "Maybe you got something there. We can just do that. . . . But we better do it damned quick. Look . . ."

I put my hands over my eyes and looked down the clearing. Coming towards us, with their guns drawn, was the fat man in the long coat and the Indian with the limp green feather.

"Awww shit!" I said. "I'm too young to die."

"Follow me," said Annie.

"Hey, you kids," shouted the Indian. "Get away from here. Get away . . ."

"Goddamn, Annie, run," I said.

Then we was kicking our horses hard and heading down around the Pinkertons, toward the road. It was a steep incline and suddenly behind us I saw a couple of them yellow-skinned young kids moving toward us, and I kept kicking Jake and he kept following Annie and Blackie down through the green leafy trees and over the rocks and then we was almost down on the road when I heard shooting and looked up on the other side of the mountain and saw the glint of rifles, and I wanted to take off my cowboy hat and pull down my hair, and scream, "It's *us*, the women. We are saving your asses, you idiots, so don't *shoot*!" But I was too busy holding onto the reins, and now bullets was flying down on us and we was almost down to the hill and I pictured both sides just shooting us into mincemeat, when all of a sudden I seen the stage come around the corner and Annie is heading right towards it, pulling out her huge old Colt with one hand, and I am right behind her as we head for the driver and behind us I can hear the Pinkertons screaming, "Shoot 'em, shoot 'em!" and I see Annie aiming her gun, but then her horse hits a rock and she is flying up and over, and behind the stage is three riders, bringing up the rear with guns drawn, and one of 'em is coming right at me and I am trying to think what the hell to do . . . pull up and away . . . make it to the other side and pray the Doolin-Daltons don't get me, so I pull Jake's reins, but like I said before, I ain't no born horsewoman, and by this time Jake, who ain't used to gunplay, having never heard a gunshot in his short life, well he just keeps right on heading for the stage guard, who is aiming at me and yelling, "Halt now, you bastard!" and I think, "Shit, Jake is gonna hafta veer off pretty quick or he is jes gonna run head on into that son of a bitch," and to my left the stagecoach guard is falling off the stage, nothing fancy, just like he's flopping down in bed, only there's blood dripping from him and now we are only two feet away from the guard and Jake keeps right on going as the guard shoots his gun. I am so low he can't hit me, then I hear a terrible thud, and see the two horses hit head on, and fall over . . . and the guard is flying through the air and I am flying head over Jake, who is lying on the ground unconscious, and somehow I land on my arm and roll over and end up half sitting up, with only a terrible pain in my wrist, and all around me horses are screaming and the stage looks abandoned and there are gunshots being fired from the cliff in front of me and from the smaller hill I see the Pinkertons starting to get on their horses, and I see the big man with the black hat stop and scream, "I will personally shoot any man who attempts to leave this scene," and the yellow-skinned boys look at one another for a second, but another hail of fire comes down on them and two of them fall over and then all of them are turning away from the fat black-moustachioed man, and the green-feather Indian and the Pinkertons are riding hell for leather off into the woods . . . and I hear the fat man say, "Damn it to hell," and he sounds jes like a little kid. I watch all this just like I was in a safe box at the balcony of the theater, when it occurs to me that I am sitting in a pile of dust, right behind the stagecoach and all around me are wounded and angry stage drivers and guards who would love to break many of my cowgirl bones. Then I remember Annie sailing off her horse and I feel a terrible fear. What if they . . . I stagger to my feet and look around when I feel a clutching finger on my neck, and I scream.

"Shut the hell up, girl, for Chrissakes," says Annie. "We got to get out of here. . . . See if you can crawl under the stage and make it over to them rocks. . . . We got to get up there with the Gang before they shoot us."

"Right," I say, falling to my belly and crawling like a gila monster under the stage.

We are halfway under the stage when I hear someone moaning, and when I look outside I see a man with a hole in his neck and blood seeping out like tomato juice.

"Annie," I say, "Jesus . . . Annie. We got to help him."

I am stopped dead, staring at this man whose eyes are meeting mine, and such terrible and hurt eyes they are, too. I feel a wave of terrible fear coming over me, as if the earth has opened and I have fallen clear through.

"Keep on moving, now," says Annie. "We got to think of our own asses. He's a goner!"

"A goner!" I said. "A goner! Annie . . . look at him."

The man was reaching out toward us now, trying to crawl in our direction. His eyes was all puffed out of his head and his tongue moved back and forth. He looked like a snake that had fallen on spikes.

"Jesus," I said.

Now Annie began to pull me hard and I moved with her, too terrified to stay around. Yet I could not take my eyes off the man.

"All right," said Annie when we reached the other side of the stage. "We got to run for it now. You ready?"

I turned away from the man and thought of him crawling toward us. I began to cry some and Annie grabbed my shoulders.

"Listen," she said. "Listen, you got to make your move."

"I can't," I said, as the tears came down and my stomach welded into a huge knot. "I can't go . . ."

"Why?" said Annie. "What is it? Are you shot?"

I shook my head and grit my teeth.

"What is it then?" said Annie.

"He's got my ankle!" I said.

Annie turned and let out a gasp; then I turned and looked down at the gray-eyed man. He had his cold hand on my ankle and was holding it in a horrible grasp. I felt all the sympathy I had for him just vanish like smoke, then I felt such a cold fearful rage that I thought of nothing, but simply began kicking him in the face, over and over again. Each time I kicked him he moaned a little, and now when I think of it I know how bad he must have suffered, but at the same time all I could think of is, "If that son of a bitch don't stop moaning, what's left of them Pinkertons is gonna come do some very bad business to us," so I kicked again and he finally gave out a very frightening yell and fell over on his back, his big belly heaving in death agony.

"Now," said Annie, pulling me to my feet, "let's get up that hill."

We started scrambling forward into the rocks and for a second it looked as though we were going to make it. But just as we got into the trees another man come toward us, blood dripping down his head. He had lost his rifle from the confusion, but right near him lay someone's pistol.

"All right, you two," he said. "All right. . . . Now you've had it!"

He stood in front of us, the blood dripping from his eye, his feet shaky.

87

"We didn't do you no harm," I said. "Let us go!"

"You darn kids," he said. He staggered a bit then and shook his head. "I am gonna plug both of you!"

I looked at Annie and in her hands was the knife Dalton had given her.

"Annie," I said. "Don't . . ."

"I hope I learned to throw this thing!" she said.

Then she coolly stepped back, cocked her arm behind her ear, and let the knife fly toward the wounded guard. I watched it fly toward its target, straight and true. That it was straight and true until the last few feet . . . then it took kind of a dive, and when the guard tried to dodge, he moved right into it. . . . But not the point.

Instead the blunt end caught him right in the crotch and he doubled over in pain, screaming terrible language and holding his private parts.

"Bull's-eye," said Annie, as we ran around him into the forest.

"Jesus," I said. "Oh Jesus . . ."

"C'mon, girl," said Annie. "Jesus don't live around here. You got to pull your own weight!"

And pull I did. We both did. Up the steep boulders and then through the trees and finally, after what seemed like a very long climb, I could hear the voices of Dalton and Dick Whisper just over the other side of the rocks. I wanted to go right around and hug them, but Annie was smiling and held me back.

"Listen," she said. "This might be interesting."

"Oh hell," said Dalton. "Jesus . . . if it hadn't a been for them girls . . . I don't know."

"Them girls was real cowboys," said Dick Whisper.

I turned to Annie and we was both smiling like the sun.

"Look through here," Annie said, moving over a bit. There was a good little hole in the rocks and we could see pretty well. Now the rest of the Gang was walking around, kicking up dust. Dalton looked like he was gonna cry and Bittercreek kept rubbing his nose, and sobbed once or twice. Doolin just sat next to Whisper and even Raidler and Dan Clifton stared down at the dust.

"If it hadn't a been for them, we'd all be six feet under by tonight!" said Dalton, in a high cracky kinda voice.

"Either that or worse," said Doolin.

"At the end of a rope!" said Bittercreek. "Ah, Jennie . . . I was jes getting to know her. . . . There was a sweet kid."

"Hey," said Whisper, in a real mortician's hiss. "Do you suppose that they . . . mighta . . ."

He couldn't bring himself to finish the sentence. The rest of the Gang didn't say nothing but stood there, with their Adam's apples going up and down, and wiping their eyes.

"Awww shit . . ." said Dalton. "I can't bring myself to go down there . . ."

"Me neither . . ." said Doolin.

Annie started to giggle insanely, and I must admit I felt as warm as I had felt cold when we started.

"I can't stand going down neither," said Bittercreek. "But we got to."

Suddenly I heard Annie pipe up: "You boys shoulda never left them two helpless girls all alone. You are gonna be haunted the rest of your lives . . ."

Dick Whisper jumped back into Doolin's arms. Doolin dropped him like he was a bad habit.

"We help you boys?" Annie said, standing up and pulling me up with her.

"Yeah," I said, scrambling up and over the rocks. "We got nothing to do since we're dead. Maybe we could help you bury them courageous girl outlaws what gave their lives for the likes of a mangy group such as you."

Then we were both over the rocks and the Gang was all over us, pounding us and picking us up and I began to cry and hug Bittercreek, and Annie began to cry and hug Dalton, and Doolin, like a great black bear, was racing around like a kid, hugging all four of us and lifting us up into the sunshine and the good clean air. "Awww shit," he kept saying, shaking his huge, handsome old head. "Awwww shit. . . . You just got to praise the Lord. Awww shitttt!"

CHAPTER
XII
TALKING WITH BILL

THAT AFTERNOON WE WERE IN HIGH SPIRITS FOR QUITE A WHILE. I don't ever remember feeling closer to a bunch a boys in my life and doubt if I ever will again. When we rode down outta the hills, with the birds soaring around us and the sun shining, it was just better than any amount of gold. We was all like one . . . and for an hour or so, as we made our way through the woods, it was jes like we had pulled off the robbery and was set for life. There was almost a visible rope between us . . . or between our spirits, and I know that everyone felt like we was never gonna be alone again. After we had rode for about an hour, Dalton suggested we make camp for the afternoon and go swimming in a place called the Miracle Valley. Well that was all right by me and Annie and Bittercreek, too. In fact, there was nothing I wanted more than to spend some time alone with Bitter and I know Annie wanted the same with Bill.

So, we came to the Miracle Valley, and what a place it was, too.

Though I woulda never said so to Annie, the look of the trees and the way the sun came down through the leaves and being able to see deer drinking at a pool . . . well it seemed just like a fairy book I'd read and for a while I felt like a queen who had fallen on hard times and was forced to act like a beggar . . . and I wanted to tell that to Annie or to Bitter, but then I became afraid to say it. What if they laughed at it, or worse, started thinking of me as a softheaded idiot? And as far as that last score went, maybe I was a softheaded idiot cause I couldn't seem to get that dying man's face out of my head or the feel of his deathly fingers offa my leg. Even now, as we pitched camp and the boys went running down a trail where they said they could find a stream . . . well even with all my joy at finding this beautiful place, I could not forget the way the man's fingers felt on my flesh . . . five cold spots to be exact, and I began to feel the whole leg go numb. Suddenly, I felt like I was going to faint dead away, and I didn't want Bitter or anybody to see me, so I sort of went over by a boulder and crouched down, holding the spot. Out by the fire I could hear Annie and the rest of the gang whooping it up and I caught a glimpse of Bitter jumping about and I began to feel worse than ever . . . kinda sick to my stomach. Of course it was my own damned fault for thinking and feeling like a girl . . . when I wasn't supposed to be one at all, but a cowgirl-outlaw-desperado-type woman . . . a real wild west mama . . . But just the same I couldn't help feeling a little ornery at Bittercreek. Here he'd had his way with me and claimed to love me and he just let me sidle off into the rocks with my dead man's leg and with my stomach feeling like it just got offa bronc, and you'd of thought he would have just come over and asked me how I was doing. But nothing like that happened. He was drinking whiskey now. I could hear 'em all yelling and laughing, and then someone said, "Let's go down to the stream and go skinny-dipping," and someone else said, "Where's the girls?" and I thought Bitter might come over then, or at least ask, "Yeah, where *are* the girls?" but he done nothing at all but say, "Let's go to the creek. They are probably already down there." And then there was a big to-do, lots of yelling and whooping and all of a sudden I felt very far away from it all. I don't mean physically far away . . . but sort of inside far away, as if I were on a mountain top somewhere, and their cries was just small, hot little peeps that come from way down the bottom of the mountain. It was a right scary sensation and I couldn't help feeling those damned cold blue imprints on my leg and I began to shudder a bit, when all of a sudden I looked up and there was Bill Doolin staring down at me, with his old big moustache and his long, scraggly hair and his big, green eyes.

"Well," he says to me, "just what do we have here?"

"Leave me alone," I sort of mumbled, sounding for all the world like an infant brat.

"Leave you alone? Leave alone a poor little creature huddled all up in a knot and rubbing her leg like she has been bit by a rattler? Now that would hardly be manly of me, would it, Jennie?"

He smiled a bit and I tried to smile a bit, but instead I began to gush tears like I was the original waterfall of paradise, and I woulda felt embarrassed if I hadn't felt so sad, scared and awful.

In another second he had knelt down and taken me in his big ole arms and was holding me to his breast.

"Now what's a matter?" he said. "What is it?"

And I began to tell him everything. How I was afraid of the killing and how I never belonged nowheres, but felt like I might like to belong here but was afraid that someone I liked would get shot and was afraid that I might get shot and was afraid that I might have to do some shooting myself and was afraid of the dead man's hands, which were still clinging to my legs and that I was afraid of being afraid because maybe he would think I wasn't desperado material after all and would send me back to Morgan's Hash House.

After I got all of that out, I felt a little better and Doolin patted me on the head and kinda pulled me out from behind the rock and sat me down next to the campfire and rolled a cigarette, while behind him the sun was blazing.

"Being scared," he said, "is what I would expect. If you wasn't scared when you was out there, then you are certainly crazy as hell. But you go through stages in this job . . . that is, men do, and I reckon it ain't much different for women. I mean to say, at first, all you are is scared. Did I ever tell you about my first job?"

"No, sir," I said, sniffling and hunching myself up against a tree.

"Held up a circus," Mr. Doolin said, winking at me. "This here sadassed circus come to our town. They advertised a dancing bear, a real genuine buffalo and the King of Beasts. . . . They also said they had clowns. Well, I had heard this here circus was coming to town for near two months and I had worked my tail off around the barn, doin extra chores so's I could see it. There was nothing in my life, before or since, I wanted more. I still remember looking at them wall posters, with the crazy pink-colored clowns, and the King of Beasts being backed up against a cage wall by a tall, thin fella in a top hat. I can still see the whip . . . the way it was held in the air and the fella's black moustache, which was as thin as a snail. . . . There just wasn't nothing like it. . . . I used ta sit up nights waiting for that circus to arrive. And arrive it did. They set up their tents on the outside of town, two big ones . . . and they had a sign that went clear around both tents with pictures on it. And these pictures was even more dramatic than the ones that they'd sent to town in advance. Oh, say, you never seen anything quite like it. Pictures of giant tiger mouths and pictures of beautiful bareback riders. . . . Wheww! It made my temperature go up jes seeing it, I'll tell you. . . . Yeah . . . it was something. . . . If only the actual circus itself had been anywhere near as good as the pictures they showed, well I might never have had to hold it up."

He smiled and took a long drag on his cigarette and I watched the smoke pour out of his mouth. He looked like a great big old dragon.

"You see," he said. "When me and my friend Riley got inside this place, we seen a bear in a cage . . . jes like they claimed. Only the bear has been left out in the sun so long he is just about panting himself to death. His tongue is hanging out and his ribs are exposed and he is about as ferocious as a snail, and a lot slower. Well, I was deeply disappointed, but Riley, he was plumb crazy. For weeks he had been talking about getting in the cage with the bear, watching this giant black killer and stuff like that. The lion is about a shade poorer than the bear. This toothless old thing might gum you to death but that's about it. Her coat was so covered with flies she looked like the buffalo, which died the second day. . . . The clown, one Mr. Hezekiah J. Lipton, tried to make these beasts into greater than life, but even he didn't have it in him. I remember leaving that day and thinking, 'It ain't right. It ain't right at all.' Riley didn't stop to think a whole lot. That night he come round my house, all dressed up like a clown. His argument was that Mr. Lipton had gotten just about every kid in town's five cents, so it was up to us to sort of get it back again. . . . We was gonna be sort of like . . . knights, if you know what I mean. I remember riding out there all dressed up like a clown . . . with whitewash on my face and a big red nose. . . . We rapped on the door of the place and Mr. Hezekiah Lipton answered, and in a few minutes we had jumped him pretty good. . . . We got his strongbox and then started out, but he tried to go for his gun and Riley hit him over the head and knocked him out cold. We both started laughing then. It was like we was going to the circus we had dreamed about if you know what I mean. . . . *Robbing* was the real circus, the real fun, and I remember seeing them animals all different this time . . . as if they was me, if you know what I mean. . . . They was me all locked up. . . . So we started to let them out . . . but the bear was too weak to go, so Riley shot it between the eyes, and the lion was barely able to get out of the cage . . . but she went just the same. . . . And I felt good, so damned good, and on the way out, Mr. Lipton woke up again, and we had to hit him all over again . . . and then we just took off down the trail, Riley and me . . . and we was partners for nearly a year."

"Where is Riley now?" I asked, totally forgetting my own misery.

"Now? I reckon he's down below," said Bill Doolin and he did not look like he was kidding. "He caught a bunch of bullets up in Abilene. Bushwhacked in the back by Wyatt Earp."

"Wyatt Earp?" I said. "But I always heard tell he only wounded men."

"Yeah," said Doolin, "and I always heard tell that they had real dancing bears in that circus. You see, what it comes down to is, a good outlaw is dedicated to the proposition that life ain't all that good and therefore stealing, shooting and generally raising hell ain't all that bad. We are entertainment for people. . . . We keep 'em alive. That's why they don't tell on us. Nobody really wants to see us dead, except them that already are!"

I smiled and shook my head. A smarter and crazier man I have never met. Yet there was a tinge of sadness to him, so strong I could almost taste it.

"What's wrong, Bill?" I said. I moved a little closer to him.

"Nothing," he said. "It's just when you get a little older, you lose a little something. . . . You start making mistakes . . . and you can't afford that. No sir!"

"Like today?" I said.

"Yeah, like today. I don't know how in hell they knew I was there."

He shook his old head then, and I wanted to bring him over and hug him. I felt all warm and loving and so proud to be there with him that I almost burst.

"Hey, you two," said a voice. "You are missing all the fun!"

We both turned to see Annie coming up the trail.

"What is it?" I said.

"Bitter and Bill are down at the creek. They are going swimming and stuff like that. C'mon girl . . ."

I looked at Bill Doolin, and he laid back up against a tree.

"You go ahead," he said. "I'll be resting. See you soon, Jennie."

"Yessir, Bill," I said.

I wanted to reach over and kiss him on his head, but that was probably going too far. A cowgirl has to keep herself together at all times.

CHAPTER
XIII
TAKING A SWIM

WHEN WE GOT DOWN TO THE STREAM I SEEN BITTERCREEK AND Bill Dalton smiling like a couple of skulls in a funhouse.
"Hey hey," said Bill. "I got something here jes right fer you."
"Indian happy happy happy," said Bittercreek.
He took a cigarette from Bill Dalton and laughed his ass off, took a puff and then started looking up at the clouds.
"Indian see happy spirits," he said. "Indian see great God Wahtumsecuh in sky. Wahtumsecuh is very happy. . . . His eyes are bulging from his head and his cheeks are filled with sunshine."
"You are one crazy Indian," said Bill Dalton. He grabbed the cigarette and took a deep drag and then passed it to Annie.
"White woman smoke that!" said Bittercreek. "Make you feel like passionflower. Hmmmm!"
"What the hell is that?" said Annie.
"Not in books written about us badmen," said Dalton, putting

his hands together and looking for all the world like an Indian praying to the clouds.

"Ned Buntline no get loco, don't know gods, white woman," said Bittercreek.

"Well, I'll be," said Annie, putting her hand on her hip and holding the cigarette away from her face like it was a lit stick of dynamite.

"You'll be what?" said Dalton.

"You'll be who?" said Bittercreek.

"I'll be damned," she said. "What's this stuff do?"

"Stuff do?" said Dalton. "Do stuff and see what stuff do!"

"I don't get it," Annie said, but she took a few puffs.

"Hold in deep," said Dalton.

Annie did it again, and this time held it deeply. Then she passed it to me.

"Why not?" I said. Inside I was shaking like a leaf. But hell, I'd already acted like a baby more than enough for one day. So I took a big long pull of that stuff and snorted it out like a bull, then took another pull and snorted it out again and handed it to Annie, but suddenly she wasn't interested. She was too busy hiding her face from the two boys, who were laughing hysterical like and taking off their pants.

"White women want to see Indian arrow?" said Bittercreek.

"Oh shit," I said. That was the worst joke I ever heard. Since Annie wasn't smoking anything, I just had me another little pull of that stuff and like all of a sudden I was laughing like hell.

"Arrow," I said. "I get it. You mean like Arrow . . . Oh, that's good."

The funny thing was I knew that wasn't a funny joke at all, but the unfunniness of it made it seem all the more funny. In fact, everything seemed real funny all of a sudden. The trees were a riot, the grass was a million laughs and the birds one big guffaw.

I watched them two handsome devils taking off their pants and I started taking off my shirt and my tight Levi's.

"Hey, here we go," said Dalton. He and Bitter waved goodbye

to Annie, who was standing with her hand part way over her face. There was just a little slit where she could see out.

"Now wait a minute," said Annie, looking at me, as I wiggled out of my pants. "Jennie, I never figured you . . . I mean. . . . You can't just do that. . . . I mean . . ."

Well, if I had any doubts about what I was doing, they disappeared when I saw Annie's reluctance. Like I said before, I always did want to beat her at something.

"Heck, girl," I said. "There ain't nothing to this. Smoke some of this stuff before it burns my fingers."

"No," said Annie, "and you put your clothes back on. We are cowgirls, but we still got to have some decency."

Well, that comment, lame as it was, just about brought the house down. From out in the sparkling waters Bitter and Dalton started in making faces and arching their eyebrows and acting like they was a couple of swells from Boston.

In a second I about had my pants down, and when I saw the looks of appreciation on Bitter's and Dalton's faces, it made me feel all flush and happy as a catfish.

"Three cheers for the lady who took off her britches . . ."

"Yeah. . . . She's little but she sure is fine."

"Three cheers for Little Britches. Hip Hip Hooray!!!"

I smiled and turned to Annie and stuck out my tongue, then leaped into the air and splashed into the wonderful cold water. In a second Bitter was coming toward me and we hugged and I felt as if I were going to drown with happiness.

Then we turned and looked at Annie, still on the bank.

"C'mon, Annie," I said.

"Oh, Cattle Annie, won't you come out tonight?" sang Dalton. "C'mon, honey. Come out tonight!"

Annie shook her head, then turned her back and then suddenly spread her long legs and turned around. When she did, the buttons of her shirt were undone and you could nearly see her breasts.

"All right now!" said Dalton.

"Yip, yip, yippppie!" said Bitter.

She began to sashay back and forth on the riverbank, smiling and singing.

> "Well the boys all call me Cattle Annie
> Cause I rustle up the fun.
> If you don't want your cattle rustled
> Don't you hurt me none!"

"Whooop whooop," said Dalton.

"Yes ma'am," said Bittercreek, and though I guess I shoulda felt a little jealous, it was no use. She had topped me again, and yet she had done it with such style, with such good spirits, that all I could do was sit in the river, tread the water and appreciate her act.

Now she pranced back and forth on the mossy river's edge, laughing and singing her song and dropping her shirt, untying her long black hair and then slipping out of her jeans to reveal her long, sexy legs. Dalton got so excited I thought he was going to turn into a flying fish.

"Oh, Cattle Annie, come in and play!" he tried to say, but his voice cracked.

Now Annie put her legs together and her hands on her knees and leaned over the edge into the water. She put forth one delicate toe and smiled and teased: "Should I?" she said in a wee little voice. "Do you really think I should?"

Suddenly behind her there came a huge chorus of voices: "Hell no. Stay there. The view is jes fine!!"

High on top of an oak tree, Whisper, Raidler and Dan Clifton were sitting stark naked.

"Yippie!!" Dan yelled.

Annie turned and threw her hand over her mouth as if she was terribly embarrassed, then smiled, waved and hit the pool with a perfect dive. The sun caught off her body real nice as she entered the stream.

CHAPTER

XIV

DOWN IN THE CAVE

ALL THAT AFTERNOON WE PLAYED IN THE WATER, AND HARDLY a better time coulda been imagined. Me and Bitter dove under the stream and attacked Annie and Bill, and then all four of us swam downstream where a huge waterfall emptied itself down on us. The sun shone through the haze so beautiful that I felt like I was an otter or a beaver or some strange magical animal that don't worry like people always do and don't think of the future or feel guilty about the past. . . . Rather I was just a heart and a muscle and a good clean bodily being . . . all eyes and ears and breasts and legs and sex . . . (I hope Mrs. Patterson don't see this). Especially the latter . . . I felt fires burning in between my legs and as we swam up under the water, and I looked at Bitter standing in the mud, his great long penis hanging down in front of him and his strong muscular thighs . . . God, I bout went out of my mind with yearning. . . . I know Annie and Dalton felt the same way because they kept playfully going under the waterfall and I could hear her cries . . . first little squeals and teases, then long happy moans which echoed through the valley and must have give even the forest creatures reason to be jealous. (Now, here at the school they tell me what we did was sinful and wrong, and I've already felt that, perhaps I even felt it that day under the water. But I also felt good and freed of sin, and like I say, I pictured myself as an animal who only answers to his own blood and mine was racing that day. Oh Lordy, wasn't it . . .)

After a bit Annie and Bill came out of the water and went up on the beach and lay down in the grass, staring up at the sun. They never looked more beautiful, neither of them. Annie's black hair falling round her shoulders and her large round breasts so firm, with the nipples sitting up straight . . . Lord, she looked like a goddess, and I looked down at my own breasts, which are nicely shaped but perhaps a little small, and I felt that right then and there was where she was superior to me. . . . She was all animal, the animal world of action was where she functioned best . . . and I began to think that everything she did was in some way related to that . . . to her wanting to become a forest creature, a creature who lived not by thoughts and ideas, but by scent and fang and sex. . . . And these thoughts scared me . . . or perhaps they have become thoughts only now, for at the time they were more jes like brief little flashes of what Mrs. Patterson would call insights. . . . Imagine that—me, Jennie Stevens, having insights . . . it's a scary thought, but exciting all the same. Exciting in a different way than that afternoon was exciting, for that became an afternoon of sheer bodily pleasures, wonderful impulses of water flowing over my body, and Bitter's hands rubbing my back and the sound of the birds calling . . . and feeling Bitter's small, muscular waist and his own arms around my back . . . and the two of us lying on a rock, and he saying to me: "Oh, Jennie, I love you so. . . . I never felt so good in my life!"

And then he moved inside me and I was pushed up against the mossy waterfall and felt him in me, and I was bucking and crying out and hearing the water rush over me, and he was plunging inside me again and again, and then he took it out of me, and I fell down below him and took his cock inside my mouth, and he thrust it in me and stood up above, and I held my hands on his flat strong ass, and when he came I cried and he cried, and the water rushed down over both of us, good and clean and cold. Oh, there was nothing like it . . . nothing . . . (and I hope Mrs. Patterson could understand this. I hope she had a moment sometime in her life like my moment that day with Bitter, for I hate to think of her as always being corseted up with the three inches of rouge on her face and her eyebrows looking like they was stitched up on her forehead and her mouth stitched down like a forever-sad rag doll. Oh, I hope she felt this and felt good . . . because no matter what they tell me now about my outlaw life, I ain't never gonna forget how good and fine that day was).

Nor the night, in the dark, glistening cave with Bittercreek. We had smoked some more of that marijuana plant and we had all set around the fire eating cornbread and smoked ham and beans, a meal Annie cooked to perfection, and then after we had passed around the bottle a little, Bittercreek and I decided to sneak off somewheres and be alone again. Oh, the thrill I felt that night, a real rapture, yessir, as we made our way through the sticker bushes and the low-hanging boughs of the trees and down a narrow pathway to the mouth of the cave. The entrance was small and dark, and looking at it I felt fearful, but Bitter held me close and said we only had to crawl a little ways in, and then the place would become wider and there was a natural stream what ran through it. So I shook my head yes and followed him in and Lord it was dark in there, darker than a night with no moon, darker than a blanket draped over a coffin. Bitter led the way and I held onto his ankle (and thought of the dead man holding onto my ankle, and felt like standing up and screaming), and we made our way through the narrow passage.

"Up here," Bitter said after a while. "It ain't much farther now. Keep on going."

Which I did, though my hands was getting cut up on sharp little rocks, and ever so often I would have a terrible fear that I was going to come to the end of the earth and just fall off . . . but then I figured that if that was going to happen Bitter would go first, which is a strange thing to admit since I was in love. Still, it was them kind of feelings which kept me moving forward.

"Here, here we are," said Bitter, and suddenly I saw him lighting a match and setting it in a lantern he had carried along, and lo and behold, he was standing in a whole cavern full of beautiful sharp-pointed diamonds. . . . I believe the term is stalactites or some such, but they didn't look like that to me then, cause I didn't know what to call them. They was long and pointy and white and dripping this soft blue water, and I felt something come over me staring at them, standing out of the wall and the lantern burning, and Bitter spread-legged over me, taking off his shirt now and smiling at me in this slow, Indian smile, his dark hair and dark eyes glowing almost blue in the strange white-red light.

Then he was on top of me and we made love like we was from some other world, and we was scratching and holding one another, and he thrust his long lean cock inside of me, and I shut my eyes and thought of the walls, all of them thrusting inside me, and I wondered when he finished, would he leave that strange smoking liquid up in me. . . . And I started to moan, and the moan was echoed all through the cave, and Bitter started to moan in harmony to my moan, and that got echoed all about, and it seemed like the walls themselves was making love with us, and oh, it was the strangest, wildest feeling, like nothing else in this world or out of it. . . . And then I felt him hitting at me, harder and harder, and I could feel myself bursting forth, it was like I was dead, dying, and I said, "Ah ahh ahhhh, Bittttttttter," fairly screaming out his name, and then I was exploding inside, all of me just afire, and I burned like the lantern, and wondered why we didn't melt the whole damned cave, and drown in a sea of ice cold water, millions of years old.

Afterwards we lay still, without saying nothing, but touching each other, and I knew I was so deeply in love with him that it didn't matter what he was or what might happen. I was his and I trusted him and knew he was mine.

Then I started to say something, but before I could get it out, I began to hear this tremendous moaning and screaming, and Bitter and I both jumped up, and it seemed to be coming from somewhere back in the cave, and I knew right from the git-go who it must be.

"It's Annie," I said. "Annie and Bill. Oh, damn it."

"What's wrong?" said Bitter.

"Well," I said. "I just thought we was alone."

"Ahhhhh, Billll," came the sound, and I started to giggle a bit in spite of myself. Love is magical and wonderful and like the crazy moon when it's you. When it's somebody else, it reminds me of a couple razorbacks grousing in the mud.

"Come on," said Bitter. "Let's see!"

"We shouldn't," I said.

"We can't afford not to," Bitter smiled.

"Oh hell," I said.

Then we was crawling through the rocks and hardspace and soon we was at a lagoon, an underwater lagoon, with strange white rocks which jutted out of the earth like they was trying to escape, and down on the bank we could see Annie riding on top of Bill Dalton, swaying and crying and calling out his name, and then she screamed and fell down on top of him, and I looked at Bitter and him at me, and I knew I should feel guilty and awful for watching but all I felt was a great hot desire to have him on me again, and I never felt no shame. In fact, looking at her there I loved her, and Dalton too, and it seemed that nothing would stop our closeness, and yet I was going to say, "We ought to leave them alone," except I didn't say that. Instead I found myself walking down among the rocks, and Annie and Bill saw us, and they looked startled at first, but then Bitter came up with me and we all sat on the river's edge talking to one another about how happy we was and laughing about the robbery, and it all seemed so natural and good and real that I felt like I was going to cry . . . and Annie seemed so damned happy to see us. She began laughing and standing on the edge of the rushing underground river.

"Ain't this place the greatest!" she said, and her words was echoed throughout the entire cavern. "Boy, jes listen to this!"

Slowly, Annie's face assumed a kind of stagey look . . . her eyes got all serious and she looked at Dalton and Bittercreek and me and she climbed up on a white rock. Then she placed her right hand over her breast and looked up to the dripping ceilings: "Oh Romeo, Romeo, wherefore art thou, Romeo? Deny your father and refuse your name . . ."

Her voice echoed real sharp all over the place and Bill Dalton looked like he had seen a winged horse.

"Damn, Annie," he said. "What was that?"

Annie stepped back down and smiled cockily: "That, Mr. Bill Dalton, was William Shakespeare."

"Oh yeah," said Dalton, looking at the ground, "I heard tell of him. He's a local boy, ain't he?"

Annie laughed a little and turned to wink at me. "Sure," she said.

Dalton took the bait real good: "Yeah, I thought so. . . . He's from Dallas. . . . I seen his name on a theater marquee down there."

Annie laughed and rubbed Bill on the back.

"You are crazy," she said. "Shakespeare is from London, England. . . . He is the Bard of Stratford and Avon . . ."

Well, Dalton got a little angry at this: "No. . . . Well where did you learn that stuff anyway?"

Annie stood back up, and I realized again suddenly that she was naked. That we was all naked . . . and I felt a little embarrassed, and a lot excited. "My daddy taught it to me," Annie said.

"Your daddy?" said Bittercreek. "I thought he was a dirt farmer."

Annie nodded, and then her eyes got cloudy and she looked as though she was hearing voices from deep inside the cave. "He was a dirt farmer," she said. "But he had a dream. He wanted to be a great actor on the stage. He knew every play of Shakespeare's by heart. But we was too poor fer him to do anything with it. The only actresses he had to work with was me and Ma. You know, sometimes at night he'd get that old book of plays out and we'd read it and act all the parts . . . like Juliet and Puck."

The way she spoke so softly, so longingly fer her dad, made all three of us get real quiet. Finally Dalton said: "Whatever happened to your dad anyways?"

"He got killed by a bottle," Annie said. "But I'll always remember the lines he taught me. That and one more thing."

"What's that?" Dalton said.

Annie turned and looked at us all now. Her eyes was blazing: "He told me, 'Don't do like I did, Annie. Don't let 'em trap you. Live, girl, live.' And I aim to!"

Dalton sucked in his breath and held out his hand to Annie and she sat back down.

"You are living, honey," he said real tender like.

Annie turned then and looked at me and Bitter.

"We all are," she said.

Then she reached over and took my hand, and I held her fingers tightly, and Bitter took my other one, and we was all silent and smiling and I could feel a kind of radiance which shone off all of us, and Annie started to laugh, and Bitter and Bill joined her, and the walls seemed to shower the good sound back to us, and that second we was all together . . . rocks, trees, cold blue icicles, and we stayed there for the longest, yet the shortest time. Just sitting there with one another, everyone part of one fine thing.

CHAPTER

XV

DALTON SPINS A YARN

DURING THE NEXT FEW DAYS, BITTER AND I AND BILL AND Annie spent a lot of time together, both on the ranch and in the nearby hills. We went fishing in a clear brook and went for picnics and we had a hell of a time. Naturally I fell more and more in love with Bittercreek and he did with me . . . and told me all about his past in Texas and I told him all about my own past, living with my grandmother, who was a terrible religious old cuss, like to sit on the porch, knit her shawls and cuss the heathens, of which there was no short supply.

"Every one of them rascals was a heathen," I told Bitter, Annie and Bill one day, while we was out shooting us some deer.

"There was heathen drunkards and heathen judges and heathen lawyers. . . . Oh, she hated them a might more than most. . . . And worst of all was them heathen redskins."

"Owwwwwww," said Bitter, jumping around the field like he was just plugged by a Winchester.

Annie and Dalton laughed too, and then Bill got a little quiet and said his brother Grat was kind of religious too, but in a different way.

"Grat used to like to take long walks and have talks with Jesus," Bill said. "He took a heck of a lot of kidding about it, too."

I looked down at my shoes and felt a little skittery, cause Bill Dalton never talked about his brothers no more. Bitter had told me that it was best not to mention the old Dalton Gang, cause since they got hit in Coffeyville, Dalton was never able to speak of them without getting powerful drunk and ornery. But now, as we sat on the grass, with our rifles in our hands, he looked at us with his blue eyes, dropped his head and just started talking as if he'd kept it in very long and needed to get it out. Annie sat real close to him with her green-checked shirt on and her high boots, and she looked at him real thoughtful like, or so I thought at the time.

"Grat was the religious guy, all right," Dalton said, picking some grass with his left hand. "But Bob was the smartest one of the lot. Oh, there was never nobody smarter than Bob, that's for sure. He was the one that got us into the Texas Rangers . . . and when he realized that we was gonna spend our lives broke and probably end up real dead real fast, he was the one that told us we had to change horses in mid-stream."

"Where was that?" Annie said, putting her hand on Bill's.

"That was in Waco," Bill said. "He come in the house one day and he said to me, 'Bill, we are all real fast and real young, and if we stay here with these boys we is gonna end up old and slow —that's if we are lucky—old and slow and dead broke. You think any of these rich folks is gonna care about us then? You know as well as I do—old folks who are poor are no better than Mexicans or niggers.' And I shook my head like a dumb oaf and said, 'Yeah, so what?' and he smiled and said, 'We keep waiting for the stage to come in,' and I said, 'Sure,' and he said, 'Let's get acquainted with the driver,' and I said, 'Sure,' and we went and got the other brothers, and that very afternoon we robbed our first stage. . . . It was a good feeling . . . real good. . . . For the longest time folks couldn't figure it out. Nobody had ever heard of Texas Rangers robbing folks before. The real work of the Rangers was to protect the big spreads. Lynching Mexicans was the chief occupation. It didn't matter which one—as long as his name was Pedro, that was good enough for the cattlemen."

Annie smiled now, and what I saw made me feel real strange. It was such an "old smile," as if she was a saloon owner who has just seen a whole bunch of range hands come in with their pay.

"The Daltons was the greatest gang ever," she said.

Bill Dalton smiled and sat back and stared up at her, then gave a funny little twist of his head and rubbed his nose.

"The second greatest gang ever," he said. "That's what done us in, I guess. Jesse James was getting all the publicity, and Bob couldn't stand for it. Every time we would hold up a stage or rob a train, Jesse would rob a bigger stage or a richer train. It seemed like he was watching us and waiting to see what we did, just so he could go out the next day and top it. Finally, it got to Bob . . . well hell, I can't blame him . . . it got to all of us. You see, we learned real fast that though outlawin was more fun and got you prettier women than did Rangerin, well truth was there wasn't a hell of a lot more money in it. Cause you lived faster and burned it up as quick and half the time you had to pay off friends for putting you up, and they was always wanting a little more for their kin so's their kin wouldn't say they seen you at the farm, or at the dance . . . you know? One ole boy we had in the gang, Jake Weatherspoon, he jes wanted to shoot everybody who threatened to turn us in, but that woulda burned down the whole barn sure as hell . . . plus, since we was billed as Robin Hoods, it got embarrassing to keep explaining to people we was only in it for the money, so we kept having to act like Robin Hoods, buying people drinks and sending kids to the store with candy money and giving the moms and dads some liquor . . . that Robin Hood shit was Bob's fault . . . he jes naturally wanted to make everything like it was bigger than life . . . but again I can't get sore over it, cause that was the way outlawin was supposed to be, and only Jesse James and the Daltons was really living up to it all. . . . Anyway, ole Jesse kept topping us, and finally, finally he goes out to Northfield, Minnesota, and robs two trains in one afternoon and gets his ass shot off, bout loses all his gang . . . but you shoulda seen the papers. Oh Christ . . . they was all singing his praises. Everybody from here to California had heard of him. Brother Bob couldn't hardly stand that, so he says we are gonna rob two banks on one afternoon at our old home town, Coffeyville, Kansas, and even though everybody knew it was crazy as hell . . . well, it just seemed like a damned good idea. . . . So off we went . . ."

"Was Bill Doolin with you?" Annie said. She was leaning forward now, so excited that her eyes was popping from her cheeks.

"Yeah, he was there," Dalton said. "But lucky for him his horse come up lame as we was going in, or else he wouldn't be here today. Oh what an afternoon. It was blazing hot and there wasn't hardly a soul on the streets. The sheriff of Coffeyville, Bill Martin, was away for the afternoon, attending a political rally. I heard tell he had ambition to become governor, but he got the liver warts and died before he could make it. So we come into town and half of the gang goes in to the First National Bank of Kansas and the other half goes into the Coffeyville Bank. . . . I was in the second group. I'll never forget it. We walk in and pull out our guns, and a woman faints dead away and another man goes for his gun, but Grat hits him in the neck and knocks him cold, and we march the teller toward the vault and say, 'All right, open that damned vault,' but the guy looks at us through these little runny eyes . . . they was like a rat's, and he says, 'This here vault don't open, see? It's a time-lock safe!' Well, this here is too much for Grat, and he starts talking to the Lord, saying, 'Jesus, I know you want me to blow these here boys away. That is why you having them speak this here nonsense to me.' But the bank manager comes out, this little guy with a felt coat on, and he starts saying, 'It ain't nonsense, boys. That there is the first time-lock safe in the town of Coffeyville.' He then goes on to tell us that it was closed and locked by a 'secret mechanical magnet' which can only open when a twenty-four-hour period is up, and that period ain't going to be up for a full fifteen minutes, so we may as well leave.

"This here news didn't set too well with Grat, who began saying the Twenty-third Psalm and started slobbering on hisself a little, and it didn't make Brother Bob happy either, cause the other boys had already robbed the bank across the street and was out back on their horses, waiting for us to come out. Grat, he gets all excited now and starts saying things like, 'Cain slew Abel,' and 'The Devil lives in the cities,' and other such Bible stuff, some of which applied and some of which didn't . . . which didn't particularly matter to Grat, as long as he could do his Bible talk he was somewhat mollified. . . . But jes the same, we was all getting a bit nervous, so I says to Bob, 'Hey, Brother B, don't you think we ought to leave these parts . . . real quick,' and Bob looks at me and says, 'You got to be kidding. Would Jesse James be stopped by some goddamned magical magnet? Son of a bitch, no, he would not!' and then he declared that we would jes sit there for as long as it took and wait for that goddamned devil of a safe to open! Well, I'll tell you, I started to sweat then. . . . There wasn't nothing I could do, as he had his mind made up . . . and Grat was walking around the room asking people if they was ready to meet their maker, and the other boys was breathing so hard I thought the whole bank was going to turn into a balloon and float away, and what's more I wished it would . . . and so we waited . . . and waited, and finally the safe opened, and we got out about ten bucks when the shooting started out back. I took one look out the window and knew we was done for. Brother James was shot right through the head, and before he fell he held his ear, then looked at his hand, then his whole head gave way, like his skull was a dam what had burst, and brains and blood come out so hard that they hit the window in front of me. . . . Bob and Grat started screaming and shooting out the windows, and then both of them run outside and was hit almost immediately . . . and I run out trying to help Bob, who fell back in my arms, saying, 'Fucking magnet!' and then he died on me, and I started whirling and shooting and got hit with something that felt like ten million tons of pebbles, and my leg was numb and bleeding and I crawled away, back into the bank . . . and went through it to the front door, and somebody come toward me, and I shot him and got on a horse . . . and somehow kept going straight out of town . . . and back to where Bill Doolin was still working on his horse, as quiet as you please in the noonday sun. Nobody else made it. That was the end of the Dalton Gang . . . but to me it wasn't jes no gang. It was all my brothers and they was dead . . . and I never give a shit about much else since then . . . until this day."

Dalton stopped talking and there was such a silence that it caused all of us to stop breathing. It was as if even the birds had heard him, and Annie shook her head and a tear was in her eye, and Bitter had a lump in his throat and gave a deep breath, and finally Annie said: "But now you are with the Doolin-Daltons, and there ain't nothing that can stop us. Nothing!!"

"Right," Dalton said, hugging her a little. But it was the weariest "right" in the world, and that ended our little picnic for the afternoon. Still, as we parted, I could see something very great in Dalton. . . . He wasn't slow or stupid at all, and I felt myself admiring him and thinking that I understood, finally, what Annie loved about the man. But I was never more wrong in my life.

CHAPTER
XVI
ANNIE REBELS

IN FRONT OF ME AND ANNIE WAS A HUGE BLACK KETTLE. Steam rose from it in huge puffs and got on our faces and singed the ends of our hair. Underneath, the firewood was crackling, and since the day was already hot, it wasn't no picnic out there washing men's clothes.

Annie looked down at her raw, red hands, and then back over at me. "Hey," she said. "This remind you of anything?"

"No. What?" I said.

"Morgan's Hash House, that's what!"

She sighed deeply and threw her scrub brush up in the air. I went on with my business and hung up a couple dresses we had found in our trunks. Dresses we had planned to use for good times but was now getting musty and a little tight around the hips.

"Damn," Annie said, sitting down on the fence post. "Look at them out there. I thought we was dealing with a bunch of outlaws!"

I looked out in the yard. Dick Whisper and Bill Raidler were playing mumbly peg with a jackknife.

"Do they look like desperados to you?" Annie said.

Over on the fence opposite from us Dan Clifton and Bittercreek were sitting and drinking whiskey.

"They look like a bunch of chicken farmers," Annie said, her voice getting more and more irritable.

Dalton and Doolin wasn't much help either cause they sat not ten feet in front of us on opposite sides of a checkerboard.

Annie jumped down and began to walk around in circles, kicking the dust.

"I know what it is," she said. "I know jes what it is."

"Well," I said, "I wouldn't get all excited. The boys is jes resting . . . thinking up another robbery . . ."

Annie stopped and looked at me with her mean little squint: "No they ain't," she said. "I overheard Doolin and Dalton talking last night. Doolin ain't got no confidence. He thinks Big Bill Tilghman has the Indian sign on him. Knows his every move."

"Well, hell," I said. "What can we do about it?"

I knew I shouldn't say nothing of the kind. But truth be told, I was getting a little tired of playing slave to the Gang. We come out here to escape drudgery and they was only too eager to get us right back into it.

Now I saw Annie smile and I felt a little chill, even through all the heat. When she picked out a pair of Raidler's dirty pants and threw them over a tree, I knew something was cooking.

"I'm glad you asked that," she said. "Cause as soon as them dresses are dry, you and me are going to take a little trip to the Cattleman's Bar in Tulsa. . . . And we is gonna look ever so fine!"

I started to say, "Now hold on," but I could see from the way her mouth was set it weren't no use. We was on our way to trouble, sure as hell, and though I was scared, trouble was jes what I was aching fer.

All around us was men, big men with stomachs that hung over their belts, little dried-up farmer men with faces like raisins, short men with guns that came nearly clean down to their ankles and tall men with rifles sitting up against 'em, both of 'em so thin you could hardly tell the gun from the drunk. Me and Annie stood at the bar, fanning ourselves and trying to look like the two other "saloon gals," who were leaning on the bar like they was holding it up. It wasn't easy to model yourself after the likes of these babes . . . for they were two of the meanest-looking females I have ever laid eyes on. The one had kind of green hair and skin what looked like day-old grits, and the other wore a piecrust of red rouge. Of the two, she was a good deal more awful; her cheeks reminded me of a dripping candy apple which has been left out in the sun. What I mean is, these two was far removed from the kinds of gals you found in Annie's Ned Buntline books . . . the gals with the auburn hair and green cat eyes and the slightly weathered but handsome faces all full of character and deep sentiment. The only thing these two, whose names I learned from the bartender were Flo and Rose, was full of was cheap whiskey and bad jokes. I sat there at the bar staring at 'em in a kinda fascination, the same kind you have at a funeral parlor when you can't take your eyes off the corpse. First Flo would tell a joke (there was a couple of "boys" hanging around 'em . . . three of 'em looked ninety-five years old. One poor devil was especially sadassed, what with big black moles growing over his face like some terrible weed patch) like, "Why did the chicken cross the road?" Then she'd open her eyes, stick out her tongue whilst Rose clapped her hands like an idiot child. Meanwhile, one of the old boys would stare down in the general direction of his feet, which pointed in opposite directions. "Don't know, do you?"

said Flo, tossing her hand through her green hair. "Well, here's the answer. He was being chased by a two-hundred-eighty-five-pound nigger!" At this the boys would break up, slapping their knees and sending out clods of dust, which was big enough to choke a mule. Watching and listening to these poor old hags at first made me sick. . . . I mean I felt they was repulsive. . . . But then the whole scene touched me with a kind of awful sadness, and I began to feel like I had to get out of there. The only thing that kept me standing there was Annie, who had already struck up a conversation with one of the younger guys, a farmer named Freddie, who was kind of fat and shy. He had come up to the bar with his friend, Nelson, a poor sheepherder who wasn't bad looking but seemed not to be able to talk at all. Instead, he bought me a drink and just stood up next to me, kind of rubbing up against my arm and occasionally staring and smiling. The staring I didn't mind so much, but when he smiled, he gave off this particularly hideous stench of sheep shit . . . and I began to gag a little and tried not to think about it, less I come up with some pretty horrifying conclusions. Pretty soon, Flo began to sing a song all about a nigger that tried to have sex with a monkey and I started to feel real poorly and wanted to get out of there in the worst way, but Annie and Fred was having fun talking and giggling, and then she started kicking me in the shins and saying stuff like: "That's right, we are just a couple of traveling actresses on our way up to St. Louis. We come from Texas . . . where the men are big and bad!"

Well, I knew that kinda talk was bound to get us in great big heaps of trouble, so I hit her on the arm and she smiled and hit me on the arm, twice as hard. Oh, that girl was tough . . . and then she went right on with her babble: "So we come here looking for some excitement. And we heard that the place you get it in is none other than the Cattleman's Bar. So here we are looking for fun!"

Well Fred, he nearly gets the Saint Vitus's dance at that. This fat old blob of a boy is twitching and salivating just like a hog in heat, and I feel myself getting pressed in by Old Sheep Dung, tighter and tighter. Finally, Old Sheep Dung, who up till now ain't said doodly-squat, starts just reaching over and grabbing my breast. I jumped back and gasped: "Get your hands off me now, Nelson. I ain't no little lamb!"

But Nelson drains his fourth rotgut whiskey, winks like he is on to something good and opens his mouth. "You are a LOOKER!" he says. "You are the best-looking woman I have ever seen. I'M GOING TO GET ME A PIECE OF ASS TO-NIGHT, BOYS! Yessssssssssssir!"

"You talking about my ass?" I said, shaking and trembling like an eighty-five-year-old spinster with her death of cold.

"You damn right!" Nelson says, opening his mouth and revealing a set of black teeth that look like the fence around a graveyard. "Come here, you!"

"Hold it," I said.

But he weren't "holding it," no sir, he was holding me. He was holding my breasts and my stomach and my crotch and my legs and my ass . . . that boy had hands everywhere and fingers like iron claws. . . . I was trying to keep my cowgirl demeanor, but it wasn't no easy proposition.

Finally he started to pick me up and carry me upstairs. It was then that somebody come up behind me and sort of picked me up light as a feather . . . and sat me down . . . on the floor. I felt like a lump, and when I looked up, I seen a huge heavy man moving over me . . . more of a force than a man. He wore a long black coat and he had these huge hands . . . which balled into fists the size of a cow's head.

"Boy!" the man said. "You should apologize to this girl. And I mean now!"

Nelson opened his mouth and gave off the smell and the big man kind of backed off a bit like it was too much for him. That musta convinced Nelson that this hombre's bark was worse than his bite, for he stepped forward and swung from the heels and caught the big man clean on the head. It was a right powerful punch and the big guy went down as I come up and moved back next to Annie, whose eyes were like a frog's.

The big man got up fast, faster than I would have ever expected, and charged Nelson, caught him in the stomach and picked him up and held him over his head. Now it was Nelson's turn to be surprised, and for a second he was just that . . . flabbergasted. Here he was, King of the Sheepmen, hanging in midair, above the man's head. He wasn't dazed fer long though. From up on his lofty perch he had only one target, and that was the big man's head. So he started in on the big guy's eyes, just scraping at the lids like he was about to dig them out of the man's skull.

This caused the big man to bellow a bit, which sounded like a whole pen of horses caught in a barn fire . . . and not being able to see real good, he simply chucked Nelson like a sack of flour . . . right into Annie. . . . Both of 'em, Annie and Nelson, went down in a huge crash . . . and before anybody could say a word, the big man had gone over and stuck one boot on Nelson's head and pressed down hard, until it sounded like bones was cracking in his skull. Without so much as looking at poor Nelson, the big moustachioed man reached down, pulled Annie to her feet and smiled at her.

"Hello," he said. "I'm sorry for all this trouble. It ain't often we get good-looking women like yourselves in town. My name is Big Bill Tilghman."

"Pleased to meet you," said Annie, as if nothing had happened. "My name is Sussette La Range, and this is my friend, Madeline Eiffel. We are actresses on our way to St. Louis. We certainly appreciate your helping us out."

Tilghman smiled courteously in my direction and then signaled to the end of the bar. An Indian came forward, a tall thin man with black skin which hung off his face like an old hound dog's. It weren't no doubt it was the one we had seen at the stage.

"My friend, Tim the Indian," said Bill Tilghman.

"Tim?" Annie and I said all at once.

"Hi," the Indian said. "I see fatty worked this fellow over pretty good. But don't you think you ought to step off his head, Bill?"

Tilghman looked down at Nelson, whose tongue was hanging out and whose complexion was blue.

"Hell, I forgot about him," Tilghman said. "I thought I had my foot up on a barstool."

"There ain't no barstools in this town," said Tim.

"Shit," said Tilghman. "Well, I guess I will have to go right on using this kid then."

He smiled, picked the kid up and threw him in a chair. The chair turned over backwards, and some of Flo and Rose's old boys dragged him out to the street.

"There," said Tilghman, smiling. "Now what say we all get a room upstairs and have us a little get-acquainted session."

I felt my skin run cold, as Tim the Indian stared at me with his beady yellow eyes.

"I thought you saved us," said Annie, smiling and putting her arm through Tilghman's. "But you, you rascal . . . you just plan on doing bad bad things!"

Tilghman smiled and winked at Annie.

"At my age, honey," he said, "you are lucky to get to the planning stage. But we gonna give it a whirl anyway, ain't we, Tim?"

"And how!" said Tim, grabbing me and laughing up a storm.

"And how!" Tilghman said, patting Annie on the rear end, pulling her along like she was a rag doll. "And how! Whoooooo, boy! This here Tim is a funny redskin. Did you hear that? And *how!*"

I looked at the Indian and he opened his hands modestly, as if he had only touched the top pearl in a treasure chest of wit.

"Tim is a funny man," he said.

"Ha ha," I said, and followed him up the stairs.

* * *

Pretty soon we was all four of us in this big room, one of the strangest places I have ever seen. There was mirrors everywhere, mirrors with strange little carvings on them, like a big man eating a baby . . . or at least putting the baby's head in his mouth (Tim the Indian said he was jes gonna lick the baby's head to wake him up), or like a winged woman, who was leaning from the mirror over the bed, jes like she was aiming to turn into flesh and fly around the room. And speaking of the bed, it was the biggest damned thing I have ever seen, certainly big enough for two drunk buffalo . . . and that made me a little nervous. There was also these here wall hangings (which I have learned is called "tapestries"), with pictures of little nude girls on them . . . girls with golden hair who weren't a whole lot younger than Annie and me . . . well, that made me even a little more nervous . . . and finally there was a big table near the bed, and Bill Tilghman and Tim the Injun says we should all sit down and get to know one another . . . so we do just that, Annie and Tilghman on one side, and me and Tim on the other.

The conversation, I might add, was not scintillating.

I started off with, "Well isn't this nice!"

My voice, however, sounded like it was a peep from a baby chicken hawk, which is about as pretty as chalk rubbed over a slate.

Annie then picked up the slack, batting her eyes and telling the most monstrous lies.

"You see," she said, "we girls is classically trained actresses. We know all the parts of the plays of Mr. William Shakespeare and are on our way to the St. Louis Repertory Company. We are going to play Cordelia and Goneril in *King Lear*."

Tilghman scratched his head and lit a cigar. His face was big and beefy, and I was hoping it was going to be ugly as well. I was hoping that because him being the man that was chasing down Bittercreek, well, I wanted very much to dislike him, to see him as some hunchback armadillo who was only out for the sheer nastiness of it. But truth be told, he had such twinkling blue eyes and such a friendly laugh (even if he did laugh at the horrid jokes of Tim the Indian) that I found myself kind of liking the man. In fact, after a few drinks and a few lines of *King Lear* and then a few more of *Hamlet,* I began to feel right friendly and all but forgot what the hell was going on. The whiskey was bad, but in a very few minutes I was drunk enough to pretend it was good.

And Annie was terrific. Watching her go into her act, I began to realize that she was capable of anything. Just let her have a stage . . . let her have an audience, and she could be anything or anyone. And that night, I remembered what she had just told me about her daddy and his little theater group, and about Mike Morgan, who I had assumed was always the moneygrubbing bastard he seemed to be now. But it weren't true. I had things wrong . . . or at least partly wrong, for though Annie probably had waited to tell me the story of her past when it would do her the most good, the story itself must have been the real McCoy, for now suddenly she was up and walking across that giant bed . . . trailing her white satin gown and smiling at the three of us as if she were a queen and we her subjects.

"I love Shakespeare's comedies," she said, smiling. "There is nothing like them anywhere. I want to do one of my favorite speeches from *A Midsummer Night's Dream.* It's Lysander talking . . . and he's . . . well, I won't tell you about it . . . just listen."

So saying she began to spring around on the bed until she had her right position. Then with her head arched back and her eyes staring at the mirror on the ceiling (the one with a dragon with a long, bronze tongue), she began to quote the lines:

> "Or, if there were a sympathy in choice,
> War, death, or sickness did lay siege to it,
> Making it momentany as a sound,

Swift as a shadow, short as any dream,
Brief as the lightning in the collied night,
That, in a spleen, unfolds both heaven and earth,
And ere a man hath power to say 'Behold!'
The jaws of darkness do devour it up:
So quick bright things come to confusion."

When she was done, both Tim the Indian and Bill Tilghman sat back with their mouths hanging open like they was waiting to let the words fly inside 'em.

"That was one hell of a thing," said Tilghman. "There was never nothing like that. Especially that part about the darkness and the confusion. Hell, I don't know what all the rest of it meant exactly, but by God, I can understand that sure enough. Miss La Range, you are certainly one heck of an actress. . . . I'm gonna come see you sure as hell. Boy, the 'darkness' and the 'confusion,' wiping out the 'bright things.' That does make a man think . . ."

With that, Bill Tilghman, the head of the Pinkertons and the meanest lawman in the West, shook his head and went into the real brown study. He stared down at his glass, gave a long sigh and then stared some more. It took a war whoop from Tim to get him going again.

"This sure is a hell of a place," I said, trying to get the party rolling.

"Yes, it is," said Tim. "And in the room next door they have food. You have to pay a bunch to rent this place, but the guy who owns it keeps it real special. He's been to Europe and places like that. His name is Shorty but he can speak French. . . . Hey, maybe I ought to have him come up here. . . . We would love to see you two act out a scene together!"

"Aha," I said. "That is a real nice idea . . . but I'm awful hungry. Maybe we could go next door and get some food."

I looked up at Tilghman, but he was still staring at himself, mumbling "darkness and confusion" over and over. Annie sat down beside him, poured herself and him a drink, and put her small soft hand on his big scarred knuckles.

"I think Bill and I will stay here. You and Tim go next door and get some food."

"Sure," said Tim, smiling and helping me up.

"You sure you don't want to come?" I said. But one look from Annie told me I should keep real quiet.

"OK, Tim," I said. "Show me the way to the vittles."

We went down the hall and Tim opened the door for me. I stepped inside another room, this one bare as a dungeon and twice as smelly.

There was an old four-poster with a torn canopy and a night table with an old cracked white porcelain water pitcher.

"Hey," I said, as I hear Tim the Indian lock the door, "just where is this big feast?"

"I am the big feast," said Tim the Indian. And so saying, he reverted right to his heathen redskin ways and soared like an eagle across the room, landing on me and throwing me roughly down into the bed. In no time at all he half pulled my dress off and I was hard pressed to keep my white britches up.

"Listen here, Tim," I said, panting and wrestling with him on the lumpy old mattress. "This is no way to treat a lady."

"I love you," said Tim the Indian. "I want to marry you and take you to New York City.

"I thought you was an Indian," I said.

"New York is full of Indians," said Tim, breathing hard and biting my neck. "They have teepees in the streets in New York. The entire population of someplace called Greenwich Village is all Indians. There are parks full of them. . . . It is a wonderful place . . . my love . . . oh my dear love . . ."

The Indian was as looney as any man I've ever met and now he was pumping up and down on me and making very bestial Indian grunts and speaking in some kind of Cherokee and broken English about the great island of Manhattan, entirely owned and operated by Indians . . .

"Please, Tim," I said. But I may as well been talking to the moon.

Besides, what can you expect from a damned heathen named Tim.

In no time at all, he had my blouse all ripped off, so I was in my slip, corset and bloomers.

"Oh, please stop . . ." I said, thinking of Bitter and starting to get a little upset for real. No damned Indian was going to take me against my will, and so I began to wrestle back a little.

I grabbed his hand.

He grabbed mine.

I grabbed his other hand.

He twisted free with the first hand and pinned down both my hands.

At least he didn't have no more hands to do business with. But that didn't stop him much. He started nuzzling my breast with his nose, and in spite of myself . . . oh, I am loathe to admit this . . . in spite of everything . . . his yellow skin, his name and his bad manners . . . that Indian began to get me excited. I started to pant a little, and the more I panted, the more I remembered Bitter, and the guiltier I felt, and pretty soon, I had worked up a good case of the guiltiest sweats imaginable, and then I started to really fight back. He was nuzzling my legs now with the top of his head, mumbling stuff that sounded like Indian prayers of thanks, and I saw my chance and managed to throw one leg around him and rolled the wiry bugger off the bed. He fell pretty hard and then I was up and out of the room before you could say Doolin-Daltons.

Once out in the hallway, though, I had no idea of where to go. I thought of Annie! I figured I must get her out of there. Bill Tilghman was a lot bigger than Tim, and Annie was in real danger. I knew I couldn't go back downstairs so I went two rooms down from my own, opened the door, slid inside and locked it good.

From there I saw a window which led to a small balcony on the roof, and in sheer panic I made my way out on it, in my slip and bloomers. Luckily it was dark out and down below the boys was laughing and drinking and a couple of people was fighting, so nobody much looked up my way.

In my head I kept one thing in mind—saving Annie from her bout with Bill Tilghman. And so, slowly I crept up to her window to see how she was doing. If things was real bad, I'd have to formulate a plan, like maybe lighting the curtains and yelling, "Fire." That would get 'em out. Damned fast too.

But lo and behold, when I looked into the window, there was already a fire going. It wasn't no cigar neither. For there on the giant bed was old Bill Tilghman, still in his cowboy boots and his big black hat, and underneath of him, with her long legs wrapped around his big old hairy waist, was my friend, the great Shakespearean actress and all-round cowgirl, Miss Cattle Annie. Together they was straining and sweating and from the look on my dear, wild friend's face, she didn't mind consorting with the law. Not at all.

CHAPTER
XVII
ANNIE SPINS A YARN

I WON'T BOTHER YOU NONE WITH DRAWING OUT HOW I WAITED on the roof of the Cattleman's Bar till a darned mean wind started up. I huddled in my torn dress and bloomers, my knees knocking so they sounded like Mexican castanets. I won't go into how scared I was that crazy Tim would find me up there and get me where there was no place to run to and do me his meanest. Suffice it to say that my two-hour wait for Miss Annie was not a comfortable one, especially since I had to finally summon up my nerve and sneak down to the balcony, assess that Tilghman was no longer in the room, then rap on the dirty window and tell Annie to meet me around back with the horses. Which she did, pronto. It was near dark when we finally began our ride back to the ranch, and I was shook so badly that I felt like I had been shot again. In fact, I felt worse than when I had been shot. Strange and violent emotions ran through me, and I felt like crying and shouting and laughing with Annie . . . all in one bundle. It wasn't no joke at all, but to see Annie riding along, her little back shaking not a bit and a slight smile on her face, well it made me all the more upset.

"Why on earth did we ever get involved with these guys?" I said, breaking the ice as we headed back up toward the ranch.

"It was a real educational experience as far as I'm concerned," Annie said. "One I wouldn't trade fer nothin!"

"Sure," I said. "But what on earth did you tell Tilghman? Ain't he gonna get suspicious?"

"No ma'am," said Annie. "The truth is he had drunk so much he fell asleep in the toilet and nearly drowned. The old boy can't hold his liquor as well as they said he could. I already told him we was thinking about pushing on to Fayetteville, where I got a cousin . . . so when he awakes he will only find my little heart-felt note, and I reckon he will hold that to his tearful eyes . . ."

Annie was laughing now and when she turned and trained her black eyes on me she smiled even wider.

"So that Injun gave you a time, did he?" she said. "You shoulda heard the terrible racket he made when he discovered you was gone. He went down into the bar and asked Flo and Rose where you was, and then he accused that poor critter Nelson of taking you away, and pretty soon they got into a terrible brawl and then the sheriff come and I think they both got thrown into the slammer for the evening."

"You're kidding?" I said, laughing in spite of myself. I loved picturing the Indian Tim and Nelson in the same cell, scratching one another's eyes out and smelling of sheep dung. Now that we had gotten the hell out of there, well, the whole thing did seem like a crazy, dangerous dream that you sweated and hooted through, but was glad to tell to your friends come sunup.

We was riding along at a pretty good clip now and the moon was coming up and all around us there was the sound of night-birds and crickets and the deep breathing of the horses. It was as good and clean a feeling as I ever hope to have. Yet, some of it was spoiled because I could not get Annie and Tilghman out of my mind. I wanted to . . . needed to talk to her about it all, but didn't know how to bring the matter up without sounding like some kind of horrible prig, or worse. I was actually afraid that talking about it might make me burst into tears, which was no way at all for me to be, and I kept thinking of my grandmother at the same time. How she had railed against the sinners and the "flesh" . . . how she had opposed me even going to the circus when it come to town because they was supposed to have a strongman who dressed up in a skimpy leopard skin . . . and how I'd gone anyways and seen him there all glistening and beautiful, and yet when I went home felt soiled and dirty and small . . . I mean all these images was going through my head at once, but mainly Annie, my own sweet, crazy, loving Annie, hunching under the gigantic weight of Big Bill . . . well, it was all a little too much for this cowgirl, so I vowed to myself that I wouldn't say nothing at all about it. If Annie wanted to bring it up on her own, that was OK by me, but I wasn't about to start nothing. After all, I figured she had a right to do whatever she wanted . . . but I jes couldn't see how she could square it with Bill Dalton. Still, I said, as we rode through the winding hills, the stars above us like eyes . . . still, it weren't none of my business . . . not at all.

So we rode on, a kind of strained and unpeaceful silence between us. (Ain't it strange how a situation can be tense between two people even without an ill word being said? It's almost like thoughts carry their own weight, beyond words all together . . . and each party, especially parties close to one another . . . each party can feel it, like a stone on his neck.) Finally, as we come to a bluff where the view was breathtaking, Annie stopped and got down offa her mount.

"We ought to take a break here," she said. "We can't make it all the way back at one clip. The animals will keel over."

"Right," I said, not liking the sound of my own voice. I had wanted my words to sound normal, easygoing, but even "right" was filled with accusations.

Annie stood out on the bluff, staring at the stars. She stretched and pulled out some tobacco and rolled a cigarette, real deft like, and blew the smoke out into the dark space.

"This was one of the most important trips of our outlawin lives," she said. "This one here has made us both into real women . . . do you realize that, Jennie?"

"Well ah . . ." I stammered.

She turned and looked at me, her eyes as bright as the stars that shone down on us.

"You see," she said, "on this trip I have found out so many things. I have found out . . . it is hard to put into words . . . but I have found out that men ain't as tough as we had been led to believe. This Big Bill Tilghman has told me his whole life story. What's more, he ain't such a bad guy as all that . . . jes like the Doolin-Daltons ain't near so good as we have heard. I mean when I think of it . . . you and me is looking better all the time. We may be as good criminals as any of 'em, and better people to boot. Still, ole Bill wasn't really a bad dude. He was a gunman hisself, you know. He switched over to the good side cause he figured that outlawin was going to end him up in Boot Hill. Jes the opposite of the Doolin-Daltons. Ain't it strange?"

"Yeah," I said, turning my back to Annie and staring down at some rocks. "That's real interesting. . . . I wish I could say I found out such interesting stuff from the Indian named Tim. But he was too busy pawin' me. . . . Didn't you have no trouble with that kinda stuff with Big Bill?"

Annie snorted a little, but she never lost a beat.

"Nah," she said. "Not a bit of trouble. You see he got pretty drunk pretty darned fast, and after a while he just wanted to lie in bed and talk. At first I was real worried like . . . I thought he was going to get all . . . well, you know . . . kinda personal . . . but he was as tame as a lamb."

"He was?" I said, grateful for the curtain of darkness between us, so she couldn't see how badly I was shaking.

"Yes, ma'am," Annie said. "Hey, you don't think I would want to roll around with an old goat like that, do you? He ain't my type at all. No, Jennie, I guess the truth is, I am, and always will be, Bill Dalton's girl."

"You think so?" I said, sounding as weak as a bird.

"I know so," said Annie. "Bill Dalton and I are so much alike. He lost his brothers and I lost my dad. There ain't no bond as close as that of two outlaw orphans. We are like each other's opposites. Bill's only problem is he listens too much to Doolin. Tilghman and the Pinkertons ain't got no hex on them boys. But Doolin thinks they do, which is half the battle. I can barely wait to get home and tell Bill and the others jes what I found out!"

I was going to ask jes what *that* was, but by now I felt powerful confused and disturbed. I had never known Annie to lie to me before. Though she had done many a crazy and unexplainable thing, I had always assumed that, as her best friend . . . as her sister really . . . she would never lie to me. But now, as we stood there, I knew how young I was and how deep and strange Annie was. More, how deep and terrible and strange the world was, and I wanted to cry out and lay my head on someone's shoulder. Someone I could know and trust. But who might that be?

I guess I knew right then, as I got on Jake, that things was changed between us . . . changed in a way that was beyond fixing, and as we rode off into the night, toward the ranch, I sucked in my breath and thought, "Well she is right about one thing. This here may be the biggest day of your young life!"

CHAPTER

XVIII

WE TRICK THE GANG

WE GOT BACK TO THE RANCH HOUSE AT WELL PAST TEN O'CLOCK. I must say it was a comforting sight to see the smoke curling from the chimney like it was, and the pigs, horses and Fred outside. I was all set to ride on in, see my darling Bittercreek and forget our whole crazy misadventure (or what I could of it). But as we started down the timberline towards the house, Annie stopped me and held my arm in her hot little grip.

"Now listen here," she said. "This adventure ain't quite over yet. I want to play a kind of joke on Bill."

"Doolin or Dalton?" I said.

"Dalton," Annie said. "It's important he thinks I was injured. It'll be ever so much fun, and it ought to get him real . . . sympathetic to me, if you know what I mean?"

"No," I said, a little irritated and still as bewildered and hurt as ever. "How will playing a trick on someone make 'em sympathetic to you? It seems to me we have played jesta about enough tricks in the last few hours!"

137

But Annie shook her head, making her black hair bounce around her cheeks.

"No," she said in a raspy voice which sent shivers down my spine. "It's too much to explain. Just go along with whatever I do, will you? It's for the good of the Gang. Believe you me, when I tell you what I learned from Tilghman, you will be very proud of your old buddy!"

I was about to say no, but then I thought of the consequences. Already I was a kind of partner in crime with her. I couldn't tell Dalton I'd seen her with Tilghman. It would be too much for him to take and it would finish off our friendship. It would also probably finish off Annie and me. But what I could do, and desperately wanted to do, was tell Annie I knew. I wanted to ask her why, how, she could do it with a man who was not only not her boyfriend but was swore to kill her boyfriend? My grandmother's warnings about the flesh was still riding in me . . . and while I realized they was nutty, that didn't make them any less real. It was almost as if the tortured old lady was inside me, running through my blood, spoiling my fun . . . and then I thought of Annie at the swimming hole. She had been so modest, so shy at first. . . . It had been me who had first taken off my clothes and displayed myself, and it had felt good . . . even if I was a little afraid. . . . Annie seemed only to be able to go ahead with it when there was some kind of stake involved. Like topping me . . . or tonight . . . like getting the information. I could understand that. I wanted to shine, too . . . like a star. But still, I wasn't ready to do anything for what I wanted. No matter what, I wasn't going to sleep with no Indian named Tim. But Annie . . . my head whirled with all these speculations which I didn't understand, and the net result of it all was me saying: "OK, I'll go along with your little game."

Annie squeezed my hand and we rode down and got off our horses, about a hundred yards from the house.

"Listen," said Annie. "What we got to do is rip up my dress

a little. You know, tear it here and there, like this . . ."

Without a second's hesitation, she ripped the sleeves off her pretty satin dress.

"Get the bottom a little," she said.

"Annie?" I whined.

But it was no use. In a second more she had me ripping the bottom of her dress. Then she laughed, winked at me and gave me a little hug.

"You are the best friend in the world, Britches," she said. "I will always love you!"

"Oh," I said, squeezing her hard.

"Now watch this," Annie said, pushing me away, falling toward the house and rolling in the dirt a little.

"What in the hell are you doing?" I said.

"The same thing you are going to be doing," Annie said.

"Huh?"

"Getting down and dirty," Annie said.

She pointed at the dirt, and sure enough, like a good slave, I found myself rolling around with her, both of us smudging up our faces and her ripping her dress a little more.

"You may as well reap the benefits of this, too," she said. "Bitter will love it and it'll get the gang real good and angry!"

"What will?" I said.

Annie smiled and ripped her dress a little more.

"Jes do whatever I do and say whatever I say," she said.

"Jesus!" I said.

"Oh, hallllp," Annie said, looking in the direction of the house. "Oh, pleeeeeease heallllllp! Oh, Bill, haaaaaaalp!" said Annie. "Oh, Big Bill Tilghman . . . he almost got us. . . . Haaaaaalp!"

"Oh, pooooooor me," I screamed, getting in the spirit of it all a whole lot more than I was willing to admit.

"Ohhh me," Annie screamed.

"Oh my," I yelled.

"I'm passing out!" Annie yelled, starting to laugh like a jackass.

"She is passing out!" I screamed, barely able to hold my sides, I was laughing so hard.

But to the boys on the porch all this was no laughing matter. One and all, the Doolin-Dalton Gang come running out of the house toward us. Doolin was in his long johns, and seeing him rushing toward us, his big belly hanging and swaying and his old black hat on, I couldn't help but think of Big Bill Tilghman. The two of 'em looked that much alike. Behind Doolin was Dalton, and then Bitter run by both of them, toward me, jes like he did the day he had accidentally plugged me.

"Jennie," he said. "Oh, my Jennie. If they have hurt you!"

"Agh agh," I said, sounding like a weak little squirrel with a bad cold.

"Annie," said Dalton. He was trembling all over, and on his face was the deepest concern. Looking at him, all worried and caring for Annie, took all the joy out of the ruse for me. In fact, I began to feel downright low and mean, which only added to the effectiveness of the joke.

"Look at her," said Bill Raidler, staring down at us with his little wolf eyes. "She looks like she's been beaten up bad!"

"Annie's out cold!" said Dalton.

"Get 'em both into the house," said Dalton.

"What happened?" said Bitter.

"I don't know," I said, beginning to cry for real, and for so many reasons that I couldn't name 'em all.

After a few minutes, Annie came around and began telling the Gang of our "adventure."

"It was like this," she said, waving her hands around and moving her head kind of hysterical like, as if she wasn't too sure where she was.

"We was going into town to meet Big Bill Tilghman and his boys. We figured we would pose as actresses and fool everyone.

And it worked, too. Only the Pinkertons tried to take us upstairs and . . . and . . ."

With that, she broke down and looked over at me, as if I was supposed to break down too. But I felt so ashamed at her lying that I held my ground and looked straight at the floor.

Finally Dalton's kisses and Doolin's encouragement got her started again: "Anyway, the Pinkertons tried to take our clothes off. I guess we played the party girls too well. If it hadn't been for Big Bill Tilghman we woulda been in their clutches even now. But he come in and knocked his men right and left. He almost killed an Injun named Tim."

"Tim the Injun is a bad hombre," said Dick Whisper.

"He sure is, Whispy," said Annie. "But Tilghman stopped 'im. Then he and Jennie and I talked, and he told us all how he was gonna stop you all cold, cause he knowed how you thought, Bill."

Doolin moved forward, wiping his eyes, and looked sincerely at Annie the same way I seen the minister look at a porcelain figure of Jesus Christ.

"You see," said Annie, "recovering" quickly now, "he said you had fallen into a pattern. A stage, a train and a bank. He said you tried to get a stage the other day, so there was a good chance you would hit that train coming up tomorrow . . . the one called the Redrock Special. . . . He even thinks he knows where you are going to hit it . . . right there at the Carstairs Pass, when it slows down."

Doolin looked confused and hurt. He bit his lower lip, and I felt like holding his hand.

"I'll be damned," he said. "He was right again!"

"He said something else, sir," Annie said.

"What!" Doolin thundered at her.

"He said you used to be a real sharp thinker, Mr. Doolin. Always had real original plans . . . but now you git all your stuff straight from the papers. He said he reads the same papers as you do."

Doolin bit his lower lip so hard I was afraid he'd begin to bleed.

"He did, huh?" he said. "He said that?"

"Well, it ain't true," I said suddenly, wanting to smooth things over. "There's not a lick of truth to it. . . . We'll show 'em, Bill, tomorrow, when we rob the bank over in Tulsa instead."

"Yeah!" said Bill Dalton.

"Damn straight," yelled Bittercreek.

Then the rest of the Gang cheered and picked us up, and carried us toward the house. Everybody was whooping and carrying on. Everyone but Bill Doolin, who stood outside, staring blank faced at the porch.

CHAPTER
XIX
HITTING THE TRAIL

THE NEXT AFTERNOON AT HIGH NOON WE HIT THE NATIONAL Bank of Tulsa. It was the first time I had ever been in a robbery in my life, and I can't tell you how it went exactly . . . it all seems like a blur. But a good blur fer sure . . . one that left you feeling great. It was then that I began to see the appeal of leading an outlaw's life. What I do remember is the Gang getting off their horses and walking real slow up to the bank door, and me and Annie in the back a ways. It seemed like they would never get up there in a million years . . . it was all happening so slow like. . . . But don't think it was dull. . . . Not fer a second. The slowness made it feel faster inside. Oh how my heart beat as Bitter and Dalton went through the door with the rest of the Gang just behind them. We was supposed to stay with the horses, but Bill Doolin, who was covering the door, come out and looked up at us.

"Come in," he said. "If you're gonna be outlaws you at least ought to git in on the good stuff."

Which we did, sneaking up to the door and peeking through, and goddamn Almighty Jesus . . . there they were, my friends, Bill Dalton and Bittercreek and Raidler and Dick and Dan . . . except it wasn't the guys I knew at all. No, this wasn't no ragtag bunch of colorful drunks or even lovers—this here was the Doolin-Dalton Gang! Oh how beautiful they looked as they stuck their guns into the face of the bank teller, and grabbed the money sacks. . . . And the looks on the faces of the people in the bank . . . such awe and respect . . . There was never nothing like it, I swear.

"Goddamn," said Annie. "This is it. This is what I been telling you about."

I didn't say nothing, but held my breath as the Gang smiled at one another, all confident and cocky and alive. It was as if they weren't really alive before . . . or that they had stepped into a kind of a dream and made themselves over in a way. For as they come out the door, backing out with their guns drawn, they were truly transformed, bright and beautiful shining creatures that didn't answer to nothing but their own blood. As we rode out that day I felt such a surge of pride, such exultation, that I was amazed. The only other time I had felt such happiness was once when I had gone to church with Granny, and they had gotten the whole congregation together singing "Amazing Grace." It was as if I had been lifted from my mortal cares and lived somehow outside my body, in an eternal space. This day, after our first real good robbery, was a whole lot like that, and I felt as we circled up into the mountains that we could ride our horses right off the trail, up a long cloud to the sun.

Not only was the robbery good (we got over ten thousand dollars!), but the next day a neighbor friend of Doolin's came out from town. He was drunk and laughing, and as I brought him some sipping whiskey on the front porch, he told us what he had heard about Tilghman.

144

"It was wonderful," he said. "Ole Bill thought he had you all. Him and Tim the Indian and the other Pinkertons waited all morning up at the Carstairs Pass. . . . They had it all fixed up. There was soldiers in the train and Pinkertons ready to swoop down on you all. Well, from what I heard at the Cattleman's, Tilghman is laughing it up and telling Tim, 'We got 'em this time. We got 'em dead to rights!' But you shoulda seen his face when the train went by. Oh, he let out a string of curses and that damned Indian musta given it to him pretty damned good. That's fer sure. . . . Cause Ole Bill got pretty damned drunk last night. He kept standing at the bar, saying, 'I jes can't figure it. It don't make no sense . . .'"

Well, you shoulda seen the Gang when they heard it. There was joy all around, and even old Bill Doolin let up a bit with his long face and got drunk.

"Had him talking to hisself, Britches," he said to me as we sat on the porch. "Had him talking to hisself. Yessir. Now maybe he knows what it feels like. Yeah, I think things is gonna be all right."

"I know they are, Mr. Doolin," I said. "Things are gonna work out jes fine."

Which was true on our next job too. We hit a gambling casino in Fort Smith, Arkansas. This was the biggest job the Gang had pulled off in three years. The place was called Slim Jim's, and there was more money in the joint than in most banks. We had it planned real good too. Annie would go in first (her hair up under her hat) and get to the back of the room and play some roulette. Bitter would act like a drunk and stagger over to the bar. Meanwhile Bill Doolin would be across the room playing poker, and the rest of the Gang, including me, would be near the front, so nobody could git out fer help.

Everything went like clockwork. On a signal from Doolin, Annie, Bitter and the rest of us pulled our guns and started lining people up. Now the whole damned thing was really speeding up fer me. A change come over my voice . . . in fact, it didn't sound like my voice at all to me but the voice I woulda imagined it being if Ned Buntline was writing about me. I could hear his words:

> Little Britches barked her commands at the terrified gamblers. Her soft child's voice had given way to a sharp metallic growl which sounded like a curse. After the robbery, those present said she was more terrifying than any of the older men.

It might sound a little corny now, but that's how it was. . . . I could feel it happening to me. The fever of being an outlaw was surging through me. And what's more, it seemed to be a fever which spread to our victims as well. For as Bill Dalton went down a row of men with his hat in his hand, collecting their wallets, the last man on the line dropped in his cash, then produced a copy of *The Amazing Exploits of the Doolin-Dalton Gang* and a pen.

"Please, sir," he said. "I want your autograph!"

Dalton promptly obliged him, and we began backing out. Everything looked like it was going to be as simple as the flight of a hummingbird.

Only it didn't turn out that way. For as we hit the boardwalk in front of the casino, Bill Doolin's boot hit a crack in the board and he fell heavily backwards and rolled off the deck, three feet to the street.

"Get up, Bill," Bitter screamed. "Hurry."

But Doolin was holding his back and his face was twisted in pain, and he was having trouble rising.

"My damned back," he said.

"Bill, watch out!" screamed Bitter. He was looking down the street, where we saw a man with a badge coming fast toward us.

"The sheriff!" screamed Dalton.

The man was carrying a rifle. He took one look at Doolin staggering to get to his horse, aimed his rifle and fired.

Doolin was hit in the arm, and I screamed and felt my blood run cold.

"Oh God!" I screamed. "Oh God!"

Annie was openmouthed, but as she was pulling out her gun Dalton and Bitter had already started firing, and the sheriff was hit, dropped his rifle, and crawled into a doorway. That gave Doolin the time he needed, and in a moment he had made it to his mount and we were off through the town, firing bullets at anyone who came out into the streets.

That night I bathed Bill Doolin's wounds. The flesh wasn't too badly ripped, and he took it like the old gunman in the books—calmly and philosophically. I didn't take it nowhere near as good. I kept thinking of him there . . . a sitting duck . . . and I knew a fear that up till then had only been hearsay. . . . The real fear. When everyone else had gone to bed, and I was fixing up a sling for him, I managed to talk some about how I felt.

"That's all part of it, honey," the old walrus said to me. "It's like that. When you accept outlawin as your way of life, you got to realize that everything you feel is gonna be extreme. You get the best and worst of it. That's why it wears a man down so. . . . There ain't many people who can afford to live excitin lives. It ain't natchural . . . on the other hand it ain't dull. It ain't never dull when you is getting shot at."

Apparently, it wasn't so dull for Big Bill Tilghman either. A couple days after our casino robbery, Dalton come in with a paper he had gotten hold of. We was all setting round about, ready to eat dinner when he arrived. The smile on his face lit up the whole damned room.

"Here," he said. "Read this . . ."

He gave the paper to Annie, and she stood by the crackling fireplace, and read loudly.

" 'Big Bill Tilghman has a bad case of the blues,' " she read. " 'He has been unable to catch the rejuvenated Doolin-Dalton Gang, who have staged two highly bold and successful robberies in the past week. The first was at the National Bank of Tulsa and the second at Slim Jim's Gambling Casino in Fort Smith, on Monday,

147

June 2. In an interview with the *Gazette*, Tilghman explained he "was not worried, and that he was certain he would nab them on their next escapade." But sources around the Grand Old Man of the Pinkertons say that he is vexed by the Gang's moves. A person who asked not to be named said, "The other day Big Bill and the Pinkertons waited two hours in 108-degree heat on a rooftop overlooking the First National Bank of Rogers. . . . They finally saw dust coming from the North and got their guns ready but when the dust cleared all they had was Nelson Greer, a sheepman with five hundred head in Main Street. Tilghman cussed a streak, and went out and got drunk." ' "

When the Gang heard that, they began to laugh and scream. Dick Whisper and Bill Raidler hugged one another and Annie and Bill Dalton did the same. Bitter brought out the moonshine and toasted "Big Bill Tilghman and his herd of sheep." Then after the roaring grew silent, Bill Dalton got up and said he had to have our attention.

"We've really got his goat now," he said.

"His sheep!" yelled Bitter, and everyone roared again.

But Dalton raised his hand and silenced everyone: "Right . . . his sheep. But now we are going to pull off something I've dreamed about for a long time. . . . Ever since Coffeyville, Kansas."

The silence in the room was stunning. There wasn't no need for him to go on. Everyone knew what he was going to say. We was going to try and do what had been the downfall of the Dalton Gang. We was going to rob two banks at once. Tomorrow. In Fayetteville, Arkansas.

I can't say I slept real good that night. As I was lying there next to Bitter (who slept like a dreaming cow), my mind kept shooting pictures through my head. First I would see Coffeyville, Kansas . . . on a bright yellow afternoon. The streets was all brilliant yellow . . . lighting up the sky . . . and the stores along Main Street was all deep orange or scarlet . . . as if they was about to burst into flame. Then I saw the Dalton Gang riding into that terrible place, and saw them get off their horses and walk into the buildings, which was already burning . . . and I was there too, and I kept trying to warn them . . . stop, look out, no, wait . . . but they didn't hear me. But the strangest part of the dream (a waking dream really) was that Annie was with them . . . and she seemed to be opening the doors for them . . . and she was dressed like Little Bo Peep . . . right out of one of the fairy books my granny had. Finally, the Gang went inside, and as soon as they shut the doors, the scarlet-hued buildings began to burn and burn . . . and I jumped and felt crazy as hell. . . . I don't have no idea to this day what all that coulda meant, unless I was getting some kind of ghostlike warning from the dead Daltons. Anyway, that's what I thought at the time . . . but I dared not tell it to no one. What could I say? "You are all falling into a trap. I just got a message from the grave!" Them outlaws woulda thought I was taking too much jimson weed. And truth was I felt so myself. It was just cold feet. That's what I thought then. Cold feet. Afraid of really taking the big risks. Suddenly, I felt very small and very alone, and I wanted to race out of the house, git on my horse and go back home. . . . But then I thought of Annie, who seemed so cocky, so confident, and I said, "You are tough, too. You are an outlaw. You are a member of the greatest gang in outlaw history, and you should be right proud, instead of acting like you was snake-bit." So I climbed back into bed, huddled up next to Bitter and shut my eyes. But I still didn't sleep.

The following morning at ten-thirty, the Doolin-Dalton Gang struck the Farmer's Bank and the Whitehead Savings and Loan, both of Fayetteville. As we rode into town, there was such complete silence throughout the Gang that I could barely stand it. So I began to cough. Annie shot me a look, though, so I stopped. Then I began to feel a kind of huge resentment at her for acting that way toward me. She was beginning to have a right prideful attitude toward me, I told myself as we came into the streets. I'd talk to her about it if we didn't get killed. . . . Now I know I was glad she had given me something else to think about cause if I hadda thought about what we was really doing . . . it woulda been the end of me. I mighta fallen apart. For this was sheer madness, no other way to describe it.

"All right," said Bill Dalton, stopping at the Whitehead Bank, up on the town square. "We're going in here," he said. "Remember not more than ten minutes. Then get back out here, fast."

Dalton, Annie, Dan Clifton and Bill Raidler got off their mounts and started inside.

We went on around the town square and in a second was at the other bank. People on the street looked at us as if we was a mirage. One man, with a giant nose like an old turnip, turned and ran into a store. I was certain he was getting a gun, and I wanted to scream in fear. But I remained very calm on the outside.

The rest came off like a dream. Suddenly, we was in the bank itself, then suddenly they was handing over the money and opening a safe, and before you could snap your fingers (not that I could—mine was drenched in sweat. It was all I could do to hold my gun. But hold it I did, and right on three tellers), we was outside and backing down the street, our guns drawn. As soon as we hit our horses, the other half of the Gang came riding toward us. We started to mount our horses, and everything seemed to be going smooth, when suddenly the turnip-nosed man comes running out of his store, holding a pistol.

"Come on," he screamed. "It's the Doolin-Dalton Gang!"

Down the street a couple of other men started toward us. They had rifles out and were already firing, though none of the bullets hit nobody. But the turnip-nosed man was real close, and he took a bead on Bill Doolin, who was a mite slow getting on his horse. . . . When he did finally climb on, he saw the gun trained on him, and tried to dodge the bullet, but his sling got tangled up in his saddle horn, and the turnip man got off a shot.

Doolin seemed to panic . . . His face was trembling, and he tried to lean far over on the right to avoid being hit. But he leaned too far, and fell off the horse.

"Get that guy!" I screamed, firing my gun at the turnip.

But the son of a bitch had got himself wedged in between a barrel and an overturned bench and had pretty good cover. Now I looked down the street, and all I could see was the sun glinting off of rifles.

Dalton and Bitter and the rest of the Gang had their guns drawn and were firing everywhere, wheeling right and left, trying to keep the townsfolk back. But we was in a world of trouble . . . that was fer sure. . . . Now it seemed the quiet town square was just overflowing with people. Everyone was getting in the act. I could see little kids with six-guns, shutting their eyes and firing at us. Meanwhile Doolin seemed to be lost, as if he was sleeping walking. . . . He couldn't get up right . . . tripped, almost fell again. Dalton turned his horse and headed fer him.

"Come on, Bill," he said. "Grab on."

He reached down and offered Doolin his arm, and Doolin seemed to come awake. Suddenly he was moving fast, and he reached up and threw himself up on Dalton's horse, and hung on. God, it was something to see. . . . He was so light on his feet; just for a second he seemed young again. But the moments we had lost were costing us now. For the bullets was flying thick as gravy. . . . And then I saw Bill Dalton's mouth fly open, and he reeled back and grabbed his shoulder, which was suddenly covered with what looked like a squashed tomato. Only it wasn't no vegetable. It was flesh, and I felt sick and only wanted to run. . . . But somehow I waited and kept reeling and firing, though I didn't see nobody fall. Beside me Annie was shooting and turning and Bitter was too, and then we started out of the town, riding low and hard and fast, and kicking up dust, which made us harder to see . . . and somehow, through sheer luck and the help of Jesus, we made it out of there with no more in-

151

juries. It wasn't till we was safely up in the mountains and headed back to the ranch that it really dawned on us what we had done. We had made it. Robbed two banks in one day—something no other gang had ever done. But no one yelled or said much of anything about it all the way home. . . . Instead there was a kind of reverent silence, the strangest silence I have ever felt. . . . It was a whole lot like being in church, and as we rode I was aware of the cleanness of the air, the blueness of the sky, the beautiful smell of the pine trees and of a huge, ambling tarantula which crossed the road at his own pace, not in no particular hurry to get nowhere.

The partying, of course, came that evening. And what a celebration we had. Bill Raidler and Dick Whisper got us a huge tub of pure grain alcohol, some more of that marijuana plant, and about forty bottles of red-eye. Annie cooked up a couple big chickens and potatoes and fresh vegetables, and we all sat out in front of the house, laughing and jumping about, and then someone said it was too bad Dan Clifton had forgot about how to play the guitar, and he said, "Who the hell forgot?" and got out his old six-string, and began to play cowboy songs and dance hall tunes, as good as you like, and Dick Whisper got out a fiddle, and he started to join in, and I watched Annie and Bill Dalton standing in front of the strongboxes, counting the money out, and then we was all laughing and hugging one another, and pouring pure grain alcohol and money over one another's heads and yelping like coyotes, and up above us the moon was full and friendly, and God I felt good. . . . This was the moment I had waited for, the Gang's greatest day of triumph. And Annie came over to me and hugged me, and I hugged her back, and thought I'd be able to forget the things that bothered me so . . . for she was an outlaw, and had helped provide the spirit that got me moving and the Gang . . . and then Dalton come over, and Bitter, and we all squeezed one another . . . and Annie said, "Now don't hurt Bill's shoulder!" and I was touched by her concern and felt small for condemning her. Then I heard the fiddle music getting louder, and me and Bitter began whirling about while the Gang yelped and clapped and stomped their feet, and as we whirled faster and faster, I could see the smiling faces of them all . . . Bill Raidler, who didn't look like no weasel to me no more, and Dan, with his big friendly grin, and Dick and Dalton and Annie, and I felt full up inside, and I almost wanted to cry from the beauty of it. . . . But as the dance ended and another began, I sort of fell away, as it occurred to me that Bill Doolin wasn't there.

"Where you going, Britches?" Bitter called.

"Up to the house to bring out some more food," I said, smiling.

Then I hurried up the path to the dark house.

He was sitting at the end of the long oak table, his face in his hands. Next to him was a bottle of whiskey and a shot glass. But it didn't look like he had made much use of the glass. Before I could say anything, he turned and looked at me with the tiredest eyes in the world.

"Oh, hello, kid," he said.

"They're having a heck of a party, Mr. Doolin," I said.

Doolin looked down at his boots, which was splattered with mud.

"Yeah, I know," he said.

I moved toward him a little and talked real soft.

"Maybe you'd feel better if you came out and joined us, sir," I said.

Doolin seemed a little perturbed by this. His voice rose, as if he was making an effort to be angry.

"What makes you think I feel badly?" he said.

"I can tell, sir," I said, ever so soft. "My daddy used to sit by hisself. Late at night. He'd drink . . . till sun come up."

Doolin started to lift his bottle, but then he looked at me, sighed hard and put the bottle back down.

"Your daddy? What happened to him?"

I started to tell him, but suddenly it all seemed terrible to me, and I couldn't say a word.

"I'm sorry, Britches," Doolin said. "Was he a nice man?"

"Yes sir," I said. "He was ever so nice. You would have liked him. But I could never understand why he drank so much . . . sitting all alone like that."

Slowly I sat down, right next to Bill Doolin. He looked into my eyes, and he seemed very very tired, very remote . . . as if he weren't in the room at all. His hands gripped the bottle tightly.

"That's hard to say, kid. It's sort of like music," he said. "Booze, I mean. You know why you like a song. You *know,* but you can't tell anyone else."

"Is it really like that, Bill?" I said.

Doolin opened his eyes a little and smiled wearily.

"No," he said, shaking his head. "I guess not. Maybe drinking is what you do when you stop hearing the music."

I began to feel worried when he said that. Real worried. There was such pain in his voice.

"But, Mr. Doolin," I said, weakly. "The Gang has never done so good."

Doolin nodded quickly.

"Yeah, the Gang . . . is doing fine. It's just that I ain't in the Gang no more."

"Don't say that, sir," I said, reaching out and touching his hand.

But Doolin really didn't seem to be hearing me. He looked into the darkness and spoke like he was in a play: "I almost got my ass . . . myself killed today. That ain't so bad. Not really. But I got Bill Dalton shot up too. I nearly killed my best friend."

"It wasn't your fault, sir," I said. "You was trying to dodge a bullet and ride with a sling on. . . . It coulda happened to anybody!"

Doolin smiled at me again, but there wasn't no pleasure in it.

"Yeah," he said. "It was my fault. It's jes that I'm too old, honey. Just too damned old."

I could say nothing. Tears was starting to come, and it was all I could do to hold them back.

"Hey," Doolin said, putting his old leathery hands over to my face, and holding it. "It's all right. Outlaws ain't supposed to git old. Jesse James was dead at thirty-four. . . . I'm forty-two and I am so damned tired."

"You don't seem old to me, sir!" I said, feeling desperate.

Doolin patted me on the head and got up. He winked at me and turned away and went out the door.

"Hey," I said, "wait, Bill. . . . Where you going?"

I heard his voice, already halfway down the hall.

"Going to Hot Springs," he said. "I need a little vacation down in the steam baths."

I jumped up fast then. This was serious. He couldn't go there alone. There was probably a thousand men looking for us.

"Mr. Doolin," I said, chasing him through the back to the kitchen door, "they are out combing the hills. . . . I mean you can't go there alone."

But when I got outside he was already mounted up.

"You take care, honey," he said.

"No, wait. . . . I'll come too."

He just shook his head at that.

"See you, kid," he said.

Then he turned and rode toward the hills.

I could feel my gut tighten up. He couldn't do this. . . . It was crazy. I started running around the side of the house. Out front the party had really started getting wild. Bill Raidler and Dick Whisper was throwing coins in the air and shooting them before they hit the ground. Dalton and Annie was laughing and banging on the guitar, and Bitter and Dan Clifton was taking turns hitting the bourbon. I ran right for Bitter.

"Hey," he said. "Here's my girl! Yessir!"

"Bitter, I got to . . ."

Before I could say a word, he had picked me up and was whirling me around.

"My girl. Little Britches . . ." he said. His breath was terrible, and I felt all giddy from his tight arms around me.

"Bitter," I said. "Let me down. Let me down!"

He dropped me lightly, and then took the bottle from Dan Clifton.

"Little Britches. . . . Yahhhooooo," he screamed.

"Listen to me!" I screamed. "Damn it!"

A couple people turned when I yelled that, but all they did was smile.

Finally, I realized I still had on my gun. Quickly, I took it out, and aimed it to the moon and fired three times.

"Listen to meeeee!" I screamed.

That got their attention real nice.

"Listen, I got something to say," I said, feeling the panic even stronger now. "Bill Doolin is on his way . . . all by himself . . . to the Hot Springs steam baths."

I thought that would git them in a state, but all anybody did was shrug and smile like loons.

"Well damn it," I yelled. "Don't nobody care? He could easily get killed. They are all out looking for him now!"

Annie stepped forward and looked at me through two bloodshot eyes.

"Aw hell, Britches," she said. "Let him go. He can take care of hisself. . . . Besides he's tired and old!"

"Let him go?" I screamed at her. "Is that all you can say?"

Annie teetered a bit, took another shot of alcohol.

"Bill Doolin is old . . ." she said again. "He's too old and he knows it."

"Too old?" I yelled at her. "Too old? Who the hell are you to say? He is the greatest outlaw in the West!"

"*Was* the greatest!" Annie said. Her face looked like a jack-o'-lantern—all lit up and smirking.

"The hell with you!" I screamed. Then I rushed at her, pulling her hair and kicking at her. She was surprised, but not for long, and she began scraping at my face. But Dalton and Dan Clifton pulled us apart.

"You are nuts!" Annie screamed. "Nuts!"

"If Doolin goes," I yelled at her and anybody else who was listening, "then I'm going too."

I started off to my horse, running through the grass.

There was silence for a second, then I heard Bitter.

"Oh hell," he shouted to the Gang. "This is a fine mess. She's going to take care of Doolin. And now I'm going to have to take care of both of 'em."

I slowed up a little till he caught up with me.

"Come on," I said, when we got to the horses. "We got to catch up with him."

"Aw hell," said Bitter.

Then we rode off.

CHAPTER

XX

A HOT BATH

WHEN WE COME INTO THE TOWN OF HOT SPRINGS, THE STARS was out like fox eyes in the sky. All around us was the cobblestone streets and walls of the place. You went down one winding street and you hit another. It was ever so charming, and even though I was plumb tired from the long journey, I felt a surge of excitement sweep over me. I was nervous, too, and hoped putting my hair under my hat and squinting my face up real mean made me look like a boy.

"You are gonna love this place," said Doolin. "Old Tom Bryant runs it. I hear tell he's got it all fixed up new like. . . . They say that this place is gonna become some kind of vacation spot. . . . Old Tom and me run together up in Kansas . . . had us some wild times."

"Where is it, Bill?" I said.

I was getting impatient kinda, looking all around trying to find the right place. There was banks and a faro place called Hot Lizzie's Gambling Casino, and a place called Moon's Club with a big yellow sign and another called Big Jim's Casino that had a sign decorated with a picture of a huge man with a red-and-black shirt on and a smiling cardboard face and a giant finger which pointed inside. As we rode past it, two girls was having relations with an hombre on the porch. Then I heard them cackle loudly and throw him into the street.

"Jesus," said Bitter, looking at me. "If the women are that tough around here, we are in real trouble."

"Don't worry," I said. "You got me to protect you."

Doolin rode up ahead a little and we turned the corner and saw a place with a cavelike-looking entrance.

"Here it is," he said. "This is the place. Boy, is it different!"

Over the mouth of the cave there was a huge yellow sign: "The Mineral Caves—Relax and Rejuvenate."

"Boy that do sound like *it*!" Doolin said. "Old Tom must be quite a guy to pull off something like this. I never knowed him to have so much business sense. Just goes to show you—give a man a break and he'll *do* something."

"You sound like a fucking preacher," Bittercreek said, but not in a mean way.

"Yessir. . . . Well look here," Doolin said. "It might be better if you all waited in the Mineral Bar there. . . . Goddamn, I wonder if old Tom owns that too? Cause I don't want us all sitting down there at once. We could get recognized."

"Bullshit," said Bitter. "You just want to be the first to hit them baths."

"I need 'em more'n you two," Doolin said. "You got enough sparks between you to keep the bones warm."

Bitter and me laughed, and we all got off our horses, hitched 'em up and slapped one another on the back.

I watched as Bill walked toward the mouth of the cave. When he went under the yellow lights he seemed to get all yellow hisself, and I felt a powerful cold come over me. I musta looked like the hound of hell itself because Bitter even noticed it.

"What's a-matter?" he said.

"Nothing," I said, as I watched Bill walk inside. "Nothing that some of that good old-fashioned mineral water won't fix."

Saying that made me feel better (it's amazing how talking tough always seemed to make me tough, as if the words was forming a ball of grit in my stomach where all them butterflies used to be).

Once inside the Mineral Bar, however, my spirits begun to drop again. All around us was fine-looking gentlemen with fancy hats as high as a gravedigger's and genuine silky-looking scarves, and women with the finest-looking dresses. They were laughing and acting ever so gay, and me and Bitter looked like we was from some other world.

"What the hell is this we have here?" said Bitter to me.

"I don't know," I said. "Maybe we jes ought to wait outside."

But that got Bitter's dander up. (I loved him when he got mad. Show me a man without rage, and I'll show you a stiff.)

"Bullshit," Bitter said. "We got money. And we are gonna have a drink."

With that, he started shoving his way through the crowds of laughing gay-looking people. For a second I thought they might start in laughing at us, one man especially. He had on a black silk top hat and he wore a kind of thing around his neck which looked like it was about to cut off his windpipe (later I learned it was called an ascot), and he had on spats and shoes so polished you could see the reflections of the chandeliers in 'em. He looked at us with a cocked brow fer a second, but instead of laughing or making a funny noise, he just turned away, as if we was some kind of bad odor that he'd put up with cause it would soon waft away. It made me angrier than if he hadda made a crack, but it was a kind of anger that gets all up inside you and makes it impossible for you to say or do a thing.

"What kinda drink do you want, Jennie?" Bitter said to me, as we finally leaned on the bar.

"Oh, I don't know," I said. "I ain't sure."

"Whiskey," said Bitter. "Two doubles. Well ain't this the biggest looking room of swells you ever did see?"

"I guess it is," I said. "Seeing how it's the only one I ever did see."

Then we didn't say nothing more, and I sort of hunched up my shoulders and made my face all mean looking, and felt meanness and confusion shooting through my body jes like bad blood.

The man next to me was talking real loud: "I don't think the Harrisons understand the true nature of racing at all. They don't have the slightest conception of good breeding."

A woman with a nose which looked like it was hung onto something, hovering jes above the rest of us, nodded her head in a way that made me want to bash it.

"I quite agree," she said. "I quite agree."

"I quite agree too," said Bitter then.

The others turned and looked at him and he smiled and thumbed his nose.

The woman with her nose pointed at the chandelier rolled her eyes and turned away.

"Baaaad men," she said. "Don't you simply adore baaaaad men?"

"Sheeeeet!" I said, ready to go up behind her and give her a good pop to the back of the neck.

But Bitter grabbed my hand and pulled me back.

"Now this here is a vacation spot," he said. "And we is here on a vacation, so let's not git into any trouble."

"Your words might be cool," I said, all burned up, "but you are shaking as bad as I am. . . . I don't know who these pig's asses are, but this ain't my type of place. No sir. I thought this was an outlaw town. That's what Bill said."

"Well," said Bitter, "I reckon the outlaws is hanging out somewhere else. Maybe in Eureka Springs. Cause this place sure has changed its face."

"Speaking of faces," I said, tossing down my whiskey, "where the hell is Bill Doolin?"

"Oh, he'll be along," said Bitter. "I'm sure of it. And when he gits here, then it'll be our turn. I hear tell them hot baths jes wash all the orneriness right outta you."

"It'll take a hell of a lot of washing," I said.

The bartender come up to us and looked at me real close.

"How old are you, kid?" he said.

"Old enough to put a bad hurt on you if you don't gimme that whiskey," I said.

"That old enough for you?" said Bitter, looking at the guy like he was already tossing the dirt on his coffin.

"Sure," the guy said.

He handed us a couple more drinks, but Bitter grabbed the bottle from him. "Shit on this place," Bitter said. "I never seen such a lot of goddamned weirds in one place."

"Weirds?" I said, starting to laugh. "A lot of weirds."

Next to me I heard the man with the ascot say, "There is no trouble at all that a few more lawmen couldn't handle."

I sucked in my breath and jes tried to think of the son of a bitch as a "weird." It worked pretty good too. A "weird" ain't gonna bother you. A "weird" ain't gonna do jackshit to a grasshopper.

"This here is pretty good whiskey," I said, cuddling up to Bitter a bit.

"Cut it out," Bitter said. "You is supposed to be a boy!"

"Oh yeah," I said in the deepest voice I could muster. "Well I'll tell you . . . I think the Indians ought to be jes lynched from the highest tree, right out there with the Negras and the 'weirds' . . . like this asshole standing here next to me with that lady's garter round his neck!"

The comment caused the "weird" next to me to turn around and stare at us.

"And what species of imbecile are you?" he said.

"Huh?" I retorted.

"Mister," said Bittercreek, "you are gonna need a new face."

The guy was pretty game, I'll say that for him. He put a big pink hand on Bitter's arm.

"Sir," he said, "I contest what you have said."

"Mister," Bittercreek said, "you'd better get your hand off my arm, cause if you don't, the next time you go to buy gloves you are only going to have to purchase one."

That set the fella back a little and Bitter was all set to put a dent in his cheek, when suddenly a kid come running through the door, screaming like he was set afire.

"Everybody come see," he said. "Everybody come see. They jes captured Bill Doolin. They got him in the steam baths and have taken him to jail. Come quick. Hurry up now. They are gonna hang the baddest man in the West!"

"Jesus Christ," Bitter said, pushing himself away from the man.

I felt a kind of fog come over me and I didn't know what to say or do. When I did talk, my voice sounded as if it had been asleep for so long that it didn't no longer belong to me.

"We gotta do something. We gotta help him . . ." I said.

I started right outside but Bitter grabbed at me and once again pulled me back.

"Not now. Wait. Let's see what happened," he said.

Pretty soon the whole mob of men and women swells was rushing outside and up the curvy cobblestone streets toward the jailhouse, and we was right behind 'em.

After going up a few hilly turns, we come to a really big mob who was waiting outside the jail. In front was two armed guards, a man with a sheriff's badge and another man, with sleepy eyes, who was so thin you coulda mistaken him for a pitchfork with hair.

"All right," said the sheriff. "We have inside here . . . Mr. Bill Doolin, the notorious leader of the Doolin-Dalton Gang. But I don't want to have no damned violence. He is entitled to a trial same as any other cutthroat. Now I want all you people to know who did this, the man who was responsible for the capture. None other than our best citizen, the proprietor of the Mineral Caves and the Mineral Bar, good old Tom Bryant."

Bryant looked down at the swells and the old-timers and the youngsters, one of whom had a rope tied around another's neck and was yelling, "Say yer prayers, Bill Doolin!"

"I'm jes happy I could be part of this town," Bryant said, in a voice real low like. He looked out at us all and there seemed to be some real tears in his eyes.

"We got to have law," he said. "We been building too much for it to go on like it was. Hot Springs used to be known as an outlaw town. But not no more. No sir!"

Well this made them swells break into a tremendous burst of applause and hip-hip-hoorays, and I felt like I was going to have to pull out my gun and jes start blastin 'em front, back and sideways. Instead, though, I began to shake and Bitter pulled me aside.

"That bastard. He sold us out," he said. "I'll git him."

"No," I said, watching the wild faces of the people around me. "We can't get to Tom Bryant now. If you pull your gun out, then we'll both get shot."

Bitter didn't say nothing else but elbowed his way through the crowd, hitting people in the ribs and causing such attention to himself that I was afraid he'd give us dead away.

I ran after him, feeling fear and confusion all through me. It was like somebody had lit a candle in my stomach.

"What are you gonna do?" I said.

"Gonna take a bath," Bitter said. "That's exactly what I'm gonna do."

"What?"

"You'll see. You coming or standing around?"

"Coming?" I said. "Calm down, will you?'

"You don't look like no rock yourself," he said, stopping and staring at me.

"Well?" I said lamely, not knowing what else to say, but figuring speech was better than no speech.

"It's like this," Bitter said. "They got Bill in there. I don't reckon they are gonna waste much time with him. They are gonna give him a quick trial and a quicker hanging. That's the way it is. We gotta get back to the ranch and tell the rest of the boys. Then we gotta try to figure a way to git him out."

"But that's crazy," I said. "They are gonna be waiting for us."

As soon as I said it I felt like a coward. It made me feel as though a hand had squeezed my heart.

"I thought you loved the old man," Bitter said.

"I do, I do . . . it's jes we gotta figure a better plan. You know . . . if we jes come riding in here and try to take him out, we are gonna end up exactly like the Daltons in Coffeyville."

"I know that," said Bitter, walking like he was stalking a wild razorback.

"But what's all this have to do with you taking a bath?" I said.

"You'll see," he said. "In fact, I want you to see. You think outlawin is easy? You think it's fun? Goddamn it . . ."

Well now it was plain to see that he was taking all his rage and frustration out on me. It didn't make no sense at the time, though, and I got pretty damned upset about it.

"Listen here," I said. "I'm jes as much an outlaw as you and the others. Everybody thinks Annie's the one . . . but I'm jes as tough as her."

"You are?" Bitter said. "Then you come with me. . . . Come on."

It was then I realized where we was—right in front of Tom Bryant's Mineral Caves. And Bitter was heading inside.

"I can't come in there," I said. "They'll see me and know I'm a girl."

Bitter didn't say nothing but jes walked on inside. In front of us was a blue door, in front of which was a midget, with a head twice as big as his body, a nose what looked like a sweet potato and hair so black and flat, it looked like it had been painted on his skull.

"You boys want to take a bath?" he said in a voice that sounded like it come from a screeching bird.

"Yeah," said Bitter, all at once full of a hearty-sounding laugh. "We want to see old Tom Bryant. We jes heard tell he captured a bandit."

"Old Tom is over at the jail," the midget said. "And he did do it. Captured Bill Doolin. They was friends back when Tom was a badass. Now old Tom is straight as an arrow . . . and he conned that old devil Doolin. Now what are you boys doing if I might ask?"

"We is writers," Bittercreek said. "We come to this town on vacation, all the way from back East. . . . Got us some fancy cowboy clothes and been traipsing around in the woods, hoping to run into some real old-timers."

"That's right," I said. "You tell old Tom if he comes over here, we might write him up in a book on the Doolin-Dalton Gang. He could get real famous."

Well this sent the midget into a state of glee the likes of which I ain't never seen. He jumped up on one foot and hopped about, and spittle came out of his mouth, and his ears wiggled back and forth and his eyes crossed and he looked about as happy as a troll smoking the green leaf.

"I'll go get him," he said. "Yessir. I'll go get him. Hey, why don't you two take a bath down there . . . jes go down into the cave there, and you'll find towels and the pools. It's real nice. Writers, huh? I'll go get old Tom."

"Sure," Bitter said.

The midget run off to fetch old Tom, and me and Bitter started walking down this long, wide hallway, all covered over with limestone and strange white rocks. We could hear our bootheels resounding as we went.

"Nice place old Tom has got here," I said.

"Ought to be nicer when he gits his reward money," Bitter said. "He can afford to make all kinds of improvements then."

"Sure can," I said.

I was trying to sound cool and calm, but every part of me was tingling, jes like somebody was running ice all over my spine.

Soon we come to the bottom of the strange hall, and a kind of hot mist come up from the baths.

We went through a little wood gate and seen this real big pool marked "Gents" and another doorway with a pool marked "Gals."

Bitter walked over to some benches and started stripping down. The water looked green and mist come off of it, and in the corners it seemed to bubble. I felt it had a strange power over me, as if it were some kind of whirlpool pulling me into it, and the feeling made me tingle all over, but in a new way, exciting and hot and full of joy and fear.

"I'm having me a swim," said Bitter. "You sit over on them benches. Jes stay right there. . . . When Tom Bryant comes down here, see if you can sneak up behind him like and push him in."

"Bitter," I said, "what are you going to do?"

"Like I said," Bitter answered, cold as steel. "I'm having me a swim."

I sat over on the benches and watched Bitter as he waded down into the pool. The water covered him over, and the bubbling seemed to get stronger, and I looked at the ceiling which dripped from the moisture.

It was about five minutes later, with me half dozing off from the heat in the place, when I heard the bootheels coming down the hallway toward us.

"Bitter," I said, "here he comes."

Bitter didn't say anything but smiled and pushed his hair back with his hand.

He waded around toward the edge of the pool and both of us watched as the wooden door swung open.

"Mr. Bryant?" I heard him say, as if he was in another tunnel, very far away.

"That's right," Tom Bryant said.

Looking at him now, closeup like, I was surprised to see how old and tired and yellow-skinned he looked. It was as if he was suffering from a disease which had spread all over him.

"My name is Bill Pinkerton," Bittercreek said. "And this is my youthful partner, Jimmy. . . . This sure is a beautiful pool you got here."

"Thank you, sir," said Tom Bryant. "I have worked hard to fix this place up."

"I understand today you'll be collecting quite a reward for the capture of Bill Doolin, sir," said Bitter.

"Yessir," said Bryant, smiling a little. "That is so. I will be collecting ten thousand dollars."

"That's good," said Bitter. "Then perhaps you can fix up the side of the pool here . . . where it seems to be giving away."

"What?" said Bryant.

"Over here," said Bitter, pointing at the side of the pool and looking toward me.

I got up and smiled at Tom Bryant and walked over with him, just an inch or so behind, as if I were interested in looking at the side of the pool.

"It's cracking here," said Bitter. "Yessir . . . but with your money you'll get from the reward, and the money I aim to make you writing up your story . . . why all the fame that you are gonna get will make you a very rich man. You can build a place twice as big as this one if you have a mind to."

"Is that so?" said Tom Bryant, leaning down.

"Yes," I said, coming up behind him, "that's so, you dirty backstabbing son of a bitch."

Bryant turned faster than I expected for an old man and grabbed my arm. I felt terrified and yet something had come over me. Thinking of Bill Doolin in that jail cell and this man, his friend from way back . . . I seemed to be filled with all of hell's fury, for I didn't hesitate and kicked him where it hurts a man, no matter how big or how small.

"Owwwww," he screamed, falling backwards into the water, but holding onto me nonetheless. Then we was all in there, and Bryant came up fast, trying to use me to keep away from Bitter.

"You bastards," he said. "I shoulda known. . . . Help, help . . ."

"Get off me, you son of a bitch," I said, scraping at his eyes and trying to pull away from him.

"Let go of her," said Bitter. "Fight like a man."

"Little Larry!" yelled Bryant.

But now Bitter had leaped over me and had him. I felt Bitter's strong arm pull the old man's away from me, and then I was swimming free and was on the side of the pool watching as Bitter grabbed Bryant's neck.

"He was your pal," said Bitter, "and you turned him over to be hung."

Bitter had him around the neck now, and Bryant had fallen kinda limp. I said to myself, "I can't watch," but the truth was I wouldn't a missed it for the world.

"I got old," Bryant said. "It'll happen to all of you. You get old and you can't wait no more . . ."

"You're old, all right," said Bitter, pushing forward.

The old man tried to call out again.

"Little Larry," he said. But his voice was like the cackling of an old turkey jes before the axe.

"You worthless son of a bitch," said Bitter. "You did it all for this rotten little pool of water. . . . You gave up your friend's life fer this. . . . Now give up your own."

The old man looked up at me, his yellow eyes all teared over with fear, and I thought how I wished somehow we could let him go, but it weren't no use. He had broken the Code, and that was all there was to it. I watched as Bitter pushed him under, and held him until his arms stopped flailing, and he was limp.

"Well, that is that," said Bitter. "Now let's . . . watch out!"

I saw him looking behind me, and turned quickly, just in time to see the midget coming down on me with a chair. Moving as fast as I could I was able to duck, and he went over into the water, the chair bobbing at my feet. He came up fast, blubbering and yelling, but his huge head made a nice target, and with one swipe I smashed him on his noggin, knocking him unconscious.

"Let the son of a bitch drown," said Bitter.

But I couldn't do it. I guess it was selfish, horrible . . . but although I didn't mind Bitter hurting and killing folks, it weren't in me to do it. I guess when it comes down to it, I wasn't so much of an outlaw as I was an adventurer. . . . I wanted to see it all, but I never wanted to kill nobody myself. I felt real strange about it too, as I dragged the midget out of the water. It was like I was secretly guilty of being like one of the swells we had seen in the bar. The thought made me loathe myself, but it was there nonetheless. I wanted all the excitement without really feeling any of the guilt. That bothered me bad as we ran up the hallway toward the outside, and it bothered me worse when the sun went down and we made our way across the mountains, back to the ranch.

CHAPTER XXI

GRIEF

As we rode up into the hills the night turned cold, but it wasn't the weather that gave me the chills. I kept thinking of Bill Doolin in his cell, and of Tom Bryant, strangled in the water, and I wanted to scream. Finally I was so tired that I fell off my horse, so Bitter suggested we stop, build a fire and hole up for the night.

"But we should git back," I said. "I mean . . ."

"It's all right. Nothing is going to happen fer a couple days. We'll be better getting back tomorrow . . ."

Then I started to cry, and Bitter come over to me and sat me down, spreading his rain poncho out on the ground for me. So I lied down, trembling and shaking, and Bitter smiled and held my head.

"I'm sorry," I said. "It's jes so frightening."

"I know," he said.

"You think we will get him out of jail?"

"Sure. Gotta get the rest of the Gang and come up with a plan, that's all."

I relaxed a little and held onto him, while around us the night birds sang, and we heard the sound of animals moving through the brush.

"You really think so?" I said, as I got cold again.

"We got people outta worse spots than that. Ole Bill has nothing to worry about."

"I hope not. I love that old man."

Bitter smiled and rolled a cigarette. "He is a real outlaw."

"So are you," I said slowly, afraid to tell him how scared I felt. "You are real, and so is Annie. I don't know if I am. I couldn't kill nobody like that."

"I don't know," Bitter said, letting the smoke out through his nose. "Nobody thinks they could when they are first getting started. Got started when I was ten. Stole a pig from a neighbor's pen."

"What fer?"

Bitter knitted his brow and got a very serious expression on his face. "I had an idea I wanted to be a farmer. But my old man was too drunk and I didn't have no ma, so I figured the only way I was gonna have the farm was to kind of round up the animals on my own."

"You are kidding?" I said, laughing in spite of myself. "What did you git next?"

"A duck. I stole a local man's duck. That gave me a duck and a pig."

"Then what?" I said, really laughing now.

"Next comes a hen. I figure a duck and a hen would get along well, them being both fowls."

"What about the pig?"

"I'd lost him," Bitter said, running his tongue around his mouth and laughing at me a little with his eyes. "Lost him to my old man. He got right close to that animal."

"What?"

"He ate him." Bitter said, shaking his head as if he had just described the saddest thing in the world.

"Your old man ate the pig?"

"Yes, ma'am. That son of a bitch ate the farm as fast as I could steal it. In one week he ate the duck, the goose and the hen, and he was eyeing the cow when I got wise."

"What did you do?"

I was snuggled up right nice now, and feeling lots better.

"What I shoulda done all along. I waited till he was asleep one night. I sneaked over then, carted him off to the oven and cooked him up. Ate every damned bit of him. Best damned Christmas dinner a man ever had."

I hit Bitter some then.

"Oh, you damned liar. You liar. All outlaws is liars and thieves."

Bitter was smiling like the moon now.

"You called it. Now come on over here and let me lie to you some more."

He moved on top of me real fast, and I let him.

It was near morning when we finally pulled into the cradle of hills where the ranch lay. Just seeing it there, so beautiful and cozy through the foggy-dew morning, made me feel more like myself. And when we brought our horses into the yard and I saw old Fred tied up outside, I felt my heart bulge a little. This was my *home*, the only one I had ever known . . . and whatever my feelings, I knew I would protect it.

Well, it wasn't long before the Gang was wakened and we was sitting around the old table talking with Dick Whisper (who looked like he had been on a six-day bender—his eyes looked like a couple of overcooked cherries and his nose had veins sticking out of it like iron ore in a mine shaft) and Dan Clifton (who looked about as bad) and that little hawk-toothed

Bill Raidler, who sucked on a toothpick, and Bill Dalton and Annie, who sat together now at the end of the table, looking fit and rested and bright-eyed.

"So they got him," said Dalton. "They got him . . . well, we got to do something fast. I got a hunch they will be having Issac Parker coming in to see him, and if that happens we are all in big trouble."

"Issac Parker?" I said, trying to drink some coffee and get the damned pictures out of my head. "Ain't he the hanging judge from Fort Smith?"

"One and the same," Annie said. "He's hung over forty men. Some he has pulled the trap on personally. He's that kind of bastard."

At this, Dick Whisper began to clear his throat with the most annoying and obnoxious sound I have ever heard this side of a cow belch.

"Now listen," he said, baring his teeth and scratching his nose so the veins stuck out like rivers on a relief map. "This is my plan. We go into town fast . . . and by the back way . . . and . . . we get Dan to toss some dynamite."

"And the result of that," said Dalton, "is they blow the hell out of us, jes like they did my brothers and me in Coffeyville. No sir . . . they know we are coming all right. And the way that town is situated, we don't stand a chance with all the high walls around it. We got to come in as loners . . . but somebody has to spring Bill first. . . . Then we jes have to ride for it and use the dynamite to keep 'em away."

"But there ain't no way for us to git in there," said Raidler, switching his toothpick from the right to the left side of his mouth. "They will draw a bead on us as sure as hell."

That stumped the Gang for a bit and we all looked at the tables and chairs. I felt so tired I was sure I was hearing everything from the other side of a train tunnel.

"What the hell are we going to do?" said Annie. "We can't let 'em hang Bill."

"I don't know," I said, "I jes don't know . . ."

I looked down at my hands and started to shake a little. A picture of Tom Bryant flashed by me, his broken neck swirling like a dipper in a punch bowl. Suddenly I fell over, and if it hadn't a been for Bitter, I'd have likely cracked my neck on the edge of the table.

"Hey, there, old girl," I heard Bitter say.

Then it was very very dark, and I felt large, strong hands lifting me up.

They kept right on lifting me too, up over the house, which I looked down on from a very high distance. When I turned I saw Bill Doolin smiling at me. He wasn't dressed like he usually was. There wasn't no overalls or sodbuster boots or big black hats or Colt forty-fives or Winchester rifles. . . . Instead, he had a top hat on and his moustache was waxed and he was looking very elegant . . . like a swell, but a nice swell, and he seemed to be telling me something. That is, his mouth was moving . . . but no sound come out at all, and he motioned me closer, so I crawled across what looked like a pink cloud until I was only a few feet away from him, and I tried listening again, but this time there was even less sound. Then I noticed that he was starting to cry and I felt a terrible horror coming over me, as if my whole personality had disintegrated right there in front of him (I know this sounds plumb crazy, but that's how I felt), and I tried to tell him that I couldn't understand, so he motioned to me to listen closer. He kept putting his big right hand up to his old gnarled ear, and I crawled across the pink clouds a little further, until my ear was right in front of his mouth, and I could feel the wind coming out of his mouth, and I knew he was trying to tell me something terribly important, so I turned to tell him please try harder, but his mouth had opened, and it was as wide as the entrance to a cave, and I began to look straight down in it, and it was black, blacker than the color black, so black that it looked like ink which had gotten under your pores and was filling you up, and I tried to pull back but I tripped and then I was falling through Bill Doolin's mouth, down and down and down, and I began to scream and cry and kick . . . and then I felt I was drowning in black ink; it was filling my lungs. It was about then that I heard a voice and looked up and saw Annie sitting above me.

"Hey, honey," she said. "You listen here. It's all right now. It's me. It's me. . . ."

Well, I was pretty shook. I looked around the room. At the marigolds on the nightstand. At the orange curtains blowing in the breeze. At the mid-afternoon shadows coming in and making patterns on the quilt, and I felt so very very lucky to be alive. I thought of Bill and my feet got numb.

"Annie," I said. "It was a dream. It was a terrible dream."

"But only a dream, dear," Annie said, smiling.

When she smiled like that it was like we was back in Guthrie, still thinking of the good times that lay ahead of us, still as close as any two sisters could be.

"But this was such a terrible dream, Annie," I said. "I was falling through dark space . . . sort of inside Bill Doolin, and I felt such terrible emptiness, as if I were going to fall forever. . . . It was like I was with Bill when they took him to the gallows. That I was experiencing his death . . . or something. . . . Oh, God, it was so frightening."

Now, outlaw girl or no, I just started blubbering like a baby, and Annie comforted me and held me.

"I know how it is," she said. "I know. You are afraid, honey. You think I'm not? This outlawin business is for real. It's the real McCoy all right. Sometimes at night, after Bill is asleep, I sit there and look at him and run my hands over his back, and I think to myself, 'This is the man I read about in books. This is him. He's jes like me. Flesh and blood and muscle and bone. He is jes like me.' And when that happens I am struck with a kind of sense of . . . I don't know how to put it exactly . . . a sense of wonder. That he is jes flesh and blood but that he has become someone who is greater than that. Don't you see? It's as if he has been turned into something greater . . . like in the fairy stories we used to read. The one about the beauty and the beast. That one. A beast is actually a handsome prince. . . . Well, that's how I feel. Like a magic wand come down and changed us so completely . . . but then other times I get scared. I think of what might happen. I'm jes like you, honey . . . really I am."

"Oh, Annie," I said, opening my arms.

And she put herself down on top of me and hugged me, and I smelled her and clung to her, and took strength from her. For I knew that she had a vision of what we were doing, and that I had none at all. That no matter what happened, how dangerous things got, how mixed-up she was, she would cling to the greatness of our adventure and I wanted that greatness too. . . . I wanted it badly, I guess, for when I tried to imagine going back to the other life there didn't seem to be no choice. . . . Still and all, though, even clinging to her like that, I felt I had to ask again.

"But the killing, Annie. It's one thing to hold up a bank. I mean it was like an adventure. . . . But I seen Bitter kill Tom Bryant in cold blood. Not five feet away. It made me sick, Annie. Oh, it made me want to die to see it."

"Let me ask you this, dear," Annie said, sitting up a little and wiping off my brow. "Do you love Bittercreek?"

"I think so," I said. "I think I do . . ."

"You think so? And how do you feel about Bill Doolin?"

"I love him like he was my old man," I said, blushing.

"Yes," said Annie. "And so does Bitter and all the rest of us. You got to understand one thing, honey. This is a war we are in.

If we let a guy like Tom Bryant go . . . there will be others . . . others like those good farm folks we met at the dance. They all know about us. Sure, they are friendly enough, but the price on our heads is getting bigger every day. . . . Tom Bryant is going to keep the rest of us alive. You see that. He's a reminder to them other boys out there. You see, it is like this—they hang criminals to stop crime, so we hang squealers to stop the law. What Bitter did was execute a rat who turned in someone you loved."

"Yes," I said. "I guess I see."

Now I felt numbed-out all over, as if I had already fallen to the bottom and broken vital organs but had to go on breathing jes the same.

"We aren't killers, none of us," said Annie. "And if you didn't get sick over the killing of Tom Bryant, you wouldn't be no sister of mine. . . . But you see why it had to be, don't you?"

"Yes," I heard myself say.

Now Annie smiled and reached down behind her, and got me some lemonade, and I propped myself up and took it from her and put it to my lips, and stared at her as she smiled and patted my thigh.

"Do you feel better?" she said.

"Yes, Annie," I said, feeling very very small.

"Good," Annie said. "Because I figured a way to get Bill Doolin out of jail. Oh, it's a beauty, and it's one they are never gonna forget. No sir. Never! . . ."

With that, she was smiling again and jumping about the room like a circus clown and in spite of all the strange and jangled things that clanged together like steel bars inside of me, jes the sight of her infused me with happiness, optimism and, yes, love.

CHAPTER

XXII

TWO BAD HOMBRES

THE SUN WAS BLAZING DOWN LIKE IT HAD A PERSONAL SCORE TO settle with the cobblestone street. The bricks glistened and seemed to run together, and up ahead of Annie and me, two tough little monkeys were pushing and shoving one another around like Punch 'n Judy dolls. The first one, a big boy with a big yellow shock of hair, was poking the little one, a skinny kid with a ferret face.

"I said, I'm Big Bill Doolin," said the yellow-haired bully.

"Nah, ain't fair," said the other. "You always git to be the bad guy. Who the hell am I gonna be?"

"You are gonna be an omelet out on this street if you don't shut your mouth," said the big kid. "Besides, you can be Bill Dalton."

"Oh yeah," said the little guy, taking a slingshot from his back pocket and loosening it up a little by bouncing rocks off a nearby horse. "That ain't so bad. No. I think I might *like* to be Bill Dalton," he said.

"Ain't fair," said another voice.

Around from behind the livery stable came another kid, this one about two foot three. He had big buck teeth, which caught the glint of the sun. In his hand was a wooden gun which seemed to drag his whole body down.

"Who can I be?" he said. "Who can I be?"

The little kid with the slingshot, grateful to have somebody smaller than himself around, turned and said: "You can be either Cattle Annie or Little Britches. Them's the two girls that travels with the Gang."

"I'll tell you one thing," the kid said, so angry that spit flew off his teeth in every direction. "I ain't gonna be no damned girl. That's fer certain."

"Well, then you can play Bill Doolin," said the big kid. "After the hanging!"

With that, he dropped his neck over and fell to the cobblestones. The rest of the kids laughed and Annie touched my side.

"It is time to go, little brother," she said.

"I can't go through with it," I said. "I feel like I'm gonna die. I mean it . . ."

I looked at Annie's face, barely recognizable under her specs and hidden beneath the peak of the silliest-looking schoolboy cap in the world. Then I kept right on looking down at her knickers and her riding boots. She looked like a pompous little boy from the East.

"How do *I* look?" I said.

"Great," she said. "That's the finest-looking sailor suit I ever did see. Fix your little sailor cap now, darling, and get your little bow tie straight. And keep your damn lollipop in your mouth so you won't begin to blubber. We only got about three minutes left here."

At that exact second, I began to feel Nature's call.

"Annie," I said, "I can't go no further. I am gonna have to get to a john, but fast."

"Oh hell, girl . . . I mean, Foster . . . no more of that girl talk. Now what's my name?" she said.

"I know your damned name, Talbott," I said. "But I jes got to git me to a john, or there is gonna be one hell of a mess!"

"OK, let's go," said Annie. "But make it quick."

She pointed to a place called Sadie's Roulette Lounge and in we went, looking like two of the biggest flops ever to hit the Old West.

We wasn't halfway across the room when I heard a young cowpoke call out, "Hey look at what the dog dragged in!" and I began to quiver, but Annie went straight ahead. She looked as steady as a rock, but when I saw where she was heading I knew she was only putting up a good show. For she was heading directly for the room marked "Ladies," and I had to reach up behind her and grab her by the arm.

"In here, Talbott!" I said.

Then I led her through the swinging doors to the men's john. All around us was bad-looking hombres, combing their big black beards and fixing their hats and adjusting their gunbelts. In front of us was a row of freshly installed chamber pots, and the smell made a stockyard seem like heaven.

"Well, looky here," said one man with a Stetson and a checkered suit. "A couple of kids from the East. . . . What chu all out here on one of them dude ranch tours?"

"No sir," said Brother Talbott.

"Well what chu two doing here, then?"

"We have a uncle who lived here," Talbott said. "At least ways we *had* an uncle. Uncle Tom was his name. And we heard tell he helped capture a bandit named Bill Doolin!"

"Tom Bryant was your uncle?" the man said, all the nastiness and anger dropping away from his face like sunlight.

"That's right," Talbott said. "Me and my little brother, Foster, here, we come all the way from Boston to see Uncle Tom and to stay a bit. But now that he has gone to his great reward, well I guess there ain't much to do but go home."

"I'll be," said the checkered-suit man. "Your uncle was a town hero. You know that? Hey, when you two get done here, you come on down to the jail. . . . You ought to see the jail where Bill Doolin is being held prisoner. Yessir, you at least ought to see that."

"Yessir," said Brother Talbott, while my bladder started to burst. "We would like to see that."

The man patted Brother Talbott and me on the head, and then he and the others finally left.

"Oh, Jesus," I said, leaping into the stalls. "Annie, stand in front there. Don't let nobody look in."

"Don't worry, honey," said Annie. "How'd you like that little story?"

I didn't say nothing but paid attention to all the relief I was experiencing.

When I was all done and had managed to get back into my sailor suit, Annie said it was her turn.

She backed into the next stall and gagged a little at the odor which clogged the nostrils. Then she squatted down on the toilet and did her business.

"Hurry," I said, imagining the door opening any second. "Oh please! If somebody comes . . ."

"Don't worry," said Annie.

Then she did a strange thing. She reached down into her pants and pulled out a stick of dynamite. Using some tar tape, she quickly stuck her hand down in the hole and began working and gagging and gasping. Finally she had it stuck, and lit a match.

"That's a nice long fuse," Annie said. "I jes hope nobody is sitting on there when she blows. It could hurt a couple folks real bad . . ."

"Annie," I said. "I mean . . ."

But she looked at me with those cold black eyes and she smiled, and I thought of Bill Doolin and what she had said before. How this was a *war*. Still and all it didn't seem right, and I wanted badly to do something about it. So I reached into my pocket and pulled out my writing pen.

"I ain't blowing folks up," I said. "I just ain't. Not if I can help it."

"Christ, what will you do then?" she said. "Is there anything you will do? You got a gun in that coat. What if you have to use that?"

"I ain't using no gun, neither," I said. "I just don't think we will have to."

Suddenly the door opened. Annie hid the fuse and shut the commode. The man looked at the stall and started for it, but I smiled and winked at him.

"That one's pretty filled up, pard," I said. "Try number two."

"Jesus," Annie said.

The man went in, relieved himself and stared at me.

"Come on," Annie hissed. "We got to get out of here. Now!"

"I know we do," I said. "I know it."

We started out and I felt awful about someone who might go in there and sit on the john. But as we walked through the bar, I overheard a couple of 'em talking and it made me snap back my neck.

"I can't wait to see Issac Parker do a job on Doolin," said one man. "He likes to use a rope that'll keep 'em dangling for a while. A light gauge one. . . . Just heavy enough to break the neck but not heavy enough to finish him off."

I began to gulp, and then I thought of the dynamite in the bathroom and suddenly it seemed OK. I thought of Bill Doolin, swinging from the east to the west, the blood gurgling inside of him, his neck all broke, and I didn't know what to do. It seemed like some other part of myself had taken over entirely, for now, in an instant, I felt no pity or remorse. I only wanted to git in there and git him out. It was as if I had turned into a machine of some kind. One that had a job to do and was going to do it, no matter who got hurt.

The man's words rang in my ears as we made our way down the boardwalk toward the jailhouse. Out front the same kids was playing Doolin-Dalton Gang, and I watched them as if they was in a dream. Through the streets they moved, pulling their wooden guns, shouting out the gunshots and falling dead on the bright yellow stones.

Soon we were up to the jail, and sure enough, there was the man with the checkered suit. He was standing next to a deputy who was looking down the street like he was waiting for someone to show up.

"Won't be long now," he said. "Tilghman and the boys will be here to back us up. Then we'll see if the Dalton bunch will show their faces."

"Hello, mister," said Annie, in a very small polite voice.

"Hi ya, kid," he said. "Hey listen here, George. You know who this is? This is the two nephews of old Tom Bryant. They was the ones I was jes telling you about. They come all the way out here to see old Tom, and he gits killed."

Annie turned on the waterworks, and I joined her. Pretty soon we had us a whole cascade of tears falling.

"Is that right?" said the deputy. "You Tom's nephews?"

"Uncle Tom!" said Annie. "Good ole Uncle Tom!"

I knew that Sadie's was going to be blown all over the street in a second. We had to be in the jail by then. Oh Lord, let me cry again.

"We gotta get back East," said Annie. "Without even seeing the skunk who caught him. Without even knowing about it. . . . It's terrible. Terrible. And him in there . . . probably eating and laughing. . . . You people should jes hang him and be done with it. You hear me?"

Brother Talbott really began to moan now. I began to do a kind of harmony with him.

"Well you can't see Doolin," said the deputy. "That's out."

"Well at least we could see the jail he's in," Brother Talbott sniffled. "That would be some small consolation. Oh yessir . . ."

"That's right, Brother Talbott," I said.

A kid came up from behind me and started pulling on my sailor suit.

"Fairy. Fairy. Looks like a girl!" he said.

I turned, saw it was the kid with the slingshot, and gave him a good kick in the knee without missing a gasp or a wail.

The kid fell off the boardwalk onto the cobblestone street. But three more of the little devils started toward us.

"Oh, all right," said the jailor, at last. "You kids can come inside the jail. Just for a second. You are liable to get killed by these young ruffians out here, anyway. And I guess enough has been done to Tom Bryant without stuff being done to his kin. Come on in now."

The checkered-suit man smiled and we smiled back, and then the deputy pushed us through the door.

"You see," he said. "This is the place. That over there is the rifle stand, and that big oaf half-asleep is Ned. Ned, wake up. . . . We got visitors."

Ned awoke then. Woke right up. For there was a blast that coulda been heard by a deaf Mexican. Even though I was ready for it, I jumped like hell. Annie couldn't resist a small laugh.

"Jesus Christ, I'm sorry," Ned said, leaping up and falling out of his chair. "I'm sorry. Jesus . . ."

"What the hell?" said George. "What was that? Goddamn!"

"I was having a dream," said Ned. "I was dreaming an angel come to take me away."

"It weren't no dream, Ned," said George. "It is true enough. The whole damned street is filled with stuff. I think somebody is trying to blow up the town."

"They already blowed it up," said Annie, reaching into her coat and pulling out her gun. I reached under my navy blouse and did the same.

"And you weren't dreaming none, neither," I said. "If we don't get Bill Doolin out of here in about two seconds, you are gonna need all the angels of mercy you can conjure up. Move, boys."

"Who the hell are you?" said George. "You must be kidding. You're just a couple of kids."

He began to walk toward us, and both of us backed off.

"We are small girls," said Annie, "but these guns don't mind at all. They leave the same hole no matter who fires 'em."

"Girls?" said Ned, massaging his four chins. "George, they is Cattle Annie and Little Britches."

"That's right," I said, feeling like lightning had gotten into my arms, legs and brain. "We are your basic legendary outlaw girls, and if you don't give us Bill Doolin, you two are gonna end up right where that snake Tom Bryant did."

Even Annie gave me a look when I made this speech. It sure was tougher than anything I had ever come up with before. In fact, it sounded like it come from someone else. But I had begun thinking of Bill Doolin again, and how he had made me feel like somebody. The times we had talking together. The moments Bitter and I had exchanged tales on him. I loved the old man and wanted him out. Not to mention my own ass, which was getting hotter all the time.

"You boys better do what she says," Annie said, in a voice like it come from the grave. "If we don't get Bill Doolin out of here in a very few seconds, you can't even guess what problems you are gonna have next."

I had done backing off. Now I moved forward, and stuck the gun right to Ned's head. (All the while feeling outside myself, thinking, "She's doing this, not me. She's going to kill this fat slob, while I watch. Not me. It ain't me.")

"Lead us back there and open his cell," Annie said.

"Sure," said Ned. "Sure."

He reached behind him and took the key ring from right near the rifles. Then he got up real slow and started back. Annie pushed George along beside him.

"Hurry, get through there. Hurry!" she said.

They opened the first door, and we was in a short little hallway with four or five cells. There wasn't nobody in any of them.

"Where the hell is he?" I said. "What are you two up to?"

I wasn't even watching myself no more. It was as if everything flowed from some place high back in my head, and there wasn't no stopping it. I hadn't imagined there could be no empty cells, and when there was, I couldn't imagine what else could be.

"You see," said George, "we ah . . . we ah were jes guarding him. I mean until Tilghman gets here. You see? We was jes guarding him. There ain't nothing to worry about."

"What?" I said. "Nothing to worry about? Where is he then? I'm warning you."

I saw myself squeeze the trigger, and a bullet went right into the floor next to Ned. His chins began to dance. The bottom one danced in, and the next one danced out, and the next one in. They looked like waves breaking on his mouth.

"He's in *here,* kids," said George, pointing at another room. There was tears in his eyes as he opened a white door.

Annie stopped me as I started to rush past them to see Bill. Oh God, for that second I felt good. It was as if everything that had been robbed from me as a kid, everything I had been hunting for but couldn't name for so long was in the person of that old man.

"Bill?" I said, as we pushed the two guards inside.

"Bill . . . get up . . ."

But he wasn't moving. Instead, he was lying on a table, a long white table, his hands dangling down, all cold and pale-looking. Someone had put a white sheet over him, and I rushed forward and pulled it off and looked at him, naked, with holes in his chest, holes in his neck and one in the side of his head. His eyes was still open wide and I fell over him, screaming and crying.

"Oh my God, Mr. Doolin," I said. "Not you, sir. No, Bill . . . Bill . . . oh, Jesus Christ, Bill . . . this ain't you. . . . No, no . . ."

I felt Annie tugging at my arm.

"Jennie, Jennie," she said. "We got to get out of here. They are going to ambush the Gang. . . . We got to get out . . ."

"Get out?" I screamed. "Get out? . . . You sons of bitches. None of us are going to get out, do you hear?"

As I turned, Ned was holding his chins, but George was making a move.

"Thanks for the tour of the jail, you scum-eating dog-faced bastard!" I said, and then I pulled the trigger. When the bullets hit, they did not blast him back toward the wall or even knock him down. Not at first. At first, he stood there looking at the holes in his stomach and in his arm.

Annie grabbed me.

"Jennie? Jennie . . . have you gone nuts?" she said.

"No, not no more," I said. "I get the point now. Now it's his turn."

The fat man squealed and tried to hide in the corner. I shot the first bullet in his leg and then aimed at his head, but there was a horrible lot of noise, and when I turned for a second, Annie had me by the arm.

"Come on, honey," she said. "They're coming in the front. We got to go out the back. Fast. Come on . . ."

I was so dazed and feeling so strange and ghostlike, I hardly recall what happened next. All I know is that somehow we got out the back, and began running down the alley. We were all alone for a few seconds, running like mad, and I recall tripping over my sailor suit and seeing the cobblestones sailing by me, as if I were on horseback. It seemed like that, as if I were floating on horseback through the streets . . .

But suddenly from behind us were riders and they were shouting and hurling names at us and firing bullets. There was a little space in the wall, a kind of hole (which I guess now was the entrance to someone's yard), and we ducked in and fired back at them, which slowed them up a bit. Then we started running again, down the alley close to the wall, but they had started coming again and were gaining on us, and I heard Annie say, "We are through, Jennie. They have us." But that wasn't the way it was to be, for suddenly from around the corner, just like in one of Annie's books, came the Gang. Oh, I was never so happy in my life. The Gang. Bill Dalton and Bitter and crazy Bill Raidler, who looked as though he had been shot himself. And then comes Dick Whisper and Dan Clifton, who was hanging limp from his horse. Bitter rides right up to me, and I leap on the back of his horse, and Annie jumps on behind Bill, and then we started for the mountains. But another group come at us from the west. They was ready for this and the firing between the two groups was so fierce that I think they killed a bunch of their own men. They would have surely killed us if it hadn't a been for Dan Clifton, who lit one stick of dynamite and tossed it at a group to the right. The stuff blew them golden cobblestones in the air, and the rocks did more damage than the explosive, hitting men in their heads and knocking them bonkers off their horses. Then he turned to the group behind us and hit them too. But suddenly he lurched forward and I saw him grab his head.

"Bitter," I said. "They got him. They got Dan."

And Bitter rode his horse toward Dan, but Dan turned and waved us away. When he did I saw something fall from his head, something that looked like his ear, and I got sick on myself, and thought of Bill again, and shut my eyes and clung to Bitter as tight as I could. I started screaming then, screaming and crying and I kept it right up, all the way to the mountains. My God, Bill Doolin gone, gone. . . . Oh, I wanted to die myself. But here I was, once again, doomed to live.

CHAPTER XXIII

THE SHOWDOWN

By the time we had gotten away into the mountains, I was feeling like my mind was all wrapped up in barbed wire. Every time we bounced on up into the rocks I had another thought. . . . Like a drowning person, my life seemed to flash in front of me. But not my whole life. Jes the parts I regretted, which now seemed to overshadow all the joyous and happy days. I thought how I'd lied to Doolin about what happened to Annie and me with Big Bill Tilghman, and how maybe I could have stopped him from going on down to the steam baths. Or maybe I could have said something way before that, when I saw that he wasn't fit for outlawing no more. But I hadn't done nothing. Instead I had jes been caught up in the whole bloody excitement of it all. . . . I had forgotten the man for the big damned dream, and now he was gone. For good.

Lord, I felt ashamed and alone. The pines and the elms and the maple trees surrounded us, and all around the birds sang and the blue jays darted through the leafy trees, but now it all looked just like a dark grave. I thought of him lying there, cold and dead, and I thought of the way his hands looked . . . the fingers so brittle you might be able to snap 'em off. And the way he wouldn't laugh no more, or tell me stories, or pat me on the head. Oh God, I wanted the posse to catch up with us. . . . No, I don't mean "us." With *me*. I wanted the posse to catch up with me and make me pay for my stupid little prideful manipulations. Because I hadn't stood up and said my piece, regardless of whose feelings got hurt . . . because I had tried to sneak through life, I had been responsible for the death of the person I loved most in the Gang. I guess it was the last knowledge that hurt me the most, that made me want to throw myself off the horse and tear out my hair. . . . For I knew that even though I cared for Bittercreek and loved my romance with him, my real deep feelings, the ones I couldn't afford to lose . . . these were reserved for the man who lay in the sheriff's office, cold as stone.

After we had gotten to a good place high atop a hill, where we could see anybody approaching, the Gang got down off their mounts and spread out blankets. Somehow I managed to stop crying and went through the motions of helping with the small fire, getting the blankets out, fixing the coffee. But it was like I too was dead . . . just a moving piece of flesh with a dead soul. I made myself keep moving, asking Bill Raidler if he was all right, looking over Dick Whisper, who had been winged in the arm. I poured some water from the canteen and cleaned out the wound, tore off a piece of my shirt, and bound the area up for him as best I could.

"Thank you, Britches," Dick Whisper said. "You are a real angel."

When he said that, I began to feel as if I were going to cry again, but I kept on being busy and even managed to smile and act cheerful.

Soon we were eating dinner and sitting around the campfire, and people were trying to talk a little to one another, but all in all it was about as cheerful as a funeral. Which, of course, is what it was. Our last supper for Dan Clifton and Bill Doolin. Beans, fatback and moldy cornbread.

As the fire burned down and things got so quiet you wanted to scream, Annie slowly got up and wiped off her hands on her hips. Her hair fell in her face a little and she pushed it back and spread her legs and rocked back, to and fro.

"I want to say something," she said.

Everyone looked up. (Even me, though at one point in the afternoon I had vowed I would never listen to a word of hers again. Now I was grateful for a noise. Any noise, even Annie's voice. For only talking would get me out of my dark thoughts.)

Annie put her hands in her back pockets and rocked back on her boots.

"I want to say that I think Bill Doolin was the finest man I ever knew," she said. "I know that Jennie here feels the same way."

As she started to speak, I thought of her the night Bill Doolin had left. I remembered how much she had cared then, and I felt my fingers go numb.

"He was an outlaw," Annie said. "He killed people. But he was also someone else. We knew him, and we loved him. And now he is gone, and it hurts. It hurts right down to the bone."

She stopped there and seemed to be trying to catch her breath, and I looked around at the Gang. At Whisper, who sat with his lips pursed real tight. At Raidler, whose little ferret face was all pinched up. At Bill Dalton, who coughed and breathed out deeply, and whose fingers kept grabbing at roots in the dirt, only to let them go again.

"Bill Doolin was a kind man, a man of honor," Annie continued. "It's funny, because when I come to this Gang my only picture of him was from lousy little books. They made him out to be a kind of hero . . . a person from a story book. But the truth was, he was much greater than that. He was a person who was wild and generous, with as much bad as good in him. The thing is, he was great because he played out all the bad and all the good, no matter where the chips fell. He's dead now. Cold and dead. But no one can say that he didn't live. That was the fear Jennie and I had when we was back in Morgan's. That we would go through life without living. Bill Doolin showed us how to take it to the limit . . . do you see? He showed us how to live!"

"Amen to that!" said Bill Raidler.

The others nodded their heads.

"Which is why we loved him," Annie said. "And why the Doolin-Dalton Gang is more than jesta bunch of cardboard heroes from Ned Buntline. More than jes bank robbers. We are living together. To make Bill Doolin's life worth the effort and sweat he put into it. We can mourn Bill, but we can't sit here and act like we are licked. We're the Doolin-Dalton Gang, even if Bill is gone. He never asked for no easy life, and he never buckled under. He was an outlaw, the best outlaw to the end. . . . And lemme say one more thing . . ."

But before she said it, Annie began to cry and sniffle and I felt shivers down my back, and yet . . . yet, I couldn't tell if she meant it or not. I wondered if she knew herself what she meant.

"Lemme say this," Annie went on, the moon right behind her head, lighting her hair up like strands on fire. "That he won't be forgotten. He was a *real* man, a great man, and they will write books and songs about him . . . as long as there are people on this earth. And in that way, he'll go on living!"

I could feel something happen to me when she said that. Something mean and urgent was coming up from inside, almost like a snake worming its way through my bowels to my mouth.

But Annie went on a little more: "I can see what's on your

minds. I can see it. You are all thinking of running away with your tails between your legs. Of splitting up! But if you do that, it's like Bill Doolin died for nothing. Doncha see that? We can't split up now. . . . We can't!"

The Gang was silent, and Annie looked down on us, her black eyes challenging us. For a second I thought I was going to jes sit there, but the thing inside me, the snake, started coming out, and before I knew it I was on my feet, waving my arms like a madwoman.

"That's great," I blurted out, feeling like I had the prickly heat. "That's fine for you to say. What a great guy Bill Doolin was. But what the hell did you know about him, anyway? Did you ever talk to him? Did you ever hear about his life . . . how sick and tired he was? How he felt like he couldn't stand it no more? And if you did hear any of them things, did it ever occur to you to make him feel better? To help him when he was down? Or maybe, did you think of how he wasn't no use to the great Doolin-Dalton Gang no more, and ought to be put out to pasture like an old mule?"

"Now wait a minute," said Bill Dalton. "Wait a minute here!"

"Jennie," said Bitter, reaching up for me.

But I felt full of hellfire now and dodged aside.

"You lemme finish," I said. "I got a lot to say. Cause I loved that man. I loved him, and I helped kill him, taking him off to that steam bath and letting him go down there all alone. Goddamn it, if he had been home where he belonged, then none of this woulda happened, and we coulda all done what we shoulda done after a good bank robbery. And that's quit. Look at you. You're sick of it all. All of you. You're dead sick of it. The Gang is dead, don't you see that? The world is too small now. There ain't no place to hide. You seen them swells in that town? I hate 'em. I hate 'em as much as you. But they got everybody on their side. Even old outlaws like Tom Bryant. We fought, and we lost . . . but we ain't lost our lives yet. You all listen to Annie, though, and you can count on it . . . your life is done. And there ain't nothing glorious or romantic about what I saw on that slab in that sheriff's office. It's cold and it's bloodless and it ain't Bill Doolin at all . . ."

Now I began to cry and stutter, but I sucked it in and controlled myself.

"All you see, Annie, is a goddamned dime novel," I said. "A dime novel with you on the cover. But behind the cover . . . behind it, everyone of us will be dead. What difference does it make if we live on in somebody's song? I'm fourteen years old. Dalton and Bittercreek are twenty-three, and we got lives to live . . . *now* . . . you hear? Tell her, boys. . . . There ain't nothing chicken about it. Tell her how you want to live!"

It wasn't no use now. The tears come out of me like somebody was priming the pump.

I sat down next to Bitter, and he held me to him.

"It's true," he said softly. "Jennie and I have talked of quitting. I've been thinking about it for a long time."

I looked across at Dick Whisper. He was shaking his head back and forth, like an old mammy who has lost her master.

Then Bill Dalton spoke up, quiet but strong: "Did you ever tell Jennie about the time you did try and quit?"

"No," said Bitter, reaching over and holding my hand. "Maybe I was trying to forget it. I did quit once. Got a little place and tried farming. But it wasn't no good. I missed the excitement. But I was alone then . . . I couldn't make it alone. But now, maybe it would be different."

Again we all got quiet. It was as if everything in us was all used up, even our rage.

But one by one we looked over at Bill Dalton. The way he had spoken just a second ago made us all remember that when it came to outlawing, he was now the boss.

"There's a lot of good in what you all say," he said, stirring the ashes of the fire with a stick. "I agree with all of you. But there is one thing you all have overlooked."

"What?" I heard myself say.

"Jes this," Bill said, squinting into my eyes, as if he was trying to push through the blackness. "There's no quitting now. For two reasons. One is, to quit it takes money. Money to move, money to get started again. You understand we are gonna have to move far away. Tilghman is never gonna quit following us now. And two, if we do split up, we get tracked down separately. They let you get set and relaxed, and then they come around some nice afternoon and shoot you in your rocking chair."

That was all Dalton said, and it was all Annie needed.

"Right," she said. "That's absolutely right. We got to stick together. It's like I said!"

Oh God, she made me mad.

"Well maybe we do have to stick together for now," I fairly shouted at her. "But it's not like you said!"

But my words was no use. I knew that. For now, anyway, we all had to stick it out. I wanted to say something else, but I knew it was gonna be helpless, so I drifted away from the fire and put down my blankets and lay there smelling the woodsmoke and staring at the stars.

A few minutes later I had almost fallen asleep, but no sooner was I nodding off, when I began to see a huge, white fish with a gigantic long tail. The fish was on a long white stretch of sand . . . like a beach somewhere (which image I musta got from a picture book, cause I had never seen no real beaches), and it was trying like hell to flap its fins . . . but they wouldn't move enough to get it to water. Then I seemed to be behind it, and I began shoving, shoving . . . pushing the fish. . . . It was hopeless . . . it wouldn't move. Then I noticed blood coming out of its side, and I began to get panicky and I tried to fill up the holes with my hand . . . but the fish would not stop bleeding.

Pretty soon the fish began to moan and scream, and I wanted to stop it, to comfort it . . . so I ran around in front of it to tell it I was trying to get it back to the water . . . that once it got to the water it wouldn't bleed no more and it could swim away. . . . But when I got in front of it, the fish had on a cowboy hat, a big black one, and it had a moustache and tired, droopy eyes. It was Doolin's face, and I hugged it and said, "I'm sorry, Mr. Fish, I'm sorry." And the fish's mouth moved, a huge one . . . and it seemed to say, "You brought me to the beach for a picnic. But I need water . . . I got to get water. . . . Oh, why did I listen to you?" And I started to cry and hold the fish's face while it groaned and cried and sucked air . . . and I felt guilt and terror all through me . . .

"Jennie . . . Jennie . . ."

Someone was calling my name. I opened my eyes, still trembling, half-expecting to see that horrible sad dying fish.

"What is it?" said the voice again. And when my eyes cleared I saw who it was. It was Bitter and Annie and Dalton, and then I remembered another time they had all been hovering over me—the time when we first come with the Gang, and it was me and Annie against the world. Oh, that was a good time, it seemed to me now. Even though I had been shot, it was all still new and exciting, like out of one of Annie's books. And Annie and me was together. Together like sisters, and we always would be. . . . But now, now we was on opposite sides of the fence, and there was no mistaking it.

Even so, she stood above me, smiling pleasantly, almost like she meant it.

"Jennie, listen," she said. "We shouldn't be fighting. You know that. I love you, Jennie. My dear friend."

And she reached down and hugged me, while both the men watched.

But I couldn't bring myself to hug her back. It was as if something had broken in me toward her. Something had changed and hardened in me, and no matter how hard I tried to feel the same, it weren't no use. Still, I forced myself to go through the motions. Hugging and smiling. I was too tired to be honest.

"Listen, Jennie," Annie said. "We are all gonna be together, forever and ever . . . you see that . . . but first we are gonna take a little vacation. Get away from these parts."

"Oh yeah?" I said. "And where might we go?"

Annie smiled and looked back toward Bill Dalton.

"Show her, Bill," she said.

Dalton reached around in his back pocket and pulled out what looked like a folded-up advertisement. He handed it to Annie and winked at me, and Annie smiled and opened it up.

"Look," she said. "Look at this!"

I looked down at the advertisement. Pictured was an elephant and an Eiffel Tower and some building that looked like a palace. The poster read:

> Chicago World's Fair
> July 18–August 18
> Exhibitions From All Over the Known World
> See the Eiffel Tower (exact replica)
> See the Taj Mahal
> Ride an Elephant
> The 8 Wonders of the World!

"You see?" said Annie. "You see? We can all go. It ain't all that far to Chicago and we will have a grand old time . . . and get all this bad stuff out of us. . . . It'll make us like a new team. . . . You see?"

"The World's Fair?" I said.

I wanted to say something else, but I was so drowsy. And Bitter and Dalton was smiling. For where I lay, half knocked out and aching in every bone, it seemed like a lovely dream, and I smiled and said, "Sure, why not?" and then I fell back asleep. And didn't dream of fishes or anything else.

CHAPTER XXIV
PLANS

BUT IT WASN'T NO DREAM. NO SIR! FOR THE NEXT FEW WEEKS we barely thought of anything else. And they were pretty good weeks for us as a gang. People talked to one another and listened to each other almost like they was gentlemen. It was so damned nice at first that it was downright eerie. But all the same, the quiet and the days with Bitter did a lot to restore my spirits. In the afternoons Bitter and I would take long walks through the mountains and talk of our future, of what we would do after the Gang made a couple more robberies and split up for good. It worried me a little to talk to him about it because he had mentioned "farming" that night around the campfire. Now, if there was one thing I wasn't going to be, it was no damned farmer's wife. The thought of sitting out in the middle of some damned dust farm, trying to make a living by digging in the soil, made me get the rickets. I told him as much too, on one of the first days back at the ranch. (This was in keeping with my new policy of saying whatever come into my mind, getting it all out there so people could hear it. A policy, I might add, I didn't stick to too long. Cause since you never know what you really mean at the precise second you are saying it, getting it all out seems almost as bad as not saying nothing at all. It's like you are trying to say everything at once. Which is itself dishonest . . . since you don't believe everything.)

I might add that when I told Bitter the truth, I was afraid as hell he would look at me with his big blue eyes and say, "To hell with you. I am going to be a farmer, come what may." But instead he didn't say nothing of the kind.

"That's great," he said instead, leaning on a dogwood tree and laughing. "Because I never could stand farming. I thought I'd try it, but I didn't know what else was out there. Why there must be lots of other stuff a man could do."

"Sure," I said. "Lots of stuff. You name it."

"Hell yes," said Bitter. "I could get us a little business somewheres. Maybe open a bar. That would be great. I'd like sitting behind the old bar, swapping stories with the boys. I can see me now, a great-looking old guy with a moustache and a beer gut, and I'm telling these guys about a friend, you understand, who knew the Doolin-Dalton Gang personal like. Hell, that would pack 'em in, wouldn't it?"

I swung up on a limb and arched back my head.

"Sure," I said. "That would knock 'em out, and once the chief madam of the place came in and took care of 'em . . . they'd never forget it. Never. . . . I'd walk in with my hair tied back, and I'd sing a little song. One of them French kind of songs . . . and I'd wiggle my butt, and pretty soon the money would be plunked down. Heck, there ain't nothing to it."

Now Bitter laughed and fingered the new scab on his forehead.

"You know what else I'd like?" he said. "I'd like to be near water. I remember once I was down there in Port Arthur, and I seen this place right there in a cove like . . . you know. It was a wonderful place, with chairs. And people brought in their boats and sat around talking and eating and drinking. It looked like a hell of a fine life. I think maybe I'd like that."

It never occurred to me that Bitter would want none of this. In fact, it never had occurred to me that I'd want any of it, but like I say, something had happened to me after the death of Big Bill Doolin. It was like certain things closed down inside of me, and other ones seemed to be opening. No, that's not right. . . . It was more like they was all there, all along, but I hadn't seen 'em, because I'd been looking at the stuff Annie had put in there. . . . And what made things harder for me was I had a feeling what Annie put in there wasn't nothing she really owned neither, if you see what I mean. Though I couldn't put it into words then, like I am able to now. . . . It seemed to me that somebody else had put the stuff into Annie too. . . . Oh, the thought scared me. It was like up till then we was actors in somebody else's book. Whose? Ned Buntline's maybe. But I had a feeling that even Ned Buntline wasn't to blame exactly. Because he was only borrowing something that was floating around. . . . I wish I could say it better, but all I know is that during the time we was waiting to go to the Chicago World's Fair . . . during this time, I felt like I was a dozen people at once. That is, when I wasn't feeling like a ghost. I remember waking up next to Bitter one night, feeling like my flesh had turned to paper or some kind of satin . . . all light and airy and insubstantial . . . and I wanted to cry out, but only shook Bitter and hugged him hard, and he said, "What is it?" and I said I didn't know. But I wanted to know why on earth we had to wait to get more money. Why couldn't we take whatever money we had now and get moving? Maybe go East, where the ships were. Find us jobs in Boston or New York where nobody would know us and get us a bar when we had saved enough.

Bitter held me and patted my head (which didn't feel like a head at all, but some kind of melon) and said: "You don't understand. It costs a lot in them cities. We ain't got no education or nothing. We couldn't make enough to save any. It would be ten years before we had enough to buy the bar."

I wanted to argue, but I knew he was right. Still, I couldn't stand it. I was scared now. They would come looking for us. I remembered Dan Clifton's brains falling out in the dust. I was shaking like crazy and Bitter had to hold me a long time before I was able to fall back asleep.

The next afternoon, Annie come down to the stable, where I was feeding Fred and Blackie and Jake.

"Hey," she said, smiling at me, "old Fred is doing pretty good, ain't he?"

"Sure," I said. "He's doing great."

"Yeah," Annie said. "Hey, ain't it great the way the Gang's sticking together. We are going to get this bunch back on their feet in no time. You'll see."

I didn't say nothing but kept brushing Blackie's coat.

"Well, ain't we?" Annie said.

"Sure," I said. "In no time."

I was wishing she'd just go away. I didn't want to lie to her no more. But I didn't want to argue either. When the time came, Bitter and I would just leave. That would be all.

"Hey," she said, smiling and touching me on the shoulder blade. "Listen here. You seem to be trying mighty hard not to talk to me. I thought we was friends."

"We are," I said, lamely and wishing it were so. "I've just been busy lately with Bitter."

"I noticed," Annie said. "You two been spending a lot of time together. You always seem to be off somewheres. In a field, or up in your room. The rest of the Gang is beginning to feel you don't like us no more."

I tried to smile.

"Cut it out," I said. "It's not so. . . . I mean, we've just been

wanting to see each other. Is there anything wrong with that?"
Annie smiled now. But there wasn't any friendliness in it.

"No," she said. "Of course not. In fact, I been seeing a lot of Bill. We been planning which jobs we are going to pull after we get back from the fair. We don't want to wait too long. . . . You know . . . you can't afford to get rusty."

"Like Bill Doolin was getting rusty?" I said, in spite of myself.

But Annie was as cool as a cucumber.

"Yeah," she said. "Like that. You got to stay sharp if you are going to be a great gang. Too much of this mushy, lovey-dovey stuff might take the edge off. You know what I mean?"

"No," I said, getting angry now.

Oh, how I just wanted to say it. "We are quitting. We are through. To hell with you and your murderous little dreams." But I held my tongue, because Bitter was still convinced we needed the Gang. At least for a little while.

"You mind if I ask you a personal question?" Annie said, giving Fred an apple.

"I don't see where it makes any difference whether I mind or not," I said. "You are going to ask it anyway."

Annie put back her head and laughed, but no sound came out.

"I was just wondering if you two is thinking about walking out on the Gang?" Annie said. "You wouldn't be thinking of doing anything like that, would you?"

"What if we were?" I said. "Would you shoot us?"

Now it was Annie's turn to look shocked. She moved back and her face sagged a little.

"Jennie," she said. "How could you say something like that? Of course not. My God . . . what's happened to us. We was like sisters. Oh, I'm sorry the way I been talking to you. . . . I know I musta sounded like I was trying to be a superior snot but I wanted to talk to you again. I mean, I love you as a sister. I always will. . . . But I am afraid you are going to run out on us. . . . I am afraid for you as well as for the Gang. You don't think you and Bitter could be happy outside the Gang, do you? He's an outlaw. That's what he is good at. He would dry up any place else. . . . You got to see that. Listen, I'm not as hard as you think. I don't want to see Bill get shot. I care about him more'n anybody. But he's an outlaw. He's been nothing but an outlaw since he was a kid. He runs on a different kind of clock than regular people. You can't change nobody."

I could see that she was trying, and I wanted to too. I really did want to do or say something that would melt all the coldness between us, but I couldn't. I just couldn't do it.

"You can change a man," I said. "You can change someone if you love them. Do you love Bill Dalton? Or do you just love the idea of Bill Dalton the outlaw king? . . . Is it him you are talking about or them dime store romances?"

Now Annie came toward me and looked into my eyes deeply . . . large and black.

"It's one and the same," she said. "You don't see it? You think I am cold and calculating, and swept away by dreams. But that is what I am trying to tell you. Outlaws live by dreams, and so you can't say, 'Here's the dream, but underneath is the real man.' It ain't like that. You see, the real Bill Dalton is the dream guy from the books. You can't separate them. . . . So you gotta love the whole thing. That's what I'm saying . . ."

"Well, it's not true of Bittercreek," I said. "It's not. There is another person under there . . . somebody good and kind and somebody who could live another way . . . and maybe have kids. . . . There is. I've seen it. I don't think you can see it in Bill Dalton, cause you don't want to. . . . Oh, Annie . . . Annie . . . I'm sorry. . . . Just leave me alone."

"All right," she said quietly, softly, as if I had hurt her.

Then she turned and walked out through the shadows of the barn, and I felt myself starting to cry. She had tried. I knew she had tried, and maybe she was right. That was what scared me the most. For if she was, then everything was already lost. I sat down on a stool next to Fred, and he nuzzled up to me and I held him, patting him over and over again.

"There ain't no sense in this," I said. "Trying to comfort a mule. No sense at all . . ."

And, I knew, as I stroked his head, that it was Annie I wanted to comfort, but too much had happened and there just wasn't no way.

CHAPTER XXV

THE CHICAGO WORLD'S FAIR

"THIS IS IT," ANNIE HAD SAID, AS WE LEFT THE RANCH THAT misty morning and headed for Chicago. "We are gonna have the time of our lives."

"Yahooooooooo!" Bill Raidler had screamed.

And Dick Whisper had tried to yell himself.

As for me, I was excited about going to the fair, but it wasn't hard to see Annie's strategy. We would all have a good time at the fair and then we would come home, relaxed and ready for more shooting and killing. Well, I had already decided that wasn't going to be the case. That talk in the barn had convinced me of one thing—Annie wasn't going to give up the Gang. Her reasons weren't bad . . . in fact, from her point of view, they made sense, and I realized I had been too hard on her before. She wasn't no crazy woman. . . . Hell, she hadn't even shot nobody. I had done that. (And you may be interested to know that I never felt too badly about it, neither. I figured the scum had got what was coming to him. I don't want to make myself out no angel. I hadn't enjoyed shooting him, but I never lost no sleep on it, neither.) But whatever the reasons, Annie meant to go on with it. I was determined to get Bitter out of it and had been working on him steadily since I had talked things over with Annie. I almost had him seeing it my way. We could get away from the Gang, go to New York. Find jobs and begin anew. So, as far as this trip was concerned, it was a goodbye party for me and Bitter. Only nobody didn't know it yet. And they weren't going to, until it was all over.

The trip up through Missouri to Chicago wasn't nothing worth mentioning, except that it was ugly. I doubt if there is more mud in the world than in southwest Missouri. It's the mud capital of the world, and I felt as if we was riding into it deeper and deeper. Along about fifty miles outside of St. Louis we seen something interesting, though. Some settlers had signs up all over the place that read:

SEE JESSE JAMES' CAVES
THE REAL LIFE HIDEOUT OF THE OLD WEST'S GREATEST BANDIT

We stopped and had words with an old white-bearded guy who looked like he had lost his wits.

"This is the real cave?" I asked him.

"Yes ma'am," the old fellow said, wiping his hand on his beard. "This is the place all right. Jesse and Frank and the boys hid out here many a time."

There was some fatback hanging in the tangles of his beard.

"Twenty-five cents to see the cave," he said, smiling and sticking out his yellow tongue.

"Shit," said Bill Dalton. "This is a hoax."

"A what?" the old guy said.

"It's all cow manure," said Bill Dalton. "Jesse never stayed in these parts in his life."

"Did too," said the old guy. "I known him . . . swell fellow, too."

I looked over at Annie, who smiled and threw the old man a penny.

"You keep right on thinking that, old-timer," she said.

Then she looked over at me.

"You see," she smiled. "He really believes it. Now you tell me it ain't true. It'll be true as long as people got money to spend and stories to tell."

There weren't no use arguing with her. She was jes like a bull. So I smiled and said, "Sure," and we rode on.

We rode through the little hills outside of Chicago and then we come to the place itself, and it was enough to make you want to yell for joy, which is what we did. For there ain't never been anything as wonderful as the Chicago World's Fair. No sir. Everywhere we looked there was people. Thousands and thousands of them. In a big meadow. And there were big gleaming buildings, and wonderful new rides. I never seen the Gang so happy, and in spite of all my worries, as we tied up the horses outside, I began to feel light and happy and glad to be alive. Oh, the beauty of it, out there in the distance. The Eiffel Tower, the huge cathedrals from France and Italy, the wonderful carny rides. I felt as if I had stepped into another dream, but this time a good one.

"This is going to be the greatest day of our lives!" Annie said, and Bill Dalton picked her up and threw her over his shoulder, and we all laughed as he carried her toward the fair.

"Look at them guys," said Bitter. "They look like they got the Saint Vitus's dance."

"Damn if they don't!" I said.

In front of us was a stage, and up on it were these five guys with big turbans on their heads, and these kinda puffy shirt sleeves, and they was all crouched down jes like the old men do who hunker on the town square. But suddenly, they was springing up on one leg and laughing like banshees, then they was jumping on the other leg, back and forth. Their legs moved jes like some kinda machines . . . back and forth . . . and their arms was out in front of them, clasped together almost like they was praying . . .

"Says here," I said, pointing to a sign, "that these here fellows is Cossacks. They are some kinda Russian cavalrymen, famed for their swordsmanship, riding ability and fierceness in battle. Also says . . . let's see . . . that this here is a Cossack dance which they do when they have a battle celebration."

Bitter grabbed hold of Dick Whisper and pulled him away from a hula girl who was dancing on an opposite stage.

"Look at these guys," Bitter said. "You know what these guys are, donchu? They are Russian cowboys. . . . I'll bet they rob them Russian carriages and stuff like that. . . . Then they get all liquored up on one of them Russian drinks. . . . I heard tell of it once. . . . Made from a potato? Aw, what the hell is it called?"

"Drink made from a potato?" said Dick Whisper to Bill Raidler. "A drink made from a potato. . . . What if the son of a bitch got stuck in your throat? . . ."

"Aww shit," said Bitter. "They mash it first. You ain't got no culture at all."

"Maybe not," said Bill Raidler, pulling out a pint of rye. "But I'll tell you what. Ain't no cowboy gonna wear no damned shirts with sleeves like that. Or drink no damned mashed potato. Sounds damned strange to me. . . . Besides, I like these hula girls. . . . Look at 'em over here, Bitter."

Bitter didn't hesitate long. In a second he was gawking at them girls, who was swaying to and fro like the tropical breezes. Yessir, their hips did all the talking, and the message weren't hard to figure . . .

"Say," said Bitter, "you oughta try that sometimes, Jennie.

Where the hell is Annie? She and Bill oughta see this. Let's get us a little closer."

"Now jesta damned minute," I said. "Hey, you know what we oughta do? We oughta get us a couple of them boats, Bitter, and take us a ride through the Tunnel of Love . . ."

"Aww shit," said Raidler. "You two lovebirds jes breaks my heart. A ride through the Tunnel of Love. You gonna take one of them special drinking potatoes with you?"

"I never seen a potato drink nothing in my life," whispered Dick Whisper. "But I seen a carrot talk once, when I was smoking jimson weed. He was a damned good yakker . . ."

"You boys is drunk again," I said. "Come on. Let's all take that boat ride!"

Raidler put his arm around Dick Whisper.

"That's a good idea!" he said. "We'll go out there on the lake and see if we can scout us up some women . . ."

I smiled and turned, and there was Annie and Bill Dalton coming toward us. Annie was holding a big teddy bear and Bill was laughing and wearing a strange-looking cap, all green with a pointy top and a red feather sticking out from the side of it.

"Hey," said Annie. "This here is William Tell. He was jes over at the Swiss exhibit and they got this story about this guy who was a great archer and shot an apple offa guy's head. . . . So old Bill here jes grabbed the bow, and wham, he plugged that apple in two. . . . Ain't that something? Won me this bear and hisself a hat!"

"What the hell is a girl outlaw gonna do with a bear?" said Bittercreek.

"I might be an outlaw, but I'm still jesta sweet little thing," Annie countered, posing innocently with her prize.

"You seen the drinking potato or the talking carrot?" said Bill Raidler.

"The what?" Dalton and Annie said.

"Never mind!" Bittercreek said. "Let's go down and take a ride on the lake. From out there you can see the whole damned fair!"

"Yeah, and I bet they got a Tunnel of Love!" said Annie.

"Darling girl of mine," Bill Raidler said, hugging Dick Whisper. Dick whispered out a scream, and we all started down to the lake.

All around us was swans, and Annie kept clowning and hanging out of the boat, trying to grab 'em. The damned things wasn't one bit afraid, neither. They would come right up and peck at you, and looking at them made me feel strange as hell. For some reason they frightened me, for at a distance they seemed so beautiful, all white and wonderful. . . . But when you got closer to them, you could see the meanness in their eyes, a meanness and a wildness which made my hands shake. Plus, they had a strange odor, these swans. . . . They smelled of sweat and blood, as if they had just eaten something terrible, and its death was still on their breath.

"Hey," said Bitter, "ain't they beautiful?"

"Sure," I said. "Sure."

"Hey, I got some popcorn here," said Bitter. "You wanna feed them?"

How could I tell him that I only wanted to get away from them? I began looking at their beaks . . . the way they opened and closed, and I knew they would like to get in the boat and get a piece of me. But Bitter was giving me the popcorn, so I had to stick my hand out of the boat and drop it onto them. Oh, I felt sick, sick . . . the odor of the swans . . . I can never forget it. I thought for a second I was losing my mind. I tried to tell myself that it was just a crazy idea. Swans was beautiful. Everybody knew that. But now that one was gliding toward me, moving that big beak up and down . . . I felt as if I were going to scream. They had killed before. They would kill again. They would kill me, right here in the boat. . . . I dropped the popcorn in front of the swan and he dived down and greedily chewed it up. As he would chew me up. I knew it.

I wondered if anybody else was having the same reaction, so I looked over at Annie and Dalton. But they looked as peaceful and as happy as a couple of kids. Annie was laying back in Bill's lap. She was laughing and singing "Buffalo Gals," and Bill was rowing steadily and smiling up at the sky, as if the world was his own open bank. And behind us Bill Raidler and Dick Whisper were laughing it up. Bill was honking back at the swans, and then he would disappear to the bottom of the boat, which started going round in circles.

"Here it comes," said Bitter. "Here it comes, honey. The Tunnel of Love."

"Great," I said.

Then I knew for sure.

I knew that the two fat swans who were trailing us were just waiting for us to go into the Tunnel of Love. They wanted us there, in the darkness, and then they would come into our boat and start in shredding us to death. Oh God, I was cold, and I huddled next to Bitter, who smiled and kissed me on the forehead.

"I'm cold," I said. "Keep me warm, Bitter. Please!"

"Don't you worry none, honey," he said.

He put his arms around me as we entered the big, dark mouth of the Tunnel of Love, and I could hear the splashing of the swans as they came in behind us, and I wanted to say something . . . I felt as if I were flying apart; what the hell was wrong with me? I knew that swans weren't likely to attack, but no matter what I told myself, it come out the other way. They were going to move toward us, slowly in the dark, and then they was going to go for our eyes. Our eyes, which had seen so much death in the past few months. Our eyes, which had seen Bill Doolin lying there dead. Had seen Bitter choke the old man in the steam bath. Had seen me plug that deputy in the gut. . . . The swans were coming to me now . . . and there was nothing I could do about it. Not even tell anyone. How would it sound? A girl outlaw afraid of a bird? I started to laugh at the idea. It was ridiculous. But as I did, I felt something hitting my arm, once, twice, and I screamed and slapped at it.

"Bitter," I said. "There is something here. It's after me. It's after me now! Oh God!"

And he held me close. Then I heard him reaching out and grabbing something, and when we was through the tunnel, with me still shaking like a leaf, he showed me what it was . . . just a branch that had stuck out of the water. It musta fallen off of one of the weeping willows which overhung the lake.

"What's a-matter, honey?" he said. "You ain't scared, are you?"

"Of course not," I said. "I ain't scared of nothing."

"Then how come you are trembling so?" Bitter said.

"It ain't nothing at all," I said. "Don't worry about it. It ain't nothing."

And I grit my teeth and helped him pull the boat up to the dock while behind me I could still see them white blurs moving silently across the water.

"Well, well," said Annie, as we stopped at a big booth which was selling hot dogs and beer. "This is the greatest, ain't it?"

"Yeah," said Bill Dalton, taking a drink. "This is a hell of a lot of fun. But I jes got an idea."

"What?"

"Well, you know we are wanted pretty much everywhere," he said. "I think we ought not to stay together too much. Let's break up into pairs for a while. What you think?"

"Ah hell, Bill," Raidler said. "I don't see nothing but a couple of them park guys . . ."

"I think he is right," said Bitter. "You and Whisper go that away. Go see the Eiffel Tower over there. I hear they got some can-can girls. And me and Jennie are gonna have some real fun!"

"What are you gonna do?" said Annie, putting her hand on me.
"We are gonna go into the fun house," Bittercreek said. "I hear it's real scary!"

I thought of the darkness, of the blackness of the fun house with things popping out all over the place, and I wanted to say, "No, I can't do it," but I was afraid to say anything. For if I admitted what was happening inside me . . . then I felt as if I would crack all at once . . . start screaming and crying. . . . Oh God, what had happened to me? It was as though all of a sudden everything had come back on me at once. I knew that now. I knew it as sure as hell. My mind hadn't reacted to any of the things that had happened until later . . . it was like a delayed reaction (I couldn't have figured this out without the help of Mrs. Patterson). But what a place for it to happen. Everyone else was forgetting themselves at the fair, while I fell apart. It wasn't right to spoil their fun. They had all been through it with me. Oh God, I felt guilty, unworthy to be an outlaw. Why couldn't I be like Annie, tough and resolved, and for real. But it was no use. I wasn't. And I couldn't say a word about it. . . . So, with Bitter I stood in line at the ticket booth, while above us was a huge, horrible fat lady's face, which laughed and laughed and laughed . . .

"This ought to be great," said Bitter. "Yessir. I always wanted to go into one of these places."

He sounded jes like a little boy, and then it occurred to me, for the first time really . . . that that was all he was. That was all any of us really was. Jes little kids acting out a dream. . . . A dream which would have to end in death. And I wanted to cry that out, tell him . . . but it weren't no use, for we were going into the entrance now, walking through a narrow tunnel behind a couple of children . . . and I was shaking inside, shaking and sweating and holding onto Bitter's shirt sleeve.

"This is great, huh?" said Bitter. "Look out!"

From a dark corner in front of us, a huge face swung out. I screamed and jumped back and started to cry. Oh God, let me out of here. . . . Please let me out. I felt as if I were suffocating, and I could smell my own body . . . strangely coated with the smell of swans.

"Come on," Bitter said. "Come on . . ."

So we moved ahead into a large room, where the floor didn't seem as if it were level. We lost our balance, and Bitter fell into me and then we were climbing up the floor, inch by inch . . . toward a red door, which seemed to be above us.

"Oh God, Bitter," I said. "I don't like this."

Bitter turned and saw the tears coming down my cheeks.

"It's all right," he said. "Don't worry. It's going to be all right. Try and relax. We're on a vacation."

Somehow we got through the room and came into another dark hallway. By now I was drenched in sweat and felt as if I were going to pee myself. I held Bitter tightly around the waist until he complained he could barely move.

We felt our way around a corner, then something came down over us. A net . . . a huge net . . . and I started to scream then, not only to myself but for real.

"Get me out, Bitter, get me out. I can't take no more," I demanded.

I was flailing away wildly, but the net disappeared just as suddenly as it had come.

Bitter held me tenderly.

"What's wrong?" he said, wiping the tears away. "What is it, Jennie?"

"I don't know," I said. "I feel like the bottom has dropped out. I feel like I am falling apart. Please get me away from here."

"Don't worry," Bitter said. "We'll get out of here. It's jesta little further. You are jes tired. Maybe you shoulda stayed back at the ranch."

"Alone?" I said.

Bitter looked down at me then, and I couldn't tell what he felt.

Part of him seemed to look sympathetic. But there was a distinct look of disappointment on his face. It lasted only a second, but I saw it . . . and I sank further.

Finally we made our way around a small wall, and a huge pair of teeth came leaping out at us. I jumped, but felt nothing. It was as if everything had been drained from me; like I was dead, but had to keep right on walking.

"The door is just ahead," Bitter said. "Just ahead. Don't worry about a thing!"

"Sure," I said. "I'm not going to worry about nothing!"

But it didn't sound at all like my voice.

It sounded like Annie's, trying to be confident, cocky, ready for action.

It was just about as we swung open the two black doors which led out into the sunlight that we heard gunshots.

"Oh God," I said. "Oh God."

In front of us people were running everywhere. There was yelling and screaming, and Bitter grabbed a fat man with mustard running down his chin.

"What's happening, pardner?" he said.

"Over there at the hula place . . ." the man said. "They got a couple of outlaws holed up."

"What?" Bitter said.

But now I was pulling on him. It's strange when I think back on it. When there didn't seem to be no danger, I invented it, and a couple of innocent swans had me almost ready to throw myself in the water and drown. But as soon as I realized that there was a real threat to Bill Raidler and Dick Whisper, I seemed to pull myself back together again.

Together Bitter and I started walking toward the hula exhibit. Bitter was reaching into my leather purse for our guns.

"Here," he said, handing me a pistol. "We've got to help!"

"Put it back," I said, looking up ahead. "We can't use it now."

"Why not?" said Bitter.

But then he saw what I was looking at, and he didn't ask no more questions.

In front of us was about eighty or ninety Pinkertons, all of them in a huge circle around the Hawaiian exhibit. Their rifles were aimed and cocked, ready to fire. In front of them was the big black hat of Bill Tilghman.

But in the middle of all this was the strangest thing I ever seen. High up in a palm tree was Bill Raidler and behind the tree, holding onto a terrified girl dancer, was Dick Whisper.

"This is it," shouted Bill Tilghman. "We know who you are. Dick Whisper and Bill Raidler, give up and come down, and you will be taken into trial. If you stay up there for one more minute . . . then we will have to shoot you out."

The armed circle of men raised their guns to the tree.

The hula girl screamed and cried and begged Dick Whisper to let her go.

"I'm coming down," said Bill Raidler. "Don't shoot, Big Bill. I'm coming down. Right now."

With that, Bill Raidler began to shimmy down the tree. But underneath the tree Dick Whisper held onto the girl.

"We gotta do something," I said to Bitter.

"Like what?" he said.

"I don't know," I said. "Create a disturbance. . . . They are gonna get shot for sure."

"Maybe he really is giving himself up," Bitter said.

"Forget that," I said. "Neither one of them boys is gonna give an inch."

As soon as I had spoken, Bill Raidler made his move; swinging down from the tree, he grabbed the hula girl and began to march backwards into the little nest of palm trees which lay behind them.

"Stop or you're dead!" commanded Bill Tilghman.

"*You* stop!" screamed Raidler. "You stop or this here gal is going to be doing all her dancing in heaven! You hear me?"

"Ohhhhhhh nooooooo," screamed the hula girl.

"We mean it!" hissed Dick Whisper.

"We're going out the back way," said Bill Raidler. "Anybody that tries to stop us will get plugged and will watch this little woman get hers, too. I'm dead serious."

"Advance, men!" said Tilghman. "But slowly. Slowly."

"What are we gonna do?" I said.

"Come on," said Bitter. "Around back there. . . . Come on. We'll outflank 'em!"

And so we started around the whole group of men. But it wasn't no easy going. All around us people was running up to see what was going on. Parents with their kids, who were crying to be put up on their shoulders. Old men who looked on the whole thing with their mouths hanging open. And young boys who were saying, "Blast 'em. Shoot 'em. Get 'em."

Eventually we was able to get around to the back. But it was too late.

The entire stage had been surrounded. Rifles were everywhere, and my heart sank. I knew that without some kinda disturbance there was no hope for our pals.

"Listen," I said. "I got two sticks of dynamite in my purse. We'll try our old trick. Hurry."

Bitter grabbed the bag and took out the dynamite and was about to light it when a little kid saw what he was doing.

"Look out!" he screamed. "It's Cattle Annie!"

I guess I will never forget that.

People started screaming, "Where? Where?" and then someone else spotted us, and it was pure crazy!

"Run, Bill, run," I shouted at the palm trees.

Then I threw the dynamite toward an open spot the crowd had vacated and hoped I wouldn't hurt nobody.

The explosion and the guns went off at the same time. As Bitter and I ran, we saw Bill Raidler come staggering out of the trees, blood spurting from his chest. The hula girl tried to run out, but something hit her . . . from in front or behind I couldn't say, and she fell with blood shooting all over the desert sand. There was still no sign of Whisper . . . but a second later I saw him spinning out from the trees. He grabbed an old man and tried to use him for a shield, but the old man put up a fight, and Whisper was forced to shoot him. Then I saw Whisper get hit and turn and shoot three men and try to run back into the trees, but the Pinkertons were charging through them now, and they blasted him; first to the right and then to the left and finally he fell over for good in the stage sand.

I had been frozen, standing behind a lemonade stand. But Bitter grabbed me and pulled me along. In front of us was the Ferris wheel, and when I looked up I saw Annie and Dalton just getting off their ride and holding their guns on the pipsqueak who ran the ride. They saw us, and pointed toward the horses, and we began running as fast as we could. Bitter was pushing people aside and pulling me by the arm.

We ran by the Russian Winter Palace and saw one of the dancers take off his moustache and leap under the stage. Then we took a right at the Eiffel Tower and headed across the lot to where we had tied up the horses. But it was no use at all. The horses was guarded by about a hundred men, and they started shooting at us. I ducked and started to grab Bitter's hand, but he turned and looked at me with frightened eyes.

"I'm hit," he said, and then I saw a huge blotch on his belly that was spreading like some horrible jam.

"Oh no, Bitter," I said.

"I'm hit," he said again. "You go, Britches. Go ahead now. Hurry."

"No," I screamed. "We'll make it together. To the boats. . . . We can make it to the boats . . ."

He leaned on me then, and I started toward the hill, away from the Eiffel Tower, but Bitter's guts was coming out, and he started to scream.

"I don't wanna die!" he said. "Jennie, I don't wanna die."

"I'll help you," I said. "Hang on . . ."

But it was no use. He had fallen now, and I saw that he had been hit in the head, too. There was a chunk of his scalp gone and his eyes was glassy.

"Bitter," I said. "Bitter . . . I love you. Oh God."

"Britches" was the last word he spoke. Then I knew he was dead, and I felt as if I were dead, too. I got up, and through the smoke and the haze and the burning exhibits, I could make out Tilghman coming toward me. I started walking toward him, slowly, sucking in my wind. I was waiting for the right bullet to hit me, for surely I wanted to die.

But instead of a bullet, something else brought me down.

Whatever it was hit me from behind, around the knees, and I fell forward on my face.

"Shoot me," I said.

"Goddamn it, girl. C'mon now," a voice said.

It was my friend, Annie, looking down at me wide-eyed. Her black hair seemed to be like liquid. It flowed down her back, running both up stream and down. Her face seemed to be changing shapes. Yet, though I was out of my skull, I remember her smile —the white teeth and the sure, steady black eyes.

"C'mon with me," she said. "Hurry. We can stand 'em off . . ."

And somehow I got up again and joined her and Bill Dalton behind the ticket booth of the Eiffel Tower.

"Bitter's dead," I said in a monotone.

"Get down or you'll join him," Annie said.

But I didn't understand what she had said, and the only reason I got down was because something hit my arm, nearly taking it off.

I looked down at it, like it wasn't my arm, but someone else's arm, all covered with blood.

"Look," I said, holding it.

But Annie wasn't looking. She was busy crawling over to me,

and then she dragged me by my collar to the door of the ticket booth and shoved me inside.

"You stay here," she said. "Don't move, honey."

She hugged me tight. Tears was in her eyes and she kissed me on the head.

"I love you, honey," she said.

Then she was back outside, and I heard her say something to Bill Dalton, and I heard him yell something to her. Then I heard her yell, "Bill . . . Bill, behind you, Bill," and there was a single shot, and a terrible thud against the side of the ticket booth, and I heard Annie scream.

"Oh, Bill . . . Bill . . . God, Bill . . ."

I thought it would be over then, but a second later the door of the booth was opened, and Annie come inside and crawled over to me.

"It's you and me now," she said, sounding strangely triumphant. Her eyes were blazing, and she was smiling a little.

"We're all that is left of the Doolin-Daltons," she said.

"Yeah," I said. "We'll be in the books."

"All that's left," Annie said.

Then she huddled down next to me and hugged me tightly, and I began to cry softly, and hugged her.

"I'm sorry," she said. "I'm sorry, Jennie. But it was a good ride, wasn't it?"

"Yes," I said, not knowing what she meant, unable to breathe again, because she was smothering me.

"We're gonna go together, dear," she said.

"No," I said, pushing her away. "No . . . we are not . . ."

Annie just smiled at me and rubbed the sweat from my head with her handkerchief. The one with the little white lariats on it.

Then we heard a voice. Unmistakably the voice of Big Bill Tilghman: "All right, girls. We know you are in there. Everyone else is dead. We don't want to hurt you. Throw your guns out the window and then come out, with your hands up!"

"Let's do it, Annie," I begged. "Please. I don't want to die!"

Annie looked at me quizzically then, as if she was amazed that I still didn't understand what this had been all about.

"You want to live?" she said, with a terrible scorn in her voice. "OK. You will."

Slowly she got to her feet, grabbed my gun and took her own out of its holster, and crawled to the window. The glass was all shot out, and she dangled her hand over the side, and dropped the guns.

"Good," said Tilghman. "Now you two girls come out."

"Do as I say," hissed Annie.

"What?" I said. "We've got to go out. We have no choice."

"You go first. But just do as I say!"

Her eyes were burning furiously, and her mouth looked like a penciled line.

"Mr. Tilghman," she shouted in a feeble high-pitched voice. "Mr. Tilghman, sir . . . Jennie is coming out. She is wounded in the arm, sir. But I'm hit in the leg. I can't move. You will have to come in and get me."

"Annie!" I said. "Annie, don't."

But she said nothing, only pointed violently to the door.

"Goodbye, Annie," I said.

I got to my feet and dusted myself off and dragged myself to the door. When I opened it, I faced what looked like a thousand rifle barrels. A gentle hand came out of nowhere and swatted me to the ground. Then someone tied my hands.

Big Bill Tilghman looked down on me.

"So?" he said. "The little actress. Remember her, Tim?"

Tim the Indian looked down on me, too. He smiled and shook his head.

"I'll go get Annie now," said Tilghman. "I been looking forward to this."

I saw him walk through the open door.

I heard him say: "Well, Miss La Range. . . . Let's have a look at this leg."

Then there came a terrible cry like a screaming lion which is

227

attacking its prey, and I heard Tilghman bleat like a goat, and then there was a terrible ruckus and silence.

A minute or so later, Tilghman came out. Annie was held in his arms, her head thrown back, so you could see her long, beautiful neck.

Tilghman's arm was bleeding, and he looked like a man who had seen all the sorrows of the world.

"She come at me with a knife," he said. "I had to do her."

It was then I began to scream: "You killed her. You killed her. You killed them all . . ."

I tried to get up, but Tim the Indian shook his finger and put his big mocassin on my forehead.

It was almost dark when Tilghman carried her through the mob to his horse.

CHAPTER

XXVI

THE NEW LIFE

WELL THAT IS PRACTICALLY ALL OF MY TALE. I WAS PLACED IN jail in Chicago, then shipped back to Oklahoma for trial. During the whole time I felt as if I were hypnotized, lost and alone. Especially the latter. I was so alone, terrible alone, and when I thought of Bitter or Doolin, of Dan and Bill and Dick and Annie . . . it was as if they were figures from some book I had once read. Even the character Little Britches was nothing more than someone I had heard about in the papers. I knew she looked like me and had a lover named Bittercreek and loved an old man whom she had helped kill . . . but I felt sorry for her, terrible sorry. But, mercifully, I guess, I didn't feel like she was me. Who I was . . . that was another question. For days at a time, I would sit on my cot, or smile at the marshalls who transferred me by train to Oklahoma, or nod my head to people who lined the streets to see me.

"Who are they waving at?" I would wonder.

While another part of myself would say, "Not a chance. She's a cowgirl. She's shot people. She is dead herself. Was killed at the World's Fair."

There were long periods when I didn't recall anything. Great stretches of blackness, blackness, blackness . . .

And then awakening from that dark place, and all around me were people . . . hundreds of them, and they were taking my picture, and they were calling, "Jennie," "Britches," "Hey you, girl outlaw," and then I was sitting in a huge room, and explaining to folks what happened and who I was, and in that room . . . that long room, which I dimly perceived as a courtroom (where some poor girl was on trial, in serious trouble, and I was glad I was not in her shoes), I recall seeing Annie again. Her face had a couple of bruises on it, but other than that she looked remarkable. I remember seeing her sitting across the room from me, or was it merely across a table . . . in any case, I knew she was alive. And slowly, slowly, I began to realize that I was indeed Little Britches, that it was I, I who had lost my lover and my friends, and the knowledge buried me under a ton of grief. Oh, how I cried at night, wailing and thrashing. And oh, how I wanted to die!

But death was not in the cards. Looking back on that dreamlike period, I realize now that our case had caused such international excitement that we had somehow become the very heroes Annie had imagined we would. At the trial Annie said little, but rather was dressed as a sweet young thing, in a blue gingham dress. I was told to dress the same way, and though I barely understood why, soon I was aware that nothing much was going to happen to us at all. Our defense attorneys represented us for free. They were named Gosden and Wier, and they were very young handsome types, and at night, after hearing how Bill Tilghman found our World's Fair poster next to our campfire and guessed we were going to hold it up, at night I would dream of marrying Mr. Wier, and living a different life. A happy one, with babies in a white, picket-fenced house by the sea. I knew Annie was dreaming far different dreams . . . alone in her cell . . . I knew she dreamed of riding again. Of a new gang. Of greater risks and more blood. The blood of vengeance. For she was an outlaw, down to her bones, and had tried her best to be taken like a true desperado—feet first.

Which I didn't resent her for. But neither was she a heroine to me. I had seen too much killing, too much real bloodletting (and tried not to think of that which I had inflicted, though I found out the deputy I shot in Hot Springs was alive), and I had lost too much to see Annie as she wanted to be seen. Rather, I tried not to think of her much at all. By day I spent time in my lonely cell, counting the bugs and reading some of the books well wishers brought me. I remember them now, *Hansel and Gretel*, *Grimms' Fairy Tales* and *The Three Musketeers*. It was the Grimm book that scared me the most. At night I dreamed I was turning into a snake and that mad villagers were hunting me with knives and rakes.

Oh, it was a strange and shadowy time. Mr. Gosden and Mr. Wier talked with me. They were bright young swells, the kind I had seen in Hot Springs and wanted to kill. Now I felt nothing much for or against them. It seemed all my ideas about the world had been cracked, and now I found it hard to hate or love anyone. Now that I think of it, I guess I owe my life to Gosden and Wier's brains. They were the ones who had concocted the story of my life: my folks had been killed in a twister, leaving me with my grandmother; how Annie and me was unable to understand what was happening to us; how we was just a couple of kids who had thought it was all a great prank. Of course, there was some truth to what they said, but the few times I looked at Annie, I could see it in her eyes . . . the old glint of the con. It was obvious she loved playing the wronged innocent, and I could see her composing her life history in her mind:

Not only did she ride and shoot and kill with the infamous Doolin-Dalton Gang, but she even managed to charm the jury into letting her walk out scot-free!

Oh, how she would love that.

As for myself, I didn't relish spending time in jail and let the lawyers do with me what they wanted to. But I had no real zeal for freedom, either. I felt burned down, so tired and frail that I could hardly make it from the jail, through the howling mobs in the street, to the courthouse. My feeling was that I had dreamed a dream and somehow gotten lost inside it. It was as if it were a bubble, and I thought it would come down and allow me to float away, but instead it became another place to escape from . . . a bubble with invisible walls which wouldn't let me out . . . just like one of the fairy princesses in the Brothers Grimm.

Well, Annie didn't get her wish. Not completely. Instead of being let off scot-free, we was told we were going to have to leave the Old West altogether. The judge said that homeless girls like us needed a new kind of environment, one which would "correctly instruct us on the propriety and decency of ladyhood." I guess Mr. Gosden and Mr. Wier are to be thanked for that (though they seem to be doing all right for themselves—both of them, I understand, have successfully run for office since we got them in the public's eye).

Anyway, they took us on down to Texas, to Gulf Port, where we caught us a sailing ship. I was starting to feel a bit better by then, and I remember the cactus and sagebrush, and the loathing I felt for it all. And then the water—the sailing ships and the ocean and the big old ship named the *Tahini*, which they put us on. (When I say "us," I don't mean we was together. On the ride through Texas we was in the same stage but we weren't allowed to talk at all, which was part of our new instructions on how to act ladylike.)

I was in a room with a woman who said her name was Mrs. Brown. She was a fat lady whose eyes looked like a couple of beauty marks in a sea of fat. We shared a small room, and at night she handcuffed me to the bunk. Annie, I knew, was somewhere else on board, with another fat woman. Our destination was Boston, and a place called the Pine Manor School for Wayward Girls, run by Mrs. Louella Patterson. According to Mrs. Brown, the place would likely rid me of all my "ruffian habits" and teach me how to be a "useful and proper young woman." I could imagine how Annie would react to such news. There would be gnashing of the teeth, and she'd probably attempt to bean the old bag. But, as for myself, it didn't sound half-bad. From dreams of marrying my lawyer I had moved to dreams of having a white house by the sea somewhere. . . . I would wear a lace collar and I would listen to the waves . . . the lapping of the cool, beautiful waves. . . . Oh, if they wanted to make a proper young lady out of me, let them. Just let me forget the blood and the terror of the past year. There was nothing I wanted more than to be rid of outlawing.

But apparently folks up in Boston didn't think so. For the day we arrived at Boston's harbor, we was brought up on deck with our hands bound, and suddenly we faced the biggest crowd I ever seen. There had never been nothing like it anywhere . . . later I read that there was fifteen thousand people out to catch a glimpse of the girl outlaws. I still remember seeing Annie, pale and gaunt from the trip. But her eyes glowed and shone, and a trace of a smile played around her mouth. Then, for the first time, we were pushed together, without anyone to see we didn't talk (the police and the matrons was too busy trying to hold back the mobs to worry about what we did), and Annie leaned over and put her head close to mine.

"Look at 'em," she said. "Look at 'em. All for us. Do you believe it?"

I looked, all right.

Men with crude signs that read, "We Love You Cattle Annie and Little Britches." Children with balloons and men wearing big sandwich-type boards on their backs which said, "Love Them Girl Outlaws," and down in front a man was selling what looked like little dolls dressed up like us. Annie's face blossomed when she saw that.

"It's like I said," she whispered again. "It's just like I said."

"Yeah," I said. "Except we are in chains, and the Gang ain't here to enjoy it."

I glowered at her then, and I wished I hadn't. But I couldn't help it. She seemed selfish and hard to me, and I wanted to smash through her bull. But just as suddenly as I lost my temper, she turned and said to me, "I loved the Gang. I loved them and miss them. And I still love you, honey. You are all I got."

Then the tears came down her face, and pretty soon they were coming down mine, and I wanted to hold her and stroke her head and tell her I was sorry . . . sorry I had misunderstood. That I didn't realize that she had wanted it all, wanted to have it both ways . . . the fame and the life . . . and that deep down I knew she was as hurt and pained in her own way as I was. For she had changed, if only in that she knew it was gone. Though she didn't feel sorry, she did feel grief. And because of that, and for all her spunk and fight, it was beyond me not to love her.

But I never had a chance to hold her, for in a second the Boston police was taking us down the gangplank. Then the crowd surged forward and tried to touch us and hold us, and some people fainted at our sight and others threw the dolls to us, and hands came out of everywhere with paper and pen, and begged for autographs.

But, of course, we weren't signing nothing. Rather we was hustled into a carriage, and it was there we first met Mrs. Louella Patterson, who was surprisingly young, and not even half bad looking under her pince-nez glasses and high velvet collar.

"Hello, girls," she said. "Sit back and relax. We'll be out of this in a minute."

Neither Annie nor I said a thing, and Mrs. Patterson smiled and patted our knees.

"You may talk if you wish," she said. "Only no cursing. We are all done with that kind of thing. Where you are going you two will learn to use what I believe are very good minds. Only you will learn to use them to society's advantage, and to your own."

"Not likely," Annie said.

But I said nothing. For I was pleased. And have been ever since.

There is not much else to tell. Mrs. Patterson made good her promise. The Pine Manor School for Wayward Girls helped me change my life. I learned to cook, to sew, to read and to write, and I grew fond of naming flowers. As for Annie, it's hard to say. Right away she became a school leader, and she did well in her courses, which gave me hope. She seems to have a good head for figures and for business. On the other hand, the few times we have talked (we live in different buildings and see each other rarely) she has told me she is thinking about leaving. That she wants to get back out West, and that she has a score to settle. I gather she means with Big Bill Tilghman, which makes me sad. For by the time she gets out there, he is likely to have gone to his reward like Bill Raidler, Dick Whisper, Dan Clifton, Dalton and Bitter and Bill Doolin. For he is a part of the dream we had, the dream of badmen, hard riding, lying low and living high. Which we did, oh, how we did it. But it is gone now, all its glory and noise is brushed aside as if it never happened. It's a new world we are moving toward, a world of machines and travel and wonders at your beck and call. I want to see some of it before my time is up. I want to go to London, to Paris and to India . . . and when I leave here, I shall. I feel alive now, alive and looking

235

toward a rosy future. Ironically, it was Annie who taught me the crucial lesson, "Don't live for the past. Live out your dreams." I hope she understands her own words, for it would be sad if she spent the rest of her life trying to recover something that is forever lost.

But, in any case, she has made her mark, and I reckon she is tough enough to survive. I dearly hope so, for when the history books are written of the old Doolin-Dalton Gang, they should not forget Cattle Annie. I know. I was with her. And I can tell you true, that when it came to outlawin, Annie was the toughest, the fastest, the smartest and the most dangerous of them all.

AFTERWORD

by Mrs. Louella Patterson

THE MANUSCRIPT YOU HAVE JUST READ IS A BONA FIDE MEMOIR by my second most notorious pupil, Jennie Stevens. Or as she is better known, Little Britches. The book arrived at my doorstep April 1, 1897, and with it was a letter, which I now reprint in full:

Dear Mrs. Patterson:

I am doing pretty well in New York City, though I have had the miseries of late. A bad headache, and a terrible cold . . . but none of that has slowed me up. It is perhaps ironic (your favorite word, and one of my own now that I understand what it means) that I have become the one to write our saga. All the while we was with the Gang, Annie kept dreaming of the day Ned Buntline would do a book about us along the lines of *The Amazing Exploits of the Doolin-Dalton Gang*. It never occurred to either one of us that it might be me. But as I have little to do in the evenings here—except tend to my cold, which is hard since the room I live in is drafty—I thought I might give it a try. The more I work with people at the Houston Street Settlement, the more I realize how lucky we was. There are people on this earth—most people, I guess—who never have known a grand passion and a great adventure. Either they are too poor, like those people you have sent me to work with—and I am not complaining, there is nothing I want to do more than to devote my life to Jesus and his good work on this earth—or they are too old and too rich and too afraid to take a chance. And so with a little distance on our adventure, I can say that I am glad to have done it, glad to have been part of it all. Being the person I am now—a person saved by the good works of the Church and my new love of society—I would, of course, not ever take up outlawin again. But there was something grand and great and free about it all . . . and so I thought I would try to write it up, so that it may not be lost forever. I hope you will not be offended by this book, dear Mrs. Patterson. And I hope it will help you to understand other lost souls like I once was . . . so that you might help them see the light. Perhaps, someday, I will even find a publisher for my book.

Well, that is all I care to say now. I am working at Bellevue Hospital, helping the poor, the sick and the needy. My sewing has improved, and I am trying to lead a Christian life. . . . Yet there are moments, I must confess, when I start to backslide. I dream of Annie and me and Bill and Bitter, and old dear Bill Doolin, as we ride down the trail toward yet another adventure. Forgive me, but I am afraid there will always be a little part of me that is still, even if only in fantasy, an outlaw.

Here's hoping I find you well, and please send me any word of Annie. I hear she is married and living in Oklahoma. . . . Since time has taken away the strain in our friendship, I would love to write to her again. Just to say hello.

Take care, my dear teacher. I often think of you and the school.

Yours affectionately,
Jennie Stevens

On May 12, 1897, I received yet another letter from New York. This one from Bellevue Hospital. It was from a Dr. George Johnson, and it reads as follows:

Dear Mrs. Patterson:

I have the sad duty to inform you of the death of one of your pupils, Miss Jennie Stevens. Miss Stevens was a frail girl, and she contracted a severe case of the baffling flu disease which has stricken so many (over two hundred thousand) this year. Every attempt to help her was made, but we are at present woefully ignorant of the nature of the disease. Her death came quickly, and she did not suffer greatly. Near the end she called your name many times, and said she was "ready to meet her Maker." Her belief in Jesus was a great source of comfort to her. At the very last day, she became curiously lucid and called out for a number of people. She asked to see a Mr. Bill Dalton and a Mr. Doolin and someone named Bittercreek. Finally, she asked over and over "if Annie was coming? When was Annie coming? Had she let Annie down?" It was most distressing to us, for we assumed Annie must be a close relative. Yet we were not able to contact anyone who knew who this person might be. Indeed we were not able to get through to you . . . until it was too late.

Therefore, I am writing to you in hopes that you will contact the people I have mentioned, especially Miss Stevens's friend-sister, Annie.

I am sorry to have to be the bearer of bad news. Suffice it to say, while sweet Jennie Stevens was on this earth she was an exemplary Christian, an Angel of Mercy who devoted her whole existence to saving life.

May we all profit from her shining example.

Yours truly,
George Johnson, M.D.

Acting as the liaison between Jennie and Annie McDougal, I have written several letters to Annie at Pawnee, Oklahoma. And I have included a copy of the novel *Cattle Annie and Little Britches*. Finally, the day after receiving Dr. Johnson's most heartbreaking letter, I wrote Annie a final letter. I was certain that she would be moved to write back. Each day I waited, and yet . . . a year later nothing came. Finally, on May 1, 1904, while sitting in my office, I received a small envelope in the mail. The handwriting was childlike scrawl, and inside was a fancily printed, expensive announcement:

MR. AND MRS. BURT COOPER

OF

PAWNEE, OKLAHOMA,

WOULD LIKE TO ANNOUNCE

THE BIRTH OF THEIR DAUGHTER,

❧ JENNIE COOPER ❦

ON JANUARY 9, 1903

Underneath, written crudely in black crayon, were the words: *"Jesus don't change a thing."*
I have pondered this cruel remark, pondered it to this day, and have decided that the only recourse for Annie McDougal is prayer. And so tonight, as I go to my bed, I will pray for her, and for her daughter, who is named after Jennie Stevens. I have always felt a special love and affection for both those girls, and I will not give up the case. For deep in my heart I know that someday, Annie McDougal (like her dear friend, Jennie Stevens, God Rest Her Soul) will see the light.